VISIONS OF BELONGING

POPULAR CULTURES, EVERYDAY LIVES

ROBIN D. G. KELLEY AND JANICE RADWAY, EDITORS

POPULAR CULTURES, EVERYDAY LIVES

ROBIN D. G. KELLEY AND JANICE RADWAY, EDITORS

JUDITH E. SMITH

VISIONS OF BELONGING

Family Stories, Popular Culture,

and Postwar Democracy,

1940–1960

COLUMBIA UNIVERSITY PRESS / NEW YORK

COLUMBIA UNIVERSITY PRESS
Publishers Since 1893
New York Chichester, West Sussex
Copyright © 2004 Columbia University Press
Library of Congress Cataloging-in-Publication Data
Smith, Judith E.
  Visions of belonging : family stories, popular culture, and postwar democracy,
1940–1960 / Judith E. Smith.
    p.   cm — (Popular cultures, everyday lives)
  Includes bibliographical references (p.) and index.
  ISBN 0-231-12170-9 (cloth : alk. paper)—ISBN 0-231-12171-7 (pbk. : alk. paper)
    1. Popular culture—United States—History—20th century. 2. Arts, American—20th century.
3. Family—United States—History—20th century. 4. United States—Social life and customs—
1918–1945. 5. United States—Social life and customs—1945–1970. I. Title. II. Series.

E169.S655 2004
306.85′0973′0904—DC22

                                                                                        2003067481

Columbia University Press books are printed on
permanent and durable acid-free paper.
Printed in the United States of America
c 10 9 8 7 6 5 4 3 2 1
p 10 9 8 7 6 5 4 3 2 1

Designed by Lisa Hamm

For Ben, Sarah, and Laura

CONTENTS

ACKNOWLEDGMENTS

WHEN I BEGAN THIS PROJECT, I WAS INTERESTED IN WHAT THE FILM *Marty* could illuminate about the experience of ethnic communities in the 1940s and 1950s. As a social historian dedicated to understanding the lives of anonymous immigrant laboring families, I had inherited the "ordinary family" framework from the popular front without being fully aware of its political or rhetorical significance. In following the intellectual signs that have redefined this as a project in cultural history, I have been blessed with extraordinary friends and colleagues as teachers. Sharon Strom, Lary May, and George Lipsitz were my first guides to the history of wartime and postwar film. Tom Doherty helped locate sources and films. My fellow travelers in postwar cultural history Daniel Horowitz, Elaine May, Lizabeth Cohen, Ruth Feldstein, and George Lipsitz have generously shared research and insights. Working in American Studies with literary and cultural historian Chris Wilson and film scholar Linda Dittmar encouraged me to locate *Marty* within a literary tradition stretching back through the family plays of Clifford Odets and Arthur Miller and forward to Lorraine Hansberry's *Raisin in the Sun*. My early efforts at contextualizing Chayefsky's invention of Italianness as a white ethnicity were redirected by Mary Helen Washington and Nikhil Singh, who suggested that I look at this new formulation of ethnicity in relationship to African American writers and wartime and postwar theorizing about race. When I began to draft the book in 1997 and 1998, Michael Denning's *The Cultural Front* and Matthew Frye Jacobson's *Whiteness of a Different Color* opened important conceptual directions. When I discovered that ordinary family stories were in many cases the product of the left in the 1940s and 1950s, Rachel Rubin, Jim Smethurst, Mari Jo and Paul Buhle, and Mark Solomon helped me interpret what I found.

My expert guides through the ever expanding parameters of this research have been librarians: at the Margaret Herrick Library of the Academy of Motion Picture Arts and Sciences in Los Angeles; the University of California, Los Angeles, Film Archives; the Special Collections at the Cinema-Television Library, University of Southern California; the Museum of Broadcasting in New York; the New York Public Library for the Performing Arts; the Southern Historical Collection at the University of North Carolina, Chapel Hill; the Film and Television Collections at the State Historical Society of Wisconsin in Madison; the Harry Ransom Humanities Research Center at the University of Texas, Austin. Ned Comstock from USC's Special Collections was especially generous in cheerfully sending me additional research materials as my group of films expanded. Kristine Krueger provided expert assistance in finding film stills, and Pembroke Herbert and Sandi Rygiel lent their enthusiasm and creativity to locating additional visual materials. American Studies graduate students provided invaluable research assistance: Melanie Kuhn, Robert Macieski, Nancy Palmer, Dale Dooley, Daphne Lagios, and Michael Beckett at Boston College and Lisa Bertola and Daniel Boudreau at the University of Massachusetts, Boston. Last-minute assistance from history graduate students Abigail Bass from Harvard, Erica LeMay from the University of North Carolina, and Alison Varzolly from UCLA saved me from having to repeat trips to archival collections. The warm hospitality of Bruce Green and the late Linda Dove, Mary Yaeger and John Lithgow, Charlie and Joann Kaplan in repeated visits to Los Angeles, and of Linda Gordon and Allen Hunter in Madison, Kip Pells in Austin, and John Feinblatt in Manhattan added the gifts of their friendship to research trips away from home. Daphne Lagios's research in women's magazine helped me to position Betty Smith, Kathryn Forbes, and Cid Ricketts Sumner within popular publishing. Michael Beckett's meticulous research in the black press and his creativity and initiative in tracking leads and finding material enabled me to follow the critical reception of postwar films and drama in greater depth.

Anne Fleche, Alex Bloom, Alan Wald, Irwin Silber, Penny Von Eschen, David Levering Lewis, Gerald Horne, Kate Weigand, Stephen Whitfield, Michele Hilmes, Jason Loviglio, Susan Smulyan, David Sanjek, and J. Fred MacDonald helpfully responded to research queries. Delbert Mann, Ernest Borgnine, and Walter Seltzer met with me in Los Angeles and generously filled me in on the details of the television and film productions of *Marty*. Clarice Durham and Dorothy Burnham spoke with me about their knowledge of Richard Durham and Lorraine Hansberry in the 1940s and 1950s.

Paper presentations and individual chapters benefited from perceptive commentary from Lizabeth Cohen, Peter Filene, the late Roland Marchand, Patricia Turner, Paula Fass, Sharon Strom, Mary Helen Washington, Lisa Fine, Susan Levine, Susan Porter Benson, Ruth Feldstein, Nikhil Singh, Laura Browder, Christina Simmons, Barbara Melosh, Mark Solomon, Christine Stansell, Joan S. Rubin, Harry Chotiner, and Ben and Sarah Blum-Smith. Ben Keppel, Kevin Gaines, Mark Solomon, and Jim Smethurst were insightful critics for the chapter on Hansberry. An early version of some of the material in chapter 8 appeared as "The Marrying Kind: Working-Class Courtship and Marriage in 1950s Hollywood" in *Multiple Voices in Feminist Film Criticism*, edited by Diane Carson, Linda Dittmar, and Janice R. Welsch (Minneapolis: University of Minnesota Press, 1994). Jason Loviglio encouraged me to write an article based on part of chapter 1 that appeared as "Radio's 'Cultural Front,' 1938–1948" in the collection he coedited with Michele Hilmes, *Radio Reader: New Essays on the Cultural History of Radio* (New York: Routledge, 2002). I am grateful to both presses for permission to use this material.

Succeeding drafts of this manuscript benefited from thoughtful and discerning readings by Lois Rudnick, Rachel Rubin, Paul and Mari Jo Buhle, Matt Jacobson, Dan Horowitz, Ruth Feldstein, Sharon Strom, Barbara Melosh, Chris Wilson, Ardis Cameron, and Ann Holder. Continuing conversations with Dan Horowitz, Ruth Feldstein, Ann Holder, and Rachel Rubin provided great intellectual stimulation and the best kind of collegial support during the long process of writing. Ann Holder's acute editorial suggestions and familiarity with the project proved especially important in the final revisions. At Columbia University Press Robin Kelley's spirited enthusiasm for the project came at an especially crucial time. I also want to thank Ann Miller, Peter Dimock, Anne Routon, Revan Schendler, and Susan Pensak, for their editorial expertise and guidance, and Jim O'Brien, who prepared the index with deep historical insight and a keen editorial eye.

The skills required to develop interdisciplinary methods of analysis and the focus and concentration required for a project of this scope have not fit very well with ordinary working and family life, even spread over a period of years. I began this project working in the history department at Boston College, where the late Janet Wilson James, Virginia Reinburg, Karen Miller, and Mrinilini Sinha supported my turn to teaching film history and encouraged me to think I could work my way through the new language of cultural studies. Lois Rudnick, Rachel Rubin, and Shauna Manning, my colleagues now in American Studies at the University of Massachusetts, Boston, have been consistently excited about this work and have in different ways supported the leaves required to finish it. My long-distance extended family has lovingly cheered me on: Beth Smith, Sarah Malino, Debbie Smith, Jim Smith, Lois Feinblatt, Jeff Blum, Patty Blum. In the years of working on this book, my children, Ben, Sarah, and Laura, have grown from occasionally willing movie watchers into discerning cultural critics with whom it has been an unfailing source of stimulation and joy to discuss ordinary family stories. Ben and Sarah have both been willing to get drawn into emergency editorial consultation. Laura in particular has grown up living with the pressures of this book weighing on her mother, and the unfailing generosity she has extended to me in response has been a special gift. My housemates Noel Jette, Alan Zaslavsky, and Clara Jette Zaslavsky have resided with the piles of movies, files, and books overflowing on to the dining room table and have contributed their own clarifying insights as thoughtful and perceptive film critics and political progressives. Larry Blum has been the companion of my heart and my partner in daily life, work, and parenting. His powerful philosophical work on the moral dimensions of race and racism has helped me think through some of what I discovered in this research. His unwavering faith in and engagement with *Visions of Belonging* over many years, in countless conversations in many different times and places, has meant everything to me, in addition to his reliable enthusiasm about watching yet another old movie. My words seem inadequate to express my deepest gratitude for all this and much more.

VISIONS OF BELONGING

ORDINARY FAMILIES, POPULAR CULTURE, AND POPULAR DEMOCRACY, 1935–1945

I N THEIR EFFORTS TO ATTRACT THE WIDEST POSSIBLE AUDIENCE, THE PLAN-
ners of the 1940 New York World's Fair hired an actor as "official
greeter," someone who would personify a figure made familiar by
advertising, radio, film, and popular fiction. Their vision of the "average
American" was of "a beaming, portly" person, "the kind of fellow who is
a faithful member of luncheon clubs and doesn't mind raising his voice in
conventional quarters." The planners also designed a Town of Tomorrow,
in which two "representative American families" lived for a week in Federal Housing Authority model houses. The "families . . . selected by newspapers in various parts of the country . . . will consist of a father American,
a mother American, and two little Americans, preferably a boy and a girl."
Among the criteria for the chosen families was "racial origin." Borrowing
from the Typical American contests that had been a staple of eugenics
demonstrations at county fairs since World War I, the selection process
ensured that none of the typical Americans chosen to embody the theme
of the 1940 World's Fair—Peace and Freedom—would be poor, foreign-
born, or nonwhite.[1]

The fair's "typical Americans" reflected public images of the American
family in the 1930s as Norman Rockwell presented it in his illustrations:
rural or small-town residents, neither rich nor poor, always white. The
people who inhabited the American "norm" were less aware of its boundaries than those who were excluded, who saw themselves depicted in popularly circulated images as "types" rather than typical. Racialized, ethnic,

and working-class stock characters animated American traditions of popular entertainment, especially in minstrelsy, vaudeville, and Hollywood, conveying humor, exoticism, or viciousness. They rarely appeared in serious drama, however, and never exemplified the ordinary.[2]

The social upheavals of the Depression and fears of the fascism sweeping across Europe began to shake these conventions. Slowly, forms of popular drama attempted to make room for immigrants, and even African Americans, to join farmers and residents of Main Street as featured players on a politicized stage.

While stories of families may appear private and personal, images of what constitutes a family have public and political significance. Recognizable membership in an "ordinary" family is a marker of public respect and civic inclusion; living outside that privileged realm leaves one suspect, unprotected by basic citizenship rights and excluded from national belonging, an "other." The 1940 fair's confident selection of "typical Americans" to exemplify American Peace and Freedom may have marked the end of an era. Subsequent demands for popular unity disrupted the common assumption that white, middle-class Main Street could fully represent Americanness.

World War II reshaped the American landscape. Multiethnic cooperation was publicly encouraged—in the platoon, on the shop floor and the city block. Citizens were asked to serve their country, to put aside personal dreams, to risk their lives in the fight for democracy. Men and women encountered one another outside of former local, ethnic, and racial networks; prolonged separations and the scattering of families altered standards for male and female heroism and camaraderie and opened up possibilities for expressing homosexual desire. For a brief time the vision of a labor-led movement against fascism and Jim Crow segregation coincided with national goals, expanding the range of representative Americans as well as the meanings of community that flourished within the cultural mainstream.

The national mobilization produced a division between the military and the home front, between men and women. At the same time, it created opportunities, especially for women—many of them outside the literary establishment—to write family-centered stories that made provocative cultural claims by allowing working-class, ethnic, and African American characters to represent an expanded American citizenship and to embody new visions of national belonging. Suddenly—but only temporarily—the working-class children of immigrants, laborers, and share-croppers could also exemplify the "ordinary" American.

Visions of Belonging explores the ways in which popular stories of "ordinary" families provided a forum for competing conceptions of American democracy during World War II and into the cold war years. It shows how writers such as Betty Smith, Kathryn Forbes, Arthur Miller, Lillian Smith, Laura Hobson, Paddy Chayefsky, and Lorraine Hansberry experienced wartime and postwar possibilities in their own lives, and it explores the social visions they hoped their books, plays, and movies might encourage.

Giving literary shape in family stories to the dreams of wartime democratic promise meant that questions of democratic inclusion and racial equality spilled over from the clearly public to the potentially explosive private sphere. A racially and sexually expansive cosmopolitanism spawned in the social insurgencies of the 1930s, as well as interactions with different people and places during the war years, encouraged people to rethink parochial assumptions of ethnic and racial difference and to trespass, if with hesitation, across the boundaries of the "normal."

Audiences encountered stories of ordinary families in novels, plays, and films. *Visions of Belonging* listens in on how audiences absorbed and assessed the social implications of these works, especially the ways in which white and black readers and viewers recognized the creation and shifting uses of ethnic and racial categories. Works such as *A Tree Grows in Brooklyn, I Remember Mama, Strange Fruit, Gentleman's Agreement, Death of a Salesman, Marty,* and *Raisin in the Sun* entered the popular imagination and shaped personal aspirations, offering a standard against which to measure disappointments, uncover unsatisfied longings, or fantasize loving acceptance. These stories and the responses to them provide a point of entry into an extraordinary time, when the possibilities for social transformation seemed boundless and yet were also fiercely contested.

Stories of ordinary families that featured working-class characters were especially appealing during the war years. They provided relief from war's anxiety and fear; they also created a template for working out the terms of an expanded postwar citizenship and realigned heterosexual partnerships. Through their comforting use of a nostalgic and invented past that emphasized familial loyalty, collective support, and hard work, "looking back" stories of ordinary families, such as Betty Smith's *A Tree Grows in Brooklyn* and Kathryn Forbes's *Mama's Bank Account*—the subjects of chapters 2 and 3—addressed wartime and postwar uncertainties. Both Smith and Forbes portray the mother as the backbone of democracy and as guarantor of the republic's survival. These mothers are not the controlling, infantilizing figures common to writing of the 1920s and 1930s, nor are they feminists moving from private into public life. They provide female nurture; their stories lionize domestic commitments and domestic strength. In both novels the journey of the ethnic family ultimately results in an exchange: of poverty, parochial isolation, and female- and kin-centered working-class struggle for absorption into mainstream America, class mobility, and the reassertion of masculine social and economic authority.

To use the family as a metaphor for the nation is to risk marginalizing those outside the family; in proposing an ethnic past as a universal American past, "looking back" family stories obscured the history of discrimination that had so far excluded black families from the realm of the "ordinary." Tracing the transformation of these novels into film and stage productions reveals the rise and fall of looking back as a framework to express social concerns. These productions consciously portrayed ethnic parochialism as negative and ethnic cosmopolitanism as positive, though the latter did not address racial difference or cross racial lines.

A group of writers particularly concerned that postwar society extend the social initiatives of the New Deal insisted that "ordinary Americans" must include those previously designated as racialized outsiders. During the war and through the late 1940s Lillian Smith, Arthur Miller, Laura Hobson, Richard Brooks, and Arthur Laurents produced narratives I categorize as "trading places" stories—the subject of chapters 4, 5, and 6—that allowed characters, as surrogates for the audience, to discover that the apparently fixed racial and sexual boundaries that legitimated exclusions from citizenship were in fact permeable. Trading places stories, such as *Strange Fruit, Focus,* and *Gentleman's Agreement,* were addressed to and recognized by audiences familiar with Depression-era and wartime visions of popular democracy. The rhetoric of popular antifascism stressed the parallels between Nazi racialism and forms of segregation and discrimination in America, especially the policing of racial, ethnic, and sexual boundaries. Interracial sexuality was the most commonly named form of sexual deviancy; homosexuality was a closely related threat. In the exhilaration of the Nazi defeat, challenging these boundaries seemed both possible and necessary, given the role they had played in the fascist rise to power in Europe.

Trading places stories relied for their drama on presenting the different victims of discrimination as interchangeable in order to reveal the dangers of "domestic fascism." Thus southern arguments in support of segregation in Washington, DC dangerously provided an alibi for gang attacks on Jews in New York. Writers of these stories assumed that they could challenge racialist ideas by revealing the fallacies of anti-Semitism *or* racism, that they could show the social costs of segregation by exposing discriminatory practices in housing and employment toward Jews *or* African Americans. They experimented to find the "ideal" victim who could at the same time inspire sympathy and challenge the legitimacy of racial and ethnic boundaries.

By uncovering and asserting previously unacknowledged connections between people, especially those who resisted racism and inequality, the writers hoped to promote interracial alliances and solidarity. The effectiveness of trading places stories depended on audiences recognizing racially and ethnically diverse characters as "representative" rather than exceptional. Paradoxically, when they overlooked the variety of barriers that prevented certain groups of people from achieving full citizenship, these stories reproduced racialized categories even while protesting them.

From 1946 to 1950 a steadily strengthening challenge to New Deal social activism and an increasingly aggressive anticommunism took over the political center, singling out popular antifascism as suspect and marginalizing heretofore mainstream organizations and political positions. Antifascist critiques of racism, anti-Semitism, and sexual conformity came to signal a dangerous association with radicalism. What began as an insistence on common human concerns and an effort to build empathy across boundaries was eventually narrowed to an idea of individual belonging that bypassed questions of power rooted in history. Trading places stories would eventually naturalize the exclusionary aspects of the ordinary, providing a bridge to the Everyman narrative that would become more common after 1949.

The "everyman" stories I examine in chapters 7, 8, and 9 feature modest characters whose disappointed dreams were intended at the time they were written to serve as a reproach to the emphasis in mainstream culture on material acquisition and class mobility. The right-wing mobilization claimed a monopoly in defining Americanness; conservative anticommunists were particularly outraged at the wartime popularity of left-wing portrayals of ordinary people. Left-wing writers used the everyman framework to fight for their vision of ordinary Americans. But everyman stories also conveyed the ordinary as unmarked characters with no trace of deviation from, once again, a sharply defined norm.

Everyman assumptions of universality were not, in fact, universal. Labor activists did not imagine the opposite of working-class powerlessness to be middle-class individualism; sexual modernists and homosexual progressives did not imagine the opposite of anomie to be heterosexual married couples with children. African American progressives did not imagine the opposite of racialization to be whiteness. Since an unmarked universality threatened to make people of color invisible, they continued to envision an alternate commonality based on an understanding of racial difference as historically constructed. Langston Hughes titled his address to the 1937 Second International Writer's Congress "Too Much of Race," insisting that Negroes in America were tired of a "world divided superficially on the basis of blood and color but in reality on the basis of poverty and power." His conception of cosmopolitan racial universalism spoke to "a great longing" in the hearts of "the darker peoples of the world to reach out their hand in friendship and brotherhood to all the races of the earth."[3]

Internationally, the momentum of anticolonialism was changing the complexion of the players in world government and creating the possibility for a global standard of human rights that could oppose nationalist and colonial subjugation of racial minorities. The cultural historian Nikhil Singh has proposed the term *black worldliness* to encompass the "astonishingly wide range of writings, black cultural formations, and institutional deliberations" in the 1940s in which "black intellectuals and activists argued that they were the true bearers of universality within the United States, and within the world-system."[4]

For different reasons Arthur Miller, Paddy Chayefsky, and Lorraine Hansberry were all committed to representing ordinary families in their quest to raise, before a broad audience, questions about the limitations of postwar democracy. A family life protected from fascist threats and revitalized by postwar prosperity was the most common image associated with U.S. victory during and after the war. Combining the insights of Marx and Freud to reveal the cracks and disappointments of ordinary family life could, these writers hoped, challenge the ideology of individual family happiness and domestic consumption. Everyman family stories encouraged the exploration of social themes while avoiding the question of political affiliation. But family life always carried the danger of not seeming a legitimate subject for art or politics, veering dangerously close to a feminized world of commercial soap operas, especially if attention was directed to female rather than male disappointments: the writers of everyman stories tried carefully to balance their conceptions of masculine and feminine achievement and subjectivity.

Although Jews were regularly perceived to be a racialized group before the war and faced discrimination in employment and housing, after the war many found that they could "pass" as ordinary families. The popularization in television dramas of generically ethnic everyman characters expanded the range of those who could seem ordinary; but if "ordinary" implied both white and familial, it was encouraging both inclusion and exclusion.

Whereas in the 1940s stories claiming outsiders as ordinary carried a clear political message, by the end of the 1950s, when the cultural discrediting of social protest had effectively discouraged explorations of racial, sexual, and class inequality, audiences once again perceived family stories as a comforting retreat from politics. After Arthur Miller's *Death of a Salesman* each everyman story that became popular and represented the universal as white, middle class, and heterosexual narrowed the space for envisioning an interracial cosmopolitanism. When Paddy Chayefsky's television plays helped to stretch the category of white to include ethnicity, in many ways it became harder for African Americans to contribute to a discussion dominated by the thematic frame of immigration, assimilation, and mobility. Lorraine Hansberry reasserted racial universalism by recasting the everyman story, with an African American family as an ordinary American family. The successes and the failures of her effort mark a critical transition between postwar confidence in a unified American identity and its dissolution in the last decades of the twentieth century.

In *Visions of Belonging,* family stories illuminate the call for multiracial democratic citizenship and the censoring of that call as a diminishing of democracy. To understand the power of their appeal, we must first return to the 1930s and to the ideas and circumstances in which stories of ordinary families emerged to broadcast the wartime promise of expanded citizenship.

RADIO'S FORMULA DRAMA

Racial minstrelsy, ethnic vaudeville, and soap operas on radio set the parameters against which postwar stories featuring ordinary families would help reshape American society. The business of radio in the 1920s was, according to historian Michele Hilmes, its unprecedented power to shape cultural expression. Broadcasting directly into people's kitchens and giving popular culture its widest audience to date, radio developed its distinctive form of "mass" address through its presentation of racial, ethnic, and gender "difference" in formula dramas.[5]

The most popular show in the early days of radio was *Amos 'n' Andy*, created in 1926 by two white amateur minstrel performers, Charles Correll and Freeman Gosden, and nationally broadcast by 1929. Using a comic strip story line and drawing on social satire, minstrelsy's long history of racial humor, caricature, and vaudeville-style ethnic humor, Correll and Gosden described incidents common to the lives of blacks who had migrated to cities. Later they made explicit humorous references to New Deal politics.[6] Combining racial dialect humor with urban newcomer incompetence, *Amos 'n' Andy* became a model for both comic dialogue sketches and serial drama; what distinguished it from other radio serials, however, was its construction of racialized otherness—what Hilmes calls its representation of migration as having created a "permanently unassimilable underclass." As characters Amos and Andy would never invoke everyday American life. The show's popularity also effectively limited the roles for African Americans elsewhere in radio to those of servants and minstrels—figures that white actors, directors, and producers had popularized as "black." Minstrelsy, sometimes on an imagined plantation, provided the setup for black singing groups on radio, just as visual conventions of minstrelsy did in film production of "Southerns."[7]

The struggle for African American citizenship rights demanded more complex dramatic representations of African Americans than those served by minstrelsy; black actors repeatedly attempted to defy minstrel stereotypes by agitating for stories of ordinary as well as heroic African Americans. For a brief period in the early 1930s a group in New York broadcast on a local station weekly radio dramas about black life in the city. Organized by a young Morgan College graduate named Carlton Moss, the group included distinguished stage actors Rose McClendon and Ernest Whitman.[8] The task of representing black family life—long barred from the mainstream stage, and made especially invisible by mammy and minstrelsy caricature—was a cultural and political priority. In 1935 the New York City Board of Education broadcast a serial drama acted, written, and directed by African Americans, *A Harlem Family*, portraying the trials and tribulations of an African American family during the Depression. But these were isolated efforts amidst the barrage of white programming in radio and film.[9]

Ethnic humor was the mainstay of *The Goldbergs,* the radio serial that followed *Amos 'n' Andy* on the nightly schedule and came closest to it in longevity and popularity. The show's middle-class and Columbia-educated creator, Gertrude Berg, drew on a well-known vaudeville style of Jewish dialect humor and its harsh portrayal of immigrant life, though softened and cleaned up for radio.[10] Unlike *Amos 'n' Andy,* whose characters interacted in a variety of work and community settings and were marked as "unassimilable," Berg placed her ethnic characters and the show's dramatic crises in a family setting, with a central focus on the process of their assimilation. Berg saw herself as creating an alternative to "Jewish types portrayed on the stage" by popularizing a more loving, optimistic, family whose "American" strivings for a comfortable material existence did not jeopardize their spiritual integrity. *The Goldbergs* stressed Jewish rituals, using "daily family living" as a substitute for more public themes, such as "anything that will bother people . . . unions, politics, fundraising, Zionism, socialism, intergroup relations."[11] Although *The Goldbergs* was not constrained by the restriction against racial assimilation that defined *Amos 'n' Andy,* comic "types" shaped the narratives of both shows as well as their popular appeal. Both avoided mention of exclusion and thus were unable to represent directly claims for an expanded citizenship.

Women's daytime serials, dismissively labeled "soap operas" after the sponsors who became associated with them, shared formal qualities with *Amos 'n' Andy* and *The Goldbergs,* especially an open-ended narrative structure and a reliance on strong characterization. The first domestic drama centered on women characters and family crises went on air in the fall of 1930. Daytime soaps were very successful at attracting loyal listeners, and they offered sponsors the benefit of the smooth transitions from program to advertising. By 1940 soaps constituted the majority of sponsored daytime radio programming.[12] Although the earliest characters were described as an Irish American mother and her daughter, daytime serials soon differentiated themselves from the evening racial and ethnic comedy serials by centering on characters without racial and ethnic markings; the imagined community they conveyed was reassuringly white and middle class. Under cover of day soaps explored fissures in the family, but, classified and marginalized by gender, they were no more able than nighttime serial comedies to challenge social exclusion. Even though radio formula drama relied on different conventions, many of which also appeared in genre films of the period, their combined effect was to reinforce citizenship exclusions based on race and racialized ethnicity, class, and gender.[13]

Prohibitions on "political" content in broadcasting constrained efforts to expose the exclusions from citizenship that formula representations legitimated. Labor unions reported that they were often unable to buy radio time or gain access to national networks before 1942. Racial caricature was commonplace, but any mention of racial exclusion was unacceptably political.

By the late 1930s the power of southern segregationists to demand that radio uphold racial segregation had *increased* because of the expanded dominion of the national networks and their commercial sponsors. When civil rights activists pushed racial concerns into a proposed series on "The Catholic Church and the Negro Question," sponsored by the Catholic Church on a local Memphis station in 1935, threatening phone calls succeeded in having the program canceled. When the National Association for the Advancement of Colored People (NAACP) invited speakers in Baltimore to discuss segregation at the University of Maryland, the station management canceled its scheduled local broadcast. When the white national president of the NAACP, Arthur Springarn, departed from his approved remarks as a guest on the Southernaires Sunday gospel show in order to criticize racial discrimination, NBC canceled his portion of the show altogether.[14]

Popular narratives of expanded citizenship during the war emerged from a creative ferment generated in the late 1930s, when popular theater began to compete with radio formula drama. Writers began to enlarge their conceptions of the "political" by experimenting with representations of "ordinary people" who would speak to a broad audience. The result was a proliferation of forms, topics, and characters that included images of ethnic or working-class American lives beyond the comic stereotypes of radio and film formula drama. Few of these forms, however, bridged the constantly reinforced racial divide.

POPULAR THEATER AND POPULAR DEMOCRACY

Writers and activists affiliated with antifascist, labor, and civil rights movements in the 1930s introduced ways of talking about ordinary men and women that gained rhetorical power during the war as concrete evidence of democracy at work. The vocabularies they popularized drew attention to the prevalence of comic types and formulas. Theatrical performances inspired by these social movements produced changes in dramatic form as much as in writers, actors, and audiences. The cultural historian Michael Denning has characterized the cultural expressions associated with Depression-era social movements as a "cultural front" that influenced the construction of mass culture from the thirties on. His formulation helps to reveal the broad and transforming political vision that informed various efforts to reimagine ordinary Americans.[15]

The call for an alternative theater that would dramatize pressing social problems and organize local support for collective solutions encouraged writers to experiment with relationships between theater and daily life and to create new representations of ordinary people. Popular theater broadened the reach of local and noncommercial theater, already visible in "little theater" groups across the nation. New efforts at popular theater ranged from over four hundred workers' theater groups—loosely affiliated with the Communist Party—to the topical musical revue nurtured in the New York labor movement's summer camps. In 1934 the International Ladies' Garment Workers Union created Labor Stage, which provided an arena for amateur theater that eventually resulted in the high-spirited and long-running Broadway production of *Pins and Needles* (1937–1940). *Pins and Needles* drew on traditions of both workers' theater and musical variety revue to showcase bold and brassy representations of working-class life that were neither sentimentalized nor caricatured.[16]

The 1930s Group Theatre was another attempt to create popular theater, attracting young actors, writers, directors, some from working-class backgrounds, who hoped to live and work together to create a company with a recognizable style. The founding spirit, Harold Clurman, a middle-class Jewish theater critic, hoped the Group would express through theater "the life of our times." Committed to applying Konstantin Stanislavsky's methods of psychological realism to contemporary plays that expressed social concerns, the Group wanted to transform Broadway *and* to reach new audiences. Between 1931 and 1940 the Group presented a range of work, most prominently featuring the plays of Clifford Odets. Although in 1946 the critic Robert Warshow would provocatively categorize Odets as the "poet of the Jewish middle class," Odets's 1935 works, especially *Waiting for Lefty, Awake and Sing,* and *Paradise Lost,* conveyed, through expressive language, a broad experience of economic dispossession, dislocation, and familial claustrophobia.[17]

But even radical theater could reproduce rules of segregation that were embedded in national culture. The Group's democratic sensibility played down differences in class and ethnic origins but acceded to racial inequality. In the summer of 1931 an intrepid playwright suggested that the Group

analyze its own "racial problem . . . your amalgamation of native and foreign elements, of Anglo-Saxons and Jews." The actors rejected these
terms, insisting that they were all Americans and that calling attention to
people's backgrounds would lead to the kind of "typecasting and isolation
they had joined the Group to fight."[18] They cast two established black
actresses, Rose McClendon and Fannie Belle De Knight, as servants in
their first production of Paul Green's play *The House of Connelly*, a drama
about the fall of the old and the rise of a new South. While McClendon
and De Knight were present the first summer in Brookfield, Connecticut
in 1931, living with the other actors, they were neither included in the acting company nor invited to participate in acting classes. According to one
account, McClendon listened intently from her bedroom window as
Harold Clurman lectured the assembled company on new theories of psychological realism.[19]

Wartime family stories that dramatized an expanded citizenship drew
on the cross-fertilization of news and drama that characterized the culture
industries of the 1930s—from the tabloid journalism that pulp-writer-
turned-producer Darryl Zanuck transformed into gritty Warner Brothers
crime stories to film montage and the "stage newsreels" of the Living
Newspaper plays produced by the Federal Theatre Project (FTP). The
hybrid dramatic documentary form was at the center of the news-as-
entertainment journalism that fueled Henry Luce's empire: the news magazine format of *Time* (founded in 1923, which led circulation in its field
after 1938), the investigative journalism of *Fortune* (1930), and the block-
buster photojournalism of *Life* (1936). Luce's *March of Time*, produced by
Time, Inc., for CBS radio from 1931 to 1945, and also on film after 1935,
provided the first serious attempt to present the news in a documentary
format, using professional actors to read the voices and portray the
actions of current newsmakers. Its blend of reportage and melodrama
popularized a mode of documentary storytelling and dramatic reenactment that would be enormously influential during the war and after.

The forms of address combining news, documentary, and drama provided the audience with what media historian Erik Barnouw describes as
"vicarious experience of what they were living and experiencing. It put the
listener in another man's shoes."[20] Popular journalism, sound film, and
radio were emergent forms of mass culture that employed aspiring writers from diverse backgrounds.[21] Aesthetic forms, genre conventions, and
individual creators traveled between these media.

When these new kinds of theater drew on the oppositional energy of social engagement, the results could be explosive, as illustrated by the history of the January 6, 1935, performance of Odets's *Waiting for Lefty,* a one-act play based on a taxi strike the previous year. *Lefty* politicized domestic melodrama with a combination of labor agitprop and audience participation; two of its vignettes used a family-life format. Working- and middle-class characters shared the spotlight and found common ground in social crisis. Presented in New York to benefit the League of Workers Theatres, the performance electrified its audience and swept them up into joining its call to strike. The play generated enormous excitement about the possibilities for socially informed drama and inspired attempts at popular theater in communities across the nation.[22]

African American radicals seized the openings *Lefty* created. In the summer of 1935 the Negro People's Theatre adaptation of *Waiting for Lefty,* directed by Rose McClendon, encouraged efforts to organize a Harlem community theater. New practices of dispensing with sets, curtains, and artificial separation between actors and audience inspired poet Langston Hughes to write and stage *Don't You Want to Be Free* (1938). The young black actor Robert Earl Jones stepped out of the audience to begin the play, which ended with an interracial gesture of class unity, "White worker, here is my hand," and a rousing call to action: "Let's get together, folks, and fight, fight, fight!" Hughes's play was greeted with great enthusiasm by Harlem audiences (attendance in 1936 and 1937 set a record in Harlem) and was used to launch radical black theater groups in at least four other cities, including Chicago and Los Angeles.[23]

The four-year experiment of the Federal Theatre Project provided state support to institutionalize the experimental combination of popular theater, social drama, and direct political address. The FTP was one of several arts projects funded by the New Deal's Works Progress Administration in 1935, partly in response to the widespread popularity of community theater groups in the 1920s and 1930s. Many left-wing writers and actors who used FTP projects as a bridge between street theater and commercial media would be important in shaping postwar social drama and film. Radicals were particularly influential in shaping the FTP's most consciously social dramas, the Living Newspaper plays.[24]

Social drama was only one kind of FTP production. From 1935 to 1939 the FTP also sponsored classical American dramas, pageants and spectacles, dance drama and musicals, vaudeville, circuses, and puppet shows.

Productions in Yiddish were staged in New York, Boston, Chicago, and Los Angeles, in Spanish in Tampa and Miami, in Italian in the Boston area and New Jersey. Actors performed on street corners as well as in churches, parks, and recreational centers.[25] Not all FTP productions expressed contemporary social concerns—in fact, many of the vaudeville productions presented minstrelsy shows—but activists in the FTP who were committed to social change and equality focused their efforts in this direction. A young midwestern architecture student turned actor, Nicholas Ray, moved from New York's Theatre of Action to the FTP, where he worked with actor, writer, and director Joseph Losey on the 1936 Living Newspaper productions about the crises faced by farmers, *Triple A Plowed Under*, and workers' embattled efforts to organize the Committee for Industrial Organization (CIO), *Injunction Granted*.

Explicitly repudiating the minstrel tradition, Rose McClendon and John Houseman formed the FTP's New York Negro Theatre unit, which mounted thirty productions between 1935 and 1939. These included a production of *Macbeth* set in Haiti, directed by the young Orson Welles, and a play about the slave uprising in Haiti. For a 1938 Chicago FTP production, playwright Shirley Graham directed Theodore Ward's play *Big White Fog*, which debated Garveyism, capitalism, and socialism as black political strategies. Local Negro theater groups in Philadelphia, Chicago, Seattle, Birmingham, and Atlanta also staged plays.[26] When conservatives in Congress began to mobilize a partisan campaign against New Deal labor and interracial radicalism through the Dies Committee hearings into "un-American activities" in the fall of 1938, these socially provocative productions provided obvious targets; the conservatives succeeded in shutting down the FTP in 1939.

POPULAR DEMOCRACY ON THE RADIO

Popular theater generated a desire in its audiences for an immediacy they couldn't find in mainstream radio broadcasting and formula drama. Despite public debate and vocal opposition, commercial control of the airwaves had been institutionalized in the Communications Act of 1934. The combination of popular agitation and the act had prodded the networks to expand their noncommercial, public-service "sustaining" programs; on these shows radio began to capture some of the energy of popular theater. Both government-sponsored and network-supported sustaining programs opened the way for broadcasts that combined news, performance, and social drama. Columbia University first offered a course in writing plays for radio in 1937; by then the FTP was organizing its own radio division. The potential for popular theater on radio to introduce new ordinary American characters was demonstrated by the FTP radio division broadcast of *Waiting for Lefty* in 1938 and its dramatization of Pietro Di Donato's working-class family saga, *Christ in Concrete*, in 1939.[27]

In its announcement of a noncommercial drama series, *Columbia Workshop*, in the winter of 1935–36, CBS invited writers to submit scripts that would explore the particular dramatic properties of radio storytelling, promising them freedom from commercial intervention.[28] Writers who had overlooked radio's social and political possibilities, associating it only with its formulaic genres and commercial penetration, were excited by the chance to experiment with radio's technical possibilities as well as by its potential mass audience. After writing his antifascist "The Fall of the City," broadcast in April 1937, the poet Archibald MacLeish encouraged fellow writers to use radio to speak to "the many instead of the few" as an alternative to publishing "thin little books to lie on parlor tables."[29]

When other acclaimed poets, dramatists, and writers, including Stephen Vincent Benét, Edna St. Vincent Millay, Maxwell Anderson, Dorothy Parker, Irwin Shaw, Pare Lorentz, and James Thurber, contributed their literary prestige to radio, they provided legitimacy for a wide range of left-wing writers and themes. Dramatic performance was enhanced by the use of innovative sound technique and original music, some of which was composed by Bernard Herrmann, before he turned to writing film scores beginning in 1941. Pathways between radio drama and Hollywood film were increasingly well traveled. The early career of Orson Welles provides an example of the cross-fertilization of drama, radio, and eventually film. Welles was interested in exploring how radio's capacity for theatrical illusion could invigorate narrative forms, convey social themes, and warn of the dangers of fascism. Arch Oboler, a radio dramatist known for his horror and science fiction scripts, was also interested in radio drama's political address, writing an anti-Nazi play, "Ivory Tower," for stage and screen actress Alla Nazimova in 1939 and dramatizing Hollywood screenwriter Dalton Trumbo's popular antiwar novel, *Johnny Got His Gun,* in 1940.[30]

Historical pageants on the radio presented an opening for sketches that implicitly condemned fascist political culture by celebrating idealized traditions of American popular democracy. In the years before Pearl Harbor these broadcasts were infused with political meanings. Attempts by the radio industry to regulate political commentary encouraged the networks to produce "morale-building" programs for the home front, drawing on what Michele Hilmes has called "radio's unique nationalizing address" to promote cultural unity in the face of war.[31] Socially concerned writers frequently used references to Lincoln, abolition, and the Civil War in their work. Norman Corwin, a former newspaper movie reviewer who promoted film, edited news, and produced a local poetry show for radio, began work as a producer and director for *Columbia Workshop* in 1938.[32] He arranged portions of Stephen Vincent Benét's 1928 Pulitzer Prize–winning work, *John Brown's Body*, for broadcast in 1939. He worked with the composer Earl Robinson, who had moved with the Workers Laboratory Theatre into the FTP, to adapt Carl Sandburg's *The People, Yes* for *Columbia Workshop* in May 1941.

The *Cavalcade of America*, a show sponsored by DuPont on NBC beginning in 1935, inadvertently provided an opportunity for writers after 1940, and especially after Pearl Harbor, to reorient conventional accounts of American history. Although regulations imposed by corporate sponsors prohibited mention of war, militarism, the labor movement—and, again, African Americans—writers still managed to interject a progressive framework, referring to historical precedents for solidarity across national boundaries as an alternative to isolationism.[33] Dramatists and poets Robert Sherwood, Maxwell Anderson, Carl Sandburg, and Stephen Vincent Benét wrote individual broadcasts. Especially during the war, *Cavalcade*'s regular writers included a roster of radicals.[34]

One of these radicals was playwright Arthur Miller, just embarking on his career. Miller was born in 1915, the child of an illiterate Polish Jewish immigrant father who made and lost a fortune in the women's coat business and a widely read mother born in New York, the daughter of a Jewish clothing contractor from the same part of Poland. In 1928, when Miller was thirteen, his family's economic difficulties forced a move to Brooklyn, where they lived in a succession of smaller houses and where Miller worked as a bread delivery boy. After finishing high school in 1932, he found a job at an auto parts warehouse. Although he describes the family livelihood in the early 1930s as dependent on his mother pawning her last pieces of jewelry, he was able to save for his college tuition, enrolling at the University of Michigan in 1934. At Michigan he gravitated to the burgeoning student movement of 1935 and 1936, covering the electrifying sitdown of General Motors workers in Flint for the *Daily* on New Year's Day,

1937, and driving a friend east to join the Abraham Lincoln Brigade to fight for republican Spain later that spring.[35]

Miller's turn to playwriting was inspired by the upsurge in popular theater in the 1930s. Miller's parents introduced him early to the delights of movies, melodrama, and vaudeville shows, and in his teens he was an aspiring street performer, in his own words "a star comic" who liked to sing "the latest hits," briefly the talent for a local Brooklyn radio show. Retrospectively, Miller comments that he chose theater because it was the "cockpit of literary activity" and because it enabled him to "talk directly to the audience and radicalize the people." His dramatic influences were "one-act protest plays about miners, stevedores, and the like," which he read in left-wing theater magazines. When he returned to New York on vacations, he was "branded by the beauty of the Group Theatre's productions." He was attracted to their explicit left-wing politics, "their challenge to the system," but also to "the sheer physical spectacle of the shows . . . and the special kind of hush that surrounded the actors, who seemed both natural and surreal at the same time." His inspiration was Odets, because of his politics and his language, as "the poet suddenly leaping onto the stage and disposing of middle-class gentility, screaming, yelling, and cursing like someone off the Manhattan streets."[36]

Miller's initial dramatic success cannot be separated from left-wing cultural momentum. He won the Avery Hopwood Award in 1936 for his first play, *The Grass Still Grows*, "about an industrial conflict and a father and his two sons," earning prestige as a playwright and $1,000. Another play about a strike, *Honors at Dawn*, won him a second Hopwood Award in 1937. A revised version of the first play, entitled *They Too Arise*, was performed in 1937 in Detroit by the FTP; it won a national collegiate playwriting award from the Theatre Guild. By 1938 Miller had graduated from college and returned to New York with his girlfriend, Mary Grace Slattery. Although a number of the writers he knew from the *New Masses* were accepting jobs in Hollywood, Miller turned down an offer of a highly paid screenwriting job from Twentieth Century-Fox, working instead for the FTP. Miller briefly joined what he later described as a "Marxist study group in the vacant store open to the street" in his neighborhood in Brooklyn.[37]

Miller wanted to devote himself to becoming a recognized playwright, but it was his break into commercial radio, selling a political satire to *Columbia Workshop*, that gave him the financial security to marry Mary Slattery in August 1940. He began to write biographical dramas for *Caval-*

cade, becoming the "utility man for the show" because he could quickly produce a script based on historical research. Miller chafed against the constraints of writing on assigned topics for commercially sponsored radio, but he needed to support himself and his wife while he was writing other plays. After the war Miller would publicly disparage his work in radio, but at the time he was part of a cohort of left-wing dramatists who were contributing, despite constraints, to the project of radio's cultural front.[38]

The variety format provided another opening that progressives could use to represent their visions of popular democracy, and a few possibilities for African American participation. Topical musical revue was a staple in the labor movement's summer camps and auxiliary entertainments of fraternal organizations. Michael Denning has written about the central role of topical musical revue in musical theater such as Marc Blitzstein's *The Cradle Will Rock* (1937), Harold Rome's *Pins and Needles*, and Duke Ellington's *Jump for Joy* (1941), all of which fused political expression with musical idioms from vaudeville, Tin Pan Alley, and jazz.[39] In the fall of 1939 the head of sustaining programs at CBS asked Norman Corwin to direct a variety program to promote national self-awareness and pride. The CBS announcement read, in part, "PURSUIT OF HAPPINESS will not deal with war or with issues growing out of the war which divide our minds. Instead these new programs . . . will . . . bring us reminders that . . . we Americans still enjoy our constitutional rights to life, liberty, and the PURSUIT OF HAPPINESS." Corwin drew on these precedents as he conceived of the show as an opportunity to celebrate a multiethnic, and on occasion interracial, workingman's democracy.[40]

The first broadcast of *Pursuit of Happiness* in November 1939 signaled the ways in which variety could be politically inflected. In one skit the black comedian Eddie Green played the part of Columbus; another segment celebrated Lincoln. The fourth show's mix included a Hawaiian song, a report on American folklore, and a vignette by literary critic Carl Van Doren on Benjamin Franklin, the subject of his Pulitzer Prize–winning biography. Its culmination was an extraordinary political address—for which the shows' producers had paid twice their normal rate—by the African American sports hero, concert singer, and progressive political activist Paul Robeson. Although Robeson was already an international celebrity, he had until then very little access to prime-time airwaves. Robeson's rendition of "Ballad for Americans" elicited a prolonged and tumultuous standing ovation from the six hundred people in the studio audience.[41]

"Ballad for Americans" is a folk ballad revision of American history that emphasizes an inclusive class, racial, and gendered vision of the people. "American" is represented as "Irish, Negro, Jewish, Italian, French, and English, Spanish, Russian, Chinese, Polish, Scotch, Hungarian, Litvak, Swedish, Finnish, Canadian, Greek and Turk and Czech and double Czech American." In the final choruses the "everybody who's nobody" and the "nobody who's everybody" embrace "engineer, musician, street cleaner, carpenter, teacher, farmer, office clerk, mechanic, housewife, factory worker, stenographer, beauty specialist, bartender, truck driver, seamstress, ditch digger." The song refers explicitly to lynching and champions civil rights as necessary for a democracy whose "greatest songs are still unsung":

> Out of the cheating, out of the shouting,
> Out of the murders and the lynchings,
> Out of the windbags, the patriotic spouting,
> Out of uncertainty and doubting . . .
> Man in white skin can never be free
> While his black brother is in slavery.

Robeson's powerful baritone and his personal and political authority made his rendition of the song an insistent enactment of African American citizenship and a demand for the redemption of democracy's unfulfilled promise.[42]

Despite the excitement generated by Robeson's performance, *Pursuit of Happiness* provided few openings for material produced by blacks. It welcomed the comic routines of a garment worker turned borscht belt entertainer, Danny Kaye, and the talking blues of dustbowl ballad singer Woody Guthrie. But two scripts submitted by the poet Langston Hughes were turned down, including his musical play "The Organizer," deemed "too controversial." Hughes was able to sell a script on the apparently less controversial topic of Booker T. Washington, to be aired April 7, 1940, the day the U.S. Post Office released a stamp with Washington's likeness. Corwin expressed his frustration to the network: he saw the format of the show as "merely a new framework for old and conventional outworn elements." The series ended after some thirty performances on May 5, 1940.[43]

Even before war was declared, various government agencies sponsored radio broadcasts supporting "preparedness"—if, that is, they avoided open political debate and promoted cultural unity. Rachel Davis Du Bois, a white Quaker educator, introduced a twenty-six week series, *Americans All—Immigrants All,* sponsored by the Office of Education and broadcast on CBS in 1938 and 1939. Dramatizing the contributions of immigrant groups to American life, the series included one show on "The Negro," and another on "The Jews of the United States." Gilbert Seldes, the journalist and cultural critic who wrote the scripts, was instructed by network executives to minimize controversy. All the shows were cast within the immigrant framework, as part of a rhetorical strategy to extend the terms of who could be seen as American, blurring the distinction between ethnicity and race and fitting forms of discrimination into a generic problem of exclusion, to be solved by assimilation.[44]

Debates concerning the preparation of and response to *Americans All* suggest the different stakes in representational choices. The African Americans who were consulted—including W. E. B. Du Bois, with whom Rachel Davis Du Bois worked on the NAACP board, the scholar Alain Locke, and the NAACP's Walter White—were pleased to be more visibly represented, although they disagreed about how the program might best do that. In contrast, some Jews worried that being singled out with their own separate show would endanger them by defining them as a race or nation rather than as a religion.[45]

In August 1940 the sole black employee in the Office of Education, Ambrose Caliver, proposed a series of thirteen broadcasts about the contributions of Negroes in American life. Inspired in part by the earlier episodes of *Americans All,* he later suggested that the series be named "We, Too, Are Americans." Caliver's colleagues in the Office of Education secured private funding to prepare the series but found NBC reluctant to broadcast the show until pressed by army officials to carry a special in August of 1941 on "America's Negro Soldiers."

The first segment of the resulting series, *Freedom's People,* broadcast on September 21, 1941, highlighted African American contributions to American music, but in opening and closing comments, and with the special appearance of Paul Robeson, it reiterated the political struggle to claim meaningful freedom for African Americans. Subsequent programs featured other African American entertainers associated with progressive activism, including Josh White, Canada Lee, and the Golden Gate Quartet. Several programs presented African American cultural achievements in the arts, literature, science, and exploration. The programs on athletic achievement, education, military service, and work included critiques of racial inequality and discrimination. According to historian Barbara Savage, *Freedom's People* redefined American culture as being forged by and dependent on black cultural contributions and implicitly argued for a political agenda fostering equal opportunity in order to enrich American democracy. While these cultural interventions clearly did not break the power of segregationists, concerns for national unity and black participation in preparedness began to chip away, temporarily, at the barriers erected against demands for racial equality.

War preparedness continued to legitimate celebrations of ordinary people as the backbone of popular democracy, such as Norman Corwin's historical pageant, "We Hold These Truths," commissioned to mark the 150th anniversary of the Bill of Rights. When the show was broadcast on December 15 to an audience estimated at 60 million, just one week after the attack on Pearl Harbor and the declaration of war, its praise of ordinary citizens, especially citizen-soldiers, was especially powerful. Despite the efforts of *Freedom's People,* however, "We Hold these Truths" did not explicitly include African American soldiers. The *Variety* review of Corwin's pageant noted the way in which radio's appeal for wartime nationalism drew on familiar precedents established "on the screen by Frank Capra, on the stage by Robert Sherwood, in poetry by Carl Sandburg, Stephen Vincent Benét, and Corwin himself."[46] Congressional conservatives challenged these initiatives; after 1940 the Dies-led House Committee on Un-American Activities began to investigate the broadcast industry. In September 1941 Gerald Nye, a prominent isolationist known for his anti-Semitic sentiments, called for Senate investigation into "Moving Picture Screen and Radio Propaganda." But the logic of "preparedness" prevailed, and the hearings were quickly adjourned.[47]

POPULAR DEMOCRACY IN WARTIME: MULTIETHNIC *AND* MULTIRACIAL?

The attack on Pearl Harbor December 7, 1941, and the subsequent declaration of war made radio the critical site for creating national unity and popular support for the war. Writers with culturally and socially expansive views of American democracy were central to this project. Radio was the state's most important medium to mobilize the population in defense of American "freedom"; the themes of popular democracy provided a vehicle to promote a broad conception of American citizenship. Both the Federal Security Agency, within the Office of Education, and the Office of War Information in the War Department produced and distributed radio packages to be aired free on the networks and overseas. The war department organized its own worldwide radio network, the Armed Forces Radio Service in 1942, serving 306 outlets by the end of 1943.

The wartime goals of promoting the military effort were now nearly indistinguishable from the interests of socially concerned writers. This convergence encouraged the "dramatization of political messages" supposedly outlawed by network policy, and blurred the boundaries of partisan social protest, especially for progressives writing for radio. Many warmed to this task; as Norman Rosten wrote, "Propaganda is no longer a literary problem. It is the Idea that fights." Stephen Vincent Benét, whose 1942 radio play "They Burned the Books" dramatically evoked the threat of fascism, spoke for many writers when he wrote, "I am neither afraid nor ashamed of the word propaganda. I am neither afraid nor ashamed of the fact that American writers are speaking out today for a cause in which they believe. I cannot conceive it to be the business of the writer to turn his eyes away from life because the fabric of life is shaken."[48]

The cultural mission of the war blurred the lines between social drama and radio drama. Between 1941 and 1944 popular theater played a key role in maintaining military and domestic morale. Theater troops toured defense plants as well as military bases; soldiers took center stage as subjects, as readers, as authors. The military encouraged soldiers' amateur productions and sponsored servicemen's play-writing contests. College-educated playwrights and writers who served in the military or did war work found themselves unusually well positioned to observe and learn from their potential audiences. The United Service Organizations gave unprecedented opportunities to aspiring soldier performers, at the same time building an audience for theater. Federal Theatre productions, as well as successful musicals such as *Oklahoma* (1944), had accustomed theater audiences to the integration of American folk music into popular theater, bringing mainstream theater closer to the format of noncommercial radio drama and variety. Radio plays, written both inside and outside the military, were well represented among collections of prize-winning plays, with one critic claiming that radio drama had helped to transform dramatic practice, its "free movement" making "acclaimed stage techniques" seem awkward. The social and political slant of much radio drama contributed to the perception that "the most exciting theater productions are those about social problems."[49]

Representational conventions were being established across various media that would be extremely important at war's end. The most common breakthrough was the inclusion of regional and ethnic types as ordinary Americans working side by side in a common project: Brooklyn and Texas, Cohen and Kelly. The melting-pot list of names as a formulaic statement of democratic inclusion circulated widely, surfacing repeatedly in descriptions of *any group* supporting the war, in factories and communities as well as military units. Radio and film representations of soldiers provided the most accessible opportunities to represent citizenship as multiethnic.

But whether an expanded conception of democracy would also accommodate a multiracial citizenry was yet to be decided. Racial segregation was embedded in American life. If the melting pot was only multiethnic, it reinforced segregation, if multiracial, it implied a standard of inclusion beyond the historically segregated military and was antithetical to southern laws and to national de facto practice. Progressive writers aware of racial barriers to citizenship were primarily responsible for efforts to include African American characters as ordinary Americans and to call attention to social and racial inequality, including anti-Semitism, as barriers to the achievement of American promise.[50]

Debates surfaced in black communities in 1940 and 1941 about support of the "white man's war." Despite pressures from African Americans and their allies, the military reasserted its policy to maintain segregation in the armed forces; in practice this meant *expanding* segregation through a wartime enlargement of the military. As a concession to white supremacists, the Red Cross decided to maintain racially segregated blood banks.

In early 1941 mass protest meetings were organized in cities across the country denouncing the restrictions on black employment in the military and the rapidly expanding defense industries and pressing for federal intervention. These culminated in A. Philip Randolph's call in May 1941 for a July Fourth all-black march on Washington to "demand the right to work and fight for our country," building the pressure that finally forced President Roosevelt's executive order 8801 to ban racial discrimination in the defense industries. Black communities continued what became known as the "Double Victory," or Double V, campaign, linking victory in the war with victory against white supremacist segregation. White mainstream opinion viewed this debate and protest as verging on disloyalty, and J. Edgar Hoover's FBI threatened to close down the black newspapers especially active in supporting the Double V campaign.[51] *Freedom's People* segments on the Negro soldier and the Negro worker airing between December 1941 and January 1942 used interview segments with the nation's highest-ranking soldiers and with A. Philip Randolph himself to connect black wartime contributions to the lowering of racial barriers.[52]

Historically, black military participation had fueled claims for full African American citizenship rights, challenging the legal and social arrangements that structured disenfranchisement—with uneven success. Claims for fuller civil rights depended on acknowledging wartime military service as a performance of national citizenship. But national segregation in its many forms impeded such acknowledgment. Black contributions to national military efforts were historically underreported and continued to be so during World War II. Mainstream commercial newsreels were an important source of public information about the war, but they regularly excluded black soldiers. A 1944 survey by the Writers War Board of six hundred newsreel clips found footage of black soldiers in only eighteen. Even the All-American Newsreel, founded in 1942 to serve the black movie theater circuit, featured black participation in only one third of its footage.[53]

The question of whether and how black soldiers were pictured as participating in the melting pot platoon had enormous significance for how military service translated into expanded citizenship rights during, but especially after, the war. The related question of how the war's stated ideological purpose—to defeat Nazi racialism—would translate into the dismantling of American segregation spilled from the military into communities and war industries. Initially, these issues were raised primarily in the context of soldiering and the world of men and thus avoided their potential implications for heterosocial and family life.

REPRESENTING THE SOLDIER

Progressive writers who enlisted or were drafted in the military were glad to be presented with public license to express their antifascist and antiracist political convictions. The radio writer Arnold Perl felt suddenly freed: "I have gotten radio detectives in and out of trouble, scared children and fought straw men on so-called adult programs, but it took a draft board to give me my first chance to write something for radio I didn't mind having my name connected with." Before Pearl Harbor, he commented, "every minor blow sounded for decency and progress on the air" was "like pulling teeth." Now his military work writing for CBS's army series, *Assignment Home,* gave him a chance to dramatize war stories in the language of the battle against fascism, "the most important foe America has ever faced in her history."[54]

Representation of the military platoon as a melting pot provided opportunities on screen and radio to cross ethnic and, less frequently, racial, boundaries, generating striking representations of cosmopolitan and interracial comradeship that challenged prewar conventions and sensibilities. Previously, the melting pot metaphor had not customarily crossed racial lines. Its most common usage before the war implied the Americanization of European immigrants. Most often, the military portrayed in film remained a segregated melting pot.[55]

By the later years of the war, African Americans were more likely to be included in representations of the nation. With the help of progressive screenwriters, wartime films such as *Casablanca* (1942), *Bataan* (1943), *Sahara* (1943), and *Lifeboat* (1944) began to open up spaces for "interracial mingling," especially in combat zones and exotic settings. Office of War Information guidelines encouraged filmmakers to promote the multiethnic and multiracial platoon as a model for national unity, even if those guidelines *exceeded* the practice of military segregation. Thomas Doherty, in his analysis of films made during the war, reveals that "the hyphenated Americans who got the wittiest lines, most extended screen time, and best odds for end-reel survival tended to be prominent in assimilationist success and domestic box office influence—Irish, Italians, and Jews." But the multiethnic platoon also allowed previously unseen peoples— African Americans, Hispanics, Asians, Native Americans—to make appearances.[56]

The radio version of the multiethnic platoon also began including black soldiers—again largely through the efforts of radical writers. The effort to highlight the contributions of black soldiers included a 1943 Mutual Network broadcast, *Fighting Men,* which featured black servicemen relating their wartime experiences. William Robson, a producer of *Columbia Workshop,* also produced the popular 1943 series *Men Behind the Gun,* with one episode dramatizing the true story of an all-black coast guard unit that had sunk six enemy submarines. A 1943 series supported by the Hollywood Writers' Mobilization, *Free World Theatre,* sponsored a drama about black soldiers, "Something About Joe," written by noted black actors Milton Merlin and Clarence Muse and starring Hazel Scott and Lena Horne. In 1944 Norman Corwin, with the help of Langston Hughes, and the African American folk-singer Josh White, produced a network radio drama about the Chicago black navy messman Dorie Miller. In 1941 the navy and the mainstream press had kept quiet on Miller's heroism during the Japanese attack at Pearl Harbor, when Miller, not trained for gunnery, took over the anti-aircraft gun of a dead gunner and shot down four enemy airplanes. Miller was lionized by the black press and eulogized by Langston Hughes precisely because of his provocative challenge to the navy's practices of racial exclusion: "When Dorie Miller took Gun in hand / Jim Crow started his last stand."[57] "Dorie Got a Medal" was broadcast on CBS, featuring Canada Lee, Josh White, and the Golden Gate Quartet.

In a 1944 radio series, *They Call Me Joe,* radical writers tried to promote expanded citizenship in a multiracial democracy, representing the family histories of fictional ordinary servicemen from America's distinct ethnic and racial groups. Its theme song was taken from "Ballad for Americans." The series' writers included Norman Rosten and Morton Wishengrad, who had written for *Cavalcade.* It was broadcast within the U.S. as part of NBC's University of the Air and overseas by Armed Forces Radio Service. The opening line of each program invoked the military melting pot: "My name is José—they call me Joe," or "My name is Giuseppe—they call me Joe," or "My name is Josef—they call me Joe." The final episode asserted the citizenship of Japanese Americans.

By 1944 congressional conservatives were powerful enough to challenge Major Paul Horgan, the producer responsible for the show in the War Department's Information and Education Division. Horgan was asked to defend the use of the theme song (probably because of its links to Robeson and his provocative militancy) and the rhetorical use of "Joe" (suspected to be a coded celebration of Josef Stalin).[58] Nonetheless, the show was broadcast as planned.

The representational terms for racial inclusion remained inconclusive. The 1943 film of an Irving Berlin touring show, *This Is the Army,* its cast constituting one of the army's first integrated units, depicted a largely segregated army and conventional racial and sexual caricature, including a minstrelsy number with minstrels played by white men in blackface, and blackface "mammies" entertaining the troops. Several notable exceptions briefly interrupt these conventions. A quick scene highlights the presence of Sgt. Joe Louis, training for a fight and then being drafted to serve in the army show, along with a small group of black soldiers. A song-and-dance number that follows the minstrelsy exhibition is performed by talented black troops in army khakis, singing about their military conversion in "What the Well-Dressed Man in Harlem Will Wear," against the backdrop of a flamboyantly dressed zoot-suited man and his female companion. This scene has several close-ups of Sgt. Joe Louis and is followed by a jitterbug comedy routine performed by the lead singer and tapper, the black entertainer Jimmy Cross and his drag-gowned partner. The drag performances are constantly interrupted (wigs fall off, chests are bared), minimizing homosexual connotations. The juxtaposition of minstrelsy and military seems intended to reassure audiences that black people serving in the military would not threaten the racial status quo, just as the interrupted drag sketch suggested that an all-male army would not threaten heterosexual norms.[59]

In marked contrast, the wartime film documentary *The Negro Soldier* was shaped by its primary author, the writer and director Carlton Moss, to make every image connect soldiering to the claims of expanded citizenship.[60] Moss had been working throughout the 1930s and early 1940s to give dramatic form to oppositional political visions of racial and social equality.[61] Despite a highly contested scripting process, the film's final version managed to feature many powerful images of black heroism and pride: footage of Joe Louis's defeat of Max Schmeling, triumphant black athletes at the 1936 Berlin Olympics, a powerful montage of black military contributions to American history spanning the period from the American Revolution to the present, and a well-edited tour of army life from the point of view of a black soldier. The film was a virtual enactment of the Double V campaign demanded by the black press and civil rights organizations since early 1942.[62] Moss's strategy was for the film "to ignore what's wrong with the army and tell what's right with my people" in order to get white audiences to ask, "What right have we to hold back a people of that caliber?" The film was initially aimed at black soldiers, but Moss and others fought for broader distribution. The film became required viewing for all GIs; it was also released commercially in the summer of 1944.[63] Meanwhile, the armed forces continued its policy of segregation and the unofficial practice of assigning the most demeaning or demanding jobs to black troops.

The portrayal of blacks in *The Negro Soldier* as representative citizen soldiers contrasted with the popular representation of the "ordinary" soldier—the GI associated with the syndicated columns of the beloved war correspondent Ernie Pyle. Pyle's prewar reputation was based on columns that exuded "homespun wisdom, small-town integrity . . . clear-eyed vision."[64] His characters were more likely to be rural or small-town than city people, white and native born more frequently than either immigrants or African Americans. Pyle's war reporting singled out common foot soldiers for highest praise: "in the end, they are the guys the war can't be won without."[65] His plain, unadorned style and his use of small town, personal details were seen as hallmarks of authenticity.[66] But his columns did not look beyond white Main Street for soldiers who could represent America, and his characters did not puzzle over the war's meaning or purpose.

The differences between Pyle's style of realism and the self-conscious efforts to use the Negro soldier and the melting-pot platoon to dramatize a more expansive and inclusive citizenship were revealed in a 1943 encounter between Pyle and Arthur Miller, who was hired to prepare a screenplay for a film based on Pyle's columns. Miller was concerned that Pyle's columns effectively silenced the antifascist ideological goals of the war; he thought the columns described the war from the front as "a series of essentially disconnected incidents involving millions of men who had few things in common that could be called ideas."[67] Pyle associated praiseworthy common man heroism with *distance* from ideology; his "personal hero" column lionized Frank "Buck" Eversole, ranch hand and cowboy, who "has killed many Germans. . . . Buck Eversole has no hatred for Germans. He kills because he's trying to keep himself alive."[68]

Miller wanted to find soldiers motivated by "the belief that all men are created equal," feeling strongly that they needed to internalize the goal of social equality in order to transform the experience of being part of military units into a sustaining postwar project.[69] Miller ended up quitting the film project, and Pyle died—felled by a sniper's bullet in an island in the Pacific—by the time the 1945 film *The Story of GI Joe* was released. The film's homage to Pyle captured an unusually antiheroic, antiromantic appreciation of GIs, but, once again, the world of its ordinary citizen soldiers was all white.

THE NEW WORLD OF THE HOME FRONT

During the war nonwhite and non-middle-class characters cautiously slipped over from the military into representation of home front communities. As part of the war mobilization, fictional black soldiers crossed the color line on daytime radio. Normally the boundaries of soap opera communities were carefully policed, as NBC *Lone Journey* writers came to understand when their references to African Americans were excised. The writers merited a formal reprimand when they included in a script a comment by a white character that "Negro blood is the same as ours."[70] But at the special request of the War Department popular soap writers and producers Frank and Ann Hummert included a black soldier as a character on one of the most popular daytime serials for women, *Our Gal Sunday,* in the summer of 1942. The Hummerts also introduced a black doctor into their long-running serial, *The Romance of Helen Trent.* He rescues Helen from disaster and with her help finds work as a staff physician in a war factory, occasioning weeks of awkward dialogue on the show about "the capabilities of the Negro, his unflagging loyalty to the country, and his patience with persecution."[71] When the writer and folk singer Millard Lampell was hired to write episodes for *Green Valley USA,* a "patriotic" radio series about an American community at war, he used soap-style narration and music to dramatize problems of racial discrimination.[72]

The insistence by the Double V campaign that mobilization for war would spark confrontations with existing discrimination was to be confirmed when wartime public goals of opposing Nazi fascism broke the enforced broadcast silence surrounding demands for civil rights. After Pearl Harbor Paul Robeson addressed radio audiences not only as an entertainer but also as a representative citizen and statesman. His access had already begun to expand after his success with "Ballad for Americans" on CBS. He was the featured vocalist on another CBS music show, "Kraft Musical Theatre"; in 1940 he served as the producer and host of "Five Songs for Democracy," a program of Spanish songs performed in tribute to the International Brigades who fought in the Spanish Civil War. Speaking at the Labor for Victory rally in May 1943, and later in 1943 at a *Herald-Tribune* forum, Robeson praised efforts by CIO unions to lower racial barriers but warned that these barriers, along with economic uncertainty, restrictions on voting, and segregation in the armed forces, were generating "the bitterest resentment among black Americans." He also spoke on radio at a special program commemorating Lincoln's birthday in 1944 and at a celebration for the opening of the United Nations in April 1945. Here and elsewhere Robeson repeated his message that "the disseminators and supporters of racial discrimination and antagonism . . . are, in fact, first

cousins if not brothers of the Nazis," and he insisted that the black struggle was inextricably connected with "the struggle against anti-Semitism
and against injustices to all minority groups."[73]

When CBS was pressured by Walter White of the NAACP and the
Entertainment Industry Emergency Committee to respond to the Detroit
race riots in June 1943, the network broadcast "An Open Letter on Race
Hatred," written and directed by *Columbia Workshop* director William
Robson. This broadcast drew an analogy between the "kluxers, cowards,
and crackpots" who threatened African Americans in Detroit and the
"gangs of German youth armed with beer bottles and lead pipes" who had
supported Hitler's rise to power. A postscript to the program came from
Wendell Willkie, utilities magnate and 1940 Republican presidential candidate, who had been forced to consider American "racial complacency"
during his meetings with leaders in emerging nations in Asia and Africa.
Willkie exhorted audiences to recognize that "all the forces of fascism are
not with our enemies" and must be eliminated "at home as well as
abroad."[74]

Discussion of racial injustice was still far from routine on radio. "An
Open Letter on Race Hatred" placed Robson under scrutiny from the network. William Paley, the head of CBS, had personally to approve the
broadcast before it went on the air and required Robson to produce several versions. Affiliates were given an opportunity to hear the program
before it was aired and could elect not to broadcast it, which a number of
southern stations did.

Langston Hughes's access to radio also expanded, if unevenly. CBS
Radio broadcast a half-hour adaptation of "Jubilee," his unproduced
work written for a Negro Emancipation celebration, in September 1941.
After Pearl Harbor Hughes was asked by the Office of Civilian Defense for
a script to commemorate Lincoln's birthday. "Brothers," which racialized
Roosevelt's Four Freedoms (freedom of speech and worship, freedom
from want and fear) through the story of a black sailor coming home from
duty, was immediately rejected as too provocative. In the spring of 1942
Hughes's song "Freedom Road" was sung on a *March of Time* broadcast
in which Hughes also had a brief role. His radio play "John Henry Ham-
mers It Out," starring Robeson, was broadcast in New York in June 1943.

Hughes was the only black author on the War Writers Board (WWB)
who was significantly involved in radio work. "In the Service of My Country," his play commissioned by the WWB about interracial cooperation in
the building of the Alaska-Canada highway during the war, was broadcast

in September 1943. But "Private Jim Crow," dramatizing the humiliations of black soldiers in the army, was "placed on a high shelf." Hughes's most direct public address involved his participation on the first interracial broadcast, "Let's Face the Race Question," on the NBC radio debate program *America's Town Meeting of the Air* on February 17, 1944. Hughes's private commentary underscored the racial restrictions of radio: "I DO NOT LIKE RADIO and I feel that it is almost as far from being a free medium of expression for Negro writers as Hitler's airlanes are for the Jews."[75]

An exceptional moment when African American progressives gained access to local radio illuminated the possibilities for multidimensional racial characterization, performance of citizenship, and critique of racism ordinarily invisible and off-limits in mainstream broadcasting. *New World A-Coming*, a New York program unaffiliated with any of the major networks, began weekly broadcasts in March 1944.[76] The WMCA Sunday afternoons series on "Negro life" used the title and drew on the political framework articulated by journalist and activist Roi Ottley in his compelling descriptions of race experience and politics in Harlem, published in 1943. Ottley drew on materials collected by the Negro unit of the New York Federal Writers Project when he served as its director, and his wide-ranging book challenged racial categories by describing contemporary Harlem's diverse peoples of color, including Muslims, West Indians, French-speaking Haitians, Spanish-speaking Cubans and Puerto Ricans, black Jews, East Indians, and Chinese. Ottley celebrated Harlem's distinct cultural expressions, from rent parties and blues clubs to the Hamilton Lodge of Odd Fellows' drag ball. Ottley also dismissed equations of identity with political orientation, analyzing a broad spectrum of race-conscious politics in Harlem, from Marcus Garvey's Universal Negro Improvement Association to Father Divine's Peace Mission, A. Philip Randolph's March on Washington Movement, the NAACP, Mary McLeod Bethune and the National Council for Negro Women to Max Yergen and the National Negro Congress. Ottley's book was framed by the notion that the war and ensuing anticolonial insurgencies throughout the world were advancing the fight for racial equality.[77]

New World A-Coming relied on a variety format as well as a hybrid documentary drama form to convey its political messages. Many of the black performers on the show were publicly identified with resisting racial injustice. Duke Ellington composed the theme song; the show featured performances by concert singer Marian Anderson, actors Canada Lee,

Muriel Smith, and Hilda Simms, jazz pianist and singer Hazel Scott, and blues singers Billie Holiday and Josh White. Canada Lee became increasingly involved with the series, serving as narrator and also acting in many of the dramatic productions. The February 10, 1945, show, also broadcast nationally, honored Lee for his Broadway success as Bigger Thomas in the play adapted from Richard Wright's 1940 novel, *Native Son*. The tribute was hosted by Paul Robeson, who sang a protest of Jim Crow (written, he said, "in the spirit of *Native Son*"); singer and actress Hattie McDaniel and comic actor Eddie Anderson presented a comedy skit; Bill "Bojangles" Robinson did a live tap dance; the show also included musical performances by Duke Ellington and W. C. Handy, a telegram from Joe Louis, on-air congratulations from Richard Wright, and a scene from the play.

Other *New World* shows used the news magazine/documentary drama format to protest the obstacles facing African American performers ("Negroes in the Entertainment Industry"). They also drew attention to housing discrimination in war industry cities ("Hot Spots USA"), and linked racial segregation in the United States to its international colonial counterparts ("Apartheid in South Africa"). As on *March of Time*, historical events were restaged dramatically, sometimes including key participants: Adam Clayton Powell Jr. played himself as a minister on a program called "The Vermont Experiment," about a church project that arranged summer visits from black children in Harlem to white farm families in Vermont.

Obstacles to racial equality provided the climax for original drama written for the show. Roi Ottley intended his script "The Negro Domestic" to challenge white fantasies of the "Mammy legend," the most common characterization of African American women. As Ottley wrote in the narration, "Yes, it is true that Mammy doesn't live here anymore." In the play a black domestic worker's son, serving in the armed forces and training to be a pilot, questions the white employer family's confidence in segregation. His mother, their hired worker, finds the family's attempted defense of racial separation so insulting that she quits to work in a war factory. Dramatic adaptations of fiction also appeared, including one based on Dorothy Parker's short story about white misconceptions of black culture, "Arrangements in Black and White," and a two-part version of Howard Fast's novel of the embattled African American achievements of Reconstruction, *Freedom Road* (1944).[78] *A New World A-Coming* provided an expansive model of radio's potential for new forms of progressive political address to convey a multiracial democratic citizenship.

Most of the time, the ordinary people formulation remained stubbornly resistant to signifying a racially egalitarian citizenship. When the testimonies of common people (actually written by Norman Corwin and Millard Lampell, according to Lampell) were broadcast on an election-eve radio special paid for by the Democratic National Committee for Roosevelt's reelection, those people were all white. They included an Italian American member of the National Maritime Union from the Bronx, a female clerical worker from the CIO Union of Office and Professional Workers, and a brakeman from New York who was a member of the Brotherhood of Railroad Trainmen. A Tennessee farmer touted the accomplishments of the Tennessee Valley Authority; a housewife and mother from Michigan spoke up for price controls and rationing. A disabled veteran and a World War I navy man who had been part of the 1932 Bonus March of unemployed vets added their endorsements.[79]

Only one African American voice briefly pierced the silence: distinguished actor Clarence Muse joined Earl Robinson to sing, with an interracial call and response pattern, a song connecting antifascism with antiracism. The song, "Free and Equal Blues" placed medical science behind UN internationalism and anticolonialism ("the Atlantic Charter") to mock the racial certainties of the segregated blood bank: "Aryans . . . trying to disunite us with racial supremacy" were "flying in the face of old man chemistry." The song threw the authority of world leaders (Roosevelt, Churchill, Stalin, Eden, Hull, and Litvinov) behind the doctor's pronouncement: "Every man, everywhere is the same / When he's got his skin off."[80] The musical announcement of the "news" that its association with Nazism had discredited racialism was, unfortunately, a lone voice in the broadcast.

SOLDIERS AS VETERANS: IMAGINING THE POSTWAR WORLD

As the end of the war in Europe came into view and emphasis shifted from war to a postwar world, civilians were encouraged to sympathize with the problems of readjustment that returning soldiers would face. Women's "work" was represented as private nurture; the veteran looking for a job was almost always personified as a white male. The fight during the war to have black soldiers acknowledged did not translate into a postwar recognition of black vets. The War Department rejected a script on the employment problems of African American veterans written for a "veteran readjustment" series on CBS, *Assignment Home,* as not a "military" matter,

despite protests by the black press and the NAACP. A radio script dramatizing the peaceful acceptance of a black vet as a machinist in a postwar
factory that had never before employed African Americans in skilled factory jobs, written by Erik Barnouw for the American Negro Theatre in
association with the National Urban League, was similarly rejected for an
Armed Forces Radio Service (AFRS) series. Although the show had
already been broadcast locally in New York City and accepted by the War
Department, it was barred from reaching a wider audience by a colonel at
the AFRS Hollywood office who destroyed the master recording copy,
fuming that "no nigger-loving shit goes out over this network."[81] His reaction, while not universal, foreshadowed the intensity of the racial struggles
that would erupt after the war.

Sgt. Millard Lampell's radio dramas for an army air corps series, *First in
the Air*, which sought to prepare GIs and their families for coming home,
illustrate the limits of conscious efforts to broaden the category of military
heroes to include nonwhite soldiers. Lampell's dramas focused on how
wounded vets could be reintegrated after the war; two scripts called attention to the wounds of racial discrimination. "The Boy from Nebraska,"
about the Japanese American tailgunner Ben Kuroki, juxtaposed his personal heroism with wartime internment and incidents of anti-Japanese
harassment in California, Arizona, Oregon, and New Jersey; it won a
Writers' War Board Award and a citation from the U.S. War Relocation
Authority. "Case History" was the profile of a heroic pilot in the African
American Ninety-Ninth Fighter Squadron in Italy.

Lampell hoped that the aural, nonvisual qualities of radio's medium
would establish these soldiers' Americanness in the ears of listeners. In his
stage directions Lampell suggested that Kuroki's part be read in a "quiet
plain Midwest American" accent, and that American folk tunes be played
in a minor key after each incident of racial prejudice. Similarly he suggested that the African American character, Ashborn, have no special
accent in order that "the audience does not know the central character is
a Negro until quite late in the play," although he noted that the details—
family history, the poem Ashborn remembers, his first experience of flying—"were especially significant because they were happening to a
Negro."[82] Lampell's logic provides an example of what Hilmes identifies
as "a rhetoric of inclusion deployed strategically that *denies* racial distinction in favor of a transcendent democratic national identity." This rhetoric coexisted with a "discourse of fear that *depends* upon racial distinction
to motivate white participation."[83] Without the conscious intervention of

progressive writers, racially marked characters would have remained out-side the boundaries of citizenship.

The obstacles to representing ordinary returning soldiers as black, or to using black veterans to represent postwar citizens, inadvertently encour-aged a turn toward the disabled vet—who was symbolically, if not socially, less challenging than the black vet—and was the central character in some scripts of the CBS series *Assignment Home*. The absence of the visual from radio made it particularly well suited to dramatize physical disability; radio's special ability to "suggest rather than describe" gave it the poten-tial to elicit sympathy among civilians for veterans with shattered faces or missing limbs. The physical disability of the soldier could also serve widely accepted ideological purposes, as a reminder of "the price American man-hood paid to stop the German-Japanese conspiracy against decency."[84]

A progressive writer could try to portray the disabled veteran as stand-ing for all those threatened by fascism. After all, Hitler's version of Nazi eugenics had singled out physical disability as a threat to the Aryan nation. When Lampell received his final army assignment to write a radio play for national broadcast to commemorate the end of the war, he had just come from observing a plastic surgery ward in an army hospital. His radio play "October Morning" was narrated by Dave, a disabled veteran and a rural American "everyman," directed by the script to speak for, and in solidar-ity with, all those threatened by fascism. Dave begins his wartime elegy by remembering his close country friend Hank, who had gone to fight fas-cism with the International Brigade in Spain and died in Madrid. He next relives the moment he and his buddy Irv Friedman recited the Kaddish, the traditional Jewish prayer for the dead, when burying their fallen buddy McGee, lost in the battles in Normandy. He then salutes the heroism of Negro troops of the Thirty-Third Field Artillery, and finally mourns the Jewish, Catholic, and Communist victims of the German concentration camp at Belsen.[85]

In other treatments the disabled veteran was used to substitute for vic-tims of other forms of prejudice to demonstrate how victims' problems could be solved by psychiatry. In a prize-winning *Assignment Home* script, "The Face," and in "The Last Day of the War," broadcast twice over ABC, radio writer Sergeant Arthur Laurents's developing interests in psycho-analysis reformulated the way he narrated the social problems that return-ing vets could expect to face.[86] Laurents imagined the disabled veteran as a victim of psychologically driven prejudice. Profoundly hurt by the underestimation of his capabilities as a person, he is eventually healed by medical and psychiatric professionals, ultimately refusing to be embittered by others' views of him, and regaining confidence in his manhood. In Laurents's radio plays the emphasis on psychological barriers and encouragement for disabled vets popularized a psychological framework for resisting fascist and racist categorization, using the powers of self-imagining to will away racialist thinking and, by extension, racialist barriers. The plays proposed this psychological insight as a potential basis for solidarity among the victims of prejudice.[87]

The character of the disabled vet stands out clearly in Hollywood's most widely viewed treatment of postwar readjustment, the 1946 hit film *The Best Years of Our Lives*. Director William Wyler cast Harold Russell, a disabled veteran himself, in the role. *The Best Years of Our Lives* represented the disabled vet as an everyman returning to "Small Town USA."[88] The plot surrounding the disabled vet and his two buddies presented the important divisions between them as those of age and prewar class position. Rather than calling attention to the kinds of institutionalized discrimination confronting many returning vets or the unresolved racial and social issues stirred up by the war, the film portrays the problems of readjustment primarily in terms of heterosexual relationships and appropriate employment in the postwar economy. These could be neatly resolved, at least in narrative terms, by securing girls and jobs in the final reel.[89] Although unusually attentive to social and historical setting, the film *excluded* some of the more provocative, "better-sharpened social conflicts" intensified by the war, particularly by keeping its ordinary vets unmarked by race or ethnicity and allowing them to be healed by female nurture and cross-class reconciliation rather than postwar social change.[90]

The new social drama developed in the service of popular wartime democracy chipped away at the primacy of racial and ethnic caricature, dialect humor, and minstrelsy. The "Negro soldier" and the "melting-pot platoon" presented serious challenges to the implicit whiteness in definitions of American manhood and the ordinary GI, but a more genuine cosmopolitanism that crossed race lines competed with a multiethnic cosmopolitanism that maintained firm racial boundaries and, in doing so, upheld segregationist ideals. In the last months of the war there were already indications of profound opposition to extending even these limited new characterizations to postwar society. Especially charged was the social transformation inherent in moving from the public and crisis-legitimated homosocial world of the military to the presumed heterosociability of everyday life and the return to the supposedly private and contained sexuality of the domestic realm and the family.

The next chapters explore a surprisingly popular kind of wartime family story. Looking-back stories, for the first time, attended to and imagined working-class ethnic families, and especially women, as central to the survival of the nation. These stories offered a version of the immigrant past unfiltered through radio and film ethnic humor or exoticism, or 1930s-styled proletarian outrage. Two first novels by previously unknown authors—dramatist and radio writer Betty Smith's *A Tree Grows in Brooklyn* and radio writer Kathryn Forbes's *Mama's Bank Account*—created a new genre of "family realism" that proposed the daily losses and gains of hard-working children of working-class and immigrant parents as the universal American experience. Operating both within and against wartime conventions of representing black soldiers, military melting pot platoons, and ordinary GIs, these stories help set the stage for a postwar American order.

LOOKING BACK
STORIES

2

MAKING THE WORKING-CLASS FAMILY
ORDINARY: *A TREE GROWS IN BROOKLYN*

IN AUGUST 1943 THE PUBLICATION OF A FIRST NOVEL BY AN UNKNOWN AUTHOR caused a sensation.[1] An immediate best-seller, Betty Smith's *A Tree Grows in Brooklyn* was chosen as a Literary Guild selection and reprinted as a special armed services edition distributed to overseas soldiers, who generated enough demand for an unprecedented second printing in pocket format.[2] The book became part of a broad public conversation: Parent Teacher Associations, neighborhood groups, and women's clubs sponsored discussions of it; libraries reported that *Tree* was their most frequently requested book; ministers made reference to it in sermons. The press even covered the novel's popularity as news, reporting on an enthusiastic reading of it by a mob kingpin on his way to Death Row. By 1945 the book had sold three million copies.[3]

Smith set her story far from the home front, in the years between 1912 and 1918; but her depiction of poverty and scarcity—both resolved by wartime employment—struck a chord in 1943. The novel sketches the daily lives of a working-class Brooklyn family, the Nolans: Katie, the mother who scrubs hallways and steps to keep food on the table; Johnny, the father, a singing waiter who likes his drink too much and is only intermittently employed; their dreamy bibliophile daughter, Francie, whose coming of age frames the book; and her young brother, Neeley.[4] The novel opens when Francie is eleven, helping her brother collect papers, clothes, and bottles to sell to the junk man; it closes when Francie, now seventeen, leaves Brooklyn on her way to a midwestern university. Katie's unlettered immigrant mother, Mary Rommely, has taught Katie how to hoard pennies and instructed her to read the Bible and Shakespeare to the children. Katie's sister, Sissy, also untaught, has married often, without the benefit of divorce, but her presence makes things "gay and glamorous."

Reviewers hailed *A Tree Grows in Brooklyn* as an "authentic" and "realistic" treatment of a tenement child's coming of age, without the degradation presumed to be the lot of the poor in naturalistic fiction. The *New Yorker* critic appreciated the novel as "a welcome relief from writing about slum folk as if they were all brutalized morons." The confidence in upward mobility implicit in the novel marked a turn from 1930s proletarian fiction and documentary-style reporting informed by social protest; the *New York Times* reviewer, Orville Prescott, praised *Tree* for *not* being a "sour, sordid, sociological report," precisely because Smith "finds the great American epic of upward progress toward education, freedom, self-respect, and accomplishment still going on."[5]

Other reviewers commented upon *Tree*'s departure from the ethnic humor of radio formula drama: its depiction of family life in the tenements was not "grim" or "sappily sentimental" or "determinedly humorous," but was written "without recourse to treacle." A Providence, Rhode Island reviewer noted: "The Nolan family would have been listed among the sadly underprivileged in the case records of most communities. There was a zest for living, a joy in family concerns, a color and warmth in the Nolan home, however, which even in times of abject poverty and gnawing hunger kept it from being a center of affliction." When Orville Prescott included the book in his "Outstanding Novels" column for the *Yale Review*, he remarked that "the terrible misery, squalor, and grinding poverty of their lives are here in their unsavory detail" but that Smith also "has the vision to know that loyalty and laughter and accomplishment and pride are also part of slum life, something too many writers forget."[6] *Tree*'s deviation from family melodrama made it seem more real: "It's a plotless story, in the way that life itself never seems to offer much in the standard notions of plot," offering instead what another reviewer called "the stringing together of memory's beads."[7]

Many reviewers assumed autobiographical links between Smith and Francie, as promotional blurbs stressing the author's Brooklyn origins encouraged them to do. The *New York Times*'s Brooklyn-born reviewer, whose familiarity with Smith's Williamsburg neighborhood enabled him to recognize the candy store owner and the junk dealer by name, challenged the "publisher's decision to call the book a novel." Florence Hax-ton Bullock, writing for the *New York Herald-Tribune Weekly Book Review,* "suspects (and hopes)" that Francie "must have been" Smith. Far-ther away, the Oakland *Tribune* reviewer was convinced that "here is the stuff of actual memory." Many readers consistently assumed Francie was Smith, and even addressed their letters to her "Dear Francie."[8]

Betty Smith had in fact originally submitted her manuscript to Harper and Brothers for its 125th Anniversary Non-Fiction Contest; the editors had suggested to her that the material be reworked as a novel. In the 1940s the memoir was considered a polite and elite form of instructional litera-ture, while working-class life was the stuff of popular entertainment. In 1943 when Jerre Mangione, a college-educated journalist associated with the Federal Writer's Project guidebook series, wrote an account of his life in the Sicilian immigrant community of Rochester, New York, the pub-lisher, Houghton Mifflin, insisted on releasing it as fiction because their sales department predicted it would sell more copies in that form. Man-gione agreed only to fictionalize the names of the characters, and the book appeared simultaneously on the *New York Times* best-selling fiction list and the *New York Herald-Tribune*'s nonfiction list.[9]

Once *Tree* became a best-seller and Smith a public figure, she was anx-ious to distinguish between her character and her life. She worried about the social costs of being identified with the working-class background she had described. Her mother objected to being linked to the book's descrip-tions of poverty and frank sexuality. Smith sought to distance herself from her characters: "We were poor, but always comfortable." She was also concerned about the social costs to her daughters, growing up in North Carolina. As she wrote to her editor, it wouldn't do her children "any good socially" to be connected with Francie's background.[10]

Smith's few contemporary comments about her manuscript indicate that she was aware of creating memories and, through her writing, con-structing a particular vision of the past. When she tried to pitch the novel (before it had been accepted by a publisher) to the fiction editor at MGM, Smith suggested that it could be handled like *How Green Was My Valley,* "as the history of a place and of a certain time." Or, she proposed, "the story might follow Johnny Nolan, the singing waiter. It's about Brooklyn in the great Tammany days, and goes from about 1900 to 1916."[11] As she described her method of writing, she admitted to having elided different historical experiences. Katie was based partly on herself; Francie was a composite of her mother's and her own childhoods, along with contemporary observations (she noted to her publishers that the incident in which Francie encounters a neighborhood man who tries to molest her was based on a news item in a July 1942 newspaper).[12] In interviews, she credited Thomas Wolfe's *Of Time and the River* (1935) as her literary inspiration, with its thick description and impassioned characterization. Early notes for the novel were scribbled into her copy of Wolfe's novel. Although Smith never mentioned it publicly, her daughter later recalled Henry Roth's 1934 modernist novel of the ghetto, *Call It Sleep,* as a work that had given her mother "permission" to write *Tree.*[13]

FROM WORKING-CLASS DAUGHTER
TO WORKING-CLASS WRITER

Betty Wehner was born in Brooklyn in 1896, the eldest of three children of American-born parents, John Wehner and Katherine Hummel. Betty Smith later described their origins in an autobiographical fragment: "He was American-born Irish and she was American-born German." Her mother's parents, who had emigrated from Germany as a young married couple, had both died by the time Smith was twelve. Her father's family had been in the United States since the Civil War, but Smith knew much less about them: "They have always been a mystery to me."[14]

Her childhood resembled that of many other working-class children in Brooklyn at the turn of the last century, with the exception of her scholastic success and the economic instability connected with her father's failure to support the family. Betty Wehner had published several articles in the Bushwick School Bulletin, but her father's economic decline had already begun; her full-time education ended with her graduation from grammar school in 1911.[15] The friends who signed her autograph album suggest the mixture of ethnicities in her Brooklyn neighborhood: Dora Helowitz, Joseph Glazer, Elizabeth Barth, Martha Goldstein, Frances Mazzeo, Martha Friedlander, Olga Eisenmann, A. H. Morris, Mrs. Glazer, Harry Wetherbee, Mary Spinelli.[16]

For the next few years Betty Wehner did what was expected of working-class daughters: she went to work to help support her mother and the younger children, holding the factory, office, and retail jobs a young girl could find in Brooklyn and Manhattan. She came into contact with the efforts of middle-class social reform at the Jackson Street Settlement House, where she taught sewing, learned to dance, and acted in plays.

Between 1915 and 1917 Betty worked at night and attended high school at Girl's High School in Brooklyn, where she was editor of the school paper. When in 1918 her mother married an Irish immigrant, Michael Keough, Wehner was working for the post office (a well-paid job for which she had given up high school), where she edited the weekly newspaper of the mail order department. For the first time in her working life, she was able to keep her wages and to spend them on herself.

In 1919 Betty Wehner's life took a decisive turn. She left Brooklyn for Ann Arbor, Michigan, where she married George Smith, who was also born in Brooklyn and had enrolled in law school at the University of Michigan. Leaving Brooklyn represented a break from working-class jobs, neighborhood, and family responsibilities. For the young couple, paying George's tuition and supporting themselves was a struggle they assumed would eventually lead to middle-class social and economic security.

Ann Arbor in the 1920s offered a landscape of class aspiration and cultural change profoundly different from that of Williamsburg, Brooklyn. Wehner and Smith's marriage was "modern," entered into by two individuals without consent of family, unsanctified by religion or tradition. As George later wrote to Betty, "I have no recollection of refusing your mother to marry you in the Catholic church. As I recall, you and I were married on our own in Ann Arbor by the handiest official, and there was no thought of church either way. It was some time after that we let the families know we had married."[17] Betty worked briefly in Ann Arbor and attended high school there, again serving as editor of the school newspaper. Her husband finished law school, passed the bar, and developed a successful law practice in a small town as well as in Detroit, cultivating political connections and working for a time as a secretary to the League of Nations.

In contrast to her husband's widening opportunities, Smith's world was limited to the care of her two daughters, born in 1922 and 1924. In an early essay she describes how "marriage with its consequent child-bearing and rearing and house isolation" left her "imprisoned with petty problems, often unresolvable, mental isolation, and physical and mental fatigue."[18] When the family moved back to Ann Arbor in 1927, Betty finally managed, despite her lack of a high school diploma, to attend lectures at the University of Michigan. The university had a nursery school for the children, and Smith audited journalism, literature, and playwriting classes. She began selling recipes to the *Detroit Free Press,* and was later appointed assistant editor of the women's page.

Smith's early essays and articles suggest her awareness of the obstacles she faced as a self-educated and struggling woman writer. She was particularly interested in exposing sexual hypocrisy and in opening up public discussion of sexual mores.[19] She also began to write plays, several of which were published in anthologies or produced on campus. She won the prestigious Avery Hopwood Award in 1930 for a play about the breakup of a marriage. Francie Nolan first appeared as a character in an early play, as a young girl working in a department store whose father beats her and kicks her out of the family when she becomes pregnant by the store-owner's son, whom she hopes to marry.

Smith enrolled as a special student in the privileged circle around George Baker at the Yale Drama School in the fall of 1931. Separated from her husband in 1932, Smith moved with her daughters to New York City in 1934. In the process of getting a divorce, Smith's economic position was again precarious. Her resources included education, alimony, and child support; but she and her children relied on what she could earn as a writer. According to Smith's daughter Nancy, "Food and writing were always associated with Mother, perhaps because the writing was responsible for our food."[20]

Trying to earn money by writing brought Smith in contact with a variety of forms of cultural production, from amateur community dramatics to the burgeoning mass culture industries to government-sponsored theater. Between 1934 and 1936 she wrote "confession stories" for two to five cents a word for *Modern Romance*.[21] She also worked in summer stock, on radio, and as a playreader and editor, finally securing more steady work as a proofreader and actress for the FTP. Work connected with the FTP took her to Chapel Hill, North Carolina in 1936, where she and actor and fellow Yale Drama student Robert Finch won playwriting fellowships, wrote a weekly radio script, and cowrote one-act plays for amateur productions. Smith worked on an unproduced Living Newspaper play about southern migrant laborers entitled "King Cotton." She also edited collections of one-act plays and unsuccessfully tried to sell some to Warner Brothers in 1940.

With her divorce finalized in 1939, the future of the FTP uncertain, and amateur theater productions in wartime disarray, Smith decided to try to write a salable novel. In 1941 and 1942 she returned to material she had been working on for years, mining it for the scenes that would later come together in *A Tree Grows in Brooklyn:* short stories from the early 1930s, "Death of a Singing Waiter" and "It Could Only Happen in Brooklyn," and a one-act play, *Fun After Supper.*[22] Seven publishers rejected her manu-script: "Nobody was interested in Brooklyn, they said. The poor we always have with us, they told me. People want to get away from the poor. Nobody will read a novel about two growing kids, I was assured."[23] Elizabeth Lawrence, one of the first female editors at Harper and Brothers, was also the first to recognize the book's potential and began to work with Smith to shape the sprawling manuscript into its eventual best-selling form.[24]

REVISING 1930s RADICAL VISIONS

Betty Smith spent a number of years publicly representing the New Deal as part of the FTP; many of her one-act plays popularized New Deal ver-sions of history in the spirit of the Lincoln myth, connecting ordinary peo-ple with the progress of democracy.[25] Her fiction of tenement life incor-porates imagery popularized in Depression-era documentary-style writing and film, with many references to "the people" and "the people" as "survivors."[26] "There's a tree that grows in Brooklyn . . . which strug-gles to reach the sky." It grows even "out of cement" and "survives with-out sun, water, and seemingly without earth." Francie Nolan begins her observations by describing this tree that grew "only in the tenement dis-tricts . . . it liked poor people." At the end of the novel the tree still stands, despite attempts to cut it down and burn out the stump: "It lived! And nothing could destroy it."[27] The tree metaphor offered an urban counter-part to John Ford's 1940 film version of *The Grapes of Wrath,* which closes with Ma Joad's praise of farmworkers: "Rich fellas come up, an' they die, an' their kids ain't no good, an' they die out. But we keep a'comin.' We're the people that live. Can't wipe us out. Can't lick us. We'll go on forever, Pa, because we're the people."[28] Letters from readers to Betty Smith expressed delight with the tree metaphor and its celebration of the spirit of everyday people.[29]

Smith's working-class Brooklyn represents an important departure, however, from prewar dreams of labor solidarity and interracialism. Smith signals her disaffection from radical rhetoric when her heroine tries to express thoughts about injustice. Francie proclaims: "Intolerance is a thing that causes war, pogroms, crucifixions, lynchings, and makes people cruel to little children and to each other. It is responsible for most of the viciousness, violence, terror, and heart and soul breaking of the world." She then dismisses her own language as sounding "like words that came in a can; the freshness was cooked out of them."

After the book's publication, Smith described her style as "realism, without the all-out condemnation of the ordinary virtues of home and family. . . . Honestly I believe there is a new era in writing coming up—realism without sneering."[30] A number of readers who wrote to Smith also categorized the book's genre as distinct from protest fiction. One middle-class woman commented, "Poverty has been written about before, but never with such tenderness, and lack of bitterness, and such unfailing good humor." Other readers remarked on its "realism not determinedly sordid, but shot with hope," preferring it to James T. Farrell's *Studs Lonigan* (1935) and John Steinbeck's *Grapes of Wrath* (1939).[31]

The most powerful force for social betterment imagined in the novel is not CIO solidarity, collective bargaining, and hard-won social insurance programs, but self-help and self-improvement. The narrative details bargaining strategies to stretch precious pennies, the emotional pain of scarcity, the difficult choice between maintaining pride and accepting charity. Francie moves toward the middle class through hard work, careful saving, and public education. Smith describes the Nolan family as "individualist"; they "conformed to nothing except what was essential to their being able to live in their own world." When they finally are able to leave their railroad tenement, they take pride in having made it on their own.[32] This was an aspect of the novel commonly applauded by reviewers; one reader complained, however, that the devices required to deliver "happiness . . . on a silver platter" made the last chapters "less true."[33]

Smith acknowledges collective strategies such as labor organizing, but they ultimately prove useless to her characters. Johnny Nolan proudly wears his union membership button; after his death the family "sought the union label on everything they bought" as their memorial to him. But union solidarity—exemplified by Johnny's many hours at the union headquarters waiting in vain for work, and by the union's elaborate bouquet at his funeral proclaiming him a "brother"—does not compensate for his dramatic expulsion from the union following an alcoholic binge the week before. One middle-class reader who had only seen Brooklyn as a "tourist" was surprised by this aspect of the book's philosophy about the "poor": previously she had assumed that the poor "stick together."[34]

Smith's distance from collective strategies also shapes her depiction of relief, which she presents as a demeaning form of charity rather than a social entitlement. She sees burial and death insurance—a popular provision of immigrant mutual aid societies and one of the key attractions of corporate and state-provided insurance—as a cruel exploitation of the poor. A man from Springfield, Vermont wrote to say that he understood the author to prefer individual efforts to social remedies; he "and his lady" had both read the book and had decided that Smith demanded "an understanding of difficulty and a salute to courage—rather than the extension of charity and reform."[35]

REMEMBERING A WORKING-CLASS PAST

Smith's effort to render a distinctly working-class past through "looking back" was especially appealing to readers from working-class backgrounds. Reader after reader responded with pleasure to Smith's evocation of detailed sensory memories: the color of bricks in the school wall, the smell of fresh ground coffee, the sound of hot rye bread flaking, the salty taste of a pickle. Brooklyn readers, including the Brooklyn-born *New York Times* reviewer, were especially delighted by Smith's use of street names, description of neighborhood shops, and details of childhood games. One reader wrote that so many episodes in the book were reminiscent of her childhood in Brooklyn in the 1920s and 1930s that they substituted for her own past: "I think they happened to me and I sometimes forget they are not my own memories." Many readers felt their own childhoods in poor neighborhoods in other eastern and midwestern industrial cities were fully described in Smith's Brooklyn story. A naval officer wrote that "your book so accurately described my sister and mine [*sic*] youth growing up in the Chicago slums that our spontaneous letters to each other urging its reading crossed in the Pacific."[36]

Several of the working-class readers who wrote to Smith mentioned similarities between their own experiences and the incidents in the book when family poverty elicited scorn and humiliation from other children, teachers, patronizing doctors, and social workers.[37] The children in *Tree* are not scarred by these hurts; instead, they are prepared to move upward without having to deny their past. One reviewer's plot summary called attention to this distinctive aspect of Francie's trajectory: "A slum-bred girl rises above her environment mainly because she has the courage not to feel ashamed of it. . . . Tormented and humiliated, but resilient, she wants a better life and finds it, without becoming hardened in the process."[38]

Establishing the novel as forum of public remembering, Smith juxta-poses middle-class contempt for the poor with working-class pride in self and history. In an exchange between Francie and her English teacher over the proper subject for literature, the teacher insists that stories depict "truth" and "beauty," dismissing Francie's family history as "sordid."

> Drunkenness is neither truth nor beauty. It's a vice. Drunkards belong in jail, not in stories. And poverty. There's no excuse for that. There's work enough for all who want it. People are poor because they're too lazy to work . . .
> (imagine mama lazy!)
> . . . we have well-organized charities. No one need go hungry.
> . . . her mother hated the word "charity" above any word in the language and she had brought up her children to hate it too.
> . . . [Francie] began to understand that her life might seem revolting to some educated people. She wondered, when she got educated, whether she'd be ashamed of her background. Would she be ashamed of her people; ashamed of handsome papa who had been so light-hearted, kind, and understanding; ashamed of brave and truthful mama who was so proud of her own mother, even though gramma couldn't read or write; ashamed of Neeley who was such a good honest boy? No! No![39]

Francie's emphatic refusal to forget is a central theme in the novel. The distance required to "look back," however, implies that one no longer belongs to that particular world. At the end of the novel college-bound Francie, on the eve of her departure from the neighborhood, anticipates the coming shift in her class position; a little girl watching her from a nearby fire escape personifies the childhood self she will leave behind: "'Good-bye, Francie,' she whispered."

The book's narrative of recollection was especially compelling to readers who had themselves left Brooklyn.[40] In their letters to the author soldiers from Brooklyn whose names represent a variety of ethnic backgrounds located themselves in the neighborhoods and on the streets she depicts. "I felt it was a story about us, my friends and I," wrote Al Lewis, a "Brooklyn Kid" stationed off Saipan. "To me, it was like living my life over again," Corporal M. Mednick wrote. John Flagg wrote from Honolulu that "reading your book is like a proxy furlough."[41]

Tree's narrative of remembering made a working-class past more publicly acceptable, enabling some readers, in their letters to Smith, to acknowledge more openly origins they may have otherwise tried to obscure. One woman described the experience of recovering "buried memories of childhood" as therapeutic, providing a "deep mental purge, drawing to the light of day, dark horrible experiences that were overwhelmingly painful, and which, now revealed, have lost much of their horror." Maybelle Hoffman confessed to Smith, "You have been strong in putting down so beautifully that which I have been weak enough to want to forget." Marine Sergeant Mac Kaplan reflected that the book "taught me how to dig deep into my memory and enjoy immeasurably things I never cared to remember." A man originally from Brooklyn confided his wish to show his Williamsburg childhood to his sons, "to impress on them how much better off they are;" his wife's response was, "Williamsburg was nothing to be proud of." He had struggled to counter her view: "I believe it was something good to build on, if not to be proud of."[42]

Tree's account of working-class life and mobility resonated especially with soldiers who themselves had risen through military service. One navy lieutenant commander, Russell Smith, was moved by the idea that working-class daily life could be the subject of literature: he wrote of his thrill in discovering that "the great American novel" did not concern itself with "the revolution, the Civil War, or some war, or some farm and windmill, some Mark Twain type of thing" but with Brooklyn, where he was born and brought up and where he learned "the tough ways of life." But then he "rebelled and decided knowledge was the key to heart happiness and sought it. I made the Naval Academy and lost my accent . . . and lost Brooklyn in the bargain. I have since regretted losing Brooklyn." In the jungle where he was stationed, reading *Tree* brought back "all the things that made up my boyhood." Having committed himself to an upward mobility, "I thought I could forget them and I thought I was ashamed of them." But the novel gave him a way of rethinking his history, especially in the context of fighting the "good war": "To me Brooklyn is the world and the gymnasium of this world . . . the place to train for the big battle. . . . Everybody lived in Brooklyn, accepted its temporary hurts . . . and left and forgot. Nobody wrote about it or understood it. But you have."[43]

For these readers *A Tree Grows in Brooklyn* transformed poverty from deprivation into an object lesson. As one soldier put it, "Poverty has its compensations, and although they are certainly *not* worth the suffering and heartache, they are valuable in themselves." Another private wrote to Smith, "I am grateful to you for recognizing that in spite of their hardships they had a great nobility."[44] Another declared,

> I saw that tree all during my childhood. . . . I know the tree and I know the people I grew up among, and their indomitable spirit which they quite take for granted, and their incurable vitality and guts, and I wonder, now and again, where my own guts are. You help me to have a few more (I inherited them, didn't I) but you make me wonder whether the tree only has that ruthless vitality in its own good dirt. Thanks . . . for a piece of America that's (for my money) close to the core and heart of America. Please God, don't let all the people like you and me who are coming along have it too easy when they're kids.[45]

This last comment suggests that to upwardly mobile working-class readers the novel offered a model for a nostalgic rendering of a harsh past. When characters in the novel express this nostalgia, they imply that attaining middle-class security does not necessarily entail the wholehearted embrace of materialism; rather, that necessity encourages working-class children to develop qualities superior to those born into comfort and privilege. In one scene near the end of the novel, Smith marks Francie and Neeley's increased prosperity and changed status by having them remember the "olden times," regretting that their baby sister will not have to struggle as they did. " 'Laurie's going to have a mighty easy life all right. . . . She'll never have the hard times we had, will she? No, and she'll never have the fun, either. . . . Poor Laurie,' said Francie pityingly." One Brooklyn-born father referred to this passage when he wrote from Grand Rapids, Michigan: "Now I have three children of my own and I can afford to give them everything I didn't have as a boy, and truly I feel sorry for them, as you did for Laurie."[46]

INSTRUCTING THE MIDDLE CLASS

Middle-class readers from privileged backgrounds who wrote to Smith valued the narrative for its *lack* of familiarity. One West Point graduate "never realized any American children were ever unhappy in childhood" until reading the book. A woman from Omaha, Nebraska commented on "the emotionalism of city people, and their concern about one another's opinions," which she believed was because "their lives are so completely concerned with each other." A high school student wrote that she was fascinated "to see how people could live like that; by that I mean in such a crude way. I think you were very frank with the readers." A serviceman was made to "grow from living through reading" the book: "I don't think I'm a snob; when I have felt superior to other people it has been in abilities, not being. And yet, for the first time, I have a real understanding of Lincoln's words: 'God must love the common people, He made so many of them.'"[47] Other middle-class readers evaluated the book as an instruction in social policy. Judge Curtis Bok informed Smith that "Philadelphia has its Williamsburg and also its tree of heaven and what you have written has added to the stock of solutions I must have . . . [for] my own work." A soldier wrote from New Guinea insisting that the book be required reading for all "social welfare, sociology, social psychology, and child psychology courses in the nation."[48]

Middle-class readers who identified with Francie as the child of an alcoholic father or just as a lonely child recognized themselves in Smith's depiction of working-class childhood.[49] Soldiers from various class backgrounds remarked upon the novel's cross-class appeal. As one soldier wrote,

> I don't think any book has so captured the fancy of so many of us as has your very remarkable story. The book has circulated among so many of the men here that I have lost count of the number. . . . Some of us have come from the sidewalks of Manhattan, some of us had nursemaids who wheeled us through Central Park. None of us, Park Avenue, First Avenue, or Brooklyn, has been able to escape the charm and beauty of the story whether or not we saw a bit of our biography mirrored on its pages.[50]

Another soldier, raised with southern disdain for northern urban ways, described the story's appeal across regional lines; a "rebel of the old South," he told Smith that "Brooklyn has long been my symbol of all Yankees, thus learning to hate it, but now I've learned to love it through Francie's eyes . . . as Francie loved it." Francie was the inspiration for his future "wife," he told Smith; he hoped to hang the paragraph on the frontispiece about "the Tree" on the wall of his "dream house."[51]

These readers' letters provide eloquent testimony that a popular book such as *A Tree Grows in Brooklyn* invited multiple interpretations. A newspaper reviewer in Keene, New Hampshire commented that *Tree* offered both the "most vivid and convincing description of the way really poor people live in our own American cities" as well as a gallery of universally familiar characters, comprising "all of humanity: the good; the bad; the pitiful and the ridiculous, and those with stardust in their eyes."[52] The belief, in some of its middle-class readers, that the book conveyed a transcendent universalism, "truths of the human spirit," may have kept them from understanding its special significance to working-class readers or from recognizing how exceptional was its appreciation of the struggles and triumphs of everyday Americans.

THE ETHNIC AND RACIAL BOUNDARIES OF THE ORDINARY

Smith's novel broadened the public imagination of the ordinary family in certain ways but not in others. How did Smith herself indicate those whom she included as representing Brooklyn? How did contemporary reviewers and readers recognize and identify the book's racial, class, and ethnic social location? Whom did they include in *Tree*'s working-class Brooklyn geography?

Few reviewers identified Francie in terms we would now refer to as *ethnic origins*: "Katie Nolan was of Austrian descent"; she married "Irish Johnny Nolan." For others, the terms *tenement, Williamsburg,* and *Brooklyn* were enough to convey a recognizable type of urban neighborhood populated by poor people of various nationalities. Smith depicts specific ethnic origins as significant only to the immigrant generation. Although there are many characters with Irish surnames, the Nolan children are always identified as American-born. For Smith Brooklyn origins are synonymous with Americanness: "How wonderful was Brooklyn . . . when just being born there made you an American!" Readers responded warmly to the book's pronouncement that Americanization is conferred by residence in a neighborhood, national origins being absorbed into a generic urban ethnicity. One corporal informed Smith how frequently a "Polish boy" from Francie's Greenpoint neighborhood quoted the passage "about being an American if you were born in Brooklyn."[53]

In general, Smith devotes little attention to distinguishing among national origins. Within the novel's framework, only immigrants believe national origins to be permanent as well as racial; and they are characterized as wrongheaded. Francie's German immigrant grandfather, for example, "hated the Germans, he hated Americans, he hated the Russians, but he just couldn't stand the Irish. He was fiercely racial in spite of his stupendous hatred of his race, and had a theory that marriage between two of alien races would result in mongrel children." The older immigrant generation, in general, exhibits a tribal parochialism: illiterate, they are willing to sacrifice children's education and marital possibilities in the name of family need. Katie's father "never forgave any of his daughters for marrying"; Johnny's mother "had hoped to keep all her fine boys home with her until either she or they died."

Smith designates one "good immigrant," Katie's German mother, Mary Rommely, as the champion of an Americanization based on education and upward mobility.[54] Katie despairs that, although "born in a free land," she and her sister are not able to transcend a daily struggle for work and food. Grandma Rommely indicates the proper path: send the children to school, read every night to them, one page from the Protestant Bible, and one from Shakespeare, "so that the child will grow up knowing what is great—knowing that these tenements of Williamsburg are not the whole world." Modernize traditional religion and tales from the old country: teach the child to believe in "Kris Kringle," at least until she is six, so that she can have "a valuable thing which is called imagination. The child must have a secret world in which live things that never were." Teach her to believe in heaven, "not filled with flying angels with God on a throne" but a wondrous place "where desires come true." Practice accepting disappointment; suffering is good. Keep the house colder an hour longer; bargain for damaged vegetables; and save the pennies in an empty condensed milk can; buy a bit of land, for "once one has owned land, there is no going back to being a serf." While Mary Rommely's recipe for mobility won praise from middle-class reviewers, some readers did not find it entirely credible: "Mary seems much wiser than one would expect" and "for an illiterate immigrant, she has an implausibly fertile vocabulary."[55]

Wartime readers recognized with enthusiasm Smith's depiction of Brooklyn's ethnic mixture, which they agreed was a distinctive characteristic of working-class neighborhoods. But they could not agree on a common language with which to define groups. Readers groped for terms, using the language of race rather than nationality or what has since become known as ethnicity. A soldier from another section of Brooklyn wrote, "Maybe there wasn't a mixture of so many different races but the kids acted the same way . . . there was mostly Irish and Italian, and some Polish and Lithuanian." Another wrote approvingly of overlapping social groups: "So much of it finds parallels in my own life in Rochester. . . . We happen to be of Polish descent. . . . We had a similar Catholic background.

I grew up on the frontiers of the Polish, Ukrainian, and Jewish communities in Rochester. As a result I acquired something of a cosmopolitan outlook."[56]

The novel's rejection of ethnic parochialism in favor of a "cosmopolitan outlook" fit the ideological mission of the war, as one navy officer attempted to make explicit: "I guess that's one of the freedoms we're fighting for in this bitter war, the freedom that will assure the Francies of the world the same opportunities and privileges (or BETTER!) that millions of us have capitalized in our great country." Another soldier commented that the book's "putting into words and symbol of the things which (after peace) we have to eliminate . . . made me most impatient to return and arm myself . . . for the fight at home against intolerance and ignorance."[57]

If the cosmopolitanism Smith extolled allowed residents of a bygone Brooklyn to cross ethnic boundaries, racial barriers were certainly less permeable. Remaining within mainstream literary practices, Smith composed a scene (later eliminated from the manuscript) in which Johnny Nolan plays Santa Claus in blackface.[58] (The book Smith credited with inspiring her, Thomas Wolfe's *Of Time and the River* [1935], describes Jews as a dark and alien people and often refers to "niggers.")[59] The limits to Smith's cosmopolitanism are significant: the novel expands the category of ordinary families while maintaining exclusionary racial boundaries.

In an article entitled "Listen to America!" (c. 1927–1931), Smith articulated the racialist framework for her view of who can represent "the people." Writing most likely in response to the popularity of spirituals performed by black university groups such as the Fiske Jubilee Singers touring in the 1920s, she rejected spirituals in favor of popular songs such as "Sweet Adeline" as appropriate national folk songs. "The spirituals may be Negroid but they are not American. A spiritual means nothing to a man that works at a factory bench or to a girls [sic] that stands behind a counter. Folk songs should be songs that the common people understand and love."[60]

Smith's inventive literary strategy of looking back at the Brooklyn of her childhood circumvented racial and economic tensions of wartime working-class neighborhoods in which blacks and whites jostled for housing and employment. In a letter to her editor in 1942, she distinguished between the toughness of Williamsburg "then" and a "dreadful" and "evil" "present day Williamsburg." Like many of her contemporaries, she was nostalgic for an all-white ethnic working-class community before the appearance of, as she saw them, unknowable strangers; she blamed the deterioration of the neighborhood on black residents who had arrived since her departure. As she wrote in 1942,

> In Francie's day (25 years ago) the population was mostly Germans and Irish with Jews and Italians the next in numbers. Poles were coming into the neighborhood in 1920. But there were no Negroes then. . . . If anyone were to write a novel about the present-day Williamsburg, it would be more dreadful than Richard Wright's *Native Son*. . . . If Hitler's bombers should ever get over and if any portion of this great city has to get wiped out, it would be a blessing if it were that section. Evil seems to be part of the very materials that the sidewalks are made of, and the wood and the bricks of the houses.[61]

Other groups are also excluded from the process of Americanization Smith describes in *Tree*, even if they, too, were born in Brooklyn. Asians and Jews in the novel are presented as foreign in their physical attributes, habits, and values. A Chinese shopkeeper is an exotic stranger whose abacus, gifts of lichee nuts, and delicately brushed symbols represent "the mystery of the Orient in Brooklyn." Smith presents Jewish shopkeepers as incomprehensible, tenacious, even ferocious in their pursuit of meager profit. Elsewhere in the novel, she undermines racial stereotypes of Jews as the Nolan children question assumptions of Jewish difference. In the opening chapter Francie wonders if the Jewish expectation of the Messiah explains why Jewish women are less ashamed than Irish women of being pregnant ("each one thinks she might be making the real little Jesus"). And Neeley, recalling his father's positive assessment of a Jewish bartender as a "white Jew," tries to claim this status for a Jewish boy harassed on his way to temple on a Saturday morning. Neeley's friend disabuses him: "They ain't no such thing as a white Jew."[62] Sissy, whose children have died stillborn, finally insists on a hospital birth with a Jewish doctor because everyone knows "Jewish doctors are smarter." As a group, Jews in *A Tree Grows in Brooklyn* stand outside the boundaries of ordinary Americans.

Readers whose names suggest European Jewish origins generally inserted themselves into Smith's saga of Americanization and upward mobility. They wrote of their pleasure in recognizing aspects of tenement neighborhood life. One reader raised in Brooklyn applauded Smith: "You were correct in practically every detail. The only difference was I was a jew boy and you were the irisher. . . . Thank you so much for making me feel proud to have lived there." A Jewish doctor, born in Williamsburg and doing "his very little bit over there" in Europe, expressed his appreciation of Smith's "exact pictorial view of that melting pot section of Brooklyn." The symbol of Smith's tree inspired him to verse:

> And tho many stray far away
> To wealthy homes and gardens fair
> Still their thoughts
> Wander back—back there
> To that lovely beautiful Tree
> A Tree which can laugh, cry, and shelter misery—
> *A Tree that knows no race or creed*
> Judges a man by his honest deed
> Rooted deep in the soil of Every land
> Rooted deep in sweat and tears
> This is the everlasting Tree
> That American Tree
> Which dispels Hate and Fears.[63]

Another Jewish officer, Arnold Scheinberg, on the other hand, objected to Smith's descriptions of Jews being harassed by neighborhood gangs as well as to the mention of "white Jews." He asked Smith to "imagine a group of American soldiers reading your book and among them a few who happen to be on the other side of the *white line* you so aptly described. It makes the few feel bitter and dejected in the company of his pals" (emphasis added). To Scheinberg Smith's words had the power to "cause hatred where previously friendship existed." Her use of racial terms to define Jews made him wonder, "Just what are we fighting for? Are we accomplishing anything, fighting others away from our shores, when our own house needs cleaning?"[64] Scheinberg's concern about whether Jews fell on the right side of the white line did not question the legitimacy of the "white lines" of segregation in the armed services and American cities.

Another reader criticized Smith's general use of group terms; she wrote that Smith "slur[s] nationality: why say (Wop) when the word *Italian* could have been used as well? As for other slurs, I won't mention them as I am speaking only for myself. As an American born, of Italian descent and proud of it, I certainly was insulted. . . . Only one who is *ignorant* would write a story and slur nationality." She interpreted Smith's usage as both psychologically and politically hurtful: "Here's hoping your next story will

be more *considerate* of a *person's feelings*. . . . Remember, 'we are all, created, equally.' "[65]

Only one correspondent identified herself as African American; it is
striking that Viola Bell also chose to read the novel in a way that included
her. Writing from a small town in Missouri, she recognized herself in Francie's story because she understood it to chronicle the common experience
of the poor. She noted *Tree*'s racial limits: "Although not one word is written about Colored people, so evidently a poor Brooklyn child doesn't come
into contact with my Race," Bell nonetheless read her way across racial
exclusion to glimpse the potential for an international working-class solidarity. "Like Francie, I've read everything I can come in contact with, from
the daily paper to translations of some Foreign books. This, I've found out,
to be poor in any part of the world is much the same."[66]

MAKING WOMANHOOD ORDINARY

Reading *A Tree Grows in Brooklyn* prompted the soldiers who wrote Betty
Smith to "remember something worth fighting for at a time when remembering is all we have to sustain us."[67] At the center of "something worth
fighting for" are three females, Francie, her mother Katie, and Aunt Sissy;
their primary importance distinguishes the novel from earlier accounts of
working-class life in America. That men were away serving in the military
may have allowed people to imagine families in which women could and
did shoulder the burden of economic survival. But as Smith's enthusiastic
soldier fans testified, the women characters also served as a focus of male
fantasy of female friendship, romance, and nurture, enabling a transference that made it easier to express loneliness, fear, and grief.

Smith depicts female characters as having key responsibilities in maintaining working-class family life and conforming to modern heterosexual
values. The novel repeatedly makes reference to deep-rooted, gendered
differences between working-class women and men as well as to critically
important networks of female support. The immigrant mother schemes
to protect her daughters from the patriarchal rage of her husband; the
American-born wives struggle to supplement their husbands' inadequate
salaries. Although they "wept when they gave birth to daughters," the
women, "made out of thin invisible steel," also laugh among themselves
"about the weakness of men."

The female characters accept and even reward male weakness, while
they regulate or punish female strength. Francie suffers from feeling that

her mother favors her brother and wants to see her father—despite his alcoholism and eventual death—as a nurturing presence in her life. She is torn between a sense of women as betrayers of other women and her experience of her mother and aunts as the only dependable sources of support in her life. The novel reveals an awareness of the obstacles faced by women but also Smith's ambivalence about being enmeshed in female networks. As she confided to her (female) editor: "Coming from a matriarchal family . . . and having all aunts and few uncles and mostly all female cousins . . . one of which or whom sued me and having two daughters who sometimes make demands on me that a son wouldn't, I just get the feeling that I don't like women."[68]

The sections of the book in which Francie grows into womanhood were written after Smith signed the contract with Harper and Brothers and may have been shaped by editorial suggestions.[69] In these sections Smith links education and writing to Francie's self-assertion as a female; she must address the family's need for her wages, the priority given to her brother's education despite his dislike of school, and the lesser importance of her own schooling despite her passion for books and learning. In one scene the hard-working Katie, in labor with her third child, asks Francie to read one of her school compositions; Francie has burned all except those about her father, deemed unacceptable by her teacher. As she is hesitant to share these with her mother, she substitutes Shakespeare for her own voice. By the final pages Francie's female subjectivity triumphs as she moves toward a future of middle-class, college-educated womanhood, romantic love and self-exploration—all of which takes place outside the action of the novel. Francie's alter ego, the book-reading girl on the fire escape, signals the literary potential of "remembering."

Smith attempts to convey a working-class sexual sensibility through her depiction of Aunt Sissy as sexually uninhibited and generous. Her free expression is a source of pleasure to her and entertainment to others. In the end, however, she is tamed by deep maternal longings, her devotion to children, and her loyalty to her sister and niece. Katie Nolan is a more conventionally respectable character, but also unusually matter-of-fact and modern about sex. Katie's frank discussions with her daughter about sex read like a primer of modern sex education (the subject of one of Smith's earliest published articles), in contrast to Smith's description of her own upbringing in "a strict middle-class Victorian home where the word 'sex' was unknown."[70] In one scene Katie shoots a man about to rape Francie; order is restored to the neighborhood by the man's criminal prosecution, and Francie is told to forget the incident as a bad dream.[71] Katie's sexual modernism is most clearly revealed in her advice to Francie about whether she should have spent the night with a soldier she loves on his way to war. Katie's advice reflects 1940s wartime permissiveness rather than attitudes common in 1918. She separates her motherly warning—"Horrible things might have happened to you. Your whole life might have been ruined"—from her acknowledgment of Francie as a woman: "It would have been a very beautiful thing. Because there is only once that you love that way."

Smith's sexual explicitness offended some of her middle-class women readers, who found the book "full of muck and filth," "so much dirt," "coarse and vulgar."[72] As one reader explained to Smith, "I don't object to reading true-to-life happenings, but I do demand that the delicate situations be touched upon through vague, excellent literature." Even middle-class women who found the book "marvelous" on "economics, truth, honesty, courage, etc." wondered why the author had included "all the references and *vivid* descriptions of births, sex acts, toilets, and even the sex pervert." A number of readers commented on Katie's advice to Francie about the night with a soldier: one mother accused Smith of "boosting juvenile delinquency" but also revealed her own anxiety about competing with Katie's "modernity." "After a girl has read that, what words can a good mother say to her daughter that will not be disregarded as old fashioned and narrow minded?"[73] A soldier reader identified Smith's sexual sensibility as back-alley Irish as opposed to lace-curtain Irish "Puritans."[74]

Male as well as female readers identified with the characters of Katie and Francie. Some soldiers confessed to Smith their admiration and longing for maternal sympathy: Private John Alexander wrote wistfully that "Katie seems to have been much more understanding than my mother."[75] Some soldiers fantasized about Francie as an object of desire.[76] Others imagined themselves *as* Francie. Perhaps the special circumstances of soldiers, who were suspended in a mostly homosocial world far away from home, facilitated this transference. Some of the readers surprised themselves: one corporal wrote that his memories, "even though seen through the eyes of a boy—are amazingly the same as yours." Another was pleased to "discover himself quite often in Francie." A corporal wrote, "I too acted like sweet *Francie*." A veteran who shared "every one of Francie's emotions and sometimes cried when she did," felt it necessary to proclaim that he was "no sissy," having served in the navy in the South Pacific.[77] Civilian men, particularly those from Brooklyn, wrote in a similar manner, although with less emotion. To one reader, *A Tree Grows in Brooklyn* was "an autobiography or even more a personal diary of my life spent in Brooklyn"; another wished it had been written instead by a man, who might have called his story "A Boy Grows up in Brooklyn."[78]

HOLLYWOOD REVISES *A TREE GROWS IN BROOKLYN*

The adaptation of Betty Smith's novel allowed a team of Hollywood screenwriters to reinterpret the story of an ordinary ethnic working-class family, using Hollywood film conventions to emphasize particular themes. Smith and Harper and Brothers had sold the movie rights to Twentieth Century-Fox in 1943, within weeks of publication, when it was clear that the book would be a best-seller. The contract that Smith signed gave Fox the right to any future novels she would write about the Nolans and the right to serialize the movie in any form they wanted; as she noted to her editors, Fox could reduce it to formula comedy—"it might be like the Hardy family"—and churn out derivative sequels for years (fifteen Andy Hardy movies appeared between 1937 and 1946). Smith was not able even to ensure her billing in the film credits.[79] Opening in March 1945, the film played well for wartime audiences, momentarily boosting the celebrity of both the novel and its creator.

Hollywood studios were interested in best-sellers because these guaranteed box office receipts. Producer Louis (Bud) Lighton acquired *Tree* for Twentieth Century-Fox, following studio chief Darryl Zanuck's directive to make pictures that "have purpose and significance and yet show a proper return at the box office" by "dealing realistically in film with the causes of wars and panics, with social upheavals and depression, with starvation and want and injustice and barbarism under whatever guise."[80] By early 1943 the studios had considerably expanded their view of the kinds of films that could help boost morale during wartime.[81]

Zanuck had been associated with a style of social filmmaking since the early 1930s, developing many of Warner Brothers' gritty urban films, and then at Fox, assembling the teams that made hits from adapting epic novels of the poor, *Grapes of Wrath* (1939) and *How Green Was My Valley* (1941).[82] Zanuck did not produce *Tree* personally; but the production team that made the film was regarded as classy and well suited to the material. Lighton was a distinguished producer; left-wing screenwriters Tess Slesinger and Frank Davis had worked on prestigious productions. The theater director Elia Kazan, riding on the success of four major Broadway hits between 1941 and 1944, was hired to direct *Tree* as his first feature film.

Left-wing screenwriters in Hollywood had modest goals for influencing the final film. Although their work was likely to be revised by others, they were occasionally able to infuse Hollywood genre stories with more subtle representations of Hollywood's conventional "types"—turning women and African Americans, for example, from cardboard into more complex characters.[83] Because screenwriters were positioned fairly low in the production hierarchy, Slesinger and Davis had little power to shape Smith's story compared to Lighton and Kazan. Nonetheless, Slesinger's literary interests may explain the film's sharpened focus on the marital discord between Katie and Johnny as well as the Freudian psychological terms with which it frames the tension between the couple's memory of romance and the economic pressures that divide them. As leftists, Davis and Slesinger tried to preserve the grittiness of the tenement neighborhood Smith had created in a way that did not romanticize the lives of the poor.[84]

In contrast to Slesinger and Davis, Louis Lighton, the producer of the film, brought a distinctly conservative political sensibility to the production process. When Elia Kazan first met Lighton, the latter was actively involved in shaping the script. "He had before him Betty Smith's novel, as well as several earlier versions of the screenplay. These were being cannibalized—as they say at plane repair shops—in a search for usable parts." Conservative critics of the New Deal were gaining political momentum by 1944, making Roosevelt's fourth-term victory his narrowest. Even before Pearl Harbor, political liberals had faced opposition from Republicans and conservative Democrats who wanted to dismantle New Deal programs and block the expansion of centralized economic safety nets. Lighton's "cannibalizing" process was aimed at emphasizing the family story as an *alternative* to collective solidarity. According to Kazan, each film Lighton made

> contained the same themes, the same values. He had convictions, felt them strongly, talked about them constantly. . . . He was against the New Deal of Roosevelt, believed that a real man would not accept relief, that it amounted to pity. He despised the East Coast, its ideology, its civilization. . . . He was for the frontiersman [who] asked no favors of his neighbor. . . . Lighton despised communism but he despised "liberals" even more.

Lighton urged Kazan to shape each scene accordingly, as Kazan later recalled in his autobiography: "He talked over each scene as I was about to shoot, telling me the feeling he hoped he had put into it and now hoped I could get out of it. He talked of humanity, feeling, courage, pride, all the old fashioned 'American' values of the frontier society that he admired."[85]

Kazan described himself as following Lighton's guidance, but his family history and political convictions also shaped the film version of *Tree*. Born in Istanbul, Turkey in 1909, Kazan moved with his Greek parents to Berlin in 1911 and to New York in 1913. His father was a moderately successful rug dealer, until his business was ruined in the early years of the Depression. Kazan described his childhood as middle-class but isolated within Greek circles of family; he experienced himself as an outsider through high school and then at Williams College. He began to feel less isolated in the more bohemian circles of Yale Drama School: the decisive change in his life was his marriage to fellow student Molly Day Thatcher. As his mother put it, "Molly brought us into America."[86]

Like many young artists and intellectuals, Kazan moved toward the left in the early 1930s—making himself indispensable to the Group Theatre, throwing himself into radical theater activities with the Theatre of Action, the left-wing Nykino and later Frontier Films, and, with fellow Group members, joining the Communist Party for about eighteen months in 1934 and 1935. Anticapitalism offered a perspective that engaged him on a personal level: "[The movement] expressed all the resentment I had accumulated all my life against the Turks, the American kids, Williams College, the fraternities, everybody." Kazan retrospectively described his politics as a social identity rather than commitment to social activism. He was "mostly a middle-class boy who aspired to be a member of the proletariat; that was the pure class, I thought, the class that could not be corrupted and would not waver from its line, the revolutionary class. I always wore rough clothes. . . . It was a way of turning off, disavowing the middle class, of professing visually that you are ashamed of your middle-class heritage."[87] At the Group Theatre Kazan's exposure to "the political left, the introduction to Freud and Marx, the absolute idealistic dedication and determination toward a new world" all converged, offering him a powerful and compelling world view that guided his 1930s search for "The People."

When the Group Theatre found it could no longer sustain its members financially and finally dissolved in 1940, a huge void remained. "To everybody that had been associated with it, everything seemed inferior, diffuse, without purpose. We had been brought to life by a cause. When the cause disappeared, our lives suddenly seemed empty and futile and rather meaningless."[88] But Kazan was a survivor, and he was the first of his peers to find work as a director, winning notice and the New York Drama Critic's Award for his direction of Thornton Wilder's *The Skin of Our Teeth* (1942). By 1944 his star was rising, with repeated commercial successes on Broadway.

Kazan chose to work at Fox, turning down an offer from Warner Brothers, partly because of the opportunity to film Betty Smith's novel. "I read *A Tree* and saw in it material I knew something about, the streets of New York and the lives of the working class." Themes of immigration, Americanization, and class mobility were central to Kazan's self-described identity. He also was attracted to what he saw as Lighton's "honesty." Although his own political values were the opposite of Lighton's, the dissolution of the Group, the end of Depression-era certainty, and his brief experience overseas in the Pacific as part of a mission to set up self-entertainment units for troops waiting to be sent out left him unsure in his political convictions. Lighton had quite an effect on him: "When I listened to him, my left-wing positions seemed provincial, my convictions shallow." As director, he was "sympathetic to what Bud [Lighton] stood for, and did his best to help him realize his vision."[89]

Looking Back at a Universal American Past

The screen version of *Tree* helped to circulate even more widely the novel's wartime formulation of proud, hardworking, white ethnic people as prototypical citizens. The screen adaptation flattened the vivid social particulars with which Smith had evoked the working-class Brooklyn neighborhood of her childhood, emphasizing instead "old fashioned American values" and creating a generic vision of Smith's nostalgic urban past.

The Fox contract players whom Kazan and Lighton cast for the film guide the audience away from the book's characterizations and toward interpretations derived from the film's point of view. The actress cast as Katie Nolan, Dorothy McGuire, made her screen debut as a sexual innocent, a zany and scatterbrained young bride who didn't know the facts of life.[90] An unusually plaintive and wistful thirteen year old, Peggy Ann Garner, played Francie; well-known child actor Ted Donaldson played Neeley, her brother. Joan Blondell, cast as Sissy, spent her childhood touring in a vaudeville act with her parents, and her Hollywood career perfecting the character of a "cynical wise-cracking broad with a heart of gold." The kind Officer McShane, Katie's second husband, was played by Lloyd

Nolan, widely known at the time as a private detective in a long-running film serial.[91] James Dunn, film career in decline, was cast as Johnny.

From the opening credits, the film promotes a temporal ambiguity that conflates historical time with filmic time. The titles and credits for *Tree* are presented over sketches of an idealized urban past: tenement rooftops, the Brooklyn Bridge, laundry flapping on clotheslines strung from windows, throngs in public intersections. Instead of a conventional movie score, Kazan substituted "source music—the sound of an organ grinder" to enhance the realist effect.[92] The tinny player piano music changes with each sketch, using strains of American popular music—"Oh, You Beautiful Doll," "Take Me Out to the Ball Game," and "Bicycle Built for Two." Title cards invited the audience to merge their own memories into the film's presentation of a universal, fictional past: "For childhood, Saturday—free from school—is the most changeless of institutions, whether it is in city or village or main street or on those vital teeming streets which were the Brooklyn of a few decades ago." The period detail of the tenement rooms and street scenes submerged contemporary political referents by firmly keeping the focus on "looking back."[93]

Looking Back at Poverty

Kazan's reputation was based at least in part on the drama with which he had been associated in the 1930s; he was known for his skill in staging psychological and social realism. The focus on social context and social significance was a hallmark of left-wing cultural expression, but writers of drama, fiction, and film had not yet found a narrative structure capable of exposing the social causes for poverty and portraying its amelioration without falling into the trap of degrading or romanticizing poor people. The film adaptation softened the harshness with which Smith had portrayed middle-class humiliation of the poor, further diminishing the novel's occasional references to a larger social reality.

Reviewers who hoped the film would break new ground in the cinematic representation of working-class life were disappointed. James Agee wrote in *Time* that "the clangorous redolence of Brooklyn streets and schools and stores and tenement staircases, though reproduced with loving care, seems canned and trimmed." He likened the effect to an attempt to "recreate the life of a big city in a studio, as if under glass." To the *New Republic*'s Manny Farber the photography was the "most destructive element" in the film, as it "blankets the poverty in lovely shadows and pearly sentimentality"; the dialogue reproduced the "embarrassing, stiff lower-class speech that sounds like the talk used in the old melodramas of the South."[94]

Tree followed the precedents established in prior Zanuck-produced Fox films in emphasizing familial self-sufficiency and downplaying social institutions. The film depicts union membership as insignificant or even negative. When Katie Nolan searches for the missing Johnny in the union hall, the officials appear disinterested and powerless in the issue of most urgency, finding Johnny work. Rather than being contemptuous of the poor, the middle-class characters are indifferent in the worst cases, but more frequently sympathetic and understanding.

The film's ending emphasizes the children's final escape from poverty through their enunciation of looking back. As Francie and her brother Neeley contemplate their mother's impending remarriage to the securely employed and unfailingly polite policeman McShane, and the resulting change of income and status for their family as a whole, they voice the novel's line of regret for their baby sister: "Laurie's going to have a mighty easy life all right. . . . She'll never have the hard times we had, will she? No, and she'll never have the fun either." The promised distance from poverty was central to the film's uplifting message, noted and enthusiastically applauded by a number of the film reviewers: *Commonweal*'s Philip Hartung was sure that the film showed that "in spite of adversity people of strong character like Francie Nolan grow and fulfill their promise." *Newsweek* similarly saw the film as showing that "Francie represents the triumph of spirit over environment."[95]

Looking Back at Ethnicity

Like the book, the film conflates urban tenement poverty and generalized white ethnicity. Apparently, Kazan did not have any input on the script (and never met the original scriptwriters), but he later claimed to have encouraged Lighton "to put in a bit more of the immigration theme than he otherwise would have because it meant something to me."[96] No indication of foreignness appears for the first half hour; then, speaking with a generic foreign accent, Grandma voices the novel's firm and didactic strategy for automatic Americanization—the nightly reading of the Bible and Shakespeare. She makes the rhetorical link between immigration, education, and upward mobility and emphasizes spiritual rather than material goals:

This reading will not stop. [Close-up of Grandma, speaking.] I say this thing. To this new land, your grandfather and I came, very long ago now, because we heard that here is something *very good.* [Camera pans to Katie.] Hard we worked, very hard but we could not find this thing. For a long time, I do not understand. [Camera pans to Francie and Neeley.] And then I know. [Close-up of Grandma.] When I am old, I know. In that old country, a child can rise no higher than his father's state. But here, in *this* place, each one is free to go as far as he is good, to make of himself. [Camera pans to Francie and Nee-ley.] This way, the child can be better than their parents. [Close-up of Grandma.] And *this* is the true way things grow better. And *this* has some-thing to do with the *learning.* Which is here free to all people. [Camera pans to Francie and Neeley.] I, who am old, missed this thing. [Camera turns to Katie.] My children missed this thing. But my children's children shall not miss it. [Camera pans Francie and Neeley.] The reading will not stop. [Close-up of Grandma.]

The film leaves out explicit references to the white ethnic mixture, which had encouraged readers to imagine themselves into the book, as well as the novel's representation of the unassimilable "white Jews" and exotic Asians. The film's Chinese shopkeeper, hailed warmly by Johnny on a neighborhood walk with Francie, and references to Johnny and his publi-can as Irish—typed primarily through their association with alcohol—are all that remain. Only a few reviewers noted this "Irishness."

Remaking the Working-Class Family into a Middle-Class Ideal

Kazan left his mark most clearly on the film through the psychological interpretations his direction conveyed. The film version of *Tree* recon-structs the working-class family in effect to disempower the child, to min-imize the social and emotional centrality of the mother, and to emphasize the importance of the father—despite his inadequacies—as the primary structuring authority.

In 1944 Kazan's reading of the book was affected by his familial situa-tion, torn as he was between a stable home life with his wife and children and a passionate love affair. Previously he had read the book and had found it unengaging; "Once over, quick and light. I couldn't even remem-ber if I'd liked it. No I hadn't; not really. I'd thought it 'soapy,' a tearjerker, corny." After agreeing to direct the film he read the book again, and was overwhelmed: "I cried, and had other emotions of a most personal kind."

Kazan's new reading of the book placed the father-daughter relationship at the center of the dramatic action.

> Perhaps it was because I'd just seen my children and felt my loss of them so keenly. Perhaps it was because I saw no solution ahead for me, so was sympathetic to the man who was addicted to alcohol. Perhaps the figure of his ramrod wife reminded me of everything unyielding I admired about Molly. *This, I saw, was the first piece of material offered to me that made me think about my own life and my own dilemma.* The dilemma of all the people in Betty Smith's novel was mine and Molly's. The little girl who loved her father absolutely despite all, felt what my daughter, I believe, was now feeling about me [emphasis added].[97]

Kazan's direction made masculine approval a recurring motif and the central legitimizing framework for women's actions and emotions.

Both Francie and Katie lost substance and agency. Kazan never called attention to the appealing qualities of the mother or to the mother-daughter relationship that had so compelled readers. He adopted a time frame that "froze" Francie in childhood. Kazan characterized the film as dramatizing "a child's struggle to hold her parents together, it spoke of the pain of separation, of a young child caught between warring adults."[98]

The film's heightened focus on marital strife required that Katie's working-class materialism, her work as economic provider—conveyed in many shots of her scrubbing floors in exchange for rent—be associated with her developing "hardness." It is Katie's sexually expansive sister, Sissy, who first labels her in this way, but Katie is also made to accuse herself: "My kids is going to be something if I have to turn into granite rock to make them."[99] Her mother joins the chorus to rebuke Katie for her interest in economic security and respectability, labeling these concerns as a spiritually bankrupt materialism: "You have forgotten to think with your heart. . . . There is a coldness growing in you, Katie." Cinematically, Kazan repeats the accusations of Katie's "hardness" by visually separating Johnny and Katie, who rarely appear in the same frame. Two-shots and close-ups are used again and again to emphasize the relationship between father and daughter, the film's primary couple.[100]

Much of the dramatic tension in the film emphasizes Katie's growing hardness. This includes the central metaphor of the tree, which Johnny sees as beautiful and Katie as interfering with her hanging out the laundry and "not putting any money in the bank." Katie's material efforts for her children cannot compete with Johnny's spiritual bequest. Despite his financial unreliability, Johnny's emotional encouragement sustains Francie: he sneaks her into a school where she receives support for her writing; he celebrates her accomplishments even from the grave by arranging before he dies for flowers be sent to her graduation.

Expanding the importance of the father in the film and diminishing the importance of the mother in effect limits female autonomy and restores male authority as the ultimate legitimator of womanhood. This filmic construction reverberated with wartime and postwar social debates about masculinity and femininity sparked by a number of concerns: about male absence resulting from unemployment in the 1930s or military service during the war, about female presence in formerly male positions in factories and in the military, and widespread anxiety about the conversion to a peacetime economy.[101]

The childbirth scene is one in which the novel's construction of powerful women momentarily disrupts the film's male/female psychodrama, although even here Kazan makes the absent father an important presence. Manny Farber, writing for the New Republic, called this scene the only one with "any real terror and hardness in the faces and gestures, any drabness in the photography and any complexity of thought and feeling"; Bosley Crowther of the New York Times noted the "childbirth anguish" for its ability to "embrace all the wretched despair of the poor."[102] This scene also stands as an important departure from conventional depictions of mother-daughter relationships, providing rare filmic attention to a reconciliation based neither on maternal sacrifice nor on maternal domination.[103]

Even here, however, Katie's affirmation of Francie turns on Katie's coming to accept her daughter's admiration of Johnny. Katie asks Francie to distract her from labor pains by reading to her, and she finally acknowledges Francie as a writer by praising Francie's story about her father, "The Man People Loved." The story helps Katie to stop being "hard" and critical of her husband; she becomes instead a good wife/widow who at last appreciates her (alcoholic and unemployed) husband. Soon after, Katie's transformation is appropriately rewarded when she gains a truly good husband, the steady Officer McShane. The film's stake in propping up manhood was noted by the New Yorker critic, who commented that the phrase "a good man" was "applied to practically every man on the screen at least once."[104]

The film's final scene conveys Francie's success not as a writer but as a maturing woman who could be the object of male desire. [105] Although her sexual persona never challenges Hollywood's conventions for a female juvenile actress, the proof of Francie's growing up is signaled when a neighborhood boy notices her and asks her to go with him to the movies. In the film's final moments, after the dialogue with her brother in which they pity their baby sister the poverty and good times she will miss out on, Francie reveals that she is developing appropriate womanly concerns by asking her brother if he thinks she is "good-looking." He grudgingly concedes that she'll do. These words are spoken as Neeley looks out, surveying the world beyond Brooklyn, and Francie's eyes are directed at him. The strength of the mother-daughter bond, the authenticity of Francie's voice, and her identity as a writer all recede beside the achievement of heterosexual femininity, her value confirmed by male authority.

THE DECLINING APPEAL OF *TREE*'s SOCIAL TERRAIN

Giving her stamp of approval to the film version of *Tree,* Betty Smith was "pleased with the details of the picture—the way they have the gas plate in top of the coal range and the upper part of the windows 'window paned' and the spoons in the glass bowl on the table—the kid with the belt missing from the coat, and the middy blouse with the piece in the neck." According to an article that went out over the UPI wire service, she "wept like any ordinary moviegoer" after viewing the finished film. Although in private Smith expressed her doubts, publicly she hoped that "well, at least they know what Brooklyn is like out there, now."[106]

The film, like the book, was a success with wartime audiences, ranking as one of the top-grossing films of 1944–1945.[107] In the winter of 1945 filmgoers were never far from an awareness of the war. Prints of the film carry a message from the War Activities Committee of the motion picture industry advising "Families and Friends of Servicemen and Women" that "pictures exhibited in this theater are given to the armed forces for showing in combat areas around the world." The Los Angeles premiere for the film, which sold out Graumann's Chinese Theater, was a benefit for the Naval Aid Auxiliary. The *Los Angeles Times* reviewer, Edwin Schallert, tried to comprehend the particular appeal of *Tree*'s family story in wartime. Besides its novelty in having "naught to do with the global conflict," the film was timely, he believed, and part of "the struggle against poverty, a campaign that goes forward for throngs of people, whether or not there are war fronts of a far more spectacular genre." He assumed these qualities would appeal more to women than to men.[108]

The film version of *Tree* offered audiences an opportunity to remember the "normal" times of prewar America. Trade reviewers noted, however, a plaintive quality that particularly affected wartime audiences, who were invited to cry, to acknowledge their grief and unsatisfied longings. Some reviews suggested that the film's painful evocation of working-class scarcities were not fully resolved by the film's happy resolution, that parts of the film were quite disturbing to watch. The reviewer for *Motion Picture Daily* was especially struck by the emotional intensity of the middle sections of the film: "There is more sustained pathos and unrelieved heartache in this production than the reviewer has encountered in many a motion picture. The last half of the film offers virtually no emotional escape up to the final few minutes." The *Variety* reviewer concurred: "There have been few pictures to tug at the heartstrings as this one does."[109]

Then, suddenly, the war was over, its enormous weight lifted. *Tree's* world no longer seemed so immediate or compelling. The film opened and closed without approaching the outpouring of interest the book had generated. Although Dunn received the Academy Award for best supporting actor in March 1946, and Garner won a special award as the outstanding child actress of 1945 for her roles in *Junior Miss* and *Tree*, the film did not command the attention that the book once had.

Betty Smith did not speak again as effectively to an audience as she had with A *Tree Grows in Brooklyn*, although she did try. She returned to a Brooklyn locale and a female protagonist of Irish working-class background for her second novel, *Tomorrow Will Be Better*, published by Harper and Brothers in 1948. With a hopeful ending tacked on, the novel was a Book of the Month Club selection and immediately hit the bestseller list. Apparently many critics and readers found their expectations disappointed.[110] The novel did not depict a working-class life that enabled middle-class belonging; family ties were represented as more claustrophobic than sustaining. Lewis Gannett, reviewing the book for the *Herald-Tribune*, returned to the tree metaphor to comment on the narrowing of social promise: "Betty Smith's first novel was about a tree that grew, lush and beautiful, out of the cement of a Brooklyn back yard. Her second novel is about weeds that grow between the cracks in Brooklyn sidewalks and shrivel in the dust."[111]

In 1951 Smith tried to resuscitate *Tree* as a Broadway musical with the help of established and successful Broadway impresario George Abbott.[112] In a publicity interview Smith proclaimed her willingness to change her original framing of the story and dismissed as "dated" an earlier drama she had written about Francie Nolan: "It was bitter and tragic, an indictment of poverty. Remember? Everything was social significance in those days."[113]

The musical adaptation of *Tree* emphasized the relationship between Katie and Johnny: it was now a heartwarming if bittersweet Broadway-style romance that recalled the working-class, star-crossed lovers in Rodgers and Hammerstein's musical *Carousel* (1946). Lyrics touting working-class family life as materially impoverished but spiritually rich rang flat: "Money, success, we ain't got those things. But think of the love we hold for each other. You can't buy that."[114] Smith tried to reinstate Katie's centrality at the end of the film, spotlighting Katie, standing alone, holding Johnny's flowers and Francie's diploma, the lights of the Brooklyn Bridge coming on in tribute to her.

The audiences did not come.[115] Perhaps harsh working-class lives were not well suited to the optimism associated with the musical genre. Betty Smith eventually admitted that the connection between her fictional memories of Brooklyn and life in the present was increasingly tenuous. Her densely described drama of "making it" was no longer compelling. As she commented in 1958, "An era has come in which little advances aren't important anymore. The exhilaration that came to a family when they were able to move from one flat into another flat that cost $5 a month more, the excitement of wanting a $30 coat and finding the price suddenly reduced to $20—these things are no more. Things are too easy to come by now." Her working-class memories slipped away from readers' imaginative recollection: "I keep wondering whether readers will recognize the old ways."[116]

Stretching the boundaries of what was considered an ordinary family to include ethnic and working-class families, with complex women characters at their center, *A Tree Grows in Brooklyn* created a "literature of nationalism" in which "national unity reflects itself in family unity." Its imaginative framework overlapped with a broader cultural mission during the war, and it reverberated with powerful public sentiment. After the war it settled into a more specialized, although still popular, niche without attracting much public notice. Adolescent girls continued to plumb its emotional terrain, and its nationalist ideology linking Americanization and upward mobility recommended it as one of the first American novels released behind the "Iron Curtain."[117]

Betty Smith, her most famous book, and its film version helped to establish a public narrative in which ethnic looking back expanded the idea of American citizenship. Smith's story of an ordinary family popularized a vision of postwar citizenship in which a nostalgic version of an "ethnic past" became a universal American past. Escape from poverty became the rite of passage into middle-class belonging, Americanization took place in mixed ethnic but white neighborhoods, and female-centered working-class families were reconstructed according to a middle-class heterosexual ideal. The vision persisted long after the cultural resonance of *Tree* had faded. In the same period in which Betty Smith's novel so effectively gave voice to these beliefs, Kathryn Forbes's "Mama" stories depicted another ordinary American family and gained a comparable audience, ultimately retaining its popular relevance far longer than *A Tree Grows in Brooklyn*. Let us now turn to Kathryn Forbes' s vision of remembering Mama and her family.

3

HOME FRONT HARMONY
AND REMEMBERING *MAMA*

IKE BETTY SMITH, KATHRYN FORBES WAS VIRTUALLY UNKNOWN WHEN HER
working-class family saga appeared on bookseller lists in 1943. Like
Smith, she had worked in the culture industries, writing for radio and
beginning to sell short fiction to mass-circulation magazines. Though
Mama's Bank Account did not generate the same attention from book
clubs, PTAs, and ministers' pulpits as did *A Tree Grows in Brooklyn,* it
achieved a long-lasting success through its many adaptations.[1] First
appearing as a short story with minimal characterization in a Canadian
newspaper, "Mama's Bank Account" would, over the next fifteen years,
provide the characters and plot for a record-setting Broadway play, *I
Remember Mama;* a popular film by the same name released in 1948; and a
pioneering form of serial family drama, broadcast weekly on television
from 1948 to 1956. In each format—book, play, movie, serial family
drama—a version of working-class family life provided the framework for
dealing with pressing social concerns, with different narratives and out-
comes appealing to audiences in the shifting historical contexts of wartime,
the contentious years of the late 1940s, and the expanding consumer affluence of the 1950s. Smith's and Forbes's accounts of "domestic illusions"
both appealed to readers "against the insecurity of the world" when they
were first published; their differences help to explain why *Tree*'s postwar
revisions fell flat while *Mama*'s incarnations increased in popularity.[2]

The characters in *Mama's Bank Account* (an expanded series of
vignettes) include Mama and Papa Hansen, emigrants from Norway to

San Francisco, where Papa is employed as a skilled carpenter and has a respected role in the carpenter's union. Their children, born in San Francisco, are their son, Nels, and their daughters, Katrin (a future writer), Christine, and Dagmar. Mama's sisters have also made new homes in San Francisco; they keep boarders and visit one another. The titular head of the extended family is an uncle, the "black" Norwegian Chris, a farmer in northern California. The title story describes Mama's management of the family budget as she stretches pennies to cover the family's needs and invents an imaginary bank account to give the children a sense of security during hard times.

As a collection of short stories, at least some of which had been previously published, *Mama's Bank Account* was not reviewed seriously as literature. The *Library Journal* regarded the stories as humorous sketches to be read aloud, suggesting that their value as appropriate family entertainment was their most noteworthy quality.[3] But the stories of this "quaint" or "picturesque" immigrant family had a special significance in wartime, depicting new kinds of Americans who promised, even more than the family in *Tree*, to revitalize American democracy. The *New York Times Book Review* suggested that "if in the making of the peace after the war there could be included some people like Kathryn Forbes's Mama, it would be a fine thing," particularly because of Mama's "deep belief in security" and her being "happy to work and plan for it."[4] Note the vision of "security" being touted here: hardworking families taking care of one another and requiring little from the state.

Forbes's explicit concern with Americanization caught reviewers' attention. The *Atlantic Monthly* described how "Mama's daughter Katrin takes us into the heart of a delightful Norwegian family who are slowly learning American ways in San Francisco." The *New York Times Book Review* applauded how the Hansens "responded rapidly to Americanization while retaining the integrity and virtues of their Norwegian past." The *Book Week* review was the most political: "If there are any who may excusably be called 100 per cent American, they are people like this Norwegian family, who brought with them from the old country traits of courage, honesty, and straight thinking which we like to think make up the American character."[5]

Reviewers suggested that the Norwegian family and their "old country traits" provided a model of upstanding citizenship during the war. Mama's "domestic strength" and her working-class family were willing and enthusiastic new citizens, capable of sustaining and reinvigorating

American democratic culture. Forbes's contribution to what critic Diana Trilling labeled as the wartime development of "literary nationalism" would be selected by the government for translation into German and Japanese after the war, in support of U.S. occupation of these countries. The theory, as drama editor Virginia Wright reported it, was that "this enduring portrait of American family life will be good for our former enemies to read."[6]

How did Forbes come to write an ordinary working-class family story with such popular wartime appeal? Like Betty Smith, she had addressed other subjects before turning to stories of immigrant families. Of the short fiction she published in the *American, Saturday Evening Post, Colliers, Capper's Farmer, Redbook,* and *Ladies Home Journal,* "Mama's Bank Account" struck a chord with readers. After Pearl Harbor Forbes interrupted her writing, "feeling that if she couldn't build ships, she wasn't doing her part." She took first-aid courses and made what she termed a "feeble attempt" at writing propaganda for the government. When the "first rush" was over, however, Forbes returned to writing Mama stories. She used her radio scriptwriting as prior experience to attract the attention of a literary agent, who obtained for her a contract to publish a group of stories as a book, titled after the original story, *Mama's Bank Account.*[7]

Forbes was born Kathryn Anderson in San Francisco in 1909, the daughter of Leon Ellis Anderson and Della (Jesser) Anderson. Her mother was a California native, born in about 1875, whose own mother had emigrated from Norway. Forbes's early years were apparently unsettled after her parents divorced.[8] She attended grammar school and Lowell High, graduating from the Mountain Valley High School in San Francisco in 1925 at age sixteen.

Forbes described her educational ambitions as cut short by working: "Once I found I could use a typewriter and make money, I lost interest in college."[9] Her wage earning outside the home ended in 1926 when she, now seventeen, married a carpenter named Robert McLean and had two sons, born in quick succession. In publicity releases Forbes attributed her writing career to the development of radio. "With a couple of babies to raise, Kathryn Forbes didn't think about working for some ten years," but she thought about trying to write professionally when she became interested in radio: "listening to monologues on the air, she decided she could write better ones."[10]

In the 1930s radio shows were produced locally in San Francisco, and Forbes began writing as a freelancer for a Sunday radio program—"everything from dramas to gag shows." The name Forbes was Kathryn Anderson McLean's pseudonym, adopted for her first on-air writer credit and borrowed from her (non-Norwegian) paternal grandmother, who had lived in Forbestown, one of California's ghost towns. When the industry began to abandon San Francisco for Hollywood, the most viable commercial option for a writer in her circumstances was magazine short fiction. With the help of a fiction-writing class at the San Mateo Junior College Adult Center, Forbes published her first short story in 1938.[11]

Thus, before she turned to Norwegian immigrant material for her Mama stories, Forbes—like many female writers who had emerged through the openings created by the new culture industries—was familiar with the conventions of radio humor and formula drama, as well as women- and family-oriented mass magazine fiction. Her connection to Norwegian immigrants was at best tenuous. Her exposure to Norwegian was that she knew her mother's parents spoke it when they didn't want the children to understand.

Like Smith, Forbes elides historical time and family time, merging immigrant grandparents into immigrant parents living in San Francisco in the 1920s. Forbes's mother was born in the U.S. in the 1870s; the acculturation of Norwegian immigrants in her family would have taken place in the late nineteenth century. The device of the writer, Kathryn Forbes, creating a story about a Norwegian daughter, Katrin, who publishes her first writing by the end of the title story, also encouraged readers to conflate the generations and the timing of Americanization as well as the names "Kathryn" and "Katrin." Forbes used the opportunity in publicity interviews to stress both artifice and authenticity in the stories.[12] Calling attention to the fictional origins of Mama's family, she also recalled her aunt's response, "It's a very nice book, Kathryn, but I don't see what all the shouting's about. Anyone in the family could have written it." Forbes claimed to have called the Norwegian consul to check the spelling of a phrase, only to hear the consul's response: "That kind of a story has already been done. You'll find it in a magazine piece written by Kathryn Forbes."[13]

"MAMA'S BANK ACCOUNT" AND OTHER
ETHNIC WORKING-CLASS FICTIONS

The Mama stories constructed another powerful formula for looking back at a "history" that produced American citizens who were easily recognized as exemplary by audiences both during and after the war. According to this formula, "old-world" values—of hard work, familial cooperation, maternal devotion, and spiritual over consumerist concerns—led directly to American economic self-sufficiency, security, and social mobility, as determined by education and professional stature rather than by wealth. *Mama*'s family embodies these quintessential American values, and thus their assimilation is automatic. The fictional Norwegian family's use of a patriotic language characteristic of World War I to describe their appreciation of citizenship served as a civics lesson for readers facing wartime mobilization in 1943.

Unlike Betty Smith, who used dense description to fill out her story, Forbes relied on bare and suggestive characterization, perhaps as a result of her experience writing for radio. Leaving details to the imaginations of readers may have amplified the novel's ideological effect. One reviewer commented that its "brief pages" were enough to "tell simply and sincerely a great deal about the *spirit of a family,* something which many a longer book has not accomplished" (emphasis added).[14]

Like Smith's novel, Forbes's stories presented a working-class family as an ordinary family. The title story, "Mama's Bank Account," describes a family dependent on more than the contribution of a male breadwinner; reliance on the contributions of multiple family wage earners, in the words of historian Kathy Peiss, was "both a strategy for survival and a working-class cultural ideal." Studies of working-class oral histories and analyses of family budgets have revealed the ways in which economic pressures required families to cooperate in order to survive and that cooperation often involved bitter negotiations.[15] What appear in twentieth-century family histories as battles over how to weigh individual desires against family needs—battles that are, in *Tree,* emblematic of emotional scarcity—become, in Forbes's story, a magical system of accounting in which very little was always enough.

The war required some women to shoulder the burdens of economic survival. Forbes's family economy, managed by Mama, enables her to play a central role in filling a working-class family with sunny cooperation rather than painful disappointment. In Betty Smith's long-ago Brooklyn Johnny's unreliability as a wage earner adds to the burden of Katie's already tight budget; she becomes increasingly "hard" as a result. In Forbes's long-ago San Francisco, on the other hand, the fiction of harmony is unchallenged. Mama's budget is a loving one; everyone in the family contributes to the household; there are no competing interests, no contending claims on the money. Mama divides Papa's wages into sums for the landlord, the grocery bills, new soles for Katrin's shoes, Christine's new notebook. In order to attend high school, Nels must find an after-school job, Papa gladly gives up his only pleasure, tobacco, and the sisters promise to help out with weekly babysitting. Teaching discipline and self-sacrifice, Mama puts everything before a new winter coat for herself.

The reciprocity always comes out even: no two children get sick or require special expenditures at the same time. Even when Papa is on strike, Mama and Papa find part-time jobs to put food on their table. All these efforts enable the family to manage without drawing on their "bank account," which turns out to be a fiction (inside a fiction) created to keep the children from worrying: "Is not good for little ones to be afraid—to not feel secure."[16] Family budgeting—a material necessity of working-class life—comes to represent, in Forbes's tale, Mama's nurturing devotion, the importance of which was popularized by "experts" in the kinds of magazines for which Forbes was writing. Forbes's innovation was to imagine an immigrant working-class Mama as the model, psychologically nurturing, mother.

Forbes endows the Hansens' working-class consciousness with a spiritual critique of excessively materialist goals. The market value of women's work is secondary to, and often masked by, its family value. In the second story, "Mama and the Idle Roomer," Mama is cheated out of the income she has earned cooking and cleaning for a boarder; but she accepts the boarder's nightly readings of great literature as a substitute for the lost income. Mr. Hyde helps Nels with his homework and encourages him to stay in high school rather than going to work; the readings keep Nels out of trouble and off the street. Although Hyde leaves a worthless check, he also leaves behind his library of Dickens and Shakespeare: Mama insists that he owes them nothing, despite the domestic labor she has performed.

Mama's "old country" ability to barter for domestic goods and services also contributes to the magic of the family accounting and even compensates for momentary lapses in the family's ability to withstand the lure of consumerism. When Papa falls under the influence of an unscrupulous realtor who sells them a worthless chicken ranch, Mama manages to trade it for several rent-free months in a boarding house where the family can regain their economic self-sufficiency. When a doctor's wife refuses to let her husband perform Papa's required brain surgery for the sum that the aunts and uncles have pooled, Mama makes up the balance with the promise of Papa's labor on the doctor's home. When Katrin, eager to be admired by her peer group, wants to mark her graduation with the purchase of a fancy celluloid dresser set, Mama trades her silver heirloom necklace for it. (Katrin signifies her return to family-defined cultural values by taking back the dresser set and repossessing the necklace.) All of these efforts prevent the ups and downs of the marketplace, the economy, and commercial value systems from interfering more than momentarily with family harmony.

Mama's domesticity proves to be superior to more publicly acknowledged and economically compensated forms of expertise. Bureaucratic hospital nurses are no match for Mama when, with daughter Dagmar recovering from emergency surgery, she masquerades as a scrubwoman so that the child will not be separated from her reassuring presence. (Note that Mama gets down on her knees to clean either her own kitchen or to *pretend* to clean the hospital in order to better care for her child; she does not perform this labor outside the family, as Katie Nolan must.) When Katrin delivers Norwegian meatballs to a fancy tea at school and feels acutely her ignorance of social rules, Mama presents the meatballs as a genuine expression of hospitality that will nourish the cold and hungry teachers, classmates, and the special guest, thus transforming a formal social ritual into a meaningful interchange. Mama engineers an arrangement between an ailing elderly aunt who is a great cook but has no place to live and a younger aunt whose inferior cooking alienates her boarders. In each of these incidents the resolution of conflict between family-defined values and competing social norms preserves family harmony. Forbes creates a utopia in which family dynamics, historical change, and social change operate in perfect synchronicity.

As in *A Tree Grows in Brooklyn,* upward mobility requires education rather than wealth. In *Mama's Bank Account* belief in education is taken for granted; unlike in *Tree,* education does not drain scarce resources. "To Mama and Papa, education was the finest thing in the world, and unlike other parents we knew, they did not consider it a sacrifice to keep us all in school." Paying for Nels's high school education is the goal of the opening chapter's family accounting. When Christine decides to work in an overall factory rather than attend high school because, as she puts it, "I want clothes, and other things," Mama handles this materialist challenge to the family culture by refusing to accept Christine's wages as a contribution to the family budget. Instead, she spends them on a set of books for Christine and gently urges her to resume her education.

Redefining mobility as education rather than wealth and ending the stories with the family's achievement of financial security avoids the problem of what happens to family unity when it is no longer a requisite for survival. Although the family allots resources for Katrin to become a teacher and Christine a nurse, the pinnacle of achievement for the family is Nels's career as a doctor: "To them it was a never-ending miracle that a child of theirs had achieved such a marvelous thing." Mama explicitly stresses the importance of giving to others over material rewards: "He will be able to help people who are ill. He will save lives. . . . To be famous is not important. But to be able to stop pain—to know how to do so much good."

Forbes contrasts her version of the ordinary family with an upper-class family to make more explicit the family's critique of wealth and acquisition. Nels's high-society girlfriend pressures him to give up his medical career for a more lucrative position in her father's business. The woman's family bears a striking resemblance to wealthy families in 1930s screwball comedies. The mother is pretty, flirtatious, and cares only for position and mah-jongg parties; the father is small and bitter; the older son handsome but dissolute; the youngest son a "problem child." Like the characters who represent ordinary people in the film comedies, Mama holds her own against the superior position of the wealthy family. With hesitation she questions Nels's plans to marry Cora: "Although they are rich and handsome—the family . . . background is not good." Her choice of words reverses the conventional wisdom that "good" background is measured by social pedigree and wealth. A momentary encounter between the two families is all that is required for Nels cheerfully and independently to renounce the relationship and return to his medical plans, once again restoring family harmony.

As contemporary reviewers emphasized, *Mama's Bank Account* contains a specific account of the process of Americanization. As in *Tree,* Americanization is automatic for those born in the country; Mama proudly displays the children's framed birth certificates on the parlor wall. She identifies herself as a "San Franciscan," and then adds, "Norwegian. American citizen." Rather than stressing difference or unfamiliarity, Mama pronounces San Francisco to be "like Norway." Her pleasure in the city embraces its diverse inhabitants: she counts among her special friends an Armenian shopkeeper, to whom she gives one of her best Norwegian recipes, and a Chinatown shopkeeper, Old Sing Fat, who sends her home with gifts of litchi nuts and preserved ginger. Mama's cosmopolitan sensibility reflects the war's demands for popular unity.

Her sisters are more parochial than she, more ensconced in old-world customs and morality. Aunt Jenny is less trusting of Americans, Aunt Marta more fatalistic in accepting a child's injury, Aunt Sigrid more sentimentally attached to family heirlooms. Aunt Trina still expects the familial provision of a dowry. Despite these differences, the aunts all come through in a family crisis, contributing cash toward Papa's unexpected medical bills. Uncle Chris, the "black" Norwegian, represents another kind of immigrant, physically marked by his "singular swarthiness" and a black mustache. Forbes plays on Chris's "blackness" as distinguishing him from the blonde Scandinavian "type" and also as an indicator of his lack of respectability: he drinks, swears, lives with a woman. But his "darkness" also enhances his position as the family patriarch with certain male privileges: he publicly relishes his whiskey and teaches his nephew to swear as a manly antidote to pain. He treats his sisters (the aunts), with the exception of Mama, as children, and supersedes their authority when it comes to treating a nephew who suffers, as he once did, from a limp. His crusty exterior hides the tenderness with which he softly sings Norwegian lullabies to the nephew in the hospital. Uncle Chris is the only immigrant who shares Mama's cosmopolitanism. After his death the aunts discover he has given all his money to pay for surgeries enabling children to walk. The recipients of his charity extend far beyond his nephew, illustrating a domestic application of the military melting pot: "Joseph Spinelli . . . Jamie Kelly . . . Esta Jensen . . . and Sam Bernstein."

The public schools are the only place in which the children's Americanness is questioned. When the daughters are enrolled in a girls' grammar school in a neighborhood new to them, they encounter a xenophobic principal who, despite the Hansen children's insistence that they are native-born Americans of Norwegian parentage, calls them "Swedes." She complains about her new charges, assigning them to a status somewhere between the uncertain whiteness of Italians and Jews and the clearly racially marked African and Asian Americans: "The Vanetti girl, and the Gubbenstein creatures, and now three tow-headed Swedes. . . . Next thing you know we'll be getting Negroes, or even . . . Orientals." A teacher does not accept Katrin's name, insisting on calling her Kathryn, and ignores Dagmar's request to go to the bathroom, which results in the shame of a public accident.

These unpleasant incidents do not deter the children from either their schooling or the process of assimilation. Since they are not excluded by racialized boundaries as "Negroes or even . . . Orientals" are, members of the family can shed their "Norwegianness" (language, cuisine, social practices) as they become familiar with American ways. "Little by little, the foreignness had disappeared almost entirely from our family life. Only on special occasions did Mama make the *lutefisk* or *flatbrod,* and she and Papa seldom spoke Norwegian any more. They had learned to play whist, and often went to neighborhood card parties or shows."

As the *Library Journal* predicted, the stories' formula of family cooperation, maternal devotion, hard work, educational mobility, and Americanization sold very well.[17] Popular response to the stories attracted Hollywood interest; RKO quickly bought the film rights. But the debate about which tried-and-true studio formula should drive the screen adaptation was halted when Broadway composer Richard Rodgers and lyricist Oscar Hammerstein, fresh from their triumph in mythologizing the American West in their folk musical *Oklahoma,* bought the rights to produce a theatrical adaptation, which would precede a film version.[18] The Broadway hit play expanded *Mama*'s appeal through the 1940s and into the mid-1950s.

REMEMBERING MAMA ON THE STAGE

Forbes's Mama stories were adapted by the prominent playwright John Van Druten, who was hired by Rodgers and Hammerstein to produce a hit that did not imitate *Oklahoma* in too obvious a manner. Creating a kindred "folk play," Van Druten gave the stories a new orientation and a hugely popular theatrical life as *I Remember Mama.*[19] *I Remember Mama* opened on Broadway in October 1944 and was a smash hit, running for 714 performances (89 weeks), with additional long runs in London and San Francisco. Harcourt Brace published Van Druten's dramatization in 1945. The actors then brought *Mama* to a much wider audience with a one-time radio broadcast for *Theatre Guild on the Air* in 1946; it was the first Broadway play brought to radio by its original Broadway cast.[20] The success of Van Druten's adaptation significantly widened the reach of Forbes's ethnic working-class family, but also reformulated what made them ordinary.

By the time John Van Druten began to work on adapting Forbes's short stories he had been a successful dramatist for nearly twenty years, known for work that was characterized as short on plot but long on charm and naturalistic dialogue and situations. He had also been employed as a screenwriter by both British and American film studios. Van Druten's homosexuality may have shaped the perspective of his 1930s drawing room comedies, which probed the strictures of femininity and masculinity within heterosexual conventions. Several of these present female characters who achieve self-fulfillment through sacrifice and selfless love.[21] *I Remember Mama* was Van Druten's first departure from drawing room comedy—though here too a selfless and loving female figure appears.

Van Druten's theatrical adaptation expanded the play's representations in the spirit of wartime concerns, giving the stories the shape in which they were most widely diffused. Offering the audience images of nurture and safety rather than horror and uncertainty, Van Druten structured the play around the daughter's idealized memories of her mother; her literary success, based on these memories, defines the family's economic security. Encouraging a multiethnic pluralism, Van Druten used émigré actors to play ethnically marked Norwegians, stressing Americanization as a form of patriotism and linking old-world ethnic ties with narrowness and superstition. (Van Druten applied for American citizenship in 1944, the year he wrote and staged *I Remember Mama*.) Through specific dramatic innovations, such as featuring the daughter as both narrator and dramatic actor and imitating memory through a deliberate absence of plot, Van Druten created a prototype for looking back through ethnic nostalgia that could be adapted to a variety of postwar audiences.

I Remember Mama established a convention for the genre of the memory play by calling attention to its own loving nostalgia while inviting audiences to revel in a positive rendering of a shared past. One critic noted, "Memories can convincingly present, not the past, but an idealization of it." The daughter's narration of remembering encouraged the audience to pay special attention to the subjectivity of memory. Her moving back and forth, from adult narrator looking back to a girl whose story unfolds in the course of the play, also called attention to how family memories take shape. Although the play contained no plot, conflict, crises, or climaxes, reviewers found Van Druten's innovative staging—more than thirty scenes enacted on or in front of three revolving sets, with twenty characters and two time frames—especially effective in eliciting pleasurable "remembering" from Broadway audiences. One reviewer commented that the staging invited the audience to share its device—"let's pretend"— creating "a welcome sense of liberation from the confinements of [theatrical] realism." The revolving sets and episodic quality of the scenes were both "stylized and realistic," theatrical *and* cinematic. Several reviewers noted that watching the play approximated the intense "pleasures" of flipping through family picture albums. (One critic noted ruefully that some of the scenes were, like pictures in an album, a little blurry, while others were in superb focus.)[22]

Van Druten shifted both the time frame and characterization of *Mama*. He located the play even further back in time than Forbes had set her stories, placing its action in 1910, well before both world wars. (Forbes left the dates unspecified, but "twenty years ago" would have placed the action in the 1920s.) In his hands *all* the characters become more universally typed than in the sketches. Mama is always understanding and self-denying; Katrin must learn to abandon literary pretension and write about the familiar; Uncle Chris hides a kind heart behind his gruff exterior. The children all have labels: Nels is "the kind one," Christine the "stubborn one," and Katrin, the future writer, "the dramatic one."[23]

Van Druten's adaptation made Katrin's *literary* success the climactic achievement of "remembering Mama." The plot uses Katrin's writing aspirations, mentioned only briefly in two minor plot lines in the stories, as the central theme. The family's economic mobility is indicated in several ways: they give generous tips, hire domestic help, and are able to pay for Nels's medical school and the girls' college education.[24] But it is Katrin's writing that enshrines the memories of Mama—invoked at the start and close of the play—and successfully turns the story of family accounting into a means of supporting the family. Basing the achievement of personal success and financial reward on the act of remembering Mama is a means of containing the potential for individualism and materialism—otherwise transgressive in a female character.

The play calls attention to the gendered implications of remembering Mama. Mama herself suggests remembering *Papa,* and is initially unsettled by Katrin's turn to *her* instead. Many reviewers noted the distinctiveness of Van Druten's focus on Mama by referring to *Life with Father* (1939), Howard Lindsay and Russell Crouse's humorous play detailing the gentle decline of the father's authority when confronted with the persistent efforts of his upper-class Episcopalian wife. *Life with Father* had been selling out to Broadway audiences for five years when *I Remember Mama* opened.[25]

After it became clear that *Mama* was drawing the same enthusiastic audiences as *Father,* critics tried to analyze *Mama*'s appeal. They did not always acknowledge wartime uncertainties, although the war was a continuing point of reference. One reviewer commented on critical treatments of mothers before the war, the *uneven* praise of mothers between Al Jolson's 1927 blackface tribute to the immigrant mother in *The Jazz Singer* and Van Druten's 1944 production, noting that mothers were in "disfavor" in "times less troubled" and that Freudian thought gave mothers "a hard time of it."[26] Although reviewers did not mention them, feminist ideas circulating in the 1920s and the 1930s had also challenged maternalism as a conservative rendering of women's destiny.

The play's idealization of Mama could affirm a conservative ideological position in the heated debates in the 1940s about women's roles in society. Arthur Hopkins proposed in *Theatre Arts* that Mama's joy in serving others could serve as the solution to all modern social problems. If more women would emulate Mama, he wrote, there would be no more debate about women's place in the world, no questioning of motherhood as a sacred calling, no more children stricken by divorce, no more marriages divided by "selfish storms."[27]

Other critics connected the appeal of remembering Mama in 1944 to "the horror and anguish of a world at war." Rosamund Gilder interpreted Mama as "more than just a mother; she's a symbol of security, a potent symbol in the age of chaos." John Mason Brown labeled *Mama* a "war play" because "when the present is desperate and lonely, and the future uncertain . . . the past offers an emotional and domestic security that we all hope will come again." Brown elaborated on the wartime meaning of Mama's "security" by positioning it, like Norman Rockwell's famous illustrations of the Four Freedoms, within the private realm. Brown argued that Mama's virtues were private ones, "which can be lost sight of in the midst of public causes. She is the more comfortable because, in a world gone confusingly global, we find her thinking only in terms of her own family."[28]

Brown's comments revealed what was provocative about the turn to women and to the ordinary family as representing wartime citizenship. Because Mama "reaffirms the forgotten and once despised family focus," she was "the more welcome as the average man's symbol of security."[29] A working-class immigrant mother could now become a powerful representation of a glorified motherhood, holding together a family to stand in for the nation. But these representations of "mother" and "family" undermined any specific sense of female agency or of the particular loves and labors associated with immigrant working-class life: what recommended her were qualities expressed as universal maternalism in wartime. Maternal selflessness was a feature of *all* successful patriotic mothers.

Van Druten's story of Americanization served a similar function. Setting up a contrast between "good" and "bad" immigrants—as Betty Smith had done—and offering American citizenship as the final achievement of "remembering Mama" enabled the play to express a cultural mission of the war. Mama and Uncle Chris serve as model American wartime citizens: they are cosmopolitan and worldly, generous and productive, without being too materialistic. The reason for the family's emigration from Norway is pronounced to be family solidarity rather than material gain. Katrin asks, "But didn't you come to America to get rich?" Mama answers (according to stage directions, "shocked"): "No. We come to America because they are all here—all the others. Is good for families to be together. . . . I become American citizen. But not to get rich." Fortunately, their motives of reuniting the family and becoming Americans do not stand in the way, and may even increase the likelihood, of their amassing considerable resources—enough to own and improve property, provide higher education for their children, and, in Chris's case, to become a kind of neighborhood philanthropist. Mama and Uncle Chris form an alliance against the aunts, thus dramatizing the distinction between cosmopolitan "good" and parochial "bad" immigrants.

In Van Druten's adaptation, the aunts become negative "ethnic types." They represent immigrant women as gossip-driven, harsh enforcers of moral standards of temperance and sexuality, materialistic, and ungenerous. (Forbes's account of the aunts readily pooling their savings for Papa's critical operation is omitted from the play.) In contrast, Mama favors romance over family-centered criteria for marriage, assesses individual worth over group valuations, and withholds moral judgment of Uncle Chris, though he is still distinguished from others as a "black Norwegian" (Van Druten assumes the whiteness of his audience when Papa, responding to the aunts' pronouncement that children drinking black coffee would turn their complexions dark, makes a joke: "Maybe it would be all right if we have *one* colored daughter").

Van Druten's casting of émigré actors enabled the performances to emphasize a message of wartime Americanization and cultural pluralism. Mady Christians as Mama brought a cosmopolitan sensibility to her characterization. She had fled Berlin in 1933 to escape Nazi domination of the theater, successfully finding parts on Broadway and in Hollywood in the late 1930s and early 1940s. In 1941 she won critical acclaim as the American-born wife of a German antifascist in Lillian Hellman's play *The Watch on the Rhine.* She wrote to Rodgers and Hammerstein to ask for the part of Mama. Christians's award-winning performance in *I Remember Mama* was widely admired; when Van Druten published his adaptation, he dedicated the play to her.[30]

Christians became an American citizen in 1939, and proudly declared it; critics in turn hailed Christians's performance as stepping "over the fine line between acting and being." One critic commented, "Audiences have accepted Mama as real." Others remarked that she played Mama with a "secret chic" as well as "those subtle characteristics that come from nationality." She was described as having a "warm, sensitive personality but it is covered by a patina of sophistication which suggests old silver and good wine" rather than "chipped china and herring"—more commonly associated with working-class immigrants.[31]

Audiences had the experience of being in the theater with European-born actors and actresses whose characters reiterated the promise of Americanization and celebrated the possibilities of wartime pluralism. Christians, who reported that she based her characterization on memories of her own mother, was greeted by enthusiastic servicemen from various white ethnic backgrounds who waited for her after performances to tell her, "We weren't Norwegians at home. We were Czech (or Danish or Greeks) . . . but you remind me of my older sister (or of my mother)."[32] After the war, however, Christians's foreignness would no longer suit the requirements of representing maternalism.

THE MOTHER NEXT DOOR ON FILM, 1947–1948

By the time RKO began production on a film version in the fall of 1947, even the *brief* distance from the war reshaped the context in which the Mama stories were filmed and viewed. Home front unity had fractured into many competing narratives. Dark detective and crime stories (labeled *film noir* by French critics beginning in August 1946) were popular at the box office. They probed victory and success to unearth corruption, cynicism, rage, and violence, and set the terms for new norms of psychological "realism."[33] Motherhood was routinely portrayed as obsessive and pathological—in movies such as *Mildred Pierce* (1945)—and accused of contaminating young manhood, echoing the position popularized by Philip Wylie in his 1942 bestseller, *Generation of Vipers*.[34]

The popularity and critical success of *I Remember Mama* increased the resources RKO was willing to devote to the film adaptation. Harriet Parsons remained the producer, but studio executives now regarded the film as a major production.[35] Parsons and the screenwriter DeWitt Bodeen adapted the script, but Van Druten's theatrical conception fundamentally shaped the screenplay. Forbes publicly acknowledged this at the time of the film's release: "The play was John van Druten's idea, not mine. He wrote the play, and had he not, there might never have been a movie."[36]

Although the film intended to cash in on the play's success by casting at least some of the stage actors—notably Barbara Bel Geddes as the daughter-narrator Katrin and Oscar Homolka as Uncle Chris—Mady Christians, the biggest star, was not cast in the film. Despite Christians's numerous theatrical awards and being hailed as synonymous with the part of Mama, her activism on behalf of refugees from Nazism and with the American Committee for the Protection of the Foreign Born resulted in her being blacklisted. Before her death in 1951 she could only get roles in the independent productions of sympathetic directors, Irving Reis's *All My Sons* (1948) and Max Ophuls's *Letter to an Unknown Woman* (1948).[37]

The process of casting the film *Mama* suggested that, after the war, the interest in émigré ethnicity that enabled Mama's immigrant status to stand for a wartime pluralism soon yielded to the more standard Hollywood version of "motherliness." For a short time there were reports that Katina Paxinou, the Greek actress who had won an Oscar for her portrayal of Pilar in *For Whom the Bell Tolls* (1943) would play Mama, requiring a shift in the family's nationality to Greek. Harriet Parsons thought Greta Garbo's Swedish nationality made her suitable, but Garbo was not interested in playing a "mama." Marlene Dietrich apparently sought the role, but studio executives felt that her glamour and mysterious sensuality did not suit the part of a Norwegian mother. Irene Dunne was the actress solicited to play Mama, fresh from her success as the determined English mother in *Anna and the King of Siam* (1946) and as the endearing American mother in the film *Life with Father* (1947). Paradoxically, Dunne had achieved stardom in the 1930s through some notable "antimother" parts in romantic comedies such as *Theodora Goes Wild* (1936) and *The Silver Chord* (1933), in which she played an elegant and modern career woman challenging a mother who is overly involved with her sons' lives. Dunne agreed to play the part of Mama only if George Stevens, her director in *Penny Serenade* (1941), was hired along with her.

The casting of Dunne in the title role signaled the way in which the studio would interpret motherhood in *Mama*. Publicity news about Dunne in May 1947 commented on her as "the screen's ideal young mother type." She actively promoted a maternalist image when she appeared on a special radio Mother's Day program in 1947 and an Easter broadcast in 1948. A Hollywood columnist listed her as one of the "ten most perfect house-wives in Hollywood" as named by the Perfect Housewife Institute. Another wrote, "Miss Dunne's offscreen life is, in its routine predictabil-ity, practically indistinguishable from her cinematic one," describing her husband of twenty years, her adopted daughter, and their life as "solid cit-izens, property owners, and regular church-goers." Her publicity inter-views stressed the importance of women supporting their men: "Our main responsibility—also interest—always will be taking care of the man of the house because the man of the house needs to be taken care of—in more ways than you can shake a stick at." Dunne was also featured as the author of the advice column "You Have a Problem?" in the monthly movie magazine *Silver Screen*—illustrated with publicity stills of her as Mama interposed with Hollywood glamour shots.[38] Both prefilm public-ity and reviews called attention to the artifice of Dunne's transformation from movie star to immigrant mother, with her blonde braided wig, her padded figure, and her "cheap and rather exhausted" clothes.[39]

RKO promotional efforts contributed to conveying the film's themes of family and motherhood in the most general terms, consistent with their own development of the film's universalism. They did add "Norwegian societies" to the list of usual preview audiences. But they aimed most of their efforts at selling tickets to mothers: inviting wartime's Gold Star mothers to a screening of the film in Denver; offering free tickets for women who became mothers on opening night in Columbus, Ohio; encouraging Providence theater patrons to nominate the "most outstand-ing Mama" in Rhode Island.[40] *Film Bulletin*, published in Kansas City, Missouri, encouraged this focus: "Spread the word that this is a picture the whole family will enjoy. Stress the human interests of mother love and sell the dramatic portrayals of situations which occur in every family circle."[41]

A film that portrayed, with a documentarylike realism, family values as timeless, sustaining, and more powerful than the economy or commercial culture had profound implications in the postwar world. Hedda Hopper was one of the critics who promoted the film as supporting a conservative social vision: "It is families such as they portray that help make democracy and America great." Others made clear its political significance as an ordi-nary family story, labeling it "a poignant tender tribute to the family insti-tution" and a "warm human document of plain ordinary people—the backbone of American civilization." Several other reviewers commented with approval on Mama's lack of material aspirations: "As Mama tells it, their reason for coming over was not to make money but to be with their relatives and friends who had preceded them; she no more wants to be rich than to be ten feet tall."[42]

Irene Dunne's performance was nearly universally admired for creating an ideal Mama who embodied the values of modern maternalism. As Bosley Crowther described her enactment of a "mother's selfless love," Dunne endowed Mama with "strength and vitality," but also "softness."[43] Another critic praised Dunne's Mama as "not a matriarch but a gentle and loving wife and mother, whose only fierceness lay in defending the rights of her husband and children." A Hollywood reviewer noted the contrast between Dunne's star position on theater marquees and the way that, in the film, "she subordinates herself to everything and everybody."[44] The only dissent seemed to come from reviewers with a suspicion of motherly over-involvement. The *New Yorker* reviewer, for example, wondered if Mama's many exertions to "make ends meet, to steer the clan through sickness and health" put "rather too fine a burnish on the silver chord," adding, "I'm not at all sure that her conduct would win the complete support of many psychiatrists." Nonetheless, Mama's maternalism and her acquiescence to male authority suited the political and cultural contexts of the postwar period. Even Cecelia Anger's critical review of the film praised Barbara Bel Geddes for her portrayal of Katrin's similar womanly qualities, "sensitive responsiveness to others in her orbit," and "unassertive selflessness," rather than, for example, applauding her developing purpose as a writer.[45]

On one level Irene Dunne brought a gracious glamour to the part of an immigrant working-class Mama, inviting the audience to identify with a hardworking and loving but also cosmopolitan immigrant mother. On another level Dunne's Hollywood persona obscured markers of class and ethnic identity signified by the costumes and set design, presenting a mother with a face unmarked by lines, serenely presiding over lovely children, living with an adoring husband in comfortable surroundings. These opposing messages appeared in reviews of the film: while *Variety* identified it more as a "skillful depiction of the life of one humble obscure Scandinavian American family," another reviewer stressed how Mama was "like mothers the wide world over" as she "performs minor miracles every day in the week without a second thought." Movie reviewers in general treated the film as a recreation of Forbes's childhood, referring to it as "reminiscences" or "recollections" of family life.[46] Kathryn Forbes seems to have been a willing participant in promoting this interpretation of the film, teaching Dunne about Mama through telling stories of her grandmother and applauding Dunne's characterization of Mama.[47] But review-ers also folded the specificity of Forbes's setting and stories into the uni-versal, assuring readers that Mama could serve as a role model for how to raise children. The reviewer for a newspaper in North Hollywood stated that the film revealed "the wonderful influences of good, strong and true parents in the American home." For this reviewer Dunne's performance as Mama called to mind "the mother of a family, the like of which proba-bly lives next door, or it could be yours." The imaginary San Francisco household seemed to offer an actual "demonstration of how many Amer-ican families live, what space it has physically and spiritually to grow in, and what you can afford to spend without withdrawing your savings from the bank of Utopia."[48] *Life* approvingly labeled the film as a "folksy" pic-ture about an "eccentric Norwegian family" that made money by cele-brating "comfortable virtues of home life" instead of relying on Holly-wood's "old staples of sex and adventure."[49]

Dunne's publicity interviews highlighted the film's celebration of "nat-ural motherhood," applauding her character as "so wise in the handling of her children." She stereotyped contemporary women who may have been moving outside the domestic realm when she described how "too many mothers today play bridge and hurry home and grab a cocktail to stimu-late themselves and care very little what happens to their children, just so they are not bothered." She turned the immigrant family story in *Mama* into a didactic narrative showcasing Christian humility and upward mobility: "These people in 'I Remember Mama' came here from Norway without a cent. He was a humble carpenter but it was Mama who kept the family together, encouraging her boy to be a doctor, her daughter to be a writer." Dunne praised the film's emphasis on "the fundamental things, the real things in life" as a welcome alternative to "too many stories of social significance"—a previously and widely admired genre committed to dramatizing social forces and social analysis.[50]

In filming family memories George Stevens was venturing into territory already fixed in terms of Hollywood genres: vaudeville-styled ethnic cari-cature and soap-styled family drama. As one film critic opened his review, "Memories of happy-sad childhoods peopled with both noble and comic characters are not exactly novelties." Stevens planned an unconventional treatment of a conventional subject: "To build accumulative interest, we're trying to develop in the audience a feeling of almost possessive affec-tion for Mama and her family."[51] Stevens aimed to reveal "family portrai-ture" without crossing "from sentiment into sentimentality." This was the same emotional territory Betty Smith had sought to convey in *A Tree Grows in Brooklyn*. What was striking about Stevens's filmic "remembrance of things past" was that it avoided being "mawkish in its drama" or "outlandish in its comedy," creating instead "realism" that blended laughter and tears.[52]

Stevens was one of the most prestigious producer-directors in Hollywood at this time; *I Remember Mama* was the first film he made after the war. The child of two actors, Stevens had been working in Hollywood since the early 1920s.[53] He spent four years in the U.S. Army Signal Corps, where he had worked directing the Special Motion Pictures Unit assigned to photograph the activities of the Sixth Army. Photographing the D-Day invasion of Normandy, the liberation of Paris, and the arrival of American troops at Dachau profoundly unsettled Stevens, as he later commented:

> I hated the bastards [the Nazis] and what they stood for, *the worst, worst, possible* thing that's happened in centuries, and yet, when a poor man, hungered and unseeing because his eyesight is failing, grabs me and starts begging, *I* feel the Nazi in any human being, I don't care whether I am a Jew or Gentile, *I* feel the Nazi, because I abhor him. . . . I feel myself being capable of arrogance and brutality to keep him off. That's a fierce thing to discover within yourself that which you despise the most.[54]

On his return to Hollywood Stevens moved away from the studio system in 1946 by joining an independent production company, Liberty Films. He had not yet found a way to make films that reflected the change in his sensibilities when he was "lent" by Liberty to RKO to make *I Remember Mama*. This project attracted Stevens by offering him a "return home to the San Francisco of his youth, what he called the 'confirmed period of the past.'"[55]

Under Stevens's direction, rather than being contained within a Hollywood formula, the episodic story served to make the film "real" to its audience: as one reviewer commented, it "flows forward with some of the waywardness and unpredictability of life itself."[56] In publicity interviews Stevens justified the extra running time as requisite for this subject matter. Although most reviewers felt the film was too long, they acceded to the logic of conveying family realism through a leisurely pace: as Bosley Crowther noted, these were "common objections to personal reminiscences."[57]

As on Broadway, "Norwegianness" was not particularly important to the filmmakers in their attempt to achieve authenticity. Too much ethnic specificity would have decreased the appeal of the film, which projected the same kind of generic "foreignness" as had the film of *A Tree Grows in Brooklyn.* Although prefilm publicity highlighted Irene Dunne's "daily work with a Norwegian woman to perfect her accent," the other starring "Norwegians" improvised a variety of "foreign" manners of speech. Philip Dorn (Papa), originally born in the Netherlands, was described as "speaking with his own indigenous accent," while the speech of Viennese actor Oscar Homolka (Uncle Chris) was described simply as "loud." The radio ventriloquist Edgar Bergen, who played a small part as an undertaker from the old country, was U.S.-born with Swedish relatives and could presumably adapt any accent.[58] The "foreignness" of the immigrant generation's speech contrasts with the Americanization implied by the children's unmarked speech. (Even the children's brush with "foreignness" is safely contained when the film repeats the play's Norwegian whiteness "joke." The aunts express an old-world superstition that drinking coffee will turn the children's complexions black. In the film version it is the child Dagmar who praises the potential effect of coffee: she wants to be a "black" Norwegian like Uncle Chris. Papa tells her it would be better if she turned out to be blonde, like her Mama.)

Stevens used what he saw as the similarities in physical environment between Norway and San Francisco to justify for the audience the easy transferal of Mama's national loyalties. "I don't want to romanticize Mama but I do want to establish her affinity, perhaps unconscious, with her native Norway," Stevens said in an interview at the time. "She could never have settled in a flat land like Iowa. Mama would naturally gravitate to a city like San Francisco. The hills, the wind, the salt air, the comings and going of ships in the bay—all these things would instinctively remind her of Norway."[59] Visual emphasis on the San Francisco setting served to reinforce the family's claims of American citizenship.

As in the film *Tree,* the opening titles and credits for the film invited the audience to view a nostalgic ethnic family past as the universal American past. First appears a sketch of Irene Dunne as Mama in an ornate oval picture frame; then the camera draws the audience into the frame to view a set of sketches of an idealized urban past that foreshadow key scenes in the movie: bustling downtown San Francisco, complete with clock tower; the family, listening around the table to a reading of literature, stretching meager cash to pay for necessities. Associating the family with San Francisco landmarks of the bay, cable cars, the ferry, and the fog implicitly proclaim their American belonging.

In order to heighten the feelings of intimacy within the family and to play crowded interior scenes against panoramic shots of the San Francisco Bay—visible from windows inside the set—Stevens had the interior sets constructed within the house (normally they would have been built on a different stage). To develop the "possessive attachment to Mama and her family," Stevens relied on an unusually mobile camera. He freed the camera to create the illusion of movement in order to balance the lack of action in plot and to enable the audience to "see into" family life. As one critic noted, "The camera stalks furtively around the tiny setting of the Hansens' little house, at times eavesdropping through a stair railing, frequently taking in a large family gathering with ingeniously distributed emphasis."[60]

Family budgeting is the central motif of the film, identifying the family as working class and representing the unity (revealed in the end to rely on maternal psychological nurture) that underlies Katrin's literary success and propels the family into the middle class. In the first allocation of the family budget, Katrin's voice-over narration shades into Mama's voice reciting, like an incantation, "First, for the landlord," repeated by all the others. Some of the time the family is shot from behind in order to emphasize the audience's unusual access to a private family moment. In one significant moment Papa and Nels walk away from the table—suggesting a crisis brought on by scarcity—but quickly the family regroups, with Mama at the center: she pronounces that once again, with cooperation and collective sacrifice, everyone's needs have been met. "Is good . . . is enough . . . we do not have to go to the bank." When this scene is repeated at the end, the family again gathers around the table, this time to listen to Katrin read her soon-to-be published account of that moment. The camera begins the transition to the close of the film, following Mama's move to the window by slipping the audience back outside, moving away slowly to a panoramic shot of the fog-shrouded city, affirming one final time the family's secured place in San Francisco and America.

Because of the original stories' focus on Mama, the male performances were especially important to the film's meaning in the postwar era. Papa's part was expanded from the play to the film, and significantly it is he, rather than Mama, who confirms Katrin's adulthood. Papa rewards her expression of appropriately womanly behavior (giving up the object of her desire, the fancy dresser set, in favor of one that the family has sanctioned) by pouring her first cup of coffee. Oscar Homolka's performance as Uncle Chris adds the most masculine weight to the film. A number of the reviewers thought that he "stole the picture," saying that his "boisterous character" had saved the film from "excessive saccharinity."[61] The screenplay deleted his blasphemous curse and transformed his illicit relationship with his housekeeper (invented *for* the play) into a secret marriage. These changes did not diminish Chris's hypermasculinity, which is so secure in the film that it also provides nurture for his lame nephew superior to that of Arne's own "bad" mother, one of the parochial immigrant aunts. That Mama is the only one of his sisters whom Uncle Chris trusts provides yet another demonstration of her superior, nonjudgmental womanliness, fully compatible with his robust masculine style. Mama's triumphant circumvention of hospital rules to appear at Dagmar's bedside, and the comfort her gentle presence offers to all the children on the ward, including one African American child, emphasizes the universality of her maternal nurture.

Audiences' general enthusiasm for *I Remember Mama* was reflected in the film's box office receipts, placing it on *Variety*'s list of "top grossers" for 1948. In March 1948 it won the *Parents' Magazine* medal for "outstanding family picture" of the month.[62] But the filming of *Mama* set it on a journey increasingly separate from Kathryn Forbes, who never again produced a popular narrative. Forbes's short fiction for women's magazines applied popular family psychology to other kinds of war stories; she even sold a few more stories about the Hansen family after *Mama's Bank Account* was published.[63] Divorced in 1946, Forbes began to write about less ordinary families with less popular appeal. Her full-length novel *Transfer Point* (1947) relies on the device of a child remembering San Francisco in the early 1920s, but this child is torn between separated parents. In this "wholly different kind of book," serialized in *Good Housekeeping* in the fall of that year, the memories are not so sweet. As one reviewer noted, the protagonist of this book "had no such luck as the children in the united Norwegian family of the earlier story. In her life there was no bedrock of family solidarity on which a child could rely."[64] When the television show was broadcast in 1949, Forbes's name appeared in the weekly credits, but the character of Mama had by then overtaken her other fiction as well as her personal celebrity.

MAMA ON CBS, 1949–1956

In 1949 a serial about the Hansen family called *Mama*, "based on *Mama's Bank Account* by Kathryn Forbes," became one of the first family situation comedies to air on television. Although there were similarities, the requirements of its broadcast venue—and its context further removed from the war years—required that a serial of *Mama* would be reshaped in form and content and would cover different cultural terrain than had the movie. The television *Mama* developed a large and devoted audience and remained in the same time slot (Friday nights, from 8:00 to 8:30) with the same sponsorship (General Foods, Maxwell House Coffee) on the same network (CBS) from July 1949 to July 1956. By 1950 the Nielsen Company's early ratings system measured *Mama*'s audience share of 39.7 percent of households with televisions as the highest of any family serial.[65] Hundreds of scripts and episodes enacted over seven years embedded the ethnic working-class characters and setting in popular memory.

The television *Mama* was shaped by and against genre expectations established by radio. Unlike *The Goldbergs,* which was CBS's first half-hour situation comedy on television, premiering in January 1949, *Mama* did not have a previous existence as a radio family comedy serial.[66] Indeed, one of the *Mama* writers stressed its distance from ethnic humor by his comment that *Mama* "never did jokes."[67] But when Erik Barnouw adapted the play for a radio broadcast in 1946, he pointed out how its theatrical structure, a "series of scenes held together by narration spoken by the protagonist," was "more characteristically a radio form than a stage form." He also noted that the play's narration, "foreign to stage and screen," was "very usual in radio," where it "takes particular advantage of" radio's special ability to address the audience "person to person." His observations explained *Mama*'s easy transition to early television, which drew heavily on radio's financial resources, talent, and formats to establish itself as a commercially successful broadcast medium.[68]

Many of the people responsible for *Mama*'s distinct form had backgrounds in popular theater, wartime drama, radio, and early television drama. One of the significant "authors" of Mama was the left-wing Ralph Nelson, who had experience on Broadway as well as acting in and directing live television drama. Nelson directed the *Mama* series during its entire run on television.[69] Carol Irwin, who shared the producer credits for *Mama* with Nelson, had been a production executive for Theatre Guild on the Air.[70] The main writer for *Mama*, Frank Gabrielson, was a left-wing screenwriter for Twentieth Century-Fox before securing this job.[71] Mama was played by Peggy Wood, a versatile actress who had appeared on the stage, in a few movies in the 1930s and 1940s, and on the early live television drama Philco Playhouse in its first season. Papa was played by Judson Laire, who had first acted in live television drama on

Studio One, CBS's dramatic anthology show. Robin Morgan, cast as Dagmar, came to *Mama* from her own half-hour weekly national radio show, *Little Robin Morgan,* from 1946 to 1948.[72]

Mama's production aesthetic was derived from the conventions of live television drama, one of early television's pioneer forms. Although drama was a staple of radio programming, television's live drama anthology shows offered something different, combining for home viewers the intimacy and immediacy of radio's live broadcasting with a new view from "the best seats in the house." These shows reinforced the audience illusion of being in the actors' presence with naturalistic modes of theatrical representation: "realist" acting styles, slice-of-life stories, and psychological characterizations.[73] *Mama* was filmed live, as a continuous half hour, without any commercial break. The actors worked in a professional theatrical manner, rehearsing several times for the weekly performance. [74] Like live television drama, *Mama* was filmed with three cameras, which in effect created three prosceniums, giving the director more control over pace and mobility because "an actor never knows when a camera might be on or off him."[75] A 1949 CBS press release promoted the show on the basis of its distinctive form of "realism," claiming that "we try to give the impression that no one is acting" and citing an unnamed viewer's response that "nobody but members of a real family could talk like that."[76]

In utilizing the live drama apparatus to make a weekly family serial seem "real," *Mama* was distinct from other serial forms exploring television's entertainment potential, not a character-driven comedy show relying on vaudeville-style ethnic humor like *The Goldbergs* (1949–1954) or *Life with Riley* (1949–1958). Unlike *Amos 'n' Andy* (1951–1953) and *Life with Luigi* (1952–1953), *Mama* featured a family ensemble rather than individual performers. It did not integrate the theatricality, spectacle, and self-reflexivity common in family sitcoms headed by entertainers, such as *I Love Lucy* (1951–1961), *Make Room for Daddy* (1953–1971), and the *Burns and Allen Show* (1950–1958). [77] Actress Wood's comment that the show was "never maudlin, never sticky" distanced it from the genre of daytime "soaps."[78]

Mama's distinctive form of serial drama was preserved in tightly controlled scripts that focused on character development rather than plot twists or verbal humor. Peggy Wood said that writer Frank Gabrielson's scripts "were beautifully written and we looked forward each week to his scripts. We had a feeling of security in them because they were so right. . . . They were really solid, honest things." When Carol Irwin approached Max Wilk in 1952 to write for the show, she advised him of the show's standard: "We never go in for quick plots, with contrived twists and turns and easy solutions. What happens here is that we're dealing with honest characters, and our audience knows and identifies with them. We keep playing off their actual experiences." Wilk later described his experience writing character-driven episodes for the show: "I learned to get plot out of the characters." Director Ralph Nelson also exercised tight control over the content and look of the show: as Wood recalled, "Sometimes things were sent in, and I've heard Ralph say, 'But we don't do things like that in this family.' It would be something a writer might think of as a sure-fire formula plot—and perhaps it would have been, for some other show . . . but Ralph would always repeat, 'No . . . we couldn't do something like that here.'" Even the commercial sponsorship of coffee was absorbed into the show's dramatic themes so as to cause minimal disruption to its live-drama "realism."[79]

Compared with its film antecedent, the television series *Mama* had a narrower canvas: the San Francisco hills visible from the windows looked artificial; the number of characters had to be cut to fit the size of the screen. The family tree had already been "pruned" for *Mama's* radio adaptation, cutting one sister and two aunts. For the television series the boarders had also disappeared; the Hansen household came to resemble a model nuclear family.

Mama was distinct from other family sitcoms on the new medium of television because its action unfolded in the past. This "past" was dramatically constituted in each episode by the family album, imaginatively suggested by the Broadway staging and now rendered literally. The device of the album and the narration about "remembering" opened and closed every show. Katrin's voice-over begins the remembering; the album then opens to an old photo of a modest white Victorian-style frame house (situated next door to a similar house) labeled "our house." The camera cuts to a shot of the neat but empty kitchen, with a white tablecloth on the table and white curtains at the windows. The kitchen then fills with the actors portraying the family, who sit talking to each other around the kitchen table as Katrin's voice-over continues, with the camera panning as she speaks of each character: Nels, Dagmar, Papa, and of course, Mama. The camera lingers on Mama as the Maxwell House announcer takes over the narration, linking Mama with coffee. Katrin's voice-over also ends the story, as the camera shows her hand writing in her journal. The closing credits appear on album pages, as does a final photograph of the happy family of five.

In the second season of the show the album's elaboration of the past expanded. Now the first voice-over narration from Katrin begins with "remembering" the album itself and locating it in the house—on "the parlor table at home." The first pages in the album call attention to the immigrant status of Mama and Papa, with "the old pictures from Norway that Mama and Papa brought with them when they came to this country" suggesting a large extended family, but safely putting distance between the television family and that larger one left behind in Europe. Then Katrin remembers *her* family, and her narration accompanies a page of photos for Dagmar, Nels, and Papa. Katrin's voice-over sets up the introduction of Mama: "but most of all, when I looked through this album, most of all, I remember Mama." At this point the Maxwell House narrator links Mama's invocation of tradition, domestic skill, warmth, and hospitality through the coffeepot she is holding to the sponsor's product. Katrin's comments on the action of the episode close the show, with a shot of her hand writing in her journal, followed by the final scene of the family, narrated first by Katrin and then by the authoritative voice of the Maxwell House spokesperson.

The device of remembering Mama had been central to the play and film; the use of the album was a visual means of developing this device for the television presentation. But the show's past time frame also defines its setting of class and ethnicity. Remembering enabled *Mama's* working-class action to unfold in a time that was *not* the present and did not have to engage explicitly with the contemporary. Compare the class terrain of *Mama's* set to those used in two other early 1950s sitcoms, *I Love Lucy* (which premiered in 1951) and *The Honeymooners* (premiered in 1950). *Mama's* set revolved around a kitchen, with handmade built-in drawers and an old wood-burning stove, and a parlor with patterned wallpaper, ornate lamp, overstuffed chair with doily on the back, and a piano. These signified the family as having achieved a modest and old-fashioned comfort, especially in comparison with *I Love Lucy*. The Ricardos were renters, but of a swanky New York apartment, furnished with modern mass-produced decor: couches, lamps, desk, decorative pictures, flowers on the table. But then compare *Mama's* kitchen to the set for *The Honeymooners*. *Mama's* house looks positively palatial in comparison to the Kramdens' cold-water walk-up, consisting of a bare kitchen, nothing on the walls, no curtains lining the window that looks out on other tenement buildings and fire escapes.[80]

Like Stevens's film recreation of "the confirmed period of the past," *Mama*'s television past is a period creation—a homey, domestic past, carefully removed from contemporary signifiers of wealth and consumption, consciously invoking a simpler and leaner time, when women shopped for each day's dinner in wicker baskets and when men carried their meals to work in dinner pails. The Hansens are defined as "working class" by Papa's job as a carpenter and by his expression of the values of honest craftsmanship and solidarity. In one episode written after 1952, Papa puts down his tools and walks off the job to protest a new young owner's use of an efficiency expert to speed up production. Another marker of working-class life is the general sense of careful budgeting, scarcity, and constraint. The adult Hansens are also defined as immigrants, especially marked by their accents: some episodes engaged their European past directly. The first episode, broadcast July 1, 1949, begins with the "memory" of Mama and Papa drinking coffee in the kitchen, followed by the problem of getting Papa to go to the special school to study for his citizenship examination. The solution is for Mama to attend, later teaching Papa what she had learned so that he may finally become an American citizen.

The show's family crises often are prompted by the clash of the children's modern American consumer values with the parents' working-class immigrant ideals of solidarity. In the episode "Mama and the Carpenter," Papa declines a foreman's job because he doesn't want to be a boss; he changes his mind after hearing the children bemoan his lack of promotions and their lack of new wallpaper. He accepts the job, but shortly afterward announces he has lost the position, because he refused to fire a man. The family is reunited through their pride in his principled stand. Mama often serves as the mediator in these incidents, standing *between* immigrant and American, between Papa's craft pride and class solidarity—which often interferes with his ability to provide a higher standard of living for his family—and the children's desire to belong to the American middle class.

As George Lipsitz has pointed out, the use of commodity purchases to resolve crises helped acclimate viewers to new postwar consumer values (even if the actual commodities—a telephone or a "fireless cooker"—were not necessarily those most prized in the early 1950s) and to accommodate television itself, its place in their homes and lives, and its distinctive form of commercial promotion. The show's construction of working-class ethnic memories legitimated these new values and imbued the sponsor's product with resonant emotional associations.[81] But the show's constructed past also served the present when an episode shifted from the parents' generation to the children, so importantly American. The children's distance from their parents was continually mined for humor contrasting immigrant with American, old-fashioned with up-to-date. Nels is often jokingly critical of his father and consistently rejects his father's lack of interest in amassing and spending capital. In one episode Nels wins an expensive train set and gives it to the son of a bricklayer whose father had not chosen a higher priced model, because of his own disappointment with his father for failing to provide him with a pony. In another episode Nels decides to start a business so he can make long-distance phone calls to his girlfriend: he cautions his partner, "We can't be like my father. I don't even know what he came to this country for."[82]

One theme in episodes that revolve around the children's crises is a resolution based on enlightened, nonpunitive child rearing; postwar child-centered parenting thus acquired a rosy patina of old-world tradition. Mama is usually responsible for these resolutions. In one episode Dagmar's playmate David stutters and is shunned by boys his own age: Mama, realizing David's mother is pushing him to be brilliant, persuades her to be more gentle, thus enabling David to recite flawlessly the Twenty-third Psalm at school. In a Halloween episode Mama is lenient with street toughs who throw stones at the house, describing them as jealous of the Hansen family circle. She invites them to join the party—where they eat ice cream and bob for apples—rather than turning them over to the police.

Mama's understanding and child-centered approach to family life amplified the appeal of the program's creation of the past for audiences in the present. When Peggy Wood appeared on a popular daytime variety show, women asked her for advice about raising their children as if she were really Mama rather than an actress.[83] By this point Peggy Wood was virtually indistinguishable from Mama: when she was selected by the magazine *Women's Home Companion* as one of the six most successful women of 1953, she was cited as the "Brooklyn-born actress who plays the title role in the TV show Mama."[84]

Mama's stance, halfway between Papa's old-world, working-class ways and the children's American aspirations to mobility, undermined the show's presentation of itself as "about Norwegians." Both Nelson and Gabrielson had some connection to Scandinavian Americans in their backgrounds; Lipsitz has noted that people connected with the show emphasized the advisory role of the (Bay Ridge, Brooklyn) Sons of Norway for consultation concerning authentic Norwegian folk customs and stories.[85] But viewers paid less attention to the specific ethnicity of the family than to its more generic construction of white immigrant parents and American children. For many Americans, except those in contact with concentrations of Scandinavian populations in the Midwest, "Norwegianness" did not prompt distinct associations. As in the play and film, the family's Norwegianness was interesting or quaint and did not interfere with them assuming an identity as white Americans: Nels shows this in one episode, in which he and a friend are lying in bed, dreaming of the South Pacific, where "white men are considered as gods."[86]

THE APPEAL OF TV *MAMA'S* ORDINARY FAMILY

At a symposium on *I Remember Mama* held at the Museum of Broadcasting in New York in 1985, both members of its former audience and people connected with the television production talked about the importance to them of the Hansen family as a *make-believe* family. Ralph Nelson, from a Swedish American family, had fought with his father about the latter's racism and anti-Semitism: directing *Mama* was the first time Nelson was able to summon any nostalgia for his own ethnic family past.[87] Narrative closure in individual episodes was undermined by the lack of narrative closure in the series as a whole; characters in serials could take on "real life," which extended beyond their on-screen activities. Viewers' pleasure in the show may have had as much to do with appropriating for their own needs the reassuring stability of the imaginary ordinary family as with the action in any particular episode.[88]

Despite *Mama*'s relatively consistent production values and loyal audience, the show garnered strong ratings in its first four seasons and subsequently declined.[89] Large-scale changes within the television industry affecting production, sponsorship, and audience may have precipitated the decline. With the extension of national coaxial cable beyond the big cities where television broadcasts were first received, ratings reflected a shift in viewer preferences to new kinds of family situation comedies. The move, especially after 1955, from live to filmed broadcasting helped the new family sitcoms find a compelling visual form. This move was linked to changing relationships between the networks and the Hollywood studios, the relocation of production from New York to Hollywood, and a shift from sponsor-controlled to network-controlled programming. Both *Mama* and the live dramatic shows that had shaped its television aesthetic began to slip in popularity. At the same time, as the declining ratings of Milton Berle's show suggest, audiences were becoming less interested in flamboyant humor based on ethnic styles of vaudeville. David Marc has pointed out that suburban locales increasingly replaced urban settings, whether luxury apartments or modest tenements. Even moving from the Bronx to suburban Long Island in 1954, and from live to filmed production, could not keep the Goldbergs on the air after 1955; Lucy and Ricky, on film from the very beginning, were more successful, leaving the East Side of Manhattan for Connecticut and staying on the air until 1961. After 1958, according to George Lipsitz, network television eliminated urban working-class comedies, which did not surface again until the mid-1970s.[90]

Despite all retrospective claims that *Mama* remained "unchanged" over its eight seasons, the children did grow older; their concerns began to take center stage. With the focus increasingly on the American-born generation, the show's period past became hazier, its class and ethnic markers less distinct. The show was canceled by CBS in 1956, and although audience outcry convinced the network to bring the series back, the revived *Mama* was no longer performed live but filmed, broadcast on Sunday afternoons rather than Friday nights, with a new actress playing Dagmar. Rather than aspiring to a writing career, Katrin in the new series fantasizes about acting; in the last season she moves into what was then the most prominent paid employment for women on television, working as a secretary. Mama has shared with Katrin her hopes for her daughters: "You and Dagmar to marry nice young men and have a lot of wonderful children—just like I have."[91] In the final episode Katrin fulfills her television Mama's dreams and becomes a full-time wife, for which she is rewarded with her mother's precious heirloom necklace. Although Mama's television dreams for Nels are that he become president, Nels settles for being a doctor, with the promise of a secure upper-middle-class life.[92]

Television's *Mama* legitimized the child-centered family values associated with postwar middle-class culture in the suburbs. Family sitcoms required children's parts, but the heritage of radio comedy styles often highlighted the verbal play between the couple, with children functioning more as plot devices than real characters, the role played by David and

Rickie Nelson on early television episodes of *The Adventures of Ozzie and Harriet* (1952–1966) and by little Rickie on *I Love Lucy*. *Mama*'s focus on *remembering* served to enlarge the children's point of view and to convey an immigrant past that, like the sketches, play, and film, minimized conflict, softened scarcity, stressed loving child nurture, and eased the absorption of the children of immigrants into the American middle class. Whatever class and ethnic markers the show had originally introduced became less significant than its ability to express the new postwar suburban consensus.

Other show business families continued to dramatize domesticity: *I Love Lucy, The Adventures of Ozzie and Harriet, The Danny Thomas Show* (1953–1971). Popular new family sitcoms—*Father Knows Best* (1954–1963), *Leave it to Beaver* (1957–1963), and *The Donna Reed Show* (1958–1966)—expressed values of child-centered nurture, only now they took place in an imagined, contemporary, suburban middle-class community, where values of neighborliness, honesty, nonpunitive child rearing, and domesticity reigned, unfettered by remnants of the past, or challenges to successful male breadwinning, or any hint of scarcity. The qualities of female nurture held constant, although the family constellation around the mother shifted to featuring fathers more prominently in these later shows.[93] But *Mama*'s imagining of ethnicity as a set of traditions that could endow products with positive associations certainly demonstrated the commercial potential of ethnicity, just as Forbes had gained success by imagining the ideal, loving American family as Norwegian and Van Druten's character of Katrin had "sold" her family story for a tidy sum. *Mama*'s success on television also suggests that looking back at a simplified ethnic past, with invented memories effacing complex historical realities, was a critical aspect of becoming American, and middle class, in the postwar years.

TRADING PLACES
STORIES

LOVING ACROSS PREWAR RACIAL
AND SEXUAL BOUNDARIES

I N THE SUMMER OF 1944 THE END OF THE WAR WAS IN SIGHT, THOUGH FAR
from certain. Looking ahead, the progressive Hollywood producer
Walter Wanger declared that "the most urgent homefront problems to
be dealt with by screen and press are veterans' rehabilitation, postwar
employment, housing, interracial friction, and education." He understood the greatest challenge facing "the people of the United States" to be
"the reincorporation into our national life of the men and women of the
armed forces."[1] There was no political consensus, however, on the terms
of "reincorporation" or on the direction of initiatives concerning race,
labor, and social welfare. How would the peace be shaped by the wartime
expansion of segregation, widespread social dislocations, and disrupted
gender, racial, and sexual boundaries?

Progressives viewed racial reconstruction as critical to postwar democracy; this required exposing the public fiction that racial boundaries were
natural and calling into question practices of segregation and discrimination.[2] This, in turn, evoked the vexing and charged history of interracial
sex and interracial love. Interracial sex was an embattled public "secret,"
fought out in the different languages of legal prohibitions, political polemic, titillating fiction, sex radicalism, as well as in everyday practice.[3] To
speak of interracial love could suppress a profound history of white sexual
coercion and brutality. But to leave interracial love as *unspoken* supported
the central tenet of white supremacy that racial lines could be fixed, that
love, admiration, and desire could be effectively cordoned off. These racial

and sexual assumptions had long provided the central legitimization for race-based discrimination, segregation in law and informal practice, lynching, and sexual violence against black women.

In the best-selling novel *Strange Fruit,* the Broadway hit play *Deep Are the Roots,* and the Broadway run of *Home of the Brave,* Lillian Smith, Arnaud D'Usseau and James Gow, and Arthur Laurents produced popular fiction and drama exploring love that crossed the color line. These writers intended their work to bolster arguments demanding the immediate dismantling of segregation. They equated the "racial integrity" defended by segregationists with Nazi ideology. Aware of how the reinforcement of racial boundaries spilled over into a policing of sexual and gender norms, they wanted to imagine the ways in which social, familial, and community connections might flourish as racial and sexual boundaries crumbled. They invited audiences to imagine "trading places," to identify with interracial love, with its powerful recognition of commonality and its rejection of racial, ethnic, and, though usually less explicitly, gender dividing lines.

Some of these writers were homosexual and understood that "desires of the heart" (Lillian Smith's words) did not respect legal or social prohibitions.[4] The wartime contributions of homosexual soldiers who slipped by the military's sexual screening process challenged the idea of a fixed boundary between heterosexual and homosexual. In a report suppressed by the military in 1947, psychiatrists analyzing the war records of homosexual soldiers found that they had performed as well as heterosexuals in various military jobs, including combat. On the basis of their research, they suggested that "homosexuals should be judged first as individuals and not as a class." One 1947 *Newsweek* article did report that homosexual soldiers "topped the average soldier in intelligence, education, and rating."[5] A range of sexual expression was another public secret in cosmopolitan circles. Between 1939 and the late 1940s Alfred Kinsey was able to find heterosexual and homosexual men and women willing to speak with him about homosexual experiences, both inside and outside gay subcultures. His published writing from 1948, in which he argued that homosexuality was part of a continuum of human sexual responses, was made possible by this new visibility and, in turn, expanded it.[6]

The white antifascist writers whose work I explore in the following pages saw their work as arguing for love's power of human recognition to undermine social assumptions of difference. They believed that if interracial love could challenge the artificial boundaries of "racial integrity," it could stand in for other kinds of private sphere transgressions, the whole world of extramarital, nonprocreative sexuality stirred up in wartime. Illicit love might question the efficacy of barriers based on racial and sexual categories, although not necessarily the meaning of the categories themselves. Of course literary representations of interracial love were less dangerous than actual relationships or than bold public challenges to segregationist social practices. Ultimately these white authors were unable to achieve enough distance from prevailing ideas about race: they could not create complex and fully realized black characters or consciously transgressive interracial couples. In their varied reactions, black and white audiences show us the high political stakes raised by these love stories. Their responses revealed the possibilities and limits of trading places narratives; they exposed the inadequacies of efforts to separate love and desire from formal and political citizenship.

LILLIAN SMITH AND *STRANGE FRUIT*

When Lillian Smith published her first novel, *Strange Fruit*, in 1944, it became a surprise best-seller that pushed the crossing of racial and sexual boundaries into public view. That Smith's novel was rejected by publishers both for being too sensational and for not being sensational enough suggests that she was writing both within and against recognizable genres of fiction at the time.[7] *Strange Fruit* constructed a fictional ethnography of Maxwell, Georgia, a "cotton-and-turpentine town" near the Florida line. Setting her novel during the period after World War I—when the price of cotton was down and field hands were scarce because so many had joined the wartime migration north—allowed Smith to introduce post–World War II issues, to acknowledge their historical roots, as well as to offer a partial cover for her controversial themes. Smith's diverse characters enabled her to depict the economic, social, and political interpenetration of and distance between "College Street" and "Colored Town." At the heart of the novel is the love affair between the dreamy, light-skinned, college-educated Nonnie Anderson, who can only find work in town as a domestic, and Tracy Deen, the passive son of the town's leading white doctor—and the murder and lynching prompted by the social obstacles to their love. Smith intended the connection between Tracy and Nonnie to stand for "the story of the White South and the Negro South and their relationship to each other . . . the affectionate pull toward each other, the loss of esteem, always the loss of it just as it is about to be gained . . . the pull of cultural taboos against the desires of the heart."[8]

Smith grew up immersed in the economy and culture of segregation, the seventh of nine children in a comfortable household in Jasper, Florida, a town with roughly equal numbers of blacks and whites. According to her 1943 account, "Growing Into Freedom," her father

> owned large business interests, employed hundreds of Negroes and white laborers, paid them the prevailing low wages, worked them the prevailing long hours, built for them mill towns (colored and white), built for each group a church, saw to it that religion was plentifully supplied, that there was a commissary at which commodities were sold at high prices.

Her mother taught her directly "the bleak rituals of keeping the Negro in his place" as well as what she knew of "tenderness and love and compassion."[9] After her father lost his turpentine mills in 1915 and moved the family to their summer home near Clayton, Georgia, Smith attended nearby Piedmont College for a year, joined the Student Nursing Corps in World War I, taught in an isolated mountain school, studied music during two different periods at the Peabody Conservatory in Baltimore, and taught music at a Methodist mission school in China for three years. Eventually her family's declining fortunes and health required that she return to help her father run an exclusive summer camp for girls founded at their Georgia home.[10]

The social worlds Smith encountered through work and study experiences and her observations of missionary colonialism may have given her the distance to analyze her upbringing within a distinct and flawed segregationist culture. Her ideas also developed in the context of her loving though socially unsanctioned relationship with Paula Snelling and their shared work with children, their teaching, and writing. Smith's crossing of heterosexual boundaries in her personal life and racial and sexual boundaries in her fiction followed a literary tradition of similar crossings in an earlier period by writers such as Countee Cullen and Gertrude Stein.

"Growing Into Freedom" revealed an experience that had eroded her confidence in the certainty of racial separation. Smith narrated a story of "two children who learned to love each other and then saw each other no more" because of the instability of racial categorization. "When a small white child was found in the colored section . . . living with a Negro family," the white clubwomen in her town intervened, and "the child was forcibly taken from her adopted family despite their tears and protests" to live at Smith's house. "Julie roomed with me, shared my bed, sat next to me at our table, wore my clothes, played with my dolls. . . . Quickly a warm personal relationship grew up between us." But then, "word came from an orphanage. . . . Mother said gently, 'Julie is a little colored girl. She has to live in colored town. . . . A colored child cannot live in our home.'" Lillian tried to resist her mother's clarity: "She did live with us, I said, and she is the same little girl she was yesterday," unsuccessfully challenging the certainty that racial boundaries could hold firm.[11]

Smith and Snelling first became publicly active as literary radicals, starting a magazine in 1936 to showcase new voices, those of African American writers as well as their own, against the established white southern regional literary canon.[12] They had their first biracial dinner party with guests from Atlanta in the fall of 1936. They envisioned their magazine as reviewing works by and about African American authors and challenging the domination of southern literature by Margaret Mitchell's *Gone with the Wind* and the Agrarians. They eventually published articles exploring the consequences of caste in the South and other countries and analyzing the effects of child-rearing practices on adult racial and sexual relationships. Smith and Snelling shared Rosenwald Fund Fellowships in 1939–1940 and 1940–1941, which supported their joint literary study, traveling for the magazine, and Smith's fiction.

Especially after 1942, Smith was an outspoken opponent of southern practices of racial segregation.[13] She dissented from any arguments that proposed deferring the dismantling of segregation in order to concentrate on the war effort. In 1943 she criticized a left-wing editorial that had attacked the March on Washington movement as detrimental to the war effort, asking: "Is the war more important than the things the war is being fought for? If we are fighting this war to secure racial democracy for all people then why is it wrong for the Negro to use democratic means within his own country to win this democracy for himself?"[14] Smith won national recognition as a white southern woman who would not compromise her opposition to segregation. In 1943 she was named to a place on the 1942 Honor Roll of Race Relations, a nationwide poll conducted each year by the Schomburg Collection of Negro Literature and History in New York "to determine the twelve Negroes and the six white persons who have done the most for the improvement of race relations." In 1944 she was named to the National Council of Negro Women's Honor Roll.[15]

The publication of *Strange Fruit* dramatically expanded Smith's celebrity. Although the publishers were hopeful that the book would be "eagerly read and heatedly discussed," the book sold far beyond their expectations. By the end of its first month in release, 35,000 copies had been sold, and the book went through 15 printings in its first year of publication, selling a total of 475,000 copies by the end of 1944. The book was hailed by "educators and clergymen" as well as reviewers, and Smith reported being especially pleased by its reception from southerners. Smith's active support on behalf of Franklin Delano Roosevelt's reelection campaign in the fall of 1944, on radio, at public forums, and in newspapers and magazines promoted a political framing of the interracial love story in terms of wartime support for civil rights. The book was selling 25,000 to 30,000 copies a week even before an "obscenity" ban in Boston and an attempted ban in Detroit made reading the book "sensational."[16]

What can we learn about social perceptions of racial and sexual boundaries in 1944 from the response of reviewers and readers to *Strange Fruit?* The novel's themes—"love, passion, miscegenation, pregnancy, murder, and lynching," according to one reviewer—were the staples of a genre of fiction popular since the nineteenth century.[17] But there was something new about *Strange Fruit*'s treatment of its material. White reviewers in the North read its fictional critique as especially socially urgent, applauding what they recognized about its political framework. The *Christian Century* called it "the most important novel of the year" because of its "dealing with a problem which, more than any other, threatens the future of the country."[18]

Although white reviewers found not all characters equally believable, a number of them called attention to the interracial love affair as the book's well-realized centerpiece. What distinguished this relationship from its fictional precedents was the representation of mutual consent and volition rather than voyeuristic coercion and seduction. Malcolm Cowley revealed his ignorance of "southern readers" but threw his considerable literary authority behind Smith when he stated, "Nonnie's love affair with Tracy Deen—the episode that will shock southern readers—seems utterly convincing."[19] Struthers Burt wrote in the *Saturday Review of Literature* that Smith had "achieved superbly" the task of making "believable a love that runs beyond mere love-lust and passion, a love between a white man and a Negro."[20]

The literary critic Diana Trilling's response to *Strange Fruit* illuminated how the device of trading places could lead a politically aware reader from being concerned about racial friction to imagining interracial love to questioning racial boundaries. Trilling found herself surprised by her response to the book as "newly moving and unusual," even though "neither its theme nor its setting is new to fiction." For Trilling Smith had recast "the Negro problem." *Strange Fruit* was "so wide in its understanding that its Negro tragedy becomes the tragedy of anyone who lives in a world in which minorities suffer; when it ends in a lynching, we are as sorry and frightened for the lynchers as for the victim. Indeed, we are terrified for ourselves by the realization that this is what we have made of our human possibility."[21]

Trilling's review focused primarily on the interracial love affair. She applauded Smith's "special courage and passion" in "hanging her novel on the main thread of the love of a white boy and a colored girl." She was struck by what seemed to her more complex psychological and social characterizations of the two main characters: Tracy, "the son of the rather nice white doctor of the town, and if he is weak, it is because it served his mother's complicated emotional needs to make him so," and Nonnie, "college educated and refined, by her mother's excessive pride, beyond the point where she can ever hope to find a workable life in a bigoted city." These were not "the usual scion of southern aristocratic blood running thin" and "the conventional high spirited Negro girl."[22] Trilling identified marriage as the main dilemma Smith posed for the lovers: "They never do marry; Miss Smith knows they never could marry. Actually she never says they should marry." Trilling believed that Smith's fiction forced the issue: "yet as their love story unfolds . . . why in the world can they not marry?" Trilling had accepted both the challenge (*"what is this difference in color* which is admittedly no bar to love but so unassailably a bar to marriage?" [emphasis added]) and its implications ("even our vaunted northern liberalism begins to look unpleasantly like hypocrisy").[23] Trilling's review recognized that interracial romance—ordinarily signifying to white readers the sensational and unspoken, the illicit and inflammatory—was something postwar democracy must accept and encompass in order to fulfill the wartime promise of meaningful citizenship.

When W. E. B. Du Bois reviewed the book on the front page of the *New York Times Book Review,* his many years of scholarship and activism interrogating the historical construction of racial boundaries prepared him to recognize Smith's treatment of interracial love as a social challenge. "It is in the handling of the Tracy-Nonnie love affair that the novelist shows her deepest understanding. There is no distortion here. . . . If Nonnie and Tracy are each a symbol of their race, they are people, too." Du Bois applauded Smith's use of the relationship to represent the intertwined fates of blacks and whites across the color line: "On each page the reader sees how both elements in Maxwell ["no black messiahs here, no white devils"] are caught in a skein (economic, ethnic, emotional) that only evolution can untangle or revolution break."[24]

Strange Fruit was widely read and discussed by critics and readers in the black press. Many were disappointed by Smith's failure to depict recognizable African American characters and social life. The poet and writer Langston Hughes included *Strange Fruit* on his list of recommended "Books for Christmas" in his *Chicago Defender* column, but without much enthusiasm.[25] Letters from *Defender* readers communicated varying responses. Will H. Hart from St. Louis wrote that the book was a "true characterization of the South as I know it"; Bernice Brown, from Elyria, Ohio, wrote that although she hadn't liked the book "too much," finding it "high emotional reading," she thought the part of Nonnie might offer Lena Horne a chance to show her dramatic talent. Some could not believe Nonnie's participation in the love affair. Johnnie Monroe from San Francisco complained that it was "disgraceful" for Nonnie, "the most educated element," to "throw herself away on a sordid love affair." Many African American women college graduates found this aspect especially irritating. Others were more disappointed with the book as yet another failure to acknowledge black courage and resistance to white disregard. Lawrence W. Henderson, a soldier stationed "somewhere in the Marianas," was particularly outraged at what he recognized to be the book's depiction of the Negro as "inferior to the white man": he was sure that if Mary McLeod Bethune, who had publicly praised it, would read the book again, she would abandon her positive recommendation.[26] The young writer Ralph Ellison, close to the literary left at this time, faulted *Strange Fruit,* along with several other books, for its failure to create a "positive Negro hero . . . capable of action."[27] *Strange Fruit* was known as controversial among black readers; in his 1945 novel *If He Hollers Let Him Go* African American writer Chester Himes refers to what would have been a familiar argument about *Strange Fruit.* Differing views of Nonnie—linked to ideas on interracial love, sex, and desegregation—are presented to illuminate a class divide among Himes's primarily African American characters in a conversation between several "respectable" women social workers (some of whom are lesbians), a white male social worker, and a working-class male shipyard worker.[28]

The *Defender*'s coverage of *Strange Fruit,* written primarily by its white editor Ben Burns, called attention to differences between black and white readers.[29] He acknowledged to his largely black readership that Smith had "botched up" the Negro characters in her book and speculated that "she did not really know Negro life," referring to "bitter debates among Negroes" on the "honesty and validity" of *Strange Fruit.* Still, he ranked the book as his second "best of the year" for 1944 because of what he saw as its potential for political education of white audiences. Although he thought the book was "of dubious merit in its approach to the racial problem," he gave it credit as the first to "dare touch the problem of a southern white in love with a Negro girl" and as a "matchless chronicle of the hate and fear" in a "typical Dixie community."[30]

Commenting at a later point on how the book was being received, Burns had to admit that many readers did not share his interpretation: "to many whites . . . the moral of the story seemed to be that inter-racial marriage does not work." He salvaged some hope that "using sex as a vehicle, *Strange Fruit* gave many Americans their first contact with the Negro question, even though it did not resolve their thinking one way or another." Identifying himself as one of the original supporters of Smith, Burns continued to praise the "direct, frank approach to Negro-white love" in *Strange Fruit.* He defended the political significance of exposing interracial sexual attachments as a challenge to the belief that segregation maintained fixed racial boundaries: "by astounding many unknowing white readers with the facts of life on Dixie's front porches and back alleys, Miss Smith was able to spotlight the race problem in a more dramatic way than any street corner demonstration or March on Washington."[31]

QUALITY REINSTATES THE COLOR LINE

In addition to what Ben Burns referred to as "hollow and shallow" imitations of *Strange Fruit*—"an endless stream of literature concerned with lovers who cross the color line"—were the literary rejections of the world it espoused. Authors of other novels dramatized the segregationist credo that "a Negro girl and white boy (or vice versa) can't marry and live happily together ever after." Burns noted that even the "lush Ladies Home Journal" had suddenly discovered that "color can't cut courting," as was made clear in its December 1945 issue featuring a full-length novel, "Quality," by Cid Ricketts Sumner, on "Negro-White relationships."[32] Published by Bobbs-Merrill in 1946, *Quality* answered *Strange Fruit* with an insistent defense of segregation, a rejection of interracial love, and a call for a moderate, paternalistic, contained interracialism. *Quality* and the reception to it further illuminate debates over postwar racial reconstruction.

Sumner had already published one women's novel in 1938, and *Quality* housed its political debate about race and blood within familiar genres of passing and romance. As one white northern reviewer noted, "a handsome young doctor's love for a soft-voiced, well-scrubbed nurse" set up many popular novels. But *Quality*'s special draw was "to suppose . . . it develops that the nurse is a Negro who has been passing as white? What then?" Sumner was a transplanted southerner, born in 1890 in Mississippi but living in the North by 1910.[33] Her brief enrollment as a medical student at Cornell in 1914–1915 and her marriage in 1915 to James B. Sumner, a professor of chemistry at Cornell, may have encouraged her to write about doctors, nurses, and romance. Ricketts and Sumner had four children; they were divorced in 1930.

A photograph introducing Cid Ricketts to the readers of *Ladies Home Journal* pictured her as a white grandmother holding a baby—a pose that downplayed any political intentions or commercial literary aspirations. She claimed scientific as well as feminine and maternal authority: "I used to say I was going to be a doctor but after a year in medical school I got married and four children kept me busy." After mentioning the children, but not her divorce, she quickly slipped in her literary pursuits—"so I began to write"—before extolling domestic creativity and domestic service, to which she felt entitled as part of her white southern heritage: "I don't like to weed or iron or cook . . . in spite of having lived for many years in New England, I still like my black coffee, Mississippi style, before I get out of bed in the morning."[34]

Quality was set in 1944. Pinky, the light-skinned, mixed-race heroine, has been sent north for an education and taken for white, providing a literary device to contrast her life when passing (public respect, high educational attainments, unlimited professional possibilities) with her life lived as a southern black (public humiliation, inadequate educational facilities, limited menial labor). The novel juxtaposes stock southern characters, white and black, who promote an interracialism in which white social paternalism expands in exchange for African American deference. Where *Strange Fruit* exposed the bankruptcy of white paternalism, Sumner was committed to reestablishing it as both morally legitimate and politically necessary. She imagines a relationship between a crotchety ex-school teacher, Miss Em, living in the big house, and her faithful mammy-type servant, Granny, who lives in a meager cabin nearby. (Mammy products, including the black servant yard statue, remained popular in this period.)[35] Miss Em tended Granny in a moment of illness and now expects to be similarly cared for, although she is too cash-poor to pay Granny's wages. Sumner's other model paternalists include Doctor Joe, who recognizes Pinky's nursing skills but cannot find her a job except as a hospital maid and who comments, "When I cut through the skin of the blackest one of them, there ain't any difference I can see," and the fair-minded Judge Walker and his daughter Sue Anne, who urge moderation and caution rather than change—with special accommodation for educated Negroes, of course.

The "goodness" of the black characters in *Quality* grows in proportion to their deference: the faithful if old-fashioned and uneducated laundress Granny, religious and resigned, hardworking and devoted to her white folk, the quiet, earnest, well-educated Negro doctor, Frank Canaday, who wants to "help his people" and sees the necessity of cultivating white support to do so. Sumner juxtaposes two "bad" white characters—Melba Wooley, Miss Em's cousin and the mouthpiece for white supremacy, and Pinky's doctor-suitor, Chester, the signifier of northern racial hypocrisy, who leaves her when he learns of her racially mixed origins—with two "bad" black characters—the sexually assertive, razor-toting African American domestic worker, Rozelia, and the radical "outsider agitator," light-skinned Arch Naughton, whose organization cynically promotes legal challenges to Jim Crow practices. Critiquing an older form of mediation between southern white and black communities exchanging favors for patronage, Sumner's novel argued for a new form of moderate interracialism, which supported race uplift without disturbing segregationist assumptions and practices. In the conclusion of the novel, Pinky accedes to the one-drop rule and promises to reject passing and race militancy and acquiesce to segregation. Thus Sumner reaffirmed an enlightened white paternalism and a gradual pace of racial reform. Reviewers recognized her design: "The framework of 'Quality' is aptly contrived to illustrate all the points Mrs. Sumner wishes to stress."[36]

The drama of passing—less widely known among northern whites, more widely known but largely silenced in polite southern white society—was the novel's sensational "hook." The magazine version of the novel included illustrations that focused on racial ambiguity. The initial pages posed Aunt Dicey and Pinky hanging out the wash. Aunt Dicey, with her scarved head and dark face, attends to the laundry; Pinky, with straight hair and white skin, looks toward the reader from behind the clothesline. A full-page drawing spotlights the enthusiastic white suitor, Chester, and the reluctant Pinky, with the caption beginning on the page of text and continuing under the picture: " 'Tell me, Pat [her white name], is it true what they say about you?' Her heart began to pound sharply, as if she were already running away. 'What do they say about me?' " This dramatic hook treats the "secrets" of racial passing and sexual passing as closely related; the only explanation of Pinky's reluctance to flirt with the doctors, according to the hospital gossip, is that she must be a "man-hater." It is to put this (more dangerous) accusation to rest that Pinky entertains the possibility of a romantic relationship with Chester.

Sumner's novel utilizes the drama of passing to illuminate several "truths" about race and fixed racial difference, tenets of white supremacy. The first was that the one-drop rule defined racial indeterminacy as black and only a nonsouthern white can be "fooled": on the train to the North a white conductor who had not seen her board the train moves her from the "colored" cars to white seating; from then on she finds herself taken for white only by northerners. The second was that racial indeterminacy resulted from black women's sexual immorality and white men's inability to resist, though it also involved a positive transfer of "white" blood. The magazine version of *Quality* explains Pinky's racial heritage by making her a scion of the big house, an unacknowledged (though not unrecognized) kin to Miss Em; in the published novel her white progenitor is an overseer. When Pinky questions her grandmother, learning that her mother was also light-skinned, Granny's words imply consent rather than protest: "You got good blood in you, honey. Blood counts in people just like it do in a horse or a hunting dog. . . . My white folks is always been quality, from way back yonder. It would shame me to have my white folks anything but quality." The third "truth" is that the northern white doctor can love Pinky only when he thinks she is white. The published version expanded on Chester's abstract interest in black people—"My family has always been interested in the Negroes—I was brought up on stories of abolition days and the underground railway and all that sort of thing. I mean, it's the sort of thing we stand for"—to heighten his rejection of her when he discovers her actual black heritage. In the words of one reviewer, "the last seen of the doctor . . . he is hastening down a Mississippi road away from his fiancée."[37] The novel's refusal to entertain even the *possibility* of interracial love was inseparable from its support of segregation.

The final section of the novel envisioned a racial reform that perpetu-ated racial inequality. The plot revolves around whether Pinky will be allowed to inherit property left to her by Miss Em, which she intends to use to establish a black hospital. The will's legality is challenged; the trial provides Sumner with a venue to depict a caricatured social equality on the one hand and a mode of social reform driven by white paternalism on the other. In the magazine version Sumner suggests that the only goal of Pinky's black lawyer in such a trial would be to stir up trouble.[38] Rather than have Pinky be "used" in such a way, Sumner has Pinky fire the lawyer, withdraw her claims on the property, and personally appeal to the court. Pinky suggests demurely that the legal rights of a Negro to inherit property could be protected within the contexts of deference and social separation rather than legislation. When she promises that her plans are not to claim social equality or to use the house "to live in the midst of Miss Em's things" but rather to make it into "a hospital for my people," the fair and enlightened white judge grants her the property. White people of goodwill in the community pledge their efforts to "help out." In the book an outraged courtroom crowd threatens to lynch the black political organizer and, after the judge grants the property to Pinky, burns down Miss Em's house. Granny's parting claim is that something good will come of Pinky's establishing a hospital for black people, because "quality can do anything." The source and instrument of Pinky's special ability to serve her people is her elite white lineage—as defined by, rather than as a challenge to, segregation.

In the magazine version and even more in the published novel, Sumner ridiculed the political demands for full citizenship being circulated by African American activists in the black press during the war. She charac-terized these demands as vengeful and inflammatory, motivated by con-tempt for southern blacks as well as southern whites. Sumner depicted her "enlightened" southern *white* characters as the ones who counter pro-nouncements of white supremacy with "reasonable" proposals for racial reform. Dr. Joe and Miss Em challenge Melba Wooley's belief in absolute racial difference by deracializing blood: "blood is blood, Melba, no matter what color the skin is." They dismiss her claim that southern chivalry depended on fixed racial boundaries and produced "racial purity," while sharing with her an assumption of white racial superiority: "There's been plenty of amalgamation for the last hundred years. It doesn't make any change in the white race, but it certainly has lightened up the colored." The social welfare programs they favor would maintain inequality: "Give them a chance at health and education and all the advantages this country can offer. . . . We've got to keep segregation, we can't just turn them loose to overrun everything, but we must give them equal advantages." Sumner's white characters "win" the argument against African American activism by claiming that working *within* segregation for expanded education and health care would improve the lives of black southerners more than fighting for the vote and civil rights. The final proof of their "winning" is that Pinky ultimately comes to embrace their belief that they, rather than African American civil rights activists, know what's best for the Negro. Pinky was a 1944 model of a stock character in American literary tradition, the black protagonist who affirms white paternalism; James Baldwin would identify her in 1949 as a "reincarnation" of Eliza in Harriet Beecher Stowe's *Uncle Tom's Cabin*.[39]

When *Quality* was published as a book, it sold fairly well and was reviewed in white mainstream publications, with reviewers expressing appreciation for its political "earnestness" and "timely" theme, despite the lack of "artistry" or "craftsmanship" they identified with its popular origins.[40] White reviewers gave Sumner credit for drawing readers into sympathizing with how Pinky's "taste of freedom" heightened the contrast with the "cruel and unyielding antagonist: Jim Crow . . . in every aspect of human relations."[41] These reviewers recognized that Sumner's exposure of white racial hypocrisy and her modest acceptance of interracialism were controversial, but they accepted Sumner's presumption that she could speak for the South as a whole.

Most white reviewers did not identify the political implications of Sumner's emphatic support for segregation based on racial differentiation.[42] They applauded her proposals as a kind of color-blind alternative to white supremacy. They did not challenge her authority to speak on "the race question" or her knowledge of black experience. Florence Haxton Bullock, writing for the *Herald Tribune Weekly Book Review,* wrote that "so tender and genuine is Mrs. Sumner's love for the human race, be its skin black or white, that she is able to portray stupidities on both sides of the color line without undue venom or recrimination." So impressed was Bullock with Sumner's moderation as the "watchword for colored people" and her formulation of universalism that Bullock imagined the book could be read by Negroes with "qualified pleasure" and, in short stretches, even by "an old-fashioned mint-julep drinking southern colonel."[43]

Quality's contemptuous rejection of interracial love engendered antagonism from black reviewers, in contrast to *Strange Fruit*'s contested but engaged reception. The comments from African American reviewers largely recognized the book's version of "race relations" as inadequate, although some appreciated its public exposure of varieties of white racial antagonism and ignorance.[44] These reviewers saw the book as "anti-Negro" because of its many arguments in support of racial segregation and separation. The columnist for the *New York Amsterdam News* summarized the "moral" of the book: "Never the twain shall meet." Rejecting Sumner's "racial truths," he called this ending "the biggest falsehood ever imposed upon an unsuspecting public."[45]

STRANGE FRUIT AS FAILED SOCIAL DRAMA

The success of *Strange Fruit* increased Lillian Smith's opportunities to speak out against segregation. She wanted her message to reach the widest possible audience. Even before the book was published, Smith had already begun to imagine possible adaptations as a movie or as a play, but she was concerned that her complex themes of racial interconnectedness not turn into the "Negro-white romance doesn't work" interpretation. As she wrote in a letter to her editor in July 1943, "I know a play has a better chance of reaching the Broadway theatre than of reaching Hollywood, yet I think it will have to be worked out more carefully in order not to destroy its original values."[46] She herself adapted the novel for the stage, but, in doing so, retreated from the novel's emphasis on the boundary-crossing love between Nonnie and Tracy. Smith was concerned that the play not be interpreted through the lens of Paul Robeson and Uta Hagen's reenactment of interracial passion in *Othello* in 1942 and 1943, which had made theatrical and racial history. Smith did not want her story to become a "racial Romeo and Juliet." Rather than stressing the lovers as doomed by racial difference to remain separate or die, Smith wanted to show "a panoramic picture of human beings—white and colored—trapped by the whole mechanism of segregation."[47]

Perhaps because of these concerns, Smith's dramatic conception for her play moved toward racial transcendence rather than confrontation with racial inequality. In the spring of 1944 Smith signed a contract with José Ferrer—the politically progressive Puerto Rican–born actor and director who had played Iago opposite Paul Robeson in *Othello* on Broadway—to produce and direct a play based on her novel. Soon after, she and her sister Esther moved to New York to work on the dramatization and casting. The production hedged on crossing the color line: the white doctor's son was played by a not "conclusively white" actor and radio director-producer, Melchior Ferrer, the son of a Cuban-born surgeon and an American mother. Nonnie was played by Walter White's daughter Jane in her stage debut. Experienced African American actors were also cast: Juano Hernandez played the part of Maxwell's black doctor, Sam Perry, and Robert Earl Jones played the part of Henry McIntosh, Tracy Deen's "houseboy" and childhood friend, the lynching victim. Preproduction publicity in the left-wing tabloid *PM* described the main characters as reaching "across the barriers of color to find love," picturing them clasping outstretched hands rather than embracing. The *PM* text stressed interracialism, mentioning that Smith's "Negro friends" from Clayton, Georgia had contributed six hundred dollars toward mounting the production, with leading white citizens bearing one third of its cost.[48]

Smith later recalled the intense racial and political tensions surrounding the production and the large thirty-five member cast:

> Half were white, half (or about that) were Negro, half were northern, half southern. Imagine that mixture! Caught up in that play! and under the pressures. Of course segregationists were doing their nasty work, too; and American Nazis who at this time had stopped calling themselves Nazi; but we were surrounded by pressures of all kinds; some of the reactionary churches were pressuring us about obscenity; etc. It was really like casting and producing and rehearsing a play in a boiling cauldron.

At the time Smith's casting instructions to Ferrer suggested her hope that the production manage these tensions by avoiding direct acknowledgment of racial discrimination: "We want everyone in it—white and colored—to be the kind of folks who can forget color and remember that they are human beings. . . . It would be a wonderful thing if the cast of *Strange Fruit* could prove to the world that 30 or 40 human beings who happen to be of different color, can work together discarding color like an old worn-out costume."[49]

The play premiered in Montreal in October 1945, with trial runs in Toronto, Boston, and Philadelphia, before opening on Broadway in November. It was panned by both white and black critics and failed to find an audience, closing after sixty performances. Broadway magazine reviewers gave Smith credit for social authenticity but faulted her stagecraft. Wolcott Gibbs, reviewing for the *New Yorker,* called attention to Smith's "organic connection" between "miscegenation" and "her attack on racial injustice," but he felt that the "exhaustive" treatment of "social structure" and "political complexion" of a southern community "obscured and diminished" the central story. He, like other white reviewers, gave Smith credit for "the force of accurate observations, the dignity of an emotion deeply felt by the author, and the virtue of considering a serious problem in its actual terms."[50]

The dramatic presentation of *Strange Fruit* raised a number of issues in the black press. As befit a production that featured prominent African American actors, black newspapers featured profiles of Jane White and Robert Earl Jones and tracked the progress of *Strange Fruit* through its out-of-town tryouts, highlighting critical praise of black talent but also noting the "lukewarm" Broadway critics. Smith's "education" on "race-rationing," when she found out that no New York hotel would house a reception for the interracial cast of *Strange Fruit,* was front-page news.[51] But African American reviewers were also not enthusiastic about the production, finding the characterizations as inadequate and problematic as those in the book, and the drama uninspired. The reviewer for the National Urban League's publication *Opportunity* noted gently, "Many critics felt that the transition from book to play was not that successfully done."[52]

The director of the American Negro Theatre, Abram Hill, offered an extensive critique of the theatrical *Strange Fruit* in the *New York Amsterdam News.*[53] Hill made an attempt to distinguish between the author's "good intentions and [the] liberal minds behind them" and the play itself—"a sprawling piece of inept theatre that borders on the bore." He was not critical of the premise of the play, the "suicidal effects of segregation": the theme of novel and play was, he wrote, "absolutely important." And he liked the idea of the town as a symbol of "hundreds of nests of cultural isolation," the focus on how "race prejudice between Negroes and whites nurtures and perpetuates cultural isolation which is detrimental to both races and to the progress of civilization." Though he saw Tracy as "a weak shadow of a man" and Nonnie as " for the most part a silent, brooding love mate," Hill liked the idea of the "greater bond of love" that drew the main characters together "despite the mores and customs their respective races confine them to." But too much narrative exposition, too many characters, and too little "stagecraft" made the play a "colossal disappointment which only a miracle can make into a success."[54]

In Smith's reply to her critics she enumerated diverse misinterpretations of her themes: "It is about the Negro problem . . . the author is in favor of intermarriage . . . and this is her defense of it . . . an insult to Negro womanhood . . . a sneer at white mothers and their sons . . . an attack on the Christian church." She felt that "not one critic" had recognized "what the play was really about." Her own statement, expressing her deepest political convictions about the destructiveness of white supremacy, revealed both the breadth and the failure of her vision of a racially inclusive democracy:

> It is a play about human beings trapped and destroyed by segregation, the prevailing pattern of our white culture, but no one has said so. It is about the deep heartbreaking conflict between Christianity and White Supremacy, but no one has mentioned this. It is about the white man and his infatuation with his own importance; it is about a disease of the heart and mind that destroys all our people, whatever their color, if they come too close to it. It is a play about you and me and the profound difficulty we have in becoming sane, mature human beings, but no one has mentioned this.[55]

Public debate about *Strange Fruit* continued in New York at a forum organized by Lawrence Reddick, curator of the Schomburg Collection of Negro Literature and History of the New York Public Library, where Lillian Smith and Abram Hill addressed an audience of two hundred. Although Hill wrote the published account (Smith decided against submitting her own version), comments attributed to Smith and Hill shed light on their different approaches to the theatrical representation of interracial love.[56] Smith claimed that the play fulfilled her larger political and cultural mission to dramatize the "tragedy of segregation," not as a "Negro problem but as the white man's problem, for it is he who has more to gain by not trying to monopolize culture."[57] Smith's formulation took a principled political stand against segregation, refused to conflate the "race problem" with black people, denaturalized white racism, and hinted at a link between white supremacy and male supremacy. Paradoxically these principles had the effect of making African American experiences of segregation less rather than more visible.

Hill insisted that he recognized Smith's political metaphors, countering Smith's accusation that he wanted Tracy and Nonnie to be "heroic characters . . . on a dynamic struggle to defeat segregation." He wrote, "One doesn't miss" Smith's intention "to reveal through Tracy's weakness . . .

the weakness inherent in the white people of the town to do nothing about the dreadful effects of segregation." His criticisms echoed problems readers had with the book: Tracy's motivation was "flat" and Nonnie was too "silent, brooding . . . and most inarticulate." Hill took pains to distinguish the play from the playwright, though in somewhat dismissive terms: "Now, don't get me wrong folks. I like the material in this play. I believe in the author who has the passionate zeal of a missionary . . . but the play is very poor—hardly a play at all—but more or less an illustrated lecture acted on the stage." Smith was stung by Hill's criticism; when she sent Paula Snelling a copy of Hill's description of the forum, she wrote that "not one Negro called to express regret or apologize or anything else."[58]

Smith assumed that her outspoken anticommunism cost her the support of left-wing critics. But it was left-wing readers and viewers, black and white, who found her framework most powerful. Paul Robeson came to the play and praised it as moving and prophetic, offering a "clear warning that we can't take it any more." The progressive black actress Fredi Washington wrote two separate articles, in the New York newspaper the *People's Voice,* in which she described Smith's activism as "dynamite against discrimination," praised the play, and criticized what she termed as a "scurrilous" attack on it in the *New York Amsterdam News.*[59]

Earl Conrad, the left-wing white Harlem bureau chief for the *Chicago Defender,* also stood up for Smith and especially for her play's interracial relationship as a provocative examination of the instability of racial boundaries. Conrad praised it for stimulating public discussion, for cracking open "the silences, the uncertainties, and the fears surrounding the Negro question." He then spelled out for *Defender* readers the play's trading-places lesson, including its challenge to fixed racial boundaries. The play was at its most vital when dealing with the issue of "miscegenation," he wrote, because

few of us realize as yet that there is no such thing as miscegenation, intermarriage, any more than there is such a thing as "race." When people everywhere and anywhere marry or mate or fornicate, it is human life meeting, and when humanity gets together in bed all differences are resolved to the common denominator that nature has marked out for mankind everywhere. But of course the great gulfs between people stand, and the artificial differences that have been made so "real" that we actually believe that color or viewpoint goes beyond the physical anatomy into the "differences" that produce such a harsh and unreal term as "miscegenation."

Conrad praised the play's challenge to social inequality as "revolutionary."[60]

THE RETURNING NEGRO SOLDIER, INTERRACIAL ROMANCE, AND *DEEP ARE THE ROOTS*

The treatment of interracial love that succeeded on Broadway where *Strange Fruit* foundered was Arnaud D'Usseau and James Gow's play *Deep Are the Roots,* which opened September 1945—just a month after V-J Day—and ran through November 1946. A social problem drama in a popular melodramatic format, the play focused on a returning black soldier and his postwar experience in a southern town. A false accusation sets off a chain of events, with order restored in time for the final curtain. Crafted by two experienced Hollywood screenwriters coming off a recent Broadway success, *Deep Are the Roots* was a much more conventional play than *Strange Fruit,* the work of a first-time novelist trying to stage a sprawling social panorama. Its characters were recognizable "types"; its stagecraft followed the rules.

Deep Are the Roots was a product of the popular front left. The writers were left-wing journalists-turned-screenwriters who had recently coauthored a hit anti-Nazi play, *Tomorrow the World.*[61] They claimed that their search for a postwar theme led them to *Deep Are the Roots:* the problem of racial inequality was, in their eyes, the most "urgent problem—other than the war . . . troubling Americans." They structured the play according to their political convictions, rather than any first-hand experience of the South; as Gow explained, "If you are an alert and alive person, you become aware of racial friction, and if you live in America, you are aware of it daily."[62]

Deep Are the Roots was directed by Elia Kazan, his first project after returning from a mission in New Guinea and the Philippines to set up entertainment production units for soldiers.[63] He thought he saw GIs changed by their wartime experience—"Alive with a new realism, alert with a new interest . . . they're a lot tougher, more honest, and a lot more progressive."[64] *Deep Are the Roots* seemed to offer material that was also "tougher," and Kazan was pleased to do the play, finding himself in sympathy with the authors, whom he later characterized as "left-wing intellectuals, like myself."[65] Kermit Bloomgarden, the former business manager for the Group Theatre, produced the play, his first production since the group had disbanded in 1940.

Deep Are the Roots presented an array of characters covering a spectrum of beliefs about racial superiority. These include the upper-class Senator Ellsworth Langdon, who proclaims that "until the day I die, I'll fight for the rights and privileges of the superior person," the New South power broker, Roy Maxwell, willing to expand the space for the black community if African Americans played by the old rules and didn't threaten existing structures of power, and Senator Langdon's daughter Alice, the informal female patron of the black community who supports increased educational opportunities for blacks as long as she is the one to dispense them and they are received gratefully.[66]

The central African American character, the Negro soldier and citizen who faces the crisis of returning to the Jim Crow South, is Brett Charles, son of the faithful Langdon family servant, now first lieutenant in the army, decorated with a distinguished service cross. His experience in the war with the English, who "like us . . . don't seem to mind that our skins are dark," and with "those Italian peasants" who looked on Brett as "their savior," as well as with his good friend in the army, a white officer, has changed him: "no more humbleness" or compromise on social equality. "We've seen a little bit of fairness, Mama. And now we'll make it so white and black can live together, fairness all around." Brett's mother, Bella, also an important character in the play, represents black womanhood as controlling, watchful, and cautious, a foil to his militancy.

Act 2 is set in motion by Brett's campaign for "fairness." Offstage, he makes a speech in the black community denouncing segregation and challenges the de facto segregation of the public library by going in the front door and asking for "the new biography of Justice Holmes." These public transgressions are enough to motivate Senator Langdon to frame Brett for robbery. Onstage, Brett defies his patron, Miss Alice, by rejecting her educational beneficence in planning to further his education in the North. Instead Brett chooses to stay in town as the new principal of the black school, where he plans to put new "ideas in their heads." He insists, despite her disapproval, on attending a political "conference" in Atlanta, with "black and white folks meeting together. Discussing everything. Better schoolhouses, more of them. Abolishing the poll tax. Jobs for the soldiers coming home."[67]

Brett's most provocative challenge to segregation—a walk by the river at night with his dear childhood friend, Langdon's younger daughter Generva—takes place offstage. (They had been caught as children in an innocent reenactment of *Othello,* after which they were forbidden to play together: popular consciousness of the 1942 Robeson/Hagen *Othello* remained vivid.) In the play the walk is an expression of Brett's love for Generva, but his declarations of love contain no sexual overture or implication of marriage; they are offered selflessly and dispassionately by Brett and received as curiously devoid of social ramifications by Generva, whose response is to honor Brett's feelings for her by promising to leave town. Their walk turns Alice from patron to punisher; she calls the sheriff to arrest Brett on her father's trumped-up charges.

Act 3 explores the potential for black rage against white racism. Brett, still in uniform, is beaten during his arrest: the senator's black domestic staff quits en masse, including Bella, whom he has claimed as "closer" to him than family. Defined solely by her role as servant, Bella can express her resistance only by withdrawing her services. Enough political pressure in the black community is generated to broker a deal whereby Brett will be released from jail and put on a train to the North. Brett escapes from the train and, plunged into the depths of hating all white people, threatens race war. He is pulled from the brink by the selfless love of Generva and her genuine, though instrumental, proposal to marry him. In the final moments of the play, Alice renounces her ideas of black inferiority; Brett argues that interracial marriage is not the way to improve the world; Generva leaves "to learn to do something, get a job" in some unknown northern destination; the senator goes out to join his armed allies, presumably the Klan. The denouement features Alice and Brett shaking hands to symbolize their conversion to a new era of interracial partnership: "We're on the same side."

Presumably the authors' commitment to showing how racial discrimination was generated by economics and sustained by legal and political traditions as well as social customs led them to retreat from proposing interracial marriage as a solution to racial discrimination. Interracial marriage as imagined in the play would isolate the characters politically and socially: "We'd become an island, we could never live in the world as it is." Generva's (white, female, innocently utopian) belief that they could "make our own world" is decisively answered by Brett (as a black man and antisegregation activist): "No man and woman can create a world apart. There are no islands. There is no escape."

Dramatizing the love between a black man and a white woman, the authors challenged the segregationist stereotype that black men posed dangerous threats to white women. They use the cautious Bella, who earlier has warned Brett of the dangers of interracial love, to pronounce Brett and Generva "pure in heart," in contrast with the "real evil" of white men's predatory access to black women. The love between Brett and Generva, presumably a product of color-blind childhood innocence, never reaches the level of passion; it is more a state of mind than a harbinger of sex and is decisively rejected as a reason for interracial marriage.

Although mainstream white critics were divided in their response to the play, audiences were enthusiastic. The *New York Times* reviewer described "members of the first night audience, deep in discussion of both the play and the situation involved," crowding onto the street in front of the theater.[68] Racial themes and controversy were not enough to guarantee success in themselves, as was shown by the lack of audience enthusiasm for *Strange Fruit,* as well as the quick closing of the left-wing playwright Robert Ardrey's play *Jeb*—which concerned returning black vets crossing the color line in employment—in February 1946.[69] The critics seemed to agree on the dramatic quality of *Deep Are the Roots,* especially the "sensitive and honest" performance of Barbara Bel Geddes as Generva, the power and authority in the performance of Evelyn Ellis as Bella, and the strength and dignity of Gordon Heath as Brett.[70]

White critics recognized *Deep Are the Roots* as political theater. A number thought that an antifascist war demanded the use of social drama for racial protest. Their language documented the persistence of ideas about racial equality and popular democracy circulated by wartime progressives. Drama critic John Mason Brown of the *Saturday Review of Literature* argued that the play's indictment "confronts us with a problem which we cannot hope to dodge unless all our talk of democracy and equality, the Four Freedoms, etc. is fated to remain no more than the most hollow mockery."[71] *Commonweal's* Kappo Phelan wrote approvingly that the play "attacks our largest national problem." On a national broadcast Walter Winchell applauded *Deep Are the Roots* as an attack on the "racial prejudice personified" by the "white artists only" policy of the Daughters of the American Revolution in their Washington, D.C. concert hall.[72] After *Strange Fruit* opened, a number of magazine drama critics reevaluated the southern authenticity of *Deep Are the Roots,* but they remained positive about its premise and its drama. Some of the New York daily newspaper critics wrote more critically of the play's contrived "topical melodrama." The *New Republic's* Stark Young viewed *Deep Are the Roots* as political cliché. He termed it "theatre trash"—though it dealt with serious matters, the play was "prattling itself into rubbish."[73]

The black press greeted *Deep Are the Roots* with excitement, praising its themes, acting, and theatricality. Abram Hill thought the play the "most provocative piece of theatre on the stage since *Native Son,*" perhaps even better: " 'Deep Are the Roots' puts the stake of Negro-white relationship in a two-hour time capsule with every line and situation connotating some meaning to the life of every spectator."[74] In Hill's assessment the subjectivity of the black soldier is the central premise, answering "one of the most pressing questions facing the world today: What is the reaction of the returning Negro GI to his land of democracy?" (D'usseau and Gow had initially proposed the central question differently, with a focus on white subjectivity: "What makes decent Americans consciously or unconsciously embrace those notions of race superiority that Hitler found so profitable?") Hill highlighted Brett's status as an officer, his Fiske University degree, and his three years of service in the war as equipping him to take on Senator Ellsworth Langdon, whom Hill identified as a "sophisticated carbon copy of Bilbo the Man." Hill called attention to the citizenship of the black soldier, and to the dramatic tension his return incites: "What will a Negro who has been treated as an equal in England, been a hero to Italian peasants and slept with white women do back in the south?"[75]

Langston Hughes also endorsed *Deep Are the Roots* in his column for the *Defender* as "the best play I have ever seen about the race problem." In contrast to the "dialect-speaking illiterates of our stage and screen," the play's African American soldier hero "talks like a man, looks like a man, and expects to be treated as a man." Hughes praised the range of political positions and racial characterizations in the play: "the white reactionary, the white liberal, the white folk of good will, the meek and uneducated Negro, the decent hard-working Negro, and the modern upstanding forward-looking Negro are all portrayed here."[76] Walter White called *Deep Are the Roots* "the most uncompromising Negro-white play which has ever hit Broadway."[77]

Almost all the white reviewers took a position on the play's use of the interracial love story. Several of the New York daily newspaper reviewers found dubious, in Abram Hill's words, "the idea of a white girl falling in love with a Negro soldier." A number of the magazine reviewers liked the play's equivocation on the subject of interracial marriage. The *New Yorker's* Wolcott Gibbs observed that the play "deals sympathetically with miscegenation without precisely recommending it." He described the relationship as a "rather eccentric love interest," with the resolution that "Brett and Jennie [Generva] go their separate, rueful ways, having concluded that black and white marriages are not the immediate solution to the Negro problem."[78] In contrast, a southern reviewer described the play as advocating "complete intermingling among Negroes and whites—including marriage."[79]

Langston Hughes disagreed with the focus on interracial romance, arguing that getting "the race problem" all "angled up with sex" was at the cost of "clear thinking." He linked the play with *Strange Fruit* in this regard, arguing that interracial romance happens "in books and on Broadway stages more often than in real life." Hughes preferred to maintain a division between sexuality and political economy: "Most Negroes prefer a good job to a fine white woman. Certainly I, as a hard-working writer, would much rather have a Hollywood contract in my pocket than a Hollywood star in bed."[80]

Abram Hill, on the other hand, analyzed the interracial romance as of central importance in the plot, and he appreciated its construction as *unexceptional.* He named Brett as fighting for the "inherent dignity of man," which he defined as including FDR's "four freedoms of which love and marriage is definitely a part." He referred to Generva and Brett as "normal likeable human beings," not "special stage creations out to electrify the pros and cons of racial animosity." The way Hill described the love emphasized the intertwined lives of southern whites and blacks: "Secretly they are in love—have been since childhood." In his framing, it was the denial of the love, not the love itself, that underpinned the white supremacist worldview. The exposure of interracial love was the crisis that could unsettle the "truce" between white supremacy and democracy enabled by segregation: "When this fact is exposed, the walls of Jericho come tumbling down. The sophisticated senator . . . recaptures his innate venom, viciousness and violence. Alice reverts to the typical southern white woman instead of the patronizing liberal. . . . Brett's mother denounces and departs from the household where she had served for twenty-four years." Hill approvingly characterized Brett's stand on interracial marriage: "Brett refuses to marry Generva but in doing so he strongly condemns the bigoted world that denies love between two people whose only 'guilt' is that they belong to different races."[81]

Since interracial love remained a central point of controversy and was, after all, critical to the premise of trading places, even D'Usseau and Gow ultimately returned to the question of interracial love in defense of their play, despite their hopes that they could avoid taking a public position on this question. The authors noted that their attempt to join the "fight for economic and political equality for the Negro" by granting him "literary equality" was accused *both* of advocating intermarriage and attacking intermarriage. They attempted to clear up the issue: "For the record, let us state categorically that we have not advocated nor attacked intermarriage." They even tried to assert that the play's idea that "people who love each other have the right to decide for themselves, free from any interference, whether or not they shall get married" was based on a basic right, "guaranteed by our Constitution and laws." They were, in fact, mistaken: in 1945 interracial marriage was illegal in most states.[82]

Still, the logic of their challenge to racial prejudice did keep returning to love, even in their chosen mode of polemic rather than passion. As they put it,

> The desire to love and be loved outweighs the capacity to hate and be hated. We cannot continue forever to hate and fear and look down upon thirteen million of our fellow Americans. For the future of our nation, the salvation of our own souls—and also just because it's a damn sight easier—we'd better learn to love them and admit them to that equality of opportunity of which we are forever boasting.[83]

For D'Usseau and Gow to take an uncompromising stance in favor of social equality forced them publicly to endorse interracial love: *not* to do so would cede too much to segregationists. The terms in which *Deep Are the Roots* was recognized, praised, and condemned demonstrated the cultural authority still available to popular front radicals when they challenged racial inequality. Despite the authors' disavowals, their play firmly and publicly intertwined crossing racial and sexual boundaries.

INTERRACIAL MALE HOMOSOCIABILITY IN *HOME OF THE BRAVE*

Arthur Laurents's 1945 play, *Home of the Brave*, explored the issue of "racial intolerance" as an obstacle to military effectiveness and social peace; in his treatment the "race" issue refers to anti-Semitism and the racialization of Jews. Treating anti-Semitism as a race issue was common at the time, given the racial language of Nazism and the political context of antifascism. But it was very controversial in 1945 to call attention to Jewish racialization and victimization. The Anti-Defamation League threatened to picket *Home of the Brave* as anti-Semitic because of its portrayal of a Jewish soldier as neurotic. Laurents later noted that he had already been working with the themes of "discovery and acceptance . . . prejudice and betrayal" in radio drama and felt that he had "used" anti-Semitism primarily as a "dramatic element to propel the story and to justify the conflict in the central character, a Jewish GI trapped in a South Pacific jungle in WWII."[84]

In theory the military was a thoroughly public and civic realm within which male comradeship served national purpose, rather than a sphere of potentially explosive private interaction. In *Home of the Brave*, however, the intensity of wartime comradeship among men provides the context for and the resolution of love that crosses racial boundaries. Laurents later described the relationship of the soldier buddies as homosexual.[85] The play opened shortly after the dramatization of *Strange Fruit* and *Deep Are the Roots*, in December 1945. Like *Deep Are the Roots*, *Home of the Brave* was a production of the wartime popular front. The play was directed by Michael Gordon, left-wing actor and director, who had been stage manager and lighting director for the Group Theatre in the 1930s, with the stage manager, producer, and "half of the cast" affiliated with the left as well.[86]

Home of the Brave was described as a "two-in-one" because wartime trauma was added to the race theme, although critic John Gassner thought the "clinic" only a "half-satisfactory substitute for the soapbox." Its protagonist, Peter Coen, suffers from temporary paralysis, caused by having had "to desert a wounded buddy on a Jap-held island" and by his life-long "deep-rooted sense of difference" as a Jew; these generate crisis as they threaten the special closeness among men in wartime.[87] Laurent's play, like *Strange Fruit* and *Deep Are the Roots*, imagined love's blindness to racial categories as in some way managing to undermine them. It assumed that refutation of Jewish racialization could serve to discredit racialization in general. (This assumption also shaped another set of trading-places stories—*Focus*, *Crossfire*, and *Gentleman's Agreement*—that I will address in the next chapter.)

Laurents had been writing for radio since the late 1930s and continued to write radio drama while he was in the army. His 1945 radio play, *The Knife*, which he described as "honest about discrimination in the Army" was first canceled by the army head of radio in Washington but eventually aired and awarded a citation by a special order of Secretary of War Henry Stimson. Laurents's radio plays about disabled vets made popular a formulation of interchangeability—especially his prizewinning play "The Face," which promoted the use of psychology to heal veterans wounded by the war, to help make them see that "we're no different inside."[88] In the service when he wrote *Home of the Brave*, Laurents later attributed its outsider consciousness and antiracist sensibility as having been shaped by his childhood experiences of anti-Semitism as well as the influence of Marxism.[89]

The Home of the Brave is set in the South Pacific, its action comprehensible only in a profoundly different wartime reality in which the daily possibility of death produced intense relationships between men. The scenes alternate between a military hospital, a military office, and a clearing on an enemy-occupied jungle island where the soldiers are engaged in a reconnaissance raid. The set designer, Ralph Alswang, had just returned from three years in the army, and three members of the cast—Joseph Pevney, who played Coen; Kendall Clark, who played the commanding officer; and Alan Baxter, who played a tough and experienced soldier who had lost an arm—were actors returning from military service.[90]

The play's action follows a psychiatrist's attempt, with the use of drugs, to examine the causes of Coen's psychological paralysis. Within a flashback structure, and as a means to help Coen recover, the GIs reenact what transpired on their reconnaissance mission on the island. The play offered a simple explanation of Coen's paralysis. Hearing his closest buddy utter an anti-Semitic slur makes him angry, just as things go wrong on the mission and he is momentarily gratified when his buddy is shot. Coen is then torn between staying with his wounded friend and fulfilling his obligations as a soldier to deliver reconnaissance information. As one reviewer summarized it, Coen "loses his feeling of guilt when he is made to realize that his moment of gladness was perfectly normal—what every soldier feels when somebody else, and not himself, is hit." In the play's conclusion Coen also loses his "prickliness about being a Jew" when a one-armed soldier reminds him that there were other and far more painful ways of being "different" (the reviewer found this part less convincing).[91]

Laurents's radio plays had already signaled his interest in how physical markers served as invitations to underestimate a man's capabilities. The radio plays had also emphasized the healing powers of psychotherapy in restoring a self-confident manhood: "What a man looks like doesn't matter . . . the only thing that does matter is each man himself for what he is himself." These concerns helped to shape *Home of the Brave*.[92] The play resolves these themes through the relationships in the multiethnic platoon, especially through the love between buddies—allying the play with other works that imagined interracial love and desire as a challenge to fixed racial boundaries.

According to Allan Bérubé, the broad reach of the wartime draft created a large concentration of gay men in the military; the war brought heterosexual men into unprecedented closeness and interdependence with other men, both heterosexual and homosexual, and affirmed the love of men for men. By encouraging them to pair up and to look out for each other, the buddy system promoted men's relationships with one another to an extent far beyond the norm in civilian life. Buddy relationships, encouraging and expressing extraordinary closeness, easily moved into romantic and sexual intimacy and were hard to distinguish—from the outside— from more conscious homosexual relationships.[93]

It was in this context that *Home of the Brave* achieved its emotional intensity. The soldier's dual crisis—of wishing his buddy harm and then having to choose between his roles as buddy and as soldier—depended on the relaxing of the rules governing love in war. In the first drug session to induce a recollection of what happened, the psychiatrist has to probe Coen to acknowledge his "buddy" relationship with Finch. The relationship is confirmed by another soldier's taunting of Finch as a "kike-lover," thus connecting the crossing of sexual boundaries to racialization. Through Coen's enactment of the reunion with Finch, now dying, the audience hears Coen's expression of his love for Finch. It was after this moment that Coen could no longer "walk away."

These social relations were situated within the familiar multiethnic platoon, where special mission soldiers represent four different types, whose differences would be bridged by the end of the play. Coen, "the Jew from the city," is "sensitive" because as a child in Pittsburgh, he was attacked by a group of schoolboys. T. J., "the Sergeant who was once an executive and can't forget it—and who won't forget racism with Coney," is generally contemptuous. He is also the most reluctant soldier and the most powerful premilitary civilian, a high-paid corporate vice president. Coen's devoted buddy Finch, "the country boy from the ranch," is an "Arizona hayseed" whose connection to the West and the country must account for his general friendliness and reliability. Mingo is "the understanding older man who has had a rough deal from his wife." Identified as an intellectual by his one year of college and a wife who writes poetry, Mingo is initially labeled as "touchy" after receiving a "dear John" letter, but later his handling of his physical disability, having lost an arm, is presented as the model for reinterpreting "difference" as insignificant.[94]

Coen is "healed" by three men who give him ways of understanding the ties between men as transcending the racialized ethnic boundaries that have wounded him. His first healer is his buddy Finch, who defends him against T. J. and offers him unqualified love—"You either like a guy or you don't." His second healer is the psychiatrist, Captain Harold Bitterger, who gives him permission to have survivor guilt and to cry even though "guys don't." He helps Coen recall the intensity of his bond to Finch by locating the origins of his trauma not when he leaves but when he lovingly cradles the dying man; Bitterger removes the racial stigma from Finch's near taunt by repeating the words himself to get Coen to walk. His third healer is the "touchy" Mingo, who educates their commanding officer about how racialization operates and, after losing his wife, offers himself for postwar partnership with Coen. The dialogue in the third act reiterates Coen's need for a self-cure, insisting that he believe that "you're the same as anybody else." With Mingo's helpful perspective on his disability ("Okay you lost a wing but you're not gonna let it go down the drain for nothing"), Coen makes his breakthrough discovery: "I am different. Hell, you're different. Everybody's different—But so what? It's okay because underneath, we're—hell, we're all guys!" The words glorify a distinctly masculine framework for universality, suggesting that the love of men is what heals Coen. *Home of the Brave* operated within the unprecedented circumstances of wartime homosociability to frame its particular vision of loving across boundaries.

Home of the Brave was not an unqualified critical success, but it won several awards and stirred up the audiences that did come—one critic noted that after the performance, "crowds gathered in front of the theater to talk the play over," as they had after *Deep Are the Roots.*[95] Its real commercial success came from its 1949 transformation into a film that "daringly substituted a Negro" in the central role.[96] The film *Home of the Brave*, released early in May 1949, was the first Hollywood movie to place the subject of racial discrimination at its center; it will be discussed in chapter 6.

As stories of trading places *Strange Fruit, Deep Are the Roots,* and *Home of the Brave* each produced visions of love that crossed racial boundaries, popularizing images of social equality even when their representations fell short. Because racialist boundaries had previously relied on strictly enforced gender and sexual norms, reimagining any of these opened up the others to instability (though the evidence available in pubic sources represents male more than female subjectivity). Once the boundary is shown to be problematic, or even illusory, previously marginalized groups can move onto the stage. However, resolutions that emphasized everyone's "sameness" risked discouraging a deeper inquiry into the historical production of race and racialization. Love's blindness to categories undermined but also reified them, especially when the racial "transcendence" imagined by white authors denied racial experience. Both black and white audiences seized upon narratives of love across boundaries and the discursive arena they created; these stories helped to embody the possibilities for meaningful social reconstruction after the war.

SEEING THROUGH JEWISHNESS

NOTHER SET OF STORIES ABOUT TRADING PLACES—LESS EXPLOSIVE
than interracial love stories—attempted to challenge the legitimacy of racial boundaries by criticizing a familiar element in ethnic humor, naturalist literature, right-wing rhetoric, and fascist ideology:
the racialization of Jewishness.[1] Though American Jews did not face the
degree of racial exclusion and violence that African Americans did, or
come close to the fate of European Jews under Nazism, verbal and physical attacks on Jews grew in number during the war years, giving rise to new
concerns. Most mainstream Jewish organizations eschewed public discussion of anti-Semitism, Nazism, or, later, the death camps, because it
seemed dangerous to call attention to Jewish victimization. They
responded to the news of mass killings of Jews with generous attempts to
care for survivors, stressing their American loyalties and condemning
prejudice and bigotry generically rather than anti-Semitism in particular.[2]

Most discussions of fascism during the war did not focus on Jewish
racialization; especially after the war, the murder of European Jews was
commonly seen as one among many Nazi atrocities. But some left-wing
Jewish writers hoped that a challenge to the fascist racialization of Jewishness would reveal the fallacies of racialization in general. They thought
that "seeing through" Jewishness would be a first step toward recognizing
common bonds and rejecting racial categories.

The examples explored here include Arthur Miller's novel *Focus* (1945),
Richard Brooks's *The Brick Foxhole* (1945, made into the 1947 film *Cross-*

fire), and Laura Hobson's novel *Gentleman's Agreement* (1947, made into a film that same year).[3] Each narrative of trading places turns on a mistaken identity and ultimately reveals the instability of racial boundaries. Unaware of the formal and informal mechanisms of exclusion, the main characters of these stories initially believe that the borders around a victimized group are fixed. In *Focus* the protagonist is perceived by others to be a Jew; in *Gentleman's Agreement* the main character "passes" as a Jew in order to investigate anti-Semitism. Both novels examine home front society at the war's end. In *The Brick Foxhole* the setting is the military and there are two victims of mistaken identity: one is a homosexual civilian (turned into a Jew in the film version), the other a soldier falsely accused of his murder.

Miller and Hobson were following a literary tradition that explored the phenomena of passing and mistaken identity through the elusiveness of Jewishness.[4] Both authors had experience of being assumed to belong to a culture other than the one in which they had been raised. Both were attracted to socialist disregard for racial and ethnic identifications and intended to use Jewish racial indeterminacy to reject the wartime terms of racial integrity common to fascism and white supremacy. As they faced the beginning of the postwar period, both wanted to provide an alternative to celebrating the American victory and the American century, to keep an eye instead on the continuing threat of "domestic fascism"—the increasing political influence of conservative segregationists who, using a language of popular anti-Semitism and white supremacy, were undermining wartime efforts to extend labor and civil rights.

In *The Brick Foxhole* Richard Brooks shifted the perspective on the forces driving racialization to focus on another kind of victim, a homosexual civilian. The hypermasculinity of the wartime military, combined with anti-Semitism and segregationist white supremacy, motivate the murder of a man that is wrongly blamed on a soldier with a cosmopolitan and egalitarian sensibility. When a film adaptation was planned, Brooks consented to important changes: the homosexual victim became Jewish and *Crossfire* became the first Hollywood film to explore anti-Semitism as a form of racism and as its central theme.

As in the interracial love stories, the conflation of various expressions of domestic fascism helped to obscure significant differences. Seeing through Jewishness did not necessarily challenge all forms of racialization; conflating anti-Semitism with white supremacy may have even made less apparent some forms of American racial discrimination and their required remedies. Like other stories of trading places, these narratives relied on popular forms, hard-boiled fiction and social exposé, whose familiarity worked against their ability to challenge. The conventions of "tough-guy" literature, increasing in popularity since the 1920s, may have created the space for Brooks to suggest a connection between racialization and homophobia, but its masculine standards and shadowy back alleys could also make the victimization of homosexuals appear unremarkable. The responses of postwar audiences to these novels and films help us to recognize what was provocative and what was unconvincing at the time, to understand how these texts addressed racialized boundaries and the possibilities for crossing them.

PERCEPTION AND RACIAL BOUNDARIES IN *FOCUS*

Working on a screenplay in 1943 for Ernie Pyle's *The Story of GI Joe,* the young left-wing playwright and radio writer Arthur Miller hoped to present the war effort as a fight for equality. He wanted to believe that soldiers knew, "at least somewhere in their subconscious," not only that "America [must] win but fascism must be destroyed."[5] Writing his first full-length novel a short time later, Miller used incidents of wartime anti-Semitism to warn of the related dangers of domestic fascism. A parable about the involuntary trading of places, *Focus* is about an "ordinary" middle-class man who is mistaken for a Jew. Miller hoped to show that Jewishness was, in the words of Matthew Jacobson, "a highly unstable categorical convention."[6]

Miller was uncertain what "Jewishness" meant as a birthright, for himself or for others. He and his wife Mary Grace Slattery questioned the pull of childhood attachments. In his memoir Miller describes a progressive wartime consciousness that proposed an international cosmopolitanism as an alternative to local and national affiliation:

Mary had stopped considering herself Catholic as a high school student in Ohio, just as I was struggling to identify myself with mankind rather than one small tribal faction of it. Both of us thought we were leaving behind parochial narrowness of mind, prejudices, racism, and the irrational, which were having their ultimate triumph, it seemed to us, in the fascist and Nazi movements that were growing everywhere in strength.[7]

After Pearl Harbor Miller tried to enlist; when he was turned down because of a knee injury he chose to do manual labor connected to defense work. At the Brooklyn Navy Yard he felt he had to be evasive about his previous experience: no one in his shipfitter's gang would believe he had "given up what would have seemed lucrative work writing radio scripts in order to freeze aboard a ship in the river."[8] Miller's occupational "passing" involved him in other kinds of social passing. In interviews published in 1947 he referred to himself as "an inadvertent chameleon" because his "strong features, dark wavy hair, and brown eyes" were thought of as "characteristic of a number of national groups." "As one Italian to another," he explained, "I have been regaled with tales of Irish perfidy. Strictly between us Jews, I have been the confidential bearer of the latest 'wop' story. As one American to another, I have been told why foreigners act the way they do."[9] Working in the yard in the early 1940s exposed Miller to what he later described as "widespread anti-Jewish talk" and to Italian American workers fighting the war by beating up British seamen. These experiences made Miller more aware and more critical of how national identities came to be expressed as "parochial prejudices."[10]

Lawrence Newman, the main character of *Focus*, becomes, like his creator, an inadvertent chameleon. In the beginning of the novel Miller identifies Newman as a firm believer in the certainty of racial categories. Hearing cries for help from a Puerto Rican woman being beaten by a drunken man outside his bedroom window, Newman decides to ignore them: the woman's accent signifies to him she is "abroad at night for no good purpose, and it somehow convinced him that she could take care of herself because she was used to this sort of treatment, Puerto Ricans were, he knew."[11] Newman's job as a personnel manager requires him to identify Jewish "racial" characteristics in order to ensure that Jews are never hired. That he allows one to slip through convinces his superiors that he needs glasses, which precipitates a crisis of his own. Putting on glasses turns *him* into a "Jew" by making him "look Jewish." He is fired from his job, his home is vandalized, and he is nearly mobbed by a crowd of Christian Front activists stirred to frenzy by a priest resembling Detroit's Father Charles Coughlin.

In his novel Miller locates the increasing violence against Jews during the war years within the historical phenomenon of anti-Semitism, with its roots in political economy and Christian popular thought; his main focus, however, is on Newman's psychology of race hatred as a form of self-hatred. Miller resolves Newman's crisis through his embrace of the mistakenly accused: because he can no longer count on the solidity of racial boundaries, his own safety depends on joining other racialized victims to resist attack. As Jacobson points out, Newman comes to understand and define Jews as "people who are treated in a particular way, socially and politically; anyone so treated is 'in effect' a Jew"—including Newman himself.[12]

To conclude the novel Miller revised the opening in order to connect challenging the racialization of Jewishness with explicitly rejecting racial boundaries of all kinds. In the end Newman recalls the earlier cry for help he had not answered: "She could have been murdered, clubbed to death out here that night. No one would have dared outdoors to help, to even say she was a human being. Because all of them watching from their windows knew she was not white." He can no longer assure himself of the safety of that racial boundary: "But he was white. A white man, a neighbor. He belonged here. Or did he?" Newman tries to hold onto this elusive "whiteness"; when the crowd approaches him he directs them to his neighbor Finklestein's store, but they pursue him anyway. In the end, inspired by Finkelstein's courage to resist rather than run when threatened, Newman takes up a weapon and joins in fighting back. Positioning himself on the side of social justice, which can "break away the categories of people and change them so that it would not be important to them what tribe they sprang from," Newman marks his own metamorphosis. "It must not be important any more, he swore, even though in his life it had been of the highest importance." This is the epiphany that stories of trading places sought to dramatize: the rejection of a belief in the primacy of racial categories in favor of an understanding that they are a trivial form of human differentiation, no more significant than height or eye color.

Miller's novel sold ninety thousand copies by 1947 and went through several printings.[13] But Newman was not a very appealing character, reviews were uneven, and a proposed movie deal fell through.[14] Miller later claimed that *Focus* was the first novel to make anti-Semitism its main theme, especially the form of anti-Semitism encouraged by popular broadcasts and grassroots organizations associated with Father Coughlin and Boston's Father Edward Lodge Curran. Social conventions at the time did not readily acknowledge the existence of popular racisms; many saw the dramatization of anti-Semitism as potentially encouraging that which it attempted to condemn. Several critics did find the "anatomy of native fascism" to be the most effective aspect of the novel.[15]

But the reviewers did not agree with Miller that the novel was innovative. As one wrote, Miller had taken a "familiar" theme, "a kind of bogeyman fear that has been melodramatically thrust in our faces ever since

Hitler came into power," and made it "real and comprehensible."[16] That this critic saw Miller's theme as familiar suggests the effectiveness of popular attempts to link Nazi racialism, grassroots anti-Semitism, and racial segregation. Later printings advertised the novel's political goals, the jacket announcing "a hard hitting novel which burns to the core of race hatred in America."[17]

POLICING RACIAL AND GENDER BOUNDARIES IN *THE BRICK FOXHOLE*

Miller's novel posited one set of "perceptual misunderstandings" that led to domestic fascism, with self-analysis ultimately enabling the protagonist's conversion to antiracist beliefs. In Richard Brooks's novel *The Brick Foxhole* it is sadistic militarism and racist brutality that threaten the extension of democracy after the war. Here the protagonist only narrowly survives the violence unleashed because he is able to elicit help from a confluence of military and civilian, public and private relationships. In both *Focus* and *The Brick Foxhole* domestic fascists target characters marked as sexually marginalized and feminine: a Puerto Rican woman assumed to be a prostitute, an effete man assumed to be homosexual. *The Brick Foxhole* is an example of how a writer in the 1940s argued for boundary-crossing cosmopolitanism through the moral condemnation of its opposite. The replacement of its homosexual victim with a Jewish victim in the film adaptation *Crossfire* prompted explicit discussion of the device of trading places.

Richard Brooks grew up in Philadelphia, the son of Russian-Jewish immigrant factory workers. Before the war the new culture industries enabled Brooks to support himself as a writer—in print journalism, as a radio writer (like Miller and Laurents), and in Hollywood, where he produced film dialogue and two B movie screenplays. During the war he worked as a civilian in Frank Capra's Motion Picture Unit on documentaries, including the *Why We Fight* series. In 1943 he joined the marines, where he was assigned to a combat camera unit and sent to the Pacific. There he worked on the combat documentaries that popularized the documentary drama format, *Battle of Iwo Jima* and *Guadalcanal*. Brooks wrote, directed, and edited the combat film *The Battle for the Marianas* (1944) at the Marine facility in Quantico, Virginia. There he also worked on his novel and was nearly court-martialed for failing to follow the military procedure of submitting the book for clearance. The book was published in May 1945.[18]

"Brick foxhole" was service slang for "barracks." In the author's note Brooks explained why he had chosen the stateside military as a backdrop for his exploration of the pressures on masculinity in wartime: the brick foxhole was the barracks that housed "millions of men, men of all kinds, who have been suddenly wrenched from the normal pursuits of civilian life and thrown together under the abnormal conditions of preparations for war." Brooks's focus on the men in between—"warriors who will never fight in this war," their position "too far from the battlefront," too "removed psychologically" from the home front—allowed him to analyze the changes that militarism had wrought and to anticipate the transition from war to peace.

The protagonist, Jeff Mitchell, is a Disney animator drafted to make animated training films. He observes but cannot enact the hypermasculinity demanded of him. His friend and protector is Peter Keeley, a tough newspaper reporter who "had been over, had ribbons . . . had killed Japs." That Brooks made his "sensitive" character a Disney animator associated Mitchell with new culture industry unionism: the cartoonists had struck against Disney in 1941. Mitchell is also a supporter of civil rights who views the war as a fight against Nazism.[19] Mitchell's convictions are shaken, however, by his angst and self-loathing. He works as an artist in the midst of a war where success is measured by killing. He is worn down by the contrast between his views and racist and anticommunist attitudes he encounters everywhere: "Who the hell was Hitler? . . . The war was with the Japs. And after the Japs would come the Russians."[20] Mitchell's friend Peter Keeley is also coded as a progressive, someone who knows that the "only difference" between white and black is "their color," but unlike Mitchell he is a war-hardened reporter who served in the Pacific (as the author did).

Brooks reflected on the retreat from the family and normative heterosexuality using the characters of Mitchell and Keeley to explore the way violence alienated men from family life. As an antidote to his anxieties about whether he measures up to wartime masculinity and whether his wife Mary is faithful to him, Mitchell fantasizes an arbitrary cold-blooded killing:

> I'll kill somebody, he thought. The thought made his blood pound. . . . It was a feeling that made him forget Mary. That was the solution. It was simple. Easy. Merely kill somebody. . . . But who? . . . The girl in uniform walking through the office? He could call her over to his desk and kill her off easily. And everybody would look at him with wonder and awe and even fear.[21]

Keeley espouses a hard-boiled "truth" about battlefield killing that under-mined official wartime rhetoric: "The only way to win a war was to kill, and to kill more than the enemy, and faster and better. And he had learned that men kill better when they are blind to objectives. It wasn't true that men fought better when they had reasons. . . . If you wanted to win battles . . . the best soldiers are those who enjoy the pastime of killing." Brooks depicts Mitchell and Keeley as driven by ambivalent relationships with their wives, and characterizes the marines—the "self-advertised best fighting force in existence"—as attracting many men who had "enlisted to get away from their wives, not to make the world secure."[22]

The climactic murder takes place far from the battlefield; as in Mitchell's fantasy, it is a cold-blooded sadistic act. Instead of a "girl in uni-form," however, the victim is a homosexual civilian, Mr. Edwards. (Brooks later said he had witnessed a similar incident.)[23] Edwards is entrapped and murdered by two people in Mitchell's company: an ex-cop and marine sergeant from Chicago, Monty Crawford, and a southern sol-dier, Floyd Bowers.[24]

Brooks uses the formulation of trading places in the murder scene, where he links the aggression encouraged in soldiers and the politically driven sadistic and sexual violence that characterizes lynching. The "trou-ble had started" when the effete civilian Edwards plays a recording of Paul Robeson. Crawford pushes Bowers to elide Robeson's enactment of inter-racial passion with Uta Hagen in the Broadway *Othello* with an imagined spectacle of African American soldiers having sex with white women. Bowers then boasts of having lynched a decorated black soldier who refused to give up his seat on a train. Then both Crawford and Bowers dance "too tightly" with Edwards, who asks them to leave. Mitchell does leave, but Bowers takes off his pants and refuses to go. Crawford later admits to killing Edwards, "like he deserved to be killed"; Edwards's body is found unclothed, implying that he was raped as well.[25] Mitchell is accused of the murder, but the reader has "witnessed" Crawford and Bow-ers's staging of the entrapment, Bowers's anticipation of "beating up a queer," and Crawford's presumably insider knowledge of how to orches-trate a homosexual seduction.[26]

By the end of the novel a more cosmopolitan social order has been established, with alliances transcending former tensions between military and civilian, prostitute and wife, melting pot platoon and prewar ethnic divisions. Outside the military the rule of law is restored, when various characters, including Mitchell's wife, Mary, a tired young prostitute

Mitchell had visited, and a civilian police officer ally with Keeley and a young Jewish soldier—symbols of progressive elements in the military—to clear Mitchell. In the military good similarly triumphs over evil, but with a vigilante justice, as Keeley kills Crawford and then is himself killed.

Brooks was able to publish these provocative ruminations on wartime hypermasculinity and sadistic violence by containing them within the conventions of tough-guy literature. Detective fiction lent itself to an oppositional sensibility, exposing social and sexual hypocrisy while revealing the underside of political and economic authority, especially in the hands of radical writers such as Dashiell Hammett and Vera Caspary.[27] A contemporary critic described Brooks's characters as "straight from the tough fiction factory; a lone wolf, full of irony and pity, a true wife, an imitation Circe, a prostitute with an undersized but genuine heart of gold, a sly sadistic villain, a homosexual."[28] Endowed with the authority of his military experience, Brooks pushed against the boundaries of permissible wartime subjects by exploring the dark alleys and shadows of the city at night, the frantic intensity of a weekend leave.

To some critics, however, Brooks's depiction of a troubled masculinity contradicted the broader antifascist mission. As the 1940s progressive Walter Bernstein responded in a *New Republic* review, "It is true that we have fascists in our Army, but it is also true that our Army is fighting an anti-fascist war. It is true that the Army exerts a certain depersonalizing and even brutalizing influence on its men. But only to a certain extent and under certain circumstances." Rather than seeing Mitchell as a truth teller, Bernstein saw him as succumbing to "self pity and neuroses." The *New Yorker*'s Hamilton Basso shared Bernstein's diagnosis: critical of Brooks's description of Mitchell as one of the "few healthy-minded men in his outfit," Basso thought a more appropriate label would be "psychoneurotic." He particularly objected to Brooks's attempt to connect militarism with hypermasculinity, commenting that he couldn't see Mitchell as "a sensitive or admirable person," only as a man "who shows all the signs of having been so overmothered in his childhood that he is as useless to himself as he is to others."[29]

Other critics recognized Brooks's political analogy but did not share his sense of urgency, arguing that reliance on a genre of popular fiction made the fascist character formulaic. Basso dismissed Monty, the fascist character, as a mechanical and contrived "type" ("who despises Jews, Negroes, foreigners, and civilians") and the book as badly written. But novelist

Niven Busch, who also noted Brooks's overreliance on conventions—too much attention to the "Dashiell Hammett-style manhunt for Jeff" at the cost of the "theme"—admired the departure from progressive political orthodoxy. He agreed that the novel was "angry" but praised its "rejection of the easy catch-words and catch-thinking of a world halfway between war and peace."[30]

The connections Brooks implied between racism, anti-Semitism, and sexuality pushed popular antifascism in an important direction. Sinclair Lewis described in *Esquire* the soldiers' "hatred for Negroes and Jews and Catholics and especially homosexuals" as "hatred finally, for everyone and themselves."[31] To depict a homosexual as a wrongful victim was a step toward defending the right to sexual privacy. The investigating police officer, serving as a foil to the brutal ex-cop Crawford, suggests how American democracy would have to expand its toleration of sexual practices: a man's "strange sexual habits," according to the investigator, do not give a soldier "the right . . . to straighten him out." In effect, this is a warning against the abuse of power by men in uniform and an inchoate but recognizable argument for the legal rights of homosexuals to personal freedom, the same right that black playwright Abe Hill had invoked to protect interracial relationships.[32]

Viewing the issue of "race prejudice" as a "purely incidental" to the plot of the novel, Hamilton Basso judged Brooks to be "confused." Richard Wright, who was not persuaded by *Focus*, applauded Brooks's framework with a ringing endorsement on the book jacket.[33] In his review of *The Brick Foxhole* for *PM* Wright interpreted the murder setup as emblematic of a wartime culture that fed rather than challenged domestic fascism. He liked the characterization of the

> frenzy of wartime America on a moral holiday: the fetid rooms of crowded hotels, the poker and crap games in reeking latrines, the apartments of men who like to pick up lonely soldiers, the bars where men who have made their pile of profits out of war contracts spew hate against the world, especially against Jews, Negroes, and organized labor.

Note that his mention of entrapment—"the apartments of men who like to pick up lonely soldiers"—reversed the novel's characterization of the racist and sadistic soldiers and the homosexual victim. But Wright was clearly familiar with and sympathetic to Brooks's overall premise. He described the prose as seeming "to have been lifted directly out of the thought-processes of people we all know." Wright contributed his racial and literary authority to Brooks's achievement, praising his "fierce truth telling" and "stinging photographic realism."[34]

RECASTING THE VICTIM IN *CROSSFIRE*

As a first-time author Brooks must have been pleased when his novel was sold for the film adaptation *Crossfire,* though he would have little control over how it would be transformed in the process. He acceded to an important change—the murder victim was now a Jew—based on the idea that any victim of domestic fascism could stand in for any other victim. As he later commented, "I guess we all have the same problems."[35]

Fresh from their wartime success at producing popular feature films and documentaries, progressive Hollywood filmmakers and screenwriters were gaining confidence that filmmaking could have a social impact after the war.[36] A number of the major studios began to explore previously unacceptable topics—subject, of course, to financial considerations and to Joseph Breen's production code office.[37] Although no Hollywood film before 1947 had made anti-Semitism a thematic focus, the group of Hollywood radicals who made *Crossfire* believed it would be possible, by challenging the racialization of Jewishness, to undermine all forms of fascist racialization.

The producer of *Crossfire* was Adrian Scott, who began work on the project in 1946.[38] In Hollywood since the early 1940s, working as a screenwriter and after 1943 as a producer for RKO, his career had taken off with the immensely popular film of Raymond Chandler's detective mystery *Farewell My Lovely,* retitled *Murder, My Sweet,* in 1944. Along with *The Maltese Falcon* (1941), *Laura* (1944), and *Double Indemnity* (1944), *Murder, My Sweet* helped to define the film noir genre that by 1946 French writers viewing Hollywood's recent output would name. Much of the hard-boiled fiction on which these films were based had been popular in the 1930s, but the production code and the demands of promoting wartime morale made it difficult to turn them into film.[39] Scott was well known in Hollywood's radical political circles in the 1940s and would be subpoenaed to appear before HUAC as an alleged Communist in October 1947.[40]

The group responsible for *Crossfire* comprised the key people who achieved success with *Murder, My Sweet:* screenwriter John Paxton, who had worked with Scott as an associate editor of *Stage* in New York in the late 1930s and came to work as a screenwriter in Hollywood in the early 1940s, and director Edward Dmytryk, a child of Ukrainian immigrants who had worked his way up in the studio system, moving to prestige features in 1943 with the antifascist drama *Hitler's Children*. Dmytryk was also a prominent Hollywood radical and a member of the Communist Party until 1945.[41] In *Crossfire* Scott and Paxton wanted to dramatize the continuing threat of fascism and racism, which Scott believed had only been temporarily defeated by the Allied victory. Paxton and Scott's research file for the film contains various historical examples of this threat, including nineteenth-century anti-Catholicism and the emergence of the Ku Klux Klan.[42] Paxton thought that "a cops and robbers format might work best. The tension and menace thus created would provide the most interesting and acceptable mode of treatment for the theme."[43]

Scott's pitch to the RKO executives, in which he detailed his strategy for adapting the novel, made clear his political aims for the film.[44] His memo provides an example of how popular antifascist thinking encouraged the problematic logic of trading places, conflating widely varying experiences of discrimination. The film would circumvent the book's focus on troubled masculinity, pushing the subtext of sexuality almost out of view. Claiming to have Brooks's support, Scott proposed changing the victim from a homosexual to a Jew.[45]

> This is a story of personal fascism as opposed to organized fascism. The story, in a very minor sense to be sure, indicates how it is possible for us to have a gestapo, if this country should go fascist. A character like Monty would qualify brilliantly for the leadership of the Belsen concentration camp. Fascism hates weakness in people, minorities. Monty hates fairies, negroes, jews and foreigners. In the book Monty murders a fairy. He could have murdered a negro, a foreigner, or a jew. It would have been the same thing. In the picture he does murder a jew. This analysis, incidentally, is absolutely correct in the opinion of the author. The picture would deal exclusively with Monty's anti-semitism.

By having anti-Semitism stand for all racisms, the film erased the links that Brooks made in the novel between the killer's racism, anti-Semitism, and homophobia, as well as its portrayal of the homosexual as innocent victim. The effect of this change was to diminish the logic of the film's plot. In the popular imagination Jews were much less likely than homosexuals to be vulnerable to violence from people they invited into their apartments.[46]

Scott's politics would have made it unlikely for him to imagine filming Brooks's original formulation: whatever the private practices of Party members and allies, the Communist left did not frame homosexual rights as a form of minority rights or suggest that homosexuals were vulnerable to discrimination.[47] Even if Brooks's original formulation had intrigued Scott, it is unlikely he believed the audience would accept a "fairy" as the symbol of the victim of fascist hatred, given Hollywood's conventionally dismissive portrayals of homosexuals as well as opposition from production code strictures on homosexuality.[48]

Nor does it seem likely that Scott would propose a "Negro" victim to serve as a symbol of fascist hatred unleashed. Leftists agreed with African American activists that, within Hollywood's historical representations of race, showing a black person murdered as a result of racial hatred could invite emulation rather than outrage. The pressure on Hollywood to expand its repertoire of black characters and the precedents established during World War II had prioritized efforts to picture the "Negro as a normal human being."[49] Like Miller, Scott may have seen a Jew as a safer choice than an African American to expose racialization: in the U.S., anti-Semitic violence was a danger but did not ordinarily end in death, as lynching did.

Still, the question of who could be shown as a victim of fascism generated controversy. The conservative Breen office noted that while the story "could be defended as being a plea against all forms of racial or religious intolerance," it was "still open to the charge of being a special pleading against current anti-Semitism."[50] Representatives of the American Jewish Committee appealed to RKO executives to stop the production or to change the Jewish victim into an African American.[51] They feared the dangers of emphasizing Jewish victimization but were either unaware of, or accepted without comment, the history of violence against African Americans.

Scott developed the character of the civilian policeman as a spokesperson for popular antifascism, representing grassroots solidarity with the victims of persecution.

> The policeman, Finley. A very good cop, incidentally. He would be Roman Catholic and an Irishman. He understands anti-semitism because he's Irish and a Catholic. He understands it more clearly than other people because his

grandfather, who immigrated to this country from Ireland, was murdered in a riot against the Irish people. This actually happened in New York City and Philadelphia in the last century. He would be our spokesman.[52]

In an early draft of the script Finley's speech illuminating broad parameters of racialized discrimination explicitly made the connections outlined by Scott; it was to be spoken against a montage of images illuminating nineteenth-century Protestant attacks on Catholics and mentioned a Negro who had been lynched. Both sequences were cut in subsequent versions.[53] The filmed version settled for a visual enhancement of Finley's authority as spokesman for popular front progressivism, with the camera lingering on a large portrait of Roosevelt above Finley's shoulder.

Finally, Scott articulated a social plea informed by his understanding of anti-Semitism as racialist and his belief that recent anti-Semitic incidents and "negro race riots" were part of the same "cancer." His proposed "cure" was "heroic" social filmmaking.

> Anti-semitism is not declining as a result of Hitler's defeat. The recent negro race riots in a high school (an unheard of event in this country) is [sic] symptomatic of the whole cancer. Anti-semitism and anti-negroism will grow unless heroic measures can be taken to stop them. This picture is one such measure.

Scott promised that the focus on a social problem would add to rather than diminish the film's appeal: "This will never in our hands be a depressing pamphlet. It will have all the rugged excitement and speed of *Murder, My Sweet* and a white hot issue to boot."[54]

With Dore Schary (who was interested in "message" films) as the vice president in charge of production at RKO, studio executives approved the project, agreeing that "anti-Semitism was on the rise" and that "here was a good useful way to introduce a new subject matter."[55] By the time *Crossfire* was approved for production, studio executives were relieved to hear that Fox had acquired the movie rights to *Gentleman's Agreement* and intended to film a big-budget adaptation. Scott later recalled, "We worried more about [the script] than we thought about it. We wondered if they would really let us make it." From Scott's point of view the film's linked critique of anti-Semitism and racism was exactly what made it recognizable as a product of left-wing progressivism, already the focus of conservative political attack.[56]

Crossfire was made quickly and cheaply, and its release was timed to "steal a lot of thunder" from the "more ballyhoo'd movie version of the current best seller on anti-semitism," *Gentleman's Agreement. Crossfire* was positively reviewed, but exhibitors noticed that strong "word of mouth" seemed responsible for its drawing enthusiastic audiences. The film did especially well in big cities.[57]

Crossfire's trading-places premise did not convince everybody. Some reviewers resisted the hybrid structure of message and mystery. They complained particularly about the insertion of a "five-minute sermon on prejudice" with phrases "so patently grammar-schoolish as to be almost insulting" in the midst of the investigation of the crime.[58] One commented that Scott, Dmytryk, and Paxton dealt with their "difficult subject" with "more energy than perception, more courage than wisdom." James Agee wrote in the *Nation* that the film lacked courage, noting its failure to directly protest racial segregation and mentioning without comment its substitution of a Jewish for a homosexual victim.[59]

Some reviewers objected to the trading places formulation because they didn't think it effectively conveyed the particular dynamics of anti-Semitism. The *Life* reviewer wrote that seeing Jews as racialized justified only some forms of their social exclusion; the murdering sergeant, "a man whose feeling against Jews is so intense that it drives him to murder" was too extreme to represent "the problems of a nation whose anti-semitism is expressed largely in the insidious but less spectacular methods of social discrimination." Jewish organizations continued to insist that marking the victim as Jewish was dangerous. To Elliot Cohen, editor of the journal *Commentary,* the film's overly simplistic explanation of discriminatory hatred did not adequately explain anti-Semitism or speak out against it. He was worried that the display of anti-Semitic violence would encourage emulation, and he objected to the way the victim in the film was "a composite of many of the anti-semitic stereotypes of the Jew." Cohen quoted a *Commentary* reader who rejected the trading places premise (which he named "the old switcheroo"). Substituting the murder of "a heterosexual, a jew" for an "unoffending homosexual" was "not good enough" to explain "race hatred."[60]

Other reviewers praised the film's critique of racialized categories and were enthusiastic about the substitution. The *Variety* reviewer labeled *Crossfire* a "hard-hitting film whose whodunnit aspects are fundamentally incidental to the overall thesis of racial bigotry," noting however that

RKO's promotion featured the film as a "whodunnit, sans any anti-Semitic reference." *Newsweek* praised the "courage" of the film's "forthright attack on anti-Semitism, and for that matter, all forms of race and religious prejudice" (for once "Hollywood hasn't disguised a Sunday punch as a cream puff") as well as its "absorbing, suspenseful melodrama."[61] John Houseman wrote in the left-wing *Hollywood Quarterly* that the film's racial protest energized the rest of the film: the "intensity of feeling which sparked the creators of the picture into attacking the racial issue" heightened the drama and sharpened the conflicts. Betty Goldstein (later Friedan), reviewer for *UE News,* was glad to see Hollywood's popular commercial formulas put to use to dramatize the "problem of race hatred," previously off-limits to Hollywood films, apparently accepting the film's use of prejudice against Jews to represent the dangers of race hate.[62]

It is striking to note how most reviewers accepted *Crossfire*'s trading places premise as a familiar, though controversial, idea in the political mainstream. As a person close to the left, Betty Goldstein would have been aware that the film's "progressive" content would make it politically vulnerable to anticommunist conservatives then gaining political force. She worried that the producer, Dore Schary, would be "investigated" when the "Dies-Thomas Committee" arrived "in Hollywood in the fall—they won't like such a man directing one of Hollywood's major studios."[63]

The anticommunists did go after the film, but it was Scott and Dmytryk that HUAC subpoenaed rather than Schary. Scott and Dmytryk had envisioned a follow-up film that would take the critique of racialization to its next step, with an adaptation of the novel *Albert Sears* by the left-wing writer Millen Brand, announced in the summer of 1948. (In the novel a white man changes his allegiance from property owners concerned about declining real estate values to a black family facing a white campaign of terror.) The proposed film would have a "hard-boiled, straight-forward message dealing with the Negro housing problem [and going] . . . deep into the very foundation of prejudices and covenants as they have been practiced in this country."[64] Whether such a film could have been financed and produced in 1948 remains a question: charged with contempt along with the other members of the Hollywood Ten, Scott and Dmytryk were blacklisted, lost their access to film production, and were finally jailed in June 1950.

DERACIALIZING JEWISHNESS IN *GENTLEMAN'S AGREEMENT*

In Laura Zametkin Hobson's novel *Gentleman's Agreement,* a journalist passes as a Jew to write an exposé of anti-Semitism and discovers the unspoken social boundaries that exclude Jews. Richard Simon of Simon and Schuster was initially discouraging about Hobson's outline for the novel, though he did concede that "the great Jewish book corresponding to *Strange Fruit* has yet to be written. Perhaps you are the one to do it."[65] The novel was serialized in *Cosmopolitan* in November 1946 and generated the largest volume of mail the magazine had ever received from readers of a serial. By the time it was released in book form in February 1947, the movie rights had already been sold to Twentieth Century-Fox. Reviewers praised the book's earnestness even when objecting to Hobson's "slickness" and "women's-magazine" style; *Gentleman's Agreement* became a book club selection and stayed at the top of the *New York Times* best-seller list for six months, selling nearly a million copies in its first year.[66]

Hobson had worked in reporting and advertising and, between 1934 and 1940, in promotion for Henry Luce's news photojournalism empire, *Time, Life,* and *Fortune.* Her first published fiction was of the mass-market genre: she coauthored two serial westerns and produced popular magazine fiction through the 1930s. She was the only woman in Luce's "senior group" until she left in 1940 to avoid a conflict of interest between the Luce publications and her then fiancé, Ralph Ingersoll, one of the top editors at *Time.* Hobson turned to fiction, and published her first novel in 1943.[67] *The Trespassers* combined popular genres of romance and documentary exposé, interweaving the romance of a modern career woman and a ruthless newspaper publisher with the story of political refugees attempting to flee Nazi Germany; it was modestly successful, selling about twenty thousand copies, and served as a practice run for some of the ideas and literary techniques that would later shape *Gentleman's Agreement.*[68]

Hobson, like Miller, had questioned the meaning of Jewishness as a birthright, partly as a result of her upbringing in a family that combined immigrant radicalism and "conformity." She described her parents as "Russian and Jewish, and old-fashioned socialist, and agnostic, and internationalists, and non-sectarians, and pro-labor and antimilitarist, and hotly opposed to every form of oppression, injustice, exploitation, infringement of freedom to speak out, to write, to vote, to oppose." Expressions of the family's socialist tradition included draping their house in yards of black bunting to mourn the nearly 150 victims of the 1911 Tri-

angle Shirtwaist fire, opening their homes to the children of Lawrence tex-
tile strikers in 1912, giving away any interest accrued on the family savings
account as "unearned" and therefore tainted money, and rejecting religious practice and ritual. Her parents were also committed "to bring
up their children as total Americans, with no trace of foreign accent,
no smallest inflection or gesture that was not native to their beloved
country."[69]

Conscious of the impact of names as markers of Jewishness, Hobson
gave herself various "American" names. She evaded efforts to screen out
Jewish job applicants—a practice Miller detailed in *Focus*—by dropping
Zametkin and using her mother's maiden name, Kean, when applying for
work. She published her first short story as Laura Mount, using the name of
her former lover and writing partner, Tom Mount. Incorporating her ex-
husband's name, Laura Z. Hobson published her first "real story" in a
national magazine in 1935.[70] In public interviews in 1947 Hobson emphasized her cosmopolitan, as opposed to ethnic, identity: "I grew up in an
agnostic and broad-minded family. I think of myself as a plain human
being who happens to be an American. But so long as there is anti-semitism
in this country, so long as it remains an advantage not to be Jewish, I can
never simply say, 'I am an agnostic,' but must say, 'I am Jewish.' "[71]

Hobson's interest in setting up a trading places scenario in *Gentleman's
Agreement* differed from that of Miller and Brooks. Hobson was more
concerned with challenging racialized Jewishness and exposing anti-
Semitism as a form of racism than with questioning racial boundaries
more broadly. Hobson initially intended to address the contrast between
the horror of war and the excitement of wartime antifascist and antiracist
social movements. The cultural centrality of men who had served in the
military shaped Hobson's conception, as it did so many of trading places
texts. Her initial impulse was to develop this theme through two characters—a soldier demoralized by the return to civilian life and a lawyer who
had never been in uniform but was still fighting " 'the long war' for civil
rights in America against prejudice and injustice."[72]

But then Hobson read a *Time* magazine report of Mississippi conservative Democrat John Rankin referring to Walter Winchell—a pro-FDR
syndicated columnist and radio personality—as "a little kike" in the
course of a speech opposing legislation that would enable soldiers to vote.
Hobson was apparently shaken that Rankin's comment garnered
prolonged applause, rather than protest, from the House of Representatives.[73] Rankin, elected by a minority of white voters in Mississippi, per-

sonified the link between conservative politics, racism, segregation, and anti-Semitism.

As she thought about this incident, she had the idea of representing the bigotry and prejudice of "the long war" as anti-Semitism. Stimulated by the outrage of non-Jewish friends over this incident, she posed the question of exploring everyday expressions of anti-Semitism, "not just among the outright bigots like Congressman Rankin, Senator Bilbo, the white supremacist, and Father Coughlin on the radio with his following of millions for his nightly hate talks, but other people, people who'd never call anybody a kike, people who said they loathed prejudice." Suppose the hero were a writer; suppose he had just come back into contact with life in America after being out of touch overseas; suppose he weren't Jewish but said he was, what would he discover?

Gentleman's Agreement inherited its narrative conventions from Luce-style documentary journalism and radio and news docudrama. Into her saga of crusading journalist Phil Green (who passes as a Jew in order to "get the story" of anti-Semitism) and his romance with Kathy Lacey, a sophisticated New York divorcée who thinks she is progressive but discovers that she too has embraced many subtle forms of anti-Semitism, Hobson sprinkled recent theories deracializing Jews. She catalogued forms of discrimination Jews faced and probed the implications of polite toleration of anti-Semitism. The options that Phil rejects before finding the right "angle" for his article—to get some "first-hand experience" of being Jewish—suggest that wartime exhortations linking racism with Hitler had lost urgency. Rational arguments about culture and race, polls revealing social attitudes, or "the same old drool of statistics and protests": Phil doesn't think these would persuade a mass audience. Still, his journalistic mission enabled Hobson to slip in references to many of these arguments, helping to establish the book's authority on its subject.[74]

The passing strategy depended for its legitimacy on 1930s documentary-style reportage, which emphasized the superiority of journalistic objectivity to subjective experience. Phil had written about migrant labor by disguising himself as an Okie: with the help of some old clothes and a used car, "he'd melted into the crowds moving from grove to grove, ranch to ranch, picking till he dropped. He'd lived in their camps, ate what they ate, told nobody who he was. He'd found the answer in his own guts, not somebody else. He'd *been* an Okie." When assigned a story on mining, he hadn't tapped "some poor grimy guy on the shoulder and begun to talk." Instead, he'd been hired as a miner, "gone down into the dark, slept in a bunk in a shack." Asking miners to reflect on their experience would have been prying: "He hadn't dug into a man's secret being. He'd *been* a miner." Phil does express some qualms about his ruse ("It's glib and trumped up and fake"), only to be reassured by his editor ("there was nothing slick or fake in that [miner] series"). To pass—a conceit central to both trading-places logic and to social exposé—was to become, to know the other with supposedly greater "objectivity" than the other.

Hobson's conception of Jewishness denied that there was a recognizable "Jewish type": the few Jewish characters in *Gentleman's Agreement* are thoroughly educated and cosmopolitan. Critic Diana Trilling pointed out that, although there were no "swinish Jews" in *Gentleman's Agreement,* there were "scarcely any Jews at all"—nothing to differentiate Jews except their awareness of discrimination that most non-Jews did not see. This homogeneity troubled Trilling: "Does the liberal society that Mrs. Hobson envisages allow no distinctions between Jew and Gentile? For that matter, it allows no distinctions between human beings." Trilling's response to the erasures in *Gentleman's Agreement* was to want, "if only for the sake of variety, to underscore rather than eliminate minority differences." She was aware, nonetheless, of "the complex political business of cultural pluralism" and its tendency to "create social problems perhaps faster than it creates social values."[75] Another problem is that Phil never *really* passes. He has to announce his "Jewishness" to provoke the assumptions Hobson meant to challenge, while hostile strangers immediately identify his friend Dave Goldman as a "yid."[76] The many offhand, anti-Semitic comments uttered in Phil's presence assume he is *not* a Jew.

Hobson's passing device did successfully highlight a particular discourse of "polite" anti-Semitism among the upper middle class. It was this focus—not the "spontaneous pogrom" or psychopathic "kike killers" but the "nice people" who "advertise their lack of prejudice" and are "accessories to the social crime of anti-Semitism"—that was, in the assessment of left-wing writer Budd Schulberg, new in American fiction.[77] The novel suggests ways to oppose discrimination: using public disclosure of discriminatory practices to change anti-Jewish hiring policies and anti-Jewish strategies used by realtors.

Hobson has Green's editor explain that the series is important because "there isn't anything bigger as an issue" than "beating down . . . commonplace . . . prejudice"; she also wanted to disassociate the issue from the Communist left. Hobson identified with the anti-Stalinist, anticommunist left, which divided her from her sister and brother-in-law, both active in Party circles. Emphasizing the fight against racial prejudice as a weapon against Communism often entailed abandoning a political and economic analysis of race, racialization, and colonization, because of their association with left-wing progressivism, in favor of personal psychological explanations.[78]

Hobson's vision of the sameness of Jews and non-Jews in effect ratified rather than delegitimized racial boundaries associated with color differences. The same anthropological authority that Hobson cites to question Jewish racialization offers an intellectual and scientific framework of racialized biological distinction, referring to the "three great divisions of mankind, the Caucasian, the mongoloid, the Negroid."[79] Hobson's representation of interchangeability also depended on men as figures for the universal; women may be able to pass individually but, as a group, women were rarely selected to signal the potential sameness of "mankind." Hobson playfully contrasted the "natural" and "biological" difference of gender to the "false" difference of Jewishness when she has Phil Green joke that his next series will be "I was a Woman for Eight Weeks."

Still, it was possible in 1947 to read Hobson's critique of polite anti-Semitism as an insistent and optimistic call for a movement to resist postwar conservatism. To those who sought to keep progressive coalitions alive, the erasure of boundaries was understood as a precondition to equality. If audiences were familiar with the terms of popular antifascism and fictional and film narratives of social exposé, the formulation linking "anti-semitism, and anti-Negroism, jingoism and anti-unionism" could offer a hopeful political synthesis. W. E. B. Du Bois, reviewing the book for the *New York Times Book Review,* called the book a "Grade-A tract . . . cleverly camouflaged as a novel"; he seemed moved by Phil Green's uncovering of "a great deal about the innate savagery of his fellow-man." Du Bois termed the book's "polemics" far better than "its probing of the verities." Yet he appreciated Hobson's renunciation of the postwar imperial vision articulated by her former boss, Henry Luce. He ended his review by quoting from the book: "It might not be the American century after all . . . or the Russian century, or the atomic century. Perhaps it would be the century that broadened and implemented the idea of freedom. All the freedom. Of all men."[80]

Looking for projects that could "be part of the solution to the problems that torture the world," Twentieth Century-Fox's Darryl Zanuck bought the screen rights to *Gentleman's Agreement* while it was still in galleys.[81] Zanuck was interested in the book even before its best-seller status would have made a movie deal automatic, partly because its liberal worldview corresponded to his own, but also because its framework of social exposé was well suited to his style of filmmaking in features such as *I Am a Fugitive from a Chain Gang* (1932) and *Grapes of Wrath* (1939). Zanuck's social problem films used a strategy similar to that popularized in 1930s documentary journalism: the personal drama of a central character suddenly exposed to forms of exploitation and discrimination, relying on expository dialogue and a plot that strung together dramatic narrative incidents to represent broader forms of injustice.[82] Zanuck was the Hollywood spokesperson who publicly defended the industry's late 1930s anti-Nazi films against conservative charges of prowar propaganda in government hearings in September 1941.[83] He selected *Gentleman's Agreement* as his personal production, working on the script with Moss Hart, overseeing the editing, and concentrating studio resources on its production and promotion.

Gentleman's Agreement seemed unlikely as movie material, given that it was, in Zanuck's phrase, "eighty percent talk and twenty percent action."[84] There was also opposition to plotting a film about anti-Semitism. Elia Kazan, Zanuck's choice of director, and Moss Hart both related stories of a meeting at Warner Brothers in which studio executives expressed their reluctance: "For chrissake, why make that picture? We are getting along all right. Why raise the whole subject?"[85] Despite objections, the project moved forward, propelled by Zanuck's personal commitment, the excitement generated by the book's popularity, and an unprecedented number of readers who wrote to the studio to plead for a straightforward adaptation that would "make its audience think."[86] These were years of optimism about "progress" in human relations and the social power of filmmaking.

The film adaptation followed the original novel closely. Hobson's agent tried to protect the integrity of the book by rejecting the "based on" credit that gave producers the right to change anything in the original text; Hobson was present at the studio for much of the filming. Hart's screenplay sharpened the storytelling but preserved both the virtues and flaws of the novel.[87] The film was commercially successful, with extended runs generating a significant profit for the studio and many awards, including Academy Awards for best picture and best director.[88]

The filmmakers had to cast characters meant to look Jewish and non-Jewish at the same time, and so had to address some of the narrative's unanswerable questions: who could pass as non-Jewish, and who was unmistakably a Jew? Phil Green didn't pose a problem: his Jewishness was, after all, fictional. Gregory Peck appeared to be the perfect choice for the crusading journalist because he was "young, handsome, himself a decent man protesting prejudice." But how should Phil's friend Dave Goldman be cast? According to Kazan's account, Richard Conte was to play Dave until Kazan suggested John Garfield, who "was like a regular WASP, nobody could look nicer than him to the audience, he had no defects." Hobson remembered Zanuck telling her that some people argued against casting Garfield, "saying that his speech had something of New York in it, something Jewish, and that the audience might not believe they had grown up together in California."[89] Critics' responses to John Garfield's "performance" of Jewishness continued this debate. Bosley Crowther termed Garfield's portrayal "too mechanical." The *Daily Mirror's* reactionary columnist Lee Mortimer sneered that Garfield "played the part of a professional Jew ad nauseum."[90]

Critical discussion of the film pointed out that the film's effort to erase Jewish difference denied the possibility that "Jews might be proud of their Jewishness and wish to defend the just and good things for which they stand." One critic quoted a widely circulating tale (attributed to Moss Hart) about a stagehand's reading of the film's "lesson" about interchangeability: "I am always going to be good to Jewish people because you can never tell when they will turn out to be Gentiles."[91]

Other critics groped for a broader language in which to challenge the film's erasure of difference. An editorial on anti-Semitism appearing in the *Life* issue with Gregory Peck on the cover questioned the film's assumption that "the only solution to the Jewish problem is for Jews to be assimilated into the dominant white Protestant American culture." The editorial quoted *Commentary* editor Elliot Cohen, who hoped for a society in which people learn not only

> to permit but to prize the varieties and values of the kind of American who never appears in advertisements—the Pole, the Italian, the Irishman, the Seventh Avenue dress manufacturer, and the bearded orthodox rabbi, the grimy sweaty workmen and the men of other eye-slants and skin colors. America . . . was not meant to be a country club for people "just like us."[92]

Hermione Rich Isaacs, writing for *Theatre Arts*, also criticized the film's resolution, offering in its stead a vision in which "we cease to deny the differences among nations, races, religions, and spiritual traditions, and begin to cherish them instead, knowing them for what they are, variations in kind, not in quality."[93] Using terms popularized by the interracial love stories explored in chapter 4, one *Life* reader criticized the boundaries between public and private maintained in *Gentleman's Agreement*. The film's discussion of anti-Semitism had "either consciously or unconsciously" missed the opportunity to answer "racial prejudice" with "racial intermarriage" as the most insistent challenge to "racial integrity," which was, in his view, responsible for causing "most of the world wars and other problems."[94]

Despite its erasures, *Gentleman's Agreement* had a political resonance that astonished even the most experienced of movie reviewers: "There is film realism in *Gentleman's Agreement* the likes of which has not been seen or heard or discussed or shown, ever."[95] The reviews were nearly unanimous in their applause for the film's joining with *Crossfire* in breaking a long tradition of Hollywood silence on racial and religious prejudice. In her review for *UE News* Betty Goldstein termed *Gentleman's Agreement* "sensational" for dealing "squarely with the issue of racial discrimination as a festering sore under the surface of American democracy" and praised its highlighting the "reactionary pattern that can become fascism."[96] Critics in the black press joined this chorus. Jewell Carter described the film for the Baltimore *Afro-American* as a "strong attack on colorphobia," a "headlong attack against modern racial or sect prejudice," and a "splendid effort" to use film to criticize "the prejudices and hatreds which militate against efforts for world peace and interracial accord."[97]

A number of critics identified the calling of real "abuses by . . . their proper names" as an important social contribution of the film, a significant step away from visual stereotyping. John Mason Brown wrote of *Gentleman's Agreement* and *Crossfire* that "the surprise, more truly the shock, with which one hears such everyday words as 'Jew, Catholic, and Protestant' emerge from a sound track in a darkened movie palace is no compliment to the motion pictures." The *Chicago Defender*'s Lillian Scott appreciated Peck's broad condemnation of racial name-calling, quoting the film's dialogue: "I don't like names like 'Yid,' 'Heinie,' 'Kike,' 'Nig,' 'Nigger,' no matter who uses them." Bosley Crowther praised the film's "intrepidity" in naming "Bilbo, Rankin and Gerald L. K. Smith" as promulgators of domestic fascism. The New York *Daily News* critic Kate Cameron was even more enthusiastic about the efficacy of the film's public discourse:

Any prejudice which might be expressed by some portion of the citizenry against a minority group must be stamped out by shouting it from the housetops. . . . The screen is a much more effective platform than a roof might be, as the words ring out with such clarity from the Mayfair Screen, and there is no mistaking their meaning.[98]

The narrowed range of the film's social analysis of racial discrimination did not pass unnoticed, however. The *Los Angeles Times* critic Edwin Schallert contrasted the film's "mental persecutions" with the "far more bitter, far more horrible examples of real persecution" in Nazi-occupied Europe.[99] Crowther identified its focus on upper-class anti-Semitism and "petty bourgeois rebuffs" as only "the upper fringe of the really vicious and hurtful sanctions that are practiced against Jews and other minorities in certain areas of this free land."[100] A *Life* editorial noted that while Jews were discriminated against in terms of equality of opportunity, they were *not* disadvantaged in personal safety, citizenship, and freedom of conscience and expression, as other minorities were, "notably Negroes."[101] While Betty Goldstein especially liked the film's demand that "unless you fight [discrimination] in your own life and daily actions, you're helping to keep it alive," she was concerned about the film's exclusive focus on the " 'station wagon set,' as if racial discrimination mainly exists in high society." Jewell Carter asserted that "all the details" of the "experience and hurts Jews suffer because of anti-semitism" reflected "the anti-colored circumstances under which colored Americans experience hardships and oppressions more widespread and disastrous than that suffered by Jews."[102]

Hobson seems not to have paid much attention to how the kinds of discrimination faced by other minority groups may have differed from those faced by Jews. She did not consider the dangers of allowing particular forms of injustice, and the solutions she proposed for them, to stand for all forms of injustice and all manners of remedy. Her confidence that she could speak for others without considering the limitations of her own perspective, as well as her willingness to promote the struggle against racial injustice to serve the cause of anticommunism, were revealed in a statement that appeared after the novel became a best-seller (but before the film was released):

It's more exciting to be Jewish or Negro. . . . We who are of the minority wake up every morning, not just looking forward to another day but knowing we have another fight on. The stakes are for the future of this country. . . . I tell you—and I'm positive that I am right—that if this habit of discrimination against minorities is not checked, you're going to lose the freedoms that you're proud of. You're going to see terrible changes in what you, perhaps, call the American way of life—a phrase that I don't find quite pretty because the American way of life is not so damned wonderful for a lot of us who are Americans—and you'll be left with two alternatives—Communism or fascism. They are the logical ends of discrimination. That has been proved.[103]

Hobson assumed that, as a Jew, she could speak for "the minority." She was only one in a long line of Jewish producers of popular culture who envisioned themselves as representative Americans with a special "right to sing the blues."[104] The film's critique of Jewish racialization was not adequate to reveal the extent of racial exclusions more generally or to promote racial equality. One legacy of Hobson's strategy for deracializing Jewishness in *Gentleman's Agreement* would be to further legitimate racialized boundaries for other groups.[105] Within a few years resurgent anticommunism would shut down trading places efforts altogether, mobilizing the cultural force to limit the terms of racial protest and the political clout legally to harass and disrupt organizations supporting civil rights. But in 1947, using terms recognizable to the broad alliances grouped together by wartime antifascism, the popular films *Crossfire* and *Gentleman's Agreement* represented new possibilities for popular culture to promote claims of expanded citizenship for all minorities. As Jewell Carter wrote, "We are fortunate to have help from the theatres in this great cause."[106] When *Chicago Defender* columnists assessed Hollywood's 1949 turn to "fingering of the minority theme," the subject of the next chapter, they placed *Crossfire* and *Gentleman's Agreement* in the history of "race-themed" films.[107]

HOLLYWOOD MAKES RACE (IN)VISIBLE

OLLOWING THE SUCCESS IN 1947 OF FILMS THAT EXPLORED THE THEME of Jewish indeterminacy, progressive Hollywood producers and writers began their efforts to bring a discussion of race onto the screen. Responding to demands for more complex representations of African Americans than those suffused with white supremacy, racial condescension, and minstrelsy, filmmakers again employed the framework of trading places to question the legitimacy of previously accepted racial boundaries. Their productions appeared in quick succession: Stanley Kramer's *Home of the Brave* in March 1949, Louis De Rochemont's *Lost Boundaries* in July of that year, Darryl Zanuck's *Pinky* in September, Dore Schary's *Intruder in the Dust* in December, and Darryl Zanuck and Joe Mankiewicz's *No Way Out* in June 1950. These first efforts to present black characters as ordinary attempted to break with segregationist conventions by pointing, at least briefly, to the historical dangers of exclusion.

Stories of looking back had affirmed immigrants' Americanness by constructing an ethnic past that led inevitably to assimilation and class mobility. The construction of an equivalent racial past outside the framework of white supremacy would require exposing a history of discrimination as well as a history of survival and resistance. Stories of trading places attempted to enlarge existing sympathies in their audiences, beginning with narratives of interracial love; the provocative sexuality of these stories suggested the racial stakes in the transition from the wartime public world of men to the postwar private and domestic world of men and women. The stories of Jewish indeterminacy that followed shifted the context back to the public sphere; there Gregory Peck's Phil Green exemplifies the postwar antifascist hero: likeable, principled, confidently masculine, he exposes and protests discrimination.

Both producers and audiences understood the 1949 race-conscious films to be operating within the narrative terms of trading places texts, especially the dramatic device of passing proposed by *Gentleman's Agreement*. The social and political issues associated with popular antifascism—opposition to lynching, police brutality, economic exploitation, political injustice—continued to shape the stories. Beginning in 1948, however, expressions of racial protest and outrage were closely scrutinized for statements of American disloyalty. A resurgent anticommunism discouraged organizations from attaching demands for civil rights to criticism of American politics, economy, or foreign policy—effectively limiting analysis of the structural causes of racial discrimination. At the point of firmest belief in the social potential of film, a new round of conservative attacks on Hollywood progressives and social filmmaking began. Arthur Miller later described 1949 as "the last postwar year."[1] The 1949 race-themed films and audience reactions to them reveal the emerging tensions between the antifascism of the 1940s and the anticommunism of the 1950s.

Stories of racial passing made the most explicit use of the trading places device; this theme shaped the plots of *Lost Boundaries* and *Pinky*. Passing stories required racially indeterminate characters—and implied the instability of supposedly fixed racial boundaries. Conscious that they were straying into new and contested territory, producers attempted to contain the connections their films made between race and sexuality. In widely discussed casting decisions, they placed white actors in the "black" roles intended to carry the burden of viewer identification; when black actors were cast as heroes, they generally appeared outside the context of a family. In these films reconciliation of racial difference is symbolic and psychological and depends on white protectors and intermediaries.

If passing narratives all rely on the device of mistaken identity, white and black writers had differed in their interpretations of the largely unspoken history of interracial sexual mixing. White writers, on the one hand, frequently imagined the passing character as a tragic mulatto or a racial and sexual provocateur and resolved the resulting chaos either with death or a revelation that racial and sexual boundaries had not been crossed after all. Black writers, on the other hand, often presented the passing character as a historical product of white domination and sexual exploitation who sometimes stood outside the black community but who also embodied human potential in the absence of racialized restrictions. In passing stories racial indeterminacy is used both to challenge racial barriers and to claim elite privilege, a contradiction widely discussed in the postwar period.[2] Actual historical experiences of racial passing were much more complex than these written and film texts, which relied on narrative framing that attempted to rein in the most provocative implications of racial indeterminacy.[3] Nonetheless, audiences recognized postwar passing stories as explicitly challenging the ability of Jim Crow laws and practices to enforce racial separation; they knew they were participating in a broad public debate over segregation.

Wartime questioning of racial boundaries, and especially wartime debates over blood, both literal and figurative, shaped both the writing and the reading of fictional accounts of racial mixing. Anthropological research disproving biological theories of racial differences developed a brief against Nazi theories of racialization. The work of Charles Drew, a distinguished African American doctor, made it possible to preserve blood plasma and was critical to the military's ability to care for people wounded in battle. At the same time, the Red Cross's decisions to segregate military blood banks acceded to the white supremacist notion that blood had distinct racial characteristics, and that racial boundaries could be firmly fixed and policed.

Scientific thought in general, and medicine in particular, had long been used to legitimate white supremacy; allied with antifascism, however, both offered ways of seeing through racialized categories and challenging "racial integrity" and racialization.[4] As the 1944 "Free and Equal Blues" refrain reminded radio listeners during the 1944 Democratic National Committee Election Special:

> The doc's behind the new brotherhood of man
> As prescribed at Casablanca, and Cairo, and Moscow, and Teheran
> He agrees with Dr. Roosevelt, Dr. Churchill, Dr. Stalin, Drs. Eden, Hull,
>   and Litvinov
> Everyman everywhere is the same, when he's got his skin off.[5]

The term *doctor* in the song refers to both medical and general authority: unless otherwise identified, a doctor in the expert position was presumed to be male and white. In this context the black doctors and nurses in three of the new race-conscious films, *Lost Boundaries, Pinky,* and *No Way Out,* symbolize more than the elite of the black community. Though white doctors play a role in their certification, their achievement stands for the collective accomplishments of black families and communities. Black adoption of medical professionalism signaled the potential for nonracialized and interracial public interactions contributing to a larger social good. It is the black doctor in *Strange Fruit,* discussed in chapter 4, who voices the novel's most articulate and forthright protest against racial injustice.

Racial boundary crossing in *Home of the Brave* remained within the world of men and crisis of war, featuring a lone Negro soldier, isolated from the black community, whose expertise and service admitted him temporarily into a multiethnic platoon on an island in the Pacific. *Lost Boundaries* and *Pinky* explored the potential for racial boundary crossing in postwar black employment and residential life in the North and the South. Leaving the public and homosocial world of the battlefield and making the move to the home front, especially to the sphere of family, these narratives threatened to destabilize the racialist boundaries that depended on the policing of sexual and gender norms.

Expanding their narrative function beyond *Crossfire* and *Gentleman's Agreement,* the women characters in *Lost Boundaries* and *Pinky* actively participate in both enforcing and transgressing racial boundaries. The films were careful to maintain white silence on the prior history of sexual coercion and brutality responsible for much racial indeterminacy. Their resolutions affirmed visible racial difference but minimized its importance and effect, stopping safely short of a fundamental challenge to racial categories.

The portrayal on film of even qualified racial indeterminacy at a time when segregation was being challenged was in itself provocative. Love and romance that crossed the color line—previously imagined only on the page and enacted temporarily and with qualifications on the stage—suddenly appeared on screen, provoking local censors to demand cuts and monitor screenings and igniting public debates on race and sex.

The last two pictures in the 1949 Hollywood race cycle—*Intruder in the Dust* and *No Way Out*—introduced racially marked heroes, a southern independent farmer and a northern urban doctor, and they were able to break free from some trading places conventions. In unsettling racial categories, however, they were no more successful than their predecessors, and they failed to reach the audiences garnered by the first three. All the trading places narratives failed to build cross-boundary empathy that would include racialized others within the universe of ordinary Americans. Instead they helped to naturalize the exclusionary aspects of ordinariness. Looking more closely at these narratives and their failures will help us to understand what was at stake in visualizing an expanded racial citizenship.

"A GREAT STEP FORWARD": THE FILM *HOME OF THE BRAVE*

Wartime popular front radicals were responsible for the film production of *Home of the Brave,* as they had been for Arthur Laurents's play of the same name. Producer Stanley Kramer—who had worked with left-wing screenwriter Carl Foreman at the Army Photographic Unit at Astoria, Queens during the war—saw the play *Home of the Brave* shortly before it closed and purchased the film rights directly from Arthur Laurents in 1945.[6] According to a later account, he immediately imagined changing the Jewish soldier to a black man, claiming that the play had failed "because it depended on a great deal of talk about a man being different. But what was so different? For the dilemma to be understood, the character had to *say* he was Jewish."[7] Kramer's formulation assumed the premise of both Miller's and Hobson's trading places stories—that audiences would come to see through Jewish racialization.

Kramer filmed *Home of the Brave* in relative secrecy and with great speed, claiming later that he didn't want antiblack pressure groups to disrupt filming and that he wanted to get his picture into theaters ahead of the three other Hollywood films about racial discrimination. Unlike Lillian Smith, who staged *Strange Fruit* in the presence of black critics, Kramer avoided scrutiny from African Americans. He swore the crew of nearly six hundred to an oath of silence and asked the actors to come into the studio through the rear gates. He concealed James Edwards, who played the lead, as a sleep-in janitor. The actors rehearsed for two weeks; director Mark Robson began filming in February 1949; a final print went to the distributor, United Artists, at the beginning of April.[8]

When the secrecy broke down at the end of February, the transposition of a black for a Jewish character was the subject of much discussion. *Variety* framed the substitutions in terms of industry and financial considerations and competition with the two other film projects already announced, Louis De Rochemont's independent film *Lost Boundaries* and Twentieth Century-Fox's production of *Pinky.* The theme of anti-Semitism in *Crossfire* and *Gentleman's Agreement* had enabled the turn toward discrimination faced by African Americans: "with anti-Semitism explored by Hollywood films during the past couple years, 1949 is definitely lining up as the year of the Negro problem pic."[9]

In a published interview at the time, Kramer contrasted Jewish indistinguishability with racial distinctiveness rather than questioning racial boundaries more generally:

> We think the power of [*Home of the Brave*] is due to the fact that five men went to an island—one *happened* to be Negro. . . . Originally the play dealt with a neurotic Jew, and the question always is to anybody, how different are you anyway? But using a dark colored boy who was physically different in front of a mass audience gave us a chance to say, dramatically, this should hold water.

Kramer claimed the authority to understand difference from growing up in Manhattan's Hell's Kitchen, where his "associations were with all kinds of people." But he insisted that his own consciousness was color-blind, produced by "growing up and reading" and manifest in his support for New Deal social policies: "politically, I was somewhat of a Rooseveltian."[10]

The change from Jewish to black soldier profoundly transformed the film's representational claims. The part of Mossey—named after Carlton Moss, the left-wing actor, activist, creative force behind *The Negro Soldier* and a friend of screenwriter Foreman—was the first starring role for a black actor in a dramatic film produced by Hollywood. James Edwards had been a steelworker and CIO activist and had served in the infantry and the Signal Corps as a commissioned officer in World War II. He appeared for his first New York stage audition in the flamboyant dress of wartime resistance, a purple zoot suit and yellow coat.[11]

The play's resolution denied the importance of difference; the project of condemning discrimination and exposing the bitter history of racism in the film filled it with contradictions. The relationship between Finch and Moss in the film begins as a high school friendship, a change that limited the intimacy they could achieve in wartime by showing how segregation had already come between them. Film historian Thomas Cripps credits Foreman's script with adding Moss's "lifetime of repressed rage" (which implicated Finch as an old friend and as the speaker of racist words in the tensions of battle) onto the play's commitment to therapeutic healing and the scientific view that all men are "the same."[12]

Even as the film stepped back from the play's homosocial intensity, *masculinity* remained central to the linking of psychic health and interracial cooperation. Love between men prompts the pain of Finch's racist remark, the terror of abandonment, and Moss's paralysis after his embrace of the dying Finch. Wartime "buddy" culture was familiar enough to provide a legitimating framework for love between soldiers.[13] But invoking the history of racism dramatically shifted its emotional register; the buddy relationship between Finch and Moss and the postwar partnership between Moss and the disabled Mingo promised far less than the play had.

The press kit signaled the film's challenge: "Mossy understood the sameness of men, and in understanding the sameness, was prepared to fight the artificial barriers." Some reviews in the left-wing press did voice concern that the "sameness angle" would make it "easier for an audience to ignore the special character of the oppression of the Negro people."[14] While they saluted *Home of the Brave* for breaking important ground as the first Hollywood film to explore "the race problem," many of the film's mainstream reviewers questioned the film's promise of psychiatric healing and its quick resolution of racial issues. The *Time* critic blamed the original play for the tension between the film's "arguments against discrimination and the abracadabra of psychiatry," while the *Newsweek* critic complained that the "mechanics of the psychotherapy" diverted attention from "the racial theme." But their reviews also praised the film's "novelty, emotional wallop, and the excitement that comes from wrestling with a real problem."[15]

Reviewers in the black press were exhilarated by the film's accomplishments, although they also perceived its limitations. The *Chicago Defender*'s reviewer wrote that the film came "closer" to the "true story of the Negro-white problem as developed in this country" than any other Hollywood film had, noting that its "powerfully presented smash at prejudice against the American Negro" and its "boldness of script and action" far surpassed the "real messages" about anti-Semitism carried by award-winning films *Crossfire* and *Gentleman's Agreement*.[16] James Hicks wrote to black GIs in the *Afro-American* that the film "tells the world what you have wanted to tell for so long—the story of how you had to fight two wars while your white comrades in arms were fighting one." The radical sociologist Horace Cayton described watching the film as having been "hit by a sledgehammer": the film's treatment of a black soldier brought to life "all the cruel forces of race prejudice—the rejection, the senseless useless hate, the unexpected slaps and blows." The reviewer for Oklahoma City's *Black Dispatch* admitted that the film wasn't completely convincing, but felt that the story "leaps from the screen," dramatizing "the sufferings a black man must endure, in and out of uniform, in a free land, for no other reason than he is black."[17]

Edwards's performance was widely praised in the white press; the black press hailed him as a hero. His handsome and brooding persona and his dramatic success signaled new possibilities for black male citizenship. To be "the first Negro to play a completely non-Jim Crow role in a big time Hollywood movie" was a counter to racist stereotyping pervasive in all the popular media.[18] Articles about the film in the black press were often accompanied with production stills that pictured Edwards in uniform and, in one preferred pose, aiming his rifle at a Japanese sniper.[19] Coverage of Edwards's publicity trip to New York in June 1949 pictured him in the company honoring the United Nations negotiator Ralph Bunche at the Waldorf Astoria.[20] An *Amsterdam News* editorial encouraged readers to view Edwards's success as a collective accomplishment, reminding them of "untiring efforts of courageous men and women, who, regardless of what roles they played, were never satisfied with their lot and place in the movies, on the stage, or on radio."[21]

Black writers assessed the film's representational breakthrough within the context of the ongoing struggle to dismantle racial segregation. Ralph Ellison noted the dissonance between the film's depiction of racial discrimination and its attempt to banish racism with the therapeutic. Ellison referred to debates within the black community about whether to support the war effort while Jim Crow stood intact: psychiatry could not answer the question whether "Negroes can rightfully be expected to risk their lives in an army in which they are slandered and discriminated against."[22] An editorial in the *Defender* juxtaposed attention to the film with *inattention* to attacks on blacks in Atlanta and Birmingham who were attempting to exercise their legal rights to find housing in white neighborhoods—rights newly enunciated in the 1948 Supreme Court decision outlawing racially restrictive real estate agreements. The editorial wondered if "in the South, or anywhere within the boundaries of this nation, there is a 'home of the brave' for all men."[23] The *Amsterdam News* reprinted an article from the Associated Negro Press service on how the film's theme provided an opportunity to challenge segregation in movie theaters. In Washington, D.C. representatives of fourteen organizations confronted the Trans Luxe Theater Corporation, trying to gain admission for an "interracial theater party" to view *Home of the Brave* and demanding that the picture be shown to audiences on a "policy of nondiscrimination."[24]

Home of the Brave was seen by rural and urban, black and white audiences in the North and South. The *Chicago Defender* interpreted the film's popularity as evidence of audiences being receptive to the film's protest against the psychic costs of discrimination; the evasion of censorship demonstrated a momentum toward racial equality. By the end of July 1949, the paper reported "record-making runs" across the country.[25]

The citizenship claims of *Home of the Brave* were articulated within a public, all-male sphere, far away in the South Pacific, amidst the crisis of war, with family and community nowhere in sight. But the film seized the opening created by a vision of interracial male comradeship ("Hell, we're all guys") to represent the Negro soldier as "ordinary American." Although his psychiatric crisis compromises the heroism of the black soldier—he's on his back under the paternal care of the white psychiatrist for most of the film—audience response helps identify the openings created within the film's efforts to name and protest racial discrimination.

LOST BOUNDARIES: RACIAL INDETERMINACY AS WHITENESS

Cid Ricketts Sumner's novel *Quality*, discussed in chapter 4, proposed its story of racial passing as a revisionist history that supported the maintenance of segregation. *Lost Boundaries* provided another version of racial passing as revisionist history, substituting a postwar color-blind pluralism for a more forthright racial equality. Its "true" story of racial passing deemphasized racial significance by revealing race as a secret behind the facade of a storybook white New England town, a skeleton in the community closet common to "romance, mystery, and even tragedy . . . legends and ghosts." The passing narrative of *Lost Boundaries* highlighted racial indeterminacy in a way that minimized its historical origins, folding historic and contemporary practices of discrimination into universal color prejudice, which it answered with a plea for tolerance rather than a demand for racial equality.

Soon after the war, *March of Time* producer and filmmaker Louis De Rochemont met the son of a mixed-race doctor, Albert Johnson, who had been living as white in a small New Hampshire town near De Rochemont's summer house. When De Rochemont heard his account of the family's passing for white for twenty years until the doctor was first recruited and then rejected by the navy, he recognized its commercial potential as a parable of an ordinary family in an expanded wartime democracy. He arranged for the Johnsons' story to be written up by popular journalist William L. White. An excerpt from *Lost Boundaries* appeared in *Readers Digest* in December 1947, with publication of the book in March 1948. De Rochemont's announcement of plans to adapt and film the Johnson family's story signaled the first publicly announced Hollywood "race film" (*Home of the Brave* was produced in secret in early 1949). In De Rochemont's hands, the material would be arranged to extend wartime pleas for cultural pluralism.[26]

De Rochemont's style of dramatic reenactment shaped the filming of the Johnson story. Since the 1920s, his feature newsreel films had recreated historical events; staged with realist effects and professional actors, they were concerned with topics one historian has described as "consistently liberal, progressive, and militantly anti-fascist." Depression-era efforts at documentary suggest broad interest in experimenting with form to capture the "real." Working on feature films independently of Hollywood-style filmmaking, De Rochemont relied on location shooting and non-professional actors to create a "synthesis of the realism of factual reportage and the intensity of dramatically conceived narrative." He believed that "the essence of good drama is an illusion of reality. Shooting in real places is the best way to get that illusion."[27]

The historical experience of the Johnson family was considerably more complex than the popular retelling of their story in the film *Lost Boundaries*. Albert Johnson was categorized as "white" on his Chicago birth certificate, although his family heritage was part black and part Indian. He was one of two black students in his class at Wendell Phillips High School in Chicago and was admitted to his class at Rush Medical College under a racial quota. When officials at Maine General Hospital in Portland accepted his internship application without inquiring about his race, they presumed him to be white.[28] Thyra (Baumann) Johnson was born in New Orleans and grew up in Boston. Although her son described her as "looking as Irish as any of her neighbors," her family heritage classified her as one-eighth black, and she was categorized as "Negro" on her birth certificate.[29] The Johnsons married when Albert was in medical school, and they had four children. In Gorham, New Hampshire both Johnsons were active in church and local civic and professional organizations. The family moved to Keene, New Hampshire in 1939.

The Johnsons were publicly reracialized during World War II. In 1940 the navy, looking for radiologists, recruited Dr. Albert Johnson, one of only twenty-two hundred trained radiologists in the country. After Pearl Harbor Johnson applied for a commission, which the navy later withdrew, after army intelligence authorities questioned him about reports that he had "colored blood." (The grounds of their rejection stated that he was unable to "meet the physical requirements.") The Johnsons had maintained the fiction of whiteness by raising their children to think of themselves as white, but now, publicly confronted with an obstacle generated by racial segregation, Dr. Johnson and his wife told their children of their mixed-race heritage. Because Dr. and Mrs. Johnson had grown up and lived in various racially diverse communities, they had learned to negotiate the terrain of racial discrimination. The sudden encounter with his father's discriminatory rejection by the navy unsettled Albert Johnson Jr., who left college, served briefly in the navy, and traveled around the country visiting his newly discovered black middle-class relatives in Chicago and Los Angeles. According to White's account, these relatives introduced Albert Jr. to a wide range of black experience.

Stressing northern inattention to racial difference did not require critical exploration of northern assumptions of white superiority. Accounts in both *Reader's Digest* and *Ebony* stressed that the family experienced virtually no social backlash or economic discrimination in Keene. The *Ebony* story that accompanied the publication of the book described the seventeen-year-old daughter's parties as "still popular" with her peers in Keene. "Disclosure she's colored meant little. The boy I go steady with, Ann said, told me it didn't make any difference." The article also stated that "New Englanders . . . feel, as Mrs. Ensign Barrett, Keene's druggist's wife, that "whatever Dr. Johnson is, he's a very nice man." (Dr. Johnson's practice continued to grow until he accepted a lucrative offer to move to Hawaii in 1966.)[30]

Publicizing their story of passing ended the possibility of racial indeterminacy for family members. No matter how many times accounts repeated the claim that "disclosure . . . didn't make any difference," there are suggestions that it did. After his initial uncertainty, Albert Jr. came to embrace a public identity as a Negro and to protest racial discrimination, eventually publishing an essay in the *Survey* on the subject. Dr. Johnson resigned from the all-white Rotary Club and stopped going to the Masonic Lodge, admitting sadly, "I guess I've become morose." According to White's account, by 1947 Dr. Johnson expressed despair about race relations and the way in which the war had nationalized Jim Crow: "In recent years there has not been an advance, but a regression . . . it has become worse in the North." He also felt that his racial personhood was more invisible: "Whatever I do, my race gets no credit." The *Los Angeles Tribune* quoted him as saying that "his revelation 'helped things' " in the battle to establish racial equality, although he doubted "that conditions for the race are improving." In an interview with Bob Ellis for the progressive black newspaper the *California Eagle* when the film was released, Dr. Johnson said, "In spite of all that I have accomplished as a white man, I have, more or less, an empty life."[31] Unable to claim his accomplishments as undermining racial discrimination, which to him seemed to be expanding rather than diminishing, he publicly disparaged his "white" success as hollow, individual, and temporary.

From the first announcement of the film, the script engendered debate. Ralph Ellison was concerned about whether a passing story could ever effectively convey protest against racial discrimination. His comments to De Rochemont, soon after the project was made public in 1948, focused on the limitations of the genre. Only by stressing "the will to assert their own identity," would the film enable audiences to "to feel the ambiguity with which racism tinged all social intercourse" and to understand how notions of white superiority dictated the need to pass. Ellison, always insistent that black cultural contributions be embraced as American culture, later mocked the film's theme: "Have mulatto Negroes the right to pass as white, at the risk of having black babies, or, if they have white-skinned children, of having to kill off their 'white' identities by revealing to them that they are, alas, Negroes?"[32]

To Hollywood, the racial indeterminacy Ellison saw as a strategic limitation was tempting but also potentially explosive. With ticket sales beginning to decline from their wartime high by 1946, the studios were especially worried about forms of representation that could antagonize segregated southern audiences. Two white southerners who worked for *Reader's Digest* offered opposing views of the risks the film could take in criticizing northern presumptions of white racial superiority. One was concerned about the social ramifications of exposing northern racial hypocrisy, worrying that a script critical of their attitudes would "damage" whites. Another encouraged the challenge to northern racial complacency, writing that the " 'damage' might be beneficial." Studio personnel at MGM were not optimistic about being able to make a commercially successful film out of material on which so little consensus existed. The studio undertook a survey to resolve their doubts; by early 1949 they withdrew their support, citing De Rochemont's "handling of the Negro theme."[33]

Lost Boundaries was eventually independently produced and distributed by De Rochemont and financed on a shoestring budget, going through several writers and scripts.[34] Although the final film took liberties with the Johnsons' story, De Rochemont publicized his work as a "drama of real life," a claim that made some of the film's black critics especially irate.[35] In its credits and opening narration the film claimed its "real-life" origins; a title card for "additional music by Albert Johnson, Jr." implied that at least one member of the family had participated in the film's production.

To cast racially indeterminate characters rather than racial stereotypes presented a challenge to the makers of *Lost Boundaries.* The selection of Mel Ferrer, who was part Cuban and had played the white male lead in the Broadway production of *Strange Fruit,* and other white actors to play the passing family members, equated racial indeterminacy with whiteness; it reproduced the white southern claim that "real" mixed-race people, actors and others, couldn't really "pass" as white. These casting decisions were broadly condemned in the black press. As Fredi Washington— widely praised for her performance as a light-skinned passing character in Universal's *Imitation of Life* (1934)—observed, they signaled "retrogressions rather than progress." The cofounder of the American Negro Theatre, Frederick O'Neal, pointed out that "these pictures are supposed to be clarifying race relations and yet they are all doing the same thing they are preaching against."[36]

In response to the objections raised in the black press, the director of *Lost Boundaries,* Alfred Werker, offered a defense of the film's casting. Werker, a Hollywood studio craftsman who had been directing B movies in various genres for Fox since the mid-1920s, insisted that casting a relatively unknown and *white* actor was necessary in order to maintain the film's "illusion": "If we used a Negro actor, he would have immediately been spotted by the audience as colored and our illusion would have been gone." Werker then conflated black actors with the demeaning stereotypes they were forced to perform, declaring that the "majority of Negro actors are of the Uncle Tom minstrel show, shuffling dancer type of performer." Displaying his ignorance of the diversity of the black community as well as his lack of understanding of the phenomenon of passing, Werker stated that only white actors could depict Negroes as fully realized citizens: "We were trying for quite the opposite effect: the idea that Negroes, too, are intelligent, that many are cultured, refined, and are good citizens, that some can live for twenty years besides white neighbors without anybody thinking they are any different."[37]

The left-affiliated Committee for the Negro in the Arts circulated a response to Werker in the black press that focused on the history of discriminatory practices in the entertainment industry. Challenging his proposition that most black actors were "of the Uncle Tom minstrel show, shuffling dancer type of performer," their statement listed a variety of organizations featuring talented black actors:

> If you had contacted the Negro Actor's Guild, the American Negro Theatre ... the Hollywood Actors' Lab ... the Gilpin Players, the Intercollegiate Dramatic Association ... our own Committee or any similar organization, you would have found Negro actors who are "cultured, refined, and good citizens." ... The majority of Negro actors, regardless of the roles they are forced to play, have these virtues ... and only play caricature-roles because they are permitted to earn their living only in this manner.

The tradition of minstrelsy had distorted the perceptions of casting directors: "We have in our files numerous Negro actors and actresses who have been turned down for roles on the gossamer excuse that they are too fair, too intelligent, too modern looking, etc."[38] The committee identified the ways in which these casting decisions expressed contempt for black culture: "Until such time as you are willing to look squarely into the face of black America and utilize their cultural attributes as you do the white Americans, the Committee for the Negro in the Arts will continue to fight to put the lie to your acid Anti-Negro approach to the Negro artist." They also criticized Werker's claim that a Negro actor could not convincingly convey whiteness because white people could always identify racial indeterminacy: "You dared not show that Negroes do pass freely among white Americans AS White Americans—without the white Americans knowing this." Finally, their statement reasserted an African American understanding of racial indeterminacy as a challenge to the supposedly fixed racial boundaries underlying segregation: "It is only when the Negro reveals it that the white really knows. Thus putting an end to the myth that the white American is superior in his 'knowing how to keep the Negro in his place' as he pretends."[39]

The film introduces the hero, Dr. Carter, at his 1922 medical school graduation. The camera lingers in close-ups on a racially distinct black graduate as well as a white graduate and on the black doctor being awarded an honorary degree. The medical school "just outside Chicago" is presented as a paragon of pluralist integration in which achievement is rewarded without reference to color.

The film's first mention of racial passing establishes the passer as a "tragic mulatto" guilty of social climbing. Mrs. Carter's mother describes her passing husband's stance: he "won't admit even to himself that we're Negroes." The "tragic mulatto" references are made more explicit when a black staff doctor at a southern hospital turns Carter down after he appears in person to claim his internship; the film proposes *intraracial* prejudice as the cause of color discrimination. As Ralph Ellison pointed out, "In real life, Dr. Albert Johnson . . . purchased the thriving practice of a deceased physician in Gorham, New Hampshire, for a thousand dollars," but in the film "a fiction is introduced wherein Dr. Carter's initial motivation for passing arises after he is refused an internship by dark Negroes, in an Atlanta hospital—because of his color!" Ellison noted the absurdity, "since there are thousands of mulattoes living as Negroes in the South, many of them Negro leaders."[40] In the film's fiction the rejection of the light-skinned Carter by blacks explains his eventual "integration" into the white community: no political militancy is required; blacks are more color conscious than the film's good (and innately superior) white characters.

Lost Boundaries presents various motives for racial passing. Dr. Carter's father-in-law is a status-conscious member of a light-skinned elite, driven to pass as white by his contempt for black people. Dr. Carter's black associates debate racial passing as an individualistic economic strategy, contrasting passing in order to find work with "needing to be black if a man wants to help his race" and coming to the consensus that "each man has to work it out in his own way." The film explains Dr. Carter's own decision to pass as driven by his difficulty in finding work. Carter works briefly as a machinist until a white medical school classmate finds him an internship at a white hospital; he is willing to work "as a white man" for the internship year because his wife is about to have a child. When a white doctor offers him a medical practice—on condition he works as a "white" doctor—Carter initially demurs, on the grounds that he wants to practice as a Negro. The white man convinces him to accept the offer and become a *good* doctor, contrasting a racially identified practitioner with a color-blind professional. Later scenes depict Carter, his wife, and their two children earning respect as "white" participants in the quintessential American town in which no one, "not even his children," know that Carter is a Negro.

The film introduces the themes of wartime segregation of the military and the blood banks in order to shatter the facade of the Carters' passing. When Carter tries to stop a nurse from separating out the "colored" blood donated by a chauffeur, she drops the vial rather than risk what she conceives as racial mixing, despite Carter's warning that "some fighting man may lose his life." Dr. Carter's son, Howard, first hears of racial obstacles when his black roommate at college (William Greaves) chooses not to join him in applying to the navy's midshipman's school, since in the navy all "colored" men could do was to serve meals to officers. Dr. Carter's own blood comes under scrutiny when he responds to a navy recruiter's visit by applying, like other doctors, for a commission. The navy deems his scientist's claim that "we all have the same blood in our veins" no more convincing than does the clinic nurse.

These brief incidents critiquing military segregation quickly recede when the children discover that their white identities can no longer be taken for granted; now the film falls back on familiar racist stereotyping. Howard, dazed, wanders around a hostile and threatening Harlem, as his sister, Shelley, carefully and painfully acknowledges her acceptance of interracial sexuality taboos by breaking up with her white boyfriend, despite his insistence that nothing has changed. Watching these scenes, some black critics were appalled by the narrative use of Harlem. Like so much white writing on "the race problem," the Harlem scene undermined the film's questioning of racial boundaries by positioning visible racial difference within the context of urban poverty and pathology. Turning the son's search for his black family into a nightmare of urban violence, the film then offers its "street wisdom" from the mouth of an African American character. Playing a veteran police officer on the beat, the distinguished Canada Lee delivers advice that first attempts to diminish the significance of race: "You'll find gangs like that in every slum section of the city . . . these kids, they'll kill or steal because they're caught in a trap . . . whether they're white or black, people are pretty much the same." Then Lee's character elides race with poverty, blaming the victims rather than institutionalized racism: "Can you honestly blame anyone for trying to cross over into a white man's world? If you'd seen something like I have, then you'd see that your father was only trying to buy you and your sister a happy childhood, free from fear, and hatred and prejudice." Ellison pointed out that the family's "white" life in New Hampshire was framed by "painting Negro life as horrible, a fate worse than a living death."[41]

The film restores order and achieves a narrative closure not by over-turning racial discrimination but by redefining racial indeterminacy as *whiteness.* Dr. Carter reassures his son that "I brought you up as white" and there is "no reason why you shouldn't continue to live this way," promising his daughter, who worried that "everything was so different now," that "you'll never be different." Although rumors fly and an exclusive group of neighbors on their way to church snubs the Carter family, the parents and their son are reclaimed as citizens of white Keenham by their minister (played in the film by the minister of the De Rochemont family church). He reminds congregants unsettled by the Carters' "black" blood that although a screen of "hate, fear, and especially of ignorance" may have temporarily blinded them, "in the light of God, all men are brothers." Then he buttresses God's color-blindness with federal author-ity, announcing the "news" from Washington that "commissions as offi-cers in the U.S. Navy will be extended to all qualified citizens regardless of race or color." Racial categorization, limited in the film to the wartime navy, could also be solved by the postwar navy. In white Keenham the minister reassures his flock, "We are all God's children" and Dr. Carter is "our doctor." Only the daughter leaves the church by herself, her visual isolation reiterating a tragic mulatto fate. The final images are of the white clapboard; in the last dialogue the narrator concludes this "drama of real life" in which "the characters are real people" by repeating that "Carter is still our doctor."

To turn a story of the disclosure of racial passing into a largely tri-umphant tale of white assimilation required the silencing of alternatives to its color-blind framework and denying the persistence of institutionalized discrimination. The character of Dr. Carter cannot show audiences how "to feel the ambiguity with which racism tinged all social intercourse," in Ellison's phrase.[42] The upbeat assimilation promised by the ending of the film could not include the daughter, and of course it contrasted with Dr. Johnson's actual experience of the postwar period, when, as he put it, "there has not been an advance, but a regression. . . . It has become worse in the North."[43]

Lost Boundaries was the second "race-themed" film to be released, shortly after *Home of the Brave:* according to a later account, the predom-inantly white audience sat in "stunned silence" after its New York pre-miere.[44] White reviewers reinforced the film's tragic mulatto logic by reading its elite passing as racial isolation. The *New York Times* reviewer Bosley Crowther praised the film for exposing "one of the many bitter aspects of racism in our land—the in-between isolation of the Negro who tries to pass as white."[45] The reviewer for the *Richmond Times* repeated the film's valorization of passing as "whiteness," describing *Lost Boundaries* as a "clear, unbiased account of the . . . tragedy [of the Negro] imprisoned in the no-man's land of his ancestry."[46]

By the time the film opened, readers of the black press were familiar with the Johnson family story from articles related to the original piece in *Reader's Digest,* and black commentators greeted the film with hope. The Schomburg Collection of the New York Public Library announced the acquisition of the *Lost Boundaries* screenplay as the beginning of a "collection of movie scenarios on the Negro" and displayed for library visitors the script, the original sketches for sets and costumes, stills, newspaper clippings, and the *Reader's Digest* article.[47] The NAACP's Walter White described tearing up several times in a preview screening. He hoped that *Lost Boundaries* would mark a turn toward films representing African American citizenship, describing it as an "honest" picture in which "Negroes are portrayed as normal human beings," replacing conventional Hollywood practices showing "colored people as witless menials or idiotic buffoons."[48] The *Chicago Defender*'s Lillian Scott read the film as exposing the country's white supremacist commitment to the one-drop rule: the audience "can never forget," she wrote, "that the difference between light skins and dark skins means so much only in *this* nation" (emphasis added).[49]

Still, their hope did not stand in the way of some reviewers challenging the "false" premises of the production, especially the casting, the depiction of intraracial prejudice, and the contempt for black culture. Writing in the Baltimore *Afro-American,* Al Anderson parodied the film's final homily: "Let us be tolerant. . . . These people cannot help how they were born. Let us sympathize with them in their great misfortune and treat them kindly." Anderson insisted on the rights of all citizens in a democracy: "This, naturally, distorts the entire point. There is nothing to be 'tolerant' of. All people should be treated equally not because it's the 'nice thing to do,' but because they *are* equal."[50]

The publicity for *Lost Boundaries* framed racial indeterminacy as a sensational and shameful "secret" rather than a historical product of crossing racial boundaries. Advertisements pictured the son looking at his hands, with the tag line "Why didn't they tell me I was Negro?" The film attracted white and black audiences in northern and midwestern cities. Even this story of secret passing in the North was too close to a performance of social equality for the censors in Atlanta (where the film was declared "contrary to the public good") and Memphis, but the film attracted audiences in other southern cities, including Norfolk, Richmond, Louisville, Raleigh, San Antonio, Houston, Miami, and twenty-five other "Dixie towns."[51] But the "real-life drama" of crossing the color line primarily worked to affirm it. The Johnson family could not represent an African American family as an ordinary American family within a framework that recast racial indeterminacy as whiteness.

PINKY: RACIAL INDETERMINACY AS BLACKNESS

Twentieth Century-Fox studio chief Darryl Zanuck was riding the crest of success of *Gentlemen's Agreement* when he acquired the screen rights to *Quality*. Although Cid Ricketts Sumner's controversial novel had prompted neither the commercial response nor the critical acclaim of *Gentleman's Agreement,* Zanuck may have been drawn to the possibilities of its narrative structure.[52] Like trademark Zanuck films, *Quality* was a drama of passing and return in which a central character is suddenly exposed to forms of exploitation and discrimination; the expository dialogue and dramatic incidents of the film place these events in a broader discussion of injustice. By March 1948 the studio had a script in development.[53]

The *New York Times* report of Zanuck's acquisition highlighted the unlikely coincidence that the two race films then in production shared the theme of racial passing. Zanuck differentiated his work from that De Rochemont by his focus on passing as an *individual* act. "It is the personal adventures of this girl which interest and fascinate me," he insisted. Zanuck attempted to distance his film from raging political debates over segregation: "I don't believe you could ever get me to read a book which was strictly about segregation of Negroes in America. Factual as it might be, I simply would not be bothered with it, and I am sure 99% of the American people would feel the same way." He contrasted De Rochemont's documentary-style approach with his own, "pure entertainment in terms of the adventures of Pinky."[54] A demure female heroine who first appeared in the pages of the *Ladies' Home Journal* offered an unthreatening familiarity: for white audiences she would not raise the red flag of civil rights.

Despite Zanuck's talk of "entertainment" and "adventures," a memo from progressive screenwriter Philip Dunne warned him that challenges to a race-themed film were likely from "professional leftists" associated with civil rights militancy as well as "Negrophobes."[55] The novel *Quality* had already generated controversy, and negative comments from black readers, but, as De Rochemont had discovered when making *Lost Boundaries,* the public announcement that Zanuck was making a "race-conscious" film engaged him directly in an unprecedented dialogue with an additional group—African American activists poised to demand what a race-conscious film could and should represent. Walter White had been pressuring the film industry since 1942 to abandon racist caricatures and incorporate "Negroes naturally and easily in a script in parts which are not stereotyped."[56]

Because he was addressing the race theme during a time of intense political debate about race, Zanuck was approached by and sought the advice of Walter White, who commented extensively on proposals and drafts of the *Pinky* script; eventually his daughter, the actress Jane White (who played Nonnie in the stage adaptation of *Strange Fruit*) was hired to revise the final version.[57] This "collaboration" was unequal, with Hollywood representational traditions, studio resources, and moviemaking expertise arrayed against White and his colleagues' demands in the name of racial justice. White was also aware that there was no political consensus within black communities on how to represent racial affiliation, racial barriers, and racial discrimination.[58]

By June 1948 Zanuck had assembled a production team he hoped could combine social significance with "pure entertainment." He hired Oscar-winning screenwriter Dudley Nichols to work on a script and John Ford to direct. Zanuck admired Ford's work on *The Grapes of Wrath* (1940) and *How Green Was My Valley* (1941). Nichols had frequently worked with Ford and was a respected screenwriter as well as a Hollywood progressive and supporter of his embattled fledgling union, the Screenwriters' Guild, in the 1930s and 1940s.[59] In response to criticism from White and others, Nichols attempted to even the sides represented by white paternalism and black confrontation. Nichols saw Pinky's "choice" as "whether to turn the plantation house into a clinic for poor black people or to sell it and use the proceeds politically, becoming a black militant under the guidance of the NAACP." Everyone involved knew that the ending would be seen as a comment on the future of race relations in the United States. Nichols's script favored the clinic, a resolution that White and others from the NAACP rejected.[60]

By July 1948 Walter White and his associate Roy Wilkins demanded that the script include material referring to the wartime call for an end to racial discrimination. They also demanded cuts of material that encouraged suspicion of civil rights agitation and militancy and acceptance of segregation. In August Zanuck reminded people who was in charge by announcing in *Variety* that the production of the film had been "virtually abandoned." Privately he wrote a long memo to White and others conceding that it was possible to allow Pinky to confront Miss Em's paternal influence, but also insisting that the picture's success depended on its appeal to white audiences.[61]

Determined to steer the script away from contemporary debates toward his style of storytelling, Zanuck turned the screenplay over to screenwriter Philip Dunne in the fall of 1948.[62] Dunne was concerned that the story fell apart at the end. As he pointed out, "to have a complete and satisfactory ending, you would have to solve the entire race problem in America." Nonetheless, he had an idea for reorienting Pinky's "choice": he envisioned her as "a very special colored girl who *could* pass for white, who has made up her mind which race she will belong to, who finally makes the hard decision to live as a Negro, and who is *then* subjected to persecution and slander *because* of that decision."[63]

Dunne's solution for the ending was to heighten the drama of the interracial love story as the context in which Pinky makes her choice; he could not fully imagine a love that crossed the color line, but only love that depended on the illusion of passing:

> Suppose the white doctor doesn't run away. Suppose he decides he wants Pinky in spite of her background, but only on the condition that she will continue to pass for white. They'll sell the old plantation house, move out West somewhere where they aren't known, and live happily ever after as spotlessly Caucasoid man and wife.

Dunne debated this idea with Nichols; he later wrote that Nichols couldn't conceive of a "white man ever agreeing to marry a girl with even a drop of African blood in her veins." In Dunne's conception the love story made Pinky's choice "much more moving and dramatic: shall she go through life denying her heritage, or shall she proudly acknowledge it, open her clinic, and devote her life to serving her own people?" In a story conference with Zanuck he presented Pinky's speech to her fiancé as a straightforward sacrifice of love for service to the race, the convenient by-product of which was reracialization: "I'm not going with you. I love you. I'll love you until I die, but can't go with you. I am a Negro. This is my place. This is where I'll stay."[64] In his review of the film Ralph Ellison parodied this dilemma: "Should white-skinned Negro girls marry white men, or should they inherit the plantations of old white aristocrats (provided they can find any old aristocrats to will them their plantations) or should they live in the South and open nursery schools for black Negroes?"[65]

Jane White read and commented on Dunne's script in January 1949. In her view Pinky's decisions were shaped less by personal and individual choice than by historical forces and social change. White rejected as not "credible" the reimposition of racial separation implied by Dunne's ending. The "creation of a Negro children's hospital" was "not compelling enough" for her; she wanted to see signs of the momentum toward racial equality. White rejected the script's association of visible race with the South, premodern backwardness, and accommodation to segregation, calling attention to its use of racial stereotyping in the characters of Granny, Jake, and Rozelia. She introduced the subject of Pinky's relationship to the black community in the North: "Did she live with whites or Negroes in the North, did Negroes try to dissuade Pinky from passing?" The implication that only a racially indeterminate heroine from the North could challenge racial injustice ignored, in her view, southern grassroots struggles for civil rights; she wanted to see "a dark-skinned Southern Negro character to manifest the forthright militance" that the novel had attached to its racial progressive, "someone who has grown up in the South but undefeated by discrimination there."[66]

Zanuck wrote to White that he "disagreed with most points" in her report. Her critique seems to have had a greater effect on Dunne, who warned Zanuck that the foreign press and audiences might be "tough judges" and that racial definitions based on the white supremacist "one-drop rule" were not widely accepted in the rest of the world. "In Brazil, Pinky is white, in France, the question of mixed blood is not a concern." Even the English found American concepts of race a "puzzlement."[67] Dunne also acknowledged, in order to deny, the racialist assumptions about blood and racial boundaries that he had written into the script: "There is an implication that we think that having Negro blood somehow sets one apart, that it makes one *internally* as well as externally different, that the possession of a trace of Negro blood makes one feel a mystic identity with that race." Still, he could not imagine Pinky with family and community ties, assuming that "before Pinky knew of Negro blood, she felt no connection to Negroes."

Dunne may have thought that he was avoiding white supremacist racial determinism. He wrote that by enabling Pinky to *choose* either to "live without pride" as Chester's white wife or to use Miss Em's house to serve her race he was providing an alternative to a motivation based on an "inner compulsion" or "acceptance of convention as fact." The resolution of Jewish indeterminacy in *Gentleman's Agreement* was clearly the model for Dunne as he proffered individual choice as an alternative to racial determinism. In his script the "key point is that she doesn't say she *is* a Negro, but that she chooses to be one. The point is that she has a choice. And that—her freedom to choose—is after all the theme of our entire picture."[68] The belief that racially indeterminate people could "choose" was contradicted by the decision (as in *Lost Boundaries*) only to consider white actresses for the part of Pinky.[69]

Zanuck grew increasingly committed to *Pinky,* linking his own reputation with the picture's bid to deliver a commercial success with a racial theme. He suppressed the connection to Sumner's novel and highlighted his use of the trading places formula; he wanted *Pinky* to make the "Negro question" as visible as anti-Semitism had been in *Gentleman's Agreement.*[70]

Zanuck and De Rochemont adopted opposing positions on racial indeterminacy: where De Rochemont was determined to define racial indeterminacy as white, Zanuck leaned towards defining it as nonwhite. He shaped all characterizations through his concept of the story line, pasting onto the shooting script an emphatic declaration:

> THIS IS NOT A STORY ABOUT HOW TO SOLVE THE NEGRO PROBLEM IN THE SOUTH OR ANYWHERE ELSE. THIS IS NOT A STORY PARTICULARLY ABOUT RACE PROBLEMS, SEGREGATION, OR DISCRIMINATION. THIS IS A STORY ABOUT ONE PARTICULAR NEGRO GIRL WHO COULD EASILY PASS AS A WHITE AND DID PASS FOR A WHILE. THIS IS THE STORY OF HOW AND WHY SHE, AS AN INDIVIDUAL, FINALLY DECIDED TO BE HERSELF, A NEGRESS.[71]

Both productions refused to consider any real possibility of racial indeterminacy or to explore its history in interracial sexuality, coercion, and exploitation. Francis Harmon, a southerner who worked for the production code office, wrote to Zanuck in a March 1949 memo that, based on his reading of the script, "to be true to life in the South, it seems to me that Pinky should be shown to be the daughter of one of Miss Em's male relatives"; he knew "case after case where just such a situation arose." Harmon pleaded with Zanuck to add this explanation to the film (and enclosed sample pages he had written to make this point), arguing that the producers and director of the picture would "miss a great opportunity if the picture fails to drive home the point that the very people who attack social equality on the level of virtue continue to accept illicit sex relationships, of which Pinky and her kind are innocent and tragic victims."[72]

Zanuck posed the question of race as one of personal choice. Wanting to avoid "the illicit miscegenation angle," Zanuck wrote that the "larger good will accrue by making this a picture dealing with *tolerance.*"[73] To build identification with a "black" character, however, required the casting of a white actress. As the response to *Lost Boundaries* revealed, black critics saw this focus on "tolerance" as a call for interracial civility rather than racial justice, an avoidance of the history of distinctive black experience.

When Jane White helped Zanuck and Dunne see racial stereotyping in the characters of Granny, Jake, and Rozelia, Dunne agreed to remove certain lines that would encourage "Negrophobes."[74] Director John Ford's description of *Pinky* as "a warm personal story about a girl who runs counter to racial prejudice . . . with the emphasis on the emotional life of the girl" suggested that he, too, relied on the racially unmarked character to carry the film's racial message, leaving him unprepared for new public scrutiny of the black characters.[75] Zanuck later described how Ford's direction of black characters seemed dated in the charged atmosphere of the time: "Ford's Negroes were like Aunt Jemima caricatures. I thought we're going to get into trouble. Jack [Ford] said, I think you'd better put someone else on it." The famous blues singer and stage actress Ethel Waters, cast as Granny, remembered Ford as "a shock treatment" and so cruel that she "almost had a stroke."[76]

The trade papers announced that Ford had "taken sick" and that the film would be finished by Elia Kazan, popularly associated with trading places stories and "message" films. Assuming his position one week after filming had begun, Kazan had less ability to shape *Pinky* than would have otherwise been the director's prerogative. Dunne later recounted that Kazan "flew out from New York on a Saturday, went over the script with Zanuck and me on Sunday, and started shooting on Monday with John Ford's cast, on John Ford's sets, assisted by John Ford's crew. Not one word in the script was changed." Also on the set was a representative from the NAACP, who pressed Kazan to modify props associated with Hollywood racial coding, substituting a knife for Rozelia's razor and eliminating Aunt Dicey's bandana.[77] Critics credited Kazan with creating psychologically honest performances—especially from Jeanne Crain, Waters, and Ethel Barrymore—and for his attention to dramatic effect, having "pumped conflict into every scene and sustained the excitement throughout even the talky stretches."[78]

Recollections of the novel *Quality* encouraged African American journalists to keep their distance from the *Pinky* production; as the *Pittsburgh Courier*'s Marjorie McKenzie wrote, "having read the story on which 'Pinky' is based, I shudder to think of its release."[79] They condemned the casting of white actress Jeanne Crain ("Fox's Miss Homespun America") as Pinky; noted the publicized disagreements over the script ("seems like they can't make up their minds as to whether to make it pro-Negro or follow the same old Hollywood trends in dealing with the subject"), and minimized the film's social and political aspirations ("the flicker can hardly be considered a problem play of the 'Deep Are the Roots' variety").[80] Features focused on *Pinky*'s black actors: the renowned Ethel Waters, prominent stage actors Nina McKinney and Frederick O'Neal, the former UCLA football star Kenny Washington, and the more than two hundred black children with walk-on parts, commenting that " 'Pinky' feeds a lot of Negroes even though it may not satisfy a lot more who'll view it on the screen."[81] They called attention to the high stakes, crediting film representations with either helping "to eliminate or make worse the problems of racial and religious prejudices in America."[82]

The film producers tried to influence reaction to the film by encouraging audiences to view *Pinky* in relation to *Crossfire* and *Gentleman's Agreement*. Dunne's statement, "Approach to Racism," appeared in the *New York Times* as well as promotional materials and linked *Pinky* to a wartime idealism: "The experience of the war has taught us . . . what we say and do on the screen can affect the happiness, the living conditions, even the physical safety of millions of our fellow citizens." Along with the films of 1947, Pinky was defying "the long-standing taboo against films dealing with the problems of racial and religious prejudice" and constructing a genre of postwar realism "fashioned from the raw materials of contemporary life." He attempted to remove any suggestion of political partisanship (or increasingly dangerous affiliation with the left), claiming that there were a "variety of ideas on the subject of race in America," held by "every

American citizen, white or Negro," and that views on race were always colored by "passion and prejudice."

Above all, Dunne presented *Pinky*'s representation of an ordinary American as a "completely personal story" in which "Jeanne Crain, as Pinky, portrays not a race, but an individual." Dunne admitted that Pinky's problems do not stem from individual causes—"the tragic dilemma of her life is induced by the facts of racial prejudice"—but he insisted that "the solutions she finds are her own and affect only her." Stories of trading places revealed incidents of racial discrimination, but their resolutions relied on individual character and conversion. Dunne wrote that the filmmakers "neither deny nor condone the bitter facts of racial prejudice" but then backed away from any protest against racial prejudice: "we simply try to dramatize its effect on a girl who might be anyone's daughter, sister, or sweetheart." He attempted to distance the film from social goals, especially those identified with the antifascist left. "We are propagandists only in so far as we insist that every human being is entitled to personal freedom and dignity." Without showing the historic obstacles to the achievement of these, Dunne illuminated a hollowness at the heart of the story, removing *Pinky* from any connection to the unfolding struggles for racial justice shaping the political context in which the film was conceived.[83]

When the film was released both Kazan and Jeanne Crain argued that trading places conventions enabled Pinky's unmarked racial character to convey African American racial experience. In statements published in *Ebony* Kazan asserted that Pinky was a "real Negro . . . not a fawning person but the average Negro who, I think, is bitter, goes around thinking that white people don't like him, and who is a fighter." Jeanne Crain claimed her resemblance to Ethel Waters: "our features tied in. We were believable as a grandmother and her granddaughter." She reported that she prepared for the part by reading a book about passing and by asking herself "how a young Negro girl would feel most every day." Confident that she could engage in her own form of trading places, she recalled "those times in school when I was humiliated horribly," adding that she thought "everyone has experienced what colored people face daily." She was also confident in trading places as a strategy for appealing to her audience: "so many people have told me not to stir anything up that I feel we've got to really move them into feeling for Pinky and her problems."[84] Ethel Waters also publicly supported the picture, with a statement pronouncing it a "very human and exciting story about one particular girl and her emotional conflicts as she runs up against old intolerances in her struggle to find love and happiness."[85]

The film relies on clear oppositions—between South and North, acquiescence and resistance, black and white. From its opening shots—of a train disappearing into the landscape and the figure of a lone woman walking down the road, pausing to remember the big house surrounded by dirt-floor cabins—*Pinky* contrasts the claustrophobia and ritual humiliation of segregation in the South with passing (and its attendant opportunities) in the North, invoked by the motif of the train whistle. In Pinky's encounters with the southern black community (represented by her grandmother, Aunt Dicey, Jake, and Rozelia), the filmmakers enumerate her options: to be deferential or to be cagey in negotiating the system of white patronage. Pinky's encounters with white southern justice, joy-riding good ol' boys, and small-town storekeepers provide examples of the civil treatment she receives when perceived as white and the brutality, attempted rape, and price gouging she experiences when identified as black.

As a black woman trained as a nurse, Pinky has stepped out of the place defined for her by segregation—unlike the black doctor in town who has accepted the conventions of racial separation. But without the authority of the Negro soldier in the melting pot platoon of *Home of the Brave,* or of the Negro doctor healing a white community in *Lost Boundaries,* Pinky struggles to assume the mantle of expanded citizenship. Her family is represented by the premodern Granny—illiterate, enmeshed in, and defending white paternalism. Miss Em's interactions with Pinky and Granny symbolize the relationship of white mistress to black female servant, with its daily proximity, limited personal familiarity, and economic exploitation. The courtroom scene provides an opportunity to counter Melba Wooley's unreconstructed arguments for white superiority with the promise of democratic justice. But by the end of the film Pinky passes back into segregation, leaving the color line intact as she assumes the position of surrogate mother in a hospital and day nursery where she trains black nurses and serves black children.

Discussions of the film often touched upon interracial romance. Relying on the language of Pinky's "choice" obscured the film's rejection of interracial sexuality (and the white supremacist implications of that rejection). Using a love story to disguise a modest exposé of racial discrimination confused some white critics who already found it difficult to see a female character as a representative citizen. Edwin Schallert commented that "showing the feminine side of the case" from the "viewpoint of a young girl who ultimately must face life as a Negro even though she may pass as white" could not represent society; it lacked "the panorama of effects on various lives which obtained in *Lost Boundaries.*"[86]

Pinky's renunciation of her white lover relied on conventions of female self-sacrifice popularized by the genre of the women's film as well as on the fixing of Pinky's racial indeterminacy as Negro. Although Jane White thought the ending "not credible," the reviewer for the *Hollywood Reporter* seems to have been convinced: "Pinky resolves the purpose of her life by sending away the white doctor and opening a nursery school as a wise, gifted, and beautiful woman proud of her Negro heritage."[87] The familiar female "choice" of self-sacrifice made more of an impression on some reviewers than the film's racial protest. The *Commonweal* reviewer wrote that caring for Miss Em helps Pinky understand the "meaning of integrity"; she "learns the meaning of life and . . . finally sees that her own happiness is not the important thing." An article in *Life* entitled "A Woman's Problem" removed *Pinky* from the cycle of race films altogether, placing stills from *Pinky* in between those from adaptations of Gustav Flaubert's *Madame Bovary* and Henry James's *Washington Square* (both 1949).[88] The *New Republic*'s Robert Hatch conveyed his contempt for popular women's narratives in his assessment of Pinky's choice: "Pinky renounces her man to become a ministering angel, beloved by all." Because he saw the film as "standard soap romance," he viewed its "race" angle as suffused with "sentimentality and falsehood."[89]

In the contested political atmosphere of 1949 some mainstream publications marked *Pinky* as a departure from social message filmmaking. *Variety* credited Zanuck with making a "dramatic bombshell . . . with preachment . . . secondary to the sweeping drama" and putting "entertainment above soapboxing." The *Time* reviewer identified its moderate political stance more precisely, depicting the political strategy of the film as an alternative to more combative public protest: Pinky fights inequity not with "the slimy tactics of Communists and their front organizations but in the clean fighting American way in the courtroom." This reviewer was pleased that the film might "irritate both professional Southerners and professional champions of racial equality."[90]

Other reviewers help us see what was striking in *Pinky* at the time: "plunking the Negro problem in the South's backyard, instead of in the South Pacific or New Hampshire." Bosley Crowther noted the way in which the film illuminated "the discomforts of poor housing, the ignominy of police abuse, the humiliations of Jim Crowism, and the sting of epithets." The weekly *Variety* reviewer ranked the attempted rape sequence for being filmed "as clearly as has ever been shown on the screen."[91] The reviewer for the left-wing *Daily Compass* also singled out the rape scene and the scene with the police as showing "what no Hollywood movie has ever shown—some of the pain and humiliation inflicted on the Negro in the South."[92] These particular scenes resonated for viewers familiar with the left-wing campaigns of the 1930s and 1940s to publicize cases of southern legal injustice. When searching for something to praise in the film, black critics often singled them out as well.[93]

Even mainstream white reviewers noted the absence of the forthright critique of racial injustice associated with pre-1948 civil rights campaigns. The *New Yorker*'s John McCarten was not convinced by "Negroes who know that, deep down under, most white folks are pretty fine people. . . . The message of 'Pinky' seems to be that colored girls, however fair, will find more happiness conducting themselves as Negroes in the warmhearted South than they ever could find passing up in Boston."[94] Bosley Crowther found fault with the extolling of "old Mammy" sentiment, with the "passion for paternalism" at the film's core, and for its failure to offer "genuinely constructive thinking on relations between blacks and whites." In a second discussion he stated his concerns more strongly, writing that the story "comes perilously close to denying the very equality it seems to espouse by accepting paternalism as the easiest and the happiest way out," especially given that Pinky's benefactor "clearly supports the doctrine of white supremacy." Crowther questioned the absence of a more militant articulation of civil rights, noting that there was not an "enlightened or progressive person in the lot."[95]

Nonetheless, the trading places drama in *Pinky* struck Crowther as "the kind of story the screen does best, a pictorial novel with a factual basis . . . and that all-important element of self-identification." He felt the film drew "white man and Negro" into earnest reflection: "What would I do under the same circumstances?" He applauded the effort to gloss over Pinky's subjectivity by making "the girl . . . a figure of gentle aspect with whom the audience can 'identify' . . . so that each blow and knock she receives is soundly transmitted to the audience, which is prompted to think and feel for her."[96]

Black reviewers were largely critical of how *Pinky* could "reinforce" white audiences' "faulty reasoning on the so-called race problem," although they applauded the performances of the black actors in the film, gave the film's producers credit for improving on the book, and tracked the film's promotion and ticket sales. They objected to what they saw as *Pinky*'s demeaning of black culture, its scorn of black resistance, and its stereotyping of racially marked characters.[97] Despite his involvement in the film, Walter White roundly condemned the finished product because from it "one would never know . . . that Negroes, even in the most backward areas of Mississippi, are not resigned to their place and are not only working but making progress against the kind of conditions portrayed in 'Pinky.' " White's chief objection was what he saw as the film's acceptance of the "philosophy that the Negro has his 'place,' that he accepts that place, that all white people are united in agreement that colored people must forever stay in a position of inferiority." Lillian Scott enumerated the film's "fallacious concepts" as suggesting that "a protesting Negro does not want to live among his own" and that a desire of a Negro to achieve stature as a human being should be treated scornfully as an attempt "to get out of his place." She objected to the film's depiction of white and black defense of racial boundaries, describing Pinky as "figuratively and almost literally beaten over the head by the small Alabama town's prejudiced whites on the one hand, and by her dark-skinned granny, on the other." She criticized the film's sympathy for both white and black paternalism, describing Miss Em and Granny as subjecting Pinky "in a subtle and sometimes brutal series of humiliations in their efforts to mold her into a more submissive person."[98]

Black critics reiterated Ellison's concern that a passing drama could not adequately make the case for racial equality. Cab Calloway wrote that the focus on the "specialized problem" of "passing the color line" kept *Pinky* and *Lost Boundaries* from being able to address "the Negro problem as such." He noted how the passing films substituted color for equality because they failed to consider the "darker Negro who wants acceptance not 'because he looks white' but because his color should not restrict him from living as other men do."[99] Reviewing the film in the voice of her character, the savvy domestic worker Mildred, the left-wing actress, dramatist, and writer Alice Childress sniffed, "I guess the people who make the movies think that Jim Crow is all right for darker people but is awful unjust if it happens to somebody who is light-complected." The people who attended the invitation-only *Chicago Defender* benefit premiere were less critical, but they also questioned the film's focus on passing. One woman called for secrecy: "I'd rather keep [whites] in the dark about the 'Pinkys' of our race, many of whom have made a successful and satisfactory adjustment. I'm afraid [that] to enlighten them will cause them to become too curious." Another questioned the assumption that passing implied white superiority: "The Negro 'passes' only for economical reasons. When it comes to our personal lives we are happiest among our own."[100]

White and black reviewers differed on the significance of the film's connection between passing and interracial romance. This was central to the studio's advertising campaign, explicit in promotional taglines ("I want to marry you anyway—no one will ever know our secret" and "The love story of a girl who passed for white"), and reiterated visually (a thin diagonal line superimposed between actors; letters shading from black to white).[101] White reviewers commented on the film's avoidance of interracial sexuality. One of the New York daily newspaper reviewers connected the film's "final rejection of racial intermarriage" to its general political stance: "Let each race stay on its own side of the fence and let the Negroes depend on the good, well-born white folks for justice." Kazan tried to claim that the film was personal, not political:

> I'm worried because people might think we're saying Negroes and whites shouldn't marry. We solve this story in personal terms. This particular boy and girl shouldn't get married. If the doctor had been more perceptive, we should have had a different story. But we don't mean this story to be true of all people with colored and white skins.[102]

Black critics insisted, however, that the film's rejection of interracial marriage compromised its racial protest. The first item on Lillian Scott's list of "fallacious concepts" was the proposition that "interracial marriage is out of the question." Alice Childress's Mildred linked the film's moralizing ("white people will come to the rescue and point out to the 'passer' that it is more honorable to *be what you are* and improve yourself in spite of the fact") to its evasions on interracial sexual encounters, which she positioned within the history of white sexual coercion: "Everyone feels real happy in the end 'cause the whites can go away feelin' no fear of bein' married to, bein' the son of, the mother of, or the wife, sister, aunt or cousin of a Negro who lacked the *honor* to inform them of his race. Girl, you know that we know better than that!" Ralph Ellison also mocked Pinky's "choice" to reject interracial marriage: "Pinky wins the plantation and her lover, who has read of the fight in the Negro press, arrives and still loves her, race be hanged. But now Pinky decides that to marry him would 'violate the race' and that she had better remain a Negro." Like Childress, Ellison called attention to the evasion of the South's long history of non-consensual interracial sex: "Ironically, nothing is said about the fact that her racial integrity, whatever that is, was violated before she was born. Her parents are never mentioned in the film." Joining others, Ellison protested the very grounds of the film's refusal of interracial marriage: "In real life, the choice is not between loving and denying one's race. Many couples manage to intermarry without violating their integrity and indeed their marriage becomes the concrete expression of their integrity."[103]

The film's careful avoidance of interracial sexuality did not convince local southern censors. In Atlanta they demanded thirty-four seconds of cuts consisting of parts of the attempted rape scene and the final scene showing the principals kissing (they also excised the slapping of Pinky by a white policeman). In Marshall, Texas censors ruled that screening *Pinky* would be "prejudicial to the best interests of the people of the city" because it depicted "1) . . . a white man retaining his love for a woman after learning she is a Negro 2) . . . a white man kissing and embracing a Negro woman 3) . . . a scene in which 2 white ruffians assault Pinky after she has told them she is colored."[104]

The censors encountered resistance. A Marshall, Texas exhibitor pressed for the right to show the film through a legal challenge that went to the Supreme Court. He was aided by the legal resources of the industry lobby, Motion Picture Producers and Distributors Association, which tried to prevent local censors from interfering with its oversight of film content. The final court decision in 1952 upheld the exhibitor's right to show *Pinky* without censorship of its representation of interracial sexuality as constitutional protection of speech.[105]

Lavishly promoted, *Pinky* was a smash hit for Fox, the largest money-maker for the studio in 1949. It was exhibited widely in both the North and the South, attracting black as well as white audiences. Prints were made with subtitles in twenty-seven different languages for foreign distribution. The black press covered its distribution, reporting that in one Atlanta theater accommodating all the viewers who wanted to see it required the expansion of "Negro seating" from a few rows to the entire balcony.[106] In his survey of *Home of the Brave, Lost Boundaries,* and *Pinky,* A. S. "Doc" Young referred to Hollywood's "black gold."[107]

Despite the elisions and evasions of these films, Young was hopeful that their commercial success would change Hollywood racial representations forever: "California's sunshine . . . may never rise again on the old stereotypes," he wrote, although "it is still a long way from shining on a film about interracial marriage."[108] Racial equality was central to the political and social issues linked by wartime popular antifascism; producers and audiences alike recognized this frame of reference. The *Afro-American*'s Al Anderson cautioned that "Hollywood's sudden awakening" was the result of civil rights pressure, "the vigilance and fight put up by colored people and their progressive white allies in urging Hollywood to come of age."[109] The momentum toward racial equality, now in motion, seemed to him unstoppable.

Perhaps the most eloquent statement of hope was that of the Negro Critics Circle, formed by black press critics to recognize annually those "films, plays, books and other creative efforts both by Negroes and dealing with stories affecting them." The critics assumed that they were present at the creation of a new era of cultural production by and about people of color. They believed that cultural expression had a role to play in political change: "motion pictures and the theatre are strong influences on the processes of people and a democratic process at work." Their own critical insights would be a crucial resource in envisioning racial inclusion, might help "extend, encourage, and develop opportunities . . . to assure full purposeful participation of Negroes in the motion picture industry and theater on a high level and plane." For 1949 the critics ranked *Home of the Brave* over the passing movies as the film that "dealt with the problem [of racial relations] in the most straightforward manner without offense or apologies." They looked forward to the openings of the other announced race-themed films, *Intruder in the Dust* and *No Way Out*.[110] They could not have anticipated that Hollywood's efforts to make films of racial protest would end so abruptly.

TRADING PLACES OR NO WAY OUT?

The reliance of the passing films on white casting and the fixing of racial indeterminacy as either white or black avoided representing the universal through racial experience. But even their hesitations encouraged the making of other films that experimented with more explicitly racially marked heroes. The last two films in the 1949 Hollywood race-themed cycle, MGM's *Intruder in the Dust* and Fox's *No Way Out*, feature dark-skinned protagonists who stand up to racial injustice and terror with the help of white allies who can "see through" race. The accomplishments, as well as the narrative and commercial failures of these films, mark the end of postwar confidence that stories of trading places could represent the possibilities of a racially inclusive and cosmopolitan citizenship.

The MGM production of William Faulkner's novel *Intruder in the Dust* was shaped by what we may now recognize as the usual suspects for a trading places film. Director Clarence Brown, a southerner, said that making the picture was "as little as I could do to make up for Atlanta," referring to race riots he had witnessed in his youth. The producer was Dore Schary, associated with *Crossfire*. The left-wing writer and poet Ben Maddow wrote the screenplay to focus on Lucas Beauchamp, an independent farmer, played by the renowned radio and stage actor Juano Hernandez, recently on stage as the angry doctor in *Strange Fruit*. The script was submitted to the NAACP for approval, and the production was filmed on location in Oxford, Mississippi, with town residents as extras in the crowd scenes and realist sound effects in place of conventional "mood music."[111]

That he is the progeny of master and slave explains why Beauchamp owns his land and why he refuses to defer. He wears a hat, chews on a gold toothpick, and carries a gun. The young white boy, Chick, voices the town's frustration at being unable to "make a nigger out of him once in his life." Amidst a town of whites who gather in anticipation of Beauchamp being lynched (he is accused of a white man's murder), the first shot of Beauchamp is his shackled hands—an iconographic representation of the miscarriage of southern justice for black men in the 1930s. Black critics were excited by the appearance of Lucas Beauchamp: "Something new and distinct . . . is this strong, unbending, and unprovoking character . . . [who] never cringes or bows to white folks." They credited Hernandez's "splendid" acting for creating a "wonderful character, proud, watchful and manly." Ellison wrote that *Intruder* was the only film in which "Negroes can make complete identification with their screen image."[112]

The film's sympathetic characters, who could "see" Lucas Beauchamp outside a racialized framework, live at the social margins—the oldest white woman in town, Miss Habersham, the last living member of a once prominent family, and the interracial pair of boys, the white Chick Mallison, obligated by chance to Beauchamp, and Chick's boyhood friend Aleck, the son of Chick's family's black domestic servant. No Gregory Peck–type audience surrogate here. To prove Beauchamp's innocence, they must disinter a white body, wake the dead. By the end of the film the unbowed Beauchamp is free, but he remains outside the body politic, his social citizenship reduced to being the "keeper of our [southern whites'] consciences." Both white and black critics lauded the effort, but the audiences didn't come.[113]

The production team of No Way Out also included people from Hollywood's left-wing roster: Darryl Zanuck, who promised a picture "as real as sweat . . . deal[ing] with the absolute blood and guts of Negro hating," and the Hollywood progressive writer and director Joe Mankiewicz, at that time president of the Screen Directors' Guild.[114] Like Lost Boundaries, it represents claims for citizenship in the figure of a black doctor; as in Intruder, the crossing of racial boundaries does not rely on racial indeterminacy. The doctor, Luther Brooks, is played by Sidney Poitier in his screen debut; he portrays the first African American intern in a big-city hospital, caught between the demands of middle-class color-blind professionalism and the need to defend himself against racial violence.

In quick succession No Way Out showed working-class whites planning a racial attack to avenge the death of a white patient under the black doctor's care and then a long shot of armed blacks defending their community, with dialogue suggesting that the white perpetrators caught the worst of the exchange. Black press reviewers thought No Way Out the "boldest film" of the cycle because of its "out and out blast against racial discrimination in everyday American life," expanding the other films' focus on "passing, Army Jim Crow, and lynching."[115] A white critic identified No Way Out as making the strongest case for considering "the Negro as an everyday citizen in the white everyday world of a large American city."[116] As in Intruder, the dark-skinned protagonist barely escapes being lynched for a death he did not cause, and a white body must be disturbed to perform the autopsy required to prove the doctor's innocence. Moving the locale from Mississippi to the urban North enabled the film to make the case that segregationist practices of racial injustice and exclusion were national, not regional. Now the outraged censors were in Chicago, as well as on local boards in Pennsylvania, Virginia, and Ohio. They demanded that the riot scene be cut.[117]

In No Way Out the character who most clearly views Luther Brooks outside of a racialized framework is his teacher and supervisor, Dr. Wharton. Wharton offers professionalism as a "scientific" antidote to racialization, describing himself not as "pro-Negro" but "pro-good doctor, black, white, or polka dot." The film assigns the defense of fixed racial boundaries to urban white working-class men in the North, stereotyped as racist hoodlums and personified by Ray, played by Richard Widmark.[118] A white working-class waitress, played by Linda Darnell, is caught between her family ties to the racists and her egalitarian class consciousness, indicated by her comment that there is "no difference in people except the size of their tips." Though the film attempted to avoid paternalism in the relationship between the doctors, its careful demarcation of separate black and white domestic worlds reflected suburban middle-class participation in postwar residential *resegregation.*

Racial antagonism in the film eludes a realist resolution; it is not surprising that the production team had difficulty choosing an appropriate ending.[119] In the final version Brooks works to save the life of the man who has been trying to kill him. Momentarily interrupting the film's illusion of color-blind professionalism, Brooks calls attention to racial difference with a rhetorical reversal—"Don't cry, white boy"—before asserting his class-laden medical expertise, "you're gonna live." Mankiewicz defended the lack of narrative resolution: "Even Hollywood does not have the right to offer a solution to the problem which has baffled this country for 175 years."[120]

These films gestured toward crossing between the public and the private spheres, briefly revealing their racially marked heroes to be part of families and communities. A flashback in *Intruder* introduces an aging black woman as Lucas Beauchamp's wife, and the *No Way Out* production team planned a special scene to show a modern black family: "We'll go into Luther's home. We will see real Negroes and how they live, as human beings."[121] Stage actors Ossie Davis, Ruby Dee, and Mildred Joann Smith made their film debuts as this family, whose collective willingness to support the education of a black doctor, and the resulting ability of the black doctor to support a middle-class family life, expressed the promise of expanded postwar citizenship. A quick embrace between Luther and his wife provided a glimpse of a heretofore forbidden "love scene between Negroes." Making their case, Cora says to Luther: "We've been a long time getting here. We're tired, but we're here, honey. We can be happy. We've got a right to be." But ultimately these films also retreated from connecting family, community, and citizenship. The endings show the heroes standing alone, with racial boundaries for the most part reaffirmed, the terms of redemption individual and psychological rather than social and political.

The studio attempted the same promotional push for *No Way Out* that it had arranged for *Gentleman's Agreement* and *Pinky:* ringing endorsements from Walter White and from Frederick O'Neal of the American Negro Theatre ("the greatest step forward in the fight against racial prejudice since the Civil War") as well as a range of civil rights, Jewish and labor organizations, including the NAACP and the Urban League; "Picture of the Month" features in *Redbook, Esquire, Modern Screen,* and *Seventeen;* photo spreads in *Look, Newsweek, Cosmopolitan,* and *Good Housekeeping.*[122] But northern censorship boards objected to the race riots and use of racial epithets, which also bothered some black viewers. Exhibition was limited but, most important, the audiences stayed away.[123]

Stories of trading places did not live up to their promise, as ultimately they were unable to imagine overturning racial barriers to include racial others in the universe of ordinary Americans. They could not find the means to convey how racial discrimination and danger excluded African Americans from the realm of the ordinary. After 1949 anticommunist conservatives were in the ascendancy; antifascist coalitions that had supported demands for racial equality—and had produced both the framework and the creators of trading places stories—came under fire.

The momentum to dismantle segregation was not stopped, although civil rights organizations became more vulnerable when conservatives, under the aegis of anticommunism, increased police surveillance and arrests to obstruct desegregation campaigns. HUAC's attack on the Hollywood left meant that the people most likely to produce films questioning racial boundaries could no longer find work. Weakened by the fallout from the Paramount decision severing corporate control of production from exhibition, the industry was polarized by bitter labor struggles. After the failure of appeals by the Hollywood Ten, studio heads actively enforced an anticommunist blacklist, some with enthusiasm and others, such as Darryl Zanuck, with reluctance. Themes that suggested a connection to popular front concerns came to be seen as too controversial rather than socially relevant.[124]

Civil rights organizations continued to pressure Hollywood for new racial representations, but civil rights demands compatible with anticommunism had to celebrate, rather than critique, American democracy and could not refer to analyses of injustice associated with the left. The social practices that had supported second-class citizenship—economic discrimination, socially sanctioned lynching, police brutality, and rape—as well as depictions of black community resistance and interracial political alliances virtually disappeared from the screen.

A glimpse at *The Jackie Robinson Story* (1950) suggests how anticommunism could reshape film representations of racial citizenship. This low-budget feature received positive attention in the black press and attracted the audiences to make it a commercial success. Here Robinson is an all-American boy, his achievements an American story of success, the desegregation of baseball "the triumph of democracy and of Americans of goodwill." The film portrays an all-white world encouraging young Robinson to play baseball; his childhood teammates were in fact African American, Mexican American, Japanese American, and white. Rewriting Robinson's family history, the film minimized the influences of his mother and wife and focused on the paternal authority of Brooklyn Dodgers general manager Branch Rickey. Each incident of white opposition to Robinson is balanced with a white-sponsored opportunity. The film turns Robinson's experience in the army, where he faced a court martial for resisting segregated practices, into the source of his first coaching job.

The climax of the film turned Robinson's "fight" to desegregate baseball into a fight against communism via his testimony to the HUAC hearings. Robinson's actual performance in front of HUAC in July 1949 was staged as a public condemnation of Paul Robeson, the most visible figure of the black left, long a supporter of the desegregation of baseball; Robinson tried to use the hearing to protest segregation and to distance himself from Robeson without denying Robeson's right to dissent. The film Robinson proclaims all threats to freedom as external, all fights for democracy as the fight against communism.[125] In prefilm publicity Robinson admitted that the film "watered down" some of the problems he faced, but he still hoped it would "tell more of racial problems than Hollywood's other pictures about Negroes."[126] But displacing family and community, excising the collective struggle against segregation, and subordinating the right to protest racial inequality to the loyalty requirements of opposing communism was a high price to pay for a racial story to become an American story.

Between 1945 and 1949 trading places narratives offered a range of stories that called attention to racial boundaries as part of a political insistence on the universality of human interests. Briefly, these stories raised questions of power but then set them aside. Ultimately the attempt to build empathy was unable to sustain a racially or sexually cosmopolitan alternative to normative standards of the ordinary; their failures were followed by a retreat to individualism. When the everyman stories—explored in the next section—picked up the effort, their representations of the universality of human interests made it increasingly difficult to make racial experience visible, especially for an audience no longer familiar with the concerns of 1940s antifascism.

1 A picketer demands that black military service during World War II translate into postwar desegregation in Chicago, July 1941. *(John Vachon photo, Library of Congress)*

BUY WAR BONDS!

She lives on a police widow's pension in a little house in Brooklyn in the section where Williamsburg starts to be Greenpoint. The front room . . . used only on rare and important occasions . . . is her pride and joy.

"And how's your front room?" I asked the last time I saw her.

"Wonderful it is. Only tain't the front room now. 'Tis the War Bond room. It's this way, see? I think about this Hitler; what he's doing to people over there—especially us Catholics. I want to buy War Bonds to help lick him. But I can't do it on account of no money, see? Then that there factory up the street opens up. There's no place for some girl workers to stay. Rooms is scarce, see? So what do I turn around and do but rent out my front room to two girls for $18.75 a month! I feel *I'M* helping our War by fixing a living place for two war workers. The girls is happy knowing their rent money buys a bond a month. And that grandson of mine is getting helped through college ten years from now, see? These here Bonds is the best college insurance there is. Am I right?"

You bet she was right! And I told her so, too.

Betty Smith.

Author of *A Tree Grows in Brooklyn*

2 Writer Betty Smith in the 1940s.

3 *A Tree Grows in Brooklyn* (1945), directed by Elia Kazan, and the promise of upward mobility: Grandma Rommely (Ferike Boros) instructs Katie (Dorothy McGuire) on the virtues of reading Shakespeare and the Bible. *(Academy of Motion Picture Arts and Sciences)*

4 Katie (Dorothy McGuire) and Neeley (Ted Donaldson) argue with Francie (Peggy Ann Garner) and Johnny (James Dunn) over Johnny's plan to place Francie in a better school. *(Academy of Motion Picture Arts and Sciences)*

5 John Van Druten's *I Remember Mama* (1944) on stage: Mama (Mady Christians) challenges her brother Chris (Oscar Homolka), the "black" Norwegian. *(Billy Rose Theatre Collection, New York Public Library for the Performing Arts, Astor, Lenox and Tilden Foundations)*

6 *I Remember Mama* on film (1948), directed by George Stevens: Papa (Philip Dorn), Mama (Irene Dunne), Nels (Steve Brown), Christine (Peggy McIntyre), and Dagmar (June Hedin) listen as Katrin (Barbara Bel Geddes) reads from her account of Mama's "magical" family accounting. *(Academy of Motion Picture Arts and Sciences)*

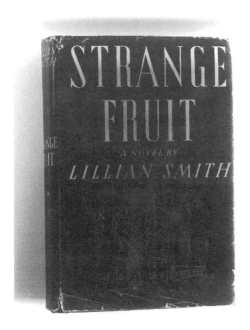

7 Lillian Smith's title *Strange Fruit* (1944) addresses lynching as the consequence of slavery and segregation; Cid Ricketts Sumner's title *Quality* (1946) refers to a southern term used to denote white ancestry visible in interracial sexual mixing.

8 Interracial romance on Broadway in Elia Kazan's production of *Deep Are the Roots* (1945): Generva Langdon (Barbara Bel Geddes) proposes marriage to her childhood friend, returning solider Brett Charles (Gordon Heath), who refuses her. *(Billy Rose Theatre Collection, New York Public Library for the Performing Arts, Astor, Lenox and Tilden Foundations)*

9 Playwright Arthur Miller in the 1940s. (*Billy Rose Theatre Collection, New York Public Library for the Performing Arts, Astor, Lenox and Tilden Foundations*)

10 The troubled world of men at war in *Crossfire* (1947), directed by Edward Dymytryk: Jewish civilian Samuels (Sam Levene) comforts Corporal Jeff Mitchell (George Cooper) in the ominous presence of Mitchell's commanding officer, Sergeant Monty Crawford (Robert Ryan). (*Academy of Motion Picture Arts and Sciences*)

11 The temporary alliance between Finlay (Robert Young), Mitchell's wife, Mary (Jacqueline White), and Ginny, a tired young taxi dancer (Gloria Grahame) suggests the potential for a cosmopolitan social order after the war. *(Academy of Motion Picture Arts and Sciences)*

12 *Gentleman's Agreement* (1947), directed by Elia Kazan, undermines its premise of Jewish indeterminacy: Dave Goldman (John Garfield), a "real" Jew, is called a "Yid" by hostile strangers as the "passing" Jew, Phil Green (Gregory Peck), looks on. *(Academy of Motion Picture Arts and Sciences)*

13 The attempt to represent racial citizenship in *Home of the Brave* (1949), directed by Mark Robson: Engineer Peter Moss (James Edwards) is warmly welcomed by his high school buddy Finch (Lloyd Bridges) but immediately faces resistance from the major (Douglas Dick). *(Academy of Motion Picture Arts and Sciences)*

14 Models for the Carter family in Louis de Rochemont's *Lost Boundaries* (1949): Thyra and Albert Johnson, and their son, Albert Jr., of Keene, New Hampshire. *(Photographs and Prints Division, Schomburg Center for Research in Black Culture, New York Public Library, Astor, Lenox and Tilden Foundations)*

15 Representing racial indeterminacy as white, in *Lost Boundaries:* Howard Carter (Richard Hylton), Dr. Scott Carter (Mel Ferrer), and Mrs. Carter (Beatrice Pearson). *(Photographs and Prints Division, Schomburg Center for Research in Black Culture, New York Public Library, Astor, Lenox and Tilden Foundations)*

16 Representing racial indeterminacy as black, in *Pinky* (1949), directed by Elia Kazan: Dicey (Ethel Waters) and her granddaughter Pinky (Jeanne Crain). *(Publicity still, Movie Star News, author's collection)*

17 White men offer to protect Pinky until they discover she lives in the black neighborhood, and then attempt to rape her. *(Academy of Motion Picture Arts and Sciences)*

18 William Faulkner's *Intruder in the Dust* (1949), directed by Clarence Brown: Chick Mallison (Claude Jarman Jr.), out fishing with his friend Alec (Elzy Emmanuel), finds himself indebted to the proud Lucas Beauchamp (Juano Hernandez). *(Academy of Motion Picture Arts and Sciences)*

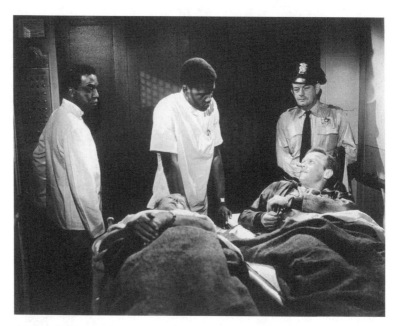

19 *No Way Out* (1950), directed by Joe Mankiewicz: doctor Luther Brooks (Sidney Poitier) and orderly Lefty Jones (Dots Johnson) absorb racial insults from hoodlum Ray Biddle (Richard Widmark), while his brother George (Harry Bellaver) depends on their care. *(Hollywood Museum Collection, City of Los Angeles, Department of Recreation and Parks)*

20 Director Elia Kazan in the 1940s. *(Billy Rose Theatre Collection, New York Public Library for the Performing Arts, Astor, Lenox and Tilden Foundations)*

21 Arthur Miller credited Elia Kazan with interpreting *Death of a Salesman* (1949) as a love story between father and son, Willy Loman (Lee J. Cobb) and Biff (Arthur Kennedy). *(Museum of the City of New York)*

22 Jo Mielziner's spare and expressionist design for *Death of a Salesman* allowed the scene to shift from Willy and Linda (Lee J. Cobb and Mildred Dunnock) in the kitchen to Biff and Happy (Arthur Kennedy and Cameron Mitchell) in their bedroom. *(Museum of the City of New York)*

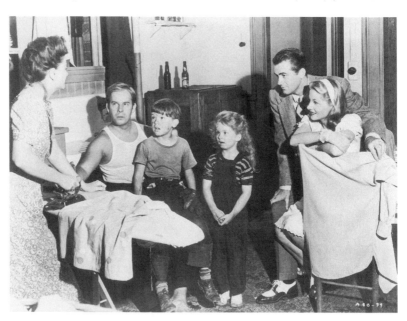

23 *From This Day Forward* (1946), directed by John Berry, contrasted the modern couple, Susie and Bill (Joan Fontaine and Mark Stevens), with their contentious relatives Hank and Martha (Henry Morgan and Rosemary DeCamp) in a crowded tenement with their children. *(Academy of Motion Picture Arts and Sciences)*

24 *The Marrying Kind* (1952), directed by George Cukor, uses claustrophobic compositions, such as in this scene with Florence and Chet (Judy Holliday and Aldo Ray), to convey class-inflected marital conflict. *(Academy of Motion Picture Arts and Sciences)*

25 Middle-class standards of consumption and glamour, on prominent display in magazines, remind Chet and Florence (Aldo Ray and Judy Holliday) of the world beyond their reach. *(Academy of Motion Picture Arts and Sciences)*

26 Paddy Chayefsky's television play *Marty* (1953) presents the aimless barroom chat of the butcher (Rod Steiger) and his friend Angie (Joe Mantell) as a "latent homosexual" alternative to sexual modernism. *(Kobal Collection)*

27 *Marty* (1955), directed by Delbert Mann, criticizes male peer culture and the sexual objectification of women: Marty (Ernest Borgnine) and the guys pore over a girlie magazine. *(Academy of Motion Picture Arts and Sciences)*

28 Marital realism in *Marty:* Clara (Betsy Blair) wants to respond to the warmth and sexual initiative of Marty (Ernest Borgnine) without losing her self-possession. *(Academy of Motion Picture Arts and Sciences)*

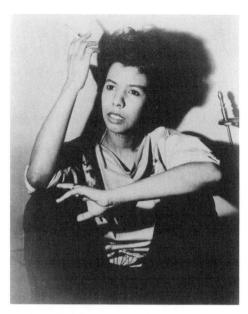

29 Playwright Lorraine Hansberry in the early 1960s. *(Ginn Briggs Photo, Estate of Robert Nemiroff, Photographs and Prints Division, Schomburg Center for Research in Black Culture,, New York Public Library, Astor, Lenox and Tilden Foundations)*

30 The clashes between Lena Younger (Claudia McNeil) and her daughter Beneatha (Diana Sands) reveal multiple stances of survival and resistance in *Raisin in the Sun* (1959), directed by Lloyd Richards. *(Photographs and Prints Division, Schomburg Center for Research in Black Culture, New York Public Library, Astor, Lenox and Tilden Foundations)*

31 A rare scene outside the tenement in *Raisin in the Sun* (1961), directed by Daniel Petrie, reveals the limited employment available to Walter Lee (Sidney Poitier). *(Publicity still, Movie Star News, author's collection)*

32 Drawing on "the strength of an incredible people, who, historically, have refused to give up": Beneatha Younger (Diana Sands), Ruth (Ruby Dee), Lena (Claudia McNeil), and Walter Lee (Sidney Poitier). *(Photofest, A Raisin in the Sun, Columbia Pictures)*

EVERYMAN
STORIES

COMPETING POSTWAR REPRESENTATIONS
OF UNIVERSALISM

A TTEMPTING TO COUNTER THE POSTWAR POLITICAL RETREAT FROM social reconstruction, Richard Durham, then living on Chicago's South Side, and Arthur Miller in Brooklyn turned to writing popular drama—Durham for local radio and Miller for the Broadway stage. Both writers came of age during the heyday of the 1930s popular front, worked in federal arts programs and radio drama, and were committed to continuing the unfinished work of the antifascist left. While Durham's work remained largely unknown outside of African American and left-wing circles, Miller's play *Death of a Salesman* became a household name.

Durham and Miller offered competing versions of universalism during a time in which conservatives were attempting to monopolize the definition of American belonging. In his radio dramas Durham proposed black protagonists to represent the universal and to articulate his broad conception of human rights. In contrast, Miller represented the universal through the figure of an American "everyman" disappointed by the false promises of the American Dream. Durham's radio voice would be silenced; Miller's strategy, with its unintended consequences of limiting who could be recognized as "the people," became the model for postwar family drama.

THE "TRULY UNIVERSAL PEOPLE": RICHARD DURHAM'S
DESTINATION FREEDOM

A powerful expression of racially inclusive universalism was broadcast on Chicago station WMAQ from June 1948 to September 1950: Richard Durham's radio drama series of black history, *Destination Freedom*. The scripts presented African American progressives as heroes fighting white supremacy in the U.S. in the context of global opposition to fascism and colonialism. Reversing the trading places conventions popularized in Hollywood films in which the "different" protagonist turns out to be just like everyone else, Durham's heroes are black people who confront injustice and whose protest against racialized boundaries extends to all excluded groups. According to Durham, finding "the common denominator" meant discovering the links "to every man who needs to change the status quo."[1]

Although the spirit of wartime unity had resulted in fledgling attempts at black programming for black and general audiences, radio in 1948 and 1949 remained a medium in which America was white and the nonwhite was "other." During a left-wing campaign in 1949 protesting racial minstrelsy on the radio and discriminatory employment practices in the broadcasting industry, actor Canada Lee demanded to know: "Where is the story of our lives in terms of the ghetto slums in which we must live? Where is the story in terms of the jobs not available? *Who would know us* only by listening to Amos and Andy, Beulah, Rochester, and minstrel shows?" (emphasis added).[2]

Richard Durham was ready to offer another way of knowing African Americans. Born in 1917 in Raymond, Mississippi, where his mother worked as a schoolteacher, Durham was one of seven children. He was raised on the South Side of Chicago, where the family moved in the early 1920s, his father finding work as a laborer in a printing plant and his mother as a waitress in a hospital cafeteria (in Chicago she was able to finish high school and begin a college course at night). Durham's mother encouraged his pleasure in books; he graduated from Hyde Park High School in 1937 and attended Northwestern University between 1938 and 1940.[3]

Durham was a participant in the mixture of black racial protest and interracial radicalism characteristic of Chicago's black and interracial popular front.[4] Durham worked as a dramatist for the Chicago Writers' Project branch of the WPA, and through his friendship with the writer and actor Robert Davis he was in touch with the literary radicals who had joined Davis in what remained of the late 1930s South Side Writers' Group that had encouraged Richard Wright, Gwendolyn Brooks, and Margaret Walker. Durham was also associated with the W. E. B. Du Bois Theatre Guild, an interracial group of progressive actors and writers, including African American actors Oscar Brown Jr., Jack Gibson, and Janice Kingslow as well as the young radical lawyer and aspiring actor Studs Terkel.[5] This group produced three or four plays, including *Waiting for Lefty,* in 1946. Durham later identified as his literary models acclaimed works of the antifascist left: Lillian Hellman's *The Little Foxes* (1939) and Richard Wright's *Native Son* (1940)—"two teachers I always kept with me."[6] At a writers' workshop in 1941 Durham met Robert Davis's sister, Clarice Davis, whom he married in 1942. Sometime after 1942 editor Ben Burns hired Durham to work for the *Chicago Defender.*

The black press was then at the height of its authority, prominent within black communities, and more visible outside the black community, because of its leadership of the Double V campaign ("the first V over our enemies from without—the second V for victory over our enemies from within") and its defiant publicizing of black protest against segregation in the military.[7] The *Defender* doubled its circulation between 1940 and 1946, featuring articles that insistently linked national to international issues, domestic demands with anticolonial initiatives.[8]

As "star investigative reporter and feature writer," Durham found "a freedom I'd never had before, except in poetry. We did things on the *Defender* then no one had ever tried before."[9] Durham eventually left the paper, but one of his final assignments was to cover the founding meetings of the United Nations. There African American journalists and activists were monitoring postwar commitment to wartime anticolonialism, "how far democratic principles might be stretched to embrace the rights of our brothers in the colonies," as well as its domestic applications to oppose segregation, questioning "to what extent the American Negro's own security at home will be guaranteed."[10]

Durham had been interested in radio since childhood; as a boy he won a contest sponsored by the Lone Ranger and later wrote scripts on a freelance basis for radio shows in Detroit and Chicago. The black press attempted forays into broadcasting in the 1920s and 1930s, although their limited resources made these hard to sustain.[11] After World War II Durham persuaded the *Chicago Defender* to join with Chicago station and CBS affiliate WBBM to sponsor a fifteen-minute weekly drama series,

Democracy USA, for which he produced the scripts. From 1946 to 1948 this series profiled famous African Americans and won twenty-two awards for its quality. Conflict between the station and the *Defender* ended *Democracy USA;* Durham had been dissatisfied with the show, describing its approach to the "Negro problem" as "vague and patronizing."[12] At the same time, he also defied the conventions of white address on radio with a pioneering soap opera about a black family, *Here Comes Tomorrow,* set in Chicago's South Side. Durham wrote all the scripts for this show, which was broadcast on WJJD for nearly a year in 1946.[13]

A harsh critic of popular commercial representations of black life, Durham sought in *Destination Freedom* to expose "the camouflage of crackpots and hypocrites—false liberals and false leaders—of radio's Beulahs and Amos and Andys and Hollywood's Stepin Fetchit and its masturbation with self-flattering dreams of passing for white such as *Pinky* and *Imitation of Life.*"[14] He wanted to produce stories that "cut through the lies, the distortions, the falsehoods, the stereotypes, and slanders that clutter up the field and hide the true nature of Negro characters." His literary goal was to "find the kernel of Negro life" and to "plant it in the sunshine of some artistic form" that would let readers and audiences recognize African American life rather than its minstrelsy stereotypes, "its inner beauty—its depth—its realistic emotions—its humanness." Durham placed himself in a tradition of literary humanism, linking his efforts with those of "Balzac with the Frenchmen of his day, Dickens for the poverty-stricken English, Gorki and Chekov for the Russians."

Rejecting the idea of the "Negro" as "problem," Durham offered instead a foundational narrative of American culture: "In this ocean of Negro life, with its cross currents and under-currents, lies the very soul of America." He saw more "drama and world implications" in resistance to segregation and white supremacy than in the diminished field of media representations. "All the stereotypes Hollywood or radio can turn out in a thousand years" could not approach the dramatic power of "the real life story of a single Negro in Alabama walking into a voting booth across a Ku Klux Klan line."[15]

Holding the copyright for both title and concept, Durham had unusual artistic control over *Destination Freedom.* He persuaded the *Chicago Defender* to sponsor its first thirteen weeks as a half-hour Sunday afternoon series on the Chicago NBC affiliate WMAQ. The station then carried the show, with several programs in 1950 sponsored by Urban League of Chicago.[16] Durham wrote all the scripts, reading histories by Du Bois and Carter Woodson and spending hours in libraries to piece together fragmentary historical accounts. He recruited actors from the Du Bois Theatre Guild.[17] In most cases he was able to resist NBC staff writers' efforts to doctor his scripts.[18] His experience in radio and his understanding of the cultural stakes prepared him to defend dramatic characterizations that reflected his historical and political interpretations. In a lengthy memo concerning the first *Destination Freedom* broadcast, a profile of Crispus Attucks—the first American killed by British soldiers in the Boston Massacre of 1770—Durham wrote: "A Negro character will be rebellious, biting, scornful, angry, cocky, as the occasion calls for—not forever humble, meek, etc. as some would like to imagine it." Direction that stressed the humility of African Americans, intended to reassure white listeners, reinforced racial stereotypes and rendered Attucks insignificant: "All of the fight, the anger, the effect of a man who'd give— and gave—his life for freedom—was torn off." Durham wanted to emphasize Attucks's agency in resisting the British in order to convey his humanity.

> Attucks picked his own destination—others didn't pick it for him. . . . Consequently, whether or not people "lose sympathy" with him is out of the question. . . . Your Attucks had somewhat the approach of an intelligent Pullman porter. Not the biting, fighting hero which would have carried the audience with him.

It was of vital importance, Durham believed, that both white and black audiences see the figures he portrayed as leaders whose authority was broadly respected: "to portray them as they are will give a greater education (to the audience) than a dozen lectures. . . . These characters (the lead ones) are leaders, initiators of historical movements—not accidents." And their leadership extended beyond the black community: "In most cases in their times they were leaders of white groups as well as Negro groups—as in the case with Attucks or Frederick Douglass."

Radio stereotypes of black women as devoted to domestic service or religious solace were also historically inadequate. "To present Harriet Tubman as a sort of refined version of Aunt Jemima would be criminal. To present her as a sort of religious fanatic would be far-fetched," Durham wrote. He wanted instead "to present her as so many Negro women are, dauntless, determined, who have a healthy contempt for people who live by race prejudice and who are quick to recognize and extend a warm hand to other humans." Durham's characterization of Tubman made her an ideal spokesperson for racial universalism.

Reminding network personnel that there would be no return to the prewar racial status quo, Durham warned against white self-deception:

> Negroes in general believe that their complete full-scale emancipation is *inevitable*. No amount of demands for abnormal subservience, segregation, or denials can stop it. They take equality (which in some circles is still controversial) as a matter of fact—as most people take the fact that two times two equals four.[19]

Durham used the history of African American resistance from the slavery era through the postwar period to show the long tradition of fighting for social equality and to place American resistance to racial discrimination within a worldwide struggle against fascism and colonialism.[20] Many of the scripts emphasized that these African American heroes consistently turned down individual privilege in favor of modeling a principled stand against all forms of discrimination. A 1949 chronicler of the show noted that "none of these Negro protagonists were ever given 'a break' in his struggle for freedom" and that "the writer [Durham] never showed— under any circumstance—that the status quo was satisfactory."[21]

Against the widespread assumption that humanity was white and people of color were the "problem" or the "other," Durham argued that African Americans were the "universal people," precisely because of their experience in resisting racial oppression in the U.S. "There has come to be created in America a people whose emotional fabrics and repeated experiences bring them very close to becoming in this atomic age the universal people." Durham acknowledged that "some leaders may have difficulty identifying their lives with this main life-stream—a Negro personality undergoing the experiences of sharecropping and segregation." To him African Americans *were* the "main life-stream."[22]

Durham imagined the mutual recognition of those facing southern white supremacy and those resisting other forms of exclusionary racialization and economic exploitation caused by imperialism and colonialism. "A Negro character confused by the caste system in the land of his birth is instantly identifiable with the 450,000,000 Indians in Asia, with Burmese Malayans, with the Jewish people whose identical struggle had led to the creation of a new nation," as well as with "millions of Europeans and white Americans who also want to uproot poverty and prejudice," he wrote. Durham singled out women as ideal allies, stressing a common break with paternalism: "One half of the population of the world—the women of the world of all races and creeds in their upward swing toward a real emancipation—find it natural to identify their striving with the direction and emotional realism in Negro life today."

Destination Freedom would reveal the "growing identity between individuals and groups" by creating "new types of human beings who have never strutted across a stage or been portrayed in a radio program or in a novel." To "break thru the stereotype—shatter the conventions and traditions" would enable Durham to show the people left out of radio and film genres, "materials from the history and current struggles for freedom." Durham was attempting to represent "ordinary Americans" by drawing on "stories we see constantly around us." His dramas showcased everyday people resisting racialized political and social exclusion: "It is in these people—the truly universal people . . . in the infinite variety that exists within the human family all across the continents—wherein lies the key to the essential meaning of life for the men and women of our day."[23]

Durham's conception of racial universalism shaped his construction of the radio stories of black heroism. In the program on the defeat of Reconstruction-era interracial alliance between freed slaves and poor whites, for example, Mississippi State Senator Charles Caldwell proposes legislation that would "abolish all segregation in the state of Mississippi . . . fine any railroad . . . guilty of Jim Crowism . . . recognize the property rights of women . . . establish free public schools unsegregated as to race, creed, or color." Later Caldwell appeals to white allies by arguing that, if Negroes lose the right to vote, "what's to stop them from saying it's not for Catholics, Jews, Irish, the foreign born? If the right to rule is for white men only, what will you say to the majority of the world who is not white?" Durham ended the script with Caldwell reminding his opponents that Reconstruction's defeat would be temporary, toasting the future: "for tomorrow when the whites and Negroes in my state will again try for the civil rights I tried to bring them."[24]

A number of Durham's scripts use racialized discrimination against African Americans and Jews as interchangeable signifiers of racism and assumed that a common fight against discrimination could build solidarity between African Americans and Jews.[25] The speech he wrote for Illinois congressman Oscar De Priest—elected in 1928 as the first African American to serve in Congress since Reconstruction—declared, "Freedom belongs not to a group of men, nor to a clan, nor to a single party, but to the black and white, Jew and Gentile who have earned it in wars and work."[26] Durham's script on Ralph Bunche, "Peace Mediator," begins with a description of his skill at mediating between Arabs and Jews in Palestine arising from his familiarity with both "the struggles of colonial people and of racial minorities." The "biggest story of his life" is Bunche's brave identification, as a high school student, of three white vigilantes who killed a Jewish storekeeper in Los Angeles. Durham contrasts Bunche's sense of solidarity with the narrow parochialism of his white editor, who advises him to keep the story quiet: "Some things, boy, you can't mess with. Rose was Jewish, moved into that restrictive covenant area. Them vigilantes been after him ever since." When Bunche defends the citizenship rights of the Jewish storekeeper, the editor responds, "Some citizen's here got more power'n others." In Durham's account Bunche's principled intervention catches the attention of the mayor of Los Angeles and leads to a scholarship in political science at Harvard and Bunche's future illustrious career.[27]

In another 1949 script Durham represents Mary Church Terrell's stand against discrimination as a rejection of Nazi-like racialization of Jews.[28] When a German school questions her about her "race," assuring her that her color is no issue, she declines to study there on the grounds that "once one accepts discrimination against another, he's preparing the way for his own slavery." Later in the script Terrell says that she encourages women to teach their children to be "true fighters for freedom and humanity . . . for their neighbors, Jews or Negroes."[29]

"Segregation Incorporated" (1949) is an exposé in which Durham links white supremacist segregationist practices in Washington, D.C. to the Nazi racialization of Jews. In this script he also shows residential exclusion as economically driven, affecting Jews, Catholics, and Mexicans as well as Negroes. Although the station censored Durham's claim that racial segregation promoted a "master-race" philosophy in the U.S., the script emphasized the irony of American Occupation laws in Berlin that outlawed Nazi discrimination on grounds of "race, creed, or political opinion" and enabled "the citizens of Berlin to enjoy more freedom than the Negro citizens of Washington, D.C."[30] In a 1983 interview Durham articulated the beliefs that informed these scripts:

> Racial animosity is essentially an artificial thing. It has to be artificially imposed and artificially maintained. Unless it's constantly supplied, it can't last in a person's normal going-about. . . . There has to be a constant resup-

ply of some motivation for the animosity, or for the separation, or for the isolation of a particular group—or it will break down.[31]

Although *Destination Freedom* was recognized and honored, Durham's extraordinary broadcasts never reached beyond the frequencies of WMAQ; in 1949 and 1950 the programs were attacked by local chapters of the American Legion and Knights of Columbus.[32] Durham described the pressures on him and the changing political environment in a letter to his friend Langston Hughes in December 1949. The series was still "going strong," although "censorship drops down on me unexpectedly. . . . Recently I took the tactic of refusing to blue-pencil anything that I felt was healthy for inspiring Negroes to a more militant struggle." The network staff "threatened and cajoled," but Durham "held pat." His anticommunist accusers turned up the heat: "Then they said I 'must be a Red.'" Hughes himself had faced vicious attacks since 1940 for publicly espousing left-wing positions, and Durham joked: "Can you imagine that? White folks will call you red in a minute, won't they?" Durham was pushed to write in the occasional "neutral character," but he "still put words like this in the mouths of some of my colored women characters (when they're giving advice to white women): 'any white woman who accepts white supremacy is getting ready to sleep with fascism.'"[33]

By August 1950 Durham's *Destination Freedom* was canceled; the station appropriated the name for a series celebrating the victors in American history. Hosted by a fictional Paul Revere, the new *Destination Freedom* profiled white American war heroes such as Nathan Hale and Dwight D. Eisenhower alongside stories of "average people."[34] Durham would not be silenced; he continued to write in many different venues in the years to come.[35] But the replacement of *Destination Freedom*—and its rich vision of racial universalism—with so diminished a version of Americanism was a warning of things to come.

THE EVOLUTION OF ARTHUR MILLER'S ORDINARY FAMILY

Opening in New York on February 10, 1949, Arthur Miller's *Death of a Salesman* set new standards for what constituted American, what would be commonly depicted as the family, and what could represent universality. The play was embraced by audiences, hailed by critics, and published in book form, becoming one of the most widely seen, read, and performed plays in the twentieth century.[36] Audiences greeted *Salesman* in 1949 with excitement at least in part because the success of *All My Sons* in 1947 had reawakened dreams of a socially engaged theater, making Miller the popular social dramatist of the postwar years. Many of Miller's fellow left-wing playwrights had abandoned the theater for Hollywood screenwriting, believing that film was the most effective medium through which to "reach the people"; *All My Sons* showed that popular theater still had that power.[37] It established some of the parameters of *Salesman,* though the later play experimented more substantially with theatrical conventions.

Miller had been inspired by the 1940 New York production of *Juno and the Paycock* by the Irish Communist Sean O'Casey, about a family whose disintegration parallels a national political crisis.[38] In *All My Sons* Miller uses the family drama to expose the tensions between parochial and cosmopolitan forms of solidarity, between fathers and their battle-weary sons in World War II, between wartime sacrifice and profiteering. The Keller family—midwestern, white, ethnically unmarked, middle class—represents the ordinary American family. Joe, the self-made father, has shipped defective airplane parts to the military and let his business partner take the rap and go to jail. Chris, the son, is thirty-two (Arthur Miller was the same age at the time the play was produced); Miller describes him as a man "capable of immense affection and loyalty." The mother, Kate, resembles the domineering mother Philip Wylie critiqued in his 1942 best-seller *Generation of Vipers,* described as a woman of "uncontrolled inspirations and an overwhelming capacity for love." Chris returns from the war the only survivor of his company. He wants to marry Annie, the girl next door, formerly engaged to his brother, who has been reported missing for three years. Kate discourages the marriage: to acknowledge her older son's death would be to reveal her husband's complicity.

The younger generation (represented by Chris, Annie, and Annie's brother George) expresses the play's central theme—how to reconcile the dissonance capitalist profit put between war's holy purposes and profane practices. This was an issue hotly debated since the 1930s Nye Commission's investigation into the corporate and financial interests that influenced the U.S. decision to enter World War I had confirmed socialist anti-war rhetoric. Miller's interest in exploring the intertwining of social and psychological denial helped him create recognizable characters who expressed wartime's contradictions in their everyday family interaction.[39] The play was published in book form to coincide with its Broadway opening in January 1947.[40] Lines forming around the theater box office testified to the immediacy of the play's success.

The 1947 staging of *All My Sons* was a postwar reincarnation of the glories of the prewar theatrical left. Former members of the Group Theatre shaped the production: producer Harold Clurman, director Elia Kazan, set designer Mordecai Gorelik, and actors Arthur Kennedy and Karl Malden, who played the sons. Productions by the Group in the 1930s had first inspired Miller to write for the theater; he was pleased for his play to be produced by people associated with the "mixture of Stanislavsky and social protest" that characterized "the best theater we ever had."[41]

Theatrical power in 1947 was seen to emanate from the playwright, in partnership with a director and the actors who would realize his vision. Miller later tried to capture an attitude toward his "pridefully tough" profession in the 1940s: "no sissy literary nonsense in cranking a play together but a job for cigar-chewing mechanics serving—according to the going myth of the time—the whole American people."[42] The writer-director partnership in *All My Sons* began an important relationship for Miller and Kazan, both professionally and personally.[43] Kazan later remarked that "the professional standing of a director depends on the plays he's able to attract"; he was intrigued by Miller's play. He was also competing with his partner at the time, Harold Clurman: "[Miller] wanted me to direct his play. . . . Art admired Harold but felt closer to me."[44] Kazan was pleased that Miller admired the Group Theatre and described their strengthening rapport:

> We were both out of the Depression, both left-wingers, both had problems with our fathers, considered their business worlds antihuman. We were soon exchanging every intimacy. I was to find that Art had many problems similar to my own in his home life; he'd been maritally unsteady, as I had been all my married life, but he'd been bound down by his inhibitions. He frequented our household. . . . Art was like a member of my family; I saw him almost daily, and usually at my home.[45]

To Miller, Kazan was the famous director connected with the Group Theatre, the "real glamour."[46] Miller's memoir highlighted Kazan's status as a left-wing celebrity: "Though he never mentioned political people or ideas, it was assumed that he identified himself with the idealism of the left, and that his emotional and intellectual loyalties lay with the workers and the simple and the poor." For Miller, Kazan personified the affiliations of left internationalism: "like Odets, he wore the faded colors of the thirties into the forties and fifties, the resonance of the culture of antifascism that had once united artists everywhere in the world."[47] Miller was more guarded in describing their emotional connection—he "felt a partnership without ever forgetting that it was an illusion"—but also acknowledged their intimacy: he "loved [Kazan] like a brother."[48]

In January 1947 New York critics recognized *All My Sons* as a new manifestation of left-wing social drama, praising actors "as true as if this was the Group all over again" for bringing serious issues to light: "no star parts . . . story and characters are evenly balanced in a vibrant play about vigorous people . . . actors play to each other not to the audience."[49] Although one Boston critic published an attack in a Hearst paper on *All My Sons* as "communist," he was unsuccessful in stirring up popular outrage. The designation of antifascist, antiracist, pro-labor groups as "subversive organizations" by the attorney general would not be announced until March 1947; HUAC's investigation of the film industry would become public in October 1947. The conservative Boston theater critic Elliot Norton praised Miller as the dramatic "catch of the season."[50] Even critics divided on the merits of the play continued to affirm its social themes; they cheered the play's "emphatic statement" about "postwar problems."[51] Coming from a range of political affiliations, critics identified the play's political concerns as an integral aspect of the drama. *Time* thought the play expressed "passion . . . without soapbox oratory."[52] The *Daily Worker* applauded Miller as a leading playwright in the quest to "restore and deepen social drama in America."[53]

Stage instructions for *All My Sons* establish its setting as a backyard "in the outskirts of an American town," in "August of our era." Critics applauded Miller's choice of "a typical American backyard of a typical American home" as the scene of an unfolding "tragedy."[54] Since 1939 the characters in Miller's plays had been moving from the ethnically inflected East to the Midwest, which Miller later remembered identifying as the "real America."[55] To Brooks Atkinson of the *New York Times* Miller had a "special gift for creating characters who are people and not merely points of view."[56]

Miller and Kazan's commitment to Method acting—which critic Steve Vineberg encapsulated as "making the theatrical familiar and the familiar dramatically interesting"—was reflected in their casting of Method-trained actors as Chris and George, the play's truth-telling younger generation, and actors associated with genre and theatrical artificiality as the deluded older generation, Joe and Kate Keller.[57]

Although Miller used the "normal" to encourage the identification of his audience, in the play's crisis social solidarity and responsibility conflict with traditional family claims. The critics seemed comfortable with Miller's depiction of family loyalties as parochial and narrow. His left-wing and masculinist focus drew the boundaries between public and private in such a way as to contrast, in the words of the *New Masses* reviewer, "the smaller less strenuous loyalty" of "decent family life" against what was imagined to be a more strenuous loyalty to "society." William Hawkins of the *New York World Telegram* saw "the strength of the play" as "its revelation that a wide horizon is becoming a necessity for intimate happiness"; the *New Masses* reviewer heard a similar message, that "self-fulfillment is possible only within a social frame."[58] *All My Sons* expressed an antidomestic sensibility; superior to the private loyalties of the family were the social bonds exemplified by the potential for solidarity of the CIO labor movement and within the shared national purpose of the war against fascism.

To portray family loyalties as constraining, Kate Keller must be neurotic and controlling. Miller greatly admired Sidney Howard's play *Silver Chord* (1926), its title becoming the term that entered the language denoting mothers as domineering and committed to preventing sons' romantic attachments.[59] The "bad" mother in *All My Sons* was a departure from the heroic representations of working-class ethnic motherhood that Betty Smith and Katherine Forbes produced during the war. Contemporary critics noticed how Beth Merrill's characterization of Kate Keller departed from the gallant and sustaining mothers they had become accustomed to seeing in wartime narratives: they described her character as "neurotic and dominating," "half-insane," "desperately ruthless," "living in a mental twilight . . . her motives based on dependence rather than morale."[60]

In Miller's play members of the family achieve their heroism as they adopt public and masculine loyalties. The "kindly loving mother who wants her brood to be safe and her home undisturbed" turns out, according to Clurman, to be "the villain" in the play, the embodiment of parochialism. The play proposed a more "strenuous" kind of loyalty in which "everything in the family and neighborhood life as well as many things in national and international life ties these characters into a tight web of relationships."[61]

All My Sons earned Miller two thousand dollars a week in royalties and confirmed his stature as the new star playwright on Broadway. In April

1947 *All My Sons* won the New York Drama Critics' Circle Award over its chief competitor, Eugene O'Neil's *The Iceman Cometh*.[62] By June the play had been sold to Universal-International for a film production, suggesting that left-wing social drama continued to be seen as commercially viable.[63]

The fate of the film demonstrates the vulnerability of politically inflected family drama as well as the sophistication of an audience able to recognize its political critique and protest its suppression. The film production was dominated by people affiliated with Hollywood's progressive and antifascist left who attempted to remain faithful to Miller's drama. Bowing to directives from the production code office, however, they rendered Keller's climactic suicide "acceptable" by showing him to be mentally unbalanced; paring down the play's social analysis, they narrowed the explanatory framework for Joe Keller's selfishness. In their Hollywood surveillance files the FBI remarked on the play's left-wing focus and noted the "open attack" on the family in *All My Sons* as particularly "sickening."[64]

When the film opened in March 1948, in spite of its narrative evasions, many reviewers still heard the play's social message; they recognized its dramatic realism as related to wartime and postwar political debates. Bosley Crowther blamed HUAC investigations for producing such "desperate caution" in the film community that the play's "sharp and unmistakable point" questioning a system of war profiteering was blunted; in the play a whole "social structure which tolerates and even encourages private greed" and war profiteering is reduced to "the greed and narrowmindedness of one man."[65]

MILLER'S SEARCH FOR "THE PEOPLE," 1947–1948

Though audience enthusiasm assured Miller he had succeeded in using drama to "reach the people," his sudden financial success unsettled his sense, formed by his family's economic decline in the early 1930s, that he was one of "the people." He prided himself on having had "more than a taste of life at the bottom," and on living in such a way that he remained ordinary. In a profile for *PM* he described "getting away from people involved in cultural work" by working as a steamfitter in the Brooklyn Navy Yards during the war, "just to be around other people."[66] Weeks after the opening of *All My Sons* Miller found a job in a factory, assembling beer box dividers; he lasted there about a week.[67]

Already known for his support of the CIO labor movement, his opposition to the Taft-Hartley bill, and support for Henry Wallace's "One

World" alternative to the emerging cold war, Miller contributed his new celebrity to other radical causes.[68] He joined other "prominent Americans" in signing statements issued by the Civil Rights Congress, which defended the Communist Party as a legitimate political party and condemned HUAC for its investigations of left-wing activism; these investigations constituted, according to the statement, "the initial phase of a sweeping attack upon the entire labor and progressive movement in the U.S." In September 1947 Miller donated the proceeds from a Polish production of *All My Sons* to a relief drive for children sponsored by the League of Women in Poland, affiliated with the left-initiated Congress of American Women.[69] Miller also attended a series of meetings of a Communist writers' group in 1947. Explaining his presence at "four or five" of these meetings to HUAC in 1956, he acknowledged that "by then I was quite well-known" and had attended meetings in order to locate "his ideas in relation to Marxism."[70]

Still searching for the "people" and restless in his marriage, which he later called a "fraudulent pretension to monogamous contentment," Miller took to wandering the streets of Brooklyn.[71] The world he stumbled into in the winter of 1947 was the "gangster-ridden unions, assassinations, beatings" of the Brooklyn waterfront. He was intrigued by the story of a young longshoreman who had attempted to lead a rank-and-file revolt within the union and had then mysteriously disappeared.

Miller could not break into the working-class culture of longshoremen on his own, but his interest in doing so, combined with his left-wing literary celebrity, gained him two new friends and guides. Mitch Berenson, an organizer for the International Ladies Garment Workers' Union from the age of fifteen, was the first "authentic" working-class radical Miller had encountered. Jimmy Longhi, a young lawyer-protégé of Vito Marcantonio (the radical Congressman from East Harlem and leader of New York's American Labor Party), had ties both to the Italian working-class families in the waterfront district and to "Tough Tony" Anastasia, who ran the International Longshoremen's Association local and was involved in the mob skimming of commerce that went through the port.[72] To Berenson and Longhi, Miller was a source of contacts, funds, and support for a new longshoremen's movement.[73] For his part Miller hoped to gain access to the "mysterious world at the water's edge" and to find political continuity with the radicalism of the late 1930s and the war years in the company of his new friends, "unambiguous men striking out heroically against unjust power." What Miller found was a "cultural shift that was completely new" in his experience; a "certain rising ambiguity" would infuse his political sensibilities and his next creative work. Looking back on this period, Miller commented that postwar America "was becoming suspiciously unreal."[74]

With his new friend Longhi, Miller found still more ambiguity when he traveled to France and Italy in February 1948. The view from Europe, where a new postwar American empire seemed to be taking shape, was strikingly different from Richard Durham's exposure to debates in the United Nations over the future of colonialism. Rather than inspired, as Durham was, by the momentum of a new world majority breaking away from a colonial past, Miller was troubled by what he read in the papers of Europeans "relying on America to rearrange a new civilization." The Marshall Plan, announced in the U.S. in June 1947, its implications for the postwar realignment of Germany with the West, and the new demonization of Russia were in the news every day. Italy's Communist Party was the largest in Europe, but Miller found that its leaders were quietly encouraging people to vote Christian Democratic in order not to jeopardize American food shipments. Looking up relatives of Brooklyn longshoremen for Longhi's election campaign on the American Labor Party ticket, Miller found oppositions that appeared irrevocable: "Europe was full of relatives and in America the pull of the blood connection was gone." On this trip Miller was also sobered by his distance from Jewish survivors of the German death camps, whom he encountered in Bari trying to get to Palestine. Like George Stevens, he was later upset by his "failure to recognize myself in them." Miller did not write in his memoir about the decisive loss of the Progressive Party in the fall of 1948 and mentioned only in passing Jimmy Longhi's electoral defeat. Both events marked, however, an important shift in the broader political and cultural context for his work.[75]

Miller's ongoing search for a language with which to animate the people was transformed by attending a preview of Tennessee Williams's *A Streetcar Named Desire,* directed by Kazan in December 1947. Miller and Williams inhabited the same cultural and political world and had seen each other "on and off" in 1947, according to Miller. He was drawn to *Streetcar* with "envious curiosity," even though he disapproved of the title as "too garishly attention-getting."[76] Miller recognized a desire to "change the world" and a concern for psychological realism akin to his own, but understood that Williams used language in a lyrical and newly fluid way. *Streetcar* demonstrated that dialogue did not have to be instructional, to tell the story. "With *Streetcar*," he later acknowledged, "Tennessee had printed a license to speak at full throat."[77]

THE CREATION OF AN ORDINARY AMERICAN TRAGEDY: *DEATH OF A SALESMAN*

A common literary subject and familiar to Miller since childhood, the figure of the salesman first appeared in Miller's writing when he was seventeen.[78] "In Memoriam" (1932) is a portrait of Schoenzeit, whose profession—"if one may call such dignified slavery a profession"—is that of salesman for Miltex (the coat manufacturing company owned by Miller's father). One day Miller helps Schoenzeit carry samples to a Bronx buyer and sees "Schoenzeit's soul crumpled and broken beyond repair" when he is forced to ask Miller, the boss's son, for subway fare. Schoenzeit fails to make the sale and is "profusely maltreated" by the staff at the buyer's office. Miller ends the sketch with an ambiguous response to hearing the news that Schoenzeit has thrown himself under a subway train: "My only recollection of that second when I heard those words is a slow exhaling of my breath and a cool, soft, glowing smile within my soul."[79]

As early as 1937 Miller wrote sketches of Willy, Hap, and Biff, and pages of what he thought of as realistic dialogue for them. Miller attached the name "Loman" to the salesman sometime between 1942 and 1947, remembering the name as inspired by a verbal reference attached to a "terror-stricken man calling into the void for help that will never come" in Fritz Lang's 1933 film *The Testament of Dr. Mabuse*.[80]

To Miller the salesman's "profession" exemplified the paradoxes of capitalist possibilities and alienation: the necessity for charisma and enterprise and the promises of mobility and accumulation, the burden of persuasion, the vulnerability to executive coercion and economic vicissitudes, the potential for masculine failure and anomie. The generic category of salesman allowed Miller to allude to everyone from modest peddler and ill-compensated commercial traveler to highly paid corporate trader and advertising pitchman. Miller protected the elasticity of his symbol by not specifying the salesman's wares. In the early short story Miller does not specify the age of Schoenzeit; to Willy Loman's dilemma Miller adds the special indignities of aging and the vulnerability of the consumer who "gets stuck" with other salesmen's products, such as the refrigerator that falls apart before he has paid for it.

Miller chose the title before writing the play: from the beginning the salesman was headed toward his death. He represented the salesman's failed dreams through their cost on the family. He recalled wanting to critique the hollowness of the so-called American Century, to challenge the illusions of the new American empire by setting "before the captains and the so smugly confident kings the corpse of a believer."[81]

Careful to avoid what he saw as the female terrain of the domestic sphere or the mannered interplay of the drawing room, Miller attempted to simulate, with a nonlinear and dreamlike dramatic structure, family life as it is lived. With Kazan's innovative staging and set and lighting by designer Jo Mielziner, Miller sought to convey historical memory in a new way.[82] The spare and expressionist staging marked the play as less domestic and more masculine.[83] Unlike *All My Sons,* in which the past unfolds as the action of the present moves forward, *Death of a Salesman* allows the past to be as real to the characters as what is happening in the present. In his notebook fragments Miller wrote: "Life is formless. Its interconnections are concealed by lapses of time, by events occurring in separate places, by the hiatus of memory. We live in the world made by men and the past."[84] Combining insights from Marx and Freud, Miller roamed freely between the voices of children and adults, speaking concurrently on several levels of time and memory. Contemporary critics described Miller's dramatic technique as cinematic; a few also identified its debts to radio technique, especially the use of overlapping voices in changing scenes.[85]

This spare and, to Miller's mind, masculine staging was central to his conception of the play's revelation that the salesman's is a "pseudo life." When he wrote about the play Miller emphasized his distance from the character, although as soon as it began to be performed he reported himself to be surprised by the audience's response—"*too much* identification with Willy, too much weeping." Writing about *Salesman* after a year on Broadway, Miller ascribed distance to the male and identification to the female: "I can see my wife's eyes as I read a—to me—hilarious scene. . . . She was weeping. I confess that I laughed more during the writing of this play than I have ever done." At this point he was willing to pronounce the "moral" of the story:

> The tragedy of Willy Loman is that he gave his life, or sold it, to justify the waste of it. It is the tragedy of a man who did believe that he alone was not meeting the qualifications laid down for mankind by those clean-shaven frontiersmen who inhabit the peaks of broadcasting and advertising offices.

Miller recalled thinking that the "play's ironies were being dimmed by all this empathy. After all . . . I had written it for three unadorned black platforms, with a single flute in the air and without softening transitions—a slashing structure, I had thought."[86] Looking more closely at how Miller made the Lomans familiar may reveal why the play evoked the empathetic response that so surprised him.

In order for theater to "change the world" Miller wanted to reach "beyond the small alienated minority . . . already converted" to the aims of the avant-garde to "those who accepted everything as it was."[87] To begin he provided Willy with a prototypically "American" genealogy before inverting his American success. Unlike *A Tree Grows in Brooklyn* or *I Remember Mama,* in which being born in Brooklyn or San Francisco makes you American, in *Salesman* Americanness is associated with the frontier. Willy's father, a restless inventor who crossed the continental U.S. in a wagon, suggests the entrepreneur; in the character of Willy's brother Ben Miller links the frontier with imperial adventure. "Why boys, when I was seventeen I walked into the jungle, and when I was twenty-one I walked out. And by God I was rich!" Ben sets down the rules: "Never fight fair with a stranger, boy. You'll never get out of the jungle that way." He admires the "fearless characters" who fill the Stock Exchange. Later Ben contrasts Willy's domesticated sales territory to this more virile realm: "Get out of these cities, they're full of talk and time payments and courts of law. Screw on your fists and you can fight for a fortune up there."

Thus Willy longs for uncrowded, open spaces. "The street is lined with cars. There's not a breath of fresh air in the neighborhood. The grass don't grow any more, you can't raise a carrot in the back yard." His language echoes restless settlers fleeing "civilization": "There's more people! That's what's ruining this country! Population is getting out of control." Miller links Willy's urban claustrophobia to a modest agrarian American dream: "You wait, kid, Before it's all over, we're gonna get a little place in the country, and I'll raise some vegetables, a couple of chickens."

To Willy's eldest son, Biff, the frontier offers a palliative to the emasculations of urban white-collar labor. Referring to his time in "Nebraska when I herded cattle, and the Dakotas and Arizona, and now in Texas," he proposes to "buy a ranch. Raise cattle, use our muscles. Men built like we are should be working out in the open." Both Willy and Biff associate "real" manhood with manual labor. Willy insults his successful businessman neighbor, Charley, by his insistence that "a man who can't handle tools is not a man." Biff eulogizes Willy in the requiem: "There's more of him [Willy] in that front stoop than in all the sales he ever made." Charley and Linda apparently concur. Charley: "Yeah. He was a happy man with a batch of cement." Linda: "He was so wonderful with his hands."

While Miller's definitions of "American" made his characters and their aspirations recognizable to his audiences, the everyman strategy also reinforced conventional boundaries of American nationhood, identity, and masculinity. Willy's quip that "a man who can't handle tools isn't a man" appears in the 1949 profiles of Miller that mention his building the one-room house in Connecticut in which he wrote the play. The association of manual labor and masculinity echoed a 1930s proletarian ideal; it legitimated Miller's claim to be ordinary and anticipated a new, middle-class, suburban, do-it-yourself yardstick for manhood. In one profile Miller was described as responding to his sudden success from *Salesman* by planning to "head for his Connecticut retreat and relax in manual labor."[88]

Miller's ordinary American family is unmarked ethnically and barely located geographically. Only the reference to Ebbets Field, home of the Brooklyn Dodgers, indicates the setting of *Death of a Salesman*. Unlike Betty Smith's Brooklyn, invoked with dense sensory memories, corner merchants, and ethnic cosmopolitanism, the Brooklyn of Willy Loman is stripped down, like the set itself, outlined only faintly as a place that was once green and is now built up and crowded. The one trace of a non-generic Brooklyn is Charley; unlike Linda, whose world is confined to her family and who speaks in homilies, and Willy, who much of the time uses a language of self-help and radio advertising jingles, Charley utters many of the lines that critics identified to be Jewishly inflected.[89]

Charley and his son, Bernard, a successful lawyer, are foils for Willy and his sons: they represent, in Willy's terms, a failed masculinity. Both Charley and Bernard offer neighborly concern and assistance; Charley's handouts of cash sustain Willy's family. There is no mother in the family of Charley and Bernard: family ties here are equated with fathers and sons. Miller depicts neighborliness and reciprocal assistance as a relationship between men, marking his distance from more common accounts of female support networks as well as from the territory of soap operas, with their focus on family and neighborhood.

Like *All My Sons, Salesman* establishes an embattled relationship between husband and wife. Miller originally imagined that "Willy should be small and his wife should be very big," signaling his intention to use physical size to show Willy's diminished stature in the world and Linda's overpowering presence in the home.[90] Managing Willy's meager earnings gives Linda the responsibility to make whatever Willy brings home cover the needs of the household. The Lomans' financial arguments are filled with accusations of familial and masculine inadequacy.

Willy and Linda's dialogue reveals that despite Linda's attempted reassurance there is never enough, unlike the family in Kathryn Forbes's *Mama's Bank Account*, in which Mama produces the illusion that there always is. In discussions between Willy and Linda there is a sharp division of labor: he inflates his sales, she estimates his commission; he adjusts his count, she recalculates; he asks how much they owe, she adds up the bills. As the producer, Willy is wounded by the inadequacy of his compensation; as the manager of the budget, Linda becomes his accuser, responsible for the black hole of time payments and repairs on shoddy products they have previously purchased. In his April 1948 *Salesman* notebook Miller wrote, "W. resents Linda's unbroken patient forgiveness (knowing that there must be great hidden hatred for him in her heart)."[91] Although Linda attempts to comfort Willy, her presence, and the stockings she is always mending, underscore his inadequacy.

Miller himself accuses Linda by having her voice the domestic concerns that constrain Willy and making her complicit in the delusion that so frustrates Biff. As in other twentieth-century American texts, consuming is coded as female.[92] Linda purchases the new, whipped "American-type" cheese and, duped by the largest ads, selects the faulty refrigerator. She overestimates capitalist paternalism and promises of mobility, referring to Willy's "beautiful job" and asking, "Why must everybody conquer the world? You're well-liked and the boys love you and someday . . . why old man Wagner told him just the other day that if he keeps it up he'll be a member of the firm, didn't he Willy?" If Miller thought of the salesman as living a "pseudo life that thought to touch the clouds by standing on top of a refrigerator, waving a paid up mortgage at the moon, victorious at last," it is Linda who makes the last payment on the house and echoes the words "free and clear." As in *All My Sons*, the domestic and the familial are equated with the parochial and narrow, all the more poignantly in the salesman's mélange of personal and occupational disappointments.

In his staging of *Salesman* Kazan emphasized the relationship between father and son over that of husband and wife. While writing the play, Miller reminded himself to "discover—How it happens that Willy's life is in Biff's hands—aside from Biff succeeding."[93] Here Miller was interrogating patriarchal expectations more common in immigrant and first-generation fathers than in other family cultures: immigrant experience often encapsulated regional, social, and economic changes that would otherwise have unfolded over generations.[94] Clifford Odets's Jewish family plays had explored this dynamic; Miller employed frontier imagery to suggest that the conflict between Willy and Biff was generically American.

Miller later recalled that Kazan, after reading *Salesman,* remarked on its sadness and then spoke of his own father.[95] Miller gave Kazan credit for interpreting *Salesman* as a love story, not between husband and wife but between father and son, and orchestrating its tempo accordingly, cresting with Willy's interpretation of his power to make Biff cry: "Isn't that—isn't that remarkable? Biff—he likes me!"[96] Writing about the play after its first year of success, Miller noted one cost of the staging, his disappointment that "the self-realization of the older son, Biff, is not a weightier balance to Willy's disaster in the audience mind." But Miller acceded to Kazan's focus in the introduction to his collected plays (1957): Willy finally knows "in his last extremity that the love which had always been in the room unlocated was now found."[97]

Miller and Kazan indicated their interest in the relationship between father and son by casting former Group Theatre Method-trained actors Lee J. Cobb and Arthur Kennedy for the parts of Willy and Biff. Kazan and Miller meant to spotlight Biff as the truth sayer—perhaps hoping that audiences might remember Arthur Kennedy's heroic role as Chris in *All My Sons.* They may also have believed that this focus would distance their work from portrayals of the domestic as a female realm.

The opening of *Death of a Salesman* was awaited with great anticipation because of the success of *All My Sons. PM'*s theater critic Louis Kronenberger observed that "few things in Broadway history can have had such a sensational build-up."[98] Most of the initial reviewers for the daily press and for popular magazines were enthusiastic, and, as critic Gerald Weales has commented, "*Salesman* became the play of the moment, which in the context of Broadway, means that it was given extensive attention—comment, interviews, pictures—in all the popular media."[99] Ticket lines stretched around the block, performances were immediately sold out, and sales remained vigorous for its long New York run. At the end of each performance critics described audience response as silence, then outbursts, then thunderous applause.

Recalling the opening night in Philadelphia, Miller noted an unusual depth of emotionalism instead of the ironic laughter he had anticipated:

> There was no applause at the final curtain. . . . With the curtain down, some people stood to put their coats on and then sat down again, some, especially men, were openly weeping. People crossed the theater to stand quietly talking with one another. It seemed forever before someone remembered to applaud, and then there was no end to it.

He also became aware that some in the audience heard his anticapitalist critique of the salesman's pseudo life as a call to reform corporate personnel policies.

> I . . . saw a distinguished looking elderly man being led up the aisle; he was talking excitedly into the ear of what seemed to be his male secretary or assistant. This, I learned, was Bernard Gimbel, head of the department store chain, who that night gave an order that no one in his stores was to be fired for being overage.[100]

Howard Fuller, president of the Fuller Brush Company, also became enthusiastic about the play and invited Miller to dinner in order, as Miller put it later, "to draw on my wisdom to clarify his salesmen's motives for quitting the firm so frequently."[101]

Miller had indeed written a popular text that spoke directly to the people. His play made *men* weep; their tears affirmed Miller's dramatic authority. His corporate admirers provided public and masculine legitimation while ignoring Miller's social critique. *Death of a Salesman* successfully appropriated the familial and psychological from the feminized venues of radio soap opera, popular fiction, and melodramatic film, reendowing the family story with the masculine authority of serious drama.

Miller's accomplishment was all the more noteworthy when juxtaposed to the work of his most important peer, the much less insistently masculinist Tennessee Williams. League of American Writers author Gilbert Gabriel observed that Miller and Williams shared an emotional range, especially in conveying sadness: "same sensitiveness, same gifted suggestiveness, and steeping sentimentality, the same fling of heavy-petalled phrases upon a pool of universal grieving." In Gabriel's estimation it was

Miller's depictions of "ordinary people" that made him seem to be "a much more aggressive masculine artist." Miller's characterization of the people underwrote his achievement as a "masculine artist," affirming fixed rather than fluid heterosexual norms. According to Gabriel, Miller's "characters insist on their usualness. They may have battles in the business district or wailing walls in Flatbush but not bats in the belfry. They are practically anybody's folks."[102]

Two weeks after the sensational opening of *Death of a Salesman,* and perhaps in response to the unexpected empathy with Willy, Miller published an essay in the *New York Times* entitled "Tragedy and the Common Man" in which he outlined a dramatic theory that encompassed his play as a tragedy—without mentioning it by name.[103] By orienting interpretations in this direction, Miller encouraged audiences to read his portrayal of generic American-ness and his flowing together of past and present as an *alternative* to historically and socially situated characterization.

Reading the Loman family as audience surrogates implicitly reiterated the boundaries of *Salesman*'s everyman universalism. Many New York theater critics, such as Brooks Atkinson, included themselves in Miller's conception of everyman: Miller wrote "as an American with an affectionate understanding of American family people and their family problems, and *everybody* recognizes in his tragic play things they know are poignantly true" (emphasis added). Atkinson noted Miller's authorial stance as a departure from social criticism: "Although Mr. Miller is the author, he does not dissociate himself from this simple story of an ordinary family. He participates in it by recording it with compassion." Atkinson praised Miller's representation of the people as "humane" because of its "respect for people, and knowledge of American manners and of modern folk-ways." Miller's sympathy for his flawed characters and their everyday dilemmas distinguished his play from literary representations of foolish and pretentious middle-class strivers and wretched or heroic proletarians.[104] Harold Clurman, founder of the Group Theatre, similarly credited Miller with finally achieving the 1930s dream of the people's drama. Revealing his own class and ethnic identifications, he wrote that the play could make "the audience recognize itself. Willy Loman is everybody's father, brother, uncle or friend, his family are our cousins." Clurman went so far as to refer to the play as "a documented history of our lives . . . conveyed with what might be compared to a 'Living Newspaper' documentary accuracy."[105]

The sympathetic reading of Willy encouraged a particularly uncritical reading of Linda.[106] Several male critics projected an ideal womanhood, not unlike Irene Dunne's characterization of Mama, onto Linda: "She, of all the Lomans, sees the Salesman as he is and loves him." Ignoring the requiem at the end—in which Linda asks, "But where are all the people he knew?" and repeats four times that she "doesn't understand"—Atkinson endorsed Linda as a wife who "not only loves him but understands him thoroughly." John Mason Brown's interpretation of Linda betrayed his marital ideal, of a woman who is

> all heart, devotion, and simplicity. . . . She is unfooled but unfailing. She is the smiling, mothering, hard-working, good wife, the victim of her husband's budget. She is the nourisher of his dreams, even when she knows they are only dreams, the feeder of his self-esteem. If she is beyond whining or bragging, she is above self-pity. She is the marriage vow . . . made flesh, slight of body but strong of faith.[107]

Focusing on Linda as a "good wife," reviewers called little attention to the play's "bad women." John Mason Brown explained that "[Willy] loves his wife, too, and has been unfaithful to her only because of his acute, aching, loneliness when on the road." Even when praising the performances of minor characters such as the waiter, they rarely mention the Woman, or the two "strudel" whom Happy and Biff pick up in the restaurant.[108]

The emotional intensity of the father-son dynamic helped efface the play's social critique. Actor George Ross watched *Salesman* performed by actors from the Yiddish Theater in Brooklyn; the Yiddish-speaking audience saw *Salesman* "as a play about a Jewish *family,* not about an unsuccessful salesman." Ross observed this audience's attention absorbed by "the problem of the threatened family when a son denounces his father, when a mother denounces her son, when a son and a father fall sobbing desperately into each other's arms." On the other hand, where the family dynamic was unfamiliar, the play as a whole was unintelligible, as for British drama critics Ivor Brown and T. C. Worsley, reviewing the touring production in London, who found the family falling "outside British sympathy." Brown disdained the emotional identification of New York audiences with the characters; the play seemed to appeal to a distinctly female and lower-class sensibility, which he associated with radio drama and soap opera audiences in "parlors, kitchens, and workshops."[109] Only a sympathetic left-wing critic such as John Beaufort, who had admired the critique of parochial family loyalties in *All My Sons*, could follow Miller's clues to see Biff as the character who "perceives the significance of the conflict," who repudiates "the false measurement of success."[110]

By 1949 the wartime consensus that social questions were appropriate to great drama had begun to break down. Although some reviewers, such as William Hawkins of the *New York World Telegram*, praised *Salesman* for its social concerns, others adopted Miller's everyman logic to argue that the play transcended social criticism. Striving for universality narrowed the range of social actors because only certain unmarked characters could seem representative; similarly, striving for timelessness had the effect of erasing history. The New York drama critic Louis Kronenberger wrote that the play was "not, ultimately the work of a social critic," because the burden of the play was less "that people are foolish or systems evil than that on any showing life is tough and to live is to suffer." John Mason Brown similarly juxtaposed social critique to "timeless dilemmas": "[Miller] has the wisdom and the insight not to 'blame the system' in Mr. Odets' fashion, for what are the inner failings and shortcomings of the individual. His rightful concern is with dilemmas which are timeless in drama because they are timeless in life."[111] Miller's formal innovations in representing the ordinary seemed to provide a way to read his play as eschewing "social significance."[112]

Other critics found Miller's everyman representation of the ordinary to be too limiting. Because the *Nation*'s Joseph Wood Krutch assumed that Miller intended his play as social criticism—"This being 1949, one naturally assumes that such a story is most likely to be told in order to expose the evils of our social system"—he was troubled by how Miller's interweaving of social and psychological dynamics mitigated against social analysis. "At least as much stress seems to be laid on the intellectual and moral weakness of the central character as upon any outward necessity determining his fate." Krutch found the action and the characterizations "recognizably true to life," but overly "familiar and without other than literal meaning . . . too prosy and pedestrian." He judged the play's efforts at transcendence to be the explanation for "a notable absence of new insight, fresh imagination, or individual sensibility." The *Time* reviewer found the play "less an indictment than an elegy," but "inadequate" as an elegy; though without "fake poetry," it contained no "real poetry," either.[113]

THE RISING TIDE OF ANTICOMMUNISM

The broad left-wing political and cultural contexts in which Arthur Miller had developed his identity as a citizen and as a writer were changing, just when his fame was at its highest, and he found himself and his play vulnerable to attack. Especially after Henry Wallace's defeat in 1948, antiradical political attacks, once the subject of parody, now appeared more viable and effective.

As he had done after the success of *All My Sons,* Miller tried to use his expanded cultural capital to support the left. He agreed to chair the arts panel at the proposed peace conference, sponsored by the Council of American-Soviet Friendship, that would honor the foreign minister of the Soviet Union and the thirty-second anniversary of the Soviet state.[114] Miller later reflected that in 1949 "the sharp postwar turn against the Soviets and in favor of a Germany unpurged of Nazis not only seemed ignoble but threatened another war that might indeed destroy Russia but bring down our own democracy as well."[115] He supported a relief drive in friendship with the "new China"; Jiang Jieshi's Nationalist government had retreated to the island of Formosa and Mao Zedong and his Communist Red Army had taken control of the mainland. He continued to lend his support to the Joint Anti-Fascist Refugee Committee, especially its Spanish Refugee Appeal, despite its being an early target of HUAC. His name was listed on the June 1949 call for a Bill of Rights conference sponsored by the Civil Rights Congress. This interracial conference was held in July 1949 to protest the HUAC hearings and call attention to the plight of the Smith Act Communist Party defendants whose trial for supposedly advocating the overthrow of the U.S. government was currently underway.[116]

But the circle of accusations was growing closer to him. Mary Miller had worked as a secretary to the publisher Philip Jaffe, who, as editor of *Amerasia,* was one of the first people to be arrested in June 1945 for publishing reports that predicted a Chinese Communist victory. Jaffe was the former owner of the house in Roxbury, Connecticut that the Millers bought in 1947.[117] In April 1949 *Life* magazine published an article about the coming U.S.-Soviet peace conference. The article featured Miller prominently in its two-page photo spread of "Red Dupes and Fellow Travelers."[118] When he attended the now broadly condemned conference, crossing a picket line of nuns on the sidewalk praying for his soul, he knew that more public outcry against conference participants was likely. Miller later wrote that he might not have agreed to chair one of the panels at the peace conference "had not Salesman continued to be such a universally acclaimed success. I simply felt better with one foot outside the standard show business world, and once invited, I could not refuse."[119] He also may have felt, as he wrote of the abrupt politically motivated firings from starring roles on national television series of his friends Pert Kelton and Louis Untermeyer, "we could not have believed that . . . the current of one's life and career could simply be switched off and the wires left dead."[120]

By June 1949 the critic for *Partisan Review*, which had become actively anticommunist after 1945, condemned Miller in terms of his relationship to the left. His social critique offered "nothing very original"; the scene in which Willy is fired issued "straight from the party line literature of the thirties," she wrote. The play demonstrated "an intellectual muddle and a lack of candor that regardless of Mr. Miller's conscious intent are the main earmark of contemporary fellow-traveling. What used to become a roar has become a whine."[121]

Miller did not retreat from his public support of the left. He refused to accept the premises of either liberal or right-wing anticommunism. When conservatives had in the past tried to label themes in Miller's work "Communist" he had easily deflected their charges. In 1949 the charges resurfaced, and Miller developed a distinctive strategy in response. Profiled in the *Saturday Evening Post* in July, Miller used the opportunity to state that he "didn't consider himself a communist." The *Post* interviewer noted that Miller was "angered by what he considered the unfair affixing of the communist label to many sincere liberals," but he wanted to remain identified with those resisting the injustices he saw so clearly. Like many people affiliated with labor, civil rights, and antifascist campaigns of the late 1930s and 1940s, Miller was likely to have worked alongside Communists for many years. Many of his close friendships were with people who had moved in and out of party membership, like Kazan. The Marxist study groups he had briefly attended could provide a format for considering party membership.

For Miller, holding onto radicalism was being true to himself. "Whatever my misgivings about doctrinaire Marxism," Miller later wrote, "it was beyond me at the time to join the anti-Soviet crusade, especially when it seemed to entail disowning and falsifying the American radical past, at least as I had known it and felt it." With careful language he identified himself as "a confirmed and deliberate radical," although, when asked about the criticism of his ideology at the time, he admitted, "I am a very disturbed radical at the moment." Miller claimed the stage as "the last sounding board for an independent thinker" and used *Death of a Salesman* to reframe ideological accusations in personal terms. "I wrote a play about a man who kills himself because he isn't liked. . . . It would be a little silly for me to worry about who likes me and who doesn't."[122]

But the ground was shifting. Not only were ideological affiliations less clear in postwar power alignments, as he had observed in Europe, but cultural front formations were shattering under the pressure to draw boundaries to exclude Communists, diminishing the ability for cultural producers to write social analysis for a mass audience with the confident power of a collective voice. Miller has not written in great detail about this period nor, for obvious reasons, is there an extensive public record to clarify his actions and choices. But he has recalled several incidents that may illuminate the dynamics of this erosion. An announced New York production of Sean O' Casey's play *Cock-A Doodle Dandy*, which had opened in England in December 1949, was threatened with a picket by the American Legion and the Catholic War Veterans. Miller failed to get fellow members of the Dramatists' Guild to organize a counter picket line in the event of a legion boycott.[123] Miller identified with O' Casey: a major backer had withdrawn her support, and Miller was stunned that this widely published, admired, and internationally acclaimed playwright found himself speaking into the void, a dramatist without a theater. Miller was also chilled by the response of the Dramatists' Guild: "I now had no reason to doubt that should the Legion decide to picket my next play to death, I could look for no meaningful defense from my fellow playwrights, for these were the most powerful names in the theater, and they were either scared or bewildered about how to act."[124]

Miller and other successful writers associated with the left in the 1930s and 1940s discovered that their cultural authority was ineffective against insurgent anticommunism. He joined a weekly discussion group convened by Jack Goodman, senior editor at Simon and Schuster, to combat the silencing of left-wing protest, "trying to come up with ideas for articles and even movies and plays which would call back the American public which was dancing after Joe McCarthy into fascism." The group brought together prominent people from the magazine, fiction, radio, and new television worlds, including journalist Edgar Snow, who had traveled in China with Mao's Red Army, publishing his account in the best-selling *Red Star Over China* (1937), and had covered events in Southeast Asia and the Soviet Union during World War II; at the time he was editor of

Saturday Evening Post. Other participants were Jack Belden, novelist and reporter on China; John Hersey, novelist and *New Yorker* reporter who wrote in 1946 the first popular account of the atomic destruction in Hiroshima; Richard Lauterbach of *Life;* Ira Wolfert, overseas war correspondent, novelist, *Reader's Digest* reporter, and author of *Tucker's People,* the source for the film *Force of Evil* (1948); Joe Barnes, foreign editor of the *Herald Tribune;* and photographer Robert Capa. Miller later recalled the gatherings as "twenty or thirty of us sitting around drinking and smoking and trying to conceive of a countertide in the media to the overwhelming propaganda of the right." After many months in which the group generated ideas, suggested essays, and wrote proposals none of their material had been accepted for print or broadcast. Miller described their collective discovery: "whatever our reputations, we were little more than easily disposable hired hands."[125]

Then Miller watched his own work come under fire; productions that featured ordinary Americans were a special target of anticommunists, who relied on prepared lists of people associated with the left to mobilize right-wing activists. Despite the reputation of *Death of a Salesman,* a boycott was organized against a traveling production playing in Peoria, Illinois in late October 1950. Albert Dekker, cast as Willy, had appeared in the final report of the California HUAC, commonly called the Tenney Committee, released in June 1949. Miller himself was named in *Red Channels: The Report of Communist Influence in Radio and Television,* published in June 1950.[126] One week after *Red Channels* author Vincent Hartnett gave a speech to the All-Peoria Conference to Combat Communism in which he suggested a boycott of Miller's play, the "Americanism" Committee of the local American Legion and the board of directors of the Junior Chamber of Commerce organized local pressure. They called for audiences to stay home rather than buy tickets to a production associated with "communist fronters" Dekker, Miller, and producer Kermit Bloomgarden, claiming that the play's proceeds would be turned over to the Communist Party. The Peoria American Legion group had already tried to have all films associated with the Hollywood Ten withdrawn from the public library.[127] Despite a published statement from Miller, Bloomgarden, and Dekker, and an unusual postperformance curtain address by Dekker, only a third of the seats were filled. Progressive assistance to fight the boycotts was disorganized: a board member from the League of American Writers wrote to Miller characterizing their efforts to stand up to the Peoria boycott as "pallid."[128]

Despite these ominous incidents, Miller continued to support the Smith Act defendants and publicly to condemn HUAC and the anticommunist apparatus; he even moved further to the left for a time, attending what he called a few meetings of Communist writers in living rooms. In early 1951 he still believed that his fame and connection to Kazan would allow him to communicate his ideas to a broad popular audience through film; they went together to Hollywood to pitch Miller 's screenplay "The Hook," about rank-and-file efforts to reclaim the longshoreman's union, which Kazan planned to direct.[129]

Their trip, which initially promised a deepening of their personal and political collaboration, instead resulted in their well-publicized rupture over whether to give names to HUAC. It is not surprising that their recollections of this period diverge significantly.[130] Although Kazan had recently turned down filming *Death of a Salesman* in order to do an adaptation of Williams's *Streetcar Named Desire,* Miller believed that "Kazan and I were back in the conspiracy again, two minority men plotting to hit the American screen with some harsh truths."[131] Both Miller and Kazan thought such a film, though politically controversial, was still viable, given the widely admired Italian neorealist film *Open City* (1945) as well as Hollywood social problem films frequently made both by Fox (for whom Kazan had worked) and Warner Brothers.[132] According to both men, Kazan's "hot" reputation, especially after finishing the filming of *Streetcar,* generated studio interest in the project. The reasons that "The Hook" was eventually turned down differ in the accounts, but in general they concerned inadequacies in the screenplay and pessimism about the film's commercial appeal. Both accounts agreed that Miller was pressured to revise the script in order to portray the rank-and-file unionists as anticommunist and that Miller was unwilling to make these changes. The recent smashing of Hollywood's own union challenge to local union racketeers and the U.S. military commitment to oppose Korean and Chinese Communists in Korea imbued anticommunism with local practical applications as well as national and international purpose and legitimacy. The disintegration of this film project profoundly shook Miller's confidence and his sense of autonomy and independence as a writer.

Anticommunism began to seem like an "unstoppable earthquake rolling through the political landscape," Miller later commented; "the public obloquy caused a defensiveness in me."[133] Miller's "defensiveness" produced a cloud of abstraction around *Death of a Salesman* that further expanded the terms of universality he had constructed within the play, extending into later critical assessments and Miller's own considerable commentary about his play. Miller never literally denied the social concerns of his work, and he continued to publicly oppose anticommunism, but he carefully extracted himself and his play from specific social origins and contexts.

Gerald Weales has pointed to Miller's own role in creating the "avalanche of genre-defining criticism" about the play.[134] Miller's initial reasons for labeling *Death of a Salesman* as a tragedy may have changed over time; nonetheless, by doing so he was able to remove the phrase *common man* from its 1930s left-wing context and reposition it in a dramatic theory concerning who constituted a tragic hero.

Since in his previous plays Miller had left plenty of evidence of his political concerns, another of his veiling strategies was to categorize his work thematically. The writer of the July 1949 *Saturday Evening Post* profile noted that, because *All My Sons* was "an attack on war profiteers" and *Salesman* was "in a sense a criticism of the American way of life," Miller had "been accused of communistic tendencies"; Miller now defended the plays as "variations on the same theme—man's need to examine himself and his relationship to society."[135]

Salesman's varied enthusiasts provided other forms of cover for the play. As noted, one of these fans was Howard Fuller, president of the Fuller Brush Company, whose combination of capitalist boosterism and Freudian analysis protected the play, but at the cost of pushing Miller's synthesis of Marx and Freud in a fundamentally different direction than Miller intended.[136] Fuller's reference to "the classic Oedipus complex angle" indicated how the language of psychology had penetrated mass culture; psychoanalysis was another framework with the capacity to obscure the social critique of Miller's play.[137]

Opening in December 1951, the film adaptation of *Salesman*, produced by some of the still employable Hollywood progressives, explained Willy's angst as psychological and individual. Even so, its social silences and excessive psychological focus did not prevent *Salesman* from being the first movie to be picketed by a rightwing anti-communist group financed by wealthy businessmen, calling itself the Wage Earners' Committee in an effort to compete with progressive labor alliances for labor support. The picket signs labeled Miller, Frederick March (cast as Willy), and producer Stanley Kramer as "Reds."[138]

Miller became increasingly guarded about his personal history and his relationship to the world of *Salesman.* In 1949 he had openly located himself in relationship to salesmen, Brooklyn, and the family in the play. As Murray Schumach wrote in the *New York Times* in February 1949, "virtually everything Mr. Miller put into *Death of a Salesman* came from the writer's experiences or observations." The interviewers seem to have collaborated with Miller to link the play's ordinary family to Miller's own "ordinariness."[139] Robert Sylvester's July 1949 profile of Miller for the *Saturday Evening Post* opened with a similar kind of claim that Miller was unspoiled by his financial success, "showing a stubborn consistency about being a subway straphanger."[140]

By 1955, however, Miller's writing veiled his personal origins. One essay, "A Boy Grew in Brooklyn," adapted Betty Smith's title as well as her tone, use of local color, and anecdotal humor. Populated with predominantly male characters and practical jokers who thrived in what Miller evoked as Brooklyn's village atmosphere, his account excluded anything readers could associate with labor, the left, the Depression, social analysis, or politics. In the summer of 1956 Miller was finally subpoenaed to testify before HUAC. That was the year Miller was working on the introduction to his *Collected Plays,* the final version of which made a case against an autobiographical reading of his work. Excising more of himself in each draft, he had successively replaced personal and geographical clues with comments about literature, drama, the individual, and society.[141]

Interviewed on the radio by literary critic Philip Gelb in 1958, Miller actively distanced himself from his former project of conveying the ordinary. Now he disavowed Willy's "averageness" and dismissed any interest in "averageness" as an outdated form of socialist realism, offering instead the formulation that a "really great work . . . will show at one and the same time the power and force of the human will working with and against the force of society upon it." Miller agreed with a statement by Gelb that "the best way to present a universal is in terms of a really specific story," but he denied Willy was "typical." Instead, he associated "typical" with the feminized masses:

The most typical pictures of society I know are probably in the *Saturday Evening Post,* or the soap operas. It is more likely to be typical of people to be humdrum and indifferent and without superb conflicts. When a writer sets out to create high climaxes, he automatically is going to depart from the typical, the ordinary, and the representative.

"Truly," Miller insisted to Gelb, "I have no interest in the selling profession."[142]

Whether or not he openly acknowledged it, Arthur Miller's popular triumph in *Death of a Salesman* was indebted to the cultural creativity intertwined with the political insurgencies of the 1930s and 1940s. Miller's accomplishment was a politically inflected and masculinized synthesis of family and society. In staking out this terrain, Miller endowed the play with a universality—further circulated in popular interpretations of *Salesman*—that could be apprehended only by those who, like Miller, attributed a greater importance to the "more strenuous social loyalties" than to the everyday responsibilities for children and extended family. Miller's universality was irrelevant to those who could not pass as Everyman, as Miller himself had so often done.

Rather than conceiving of universality in Durham's terms—as an inclusive category embracing all those who resisted the status quo and changed history—Miller's notion of unmarked, timeless, transcendent universality reproduced the normative and exclusionary. In the face of anticommunism Miller made use of universality as a defense to protect the play from the pressure that forced Durham off the air, separating it from Miller's political alignments and deflecting attention from his text's admittedly ambiguous social and political markers. The popularity of *Salesman* authorized its dramatic form and narrative; the play set the postwar standard for (and limitations of) family drama, with its insistently American, masculine, and white subjectivity.

By the early 1960s political changes enabled Miller to become less defensive. In 1966 he commented that it was "no longer gauche or stupid to be interested in the fate of society and injustice and in race problems and the rest of it. In the fifties it was out to mention this. It meant you were not really an artist." Miller gave "the Negroes" credit for breaking up this prejudice.[143]

In 1975 Miller interrogated the implicit racial boundaries of his conception of *Death of a Salesman*. In response to a request from a director who envisioned a production casting Charley as African American, Miller wrote that "Salesman arrives at something like myth through the detail of society, through its fidelity to a life we know." But he puzzled over how this casting would alter the meaning of his play. He mentioned having agreed to a proposal from Frederick O'Neal in the early 1960s to mount a production of *Salesman* (which never materialized) with O'Neal as Willy, and to Moses Gunn's all-black production in Baltimore, which did indicate to Miller that "some sort of social and aesthetic sense" could be made with an all-black cast in *Salesman,* although he felt that "it became basically metaphorical rather than real." But to cast Charley, Willy's best friend, as a black man "seemed impossible from the point of view of *Willy as a type in Brooklyn*" (emphasis added).

Miller's insight about the implications of color-blind casting attributed significance to race as both color and historical experience, commenting that "it is a mistake . . . to think that people are interchangeable parts, irrespective of their physical characteristics or their social history." But, within his conception, "if I had to put him in a sentence—'Charley is the system when it works'—to set a black man in this role is to set fire to this truth and leave us with a broken and inoperable thing."[144] Miller's response was serious and thoughtful, but it indicated that, within his representational system, the unmarked universality of *Salesman* could not be color-blind because it was implicitly white—and thus perhaps not so universal after all.

8

MARITAL REALISM AND EVERYMAN LOVE STORIES

Even as anticommunist blacklisting became increasingly effective and popular front coalitions splintered after 1949, left-wing writers and directors still managed to produce everyman love stories on film and everyman family dramas on television. In the formula for the good life that saturated mainstream culture after the war, personal expectations were expressed through images of family: successful male breadwinning, female-managed consumption, early marriage, frequent childbearing, and residency in the new suburbs.[1] Drawing on psychological analysis and sexual modernism associated with radicalism, everyman love stories and family dramas presented alternative images to a popular audience without raising a "red" flag. Love stories that repositioned romance, intimacy, and marriage within the context of social and economic constraints rather than individual choice intended to question, at least partially, mainstream norms. Family dramas that emphasized social forces and psychological dynamics provided an opening for radicals, still dedicated to the unfinished work of social reconstruction, to challenge the equation of family happiness with domestic consumption. They hoped that questioning the celebration of individual mobility and accumulation—which Miller tried to do in *Death of a Salesman*—would revitalize popular democratic visions of social betterment though organizing labor, creating a government-secured safety net, and expanding civil rights.

Many left-wing cultural producers questioned victory culture within the genre of film noir. Miller's masculinist challenge to postwar culture through his depiction of domestic and family concerns as narrow and parochial was also familiar to audiences as a left-wing thematic device. The political dimensions of everyman love stories and family dramas often eluded their audiences, both because of the common assumption that romance and family life were by definition private and because right-wing pressures encouraged radical cultural producers to leave their intentions unspoken. A wide range of white viewers who longed to see representations of their everyday lives were delighted to find familiar characters and situations lit up on screen. Showing romance and desire as part of everyday lives was a key aspect of modernizing family stories and making them compelling to postwar audiences. But if the world of the ordinary was limited—as it was—to white families, it encouraged simultaneous inclusion and exclusion. Anticommunist and conservative opposition to interracialism and civil rights initiatives and the expansion of postwar racial segregation in newly constructed public and suburban housing combined to keep racially marked characters out of sight and off limits. Each story that represented the ordinary as unmarked or stretched the category only to include white ethnic characters made it harder for African American characters to become visible on their own terms. Everyman universalization was starkly opposed to, rather than embodied by, the particular.

As the reception of *Death of a Salesman* revealed, everyman stories camouflaged social analysis in order to deflect right-wing scrutiny. There was always the potential for the disguise to overwhelm the critique, however, especially as audiences became less accustomed to social protest and more acclimated to the postwar celebration of family privacy and consumer acquisition. Television social drama, which seemed to offer alternatives to postwar domestic retreat, quickly hit the limits set by anticommunism, corporate sponsorship, and segregation. Independent film production offered a second chance for some of the most successful television dramas to expand their reach beyond the single broadcast. But the conservative silencing of dissent warned writers to inscribe political critique in invisible ink, making it harder for audiences to recognize the message. By the end of the 1950s the critique was barely visible. Over time, everyman love stories and family dramas on film and television would help to solidify, rather than challenge, cultural assumptions that families were private and universalism was white.

MARITAL REALISM BEFORE AND AFTER THE BLACKLIST

As we have seen, many wartime stories featured reluctantly heroic men, supportive and self-sacrificing women, and the postponement of personal and familial pleasure. The all-male world of the war provided a temporary escape from the domestic and heightened the tensions of postwar reintegration. Writer Mario Puzo, son of working-class Italian immigrants, recalled the suffocating prospect of working-class marriage:

> I was being dragged into the trap I feared and had foreseen even as a child. It was all there, the steady job, the nice girl who would eventually get knocked up and then the marriage, and the fighting over counting pennies to make ends meet. . . . But I was delivered. When World War II broke out I was delighted. . . . My country called. I was delivered from my mother, my family, the girl I was loving passionately but did not love. . . . I must have been one of millions—sons, husbands, fathers, lovers—making their innocent getaway from baffled loved ones.

During Puzo's five years in the military, he "toured Europe, had love affairs, found a wife, and lived the material for my first novel" but then walked back "into that cage of family and duty and a steady job."[2] In official stories the fight for democracy was often pictured as the fight for the promise of private family life; the loose plot linking the variety performances in *This Is the Army* (1943) centers around a woman convincing her soldier fiancé that marriage "is one of the things this war is about."[3] Rates of marriage began to rise during the war, spurred by GI allowances and full employment. But the marital and romantic sensibilities evoked in Puzo's account show how concerns about social reintegration encouraged writers to visualize new kinds of love stories.

Writers touched by popular front radicalism who worked in the culture industries after the war created alternative representations of courtship and marriage in films that I will group as a genre of postwar marital realism. Romances were the main currency of the mass culture industries; popular songs and fiction, mass-market magazines, daytime and prime-time radio drama, and Hollywood film. Working within and against the commercial genres, these writers introduced new and unresolved social and psychological dilemmas using everyday speech and conventional scenarios. They tried to depart from earlier film conventions of marital disruption and reconciliation in screwball comedies, of female sacrifice in women's films, or of marital betrayal in film noir. The working women in postwar marital realism films were imagined in terms established by popular front labor feminism in the late 1930s and early 1940s; they neither valorized the domestic nor fled from it. Venturing into terrain already marked as domestic meant that writers would have to establish marital realism as a distinct form, leaving audiences who anticipated the more familiar not knowing what to expect.

Writers of marital realism stories wanted to democratize and socially locate romance, detaching it from wealth and glamour, revealing it to be troubled but not extinguished by work and economic concerns. The difficulty came in conveying the interdependence of private dreams and social forces without glorifying personal domestic bliss or denying the possibility of marital intimacy. Postwar marital realism stories differed from the ethnic family stories of *A Tree Grows in Brooklyn* and *I Remember Mama*, discussed in earlier chapters: their dramatic focus highlighted the couple; they were engaged with the present, not set in a nostalgic and imagined past; their names and characters were unmarked by ethnic or racial difference—at least until Paddy Chayefsky created the television drama *Marty* in 1953. Focusing on love and intimacy, these stories featured men and women creating new kinds of marriage.

The meanings of marriage for individuals varied widely. Many assumed that marriage closed off the freedom of youth, that it made men and women poorer together than they would have been separately, saddling them with responsibilities for wage earning, pregnancy, and child care that would keep them from experimenting with change—different kinds of work, maybe even something like a "career" requiring an investment in training, advanced education, or travel. Depending on the extent of parental claims on a young person's paycheck, residing as a wage earner at home, without the responsibilities for housekeeping, might enable a far more extensive and carefree nightlife.

A frantic heterosexuality, expressed both in higher marriage and divorce rates, marked the 1940s, but same-sex socializing was also prominent. Acting on homosexual desire was more possible in cities because of urban life's potential for combining work with social networks outside of family life. Although wartime disruptions forced public acknowledgment of premarital and extramarital sex, the social pressures to contain sexuality within marriage and to define maturity as directed toward homeownership and child rearing also intensified.[4]

Postwar marital realism stories were shaped by writers who observed at first hand the unsteady boundaries between working-class ethnic cultures and cosmopolitan sexual modernism. A "modern marriage" promised the security of middle-class inclusion and romantic intimacy, along with freedoms not available to those in a "traditional" marriage embedded in obligations to kin and community. Sexual candor was important to the social milieu associated with radicalism, as was discussion of women's emancipation. Many male writers had working wives. Often they or members of their families had made the transition out of the working class, though in many cases the Depression economy unsettled prior gains. They grew up around people whose marriages were shaped by familial considerations and economic constraints, who took for granted a distance between male and female social worlds, and whose unrelenting efforts to bring in wages constituted their primary expression of affection. They came of age in the 1930s and 1940s, when love and romance, sexual and emotional intimacy, desire and pleasure were everywhere on display in advertisements, popular songs, advice columns, and paperback book covers. Postwar marital realism stories dramatized the tensions between these competing pressures shaping marital dreams.

The film *From This Day Forward* (1946)—based on the proletarian novel *All Brides Are Beautiful* (1936) by Thomas Bell, a former steelworker and the son of Slavic immigrants—provides an example of the left-wing effort to construct a popular story of postwar marital realism. Because of the novel's commercial success, RKO secured the rights in 1940, pitching the film as a "New York story, New York kid; social content, socially engaged young fellow."[5] The star playwright of the Group Theatre, Clifford Odets, was set to write and direct. The eventual producing unit included left-wing director and Hollywood newcomer John Berry and screenwriter Hugo Butler.[6] Butler's script structured the film as a flashback, starting in 1945 with the ex-GI in an unemployment office, thereby calling attention to the problems of returning vets and vividly invoking Depression-era housing and unemployment crises in order to highlight current shortages.

Bell's novel had been unusual among those with Communist protagonists for its attention to sexual politics: unemployed, the husband takes over responsibility for cooking and shopping and depends on his wife's wages as a bookshop clerk.[7] The opening scenes contrast the romantic aspirations of the couple with the contentiousness of her married sister's tenement life in an extended family; its conclusion proposes a partial reconciliation. The novel's account of marital sexuality, based on mutual pleasure and avoidance of pregnancy, led reviewers to note its "absolute modernity" and to predict that "a whole lot of people are going to find it shocking."[8]

Breaking through polite silences on sexuality was important to the task of filming postwar marital realism and promised commercial rewards; it also required a battle with the apparatus of Hollywood censorship. The wartime challenges to the Hollywood production code's standards of morality, as well as pressure from projects with increasingly complex representations of sexual passion, were already expanding what was permissible on screen. But the sensibilities of the production code's top administrator, Joseph Breen, were at odds with realist conceptions of modern marriage. Breen pushed the producers of *From This Day Forward* to remove what he considered "offensive sex desire" between the married couple.[9]

The promotional materials for *From This Day Forward* suggest the studio's confidence that there was an audience for a story of what happens "when the honeymoon fades out . . . and marriage sets in" as an alternative to conventions of Hollywood romance. The tag lines for the advertisements juxtaposed romance with economic constraints, promising a tale as "close to heaven as the milky way . . . down to earth as the family budget." Working wives appeared in the foreground ("when a bride works days and the husband works nights") with titillating suggestions of sexuality ("so much love, yet love's a luxury . . . to be indulged at dawn and dusk") in contemporary marriage, "so modern . . . millions are living it today." Most of the magazine ads contrasted a close-up of the bride, Susie, played by Joan Fontaine, lovingly admired by her groom, Bill (newcomer actor Mark Stevens), with their foils—the less attractive and more argumentative relatives—posed around a kitchen table, representing working-class family life.[10]

The attempt at social verisimilitude in *From This Day Forward*—especially its urban geography of Highbridge in the Bronx, subway entrances, public employment office, and tenement street scenes—indicated the filmmakers' intentions to situate romance within the lives of working people. A positive role for the union in the film substituted for the book's vision of a militant Communist movement. When a union job pulls Bill out of the unemployment that has been eroding his self-respect, the union is shown to be supporting, not competing with, marital commitments. The extended family is depicted as both a problem and a resource: they come through in a pinch, raising cash for Bill to redeem the toolbox he had pawned, gathering around Susie to celebrate the announcement of her pregnancy, but the resolution associates a happy ending with moving away.

In contrast to the altercations of the working-class family, *From This Day Forward* displays no serious conflicts between Bill and Susie; they share fears about marriage and desires for sex and romance. Bill takes over the cooking and shopping when he's unemployed, though he bangs the pots in frustration; Susan would like to take care of a house and children. They are in harmony about whether and when to have children. In a departure from the book's concern with maintaining love within marriage, the film endorsed postwar pronatalism by presenting the pregnancy as a confirmation of married love.

Reviewers and audiences were enthusiastic about *From This Day Forward*. *Commonweal* termed it an "almost perfect production"; *Newsweek* claimed that the film succeeded where others had failed in presenting "a believable story of young married love in the last decade." By May 1946 the *Los Angeles Examiner* critic described it as a "cinema bestseller" that had "crept in without much fanfare." Several Los Angeles–area reviewers approvingly identified the film's left-wing aspirations to "social relevance" familiarized by wartime filmmaking. Some New York reviewers were more skeptical; one accused the film of having a radio "soap suds" look, suggesting that marital realism stories ran the risk of verging into a genre then widely discredited as overfeminized.[11]

Another attempt at marital realism, Garson Kanin and Ruth Gordon's film *The Marrying Kind* (1952), directed by George Cukor, featured an unconventional portrait of class-inflected and conflictive modern marriage, but its reception in the face of heightened anticommunism was very different. The production team was less closely tied to the Hollywood left than the crew of *From This Day Forward,* but actively affiliated with progressive causes. Garson Kanin had been in Hollywood since 1937, working with left-wing writers and directors Dalton Trumbo, Paul Jarrico, and Herbert Biberman. Drafted in 1941, Kanin worked on war documentaries for the Signal Corps and then for the OSS in Europe. After the war he lent his support to the Civil Rights Congress and the Wallace campaign and spoke out in opposition to the Hollywood blacklist.[12] New York stage actress Ruth Gordon, who married Kanin in 1942, had been well known since the 1920s and had participated in the theatrical left in the 1930s and 1940s, supporting antifascist organizations and left-wing alternatives to postwar politics, the Independent Citizens Committee of the Arts, Sciences and Professions, and Henry Wallace's Progressive Citizens of America.[13] Director George Cukor had been working in Hollywood since 1930, and his circle included many people active in the Hollywood left, although he saw himself as less politically engaged than many of his friends. He had worked on OWI documentaries in the Signal Corps at Astoria, New York, during the war.[14] Their star actress Judy Holliday had been associated with popular front causes throughout her early career.[15] Like Arthur Miller, Kanin, Gordon, and Holliday were all identified as "subversives" in the 1950 *Red Channels: Report on Communist Influence.*

Garson Kanin's first play, *Born Yesterday,* which opened in New York in February 1946, was an extremely successful political satire.[16] Its humor depended on the triumph of its smart and spirited "dumb blonde," a Bronx-accented chorus girl turned working girl–citizen, played by Judy Holliday. With the topical references removed the 1950 film version was also a huge critical and commercial success, winning Judy Holliday the Academy Award for Best Actress. Several of Kanin's postwar films paid unusually sympathetic attention to the aspirations of women as they challenged conventional sex roles. He and Ruth Gordon wrote the Hepburn-Tracy romantic comedies *Adam's Rib* (1949) and *Pat and Mike* (1952).

Kanin contrasted *The Marrying Kind,* which he had "conceived on a different level, and executed in a different way," with the polished comedy he had been produced previously. "Its aim is realism, its tone is documentary rather than arty, its medium is photography rather than caricature." Kanin saw himself and Gordon as aiming for something unprecedented in their own work: "I think it is the closest we have ever come to 'holding the mirror up to nature.'"[17] In his public statements about the film, Kanin tried to distinguish it from *Born Yesterday* by calling it a comedy in "another key" that "deals with a young New York couple who are *as unusual as most average* people" (emphasis added).[18]

Working with Kanin and Gordon reoriented Cukor's filmmaking away from Hollywood theatricality and artifice toward postwar styles of social realism, including filming on location in "real settings" and experimenting with camera subjectivity.[19] In 1951 Cukor identified the postwar cultural sensibility that made *The Marrying Kind* seem commercially viable. What was considered "hot stuff, glamour, a few years ago" was now "dated." He observed a new social uncertainty, and alluded to "new problems." He may have been referring to his highly admired work with actresses such as Greta Garbo in *Camille* (1937), Katherine Hepburn in *Holiday* (1938), and Joan Crawford and Norma Shearer in *The Women* (1939) when he commented that "before . . . glamour meant a kind of allure, theatrical mystery." Now, it signified "much more of candor, frankness, and an owning up to human weakness, being much more average, not so extraordinary."[20]

Holliday did not fit the usual Hollywood categories of wholesome girl next door, femme fatale, long-legged dancer, or glamour queen. Her speech associated her with New York Jewish ethnicity, but in the studio's practice only comics and supporting players could be marked as Jewish. Columbia's screen image for Holliday attempted to convey her as "average" by removing any social marks of ethnicity from names or locations, although Kanin and Gordon's screenplays gave her dialogue written in a syntax suited to her cadence.[21]

The social world of ordinary marital realism films contrasted vividly with even Hollywood left-wing critiques of unattainable romantic happiness. The opening of George Stevens's *A Place in the Sun* (1951), for example, featured Theodore Dreiser's analysis of the hollow American dream updated by radical screenwriter Michael Wilson. The camera follows the gaze of the handsome but lonely hitchhiker George Eastman (Montgomery Clift) as his eye is caught first by the corporate bathing beauty advertising his uncle's company on a roadside billboard and then by the gorgeous Angela Vickers (Elizabeth Taylor), speeding past in an open convertible. The first shots in *The Marrying Kind* are of divorce court, with acrimonious couples hurling accusations at each other. A dissonant rendition of "Here Comes the Bride" accompanies the entrance of the female domestic-relations judge who is to adjudicate the case of "Keefer vs. Keefer." After an argumentative exchange between opposing lawyers and partisan family members trying to outshout one another, the judge invites the couple into her chambers to hear their stories. The film signals its intent to explore the larger institution rather than individual problems with the wife's answer to the judge's query about what makes the couple incompatible: "Because we're married."

The Marrying Kind introduces us to working people's Manhattan. A series of flashbacks reveals the Keefers' relationship unfolding in Central Park, at a drive-in movie, a modest wedding, a cheap honeymoon in Atlantic City, a bare apartment in postwar public housing. Each location situates the characters in modest and ordinary public space and uses the ordinariness to disappoint the romantic expectations of characters and viewers. Chet Keefer spells this out clearly: "The kind of love they got in books and movies, that's not for people. You've got to be more realistic."

The film is narrated by voice-overs of Chet (Aldo Ray) and Florence (Judy Holliday) telling their experience of what we see on screen. At first the viewer enjoys the humorous contrast between their accounts and what appears on the screen; eventually their diverging interpretations lead them to divorce court.[22] Although this structure calls attention to the division between male and female subjectivity, it is unusually sympathetic to both wife and husband. Florence wants intimacy and connection: "Well, I always thought if I ever got married the thing I'd never be any more was lonesome. It's a funny thing, you can even be in the same bedroom with a husband and he seems to be worrying and thinking about different things except you." Chet explains the pressures to provide for her. "But the different things are always FOR you," he interrupts. Although she wants companionship, she also feels constrained by their limited resources. Chet never resolves the conflict between the pressures he feels to provide and the kind of work he can get, with its limited pay and even more limited autonomy. When an accident puts him temporarily out of work, Florence returns to the job she held before marriage, suggesting that the wife's competence can flourish only when her husband is down, but also that reliance on two wage earners could redistribute the pressure to provide.

The wife's concerns are as poignantly illuminated as the husband's; her dissatisfactions are as fully a challenge to the success of the marriage as are his. In contrast to the use of a child's death to punish a mother's economic ambitions and sexuality in *Mildred Pierce* (1945), in *The Marrying Kind* a child's death is conveyed as a freak accident, leaving a burden not of blame but of painful loss, which falls heavily on *both* parents. The marriage relationship they implicitly seek is a genuine partnership, not the conventional bargain reiterated in *The Best Years of Our Lives* (1946), in which the efforts of good wives are directed wholly toward nurturing their husbands' self-development.

A range of class-inflected experiences of marriage are illuminated by kin and friends in this film, posing alternatives to the heterosexual couple that eventually serve to enforce its boundaries. The wife's aspiring family represents a standard of middle-class ownership and consumption of glamour and excitement that highlights the husband's lack of economic autonomy and power. The husband's more modest family provides the counterexample of traditional marriage: stuck in the old neighborhood, supported by work that is steady but has no room for advancement, surrounded by loyal if intrusive kin, and cemented by affectionate love without romance or style. The husband's jovial coworker and buddy in the early scenes of dating is transformed into the lonely bachelor in the course of the film, his presence at their dinner table serving to reinforce the primacy of marriage over single life. Significantly, all family and friends have to move offstage in order for the final reconciliation to take place.

The film eloquently critiques the model marriage characterized by upward mobility, acquisition, a male breadwinner and a female homemaker, but ends by offering only a more forgiving marriage contract. Telling their stories to the judge approximates the husband's proposal for improving their marriage: "Maybe if we could have gotten together in the right way and talked everything over." This therapeutic and interpersonal solution modestly retreats from the film's social critique.

While *The Marrying Kind* was in production, anticommunist activists were aggressively challenging popular front attempts to speak for and to ordinary Americans. A conservative Catholic attack on Kanin and the film *Born Yesterday* singled out Kanin's support of Wallace in 1948 and his active defense of the Hollywood Ten, but also noted the popular front framework of the play and film, calling it "the most diabolically clever political satire." In 1950 the film community still resisted this attack on Kanin's highly praised comedy, with Louella Parsons asserting that "if there are any pink ideas infiltered into *Born Yesterday,* they are way over my head." The groups of Catholic War Veterans who picketed the film at New York and New Jersey theaters in March 1951 had little impact on the film's critical and commercial success.[23]

Kanin and Gordon, who defined themselves primarily in relationship to the New York theater, were less vulnerable to the blacklist than those more dependent on the corporate-owned or advertising-controlled radio, television, and film media.[24] Attacks on Judy Holliday multiplied, however. Winning the Oscar for Best Actress in 1951 resulted not in offers for lucrative radio and television appearances or enhanced movie contracts but rather in a subpoena to appear before Pat McCarren's Senate Internal Security Committee. Columbia lawyers, trying to protect their investment in the film, arranged for Holliday to delay her appearance until after the opening of *The Marrying Kind* in March 1952.

When *The Marrying Kind* arrived in theaters, anticommunists were organized and the film community divided. Catholic War Veterans picketed the New York opening with posters proclaiming, "While Our Boys Are Dying in Korea, Judy Holliday Is Defaming Congress." In Los Angeles the Wage Earners' Committee, which had picketed the film version of *Death of a Salesman,* also picketed the opening of *The Marrying Kind* at the Hillside Theater.[25]

The picketers did not affect initial ticket sales. But Columbia's promotional materials suggest how a chilling atmosphere encouraged the studio to hide the film's social concerns, promising audiences either a repeat of *Born Yesterday*'s comedy or a sweet, wedding bells romance. Holliday went to some lengths in prerelease interviews to let audiences know she was not playing Billy Dawn. "This picture isn't a comedy. Not at all. It's a quiet love story about two people who've been married for seven years."[26] Columbia's publicity, on the other hand, emphatically insisted that the film was a comedy, describing it as "hilarious," "thoroughly delightful," produced by a "talented comedy team." Publicity stunts and tie-ins featured weddings, cakes, announcements, rings as well as *Marrying Kind*–inspired designs of "hostess coats" and lingerie.

Viewers expecting a "hilarious . . . heartwarming . . . wholesome record of a young couple in love" were surprised by *The Marrying Kind*.[27] If audiences were looking forward to a reprise of Judy Holliday as a dizzy, wisecracking blonde, they must have been unsettled by the depths of her character, confronting painful losses as well as mundane daily life. Some reviewers were familiar enough with the genre of marital realism to recognize the film's effort to "dissect married life, with its joys and sorrows."[28] *Variety* predicted that "audience reaction will be mixed at best."[29]

Although several New York reviewers approved of the locations conveying a modest class terrain, one viewer found limits to the film's realism: no postal clerk could afford to live in Peter Cooper Village or Stuyvesant Town unless his wife also worked. As a location, Stuyvesant Town reproduced the white boundaries of the "ordinary" through its policy of racial exclusion, which between 1947 and 1950 was actively being challenged in a legal suit brought by three African American veterans.[30] A few reviewers enjoyed the "New York types" finding their way to the screen, although others argued that these characters were "not the plain average Americans their names pretend they are."[31] Many reviewers found them too disagreeable, too contentious, and, once married, too naturalistic, "too obviously real for complete consumer comfort."[32] Without the legitimating quest for democratic inclusion, the ordinary and everyday could appear to reviewers as disappointingly "average" or even "sub-average."[33] The film's box office receipts were modest, falling far short of the success of *Born Yesterday*.[34]

Twelve days after *The Marrying Kind* opened, Holliday testified in front of McCarren's committee. With the help of Columbia's lawyers, she worked out a defense that relied on the committee's familiarity with her role in *Born Yesterday*. In what the *Los Angeles Times* termed a "command performance of the dumb blonde," she managed to charm the committee with "confused" answers that distanced her from the Communist Party without incriminating left-wing friends or associates. "The few things I actually participated in were things that I couldn't possibly have thought were subversive," Holliday insisted.[35] Still, she was personally and professionally scarred by anticommunist hate mail, phone calls, and blacklisting, and her public political voice was silenced. In interviews after 1952 she used her comic roles to define her career, making no mention of *The Marrying Kind*.[36]

Kanin quit Hollywood filmmaking after the disappointing reception of *The Marrying Kind;* he and Gordon subsequently ended their writing partnership.[37] Kanin's approach nonetheless influenced a widely seen production featuring an unmarked ordinary family in extraordinary circumstances: in 1954 and 1955 he helped Albert Hackett and Frances Goodrich with their theatrical adaptation of *The Diary of Anne Frank*, which he then directed on Broadway.[38] Explaining his political framework, Kanin argued that an unmarked ordinary family could make the most persuasive case for resistance to all forms of persecution. He linked nationalist and racialist exclusions: "People have suffered because of being English, French, German, Italian, Ethiopian, Mohammedan, Negro, and so on. I don't know how this can be indicated, but it seems to me of utmost importance." Then he argued that a broad condemnation of fascism would be the most compelling.

> The fact that in this play the symbols of persecution and oppression are Jews is incidental, and Anne, in stating the argument so, reduces her magnificent stature. It is Peter here who should be the young one, outraged at being persecuted because he is a Jew, and Anne, wiser, pointing out that through the ages, people in minorities have been oppressed.

Kanin thought that showing fascism's persecution of all minorities was the play's chance to persuade the widest audience: "In other words, at this moment, the play has an opportunity to spread its theme into the infinite." Representing the Franks as an ordinary family was a key dimension of the broadly acclaimed play and its faithful film adaptation, directed by George Stevens in 1959.[39]

THE PROMISE OF LIVE TELEVISION DRAMA

After 1949, when HUAC's political intimidation encouraged Hollywood studios to abandon social themes, social drama moved to television in the live drama anthology format and a new kind of everyman family drama gained popularity. First broadcast May 24, 1953, Paddy Chayefsky's "Marty"—in which a lonely butcher escapes from friends and family to love a lonely schoolteacher—was immediately recognized as groundbreaking in its representation of ordinary people. It elicited a spontaneous postproduction silence when the first show went off the air, followed by animated discussions in the subways, on the streets, in offices all over New York City, and more mail than any other production. Rod Steiger, the actor who played Marty, later recalled letters coming in from "people all over the country, and all different walks of life, from different races and religions and creed."[40]

Chayefsky had already won acclaim as a television playwright; when "Marty" was the first script to be acquired by Hollywood for adaptation into film, he and his character Marty became much more widely known. As a film, *Marty* won top honors at Cannes and four Academy Awards; slow-building, word-of-mouth enthusiasm from urban audiences turned the character and his dialogue ("What do you feel like doing tonight?" "I don't know, Angie. What do you feel like doing?") into common parlance.

Chayefsky and *Marty* became the primary representatives of the "drama of the ordinary" that was so well suited to television's small screen and intimate audience. But the dominance of this everyman love story as prototypical television drama was neither inevitable nor assured. Chayefsky purposely added ethnicity to the American family standard created by *Death of a Salesman,* enlarging the imaginative terrain of who could pass as American by creating nearly interchangeable Jewish, Italian, and Irish families as representative urban neighbors. Chayefsky wrote "Marty" to be the "most ordinary love story in the world," intending, like the writers of marital realism films, to challenge Hollywood's romance formulas and rebuke consumerist values.[41] Though television dramas such as "Marty" expanded the definition of *ordinary* and *family* within the parameters of multiethnic pluralism, their cultural power reinforced the racial exclusion articulated in the implicit whiteness of everyman stories. The conventions of televisual intimacy privatized the family story.

Broadcasting live drama on television promised the same expansion of mass popular audience that left-wing cultural producers had gained from radio. Many of the directors and producers associated with the era of live drama on television, notably Fred Coe and Worthington Minor, discovered the potential for popular theater within the left-wing milieu of the 1930s and 1940s. The first televised drama was a celebration of popular democratic traditions from the 1930s, an adaptation for *NBC Television Theater* in April 1945 of Robert Sherwood's frequently performed *Abe Lincoln in Illinois*. By the fall of 1948 there were six drama anthology shows on television, including CBS's *Studio One,* and the Philco-sponsored NBC Sunday night television drama; eleven more would go on the air by the fall of 1950.[42] The Group Theatre progeny, the Actor's Studio, produced a drama anthology for television, its Method-trained actors helping to break television drama out of a rigid Broadway format.[43] Popular fiction by writers on the left produced some of television drama's early adaptations, such as Tennessee Williams's short play "The Last of the Solid Gold Watches," on NBC in December 1947, and Budd Schulberg's *What Makes Sammy Run,* on NBC in April 1949.[44] But filming a play by placing a camera in an audience row provided an unsatisfactory viewing experience on a small screen; powerful television drama would require innovation in both camera and theatrical techniques.[45]

The boundaries between drama and other television genres were not yet firm, and some of the early adaptations were able to expand the range of permissible subjects beyond what had been allowed on radio. Radio writer Arnold Perl adapted the story of a white reporter's efforts to free an African American man unjustly jailed for the first television season of a radio docudrama show called *The Big Story.*[46] If "adultery, suicide, sexual love before marriage, or homosexuality" were part of an original work, they could, with skillful writing, remain as part of the adaptation. These were the grounds of Joseph Liss's successful defense of the lesbian love story in his adaptation of Kipling's *The Light That Failed* for *Studio One.*[47]

As a rule, however, early television dramas did not explore everyday life and were limited by the same exclusionary racial practices shaping radio drama. As Worthington Minor retrospectively characterized the theatrical conception on the live drama anthology *Studio One:* "It was black tie. There were no dark alleys or kitchen sinks on *Studio One.* There were evil souls and dangerous people, but they dressed for dinner. If they were raped, it was in satin."[48] Because "black tie" drama characters and settings turned out to be overwhelmingly white, this form of television drama replicated the segregation of most radio drama and Broadway theater.

Television's conception of its mass audience favored unmarked everyman characters. As Flora Schreiber, a left-wing observer of the medium, wrote in 1949, television's commitment to actors with the "clean American look," independently repeated to her by several directors, had the potential to create a new stereotype "from which is excluded, almost by definition, a face that reflects conflict, strain, exoticism, indeed all human emotions that are not suggested by this catch phrase." She worried that "middle-class living-room appeal" would be a "limiting touchstone" for both scripts and performances.[49] In 1952 Frederick O'Neal, the esteemed African American actor who founded the American Negro Theatre in the 1940s, estimated that less than four tenths of 1 percent of the actors appearing on television were black.[50] The turn to original drama and its shift thematically and stylistically toward what would be termed "kitchen sink" themes, substituting the ordinary for the elegant, would have no discernible impact on the number of black actors appearing on television.

The insatiable demand of drama anthologies on television provided unprecedented opportunities for a generation of writers and actors, but these opportunities were circumscribed by the rising power of anticommunism. Original drama began to appear on television just after various publications, including *Counterattack*'s *Red Channels* in June 1950, blacklisted the left-wing actors and writers who had been central to popular theater and radio throughout the 1940s. Already sparring with network management over the control of program content, sponsors responded to the threat of boycotts by institutionalizing the machinery of censorship. Eventually the networks themselves took over this regulatory function.[51] Mechanisms for blacklisting multiplied when HUAC resumed its hearings on the broadcast industry in 1951 and 1952; the American Legion conducted its own investigations, which resulted in the publication of *Firing Line*.

Sponsorship rules for television drama replicated the segregationist dynamic of radio, with industry norms dictated by southern prohibitions on any presentation of race outside of minstrelsy humor and domestic service. Conservative dismissal of critiques of racial discrimination as "Communist" reinforced the assumptions underlying the exclusion of black actors, subjects, and personnel already in place.[52] These limits formed the implicit boundaries shaping the sense of what was possible on network television drama.

Many of the writers and directors whose political and social sensibilities had been shaped in the late 1930s and 1940s did not want to accept these limits (Reginald Rose referred to them as "certain regrettable taboos"), and they ingeniously attempted to write around these barriers. The producer of *Philco-Goodyear Television Playhouse,* Fred Coe, attempted to shield writers and plays from interference by sponsors. Gore Vidal wrote in 1955 that "a writer could tackle anything if he learns how to dodge around forbidden subjects."[53]

The effect of these constraints was to push writers toward a drama focused on contemporary psychological themes, which were well suited to the technologies of television production and viewing. Television "realism" depended on its ability to broadcast live. Live television promoted the networks as the source of original programming. Live drama designed for television could turn technical limitations—less flexibility with focus, lighting, and depth of field, minimal sets, modest costuming—into virtues. Television's claustrophobic settings and shot compositions, over-the-shoulder close-ups, more dollying than in film to compensate for fewer camera setups, and predominantly close and medium shots encouraged the writing of interior, intimate drama. Reflecting on television as a "new idiom" in 1949, one critic perceived TV to be "a very personal revealing mirror or window."[54]

Television's placement in households also encouraged the turn to psychological drama. Calling attention to how viewers watched TV in private rather than as part of a public audience, one critic noted that television worked by "invading the fantasy life of the individual when he is alone." Inviting viewers to become participants in personal familial drama intensified television's promise of realism and intimacy.[55] One critic observed the power of this combination, suggesting that "the secret of television's hypnosis is that it gives you an illusion of actuality and of prying into the private lives of your fellows."[56] Television's "forbidden" subjects seemed all the more provocative when they appeared on a screen in the family living room.

Fred Coe began using original scripts for *Philco-Goodyear Television Playhouse* in the fall of 1950. Some of his writers came from radio; many of them, like the directors, had been touched by the aspirations of left-wing social drama to reach the people. They included Joseph Liss, who had worked on late 1930s radio documentaries featuring the "living ways and thinking ways" of everyday Americans; David Shaw, who had written adaptations for the Actor's Studio drama anthology; the "unaffiliated radical" Robert Alan Aurthur, who had been a Marine combat correspondent during World War II and had also worked as a longshoreman before selling his first story to the *New Yorker*; and Horton Foote, who had performed in the American Actors' Company with Agnes de Mille, Jerome Robbins, and Mildred Dunnock before he began writing for television.[57]

The earliest original television drama followed genres of radio drama: police reporter and crime drama, courtroom drama, documentary drama based on biography or newspaper headlines, romance foiled and then revived by twists of fate. Small-town girls confronting familial and other obstacles to finding romantically promising marriages figured in several early shows.[58] Innovative themes began to appear with the turn to original plays, which increased their emotional power through frequent performances by Method-trained actors from the Actors' Studio, including Eva Marie Saint, Kim Stanley, Joanne Woodward, Paul Newman, Martin Balsam, Ann Jackson, Nehemiah Persoff, Rod Steiger, and Maureen Stapleton.[59] Toward the end of Worthington Minor's stewardship, CBS's *Studio One* experimented with location filming and exposé documentary drama, broadcasting Joseph Liss's "Waterfront Boss," an adaptation of a newspaper series on the corrupt reign and criminal fall of a legendary longshoreman.[60]

PADDY CHAYEFSKY'S EVERYMAN ETHNICITY

When Paddy Chayefsky's first play, "Holiday Song," burst off the screen on September 14, 1952, it signaled the possibility for contemporary television drama to explore personal and familial crises driven by ethnic and class-specific dynamics but resolved without class conflict or social protest. The characters of Chayefsky's first four plays for TV were ethnically marked, in a clear departure from television's usual dramatic practice: they included a Long Island Jewish cantor who had lost his faith in God, survivors of Nazi concentration camps, an old Irish labor aristocrat who resisted the new machines that were degrading his craft, and Marty, the unmarried Italian butcher caught between the family-centered world of his relatives or the peer culture of his friends. These characters amplified television's intimate appeal and individualized realism, but Chayefsky's interest in the social and historical was limited to the setting they provided for interpersonal drama and contemporary psychological dilemmas. Rather than signifying the nostalgia of Betty Smith and Katherine Forbes, Chayefsky created an ethnic world to serve as a foil to his sexual modernism.

Chayefsky's career as a television writer was shaped by the personal encouragement of Garson Kanin and the literary influence of Arthur Miller, although his turn to ethnic characterizations represented a departure from the unmarked everyman characters who populated their drama. Eight years younger than Miller and eleven years younger than Kanin, he was also an American-born son of Jewish immigrant parents. Like Kanin's father, Chayefsky's had left Russia to evade arrest for revolutionary activities; in the U.S. he was a house painter and amateur actor in community theater. Like Kanin's mother, Chayefsky's worked in the needle trades; she was a great reader of Russian, English, and American literature. Like Isadore Miller in the coat business and David Kanin as a contractor, Harry Chayefsky achieved a level of middle-class prosperity for his family by working his way up to ownership of a dairy. But all three fathers suffered dramatic reverses in the early years of the Depression that cost them their businesses, forced them to double up with relatives and scramble to make even modest livelihoods.

As a youth, Chayefsky divided his time between parallel worlds: animated family conversations around the kitchen table about economics, politics, and the theater; school days with primarily Jewish classmates at De Witt Clinton, an all-boys public high school in the Bronx; afternoons and evenings with a neighborhood gang of Irish and Italian Catholic boys from his block. He enrolled at City College in 1939.[61] On campus the announcement of the Hitler-Stalin pact in August 1939 threw antifascist organizing into chaos. Investigating "Communism in the public schools," a New York state legislative body, the Rapp-Coudert Committee, singled out City College as an initial target and subpoenaed radical faculty for private and public hearings; many lost their jobs. Chayefsky belonged to a campus organization that came under attack; in a 1981 interview he mentioned his song mocking the Rapp-Coudert Committee ("Our local witch-hunting, Red-hunting Committee in New York") as the example of his collegiate literary efforts.[62]

Drafted right before his graduation in 1943, Chayefsky left the Bronx. His parents had named him "Sidney," but he took the name "Paddy" during basic training in the summer of 1943. By doing so, Chayefsky wrote the military melting pot into his own signature and represented himself through his mixed-ethnic urban neighborhood. In the Army Chayefsky met various people in the show business left. While he was in a London army hospital, his name and aggressive wit caught the attention of Garson Kanin. Kanin got Chayefsky reassigned to his Army Special Services Division, where Chayefsky met left-wing composer Marc Blitzstein, the Broadway director Joshua Logan, Dorothy Parker's husband Alan Campbell, and infantryman and stage manager Arthur Penn. Early in the winter of 1946, Garson Kanin and Ruth Gordon, exhilarated in the wake of their success from *Born Yesterday,* rescued Chayefsky from the only civilian job he could get (returning to his uncle's print shop as a messenger-apprentice) with a $500 subsidy to support him writing a play.

Kanin and Gordon found Chayefsky a small job in Hollywood in the summer of 1947, where he studied acting on the GI Bill at the Actor's Lab School among former Group Theatre and radical actors, teachers, and students including Curt Conway, Michael Chekhov, Jules Dassin, and Joe Papp. He met Harold Hecht and Burt Lancaster, both at that time active supporters of the Hollywood Ten, and went to parties where left-wing people socialized, at the homes of director Michael Gordon and film star Gene Kelley and his wife, actress Betsy Blair.[63] By 1949 Chayefsky was also connected to the left through his wife, a Greenwich Village modern dancer, Susan Sackler, whom he married in February of that year. Sackler's family were progressive Jews, and she had grown up in the Jewish socialist world of the Allerton Avenue Co-ops in the Bronx, where residents enthusiastically turned out for May Day parades, union drives, antifascist demonstrations, and American Labor Party candidates.[64] In August 1949 Paddy and Susan Chayefsky were among the crowds who gathered in Peekskill, New York to hear Paul Robeson sing at a fund-raising concert for the Harlem chapter of the Civil Rights Congress. In September 1949 they caught the attention of the FBI when they joined the signatories of a telegram to Truman protesting the complicity of the police in the riots against Robeson and the concertgoers and calling for a Justice Department investigation.[65] Acquaintances from that time remember Chayefsky in heated political discussions, critical of the left but from a position of shared concern about left-wing issues.[66]

Chayefsky's first dramatic work drew on his own experience and was written as a satire; he later characterized it as "part Hellman, part [Ben] Hecht," with a dash of Odets.[67] But seeing Miller's *Death of a Salesman* transformed Chayefsky's dramatic imagination. Chayefsky attended the play a week after it opened in February 1949 and was one of the men who wept, though he held his tears until he reached the men's room. Writing the notes on "Marty" for his published plays in 1955, Chayefsky described Miller's play as "the closest thing to reality I ever saw on stage." He abandoned the middle-class family satire he had been writing about the Jewish Bronx in 1945. Instead, now following Odets and Miller, he tried to probe what he saw as emotional realities through a working-class family drama set in an Italian neighborhood in Boston in 1922, opposing the dreams and disappointments of an immigrant ditchdigger father and the conflicted aspirations of his talented boxer son. By the 1940s Jewish families less convincingly conveyed the immigrant familial claims and tenement milieu associated with Odets's 1930s drama, but Italian families continued to be represented in these terms.

Chayefsky moved from radio to television in 1952, first adapting books and plays for the radio show *Theatre Guild on the Air,* then, following Miller's early path, writing docudrama for radio's *Cavalcade of America,* and finally writing scripts for a CBS weekly drama anthology called *Danger.* This show supported a number of left-wing actors, writers, and directors before the full enforcement of the broadcasting blacklist. Chayefsky's first script, about a union leader assassinated in a phone booth, was broadcast in April 1952.[68] With his CBS credits behind him, and looking for a situation reputed to be more favorable to writers, Chayefsky met with Fred Coe at NBC in July 1952.

Chayefsky developed his distinctive use of ethnic characterizations play by play. His first work for Coe was an adaptation of a *Reader's Digest* account, "It Happened on the Brooklyn Subway," which became "Holiday Song." Chayefsky's script presented a heavily inflected version of Jewish ethnicity. Its two survivors of Nazi death camps, miraculously reunited by a Jewish cantor, were among the first characters to represent that aspect of Jewish wartime experience, but all the Jewish characters departed from the modern passing Jew favored by *Gentleman's Agreement,* the unmarked everyman characters created by Miller and Kanin, and the original *Reader's Digest*'s account of a reunion of World War II refugees not explicitly identified as Jewish.[69]

The Jewishness of "Holiday Song" owed more to European film style and a Yiddish sensibility than to postwar American Judaism, especially in its attention to a generational struggle between Old World folkways and modern sensibilities. In 1955 Chayefsky named Marcel Pagnol's *The Baker's Wife* (1938) and the Yiddish writer Sholom Aleichem as his models for how to rewrite a news story as a "charming folk tale about a small

Jewish community."[70] Sholom Aleichem's work had been kept alive in the 1930s and 1940s by the Yiddish theater, with which Chayefsky was well acquainted, and by left-wing groups, including the Communist-inspired Artef Yiddish theater group, which popularized Aleichem's work as part of a politically inflected celebration of the "folk."[71]

Chayefsky's framing was apparently "too Jewish" for David Susskind, head of the talent agency and production company associated with Philco-Goodyear, who suggested removing it. But Fred Coe supported and even expanded Chayefsky's conception, broadcasting "Holiday Song" on September 14, 1952, four days before the Jewish New Year observance of Rosh Hashannah, and casting the famous Yiddish actor Joseph Buloff as the cantor (Chayefsky found Buloff to be "too strong" for the "wan little scholar" as he had conceived of the role).[72] The show received an enthusiastic response from audiences, though Buloff attracted most of the attention: "He got something like four thousand letters," Chayefsky later remembered. "I got maybe two or three."[73]

Gradually Chayefsky's distinctive presentation of ethnicity embedded in family conflicts took shape. His second television play, and his first original credit, "The Reluctant Citizen," broadcast February 8, 1953, revolves around a central Jewish character, played by Buloff, whose experiences in a Nazi concentration camp have left him fearful and dependent on his children, until a sympathetic social worker at the Educational Alliance helps him aspire to become a "useful and productive citizen." (Although only about one fourth of the displaced persons who entered the U.S. were Jewish, Chayefsky intentionally wrote this character as Jewish, and Coe cast him with the Yiddish theater star.[74]) The conflict between generations explored in "The Reluctant Citizen" appears repeatedly in his later work, where he set it in Irish and Italian families.

Chayefsky's next television play, "Printer's Measure" (broadcast April 26, 1953), explored a familiar left-wing theme—worker alienation associated with degradation of craft skills. He based this play on a short story he had set in 1939, which described a printer's helper witnessing the sudden suicide of Greenberg, a bankrupt printer, during the auction of his press and supplies. For the play Chayefsky rewrote the characters he had met in his uncle's print shop as Irish, perhaps because, as Delbert Mann later speculated, he wanted to make sure that he was not typed "only" as a Jewish writer.[75] Coe cast Pat O'Malley, a well-known Hollywood character actor, to play the Irish printer, who faced competition from an increasingly automated printing process, battling for respect in the eyes of his young apprentice.

By the time Chayefsky wrote "Marty" in 1953, the love story *was* the main story. Chayefsky chose to bring his characters to life with ethnic details, and again, as in his first serious play, he chose Italianness to represent familial claims. Coe and Mann endeavored to emphasize this ethnicity by casting Marty's mother, aunt, and his Italian customer with actresses from New York's Italian theater, Esther Minciotti, Augusta Ciolli, and Rosanna San Marco.[76]

Chayefsky's commitment to the left-wing project of marital realism stands out in his later reflections on the origins of "Marty." Exploring the world of the "mundane, the ordinary, the untheatrical," he wanted to create "the most ordinary love story in the world" and worked to capture ordinary speech—"I tried to write the dialogue as if it were wire-tapped"—in a love story unlike conventional Hollywood romances:

> I didn't want my hero to be handsome, and I didn't want the girl to be pretty. I wanted to write a love story the way it would literally have happened to the kind of people I know. I was, in fact, determined to shatter the shallow and destructive illusions—prospered by cheap fiction and bad movies—that love is simply a matter of physical attraction, that virility is manifested by a throbbing phallus, and that regular orgasms are all that's needed to make a woman happy.

He also meant for Marty's world of the ordinary to rebuke cultural expressions that uncritically reproduced the privileges of wealth and power. "These values are dominant in our way of life and need to be examined for what they are. . . . [Marty] was a comment on the social values of our times. . . . I am just now becoming aware of this area, this marvelous world of the ordinary."[77]

In the television plays he wrote after "Marty," Chayefsky continued to juxtapose economic and emotional dependence with autonomy, commercially driven romantic illusions with the episodic character of marital intimacy, especially vulnerable to familial demands.[78] Ethnicity provided a means for representing the world of the ordinary. His play "The Mother" (1954) explores the conflict between a widowed mother who wants to live alone and resume work as a machine operator in the garment industry and her married daughter, who plans to bring the mother to live with them, despite the husband's reluctance. The mother—whom Chayefsky made Irish—was played on television by a veteran character actress of the stage, Cathleen Nesbitt; the overprotective daughter was Maureen Stapleton. The neighborhood women were designated linguistically, by name and casting, as Irish and Jewish; the garment boss, unnamed, was played by David Opatoshu. Representing the postwar garment workforce provided a rare opportunity for introducing nonwhite characters into the world of television's ordinary. The women garment workers who teach the mother how to manage the work and the boss are named as "the Negro Woman" (Estelle Hemsley) and "the Puerto Rican Girl" (Violeta Diaz).[79] Chayefsky's last television drama, "The Catered Affair," televised May 22, 1955, and starring the film character actress Thelma Ritter, returned to the Bronx as the setting for a comic Irish family crisis triggered by a wedding, setting the mother's desire for a big church and community celebration against the taxi-driver father's plan to save to buy his own cab and the daughter's preference to elope with her fiancé.[80]

In interviews Chayefsky frequently asserted his expertise as an interpreter of second-generation urban working families. "I write about the people I understand, the $75- to -$125-a-week people." He described his local Bronx neighborhood as "the rich Bronx—in the Riverdale section—not the Odets Bronx. . . . The shadow of poverty did not hang over the part of the Bronx I knew and the social pressures there were not so intense." He denied any particular significance for the Italian origins of the families in his first play and "Marty" and stressed his personal familiarity with urban ethnicity in general: "I come from a mixed neighborhood. There were Jewish families and Italian and Irish families." He denied that ethnic origins constituted an important difference and stressed instead shared psychodynamics: "There is a distinct similarity between their homes—very close family ties among emotionally volatile people."[81]

Writing about family ties and emotional volatility drew Chayefsky perilously close to the feminine-infused realm of soap opera and sentimentality. Like Miller, who had remembered laughing while writing *Death of a Salesman*, Chayefsky insisted that much of his work was satire; he recalled that "in rehearsals of "Marty" for television, we all laughed like hell." (Actress Nancy Marchand didn't remember anyone laughing.)[82]

Reviewers noted Chayefsky's role in creating "the era of tears in TV drama, of very, very sad situations involving what used to be called 'little people.'" They highlighted the specificity of local settings ("He Celebrates the Bronx") and his claim to represent everyday people ("The Drama of the Ordinary"; "Marty and his Friends and Neighbors: The 'Little Man' of the 50s").[83] Several reviewers noticed Chayefsky's interchangeable representations of urban ethnicity. The *New Republic's* Walter Goodman commented on Chayefsky's characters: "Sometimes they are Irish, sometimes Italian, sometimes Jewish, but it doesn't matter. The Irish mother who seeks employment in a midtown garment factory might easily be Italian; the Italian mother urging her son to get a wife could be Jewish." He described them as working class: "All the major characters are first and second generation Americans; all must work to earn their living."[84]

Gerald Weales analyzed Chayefsky's use of ethnicity as necessary to plot conflicts driven by particular class and family dynamics, noting that "since Chayefsky deals almost completely in domestic affairs, he must present a group in which a sense of family is still strong even if the particular situation is one in which the family relationship is crippling." He also observed that Chayefsky's

> stories are interchangeable. For instance, 'The Catered Affair,' a play in which a mother wants to make up for what she thinks has been the neglect of her daughter by giving her an elaborate wedding would have made as much sense had the family been Jewish instead of Irish. Nor do Chayefsky's characters go much higher on the social scale than Marty, the butcher.[85]

Chayefsky's use of interchangeability created a generalized white ethnic type, rather than calling attention to difference, challenging fixed ethnic and racial boundaries, or creating social solidarity, as antifascist trading places stories had hoped to do.

Although they did not try to reproduce his distinctive ethnic characterizations, other television writers did emulate Chayefsky's localism and his attention to the tensions between work, love, intimacy, and familial responsibilities. Tad Mosel explored the familial dynamics of aging in "Ernie Barger Is Fifty" (1953). A woman caught between the demands of taking care of her aging father and her husband is the central character in his "Other People's Houses" (1953). Even Reginald Rose, most of whose social drama focused on community dynamics related to injustice and social responsibility in such plays as "Twelve Angry Men" (1954), wrote a play about two shy newlyweds overcoming the distance between them in "Three Empty Rooms" (1955).[86]

CONSERVATIVE AND CORPORATE CONSTRAINTS
ON REPRESENTING THE ORDINARY

Chayefsky's television career coincided with the intensification of the blacklist. Following the Supreme Court decision in April 1950 to uphold the contempt convictions of the Hollywood Ten and send them to jail, HUAC reopened and broadened its investigations. In December 1950 CBS, accused by *Counterattack* as the network "most satisfactory to the Communists," began requiring its employees to sign loyalty oaths. The new round of HUAC hearings, beginning in March 1951 and lasting for five years, encompassed television, radio, theater, music, and film. The second set of hearings focused more on individuals than on the industry as a whole, rewarded informers, and ultimately used its policing authority to destroy the broad reach of progressive affiliation. Most of the organizations with a history of resisting anticommunism were already in tatters.[87]

Chayefsky's close associates were being served with subpoenas. Larry Parks and Howard Da Silva were among the first group of writers and actors to be called before HUAC in March 1951; Chayefsky publicly supported both men, bringing Parks home to a dinner at his mother's house in the Bronx and joining others to host a rent party for Da Silva in Greenwich Village.[88] Chayefsky had written radio sketches for Abe Burrows, who was subpoenaed and testified about his Communist Party membership in March 1951. His friend Harold Hecht's name first surfaced in HUAC testimony in the fall of 1951; he was subpoenaed to testify to the committee in March 1953. Chayefsky knew Elia Kazan, who testified to HUAC in January and April 1952. With the exception of Da Silva, all these people cooperated with HUAC. On December 7, 1952, Chayefsky himself was listed as one of the suspected subversives associated with CBS and Theatre Guild on the Air in *Firing Line*. Chayefsky's son Dan, born in 1955, grew up with the awareness of his parents' sense of political vulnerability: "Every time a letter arrived from the government addressed to Sidney Chayefsky my parents were terrified. They were sure it was a subpoena."[89]

The blacklist was a constant presence at Philco-Goodyear Playhouse when Chayefsky became one of the staff writers. Initially Philco personnel had been more willing than the Goodyear advertising agency of Young and Rubicam to resist the pressure of *Counterattack;* Coe's informal strategy was to schedule controversial scripts and actors on the Philco weeks (most of Chayefsky's early plays were on Philco Playhouse). That flexibility ended when the head of Philco's ad agency began to consult *Red Channels* more insistently. Walter Bernstein's script adapting F. Scott Fitzgerald's "The Rich Boy," broadcast February 10, 1952, was the last work he was hired to do for Philco-Goodyear under his own name or using a front.[90]

Blacklist enforcement intensified quickly between 1952 and 1953. Frances Chaney, successful radio actress and progressive who in the 1950s was married to Hollywood Ten screenwriter Ring Lardner Jr., had been cast as the cantor's unmarried niece in "Holiday Song" when it aired in September 1952. Lardner had recently returned from jail, Chaney needed the work, and she was pleased to receive a note with her paycheck from Fred Coe saying she was now "an official member of Philco Playhouse." Chaney heard that she would be cast in another, bigger part, in what was to be "Marty"— but then learned that Coe had given the role to someone else. When "Holiday Song" was rebroadcast in 1953, Chaney was the only member of the original cast not rehired (the other members of the cast were so shocked that they threatened to strike on her behalf, but Coe dissuaded them). She did not work in television again for ten years. Coe used an opening created by the retirement of a Young and Rubicam executive to finesse the hiring of Judy Holliday for a dizzy-blonde part written especially for her in a script called "The Huntress" by David Shaw. The show with Holliday was broadcast February 3, 1954; it turned out to be a rare exception rather than a sustained challenge to what had become accepted practice.[91]

The power to enforce an anticommunist blacklist gave sponsors increasing control over programming and narrowed the content for live drama, especially after the filmed experiments developed prototypes for new series. The innovations of *I Love Lucy*, first broadcast in October 1951, demonstrated the appeal of continuing characters and self-reflexive humor that combined show business and everyday life; filmed westerns, such as *Gunsmoke*, premiering in April 1952, cultivated an adult audience. By March 1954 sponsor directives urged Coe to produce more of the "conventional boy-meets-girl type of light presentation," rather than the "realistic" approach of the Playhouse dramas. According to *Time*, the ad agency explicitly complained of the "lack of upbeat endings," with one unnamed advertising executive complaining: "One week there'd be a story about a blind old lady in Texas, and the next week, a story about a blind young lady in Texas." Anticommunist interest in tightening the parameters of the ordinary was revealed in the comments of one viewer, writing to the president of Philco after the broadcast of Horton Foote's "The Midnight Caller:" "Not one person in the cast was a normal American. They were all neurotics for one reason or another. It is a shame with so many fine stories available such trash is forced on the public." By August 1954 Coe himself was fired from the *Philco-Goodyear Playhouse*.[92]

The commercial imperatives of the advertising industry increasingly determined the themes of television drama, as illustrated by the rejection in 1954 of a proposal from eminent dramatist Elmer Rice for a television series based on his play *Street Scene*. Although theatrical producers were initially skeptical, *Street Scene* had proven to be a commercially successful and Pulitzer Prize-winning Broadway play in 1929, with successful touring companies in U.S. cities and popular productions in Europe and Latin America. The film adaptation, produced by Goldwyn in 1931, was also a commercial and critical success. Rice thought that "*Street Scene,* with its variegated characters, would lend itself admirably to a series of episodes, all centering upon a multiple dwelling house and its occupants." Although an important producer agreed that there was "a need for a television series which will dramatize the daily events of urban life," he found Rice's proposal unsuitable:

> We know of no advertiser or advertising agency of any importance in this country who would knowingly allow the products he is trying to advertise to the public to become associated with the squalor, depression, continuous frustration, and general "down" quality of the present conception of *Street Scene* week after week.

The producer claimed that "on the contrary, it is the general policy of advertisers to glamorize their products, the people who buy them, and the whole American social and economic scene." The producer's preferred conception was exactly what Chayefsky and the others hoped to critique: "The American consuming public as presented by the advertising industry today is middle class, not lower class, happy in general, not miserable and frustrated, and optimistic, not depressed."[93]

Writing for television was branded by these limits, which writers internalized. The tension between access to television's vast, expanding audience and the enforced political and social gatekeeping had a powerful effect. Writers wanted to protect their critique of consumer celebration and social norms, and the integrity of their artistic vision, but also to avoid cues associated with social dissent. Speaking the language of psychology and exploring the dramas of personal life seemed a safe compromise, but it could also lead to a realism suspended outside of history.

Chayefsky defended his work in a Canadian Broadcasting Company (CBC) interview in 1955, distancing himself from the 1930s theatrical left: "I just can't buy social resolutions anymore." He had embarked on psychoanalysis around the time he started to write for television. In the commentary to his published plays he explained that

> these are strange and fretful times, and the huge currents of history are too broad to provide individual people with any meaning to their lives. People are beginning to turn into themselves, looking for personal happiness. . . . The jargon of introspection has become everyday conversation. . . . The drama of introspection is the drama that people want to see.[94]

Thoughtful critics at the time who could see through Chayefsky's public denial of his social concerns noted the limitations of his style. Gerald Weales pointed out that "social pressures do affect the individual in the solving or recognizing of his own problem" although this was not the focus Chayefsky chose. Weales observed that "only in passing does Chayefsky indicate that something might be wrong with the society that puts on the pressure." Weales insisted that there was a "social as well as a psychological view of the world in the sadness, even desperation, that pervades all the Chayefsky scripts." When he contrasted the lack of friction in Chayefsky's mixed-ethnic universe with Harriet Arnow's combination of ethnic and racial neighborliness and bitter conflict in her novel of wartime Detroit, *The Dollmaker* (1954), Weales pointed out a significant breach in Chayefsky's realism. Although acknowledging that the "reduction of traditional realism to the narrowest possible limits makes . . . for vital television drama," Weales worried that in Chayefsky's treatment, "realism will be reduced to inconsequence." Writing in the *Nation* about the social themes of television drama more generally, Ring Lardner Jr. labeled the turn to "realism" as "Truth Sans Consequences."[95]

Lardner complained that nowhere was television's censorship more constraining or television drama's realism more "grotesquely dishonest" than in its treatments of the forbidden subject of racial discrimination. No black playwrights had found opportunities preparing adaptations or selling original scripts with new urban and regional perspectives. The ordinary African American was never represented within television drama's "small world of the ordinary, the world of the big city block with its carbon monoxide and small shop smells, sooty park benches, neon-lit bars and homes furnished with the not-quite-paid-for conveniences of the middle class."[96] A film critic's comment in the *Pittsburgh Courier* on black exclusion from urban film applied equally to television drama:

> Productions which dig deep into the everyday life of the country for emotional appeal . . . fail miserably when it comes to including the Negro in the American scene. Not only does this hurt him, but it lessens greatly the authenticity of the pictures themselves. It is ironic and resented when one sees a picture shot in New York, Chicago, or any other metropolis of the United States and fails to see a Negro anywhere in it.[97]

Chayefsky's pioneering use of an interchangeable ethnicity provided a model of substitutions that, pressed by racial censorship, made black characters disappear even from events in which they were principal actors. Television drama thus became associated with a representation of universality that contributed to racial exclusion.

Many of early television drama's respected writers supported the struggle for desegregation unfolding in the late 1940s and 1950s and wanted to represent racial exclusion in their challenges to postwar consumer euphoria. Reginald Rose had named lynching as one of his primary concerns, alongside genocide, pogroms, and wars.[98] His play "Thunder on Sycamore Street" (March 15, 1954)—in which he intended to probe the 1953 challenge to housing segregation in Cicero, Illinois and the resulting white resistance—explored instead what the higher-ups allowed: the plight of an ex-convict homeowner and his family facing a neighborhood's efforts to drive them out. Similarly, Rod Serling was interested in dramatizing community tensions related to the August 1955 lynching of fourteen-year-old Emmett Till on a summer visit to relatives in Mississippi and the subsequent acquittal of his abductors. Serling was advised that the conflict could not be depicted as black against white; his initial script redrew the central event as the killing of an elderly Jewish pawnbroker by a malcontent in an unspecified southern location. The malcontent was tried and released by his neighbors; as Serling described it, his story was "of a town protecting its own on a 'he's a bastard but he's our kind of bastard' basis. Thus, the town itself was the real killer." Press reports of Serling's off-hand comment that the revised play was originally inspired by the Till case mobilized extensive white segregationist protest. Subsequent pressure from sponsors required a shift in locale to New England, the victim to be a foreigner of unspecified national origins, the killer to be a decent American boy "momentarily gone wrong" before "Noon on Doomsday" was broadcast April 25, 1956. The word *lynch* was forbidden. By June 1956 *Variety* observed that boycotts by white southern consumers against sponsors associated with "Negro performers" were increasing in intensity.[99]

Serling acknowledged that censorship made "Noon on Doomsday" a "lukewarm, emasculated, vitiated kind of a show," but remembered "thinking in a strange, oblique, philosophical way, 'Better say something than nothing.'" Rose knew that the compromise requiring a "beleaguered hero" to be an ex-convict rather than a Negro would, in his words, "weaken the play," but he hoped that the "principle under observation" was strong enough to provoke an audience anyway. For the broadcast, the ex-convict Joseph Blake was played by an unmarked ordinary man, a non-professional actor who worked as the floor manager for *Studio One.* Commenting on audience reception to *Thunder on Sycamore Street,* Rose discovered that experienced television viewers attempted to decode the subterfuge required by censorship:

> It was variously felt by viewers with whom I discussed the show that Joseph Blake was meant to symbolize a Negro, a Jew, a Catholic, a Puerto Rican, a Communist or fellow traveler, a Japanese or Chinese, a Russian an anarchist, or an avowed atheist. Not one single person I spoke to felt he was actually meant to be an ex-convict.

Rose tried to turn necessity into a virtue: "This was extremely gratifying to me, and made me feel that perhaps "Thunder on Sycamore Street" had more value in its various interpretations than it would have had had it simply presented the Negro problem."[100] But the forms of discrimination identified by different viewers were not socially and morally equivalent, and Rose's unwilling complicity in enforcing racial exclusion undermined his hopeful claim. Rose continued to write plays that dramatized social injustice—and more pointedly as norms in the industry shifted. Serling would become best known for his innovative combination of fantasy and realism in *The Twilight Zone,* in which he was able to explore issues of inclusion and exclusion, false accusation and scapegoating.[101] But the success of their dramatic substitutions helped to establish, and then popularize, television's practice of exploring discrimination without mentioning race.

With the blacklist and control over content ceded to advertisers and protectors of segregation, live television drama was not able to represent racial inclusion or critique racial exclusion. Instead, white multiethnic pluralism filled up the space for dramas of "social intolerance." In 1958 Paddy Chayefsky described how writers internalized television's policing of subjects:

> every one of us, before we sit down and write a television show, makes that initial compromise of what we are going to write. We don't . . . conceive a television idea we know is going to be thrown out the window. . . . I have never, never written down in television in my life, but I never aimed very high.

Chayefsky's example of censored material revealed the logic by which television continually represented versions of ethnicity as a substitute for race. "Suppose . . . Rod Serling . . . wanted to write such a simple matter as the Little Rock story," Chayefsky explained. "You'd have to make [the character in the play] a Hungarian immigrant coming in from the other country, and the reason they didn't like him was because he looked dirty. . . . Let's face it, you can't write the Little Rock thing."[102]

Although many of the famous dramas that began as live presentations on television were still to be broadcast, the beginning of the end of the live television era was marked when *Philco-Goodyear Television Playhouse* lost its Philco sponsorship in the summer of 1955. The final Philco drama, "A Man Is Ten Feet Tall," took the opportunity to challenge industry practices of blacklisting, both its political and racial exclusions, but the play proved to be an exception rather than an opening. Robert Alan Aurthur wrote "A Man Is Ten Feet Tall" after watching Sidney Poitier play a defiant but redeemable high school tough in Richard Brooks's film *Blackboard Jungle* (1955). Poitier reminded Aurthur of a longshoreman he had known, the only black in a gang of forty men, who had befriended him when he worked as a stevedore on the New York waterfront in the 1940s; "sharp, attractive, ebullient, Tommy met flaming bigotry with awe-inspiring toughness and humor." Gordon Duff, the Philco producer, encouraged Aurthur to write the play without describing the character's race, thinking that they could cast Poitier after the script was accepted; when Philco canceled its sponsorship, Duff scheduled "A Man Is Ten Feet Tall" as the program finale. The NBC legal department demanded that Poitier repudiate his relationships with Paul Robeson and Canada Lee and sign a loyalty oath. Stormy and intensive negotiations were required in order to cast

Poitier—who refused to comply with any of these demands—in the title role that had been written for him.[103]

Directed by Robert Mulligan and broadcast October 2, 1955, "A Man Is Ten Feet Tall" contained contradictory racial themes. Tommy is the model hero, mentoring an alienated young white army deserter, offering an analysis of racial discrimination as a means of instructing him how to resist exploitation at work, and presenting the ideal family life with two children and an egalitarian relationship with his loving wife. The interracial friendship, growing out of work and extending into after-work lives, includes an ongoing discussion of racial difference. But Tommy's life has to be sacrificed in a fight protecting the young drifter, who then is inspired by Tommy's martyrdom to stand up to waterfront corruption.

After the broadcast, Philco's switchboard was jammed with calls from outraged white callers. Unaware that the series ending dulled the impact of their threats, six Philco dealers threatened to cancel their franchises and six thousand viewers from Jackson, Mississippi signed a petition saying they'd never watch the show again. (At least part of the animus was the "interracial" marriage viewers construed from seeing the fair-skinned African American actress Hilda Simms play Poitier's wife). Two southern newspapers lambasted Aurthur as a Communist. Black crowds in Harlem, on the other hand, surged toward Poitier the night after the broadcast, roaring their praise for him and Aurthur's play.[104]

The explicit racial representations in "A Man Is Ten Feet Tall" were unprecedented, embattled, and not soon repeated on television.[105] The demands that Poitier renounce his ties to actors and left-wing activists who were critics of racial discrimination demonstrated the intersection of political and racial blacklisting. That this drama, at best partial and inconsistent in its oppositional and racial stance, was so unusual shows how deeply racial exclusion pervaded early television.

FILMING TELEVISION'S ORDINARY:
MARTY'S EVERYMAN ROMANCE

With its origins in the ordinary world of live television drama, *Marty* proved to be the breakthrough marital realism film. Produced by the artistic experimentation possible before the corporate control of television had fully consolidated, and within the limits set by anticommunist blacklisting, the television "Marty" may have appealed to blacklist-era Hollywood, which had been forced to respond to decreasing audiences and shifting industry economics in the wake of the legally mandated separation of production and exhibition. These conditions encouraged the rise of independent production companies that looked to commercially successful television drama to assure an audience. For the most part, everyman conventions framing realism as psychological and interior, the family as private, and universality as white suffused the films that resulted from television drama and guided audience reception to them.

When Paddy Chayefsky's "Marty" was acquired by Hollywood for film production, its cultural authority greatly increased.[106] But Chayefsky's progressive friends Harold Hecht and Burt Lancaster, who bought the film for their independent production company, were taking a chance. No one was sure that people would buy tickets to a repeat performance of something they had seen for free on television. The blacklist hung over the production, even though Harold Hecht had named names and ingratiated himself with HUAC. Chayefsky's friend Betsy Blair had to use her husband Gene Kelly's pull at MGM to get Dore Schary to intercede with the American Legion: her name was cleared long enough to play the part of the lonely schoolteacher.[107] The production company's financing and United Artists' commitment to distribution were uncertain. Chayefsky and the television director, Delbert Mann, had demanded and won unusual control over the production, but the result was a shoestring-budget movie that departed dramatically from conventional Hollywood fare, with little plot, no stars, urban locations, filmed in black and white rather than the nearly universal Technicolor.[108]

Marty was shot in twenty days between September and December in 1954; when the first prints were ready, executives classed it as an art house film, planned limited distribution, and assumed it would make minimal profits.[109] At first in New York and gradually elsewhere, however, *Marty* found an usually appreciative audience, thanks in part to a plug from columnist Walter Winchell predicting that *Marty* would be one of the great sleepers of all time. Lines were long enough to keep the film booked at Sutton Place on the East Side for an unprecedented thirty-nine weeks. The release planned for the film was slow and selective, with extensive special previews—for ministers, shopkeepers, and physicians, and then for beauticians and bootblacks—courting those who were considered "community opinion-makers." By September 1955 ticket buyers kept the film running for weeks in San Francisco, Philadelphia, Toronto, Los Angeles, with shorter engagements in Omaha, Pittsburgh, Boston, and Dallas, although distributors reported that the film "died" in Memphis, New Orleans, and Bridgeport. [110]

Marty's reputation was boosted with the help of European directors, who may have recognized Chayefsky's admiration for European film, in particular the postwar Italian neorealism of Roberto Rossellini and Vittorio De Sica. Sent to Cannes, where no American entry had ever won best picture, in the hopes of cheap international publicity, *Marty* snagged the top prize.[111] The good news from Cannes encouraged Hecht-Lancaster and United Artists to increase the promotion budget, which in the end exceeded the amount spent on production. More advertising money helped convince distributors to take a chance on the film for runs long enough to build up a word-of-mouth following. By July *Marty* was among the nine top "Box Office Champions" listed in *Motion Picture Herald*.[112]

Like other left-inflected marital realism stories, *Marty* offered female characters their own subjectivity. Although the butcher controlled the action, the schoolteacher conveyed confidence in her own judgment. Although, as one reviewer put it, "to the nickel sports at the corner bar, she's a dog," and in the minds of the older generation "a college girl is just one step from the street," Betsy Blair's Clara managed to walk an unusual line for a 1950s female protagonist. In the words of another critic, "She's not a prude but she isn't a tramp either."[113]

Chayefsky also gestured toward a sexual continuum in which homosexuality was visible by characterizing the "nickel sports" as preferring the company of each other over forays into heterosexual intimacy. He boasted that he was able to show the "latent homosexuality in the 'normal' American male" as the "hidden—sometimes terrifying—impulses deep within all of us," without the "flagrant starkness" of the "two plays on Broadway now dealing with homosexuality" (Williams's *Cat on a Hot Tin Roof* and Robert Anderson's *Tea and Sympathy*). These comments were published at the time the film was released; Chayefsky's public musings on male sexuality must have been intentionally provocative.

> Most American men have decided homosexual impulses; the dramatic writer hardly needs Kinsey to prove that. . . . Most Americans hide from the thought of [these impulses]. . . . The man who proclaims how virile he is could very well be a man who is so unsure of his virility that he needs to reestablish it over and over again.[114]

The resolution to the ethnic family crisis created by Chayefsky promoted the values of sexual modernism and psychological analysis; his acknowledgment of homosexuality served to showcase the triumph of a superior heterosexuality.

The reviewers placed Chayefsky's "story of plain people who fall in love" squarely within the category of ordinary family stories. The *New Yorker* critic positively identified the genre's popular front genealogy, referring to *Marty* as a "new day version of the Odets of the *Awake and Sing* period." The reviewer for *Time* touted Chayefsky's origins, "born and raised in a Jewish-Italian part of the Bronx," an artist whose multiethnic pluralism helped to explain his display of the "vernacular truth and beauty in ordinary lives and feelings." The critic for one of the daily trade papers found the same quality in *Marty* that reviewers had admired in looking back stories, using the same words that had been used to describe Betty Smith's *A Tree Grows in Brooklyn*—"*Studs Lonnigan* without the bitterness"—and likening it to the "compassionate understanding of *I Remember Mama*." He identified the postwar politics of the family Chayefsky created for *Marty*: "The Piletti family, hard-working, patriotic and decent, has had nothing to do with gangsters or revolution. They are the type of people who have made this country." Hollywood attention to them was "long overdue."[115]

One New York newspaper reviewer praised marital realism's implicit critique of wealth and glamour, complaining that "Hollywood has long had the notion that the only New Yorkers who fall in love are people who live in mirrored pent houses, drive shiny Cadillacs, and visit the Stork club every night." He appreciated the film's democratic sensibility, representing people "neither wealthy nor handsome, but gentle and shy and agonizingly lonely, who grope for love in the most unsophisticated places and somehow find it." The *Nation* reviewer called attention to *Marty*'s democratic sexuality through its "rebuttal of Hollywood's repeated insinuation that sex is the prerogative of the spectacularly sexy."[116]

Catholic reviewers seemed particularly pleased with Chayefsky's "respect and affection" for the ethnic Catholic characters; one termed *Marty* "a blessed relief from the current tendency to portray the so-called average man in the ironic and patronizing caricature of *Life of Riley* or *Ma and Pa Kettle*." *Catholic View* argued that "it is to the credit of Paddy Chayefsky, who is Jewish, that he has fully realized just what faith means to the average Catholic." This reviewer thought Catholic writers might emulate Chayefsky and the "naturalism with which he makes Catholicism part of the American scene." *Marty* won the International Catholic Office of Cinema award as well as seven other major Catholic film awards.[117]

Marty enthusiasts encompassed an unusual range of political and cultural tastes. The film won citations from Jewish human rights groups, the General Federation of Women's Clubs, and the national AFL-CIO butcher's union as well as accolades and awards from film critics.[118] Exhibited in art houses as well as local theaters, the film was frequently described as a work of "screen art" and compared by reviewers to *On the Waterfront* (1954) for its similar "heart and charm" and use of inarticulateness to disguise emotion. Arthur Miller and Marilyn Monroe went to see it at a neighborhood theater in Boston at the beginning of their courtship. The left-leaning *Nation* recommended the "ordinary love story" of *Marty*: "characters neither bright nor beautiful, nevertheless they fall gloriously in love, and if it can happen to them, it can happen to anyone." *Photoplay* was equally enthusiastic; the romance would touch anyone who had "ever wished on a star for someone special of your own, felt lonely in a crowd, or looked in a mirror and despaired of finding romance."[119]

The film's extraordinary appeal across a political spectrum was demonstrated in 1959 when, as part of a cultural exchange during a brief thaw in the cold war, *Marty*'s "ordinary love story" was selected as the first American film to be shown in the Soviet Union. Praised by Soviet critics (as translated in the American press) for its story of "rebellion of spiritual purity against petty bourgeoisie," *Marty* was generally recognized as a left-influenced protest against postwar consumerist values.[120] Parodies would also attest to its iconic status as a cultural reference, appearing in various media, from television's comedy shows to *New Yorker* cartoons to *Mad* magazine riffs.

Marty's unusual ability to straddle socially located marital realism and personal romantic triumph was a Hollywood success story not easily emulated. Neither of Chayefsky's other marital realism films, *The Catered Affair* or *The Bachelor Party*, achieved anything like *Marty*'s cultural impact.[121] *The Bachelor Party* questioned marital faithfulness, treated pregnancy as a marital crisis in conflict with romance, and showed the tawdriness of the men's night out on the town; it garnered condemnation by the same Catholic film establishment that had praised *Marty* so highly.

Part of *Marty*'s extraordinary appeal may be explained by its unconventional journey toward a thoroughly conventional postwar resolution. *Marty* dramatized heterosexual romance and domestic privacy as a narrow escape from both long-term family responsibilities (for his mother and aunt) and the desultory pastimes of the street gang. The film reconstructed the meaning of marriage itself, redefining it from a relationship inseparable from familial interests, rightfully the concern of every member of the extended family and coexisting with loyalties to neighbors, friends, and family, to an arena for private romantic intimacy, defined by its opposition to extended family obligations, male friendship and camaraderie, and community sociability. This newer understanding of marriage—separated from the social and economic relationships embedded in it—added to the illusion of family privacy that was central to postwar middle-class and suburban identity.

The absorption of marital realism into marital privacy was nearly ubiquitous in the culture of the 1950s, making it harder to recognize the social critique of romance and marriage that had given marital realism its political edge. No matter their class and regional inflections, movies challenging sexual hypocrisy or showing the power of sexual longings—such as Elia Kazan's adaptations of Tennessee Williams' *Streetcar Named Desire* (1951) and *Baby Doll* (1956)—tipped the scales toward the personal and psychological and away from the social and economic components of marital realism.[122] Movies insistently depicted working-class marriage as claustrophobic, using language like that of a pregnant factory worker (Shelley Winters) pleading with her foreman boyfriend (Montgomery Clift) in *A Place in the Sun:* "You'll settle down, you'll be happy and content with what you've got instead of working yourself up all the time over things you can't have. After all, it's the little things that count. Sure, maybe we'll have to scrimp and save but we'll have each other. I'm not afraid of being poor." The look on Clift's face encourages the audience to imagine this marriage as a fate worse than death.

Social connections outside the couple were generally presented as a threat to romance. Prioritizing the couple in this way demanded a norm of social isolation and financial independence from family and friends that reiterated the values of the middle class and, like *Marty*, turned working-class reciprocity into a burden incompatible with true love. These conventions popularized by everyman love stories worked to reinforce the class and racial exclusion already encouraged by the "ordinary" idiom of television.

One film that did call attention to the social and cultural assumptions driving marital dynamics—and imagined a resolution in which marital romance, family solidarity, and community loyalties could complement rather than compete with one another—was nearly impossible to see on the screen. "Released" from conventional Hollywood genres, blacklisted directors and writers Herbert Biberman, Paul Jarrico, and Michael Wilson made the independent film *Salt of the Earth* (1953), based on what they learned from Chicano miners in a left-led union inflamed by a recent strike. In *Salt of the Earth* family networks strengthened rather than opposed risk taking and dissent; a marriage was saved by women's emancipation. The most powerful blacklist of all, set in motion by conservative anticommunist politicians with the help of the International Association of Theatrical Stage Employees (IATSE), was successful in keeping *Salt of the Earth* out of the nation's movie theaters. Insisting that the film provided "a new weapon for Russia . . . deliberately designed to inflame racial hatreds and to depict the United States as the enemy of all colored peoples," they ensured that its images of nonwhite, non-middle-class marital dynamics and its narrative critique of family privacy, sexual inequality, and racial discrimination remained outside the boundaries of popular imagination. Until, that is, Lorraine Hansberry reintroduced such themes in *Raisin in the Sun* (1959).[123]

9

RERACIALIZING THE ORDINARY
AMERICAN FAMILY: *RAISIN IN THE SUN*

THE UNEXPECTED SUCCESS OF LORRAINE HANSBERRY'S 1959 BROADWAY
play *Raisin in the Sun* challenged the white boundaries of everyman
universality. Sean O'Casey's *Juno and the Paycock,* which had
inspired Miller, provided Hansberry with the model for a drama that
revealed familial ties and conflicts, swinging between humor and tragedy,
as emblematic of national loyalties and divisions. Hansberry's political
commitments encouraged her to write about a black family as an ordinary
family and as an alternative to minstrelsy, exoticized, or criminalized representations of African Americans. She structured *Raisin* to call attention
to the unspoken assumptions in ordinary family stories—that families
were private, universality white, and blackness the "problem." Addressing
the erasure of African American experience in postwar popular culture,
Raisin proudly asserted African American families as *American* families
integral to the social fabric of American life, their inclusion requisite to
fulfilling the promise of postwar democracy.

Raisin in the Sun was the first play on Broadway to be written by an
African American woman. It was also the first production in fifty years to
be directed by an African American director, Lloyd Richards. When the
play won the 1959 New York Drama Critics Circle Award—over entries by
Tennessee Williams, Eugene O'Neill, and Archibald MacLeish—Hansberry became the first African American playwright to be so recognized by

the mainstream theatrical establishment. The play's long and profitable New York run, touring company productions, and eventual Hollywood film adaptation provided opportunities for a generation of black actors.

Opening *Raisin* on Broadway was in itself an accomplishment for left-wing music publisher Philip Rose and the twenty-nine-year-old Lorraine Hansberry, whose published writing had appeared primarily in publications of the left. Rose had been unable to attract major producers or investors, who assumed that people would not come to see a play about a black family. Hansberry recounted that when potential backers read her play they cried. "It's beautiful. Too bad it isn't a musical. White audiences aren't interested in a Negro play."[1] Money for the production was raised by many small investors and funds the actors generated from informal benefit readings.[2] The production traveled to Boston, Philadelphia, and Chicago, where enthusiastic audiences, white and black, convinced the Shubert organization to bring *Raisin* to Broadway. The critic Gerald Weales, present at the Philadelphia opening, wrote that never before had he "seen a Philadelphia theatre in which at least half the audience was Negro." Sidney Poitier thought that the unprecedented numbers of black people making the New York audiences often almost half black were mostly coming for the first time: "blue-collar workers from Harlem and Brooklyn, sleep-in domestics from the suburbs," as well as people from the smaller but expanding postwar black middle class—"professors, doctors, numbers runners, hairdressers." According to one theater historian, "members of the Negro community supported this Broadway production of a Negro play as they had supported no other."[3]

Raisin's popularity and Hansberry's celebrity was also a public vindication for the black and white left with whom she had aligned herself since 1948. Although by the late 1950s the public reach of anticommunist conservatives had diminished somewhat and federal sanctions were less frequently applied (Paul Robeson's passport was returned to him in June 1958), the FBI continued its surveillance of black radicals, including Lorraine Hansberry, as part of its harassment of left-wing dissent and its labeling of opposition to segregation as Communist-inspired. An FBI agent in the audience at the Philadelphia preview was watching for expressions of Communist ideology in the "plot or dialogue," but was unable to find them. His memo reported that "the play contains no comments of any nature about Communism as such but deals essentially with Negro aspirations, the problems inherent in their efforts to advance themselves, and varied attempts at arriving at solutions. . . . Nothing specific to the CP program."[4]

Like the FBI agent, mainstream white audiences understood the play as a celebration of the family's triumphant achievement of upward mobility, masculine authority, and postwar affluence. The atmosphere of anticommunism in the 1950s also prevented audiences from recognizing the social challenges implicit in Hansberry's racial universalism. Hence, much of the white mainstream press praised the play's "humanity" as a color-blind escape from social concerns and an alternative to racial protest. The play's attention to sexual inequality and its appreciation of family solidarity firmly inscribed social consequences into its domestic setting; for critics who refused to see the family as political, the play's having been written by a woman combined with its domestic setting to disqualify it from consideration as serious drama.

In contrast, most black critics recognized the play's racial and social protest, applauding its emotional power while still critically scrutinizing the characters. Those aware of the recent political debates within black communities noticed what the FBI agent missed: a critique of the materialistic and imperialist aspirations of the American Century, as well as of segregation, and an alternative vision of change drawing on the collective resources of black working-class women and families, African American labor, and worldwide anticolonial agitation.

Within a year of the opening, student-led sit-ins inaugurated a new phase of the civil rights movement. From that point on, the meanings of *Raisin* would be assessed through the debates that emerged from these initiatives. Soon black nationalism would popularize measures of "authentic" blackness according to which *Raisin* would no longer qualify.

Tracing the development of Hansberry's commitments to the themes she hoped to dramatize in *Raisin* offers an important perspective on the disappointed dreams of postwar democracy. Hansberry was struggling to articulate an expansive social vision that was racially inclusive without being overdetermined by racial parameters and that posited a mutually constitutive relationship between family and society without letting one overwhelm the other. The ordinary family framework delivered the popular audience, but at a cost. Difficulties for mainstream audiences in recognizing the characters in *Raisin* as both familial and metaphorical show again the distance between multiethnic pluralism and racial universalism and the powerful assumptions framing families as private.

LORRAINE HANSBERRY'S SOUTH SIDE CHILDHOOD

Lorraine Hansberry's racial and political sensibilities were influenced by the historical experience of her parents, southern migrants to Chicago who became wealthy and were active in local efforts to expand black civil rights.[5] Carl Hansberry was born in 1895 in Mississippi, where both his parents were teachers "with comfortable and respected positions" in their community. He studied at Alcorn College in Mississippi, where his father and mother had been educated and where his father taught.[6] Lorraine Hansberry's mother, Nannie Perry Hansberry, was born in 1898 in Columbia, Tennessee, where her father rose to the position of bishop. She attended Tennessee State University and was trained as a teacher.[7] Carl Hansberry and Nannie Perry went north in the Great Migration during World War I in search of a wider range of employment and public accommodations than were available to them in the South as well as the right to vote.[8] In Chicago Carl Hansberry became an accountant for Bingha National Bank, the first black bank in Chicago, and then founded his own bank, Lake Street Bank, where Nannie Perry worked as a teller. Their eldest child, Carl Jr., was born in 1918, Perry in 1920, Mamie in 1923. Lorraine, born in 1930, was the youngest.

Looking back at her childhood, Hansberry saw herself as an outsider in both her family and community.[9] As the youngest, she felt "a race apart." The class privileges that accrued from her parents' economic success isolated her in school and neighborhood. She remembered being "the only child in my class who did not come from the Rooseveltian atmosphere of the homes of the Thirties."[10]

Published autobiographical fragments also suggest Hansberry's childhood absorption of gendered differences. She wrote admiringly of a father who was accomplished and recognized as "a man who always seemed to be doing something brilliant and/or unusual." She saw him as exuding self-confidence and pride: "He carried his head in such a way that I was quite certain that there was nothing he was afraid of."[11] She described her mother, on the other hand, as "a vain and intensely feminine person."[12] Hansberry's fictional account of being required to display the family's position on her body associated her mother with the suffocating pressures of store-bought femininity. Putting on a Christmas gift of white furs (the bestowing of which earns her mother congratulations from admiring relatives), the five-year-old narrator describes herself as "exactly like one of those enormous stupid rabbits in her silly coloring books"; when she wears the furs to school in the middle of the Depression "the children of the ghetto promptly set upon [her] with fist and inkwell." Her refusal to "dress the part" became part of her oppositional identity.[13]

Housing segregation for African Americans in Chicago increased dramatically in the 1920s. When prominent and wealthy people (such as black banker Jesse Bingha) attempted to buy houses in white neighborhoods, they found themselves the targets of meetings, rallies, and fifty-eight bombings between 1917 and 1921.[14] Trying a more "polite" tactic than the racial violence in the 1910s and 1920s but with the same end of enforcing racial boundaries, Chicago's Real Estate Board campaigned during the 1920s to enact restrictive covenants, which were effective in walling off Chicago's black neighborhoods by the end of the decade. The growth of Chicago's black population put pressure on housing available within black neighborhoods. In 1937 there were some fifty thousand more black people than units available to house them, and blacks had to pay 20–50 percent more than whites for comparable housing.[15]

Hansberry's father established himself as a successful realtor. By 1936, when his youngest daughter was six, he was head of a major real estate corporation, Hansberry Enterprises. Mamie Hansberry credited their father with subdividing tenement apartments to create the kitchenette. Earning the title "kitchenette king," Hansberry "made quite a fortune during the Depression because the white landlord couldn't collect the rent and he could."[16] By 1938 the kitchenette was widely associated with capitalist exploitation of slum housing; in his play *Big White Fog* left-wing Chicago writer Theodore Ward represented a character's wrong-headed path toward capitalist accumulation as originating with a scheme to build kitchenettes. A 1941 article about the Hansberrys in the NAACP's *Crisis* described kitchenettes more neutrally, noting that Hansberry Enterprises' real estate ventures "made available to Negroes with limited income apartments within their economic reach."[17]

Lorraine Hansbery later described her father as believing that " 'the American way' could successfully be made to work to democratize the United States."[18] Both her parents were involved in Republican Party politics and were friends of Oscar DePriest, the Republican representative from Illinois from 1928 to 1934 and the first black elected to Congress since Reconstruction. Carl Hansberry was also active in local chapters of the NAACP and Urban League and a generous supporter of local causes.[19] His belief in promoting race progress through free enterprise and democratic inclusion was most directly expressed through the nonprofit Hansberry Foundation he created to support legal challenges to housing segregation.[20]

Carl Hansberry was no more able than Jesse Bingha had been to find housing that reflected his economic resources. The family lived in four different apartments from 1930 to 1938. Hansberry began a civil rights campaign to defy legal segregation when he decided to "go the whole hog" and buy a house.[21] Because of a depressed white housing market resulting from general economic instability, Hansberry was able to buy in South Park, populated by whites but surrounded on the south and west by black neighborhoods. By 1940 only three black families would live in the area, which served as a buffer zone between the black neighborhoods and the primarily white Woodlawn and Hyde Park sections around the University of Chicago. In 1938 the house stood vacant; with no other buyers interested in the property, the owner was willing to sell to Hansberry, setting up a dummy transaction in order to do so.[22] Hansbery and his NAACP lawyers determined that, despite a 1934 class action lawsuit to enforce the area's restrictive covenant, not as many white homeowners had signed the restrictive covenant as had been claimed. They hoped to argue that the specific covenant was invalid, but also to mount a full legal challenge to Chicago's restrictive covenants as an unfair restraint on trade guaranteed by the Fourteenth Amendment, as well as a negation of civil rights.[23]

The Hansberrys took possession of the house on May 26, 1937, in what Lorraine later described as "a very hostile neighborhood." Hansberry attended a school where all but a few children were white. For eight months into 1938 the family faced harassment and provocation with the help of black family friends and a hired bodyguard. Hansberry's memories included "being spat at, cursed and pummeled in the daily trek to and from school." One day when her father was in court in Springfield, Illinois, a white mob gathered, shouting insults and threats. A friend was able to disperse the crowd by brandishing a loaded gun, but not before a large concrete slab came "crashing through the window with such force that it embedded itself in the opposite wall." Hansberry remembered her mother "patrolling our house all night with a loaded German luger, doggedly guarding her four children."[24] Later describing these events from a developed left-wing perspective, Hansberry called attention to the central role of her mother, whose "great courage" sustained them in the day-to-day struggle to hold their ground, while "Daddy spent most of his time in Washington fighting his case."[25] Legal rights could not be won by men in the courtroom alone, but required women's daily acts of courage and resistance to racist practices.

Hansberry lost his original suit and an appeal in the Illinois courts; the family remained in the house until ordered to vacate by the lower court ruling. With the help of the NAACP, Hansberry appealed the case to the Supreme Court in order to get a ruling forcing the Illinois court to hear his challenge. In November 1940 the Supreme Court ruled that Hansberry was entitled to have his case heard, but the court chose not to rule on the validity of the covenant itself. Although the court gave the Hansberrys a victory that included returning their house, the precedent established in *Hansberry v. Lee* dealt primarily with defining the parameters of a class action in a property case.[26] Hansberry's victory did bring him to the attention of the FBI, with a memo describing his business success and "ardent" support for the NAACP.[27] The prominence of the case encouraged Hansberry to run for Congress in 1940, but the Republican Party despaired of making a dent in Chicago's strong Democratic showing and did not support his campaign. Despite local fund-raising and door-to-door canvassing, Hansberry was soundly defeated.

Carl Hansberry's extensive legal and political campaigns considerably exhausted his resources. During the war he and Nannie joined black and white Chicago activists as charter members of the Congress on Racial Equality in June 1942, with the goal of using Gandhian nonviolent tactics to protest racial discrimination, especially in employment and public accommodations. Hansberry was later targeted by Chicago's powerful Democratic machine and cited for housing code violations.[28]

Like Dr. Johnson, the man of *Lost Boundaries* fame who thought that during the war years "there has not been an advance but a regression. . . . It has become worse in the North," Hansberry was disappointed with the limitations of postwar "victory." He was also unnerved by the wartime military's nationalization of Jim Crow, especially as it affected his sons. Carl Hansberry Jr. served overseas in a segregated unit. Perry Hansberry contested his draft notice, arguing that he should not be required to defend his country in a segregated military that did not grant him equal rights.[29] The wartime Double V campaign was stalled by late 1945, with black industrial workers displaced by returning white veterans, the Fair Employment Practices Commission (FEPC) slated for defunding, and vicious white attacks on returning black veterans.[30]

In 1945 Hansberry decided to move his family out of the country, buying a house in Polanco, a suburb of Mexico City. Lorraine later commented that "my father wanted to leave this country because, although he had tried to do everything in his power to make it otherwise, he felt he still didn't have his freedom. . . . He felt this country was hopeless in its treatment of Negroes." As his daughter Mamie later recalled,

> Even though he would win his scrimmages and restaurants were opening up [from pressures Hansberry and others were exerting to desegregate them] . . . there was still a great deal more he could see [of racism]. He was becoming discouraged. . . . Daddy . . . loved Mexico. . . . He said for the first time in his life he felt very free. He felt like a full man.[31]

Lorraine briefly attended school in Mexico. While she and her mother were in Chicago finalizing arrangements for their move, however, Carl died of a cerebral hemorrhage on March 17, 1946, shortly before Lorraine's sixteenth birthday. Nannie reestablished herself and her daughter in Chicago, where the three elder children were running Hansberry Enterprises.[32] In 1964 Lorraine Hansberry connected her father's disappointment and his death when she wrote of her "father's early death as a permanently embittered exile in a foreign country."[33]

The Hansberry household's articulation of race pride and race progress despite racial "mistreatment" and discrimination was fortified by examples from black history and literature and further reiterated in adults' stories of growing up in the South. Personal terror and violence were part of the family's collective memory, retold through the story of one uncle, a prominent physician, on a hunting trip with his three brothers, taken off a train and lynched by a white mob in the Elaine, Arkansas riot of October 1919.[34] A summer trip to Tennessee in 1937 or 1938 was the occasion for Hansberry's first lessons on slavery in their family history. The Hansberry house was "full of books," including the "New Negro" poets—Langston Hughes, Countee Cullen, and Warren Cuney, whom Hansberry began to read intensively the late 1930s—and revelatory Negro history written by Carter Woodson and W. E. B. Du Bois. Carl Hansberry's brother Leo was a historian of Africa who taught at Howard University and frequently visited the Hansberrys, often accompanied by African students studying with him in the U.S.[35]

Hansberry's early memories of how she was taught the history of racial discrimination included an international dimension. "Ever since I was three years old, I knew that somebody somewhere was doing something to hurt black and brown people. . . . I certainly did know about Leopold cut-

ting off the hands of the people in the Congo." She was five when Italy sent
troops to Ethiopia and later recalled a sense of community anger and her
mother's outrage.[36] Lorraine was "very sensitive to such things as how the
slavery issue was discussed, even in grade school. I resented all of it." She
"extended this [resentment] to the African thing too."[37] By age fourteen
she was reading writers who explored links between racial boundaries,
sexuality, and anticolonialism, singling out Lillian Smith's *Strange Fruit*
and Pearl Buck. During World War II Buck became a leading American
spokesperson for the view that the Allies needed to break decisively with
colonialism and racism. Hansberry's awareness and appreciation of white
allies coexisted with her admiration of black heroes, among whom she
included the Haitian revolutionary slave Toussaint L'Ouverture in addition to her earlier favorite, Hannibal. Her motto, taken from Abraham
Lincoln, was "United we stand, divided we fall."[38]

Growing up on Chicago's South Side put Hansberry at the epicenter of
a black cultural renaissance unfolding between 1935 and 1945. African
American intellectuals, writers, and artists passing through Chicago in
these years included Richard Wright, Langston Hughes, Arna Bontemps,
Margaret Walker, Gwendolyn Brooks, Theodore Ward, Horace Cayton,
Frank Marshall Davis, and Charles White. The city was home to the second largest black community after New York's Harlem. Recent accounts
have linked this cultural upsurge to the receptivity of South Side African
Americans to varieties of American radicalism, especially Communism.
Through the 1920s and 1930s Marxist politics infused both black racial
protest and interracial radicalism. After 1935 much of Chicago's distinctive
radical and racial protest was supported by and expressed through an
interracial popular front, reaching from black participation in the Democratic Party and the new CIO labor movement to the cultural institutions
serving an expanding black entrepreneurial and professional class, such as
the Federal Writers' and Theatre Projects, John Sengstacke's *Chicago
Defender,* Claude Barnett's Associated Negro Press, and the South Side
Community Art Center. These were the places where Richard Durham
located himself.[39]

Hansberry grew up during the most intense years of radical and cultural
activity on the South Side. She finished high school at Englewood High,
which drew students from a neighborhood in transition from all white to
racially mixed, generating contentious relations between black and white
students. In Hansberry's senior yearbook in 1948, the high school touted
itself as a showcase for cultural pluralism.[40]

LEAVING HOME, STEPPING "DELIBERATELY AGAINST THE BEAT"

When Hansberry left home she sought venues in which black cultural assertion built on interracial and international solidarities. Her connection to African American radicalism in Chicago, especially her Marxist mentors and close friends Raymond and Romania Fergusen Hansborough, provided her with a framework for revising her family's assumption that "race progress" depended on respectability and class mobility and helped turn her perceptions of painful class differences into an appreciation of working-class racial resistance.[41] An easy political communion between race men and women and black and white radicals was unremarkable on the South Side during this period, before anticommunist battle lines were sharply drawn. Renewing her ties with her uncle Leo and the extensive coverage in the *Chicago Defender* of his former Howard student, Nnamdi Azikiwe, the leading West African anticolonial activist in the mid-1940s, may have encouraged her to view race within a world system of colonial domination and imperialism.[42] Whatever its origins, Hansberry later described the shift in her political thinking in terms of her confidence in the anticolonialism of the postwar world. Contrasting her "era" with that of her father, she would say that he "didn't feel free"; she, on the other hand, felt "so free" because "I feel I belong to a world majority, and a very assertive one." Elsewhere she would characterize this generational shift as from "aren't we all miserable" to "aren't we all moving ahead."[43]

At Englewood High School Hansberry had been one of 118 black students among 169 graduates. College-bound daughters of the black professional class usually headed to Howard, where her sister had gone; she chose instead the interracial world of the University of Wisconsin, with a largely white student body. Arriving at Wisconsin in January 1948, Hansberry lived in a women's residence hall of international students, becoming its first black resident and one of only a few students of color.[44] Here she joined the Communist Party and later became active in the Communist youth movement, the Labor Youth League.[45]

The intense excitement generated by Henry Wallace's third-party campaign in 1948 attracted Hansberry to the Young Progressives of America, in which she was elected campus chairman. Wallace's campaign was the culmination of several years of organizing an alternative to the postwar compromises of the Democratic and Republican Parties, with racial equality a central theme. Its platform included militant stands against segregation, the poll tax, and lynching, support for the FEPC, national rent control, federal aid to education, and other New Deal–style social programs, rather than increased military spending for the cold war.[46]

The Wallace movement was self-consciously interracial. Wallace had consulted with a group of black leaders—including Du Bois, Robeson, E. Franklin Frazier, and Shirley Graham—before announcing his candidacy; a central aspect of the campaign was its uncompromising language of social equality and racial justice. The campaign attracted significant black interest.[47] Stumping in the South, Wallace defied Jim Crow ordinances, refusing to speak to segregated audiences, sleep in segregated hotels, or eat in segregated restaurants. Although many African American leaders and voters, including the NAACP leadership, supported Truman, other prominent African Americans endorsed Wallace: the black newspaper publishers Roscoe Dunjee, George Murphy, and Charlotta Bass, the dean of Howard's medical school, Dr. J. R. Johnson, Bishop R. Wright, and performing artists Lena Horne and Canada Lee. The distinguished lawyer, civil rights activist, and lifelong Republican Charles Howard gave the keynote address at Wallace's nominating convention in Philadelphia, using the opportunity to call for immediate desegregation of the armed forces. Carrying a pennant supporting Wallace's candidacy was a student delegate, a recent graduate of Antioch College in Ohio and an accomplished musician and singer, the young Coretta Scott. Joe Louis contributed a hundred dollars to the campaign.[48]

Hansberry's participation in the Wallace campaign and in the Young Progressives brought her into contact with people who shared her developing racial militancy and radical politics. National momentum for Wallace was not sustained; Truman successfully courted black voters with the promise of a civil rights commission, branding supporters of Wallace as Communists. Nonetheless, local Progressive Party and related organizations would provide interracial rallying points for black and white leftists through the early 1950s.

At Wisconsin Hansberry also discovered left-wing theater. Hearing the mother's lament in *Juno and the Paycock* suggested to her the possibility of representing a race-conscious humanity, resolving the opposition between the antiheroic defiance of Bigger Thomas and the white-defined deference of Uncle Tom. "O'Casey never fools you about the Irish, you see. He shows the Irish drunkard, the Irish braggart, the Irish liar. . . . There is a genuine heroism which must naturally emerge when you tell the truth about people."[49] When Philip Rose, an aspiring singer and the future producer of *Raisin,* met nineteen-year-old Hansberry in the summer of 1949, he was dazzled by how much she knew about the theater.[50]

Hansberry read and reread Jomo Kenyatta's eloquent call for African independence, *Facing Mount Kenya* (1938), and Du Bois's *Black Folk: Then and Now; An Essay in the History and Sociology of the Negro* (1939).[51] Du Bois began with the assertion that "no scientific definition of race is possible" before disproving theories of superiority based on race with a sweeping synthesis of the cultural, social, and political achievements of African peoples throughout the world. As he had called attention in *Black Reconstruction in America* (1935) to the ways in which white historical accounts foregrounded white supremacist distortions of black efforts to define freedom, here he examined the consequences of northern European scholars elevating Greek over African cultures. "All history, all science was changed to fit this new condition. Whenever there was history in Africa or civilization, it was of white origins; and the fact that it was civilization proved it was white."[52] In contrast to her own reading and political involvement, Hansberry found her college lectures disappointing; she set out in search of "an education of a different kind."[53]

Hansberry's first published poem announced her affiliation with the left and marked the distance she had traveled from the worldview of her father. "Flag from a Kitchenette Window" appeared in *Masses and Mainstream,* the literary magazine of the Communist-affiliated left, in September 1950. A bleak commentary on the empty promise of postwar American nationalism for people without full rights as citizens, the title and poem located its narrator in housing associated with Carl Hansberry's real estate empire on a Memorial Day: "Southside morning, America is crying." Contrasting the patriotic rituals of national belonging with the daily hurts of segregationist exclusion, the narrator notes that "in our land" the paycheck taxes get paid to "somebody's government." The poem observes "black boys in a window; Algeria and Salerno," who recall black soldiers in World War II, but the flag hanging from the window "beats the steamy jimcrow airs." A statue of a fallen warrior is "the tomb of the betrayed." The rituals continue: "We lay the wreath, lift the flag, make the speech" and "dream of peace." But in the world beyond the South Side "beats the drum" of the war song. The only resolution the poem offers is to begin to walk with "our steps deliberately against the beat."[54]

By November 1950 Hansberry followed in the footsteps of many black and white literary radicals who departed the Midwest, heading "home to Harlem," the beacon of African American art, literature, music, politics, and protest. She made her way into the circles of the black left, joining the group of people committed to assisting Paul Robeson's new publishing venture, *Freedom,* which would publish its first issue in January 1951. This was a time when both state-sponsored and grassroots mobilizations against Communists were gathering steam. The coalition efforts of the late 1930s and 1940s supporting labor organizing and voter education and registration came under anticommunist investigation, including the Southern Negro Youth Congress (SNYC)—initiated by the National Negro Congress (NNC) to train college-educated activists—the Southern Conference for Human Welfare, and later the Civil Rights Congress.[55] Efforts to isolate and discredit Robeson as a black spokesperson were well underway, especially after his widely publicized April 1949 comment protesting black Americans being enlisted to fight the cold war on the side of segregation. Although Robeson faced organized opposition and was refused the use of major civic halls for his fall 1949 concert tour, he could still draw a crowd. Overflowing audiences filled the churches, auditoriums, and union halls where he did sing in 1949 and 1950.[56]

Efforts to silence Robeson had intensified in early 1950, as the foreign and domestic cold wars got hotter. In March 1950 Robeson's scheduled appearance on television as part of a panel convened by Eleanor Roosevelt on "the Negro in American political life" was canceled by NBC less than twenty-four hours after it was announced, making him the first American to be officially banned from television. The outbreak of the Korean War in June 1950 raised the stakes; Robeson's passport was confiscated in August 1950.[57]

Robeson founded *Freedom* in an effort to keep his voice, and news of the issues with which he was associated, in circulation. He and his wife, Eslanda Goode Robeson, raised money and generated support during its years of publication from 1951 to 1955. The people who worked on *Freedom* represented an unusually talented and experienced group of intellectuals and activists committed to challenging assumptions of white supremacy and publicizing protests against segregationist practices throughout the country. They constituted a stimulating intellectual, political, and cultural milieu in which Hansberry could find an "education of a different kind" and kindred spirits interested in stepping "deliberately against the beat."

THE *FREEDOM* FAMILY AND THE BLACK LEFT

The day-to-day responsibilities for the newspaper fell to Louis Burnham, whom Hansberry singled out as a mentor. She named him as the person who taught her to use language simultaneously literate and vernacular, who took her literary aspirations seriously, and from whom she learned "that all racism was rotten, white or black, that *everything* is political." She would write after he died in 1960 that Burnham imparted to her his political faith and confidence in the black community.[58] Fifteen years older than Hansberry, Burnham was a Communist Party activist with a degree in social sciences from City College and a year of law school when he left New York in 1942 with his wife, Dorothy, a graduate of Brooklyn College. In Birmingham, Alabama Burnham was executive secretary for SNYC; campaigns at the time encompassed union drives and strike support, voter education and registration, organizing against police brutality, and challenging racial discrimination in the armed forces.

Burnham was particularly interested in Du Bois's ideas, Gandhian resistance, and anticolonialism; after the war SNYC connected peace and anticolonialism with civil rights. Many SNYC leaders, including Burnham, began to work in the Wallace campaign, and Burnham became the southern director of the Progressive Party. With violence toward, and political harassment of, people on the left or connected with the Wallace campaign on the increase, Burnham closed SNYC's Birmingam office in November 1948, dissolved the organization, and left the South.[59]

Freedom provided an opportunity for Hansberry to renew her family's acquaintance with W. E. B. Du Bois. Du Bois had been writing, teaching, and agitating for fifty years, as a professor at Atlanta University, as editor of the NAACP publication the *Crisis* from 1910 to 1934 and again in the 1940s. He was the most prominent proponent of pan-Africanism and critic of colonialism. Du Bois's deepening relationship in the late 1940s with the writer and activist Shirley Graham brought him into contact with the group of younger men and women in the black left, many of whom were members of the Communist Party and later wrote for *Freedom*. In addition to Paul and Eslanda Goode Robeson, these included former SNYC organizers James and Esther Cooper Jackson, the radical journalist Marvel Cooke, the Howard University Marxist scholar Doxey Wilkerson and his wife, Yolande, and Alphaeus Hunton, a professor of literature at Howard University, and his wife, Dorothy. Du Bois and Robeson both participated in the Wallace campaign, the Progressive Party, and the Council on African Affairs (CAA), founded in 1937 to educate the American public about Africa and broadened in 1942 to agitate for decolonization and African liberation struggles. When the NAACP fired Du Bois in August 1948 because of his support for the Wallace campaign, he was encouraged by Robeson and Wilkerson to move his books and papers to the office of the CAA.[60] Although Du Bois did not have a regular relationship to *Freedom,* Robeson and the *Freedom* "family" actively supported his defense when he was indicted in 1951 for peace activism connected to a petition campaign to outlaw atomic weapons.[61]

Hansberry had avidly read Du Bois's work. In New York she studied African history and culture with him, taking his course at the Jefferson School, the Communist Party's adult education center. In March 1952 Hansberry and several others opened a related effort in Harlem, the Frederick Douglass School. In 1953 she began to teach a course in "The Literature of the American Negro People" at the Jefferson School.[62] Shirley Graham recalled that Hansberry was Du Bois's "favorite pupil" and that he was "exceedingly fond and proud of her."[63]

Other people who worked on *Freedom* included the writer Lloyd Brown, who helped to draft Robeson's monthly columns, and George B. Murphy Jr., the son of the publisher of the Baltimore *Afro-American.* Some of the support for *Freedom* came from people connected with the Committee for the Negro in the Arts (CNA), a group organized in 1947 from within the ranks of the Independent Citizens' Committee of the Arts, Sciences and Professions, affiliated with the Progressive Citizens of America. CNA built on an earlier campaign focused on desegregating radio and called for the employment of Negro talent in all the fields of the arts—music, theater, film, art, and the developing field of television.[64]

The extraordinary Alice Childress, actor, playwright, and writer, was a central figure connecting the CNA, black theater, and *Freedom* and another close friend and political mentor to Hansberry. Childress headed the theatrical division of the CNA in the early 1950s. Some ten years older than Hansberry, she had come to Harlem in 1925 from Charleston, South Carolina to live with the grandmother who raised her. Childress finished most of high school before the deaths of her grandmother and mother in the early 1930s ended her formal education. Around the same time, she met her first husband, actor Alvin Childress; their daughter, Jean, was born in 1935. Childress supported herself and her young daughter with various jobs as a machinist, domestic worker, saleswoman, and insurance agent. In 1941 she joined the American Negro Theatre (ANT), organized in 1940 by playwright Abram Hill and actor Frederick O'Neal with the hope of creating a permanent acting company in Harlem.[65]

Childress and ANT connected Hansberry to the world of black theater in New York, especially to the unfulfilled promise of a People's Theater in

Harlem. ANT's lineage stretched back to Rose McClendon's Negro People's Theatre performance of *Waiting for Lefty* at Harlem's Rockland
Palace in 1935 and to the Rose McClendon Players, organized by Dick
Campbell and his wife, Muriel Rahn. ANT was part of the theatrical left,
originally planned as a cooperative alternative to the star system (hence
the acronym), with all members sharing expenses or profits. The organization was interracial, accepting some white members and producing
plays by black and white playwrights. Childress appeared in ANT's most
commercially successful production, *Anna Lucasta*, in 1944.[66]

Childress wrote plays dramatizing a political critique of white paternalism and white supremacy, the inadequacies of mainstream representations of black people, and the invisibility of black women's labor and
political leadership. In 1949 ANT had presented Childress's one-act play
Florence, which centered on a contentious encounter between a black
domestic, torn between protecting and encouraging her daughter (the
title character), who is trying to break into theater in New York, and an
established, "liberal" white actress, well-meaning but steeped in assumptions of white entitlement to black labor and the "place" of black women.
Florence was presented as part of the first CNA theatrical offering in September 1950, along with Childress's dramatic adaptation of Langston
Hughes's *Just a Little Simple.* This play was based on his popular character
Jesse B. Simple, a southern migrant to Harlem introduced to *Defender*
readers in 1943, usually conversing at the corner bar with an educated
stuffy interlocutor.[67]

Childress's primary commitment was to writing about "so-called ordinary characters." Later she would explain that these were the characters
that "black writers could not afford to abuse or neglect" because they
"represent a part of ourselves, the self twice denied, first by racism and
then by class indifference." She named as her literary models Walt Whitman and Paul Laurence Dunbar, who "approached ordinary people with
admiration and respect," realizing their "endless possibilities," as well as
Sean O'Casey and Sholem Aleichem, who "celebrated the poor Irish and
the poor Jews, as Paul Laurence Dunbar honored the poor Black slave,
through love, understanding and truth."[68]

Childress's most visible contributions to *Freedom* were her columns
written in the voice of Mildred, a defiant, class-conscious domestic worker
(and an answer to Hughes's Jesse B. Simple). Mildred's conversations with
her friend Marge brought a black working-class women's perspective into
the political debates of the day. Childress titled her stories "Conversations

from Life," and they mostly took place in kitchens—usually in the household of Mildred or her friend Marge, where they often reported skirmishes from the kitchen workplace of the embattled day worker. Using the form of dramatic monologue, early columns featured Mildred regaling her friend with sharp observations on the self-deception and manipulations of white employers, exposed with wit and spunk, along with generous applications of the labor theory of value.

Mildred's kitchen table was a forum for sophisticated political analysis. Her conversations with Marge criticized the 1952 Democratic platform for placating southern conservatives by dropping mention of the Fair Employment Practices Commission and antilynching legislation, applauded "breaking the Jim Crow laws" in the 1952 South African Defiance campaign, and defended the civil and political rights of Communists. Mildred offered Marge new possibilities for representing the race: celebrating the determination and labor of ordinary women and men rather than famous heroes, parodying movie narratives that blamed black people for "everything that happens to us." Mildred took special pains to identify Jim Crow segregationists and their defenders as the real "troublemakers"; agitators for democratic inclusion were instead "peace makers," with concrete proposals for social justice. Her 1951 Christmas conversation, reprinted in 1952, imagined the seasonal message of "peace on earth" as black people welcomed to reside in beautiful apartment buildings, enthusiastically received at employment agencies, enjoying a cool glass of lemonade anywhere, riding the "front middle and rear" of streetcars on a return visit to "Alageorgia," where they were warmly greeted by "whitefolk" waving and crying out, "Merry Christmas, neighbor."[69] Childress's race- and class-conscious vision of ordinary people, conveyed through the commanding voice of a woman, provided a powerful artistic and political model for Hansberry.

What many hoped would be "*the* journal of Negro liberation" did not find an audience that could fully support it. The strategies for distributing *Freedom* were haphazard and uncertain, the public costs of associating with a left-identified newspaper increasing. *Freedom's* sole southern distributor was arrested in May 1952. The left-wing summer camps, resorts, unions, and fraternal associations whose advertisements subsidized *Freedom* were facing financial difficulties themselves. Robeson's fifteen-city fundraising tour in May 1952 did draw the crowds but failed to generate much income for the paper. Periodic pleas to generous readers sustained the paper, but with fewer pages and less frequent publication.[70]

Between 1951 and 1955 *Freedom* kept visible many black popular front campaigns: black and interracial trade union efforts to outlaw racial discrimination, African resistance to colonialism and imperialism, interracial defiance of conservative anticommunism and white supremacy, black opposition to the Korean War, and black political support for the Progressive Party. High political hopes coexisted with sharp disappointment. The momentum of the Double V campaign for civil rights was followed by a backlash: as blacks attempted to claim political rights, they faced state-sanctioned violence. Black migration to crowded northern cities was increasing, as were patterns of racial exclusion in housing, jobs, and schools. In the summer of 1951 Hansberry was attending meetings "almost every night." Her friend John O. Killens, a young African American writer working for the Council on African Affairs, remembered these years as a time of intense political engagement, when they discussed "the state of the world, and the nation, and especially the condition of the Afro-American people. It was a time of great excitement, when we took our convictions into the streets, a time of boycotts, of demonstrations and mass meetings at Rockland Palace and the Golden Gate Ballroom."[71]

Robeson and Du Bois, commanding presences in the 1940s, felt keenly the diminishing space in which their voices could be heard, the powerful costs of marginalization. To the eighty-three-year-old Du Bois, Harlem in 1952 was disappointingly conservative, committed to a "provincial American Negro program." He objected to the CAA moving there in 1952, writing to Alphaeus Hunton that Harlem offered neither the "contacts nor the inspiration."[72] Robeson and Du Bois's supporters in the *Freedom* circle, Hansberry among them, tenaciously insisted on keeping their version of the freedom struggle in public circulation, in Harlem and elsewhere, for as long as possible.

The *Freedom* radicals were committed to using imaginative cultural expression to illuminate political ideas and to analyzing the political messages embedded in cultural forms. Hansberry's work for *Freedom* supported her own interests in connecting theater and politics. For a Rockland Palace rally marking *Freedom*'s first anniversary in December 1951, she wrote a historical pageant on the Negro newspaper in America from 1827 to the birth of *Freedom*. She also coordinated script and music for a celebration of Ida B. Wells, the fiery antilynching, equal rights, and women's suffrage activist.[73]

Freedom writers considered the cultural power of racial representations in fiction, drama, music, and history. Hansberry analyzed the revived minstrelsy humor in the early television sitcoms *Beulah* and *Amos 'n' Andy* and celebrated the contributions of earlier black artists such as the singer and dancer Florence Mills and the blues composer Clarence Williams. She applauded the critique of white paternalism in the CNA production of William Branch's play *A Medal for Willie* (1951), featuring a mother's sharp denunciation of celebrating wartime heroism as substitute for postwar social equality. She promoted the themes of anticolonialism and antifascism in Alice Childress's work, as both playwright and actress, in reviews of the 1952 CNA production of *Gold Through the Trees*, a dramatic review of key moments of resistance in the history of the African diaspora, with scenes in the U.S., Haiti, the British West Indies, and South Africa, and as an actress in the 1953 off Broadway production of George Tabori's antifascist play *The Emperor's New Clothes*. She admired the politically inflected drama in the March 1953 production of Ossie Davis's play *The Big Deal* (later renamed *Alice in Wonder*), exploring the dilemma of a popular Negro singer who is offered a job for a major broadcasting company on the condition that he make a few statements against an "outspoken" Negro leader and read speeches for Voice of America about the "free and happy life" of American Negroes.[74]

Hansberry wrote thoughtfully about the power of cultural erasure. In her reviews she criticized Howard Fast's *Spartacus* for telling the story of a slave uprising from the perspective of the slaveholders rather than the slaves, Richard Wright's *The Outsider* for having abandoned the view that "dignity could be achieved by human struggle" and for what she saw as his "glorification of—*nothingness*," Eugene Brown's *Trespass* as "full of white supremacy," with its assumption that barriers between "races" should be maintained, and what she identified as both political and racist pressures obliging Langston Hughes to leave out mention of Robeson and Du Bois in his stories for children, *First Book of Negroes* (1953).[75] Even in an article on juvenile delinquency Hansberry highlighted the cultural starvation of black children, the emotional costs of the "historical and cultural obliteration" when Negro heritage is denied and "Europe becomes the world." She condemned the "Grace Kelly–Marilyn Monroe monotyped 'ideal' imposed on the national culture" in advertising, movies, television, and popular fiction as efforts to "eradicate all evidence of Negro culture anywhere in the world."[76]

Hansberry was especially interested in housing issues. She and other *Freedom* writers wrote about tenants organizing in Chicago and covered demonstrations to fight evictions in New York.[77] They linked the housing crisis to the increase of military spending; they called attention to the impact of planned slum clearance projects in destroying black, Puerto Rican, and ethnic working-class housing; they noted the discriminatory banking policies that prevented homeowners in Harlem from being able to borrow for repairs. In February 1954 the psychologist Kenneth Clark warned in the pages of *Freedom* that Jim Crow schools were "not confined to the South"; with increased housing segregation their numbers were growing.[78]

Freedom covered a major black initiative organized in 1951, the National Negro Labor Council (NNLC), with twenty-three local labor councils in industrial centers to fight for open employment and fair employment clauses in union contracts. The delegates to the national convention, one third of whom were women trade unionists, came from across the country, but the leadership emerged from the few remaining left-wing union enclaves, including UAW locals from Detroit and Chicago, tobacco workers from Durham and Winston-Salem, packinghouse workers from Chicago, and miners, millers, and smelters from Alabama.[79] Hansberry publicized local jobs and promotions gained as a result of a New York Negro Labor Council campaign against discriminatory practices in the city's big hotels in March 1953. But by April 1955 the NNLC pressure campaign on New York–area brewers, supported by the Urban League and a Brooklyn chapter of the NAACP, had won only temporary employment for black workers rather than permanent jobs. Campaigns for fair employment could not withstand anticommunist attacks; in 1956, called before HUAC on charges of being a "Communist-front organization" and without the resources to mount an expensive legal defense, the NNLC dissolved.[80]

Freedom publicized racial violence tolerated or supported by the state, in contrast with the silence of mainstream media. The lynching in Hansberry's family history gave her a personal connection to this topic.[81] From its first issue *Freedom* carried editorials and articles that referred to the Civil Rights Congress's extensive organizing campaigns for Virginia's Martinsville Seven and Mississippi's Willie McGee, black men accused of raping white women and sentenced to die by all-white juries. In the spring of 1951 Hansberry traveled with an interracial women's delegation to Jackson, Mississippi to present the governor with a petition of a million signatures pleading for clemency for McGee. The governor refused to receive the delegation; despite efforts and appeals, McGee was executed. Hansberry spent the night after his death at a candle-lit vigil in Harlem, in the early morning writing her poem "Lynchsong," which imagines McGee and his wife, Rosalee, as lynching victims facing "dark nights, and dirt roads, and torch lights, and lynch robes . . . [and the] laughing white faces of men."[82]

Closer to home, Hansberry wrote about the dangers facing local black activists. Her article for *Freedom* about Roosevelt Ward, a young member of the NAACP and administrative secretary of the New York chapter of the Labor Youth League, focused on the circumstances of his arrest in May 1951.[83] She covered the trials of the black Communists Ben Davis and Claudia Jones, arrested under the Smith Act, and interviewed George Crockett, the black lawyer who defended them and was facing charges of contempt. The murder by NYU campus police of an economics graduate student, Enus Christiani, was a chilling example of the high costs of challenging northern white complacency about the racial status quo. Christiani, a member of the campus NAACP and the Harlem FEPC chapter, had repeatedly requested that the white sorority and fraternity students running a dart game at a block party remove the picture of a black woman's head they were using as the target; he was shot in a scuffle with a security guard. The student paper termed the block party a success, unfortunately marred by "the incident." In contrast, Hansberry described the promise of Christiani's life, his shocked and desolate parents and young wife, the crowd of mourners at his Harlem church funeral, including a group of black and white students from NYU, and the tragedy of his death.[84]

The *Freedom* radicals encouraged Hansberry's leadership, elevating her from "subscription clerk, receptionist typist, and editorial assistant" to "associate editor" within six months. She was asked to speak at rallies.[85] Her inclusion in political delegations and conferences provided her with access to diverse people committed to leftist activism and dissent. In the fall of 1951 she accompanied a delegation representing Sojourners for Truth and Justice, a militant coalition of black women's organizations, on a protest visit to the Justice Department. The group included Eslanda Goode Robeson and the poet and actress Beulah Richardson as well as victims of legal injustice, including the widow of one of the Martinsville Seven. Hansberry's articles emphasized black women taking leadership: "Women Voice Demands in Capital Sojourn," "Women Demand Justice Done," "They Dried Their Tears and Spoke Their Minds."[86]

Part of *Freedom*'s mission was to connect local struggles for interracial reform to efforts throughout the country. The paper publicized opposition to HUAC investigations, quoting the southern black educator, activist, and founder of North Carolina's Palmer Institute, Charlotte Hawkins Brown, who refused to be silenced by being put on a "subversives" list: "No one but God can bridle my tongue from speaking out against injustices perpetuated against my people." Hansberry herself spoke out against HUAC at a mass meeting in Manhattan in 1952. In February 1953 *Freedom* reprinted an editorial from the Baltimore *Afro-American* questioning the death penalty for the Rosenbergs. From Chicago *Destination Freedom* actor Oscar Brown Jr. reported on the success of the Packinghouse Union in disrupting HUAC's scheduled hearings there in the summer of 1953. *Freedom* asked one southern reader, the young poet and college student Robert F. Williams, to report on southern Negro college students' knowledge of black left-wing organizing. The feature "News from the Color Line" provided updates on southern struggles for voting and civil rights, including Dorothy Burnham's account of efforts to organize tenant farmers.[87]

Freedom writers consistently emphasized the need for organizing to supplement legal strategies in fighting Jim Crow. Writing in June 1951, Doxey Wilkerson emphasized the grassroots struggles behind desegregation court cases in Clarendon County, South Carolina and Prince Edwards County, Virginia. After the 1954 *Brown v. Board of Education* decision, *Freedom*'s headline reminded its audience: "Popular Movement Needed to Enforce Court Decree." In the spring and summer of 1955 staff writer Thelma Dale warned that white terror was endangering the "education decree." She also publicized details of the political murder of Reverend George Lee, singled out for leading a local voting rights drive in Belzoni, Mississippi. The headlines of the last issue, in the summer of 1955, grimly prophesied the future: "Terror Grows in the South: Congress, Ike, Duck Action."[88]

International movements contesting colonialism and racism inspired writers for *Freedom*. The radical Chicago poet and former managing editor of the Associated Negro Press, Frank Marshall Davis, now a journalist in Honolulu, posted a report on how the labor movement in Hawaii was beginning to challenge forms of white privilege and racial division. Eslanda Goode Robeson reported on postrevolutionary China and the Defiance of Unjust Laws Campaign in South Africa. Hansberry contributed articles about Nkrumah's triumph in Ghana, Egyptian demonstrations against British imperialism—including a sizable contingent of women—and Kenyatta's struggles in Kenya. *Freedom* reported on the

meetings of the anti-apartheid South African People's Congress, and publicized local meetings and fund-raising activities to generate support for
anti-apartheid activities. The June 1953 issue was devoted to news of
African independence movements, and included a photo essay comparing
South African apartheid and Jim crow segregation. Reports from the Bandung Conference's efforts to gather African and Asian political leaders to
articulate a non-Western political, cultural, and economic agenda
appeared in 1955. The final issue of *Freedom* boldly juxtaposed the South
African Freedom Charter to the news of white backlash in the South.[89]

In March 1952 Hansberry accepted a request from Robeson, no longer
able to travel outside the U.S., to speak in his place at a peace conference
in Montevideo, Uruguay. By the time she arrived, the government had
officially banned the conference, but 250 delegates from nine countries
were already there, voicing criticism of the repercussions in Latin America of U.S. military and corporate imperial policies. Attending this conference confirmed Hansberry's place in the international, anticolonial left:
upon her return to the U.S., her passport was confiscated.[90]

From her affiliation with the left Hansberry had gained a new way of
thinking about women. Although frequently envisioning solidarity in
terms of masculine kinship, the Communist Party in the early 1950s
engaged in extensive discussions of "the woman question," with a special
focus on the intertwining of race and gender in response to the influential
writing of black Communist Claudia Jones. Jones proposed that black
women be seen not simply as victims suffering the effects of class, race,
and gender exploitation but rather as powerful activists. Even the politics
of respectability and good works embraced by late nineteenth-century
black women's organizations could be seen as efforts to resist black
oppression and improve the status of women.[91] Jones and her ideas were
important to Hansberry, whose shifting perspective was reflected in the
change from the early autobiographical fragments in which she rejected
the intensely feminine, associated with her mother, to the later essays and
drama in which she began to embrace and celebrate women, including her
mother, as sources of strength and exemplars of resistance.

The *Freedom* radicals operated with a principled interracialism, honoring the memory of prior generations of white allies in the abolition and
labor movements. They expected to work with white people who supported the black freedom struggle. Louis Burnham's lesson to Hansberry,
that "all racism was rotten, white or black," encouraged wariness of exclusionary strands of black nationalism or color-based hierarchy. Alice Chil-

dress wrote in 1951, in support of a "Negro theater," that the black freedom struggle would "inspire, lift, and create a complete desire for the liberation of all oppressed peoples." Principled interracialism included a rejection of what may now be termed identity politics: as Childress had written, "We must never be guilty of understanding only ourselves."[92] The *Freedom* milieu of black cultural and political activism within the interracial and international left set the terms in which Hansberry conceived the Younger family drama.

"I AM A WRITER": HANSBERRY IN GREENWICH VILLAGE

Moving to Harlem and working on *Freedom* enabled Hansberry to integrate her politics and her writing. Her most intense involvement with *Freedom* occurred in 1951 and 1952. In the summer of 1952 she also began a romantic relationship with Robert Nemiroff; they had met on a picket line protesting the exclusion of black players from the NYU basketball team. By the end of the year she had committed herself both to Nemiroff and to her developing talents: "I am a writer. I am going to write."[93] By 1953 she had ended her full-time association with the newspaper in order to concentrate on writing, although she continued to contribute articles until *Freedom* ceased publication.

Nemiroff, from a left-wing Russian Jewish immigrant family, was then a graduate student in English literature at NYU and active in the left himself.[94] He had personal and political experience of left-wing interracialism, in the 1940s attending Camp Wo-Chi-Ca (short for Workers' Children's Camp) in New Jersey. Here the African American dancer Pearl Primus was the dance instructor and noted black painter Jacob Lawrence ran the arts program and with his wife painted the murals on the camp dining room wall. Activities at the camp emphasized the roles of African Americans in American history and culture. Nemiroff had earlier been married to Alma Lopez, a Puerto Rican dancer.[95] By 1953, when Nemiroff and Hansberry married, he was working in the summers as the director of the interracial Camp Unity in upstate New York, where Hansberry, director of special events, would arrange for Du Bois to speak on political affairs in the summer of 1954.

Hansberry and Nemiroff shared a commitment to the left, to literature, and to African American culture. Hansberry's mother had been troubled by what she saw as the questionable respectability of Hansberry being single and was anxious for her to marry. When Nannie and Mamie Hansberry came to New York to meet Nemiroff, they weren't entirely comfortable; as Mamie later recalled, "At that point we hadn't done anything interracial really with someone immediately in our family." But the Hansberrys liked Nemiroff and his family and found common interests: "Their family, in their ethnic way, was very similar to our family." Nemiroff and Hansberry spent the day and night before their wedding at a vigil at the Federal Building in Chicago protesting the execution of Julius and Ethel Rosenberg. They were married at the Hansberrys' house, in the presence of their families and various friends.[96]

Hansberry's marriage relocated her from Harlem to a second-floor walk-up above Joe's Hand Laundry on Bleecker Street in Greenwich Village. Various neighborhood subcultures coexisted within the Village's celebrated bohemian culture, prizing creativity and artistic expression, flouting social convention, defending free speech, and supporting a continuum of sexual experimentation, including homosexuality. By 1949 the postwar housing shortage and the resulting inflation of rents threatened the Village atmosphere; some black residents observed a growing "hooliganism" against the "artistic type of Negro" and "colored men escorting white women."[97] Still Nemiroff and Hansberry met friends for dinner, went out to cafés, plays, and movies, and worked jobs that supported them as writers and activists.[98]

Although Hansberry and Nemiroff walked on picket lines and joined desegregation vigils, the left-wing infrastructure supporting these kinds of protests in New York was growing increasingly fragile. Hansberry's efforts shifted toward keeping dissenting African American voices in circulation. She taught a course on "The Literature of the Negro People" at the Jefferson School and spoke at the May 1954 Salute to Paul Robeson as part of a group that included Thelonious Monk, Pete Seeger, actor and singer Leon Bibb, Alice Childress, Julian Mayfield, and blacklisted actress Karen Morley.[99] But the event was only a brief interruption of what Martin Duberman has termed Robeson's "confinement." That summer Hansberry wrote to her husband of feeling heartsick about the state of the world.[100]

Hansberry shifted her attention to southern challenges to segregation as an associate editor of the Labor Youth League's publication, *New Challenge*. Her articles reported on the new militancy she had heard at a 1955 NAACP youth conference in Washington, D.C., the history of Jim Crow segregation, and the "real reasons" for the lynching of Emmett Till in Mississippi in the summer of 1955. In "Heroes of the New South" she critiqued gradualism and celebrated direct action, profiling Autherine Lucy's legal fight to gain admission to graduate school at the University of Alabama and her courage in facing the student and community mobs organized to block her in February 1956, the amazing commitment of participants in the Montgomery bus boycott from December 1955 to November 1956, and white students working to fight Jim Crow.[101]

The creative milieu of Greenwich Village helped to sustain Hansberry and Nemiroff in these years, especially the cabarets and clubs featuring jazz, theatrical pieces, and folk music. After the closing of the CNA Club Baron theater in Harlem in the early 1950s, the tiny Greenwich Mews Theatre staged black off Broadway theater. There Stella Holt mounted productions by two of Hansberry's friends: William Branch's 1954 play juxtaposing Frederick Douglass and John Brown, *In Splendid Error,* and Alice Childress's powerful 1955 critique of bankrupt white theatrical representations of black characters, *Trouble in Mind.*[102]

Hansberry was able to quit her day jobs to work full time on her writing in the fall of 1956, bankrolled by the income from Nemiroff's hit pop song "Cindy, Oh Cindy" and his job running a musical publishing firm for Philip Rose. At this time the remnants of the Communist left were reeling from the impact of the Soviet revelations of Stalins's crimes, published in the *New York Times* in February 1956, and the Soviet invasion of Hungary in the fall of that year. Hansberry had a number of writing projects underway, all of which were driven by her desire to represent something that was missing in mainstream culture: full-bodied African Americans struggling for their rights. The projects included an unfinished autobiographical novel, tentatively titled "All the Dark and Beautiful Warriors," and several plays. One, "The Final Glory," was about a trade union leader framed for the murder of an African American strikebreaker. Another was an adaptation of the African American writer Charles Chesnutt's controversial novel *The Marrow of Tradition* (1901), loosely based on the 1898 race riots in Wilmington, North Carolina that were orchestrated by white supremacists in an effort to destroy political and economic achievements by local blacks in the Reconstruction era. She was also thinking about an opera based on the life of the Haitian revolutionary Toussaint L'Ouverture, in her notes highlighting the former slave's creation of a nation "out of a savagely dazzling colonial jewel in the mighty French Empire."[103]

She turned increasingly to one play, which she originally called "The Crystal Stair"—from a line in Langston Hughes's poem "Mother to Son," in which the mother, noting that "life for me ain't been no crystal stair," encourages her son to continue her struggle. Hansberry later changed the title, turning to Hughes's book-length ode to Harlem, "Montage of a Dream Deferred" (1948), which warned that the disappointed dreams of "A New Day A' Coming," would either explode or "dry up like a raisin in the sun."[104]

It was difficult for Hansberry to claim her identity as a writer. In a December 1955 letter from Chicago, probably written while visiting her family, she remarked, "My work. It is only here on paper that I dare say it like that: My work!" Hansberry did not doubt what she had to say: "So many truths seem to be rushing at me as the result of things felt and seen and lived through. Oh what I think I must tell this world!" Her constraints were both practical and psychological: "Oh the time that I crave—and the peace— . . . and the *power!*"[105] In 1956 and 1957 Hansberry had to define a place for herself far from conventional expectations. Finding "the *power!*" depended in part on developing her awareness of the social construction of gender. This process strengthened her sense of self and deepened her already complex understandings of the interconnections between sex, race, and class exploitation.

Hansberry's unpublished writings from these years charted her move away from blaming women to analyzing the cultural texts and social prescriptions that shaped men and women's self-expectations. In an unpublished note from November 1955, Hansberry mentioned the resistance she had encountered to "so much as an itsby-bitsy analogy between the situation, say, of the Negro people in the U.S.—and women. . . . Must I hate 'men' any more than I hate 'white people'—because some of them are savage and others commit savage acts? Of course not!"[106] In a February 1956 letter to the *Village Voice*, Hansberry dissented from the reviewer's favorable account of an Actor's Playhouse production of August Strindberg's *Comrades*, arguing that "the playwright clearly hated women."[107]

Hansberry's long review of Simone de Beauvoir's *The Second Sex*, possibly written for *Masses and Mainstream* in 1957, called attention to de Beauvoir's pathbreaking analysis in what Hansberry thought might "well be the most important work of this century." Hansberry analyzed the deafening silence that met its U.S. publication—apart from gossip about de Beauvoir's personal life—and ruminated on its application to women's situation in the U.S. She invited those with a "more far-reaching historical materialist" view to address certain gaps in de Beauvoir's existentialist thought. She credited American women Communists with "lifting the woman question beyond the ordinary sphere of the 'battlefield of the sexes'-type nonsense," and identified areas for further discussion: the meaning of "insurgency" in dress, the burdens and social value of housework and paid labor, the myth of love, and the glorification of women as sex objects. Hansberry was especially critical of "how society tells women from cradle to grave that her husband, her home, her children will be the source of all rewards in life, the foundation of all true happiness."[108]

From letters Hansberry wrote to the homosexual publication the *Ladder* in the spring and summer of 1957, we know that her thinking about gender as a social category extended to its connection with the social organization of sexuality. Domestic anticommunist investigations and exposés had targeted homosexuals as security risks and moral deviants, encouraging public harassment and social condemnation. The first homophile organizations appeared in response, the male-oriented Mattachine Society, founded in Los Angeles in 1951, and the Daughters of Bilitis, organized in San Francisco in 1955, which published the *Ladder*.[109] Hansberry contrasted the accomplishment of public association in these West Coast organizations with the active but unorganized presence of homosexuals in the Village, where "a vigorous and active gay set almost bump one another off the streets." She wanted to know "what is it in the air out there? Pioneers still? Or a tougher circumstance which inspires battle?" She wrote to the *Ladder* editors that she was inspired by their "energy and courage."[110]

Although a full account of Hansberry's sexuality must await the opening of her papers, Hansberry referred to herself as speaking "personally as well as abstractly" about the "problem of the married lesbian" in one letter to the *Ladder*. Hansberry argued against a simplistic discussion of lesbianism as merely an "interest" in other women, formulating the married lesbian as "an individual who finds that, despite her conscious will oftimes, she is inclined to have her most intense emotional and physical reactions directed toward other women, quite beyond any comparative thing she might have ever felt for her husband—whatever her sincere affection for him." Hansberry identified the "problem" as "how one quite admits that to oneself—and to one's husband."[111] Nemiroff later emphasized that Hansberry's homosexuality was "not a peripheral or casual part of her life but contributed significantly on many levels to the sensitivity and complexity of her view of human beings and of the world."[112]

Hansberry connected the isolation and "intellectual impoverishment" of women to their second-class status: "I feel that women, without wishing to foster any separatist notions, homo or hetero, indeed have a need for their own publications and organizations." Her comments stressed the interconnections between issues, for example, when she thought about whether butch and femme dress was damaging to campaigns for homosexual rights. She wrote that her "cultural experience" as a Negro subjected her to considerable lecturing on "how to appear acceptable to the dominant social group," but she argued that this effort, if sometimes expedient, was ineffective:

> Ralph Bunche, with all his clean fingernails, degrees, and, of course, undeniable service to the human race, could still be insulted, denied a hotel room, or meal in many parts of the country (not to mention the possibility of being lynched on a lonely Georgia road for perhaps having demanded a glass of water in the wrong place).

This kind of thinking was counterproductive because, she argued, "one is oppressed or discriminated against because one is different, not 'wrong' or 'bad' somehow." Her political understanding led her to blame racial discrimination, not the person being discriminated against—"Social awareness has taught me where to lay the blame."[113]

Hansberry argued that women intellectuals were required to break into the previously male realm of "morality and ethics," because "equipped women" needed to "take on some of the ethical questions which a male-dominated culture has produced." Hansberry was sure that "moral conclusions based on a social moral superstructure which has never admitted to the equality of women" were inadequate. She was hoping for a theoretical insight that would reconnect gender and sexuality, imagining that women might apprehend the connections between discrimination against homosexuals and discrimination against women in the service of envisioning the terms of genuine equality and emancipation.[114]

By the fall of 1957, soon after she wrote these letters, Hansberry finished her play. The characters include three generations of a South Side black family who live together: Lena (a widow), her son Walter Lee, daughter-in-law Ruth, grandson Travis, and daughter Beneatha. Four other male characters represent external social forces: Walter Lee's no-good drinking buddy, Bobo; Beneatha's two boyfriends, George Murchison, a representative of black wealthy respectability, and Asagai, a radical, anticolonialist African student studying in the U.S.; and Karl Lindner, the polite white spokesman for housing segregation. The plot centers on the longings stimulated by a windfall insurance check and the characters' different strategies for confronting racial and social hurt, anger, and exclusion.

After dinner one night in the fall of 1957, Hansberry and Nemiroff read the play to Nemiroff's friend and songwriting partner, Burt D'Lugoff, and his boss, Philip Rose.[115] Rose immediately optioned the play for a commercial theatrical production; Hansberry and Rose knew Poitier, who agreed to play the male lead; Poitier suggested his friend and acting teacher Lloyd Richards, to direct; Harry Belafonte helped organize the group of small investors whose contributions financed the production. By Christmas 1957 Hansberry let herself dream of appealing to a popular audience and finding public affirmation: "longings, longings, longings. . . . I want the world to love my singing! Whether I am less for it or no—I want it!"[116]

RAISIN IN THE SUN: HANSBERRY'S CONCEPTION, AUDIENCE RECEPTION

How different publics understood Hansberry's drama depended on what they knew of racialized theatrical representations, racial discrimination, and social protest, whether they could recognize black characters as both family members and social actors. The last black-directed production on Broadway, Jesse Shipp's *Abyssenia,* was in 1907; mainstream audiences had never seen an African American family dealing with the costs of social and racial discrimination. Neither of *Raisin's* predecessors, the hugely successful and long-running Broadway production of *Anna Lucasta* (1944) or the modestly successful Broadway staging of Louis Peterson's *Take a Giant Step* (1953), attempted this kind of representation.

Anna Lucasta, with ANT productions in Harlem and on Broadway, was a family story that showcased the talents of its black actors, but it aspired neither to realism nor social criticism. It was widely understood to be a black-cast enactment of a Polish American story, written by a white author, Philip Yordan, and adapted by a white director, Harry Wagstaff Gribble.[117] At the time, black reviewers noted that references to the Savoy Ballroom and Harlem were added to the play to make it seem "essentially Negro"; they also pointed out its significant evasion: "no race problem [is] mentioned." Given the history of most theatrical stereotyping, the racial silence could have some positive effect; as one black press reviewer had commented, "This play isn't one of those condescending affairs about colored people: it's a play about people." The *Chicago Defender* reviewer suggested that the play's racial silence provided an opening for African American actors to be included in wartime's multiethnic pluralism: the play's family "might be Chinese, Bulgarian, Italian, Jewish—any nationality."[118]

White reviewers had in contrast posed "race," and by implication, blackness, as the opposite of "humanity." They admired the drama for showing the Negro "playing a human role rather than a racial one." They used the language here that would later be used about *Raisin*—that *Anna Lucasta* "is a play, not about Negroes but about people. The characters transcend their race and become human creatures, to suggest anybody's family." Another white reviewer's comment shows how this "no race" perspective could deny racial discrimination. Although he appreciated the historic significance of the production as the first play "to treat Negro life without a certain amused condescension," he also described it as "first play of Negro life to recognize that Negroes are individuals with pretty much the same problems as that of the whites."[119]

Peterson's play *Take a Giant Step* was a quiet exploration of the subtle forms of social isolation experienced by a black teenager growing up in a northern white middle-class community. It presented Negro characters without apology, exploring an adolescent angst amplified by the additional pressures of racial achievement and racial exclusion. Peterson described himself as "unfamiliar with the violence that often dominates dramas of Negro life"; he was "groping for a play about the Negro" and wanted to use his character to explore the problem "of growing up . . . and of being a Negro in this society." Hansberry admired the sophistication of his presentation and the subtlety of his characterization, but Peterson did not emphasize social issues or propose social solutions.[120] Brooks Atkinson hailed Peterson's play as a "landmark" because "it is a Negro play that does not follow any of the Negro formulas of protest on the one hand or racial solidarity on the other." In Atkinson's eyes, this is what made it a "play about Americans."[121]

Without full access to Hansberry's papers, we can't assess the formal, commercial, or political influences on her play. But a 1959 interview with Hansberry, after *Raisin* had opened on Broadway, offers clues to her social and artistic priorities. She began working on the characters and plot of what would become *Raisin* in 1956. A long version in the fall of 1957 was "much more of a social drama than it is now. There was heavy emphasis on Negroes moving into a white community." This may have been the draft referred to by Hansberry's biographer, ending with "the Youngers armed and awaiting the attack of their racist neighbors." Friends offered her "considerable criticism" of the script, arguing that it was two plays. Hansberry first resisted and then responded to their comments, revising her work into "a much shorter play that concentrated on characters and their intimate problems and dreams."[122]

Shortening the play, Hansberry cut vivid images: Beneatha transformed from straightened to natural hair, Travis doing battle with a rat, Walter Lee's dreams of authority and ambition unfettered by class or racial restrictions. The cut scenes highlighted physical danger, both for children growing up in ghetto neighborhoods and for black families facing bombings when moving to white neighborhoods. They attached characters to contemporary political arguments within the black community, setting conservative values of self-protection and individual mobility against a proud claiming of one's rights, contrasting liberal idealism with anticolonialism's revolutionary realism. The extra threads may have slowed the action, but they added to the complexity of the characters and sharpened the play's political references.[123]

The decision to concentrate on the "characters'. . . intimate problems and dreams" pushed the play into the realm of family psychology, heightening the theatricality of Hansberry's political analysis without waving a red flag. Hansberry's interviews at the time suggest how difficult it was to challenge mainstream conventions of black representation in a way that white critics could understand. Their repeated assertions that *Raisin* was "not a Negro play, but a play about people who happened to be Negroes," and that Hansberry herself was "not a Negro playwright, but a writer who happened to be black," showed the barriers in the way of Hansberry's effort to define new terms for black characters. Black theater reviewers, having for years evaluated the limitations of stage and screen representations of black characters, knew that when she criticized the idea of a "Negro play" she was questioning the limited range of conventional images of black people. They lauded her intention to write a play involving Negroes in which the characters would have "problems as people, problems and persons who would transcend the specifics of their being Negro."[124]

Hansberry frequently invoked O'Casey in the interviews she gave, calling attention to a political and artistic tradition with which she identified. She followed O'Casey's practice in *Juno* in constructing characters whose conflicts paralleled national conflicts and she sought to emulate his achievement of a dramatic tone of the dispossessed that easily flowed from humor to pain and back again. O'Casey had influenced other radical playwrights important to Hansberry: Arthur Miller, Tennessee Williams, and Alice Childress. If the family could stand in for the nation, then the Younger family could represent simultaneously the African American community and the American nation as a whole.

Hansberry structured *Raisin* to answer compromised representations of second-class and racial citizenship with characterizations showcasing diversity, social change, and historical strengths within the black community. As she noted to the African American journalist Ted Poston, "the thing I tried to show was the many gradations in even one Negro family, the clash of the old and the new, but most of all, the unbelievable courage of the Negro people."[125] She called attention to historical and generational change, contrasting the Great Migration mentality of Big Walter and Lena with the postwar promises and disappointments facing Walter Lee, Ruth, and Beneatha. She balanced black working-class productivity and exploitation—the hard manual labor that "wore out" Walter senior, the ill-paid and demeaning domestic work available to Lena and Ruth, the servility required of Walter Lee as a chauffeur—with the upward mobility and arrogance of George Murchison and the promise of social status for Beneatha if she became a doctor. Hansberry utilizes a rich array of language to represent different social and ideological positions, from Lena's black English to Beneatha's "hip" and educated, left-inflected rhetoric to Asagai's African diction in his use of English as a second language. She similarly celebrates a range of communal musical resources, from Asagai's African rhythms to Ruth's rhythm and blues to Beneatha's jazz. Embracing differences, she allots flaws and insights, narrow vision and great wisdom, to all of her main characters.

The black working-class characters of *Raisin in the Sun* engage with issues central to postwar society. Hansberry consciously set the play in Chicago's South Side because of its reputation as a vital, if overcrowded, black community. Insisting that she was *not* writing about her own family—"we were more typical of the bourgeois Negro exemplified by the Murchison family"—Hansberry presented the black working class as the initiators of radical change, both historically and in the future: "Whatever we ultimately achieve, however we ultimately transform our lives, the changes will come from the kind of people I chose to portray. They are more pertinent, more relevant, more significant, more important, more *decisive*—in our political history and our political future."[126]

Hansberry was intent on promoting a vision of sexual politics. Lena is the one to propose the move toward desegregated housing; she and Ruth willingly face the risks entailed. Hansberry's formulation was echoed in an editorial in the *Pittsburgh Courier* in April 1959 linking the play to a housing struggle unfolding in Wilmington, Delaware and to several other battlegrounds of desegregation, observing that "it is the Negro women who have the stiffest backbone when it comes to standing with one's back against the wall and slugging it out in the field of civil rights."[127]

Hansberry conveyed the pressures closing in on black men by making Walter Lee's frustrations and dreams palpable and impassioned, if occasionally misdirected. But the resolution of *Raisin* was careful to restore his leadership in the struggle, showing him capable of redirecting his dreams, rejoining the women, and reconnecting to his past and future. Here Hansberry departed dramatically from O'Casey, who ended *Juno* with the son dead and the father lying in a drunken stupor on the floor, any claim to patriarchal authority thoroughly discredited. Using a term from Communist literary debates, Hansberry called Walter Lee an "affirmative hero" because "he refuses to give up," despite "moments when he doubts himself and even retreats." Walter Lee expresses her conviction that "sooner or later we are going to have to make principled decisions in American about a lot of things. . . . This to me is a certain kind of affirmation."[128]

Hansberry gave her audience a glimpse of the nonwhite majority of the world when she introduced the anticolonial African student Asagai, Broadway's first educated, conscious, and cosmopolitan African character "who didn't have his shoes hanging around his neck and a bone through his nose, or his ears, or something."[129] Asagai's interaction with the Youngers linked the South Side black community to a worldwide African diaspora, suggesting that cultural exchange could place the struggles of American blacks in a wider international context, expanding their political imagination.

Hansberry's political goals had an additional dimension. If *Raisin* could rewrite the ordinary family narrative by insisting that black families were American families, with recognizable aspirations for decent jobs and housing, and social respect, then Hansberry could pass along the torch illuminated by the powerful essays of Du Bois, the fiery speeches of Robeson, and the streetwise poetry of Hughes. *Raisin* dramatized African American citizens as integral to the social fabric of American life, their inclusion requisite to fulfilling the promise of postwar American democracy, the racist barriers standing in the way of their citizenship unjust as well as destructive. What happens to a dream deferred: does it dry up, does it fester, does it explode? Drawing on a familiar plot device revolving around competing claims to family money—the choices pitting need against need in Odets's *Awake and Sing, A Tree Grows in Brooklyn,* and *I Remember Mama*—Hansberry made a claim for the centrality of the black experience in the saga of working-class migration and Americanization. Contrasting the meagerness of working-class earnings with the illusory promises of inheritance, she drew a parallel between the false dreams of Captain Boyle in *Juno,* Willy Loman, and Walter Lee. Writing about *Raisin* in the *Village Voice* soon after it opened, she hoped audiences would recognize the "simple line of descent" from "the last great hero in American drama to also accept the values of his culture, Willy Loman," to Walter Lee Younger.[130]

Raisin emphasized the black family as a collective resource. When together the characters reject a commitment to material advancement, which would come at the cost of collective familial goals, Hansberry suggested that black resources of hope, pride, and solidarity could replenish a postwar working class worn down and spiritually depleted. Hansberry wrote Walter Lee as an alternative to Willy Loman, associating a spiritual critique with black agency rather than white failure. In Hansberry's terms Willy Loman's "section of American life seems to have momentarily lost that urgency. . . . He cannot, like Walter, draw on the strength of an incredible people who, historically, have simply refused to give up." *Raisin* celebrated the rich history of black resistance and the momentum of worldwide anticolonialism as contributing to the transformation of American life. Like Hughes believing there could be "too much of race," Hansberry in *Raisin* reached for a mode of expression that revealed racial history as a source of cultural wealth and racialization as a tool of white supremacy. As the *Philadelphia Inquirer*'s Henry Murdock noted, the play's themes expanded beyond its rich "racial idiom" and investigation of "racial prejudice" to fulfill the playwright's desire to "express something about American life in general beyond race and color."[131]

From the New Haven previews, through Philadelphia, Chicago, and then Broadway openings, audiences helped to shape the performances. The first-night New Haven audience began to laugh in the opening scene, a reaction for which the actors were not prepared, and which pushed Lloyd Richards to reorient his direction to showcase humor as a form of social resilience. One reviewer termed this the "self-mocking humor that is so rich and saving a characteristic of have-not peoples." Reviewers noted hushed silence, tumultuous ovations, and raucous laughter mixing with tears, even from hard-boiled journalists. White reviewers shared the theater with black theatergoers, who probably cued the laughter and transformed opening night into an interracial public sphere. It was a new experience for blacks and whites to listen to expressions of racial anger in one another's presence. Aspiring black actors saw a new world of theatrical possibility. Black reviewers crowed over the mainstream acknowledgment, the white and black elite in attendance, the praise showered on *Raisin* by critics at big-city dailies, and their predictions of commercial success.[132]

But what was the history being made? Was it the individual success of a black playwright with a play celebrating the American dream? Was it also a cultural opening that, by imagining racial inclusion and illuminating racial exclusion, proposed new terms for social transformation? In 1959 "American values" were commonly defined as upward mobility, consumer acquisition, and family privacy—often refracted through a prism of ethnic nostalgia. Anticommunism had closed off spaces in which racial universalism could offer alternative frameworks. Liberal anticommunist support for civil rights affirmed American progress in race relations, interpreted "second-class citizenship" as anachronistic rather than as institutionalized in economic, political, and social practices, and dismissed militancy as impatience. Voicing race competed with silencing race in a vision of expanded postwar citizenship.

Raisin was the first commercially successful Broadway play about a black family, authored and directed by black artists, yet it was widely praised in terms that misconstrued or obfuscated its racial meanings. No single cultural intervention could on its own transform public debate or racial understanding; every dramatic strategy carried risks. But different reviewers saw different plays. If audiences picked up the political references to O'Casey, recognized the cri de coeur against the single-minded pursuit of wealth, or followed contemporary clashes over desegregation, they saw a play full of ideas. The Philadelphia reviewer Henry Murdock was an early enthusiast. Admiring the play's "theme of false gods and spurious ideals . . . which is probably as pertinent to our era as any," Murdock recognized *Raisin*'s "kinship" with *Juno* and John Osborne's *Look Back in Anger*. Seeing Walter Lee as a big talker like Captain Boyle and an "angry young man" like Osborne's hero, Jimmy Porter, Murdock found Walter Lee sympathetic in his "moments away from his obsession with money" and the "frustrations which dog him and his family" as the source of "something more tangible to holler about than the noisy hero of the Osborne play."[133]

If audiences were familiar with contemporary debates over civil rights, they were able to overhear an illuminating discussion. Kenneth Tynan admitted in the *New Yorker* that he was predisposed to like *Raisin* by his "knowledge of historical context," but he was quickly absorbed: "The relaxed free-wheeling interplay of a magnificent team of Negro actors drew me unresisting into a world of their own making, their suffering, their thinking, and their rejoicing." Tynan recognized Beneatha's progressive politics, criticized Hansberry's "reverent treatment" of Lena as she disciplines Beneatha's agnosticism, and was fascinated by the Nigerian intellectual's political engagement. The choice to present "white opinion" in the shape of "a deferential little man . . . puts the segregationist case so gently it almost sounds like a plea for modified togetherness." Tynan made the connection between *Raisin* and *Awake and Sing*, each suggesting ways of seeing previously racialized groups beyond vaudeville and minstrelsy stereotypes. "I was not present at the opening twenty-four years ago at *Awake and Sing* but it must have been a similar occasion, generating the same kind of sympathy and communicating the same kind of warmth."[134]

Black critics often responded to *Raisin* from a perspective of racial pride; they also had much to say about Hansberry's historic choices. To *Pittsburgh Courier* reviewer Isadora Rowe *Raisin* conveyed social change: it was "a play about Negroes which has so much of the *modern us* in it" (emphasis added). She saw the characters as the 1959 "New Negro," the play illuminating "his hopes, his desires, and his dreams." Shauneille Perry, an actress and Hansberry's first cousin, profiled Hansberry and the play for the *Chicago Defender;* Perry positioned Hansberry as a protest writer emerging from a group "making a resounding impact on the dramatic and literary world," a generation of U.S. "beats" and English "angry young men." "It is inevitable that a young Negro be found within their ranks." Perry linked Hansberry and Osborne thematically: "South Side or Surry . . . they have the courage to make an honest appraisal of our conformist society of today . . . and the skill to do it artistically and dramatically." She also called attention to how Hansberry conveyed the frustrations of living in a racist society as a "struggle against the mounting odds of a society which is manifested by slum dwellings, restricted covenants, and a no-exit kind of life."[135]

A *Defender* reviewer placed *Raisin* in the tradition of the social-problem play, although he appreciated how *Raisin*'s problem unfolds "through a side door." He noted that Hansberry referred to "Chicago's restrictive covenant and other housing problems," but he gave her credit for artistry, because a theatergoer who was "hep" to the situation was neither "bored or bloodcurdled by what goes on." She "avoids the usual rut of making everyone mad over how it happens and what is done." Still, he noted the successful resolution: "the protesting groups would appear to have lost and the protested move in." A particular black viewer who identified with Hansberry's political choices was one of the nine students who braved the white mobs to desegregate Central High School in Little Rock, Arkansas in 1957. He wrote her that had the students seen the play they would have been "prouder to enter Central because we knew we were not the only Walter Lee Youngers."[136]

Other white reviewers readily responded to *Raisin*. Informed by the logic of multiethnic pluralism, however, they did not understand the play's social protest because they were blinded to its *racial* significance. Relying on assumptions of universalism popularized in looking back stories, *Newsweek*'s reviewer described the Youngers' dreams as "those of any minority group living under pressure and bursting with the urge to better their condition" and a "touching story about a tenement family and their vanishing dream." *Time*'s critic wrote condescendingly that the play "belonged to the simple annals of the poor." These critics described *Raisin*'s "honesty" or "vitality" as an alternative to a social problem play. *New York Times* critic Brooks Atkinson assured his readers that Hansberry had "no axe to grind." The *Time* critic praised the "saving absence of racial partisanship."[137] The senior statesman of the 1930s white theatrical left, Harold Clurman, pronounced *Raisin* an "old-fashioned play" about the concerns of "humble Negro folk in an American big city," intended neither as "an appeal to whites nor as a preachment for Negroes."[138]

These critics did not see the social context shaping the play's family dynamics because ethnic nostalgia did not provide a framework that illuminated the price of contemporary exclusions. They quickly typed Lena Younger as a domineering but good-natured and hard-working matriarch, like *Pinky*'s Granny, or condescended to her as a domestic, rather than seeing her as an actor in a drama about desegregation. Brooks Atkinson described Lena as "a simple character" enhanced by Claudia McNeil's acting into "a worn woman with a noble spirit." They did not understand, and so dismissed the significance of, Beneatha's and Asagai's perspectives, which extend far beyond the family. In his first review Atkinson described Beneatha as "race conscious," but on reconsideration he pointed to her "belligerent racism, her provincial ignorance of Africa, her confusion of

Liberia and Nigeria." Their reviews tended to demean her, referring to her as "an emancipated type with all the fine-sounding guff of the very young intellectual," and to mention Asagai primarily as part of Beneatha's joke. They assumed that private family goals motivated everything, describing the housing move as simply a step up: "Mrs. Younger wants to get her family into a house that has elbowroom and sunlight," "Ruth will accept any benefice that will preserve her marriage and give their young son the sweet smell of security." Atkinson interpreted the play as revolving around "situations that test their individual characters" and thought it might be seen as a "Negro *Cherry Orchard*," sharing a focus on "how character is controlled by environment." He insisted that Hansberry "argues no cause" because he posed the play's resolution as "the pride of a family that has ethical standards."[139] Their failure to recognize Hansberry's protest revealed deep racial fault lines.

Critical backlash followed *Raisin*'s designation as the "best American play of the year" from the New York Drama Critics—perhaps because it won the prize without the votes from the drama critics at New York's seven major daily newspapers, who split their votes among plays by established literary figures: Tennessee Williams's *Sweet Bird of Youth*, Archibald MacLeish's *JB*, and Eugene O'Neill's *Touch of the Poet*. (Soon after that, *JB* won the Pulitzer Prize for drama.) Hansberry's six winning votes came from a reporter for the wire services, magazine critics, including one for a socialist weekly, and the reviewer for a horse paper.[140]

After *Raisin* received the award, certain critics heaped condescension on the play, attributing its popular appeal to "sentimentality over the Negro question," condemning it as entirely predictable and filled with theatrical clichés. They didn't recognize that the family stood for the nation, not simply because of the widespread ideological assumption that family dynamics operated in isolation from politics and protest but also because they assigned a female-authored family drama to the feminized and discredited terrain of soap opera. The *New Republic*'s Tom Driver charged Hansberry with falling into the "overworked formulas" of the "domestic" play, suggesting facetiously that Hansberry's objective in writing *Raisin* was to show that "stage stereotypes will fit Negroes as well as white people."[141] Hansberry was criticized from the left by the Chicago writer Nelson Algren, who read *Raisin*'s family as replicating middle-class consumerism: "What *Raisin* is all about is the aspiration of the new, rising Negro mercantile class . . . in short, it is not a play about human dignity but how to invest wisely. . . . Dramatically *Raisin* does for the Negro people what hair straightener and skin-lightener have done for the Negro cosmetics trade."[142] Others dismissed *Raisin* as old-fashioned, sentimental naturalism: "something close to this has been the stuff of so many novels and plays about Negro or Jewish, Irish or Italian families." These critics considered interactions and characters in terms of whether these were "authentic," "real," or "vivid" within the context of the family. They questioned whether an aspiring medical student could belong to a working-class family, whether a mother representing a "cautious and respectful" generation would have bought a house in a white neighborhood, whether the son's change of heart to resist the financial offer for the house was sufficiently motivated. Their ignorance of the interplay between familial dynamics and social change limited what they could imagine the "real" to be as well as their ability to recognize Hansberry's political agenda.[143]

The play's commercial success and critical recognition gave Hansberry sudden visibility, authority as a writer, and legitimacy as a voice for change. Because her celebrity contained the potential to distort and drown out her words, it is critical to revisit the words she used to defend, challenge, and attempt to reframe the critical misrepresentations of her play. With her experience of political censorship, Hansberry must have felt some pressure to be circumspect. Still, she accepted every public invitation she was offered as an opportunity to circulate her political ideas. She wanted to take advantage of a new mood: after "eight to ten years of misery under McCarthy, to the credit of the American people, they got rid of it. And they're feeling like: *Make new sounds!* I'm glad I was here to make one."[144] Her friend Julian Mayfield remembered her uncompromising strategy as a clear political decision to "act as if you don't expect to be invited back again, and to say what's on your mind."[145]

Hansberry aggressively answered critics who tried to deny the racial signifiers in the play and blunt her social protest. She argued that it was impossible to "set aside" the fact that the Youngers are a Negro family: "You can't say that if you take away the American character of something that it just becomes something else."[146] She knew that segregationists equated any investigation of racial assumptions with racial protest, that audiences were accustomed to white-authored theatrical archetypes: "de Emporer, de Lawd, and of course, Porgy, still haunt our frame of reference." That her characters transcended racial types did not mean that they transcended cultural specificity, Hansberry insisted: "Not only is this a Negro family . . . but it's not even a New York family or a southern Negro family—it is specifically South Side Chicago . . . so it is definitely a Negro play before it is anything else." She challenged those who misread the move to the new house as a voluntary move up, referring to significantly lower life expectancy among American blacks: "Our people don't really have a choice. We must come out of the ghettos of America because the ghettos are killing us." She reiterated the dangers facing the Youngers, answering one critic who damned the play's conclusion as that of conventional soap opera: "If he thinks that's a happy ending, I invite him to live in one of the communities where the Youngers are going!"[147] Asked on network television whether she was recognized by the Drama Critics simply because she was a Negro, she replied, "If I were given the award because they wanted to give it to a Negro, it would be the first time in the history of this country that anyone had ever been given anything for *being* a Negro."[148] When *Raisin* was honored by publication in *Theatre Arts,* she took the opportunity to criticize longstanding racial stereotyping in theatrical practice and to challenge racial exclusion on Broadway, calling for the desegregation of positions as ticket takers, program vendors, ushers, and technical crew as well as expanded employment of black actors, writers, directors.[149]

Hansberry fought to reclaim the cultural authority of social drama. She pleaded with her audience at a black writers' conference not to isolate themselves or write about racial realities without reference to a larger context of "war and peace, colonialism, capitalism vs. socialism"—the "most pressing world issues of our time." There was a "desperate need" for Negro writers to confront "the illusions of one's time and culture," foremost among them the idea that "art is not, and *should* not and, when it is at its best, CANNOT be social." She illustrated the "social" content of presumptions about class, gender, and race in almost all television, film, theater, and fiction: "Most people who work for a living (and they are few) are executives and/or work in some kind of office; women are idiots; people are white; Negroes do not exist." To silence the social was to censor discussions challenging the racial status quo: "Those who say they did not wish to have 'social' material on stage, motion pictures or TV screen are the same persons who in the past have not hesitated to relegate *all* black material, save hip swinging musicals, to the social category."[150] Hansberry argued that her play expanded realism by its social inflection, showing "not only what *is* but what is *possible,*" referring to contemporary victories against the formerly impregnable edifice of American segregation.[151]

Relying on the family to stand for the nation enhanced the political significance of Hansberry's representation of the black working-class mother not as a conservative spiritual moralist but as a risk-taking radical. She knew that she had to differentiate her conception of the strong mother from the antimaternal concepts currently circulating:

> I think it is a mistake to get it confused with Freudian concepts of matriarchal "dominance" and Philip Wylie's Momism and all that business. It's not the same thing—not that there aren't negative things about it, and not that tyranny doesn't sometimes emerge as part of it. But basically, it's a great thing—these women have become the backbone of our people in a very necessary way.[152]

Lena embodies the tradition of African American mothers; she is "the black matriarch incarnate; the bulwark of the Negro family since slavery; the embodiment of the Negro will to transcendence." Lena wears the mask as she presses forward, resists, survives:

> It is she who, while seeming to cling to traditional restraints, drives the young on into the fire hoses and one day simply refuses to move to the back of the bus in Montgomery, or goes out and buys a house in an all-white community where her fourth child and second daughter will almost be killed by a brick thrown through the window by a shrieking racist mob.

Acknowledging Lena as simultaneously tyrannical and heroic, Hansberry nonetheless believed that "the development of strong black women was a gain for the entire race, affirming that the would-be castigators of black men were not black women but the practitioners and enforcers of white racism."[153]

FROZEN IN THE FRAME: THE FILM OF *RAISIN*

Hansberry continued to fight for her political conception of *Raisin* in the screenplay she prepared for its film adaptation. She hoped to develop a visual vocabulary to show the daily indignities of racial discrimination without overemphasizing victimization or losing her emphasis on the characters' agency and subjectivity. She wrote a new opening to establish the specificity, promise, and despair of Chicago's South Side for the Younger family, with the phrases of Langston Hughes's poem superimposed over panoramic shots. Another planned scene contrasted the exploitative prices and inferior produce of shops in a black neighborhood with what was available in a white area; in a later scene the new white neighbors, some staring, some with shades drawn, suggest hostility. Several scenes dramatized white paternalism, including an interaction between Lena and her white female employer. Shots of steel mills, the stockyards, and the monument of the Negro Soldier on the South Side represented the stolen labor of Chicago's black workers; a street corner oration, with Walter Lee and Asagai in the audience, emphasized the social origins of the family's dilemma.

The Columbia studio producer rejected all these scenes on the grounds that that they might be racially provocative and drive away white audiences.[154] The only scene Hansberry succeeded in changing was a new ending that visually established Walter Lee's assumption of leadership. In the play Mama is the last to leave the tenement; in the film Walter Lee picks up the bag Lena passes along to him, and he stays in the frame as she makes her departure. Triumphant masculinity was entirely consistent with upward mobility and multiethnic pluralism. Producer David Susskind actively promoted this interpretation, insisting that "the point of this play is not about the race angle. It's about the disparity of needs and ambitions which bring a middle-class family to disaster. The fact that the Negroes move into a white neighborhood has nothing to do with it. It could be a play about an Italian or Jewish family and have the same meaning." Of course, a film about an Italian or a Jewish family certainly would not have encountered the difficulties the *Raisin* crew did filming on location in Chicago, meeting resistance both in white neighborhoods and at the University of Chicago.[155]

Hansberry was only too aware of the pressures of film adaptation to rewrite her language or revise her characterizations in line with film minstrelsy or black exoticism. She must have been disappointed not to convey fully her political perspective, but, as a writer who "took pride in what some intended as an epithet, the label popular," she wanted to reach film's expanded audience. She was relieved that the film remained true to the parameters of her play.[156] With performances by almost all the original Broadway cast members, *Raisin* did reach a mass audience. Black and white reviewers gave the film credit for its good intentions, faithful adaptation, and for powerful acting, especially from Poitier, McNeil, Ruby Dee, and Diana Sands.[157]

But *Raisin* lost something in the transfer from live performance to film. What was electrifying about its racial anger and self-mocking humor came from experiencing the play live. Watching a film in a movie theater had more potential for public interaction than watching in a private living room, but film reviewers missed the immediacy of the theatrical performance.[158] *Raisin* was filmed in the visual style of television drama, almost entirely from inside the tenement. Director Daniel Petrie, who had worked in television throughout the 1950s, relied heavily on close-ups, his camera moving around the tenement, "probing each scene for the utmost revelation of character and milieu."[159] Petrie's version created an intense claustrophobia, repeating television drama's narrative emphasis on the private and familial rather than social dynamics and external forces. Thus the visual techniques furthered the film's effect of locking in the drama rather than giving space to the rhetorical significance of Hansberry's characters and the political ideas they represented.

Hansberry knew that white audiences had difficulty recognizing her characters: "Many people are so accustomed to accepting and laughing at the stereotypes that they miss the remarkable sophistication of Negroes: they don't understand the ability of Negroes to turn things around and laugh at their own antagonists."[160] She represented the complex ramifications of the Younger family's move out of the South Side with the use of irony and dissonance, labeling the moving gifts presented to Lena as a "Mrs. Miniver" set of gardening tools from Walter Lee and Ruth and a "Scarlett O'Hara" gardening hat picked out by Travis. These ill-fitting labels were a reminder that neither the meanings of the journey nor the potentially complex dynamics of interracial neighborhoods had yet been envisioned in popular culture. The final open door "solved" the claustrophobia of the beginning scene but could not signify racial inclusion and expanded citizenship.

Film audiences were even less likely than theatergoers to recognize the social and racial implications of using the family as analogous to the nation. The film directed viewers toward seeing the characters and their dilemmas through the lens of multiethnic upward mobility, limiting its ability to depict racial resources or illuminate racial forms of exclusion. The triumphant move from the crowded tenement to the new white neighborhood overshadows the resistance made possible by Walter Lee's rejection of "very materialistic and overtly limited concepts of how the world should go." Instead of Hansberry's point that "ghettoization of any people, black or white, is lousy," white audiences associated "race" with poverty and assumed that leaving poverty meant leaving blackness. Hansberry hoped that "some day, someone else besides us will appreciate the innate dignity and persistence of the Negro people." But *Look* insisted that

the Younger family "only incidentally . . . happen to be Negroes";
America's Moira Walsh was sure that "racial prejudice is not its primary
concern."[161] *Raisin in the Sun* could not dissolve the cultural resistance to
perceiving an African American family as an American family or break
through the limits of white universalism.

Until she died in early 1965 at age thirty-four, Hansberry continued her
affiliation with struggles for freedom in the U.S. and Africa and her search
for a dramatic racial idiom that neither reified nor isolated race and
acknowledged social divisions and inequality without abandoning the
possibility for connection and transformation. Hansberry's last plays
included *Les Blancs,* foregrounding African revolutionaries while challenging racial essentialism, and *The Sign in Sidney Brustein's Window,*
about a group of Greenwich Village friends and lovers divided from and
disappointing one another but groping their way toward a redefinition of
social kinship and renewed social commitment. A tragedy of her time, and
our own, was the loss of Hansberry's expansive vision. In the postwar
period and since, civic imagination has been impoverished by the absence
of the racial and gendered universalism Hansberry sought to write into
popular culture.

VISIONS OF BELONGING

Between 1959, when Hansberry's *Raisin in the Sun* opened, and 1961, when
the film version premiered, the pace of social change in the U.S. intensified dramatically. Passions were rising, with militant young civil rights
activists insisting on Freedom Now; white supremacists reacted with violence; the federal government equivocated; mainstream whites called for
patience and a polite, ineffectual gradualism. Anticolonial agitation would
eventually rewrite the world map in Vietnam, Cuba, and across Africa.
"Race" rapidly entered everyday language. But was race a category linked
to history and political economy, the product of European colonialism,
white supremacy, and fascism's drive for political power and domination?
Or was race the same as color, simply one marker of difference, its meanings taught and perpetuated in psychological patterns of prejudice? In this
historical moment, racial meanings could not remain fixed, and the
resulting political debates took a wide variety of forms.

Audience failure to recognize *Raisin*'s racial universalism suggested the
widening chasms in American understanding of race. Hansberry's play
anticipated both the fractures to come and the pressing need to find terms

with which to expose the inadequacies of postwar democracy and imagine a more fully inclusive citizenship. For groups to remain unseen, or to be seen only *outside* the category of the ordinary American family, was an important mechanism of racial and gender exclusion. Expanding the framework of the ordinary American family, even with Hansberry's deliberately constructed analogy of the family for the nation, was not sufficient to reveal the mechanisms of exclusion, given the power of multiethnic pluralism to define the terms for inclusion. It would take a new phase of the civil rights movement and a new articulation of black nationalism to bring the culture and racial exclusion of African Americans to the forefront of national consciousness. Movements for women's and gay liberation set in motion a similar process that revealed unexamined assumptions about exclusions based on gender and sexuality.

The new black, women's, and gay liberation movements would build on as well as depart from the left-wing, cosmopolitan, and interracial frameworks Hansberry had synthesized; their challenge was to shatter accepted ideas concerning nation and family. The organizational move toward separation—black from white, women from men, homosexual from heterosexual—seemed the only way to take leadership, assert strategic pressure, and be heard. Their political vocabularies would emphasize their novelty and their distance from the historical frameworks of the 1940s and 1950s. One of Hansberry's most influential critics, the former Communist Harold Cruse, for example, explicitly attacked Hansberry's political credibility as part of his effort to recast blackness; he excoriated *Raisin* as a "glorified soap opera" and instructed the generation coming of age in the 1960s to see Hansberry as a writer with an "essentially quasiwhite orientation through which she visualized the Negro world."[162]

As recent scholarship on the genealogies of these movements has shown, the break was never complete. Cruse's call for a new black solidarity was partially inspired by what he saw as a Jewish mode of ethnic group loyalty. Hansberry's articulation of cultural nationalism had also been encouraged by Jewish comrades; she wrote of an elderly Jewish friend's useful advice that arguing for racial equality was inadequate: "You must, like us, argue that you are superior. Then you might—just might, mind you—be able to strike a deal." Hansberry did not draw a sharp line between her left-wing, interracial cosmopolitanism and the Nation of Islam's racial stance, publicly defending its antiracist intentions and political urgency. She did, however, bring Malcolm X to a rare moment of speechlessness at a social gathering in 1963 where she confronted him about his condemnation of her interracial marriage.[163] Similarly, much of the language of women's liberation drew on terms and ideas inherited from the left-wing feminism so important to Hansberry, although the rhetoric of a *new* left and the heritage of anticommunism went a long way toward leaving these connections hazy.[164]

The movements for black and women's liberation shattered postwar illusions of a unitary American identity and rewrote the terms for how American society understands discrimination, exclusion, and inequality. They exerted a profound influence on later articulations of social identities—sexual, cultural, ethnic, racial, and national. Ethnic nostalgia and multiethnic pluralism continue to be revitalized and reconfigured, however, drawing attention away from the social, economic, and political institutions driving racialization. *Visions of Belonging* reminds us of deep yearnings for cosmopolitan crossings, social kinship, and political interracial solidarity that must animate any hopes to realize the unfulfilled promise of meaningful social transformation and democratic inclusion.

NOTES

1. ORDINARY FAMILIES, POPULAR CULTURE, AND POPULAR DEMOCRACY, 1935–1945

1. For a description of "average American" contests, see Warren Susman, "The People's Fair," in *The Dawn of a New Day: The New York World's Fair of 1939–1940* (New York: New York University Press, 1980), pp. 22, 26. Robert Rydell identifies the racialist, eugenicist context for the fair's usage of "typical" and "average" in *World of Fairs: The Century of Progress Expositions* (Chicago: University of Chicago Press, 1993), pp. 56–58.

2. I use the terms *racialized* and *racialization* to emphasize the historical creation of meanings and significance associated with what are considered to be racial differences in a given period. When I use the language of *the ordinary*, I mean to call attention to the rhetorical and normative claims embedded in the term.

3. The full text of the speech appears in Faith Berry's *Good Morning Revolution: Uncollected Social Protest Writings by Langston Hughes* (Secaucus, N.J.: Carol, 1992).

4. Nikhil Singh, "Culture Wars: Recoding Empire in an Age of Democracy," *American Quarterly* 50 (September 1998). Singh names Du Bois as the developer of the framework for these ideas, especially in *Color and Democracy* (1945) and "Human Rights for All Minorities" (1945), although Singh notes that as early as the essay "The Souls of Whitefolk," published in *Darkwater* (1920), Du Bois had commented that "a belief in humanity is a belief in colored men." Penny Von Eschen uses the term *black popular front* to include a broad group of black American liberals, church leaders, and professional and middle-class organizations that supported black civil rights and anticolonial activism; see *Race Against Empire* (Ithaca: Cornell University Press, 1997). James Smethurst sees cultural nationalism, integrationism, and internationalism as characteristic of left-wing African American poets writing between 1930 and 1946; see *The New Red Negro: The Lit-*

erary Left and African American Poetry, 1930–1946 (New York: Oxford University Press, 1999).

5. Michele Hilmes, *Radio Voices: American Broadcasting, 1922–1952* (Minneapolis: University of Minnesota Press, 1997).

6. *Amos 'n' Andy*'s cultural presence depended on national syndication and its longevity on radio and later television; it also inspired a wide range of spin-offs, including comic strips and phonograph recordings. See Melvin Patrick Ely, *The Adventures of Amos 'n' Andy: A Social History of an American Phenomenon* (New York: Free, 1991); Thomas Cripps, "Amos 'n' Andy and the Debate Over American Racial Integration," in *American History/American Television: Interpreting the Video Past,* ed. John E. O'Connor (New York: Ungar, 1983).

7. Excellent surveys of radio history may be found in Erik Barnouw, *The Golden Web: A History of Broadcasting in the United States,* vol. 2 (New York: Oxford University Press, 1968); J. Fred MacDonald, *Don't Touch That Dial! Radio Programming in American Life, 1920–1960* (Chicago: Nelson Hall, 1979); William Barlow, "Commercial and Non-Commercial Radio," in *Split Image: African Americans in the Mass Media,* ed. Jannette L. Dates and William Barlow (Washington, D.C.: Howard University Press, 1990); William Barlow, *Voice Over: The Making of Black Radio* (Philadelphia: Temple University Press, 1999). Michael Rogin analyzes the Hollywood studio genre of "Southerns" in *Black Face, White Noise: Jewish Immigrants in the Hollywood Melting Pot* (Berkeley: University of California Press, 1996). Black actors performing in minstrel or servant positions—especially when performing for black audiences—did manage to undermine the most stereotypical attributes of their roles and to emphasize the distinction between performer and character.

8. Moss was born in Newark, New Jersey, c. 1910, and grew up in Newark and North Carolina. He directed a community project for the New York Public Library before he began writing for radio, creating three series for NBC. In the late 1930s Moss would write for the New York Federal Writers Project. See John Houseman, *Unfinished Business: Memoirs 1902–1988* (New York: Applause Theatre, 1989); Jerre Mangione, *The Dream and the Deal: The Federal Writers' Project, 1935–1943* (Philadelphia: University of Pennsylvania Press, 1972); "Carlton Moss, Who Filmed the Black Experience, Dies," *New York Times,* August 15, 1997.

9. Barnouw, *Golden Web,* pp. 110–111. In a 1944 survey of one hundred films with African American characters, the curator of the Schomberg collection of Negro Literature and History at the New York Public Library found 75 percent of the portrayals to be anti-Negro, 13 percent neutral, and only 12 percent positive; see L. D. Reddick, "Educational Programs for the Improvement of Race Relations: Motion Pictures, Radio, Press, and Libraries," *Journal of Negro Education* (Summer 1944), p. 369.

10. See Jeffrey Shandler, "Gertrude Berg," in *Jewish Women in America,* ed. Paula E. Hyman and Deborah Dash Moore (New York: Routledge, 1998); Donald Weber, "The Jewish American World of Gertrude Berg: *The Goldbergs* on Radio and Television, 1930–1950," in *Talking Back: Images of Jewish Women in American Popular Culture,* ed. Joyce Antler (Hanover, N.H.: Brandeis University

Press/University Press of New England, 1998), and "Memory and Repression in Early Ethnic Television: The Example of Gertrude Berg and *The Goldbergs*" in *The Other Fifties,* ed. Joel Foreman (Urbana: University of Illinois Press, 1997).

11. Weber, "Memory and Repression in Early Ethnic Television," p. 147, 152.

12. On radio's integrated entertainment and advertising, see Roland Marchand, *Advertising and the American Dream* (Berkeley: University of California Press, 1985), pp. 108–110. Hilmes discusses women's serial drama, and especially the process by which this form became classified and marginalized, in *Radio Voices.*

13. Hilmes, *Radio Voices;* Barnouw, *Golden Web;* Sterling and Kittross, *Stay Tuned: A Concise History of American Broadcasting* (Belmont: Wadsworth, 1978).

14. These incidents are discussed in Barlow, "Commercial and Non-Commercial Radio."

15. Michael Denning, *The Cultural Front: The Laboring of American Culture in the Twentieth Century* (London: Verso, 1996). I follow Denning's analysis of the "cultural front" as a historical formation rising out of the encounter between powerful democratic social movements and new forms of mass culture, rather than in terms of individual political affiliations, although where possible I try to identify these affiliations.

16. See R. C. Reynolds, *Stage Left: The Development of the American Social Drama in the Thirties* (Troy, N.Y.: Whitston, 1986). On workers' theater groups, see Rachel Shteir, "Workers' Laboratory Theatre," *Nation,* July 14, 1997, pp. 32–34; Colette Hyman, *Staging Strikes: Workers' Theater and the American Labor Movement* (Philadelphia: Temple University Press, 1997). On *Pins and Needles,* see Denning, *The Cultural Front.*

17. Wendy Smith, *Real Life Drama: The Group Theatre and America, 1931–1940* (New York: Grove Weidenfeld, 1990); Robert Warshow, "Clifford Odets: Poet of the Jewish Middle Class," *Commentary* (May 1946), reprinted in *The Immediate Experience* (New York: Atheneum, 1971).

18. Smith, *Real Life Drama,* p. 48.

19. Green's play limited African Americans' place in the South to that of servants to white people. Gender and racial exclusions were intertwined; when Lee Strasberg was chosen by Harold Clurman to direct the play, the only woman founder, Cheryl Crawford, who herself had hoped to direct it, was assigned instead to work with McClendon and De Knight, whose scenes were not deemed significant enough to require rehearsal according to Strasberg's method. Bobby Lewis, a Group actor who became friendly with McClendon, appeared to be the only one to object to these forms of racial subordination; Smith, *Real Life Drama,* pp. 36–41.

20. Barnouw, *Golden Web,* p. 151. Erik Barnouw was a participant in the new culture industries before he became their analyst, historian, and archivist. He began work in radio in the 1930s and taught radio writing at Columbia University from 1937; he worked as a writer and editor for CBS radio (1939–1940) and as an editor at NBC (1942–1944). See his *Media Marathon: A Twentieth-Century Memoir* (Durham: Duke University Press, 1996); Felicity Barringer, "Erik Barnouw, Historian of Broadcasting, Dies at 93," *New York Times,* July 26, 2001. On the relationship between documentary and drama in the 1930s, see William Stott, *Docu-*

mentary Expression and 1930s America; Paula Rabinowitz, *They Must Be Represented: The Politics of Documentary* (London: Verso, 1994)

21. On the importance of these new culture industries of the 1930s as a magnet for artists, writers, and photographers who were drawn to the insurgent social movements, see Denning, *Cultural Front.*

22. Odets offered *Waiting for Lefty* free to amateur groups and to semiprofessional groups at a reduced rate; it quickly became the most widely performed play in America, with productions in twenty cities across the country from January to June 1935; Smith, *Real Life Drama,* pp. 190–191, 197–201.

23. *Don't You Want to Be Free* was the first production of the Harlem Suitcase Theatre, opening in the second floor loft of the International Workers Order Community Center on 125th Street in Harlem. Robert Earl Jones was the father of contemporary actor James Earl Jones. Arnold Rampersad, *The Life of Langston Hughes,* vol. 1, *1902–1941: I, Too, Sing America* (New York: Oxford University Press, 1986); Langston Hughes and Milton Meltzer, *Black Magic: A Pictorial History of the African American in the Performing Arts* (New York: Da Capo, 1990 [1967]).

24. Laura Browder, *Rousing the Nation: Radical Culture in Depression America* (Amherst: University of Massachusetts Press, 1998).

25. Hallie Flanagan, *Arena: The Story of the Federal Theatre Project* (New York: Limelight, 1985 [1940]). See also John O'Connor and Lorraine Brown, *Free, Adult, Uncensored: The Living History of the Federal Theatre Project* (Washington, D.C.: New Republic, 1978); Barbara Melosh, *Engendering Culture: Manhood and Womanhood in New Deal Public Art and Theater* (Washington, D.C.: Smithsonian Institution Press, 1991).

26. The FTP's New York Negro Theatre Unit was headed by Carlton Moss after McClendon died and Houseman moved on. Denning, *Cultural Front;* Gerald Horne, *Race Woman: The Lives of Shirley Graham Du Bois* (New York: New York University Press, 2000).

27. On public battles over radio commercialization and the 1934 Communications Act, see Susan Smulyan, *Selling Radio: The Commercialization of American Broadcasting, 1920–1934* (Washington, D.C.: Smithsonian Institution Press, 1994) and Robert McChesney, *Telecommunications, Mass Media and Democracy: The Battle for Control of U.S. Broadcasting, 1928–1935* (New York: Oxford University Press, 1994). On network "sustaining" programming, see Barnouw, *Golden Web,* MacDonald, *Don't Touch That Dial.*

28. B. LeRoy Bannerman, *Norman Corwin and Radio: The Golden Years* (Tuscaloosa: University of Alabama Press, 1986), p. 3.

29. MacLeish made these comments in the introduction to the printed version of "The Fall of the City," in *Radio's Best Plays,* ed. Joseph Liss (New York: Greenberg, 1947), pp. 6–7; see also Norman Corwin, "The Sovereign Word: Some Notes on Radio Drama," *Theatre Arts* 24 (February 1940).

30. On Welles and radio, see Barnouw, *Golden Web; Orson Welles on the Air: The Radio Years,* exhibit catalog (New York: Museum of Broadcasting, 1988); Denning, *Cultural Front.* On Oboler, see Barnouw, *Golden Web;* MacDonald, *Don't Touch That Dial.*

31. Hilmes, *Radio Voices,* p. 230.

32. MacDonald, *Don't Touch that Dial;* Bannerman, *Norman Corwin.* See also *Norman Corwin: Years of the Electric Ear,* an interview by Douglas Bell for the Directors Guild of America (Metuchen, N.J.: DGA and Scarecrow, 1994).

33. No African American was featured until a 1948 broadcast profiled Booker T. Washington.

34. See Judith E. Smith, "Radio's 'Cultural Front,' 1938–1948," in *Radio Reader: Essays in the Cultural History of Radio,* ed. Michele Hilmes and Jason Loviglio (New York: Routledge, 2002).

35. Biographical information about Miller is drawn from his entry in *Current Biography* (1947), a profile in *Theatre Arts* (June 1947), and from his memoir, *Timebends: A Life* (New York: Grove, 1987).

36. Miller, *Timebends,* pp. 36, 57–60, 109–110, 119–120, 212, 230, 229. See also Christopher Bigsby's citing of a 1995 Miller interview in the introduction to *The Cambridge Companion to Arthur Miller* (Cambridge: Cambridge University Press, 1997), p. 2.

37. Miller, *Timebends,* pp. 498–499. The FTP was shut down after Miller had been on the payroll for six months, but he found short-term employment collecting dialect speech for B. A. Botkin of the folklore division of the Library of Congress in 1940. In North Carolina Miller recorded quarrymen, talc miners' wives, and "black people hanging around the town square who had nowhere to go after being fired from the shipyard they had recently built in the swampland mud." *Timebends,* p. 231. Miller's account of attending this "study course" three to four times in 1939–40 appeared in his testimony before HUAC, June 21, 1956.

38. Miller, *Timebends.* See also Barnouw's description of Miller's radio career in *Golden Web.*

39. Denning, *Cultural Front.* Henry Meyer, Jay Gorney, and Edward Eliscu's 1939 musical revue *Meet the People* is another example of radical musical theater; Patrick McGilligan and Paul Buhle, *Tender Comrades: A Backstory of the Hollywood Blacklist* (New York: St. Martin's, 1997).

40. Bannerman, *Norman Corwin,* p. 47.

41. Written by John LaTouche and Earl Robinson for an unperformed FTP revue, *Sing for Your Supper,* (and originally titled "Ballad for Uncle Sam"), "Ballad for Americans" was the product of a left-wing musical revue sensibility. John LaTouche was a poet and lyricist who wrote for left-wing cabarets sponsored by the Theatre Arts Committee. Earl Robinson was a member of the Composers' Collective, musical director of the Workers Laboratory Theatre—absorbed into the FTP in 1935—and a member of the Communist Party; Harold Meyerson and Ernie Harburg, *Who Put the Rainbow in "The Wizard of Oz"? Yip Harburg, Lyricist* (Ann Arbor: University of Michigan Press, 1995), p. 213. Bannerman notes that Robinson revised the song slightly for the radio according to Norman Corwin's suggestions; Bannerman, *Norman Corwin,* pp. 48–49. For analyses of Robeson's performance, see MacDonald, *Don't Touch that Dial;* Barlow, "Commercial and Non-Commercial Radio" and *Voice Over;* Denning, *Cultural Front;* Barbara Savage, *Broadcasting Freedom: Radio, War, and the Politics of Race, 1938–1948* (Chapel Hill: University of North Carolina Press, 1999).

42. Paul Robeson, "Ballad for Americans," 1940, on his *Ballad for Americans and*

Carnegie Hall Concerts, vol. 2, Vanguard VSD-79193, 1965. According to Robeson's biographer, the studio audience stamped, shouted, and bravoed for two minutes while the show was still on the air, and for fifteen minutes after. The switchboard was jammed with calls for two more hours and, within the next few days, swamped with mail about the performance. Robeson repeated the performance on New Year's Day and again on CBS radio in August 1940 in a special broadcast called "All God's Children." Robeson's recording of the song for Victor Records went to the top of the charts. *Time,* July 8, 1940, reported that Robeson's recording of "Ballad" was the number most in demand at the RCA exhibit at the New York World's Fair. See Martin B. Duberman, *Paul Robeson: A Biography* (New York: Ballantine, 1989), pp. 236–237, 647.

43. Bannerman, *Norman Corwin,* pp. 47–50.
44. Rachel Davis Du Bois had a significant political and personal relationship to W. E. B. Du Bois at this time, according to David Levering Lewis, *W. E. B. Du Bois,*vol. 2, *The Fight for Equality and the American Century, 1919–1963* (New York: Holt, 2000). Gilbert Seldes wanted to stress the interdependence of all the groups, but listeners resisted this message, indicating through fan mail and requests for scripts that they were most interested in the program dealing with their own nationality; Nicholas Monalto, "The Intercultural Education Movement, 1924–1941: The Growth of Tolerance as a Form of Intolerance," in *American Education and the European Immigrant: 1840–1940,* ed. Bernard J. Weiss (Urbana: University of Illinois Press, 1982). See also J. Morris Jones, *Americans All . . . Immigrants All: A Handbook for Listeners* (Washington, D.C.: Federal Radio Education Committee and the U.S. Office of Education, c. 1939).
45. Savage describes the debates over representing "The Negro," and "The Jews in the United States" in *Broadcasting Freedom,* pp. 36–52. The response to the show on "The Negro" was generally positive, including a small number of letters from African Americans who were pleased to see a "portrayal of the parts my race has played in helping to make America a better place for all groups to live in, even though at times we were somewhat discouraged by intolerant individuals who seemed to enjoy a sadistic pleasure in denying us our inalienable rights" (p. 44). The level of response to "The Jews" exceeded that of "The Negro." Jews were the most vocal group in expressing their appreciation; people responding negatively heard the show as an argument for admitting more Jewish refugees into the U.S.
46. Stephen Vincent Benét's *John Brown's Body* was adapted in 1939 by Corwin on *Columbia Workshop,* which also featured Corwin's antifascist verse play, "They Fly Through the Air with the Greatest of Ease;" a scene from Robert Sherwood's *Abe Lincoln in Illinois* was presented on the first *Pursuit of Happiness;* an adaptation of Capra's film *Mr. Deeds Goes to Town* was on *Mercury Theatre's Campbell Playhouse* in 1940; Sandburg's *The People, Yes* was adapted for radio by Corwin and Earl Robinson for *Columbia Workshop* and broadcast in 1941. The history of the "We Hold These Truths" broadcast appears in Bannerman, *Norman Corwin;* the passage from *Variety* was quoted on pp. 87–88. See also Barnouw, *Golden Web.*
47. On the Dies investigation of broadcasting, see Barnouw, *Golden Web.* The film industry mounted a strong defense: see Thomas Doherty, *Projections of War:*

Hollywood, American Culture and World War II (New York: Columbia University Press), p. 40, and Hilmes, *Radio Voices*, p. 246–250.

48. "They Burned the Book" was distributed free by the Writers' War Board to hundreds of groups for local broadcasts, used in schools, and in army camps as part of orientation. Although Benét died in 1943, his radio plays were published as *We Stand United and Other Radio Scripts* (New York: Farrar and Rinehart, 1945) with an introduction by Norman Rosten. Both Rosten and Benét are quoted by Joseph Liss, ed., *Radio's Best Plays* (New York: Greenberg, 1947), p. 137.

49. Margaret Mayorga, "Introduction," *Best One-Act Plays of 1944* (New York: Dodd and Mead, 1945), pp. v–vi; "Introduction," *Best One-Act Plays of 1945* (New York: Dodd and Mead, 1946), pp. v–vii. The 1944 collection included radio plays by Archibald MacLeish, Ben Hecht, Norman Rosten; the 1945 collection included radio plays by Norman Corwin, Arthur Laurents, and Morton Wishengrad. See Elia Kazan's observations of soldiers as performers and as audience based on his mission in early 1945 to observe GI entertainment production units in the Philippines and New Guinea, in "Audience Tomorrow: Preview in New Guinea," *Theatre Arts* (October 1945).

50. Doherty discusses these film representations in *Projections of War*. Paul Buhle and David Wagner document the contribution of progressive screenwriters in *Radical Hollywood: The Untold Story Behind America's Favorite Films* (New York: New Press, 2002).

51. Richard Dalfiume, "The 'Forgotten Years' of the Negro Revolution," *Journal of American History* (June 1968), pp. 90–106.

52. Savage, *Broadcasting Freedom*.

53. Doherty, *Projections of War*.

54. Later Perl made these connections explicit in "The Hanging Noose," commissioned by CBS to explain the hangings of Nazi war criminals at Nuremberg, to be broadcast in prime time when these took place, October 16, 1946. The play linked the ideology of the Nazis with what he called "seeds of fascism" in the U.S.: attacks on trade unions; the blinding of Isaac Woodward, a black veteran in the South; the throwing of bricks through a synagogue window during services and the painting of "kill the kikes" on the sidewalks outside. Reprinted in Liss, *Radio's Best Plays*, pp. 122, 130–131.

55. For example, the late 1941 attack on a Japanese freighter by Colin Kelley, a Southern Presbyterian, and his Jewish bombardier Meyer Levin, became an icon for a multiethnic American partnership, touted in an issue of *True Comics* and the inspiration for Howard Hawks's 1943 film *Air Force*. See Cripps, *Making Movies Black*, pp. 31, 66.

56. Cripps, *Making Films Black*, p. 31; Doherty, *Projections of War*, pp. 204–226, 139–148 (quoted material on p. 139). See also Clayton R. Koppes and Gregory D. Black, *Hollywood Goes to War: How Politics, Profits, and Propaganda Shaped WWII Movies* (Berkeley: University of California Press, 1990). Lary May analyzes these melting-pot military films as representing a problematic inclusion in *The Big Tomorrow: Hollywood and the Politics of the American Way* (Chicago: University of Chicago Press, 2000).

57. Hughes's reference to Dorie Miller appeared in the poem "Jim Crow's Last Stand," published in a pamphlet of twenty-three poems, *Jim Crow's Last Stand* (Atlanta: Negro Publication Society of America, 1943).

58. Barnouw, *Golden Web*, p. 196. The script "Japanese-Americans" was reprinted in *Radio Drama in Action: Twenty-Five Plays of a Changing World*, ed. Erik Barnouw (New York: Rinehart, 1945).

59. Comments in the black press applauded the mainstream film spotlight on Joe Louis, but "the strongly prevailing observation among "colored first nighters" attending the Atlanta premiere was that "Hollywood merely continued its policy of 'grin and jive' for Negro actors, even while directing them in a military show." See " 'This Is the Army' Is Gay and Entertaining: Joe Louis Shines," *Chicago Defender*, August 7, 1943; "Colored Actors 'Grin and Jive' in Army Picture—Sgt. Joe Louis Stands Out in His Role," *Atlanta*, August 27, 1943.

60. This film was produced as part of the "Why We Fight" series under the supervision of Frank Capra. But Moss's "authorship" has clearly been established by historians of the film: see Thomas Cripps and David Culbert, "*The Negro Soldier* (1944): Film Propaganda in Black and White," *American Quarterly* 31 (Winter 1979), and Cripps, *Making Movies Black*. On the contentious process of making *The Negro Soldier*, see also Buhle and Wagner, *Radical Hollywood*, p. 191.

61. His April 1941 pageant, "The Negro in American Life," co-sponsored by the International Workers Order and the Manhattan Council of the National Negro Congress, attracted a racially mixed audience of five thousand, who rose for a standing ovation to its star performer, Paul Robeson, and its dedication to "the Negro People and to Fraternal Brotherhood Among All." In December 1941 Moss mobilized an all-star cast of performers, including Hazel Scott, Canada Lee, Ethel Barrymore, and Douglas Fairbanks for a "Salute to the Negro Troops," which played to enthusiastic audiences both at the Apollo Theatre in Harlem and the midtown Mecca Theatre, repeating its success at the Apollo the following spring.

62. See Dalfiume, "The 'Forgotten Years,' " p. 100; see also Ottley's account of the black press campaign in *New World A-Coming* (New York: Arno, 1968 [1943]), pp. 252–253. The "Negro Soldier's Contribution to the War Effort" was also the subject of one program on NBC's *America's Town Meeting of the Air* in 1942, featuring a panel composed for the first time exclusively of African American commentators.

63. Moss, quoted in Thomas Cripps and David Culbert, "*The Negro Soldier* (1944)," pp. 637–638. Prints of the film were made widely available to libraries and schools after the war: see Cripps, *Making Movies Black;* Doherty, *Projections of War*.

64. James Tobin, *Ernie Pyle's War: America's Eyewitness to World War II* (Lawrence, Kansas: University Press of Kansas, 1997), pp. 35–36.

65. Lewis Gannett, the daily book review editor of the *New York Herald-Tribune* who served as a combat correspondent with the U.S. Army in Europe in 1944, characterized Pyle's columns as "modest, matter-of-fact, GI reporting" that brought the "monotony as well as the drama and drudgery of war into the American home." Gannett reported that Pyle's 1943 book of collected columns, *Here Is Your War*, sold 240,000 copies through its original edition, 150,000 copies through the People's Book Club, as well as 1,000,000 copies in a paperback

reprint and 100,000 copies in a dollar reprint, even before 50,000 copies were sent overseas in an Armed Services edition; "Books," in *While You Were Gone*, ed. Jack Goodman (New York: Simon and Schuster, 1946). See Pyle's entry in *Current Biography* (1941). The quotation is from Pyle's column "Now to the Infantry," May 1, 1943, reprinted in Tobin, *Ernie Pyle's War*, pp. 256–258.

66. This description of Pyle's work from a fellow journalist, Bob Fredericks of the *Miami Herald*, was quoted in Pyle's *Current Biography* (1941) entry, p. 688.

67. Miller noted the distance between Pyle's columns and his own political reading of popular wartime consciousness: "the meaning I was seeking in their lives never seemed to penetrate his columns"; *Situation Normal* (New York: Reynal and Hitchcock, 1944), p. 163.

68. Ernie Pyle, "My Personal Hero," February 21, 1944, reprinted in Tobin, *Ernie Pyle's War*, p. 260–262.

69. Miller, *Timebends*, p. 277.

70. These writers, Sandra Ford and Peter Michael, are discussed in Barlow, "Commercial and Non-Commercial Radio," pp. 196–197.

71. Barnouw, *Golden Web*, p. 161–162. Black soldiers were also introduced into *Young Widder Brown*, *Just Plain Bill*, and *Amanda of Honeymoon Hill*; Hilmes, *Radio Voices*.

72. His employer for *Green Valley USA* was Himan Brown, the original producer of *The Rise of the Goldbergs*. Lampell was a member of the Communist Party from the late 1930s until he was drafted in 1943, when he resigned his membership. "Millard Lampell" in Buhle and McGilligan, *Tender Comrades*, pp. 392–394.

73. Duberman, *Paul Robeson*, p. 254–256, 167; Barlow, *Voice Over*, p. 61–63.

74. "An Open Letter on Race Hatred," including Wendell Willkie's postscript, is reprinted in Barnouw, *Radio Drama in Action*, pp. 60–77.

75. On Hughes's radio career, see Rampersad, *The Life of Langston Hughes*, vol. 2. His private comments appeared in a letter to Eric Barnouw, March 27, 1945, quoted by Barbara Savage, "Radio and the Political Discourse of Racial Equality," in Hilmes and Loviglio, *Radio Reader*, p. 235.

76. *New World A-Coming* was on the air in New York City from 1944 to 1957, but the examples I refer to here were broadcast between 1944 and 1947, by the same station that had aired the 1935 black serial drama *A Harlem Family*. MacDonald, *Don't Touch That Dial*; Barlow, "Commercial and Non-Commercial Radio," *Voice Over*.

77. Ottley, born in Harlem, attended New York City public schools and studied at St. Bonaventure College and the University of Michigan. Returning to New York, he worked as a redcap, bellhop, soda jerker, in 1930 finding a job as a reporter, and then as columnist and editor on the *Amsterdam Star News*. In the early thirties he also studied at Columbia, New York University, and law at St. John's University Law School in Brooklyn. In February 1936 Ottley had joined with Harlem leaders A. Philip Randolph, Adam Clayton Powell Jr., and members of the Harlem Communist Party to form the National Negro Congress (NNC), determined to mobilize support for the industrial union movement, an end to discrimination in the workplace and public life, unemployment relief, and the abolition of lynching and police brutality. Ottley supervised the Negro unit of the

Federal Writers Project in New York, until the ending of federal sponsorship in 1939. Some of the writers were critical of his use of FWP materials in preparing *New World A-Coming*. The success of *New World A-Coming* encouraged its publishers to join with the Rosenwald Foundation to sponsor a trip overseas for Ottley, to gather material for a book about all "the colored peoples who are fighting on the world's battlegrounds." Ottley was also invited to work as a war correspondent overseas for Bernarr MacFadden's *Liberty* magazine, according to *Current Biography* (1943), making him the first black correspondent for a national publication. Barnouw, *Radio Drama in Action,* pp. 354–355.

78. Barlow, "Commercial and Non-Commercial Radio"; Barlow, *Voice Over;* Roi Ottley, "The Negro Domestic," in Barnouw, *Radio Drama in Action,* pp. 354–368.

79. On the making of the Democratic National Committee election special, broadcast on CBS radio November 6, 1944, see "Millard Lampell" in Buhle and McGilligan, *Tender Comrades,* p. 396; Nancy Lynn Schwartz, *The Hollywood Writers War* (New York: Knopf, 1982), pp. 214–215; Bannerman, *Norman Corwin,* pp. 140–142.

80. The song's lyricist Yip Harburg is best known for his 1930s songs "Brother, Can You Spare a Dime?" and "Over the Rainbow." The lyrics for "Free and Equal Blues" appear in Meyerson and Harburg, *Who Put the Rainbow in "The Wizard of Oz"?* pp. 215–217. They vary slightly from the broadcast version. The song later became part of the repertoire of singer Josh White, who performed it in 1945 and recorded it in 1946.

81. Barlow, "Commercial and Non-Commercial Radio," p. 192.

82. Sgt. Millard Lampell, *A Long Way Home* (New York: Julian Messner, 1946), pp. 169–170, 172.

83. Hilmes, *Radio Voices,* p. 256.

84. Liss, *Radio's Best Plays,* p. 81. The quoted comment was made by Robert Landry, *Variety*'s radio critic.

85. "October Morning" was published in Liss, *Radio's Best Plays,* pp. 105–117. The army air force radio unit that produced these plays included the former Group Theatre actor Corporal Martin Ritt and used music written by Sergeant Elmer Bernstein. Ritt would later direct theater, moving to live television after he was blacklisted; see chapter 8. Bernstein scored music for UN radio (where Corwin worked after he was forced out of CBS) between 1948 and 1951, and after 1951 for Hollywood films.

86. Laurents was born in New York City in 1918 to middle-class Jewish parents, and graduated from Cornell University in 1937. He began writing for radio in the late 1930s, producing formula drama for shows including *Hollywood Playhouse, Dr. Christian, Manhattan at Midnight, The Thin Man.* In 1941 Laurents went into the army, became a truck driver, a photographer paratrooper, a message center courier. By 1943 he was working in the army signal corps at Astoria, Queens, making training and educational films for the Office of War Information. He wrote some scripts for Robson's war series, *The Man Behind the Gun.* In 1943 Laurents was invited to produce scripts for *Army Service Forces Presents* (ASFP) and in 1944 for *Assignment Home.* Laurents was writing army radio scripts at the same time that he worked on his Broadway play *Home of the Brave,* discussed in

chapter 4. Patrick McGilligan, *Backstory 2: Interviews with Screenwriters in the 1940s and 1950s* (Berkeley: University of California Press, 1991). See also Laurents's memoir, *Original Story by Arthur Laurents: A Memoir of Broadway and Hollywood* (New York: Knopf, 2000). "The Face" is reprinted in Mayorga, *Best One-Act Plays of 1945,* and Barnouw, *Radio Drama in Action.* "The Last Day of the War" is reprinted in Liss, *Radio's Best Plays.*

87. Here Laurents reproduces popular explanations of the psychological effects of prejudice; see Ruth Feldstein's discussion of this formulation, in *Motherhood in Black and White: Race and Sex in American Liberalism, 1930–1965* (Ithaca: Cornell University Press, 2000).

88. Wyler made one of Hollywood's classiest studio-style pleas for supporting the war against fascism, *Mrs. Miniver,* the top-grossing film for 1942. He then served for two years in the army signal corps, filming air force bombing missions for what would become the widely viewed documentary *The Memphis Belle.* When Wyler returned to Hollywood, he wanted to depart from "Hollywood as usual" to make a film true to the experience of returning vets. The decision to cast a disabled vet was supported by research suggesting that audiences were concerned about wounded veterans and would probably react well to a screen appearance of a real wounded man. *The Best Years of Our Lives* was one of the highest-grossing films for 1946 and the top grossing film for 1947. Wyler discusses his use of Russell and his vision for the film in "No Magic Wand," *Screen Writer* (February 1947), reprinted in Richard Koszarski, *Hollywood Directors 1941–1976* (New York: Oxford University Press, 1977), and in Hermione Rich, "William Wyler: Director with a Passion and a Craft," *Theatre Arts* 31 (February 1947), pp. 21–24. See Jan Herman, *A Talent for Trouble: The Life of Hollywood's Most Acclaimed Director, William Wyler* (New York: Putnam, 1995); Martin A. Jackson, "The Uncertain Peace: *The Best Years of Our Lives* (1946)," in *American History/American Film: Interpreting the Hollywood Image* (New York: Ungar, 1979), pp. 151–152.

89. On the film's treatment of disability, see Sonya Michel, "Danger on the Home Front: Motherhood, Sexuality, and Disabled Veterans in American Postwar Films," *Journal of the History of Sexuality* (July 1992), and David Gerber, "Heroes and Misfits: The Troubled Social Reintegration of Disabled Veterans in *"The Best Years of Our Lives,"* *American Quarterly* 46 (December 1994).

90. Abraham Polonsky called attention to the absence of some of the "better sharpened social conflicts" in his review of the film in *Hollywood Quarterly* (April 1947), p. 260, a copy of which was kindly provided to me by Paul Buhle.

2. MAKING THE WORKING-CLASS FAMILY ORDINARY: *A TREE GROWS IN BROOKLYN*

1. For the publishing history of *A Tree Grows in Brooklyn,* see Carol Siri Johnson, "The Life and Work of Betty Smith, Author of *A Tree Grows in Brooklyn,*" Ph.D. dissertation, City University of New York Graduate Center, 1995. See also Betty Smith Papers, hereafter abbreviated as BSP, no. 3837, Southern Historical Collection, University of North Carolina at Chapel Hill, folder 7.

2. Elizabeth Lawrence to Betty Smith, September 9, 1943, BSP, folder 4. *Tree* was "far and away the most popular book with our soldier and military" among the Armed Services editions: "your book exceeds all others in popularity without even a close runner up." DBF to Betty Smith, June 28, 1944, BSP, folder 8.

3. "Talk of the Town," *New Yorker*, October 9, 1943, pp. 16–17; Johnson, "Life and Work of Betty Smith," pp. 151–152. *Tree* was the fourth most popular novel of 1943 and the third most popular of 1944.

4. Johnson points out that "Johnny Nolan" is the name used by Horatio Alger for his stock Irish character. "Life and Work," p. 143.

5. *New Yorker*, August 21, 1943, p. 66; Orville Prescott, review of *Tree* in the *New York Times*, quoted in "Chapel Hill Woman's Novel Receiving High Praise from Two Leading New York Papers," *Chapel Hill Weekly*, August 20, 1943.

6. "Tenement Story and Literary Guild Selection," *Oakland Tribune*, August 29, 1943; *Montgomery Advertiser*, September 19, 1943. Philomena Hart, "Betty Smith's 'Tree" Is a Strong and Well-Knit Tale," *Providence Journal*, August 29, 1943; Orville Prescott, "Outstanding Novels," *Yale Review* 33 (September 1943).

7. *Keene Sentinel*, August 27, 1943; Meyer Berger, "Among the Week's New Fiction: Green Sunless Weed," *New York Times*, August 22, 1943.

8. Berger, "Among the Week's New Fiction"; Florence Haxton Bullock, "Growing Up Beside the Williamsburg Bridge," *New York Herald-Tribune Weekly Book Review*, August 22, 1943; "Tenement Story and Literary Guild Selection," *Oakland Tribune*, August 29, 1943. Smith described her readers' identification of her as Francie in "Best-Seller Aftermath—A Successful Author's Lot Is a Public Life with Lovely Troubles," in *Life*, June 6, 1949.

9. Obituary for Jerre Mangione, *New York Times*, August 31, 1998.

10. Letters from Betty Smith to Elizabeth Lawrence, December 13, 1943, BSP, folder 5; Eugene Saxton, June 27, 1942, folder 1, box 1B; Elizabeth Lawrence, May 16, 1944, folder 7. Early press exposure that made Smith uncomfortable included a piece in the *New Yorker*, October 9, 1943, and in *Current Biography* (1943).

11. Betty Smith to James Fadiman, fiction editor, MGM, May 7, 1942, BSP, folder 7. MGM didn't buy *Tree*, but did offer Smith a job as a screenwriter. *How Green Was My Valley*, about a Welsh coal-mining family, was a best-selling novel in 1940; the Twentieth Century-Fox film, released in 1941, was a box office hit and won five Academy Awards. The film focuses on family loyalty and self-reliance, representing the union and the strike as both external and destructive.

12. Betty Smith to Elizabeth Lawrence, December 13, 1943, BSP, folder 5. See also entry on Betty Smith in *Current Biography* (1943).

13. Johnson, "Life and Work," p. 108, drawing on a 1991 interview with Smith's daughter Nancy Smith Pfeiffer.

14. Biographical information on Betty Smith is from her letters and other materials in her papers; her 1936 autobiographical statement; BSP, folder 503; Johnson, "Life and Work"; Smith's entry in *Current Biography* (1943); her obituary in the *New York Times*, January 18, 1972; Harriet King, "Betty Smith," *Dictionary of Literary Biography Yearbook* (1982), ed. Richard Ziegfeld (Detroit: Gale, 1983). Betty Smith's statement about her parents is in "Look Back with a Smile," p. 1, folder

346; her comment about her paternal grandparents is in "Autobiographical draft," p. 9, folder 341.

15. Poems printed in newspapers and pasted in her scrapbooks indicate Smith's early literary aspirations; BSP, folders 3, 4, and 5. At an early point the family could afford to employ a woman to clean once a week; Betty Smith to Eugene F. Saxton, September 30, 1942, folder 30. Smith's father, John Wehner, died in 1915.

16. BSP, folder 2.

17. George Smith to Betty Smith, June 1, 1942, BSP, folder 29.

18. The essay "What Good Is College?" has no date but is labeled Assignment 1 for an essay-writing class that she attended during the years in Ann Arbor, 1927–1931, BSP, folder 307.

19. Other essays Smith wrote between 1927 and 1931 include "Mr. Russell and Sex Education," published in *Plain Talk*, vol. 3, no. 1 (1928), pp. 96–98, BSP, folder 305; "I Want to Write" and "Listen to America," folder 306; "Special Matinee for Women Only," folder 307.

20. The statement by Nancy Smith Pfeiffer appeared in a press release written for the Twentieth Century-Fox Publicity Department in 1945. Johnson, "Life and Work," p. 54.

21. Autobiographical statement, 1936, BSP, folder 503.

22. Smith faced increasing financial pressure at the time. George Smith to Betty Smith, June 1, 1942, BSP, folder 29. A copy of the divorce settlement is enclosed in George Smith to Betty Smith, May 18, 1939, folder 21.

23. Betty Smith, "Road to the Best Seller," *Writer* 57 (October 1944), pp. 292–293.

24. The Harper and Brothers editors who advised Smith were Eugene Saxton and Elizabeth Lawrence, BSP, folders 1 and 2. Saxton was the senior editor at Harper and Brothers, but he became ill and died before the book was published. Lawrence, promoted to editor during the war, then handled most of the editorial changes. Viewed by her colleagues as an excellent editor with an eye for bestsellers, Lawrence continued to offer editorial suggestions that shaped Betty Smith's later work, even after Smith insisted on having a male editor. After Smith broke with Lawrence in the spring of 1947, Lawrence's suggestions were relayed through a series of male editors. Johnson, "Life and Work," pp. 116–123, 209–220.

25. See drafts of her one-act play "Hattie Stowe," BSP, folders 580–590; "The Boy Abe," *One Act Play Magazine and Radio Drama Review*, vol. 4, no. 2 (March-April 1941); " Story Told in Indiana," *Theatre Arts*, vol. 28, no. 11 (November 1944). Smith tried unsuccessfully in 1941 to pitch a book, "Out of the Prairie," based on Lincoln's early years; it was turned down with the comment that "the book market has been so flooded with Lincolnmania"; BSP, folder 24.

26. On the rhetoric of "the people" as a political and ideological response to right-wing populism as well as the official populism of the New Deal, see Denning, *The Cultural Front*, pp. 123–136.

27. All passages from Betty Smith, *A Tree Grows in Brooklyn*, 4th ed. (New York: Harper, 1943).

28. Steinbeck's novel was published in the spring of 1939; the film was released in January 1940. Denning points out that familiarity with the populist celebration

at the close of the film has largely erased popular memory of the novel's more somber ending, which includes the killing of Preacher Casey, the defeat of the strikers, and the unusual image of the new mother nursing the starving stranger; Denning, *The Cultural Front,* pp. 259–268.

29. The Betty Smith Papers contain nearly 500 letters sent to her by readers; most are dated 1943, but some are also from 1944 and 1945. Of these letters, 269 were written by men—at least 128 of whom were in the armed services—and 222 by women. Letters that mentioned the tree metaphor include those of Naval Ensign James A. Walker, November 8, 1943, folder 49; Lieutenant David Mack, May 28, 1944, folder 67; David Gerof, May 15, 1944, folder 66; Joseph A. Cicco, 1944? folder 98.

30. Betty Smith to Elizabeth Lawrence, July 21, 1944, BSP, folder 9. This letter was written when Smith was "smarting" under the criticism of Diana Trilling in "Fiction in Review," *Nation,* September 3, 1943, pp. 73–74; and in "What Has Happened to Our Novels?" *Harper's,* May 1944, pp. 529–536.

31. Letters to Betty Smith from Mary Bannerman, October 12, 1944, BSP, folder 85, and Clem Easly, March 13, 1945, folder 110. On comparison with Farrell, see letters from James A. Walker, November 8, 1943, folder 49; Adam Fiske, November 23, 1944? folder 92; Elmore Smith, February 13, 1945, folder 106. On comparison with Steinbeck, see letters from Sid Scheinbaum, October 21, 1944, folder 87, and Linda Hall Stevens, February 27, 1945, folder 100. All but one of these letters were dated after Smith's comment to her publisher.

32. Smith had initially ended the novel following the father's death and Francie's graduation from high school, with more hardship in store for the children. In consultation with her editors, however, she added the material that became books 4 and 5; see editorial correspondence, BSP, folders 1 and 2.

33. Howard T. Neary to Betty Smith, August 8, 1944, BSP, folder 75. See also doubts about the ending expressed by Rosemary Dawson in "The Charm of Betty Smith," *Saturday Review of Literature,* September 11, 1943.

34. Mary Allen Rowlands to Betty Smith, October 30, 1943, BSP, folder 48.

35. George P. Nisbet to Betty Smith, January 14, 1945, BSP, folder 101. One of Betty Smith's 1930s plays, "What Are You Going To Be?" is a sharp indictment of how "victims" of relief have no chance to become self-respecting and self-supporting citizens; see synopsis, folder 21. Smith equates insurance with exploitation in her letter to Elizabeth F. Lawrence, April 5, 1944, folder 7; see also Helen Christine Bennett to Betty Smith, March 22, 1944, folder 6.

36. On sense memories, see letters to Betty Smith from Fred Gibbs, April 18, 1943, BSP, folder 34; Reverend Hiram R. Bennett, September 23, 1943, folder 44; Catherine N. McDonald, August 30, 1943, folder 40. Readers from Brooklyn who especially love the Brooklyn details include Steve Braisted, January 24, 1944, folder 57; Sylvia H. Levin, August 9, 1944, folder 75; John R. Nelson, May 16, 1944, folder 66; George Resnick, November 21, 1944, folder 92; Stephen Cuozzo, November 12, 1943, folder 50; Michael J. Boyle, 1943? folder 54. The reader who sometimes confuses Betty Smith's "memories" with her own is Sophie Hillman, July 7, 1953, folder 142. Readers from elsewhere who felt that the Nolan family story captured their own experience include John Alexander, June 5, 1944, folder 69; Sid Scheinbaum, October 21, 1944, folder 87; Jack Forsythe, February 7, 1944,

folder 58; John P. Young, June 1944, folder 69; Eugene A. Kurtz, January 28, 1945, folder 103; Francis P. Lynch, May 12, 1944, folder 65; the quotation referring to Chicago is from Cox Lester Dreyer, July 1, 1944, folder 72.

37. For the incidences of humiliation by other children, see Smith, *Tree,* pp. 5, 97–98, 114; for patronizing doctors and nurses, see pp. 130–131; for humiliation by teachers, see pp. 135–137, 144, 289–292; for humiliating gestures of charity, see 176, 189–191. Readers who wrote to Smith about their own experiences of these humiliations include Jesse Austin, August 28, 1943, BSP, folder 40; Henry Vestotsky, September 22, 1943, folder 43; Flo Jackson, September 1, 1944, folder 79; Lida Hall Stevens, February 27, 1945, folder 108; James Somerville, June 18, 1944, folder 70.

38. "A Tree Grows in Brooklyn," *News,* August 29, 1943.

39. Critic Diana Trilling singles out this passage (chosen, she said, "at random") as particularly unlikely. Rather than the thoughts of an adolescent girl, the passage exemplifies "the thoughts and words of a mature person creating a 'literary' image of herself as an adolescent girl." *Nation,* September 4, 1943, p. 74.

40. As Brooklyn-born Howard T. Neary wrote to Smith from Alliance, Nebraska, August 8, 1944, "I feel your book wasn't written so much for people who still live in Brooklyn as it was for people like me, who though far from home and disquieted by circumstances, find Home again in reading it"; BSP, folder 75. As noted above, Smith herself had left Brooklyn long before she wrote her novel.

41. See letters to Betty Smith from Al Lewis, August 25, 1944, BSP, folder 78; M. Mednick, May 12, 1944, folder 65; John Flagg, May 28, 1944, folder 67.

42. Letters to Betty Smith from Elizabeth Winckler Cotterell, January 25, 1953, BSP, folder 142; Maybelle Hoffman, September 29, 1943, folder 43; Sergeant Mac Kaplan, July 15, 1944, folder 73; Albert E. McKay, February 13, 1945, folder 106.

43. Russell H. Smith to Betty Smith, February 29, 1944, BSP, folder 59.

44. Letters to Betty Smith from John Alexander, June 5, 1944, BSP, folder 69, and Ronald Lucik(?), November 17, 1943, folder 50.

45. Naval Ensign James A. Walker to Betty Smith, November 8, 1943, BSP, folder 49.

46. Henry Vesotsky to Betty Smith, September 22, 1943, BSP, folder 43.

47. Letters to Betty Smith from Frank Ebey, September 21, 1944, BSP, folder 82; Jane Dressler, March 5, 1944, folder 60; Lorraine Atkins, September 28, 1944, folder 83; Richard Bernstein, April 18, 1945, folder 116.

48. Letters to Betty Smith from Curtis Bok, September 23, 1943, BSP, folder 44, and Adam Fiske, November 23, 1944, folder 92.

49. See letters to Betty Smith from Margery Hanan, November 20, 1943, BSP, folder 51; Gertrude Appelbaum, February 5, 1945, folder 104; Daisy Hidy, March 4, 1945, folder 109; Edward Lyons, October 31, 1944, folder 88; Flo Jackson, September 1, 1944, folder 79; Mrs. J. K. Benbrook, September 21, 1944, folder 82; Earl T. Warren, November 7, 1944, folder 8; Francis Lynch, May 12, 1944, folder 65.

50. Franklin C. Reilly to Betty Smith, November 25, 1943, BSP, folder 93.

51. Pfc. V. Woods Kern to Betty Smith, October 27, 1943, BSP, folder 48.

52. "The Sentinel Bookshelf—Childhood in a Brooklyn Tenement," *Keene Sentinel,* August 27, 1943.

53. Corporal Robert White to Betty Smith, July 8, 1944, BSP, folder 72.

54. The good immigrant/bad immigrant dichotomy was common to narratives of

Americanization. See, for example, Sydney Taylor's popular children's books about Jewish immigrant family life (the first *All of a Kind Family* was published in 1951), in which the good, wise immigrant mama (always beautiful and well-groomed, cosmopolitan, nonjudgmental) is contrasted with her "less enlightened" relatives, especially Lena, the "greenhorn."

55. One approving reviewer was Florence Haxton Bullock (see note 8), who identified herself as "not brought up in the lower subsistence brackets." Letters to Betty Smith from Edward Lyons October 31, 1944, BSP, folder 88, and John Alexander, June 5, 1944, folder 69.

56. Letters to Betty Smith from Al Lewis August 28, 1944, BSP, folder 78, and Pfc. John Alexander, June 5, 1944, folder 69.

57. Letters to Betty Smith from Lieutenant David Mack, May 28, 1944, BSP, folder 67, and John S. McNeill, December 12, 1943, folder 52.

58. When she wrote to her editor about cutting this scene, Smith said that she "did not have a good feeling about this episode. Maybe I felt there was too much about Christmas in that portion of the book." Betty Smith to Eugene Saxton, December 10, 1942, BSP, folder 1.

59. Leo Gurko calls attention to this dimension of Wolfe's writing; *The Angry Decade* (New York: Dodd, Mead, 1947), pp. 151–159.

60. "Listen to America!" BSP, folder 306.

61. Betty Smith to Harper and Brothers, November 25, 1942, BSP, folder 31. The Williamsburg neighborhood of Brooklyn where Smith grew up was not far from the Fort Green section, across Bedford Avenue, home to one third of Brooklyn's black population from 1880–1930.

62. Thanks to my colleague Rachel Rubin for calling my attention to Neeley's ruminations on "white Jews."

63. Letters to Betty Smith from Henry Vesotsky (the self-identified "jew boy"), September 22, 1943, BSP, folder 43. The poem was enclosed with a letter from David Gerof, May 15, 1944, folder 66. See also letters from B. Perry Cohen, October 20, 1944, folder 86; George Resnick, November 21, 1944, folder 92; Marvin Gelbfish, n.d., folder 40; Harold Levy, May 28, 1944, folder 67; E. Nussbaum, March 27, 1944, folder 62; Morton Jerome Goodfriend, April 30, 1944, folder 64; Monus Weinstein, June 14, 1944, folder 70; Herbert Abrams, December 9, 1943, folder 52; Mac Kaplan, July 15, 1944, folder 73; Sid Scheinbaum, October 21, 1944, folder 87; Julius Tarnofsky, December 8, 1944, folder 94. Smith was invited to speak at the Brooklyn section of the National Council of Jewish Women, on the grounds that "our service in the community is akin to your depth of sympathy and understanding of the underprivileged class"; Alva M. Zeitz to Betty Smith, December 1, 1943, folder 52.

64. Arnold Scheinberg to Betty Smith, September 27, 1944, BSP, folder 83. Two other readers wrote to Smith with concerns about the book's potential contribution to anti-Semitism: M. Katz (a "dutchman" who came to the U.S. in 1939), May 11, 1944, folder 65; and the popular historical novelist Taylor Caldwell (author of a 1941 book about Nazi Germany, *Time No Longer*), September 15, 1943, folder 4. In contrast, a librarian from Milwaukee, Ruth Shapiro, wrote to thank Smith for

"the sympathetic handling of two subjects very close to me—Jews and labor"; February 8, 1944, folder 58.

65. Mrs. Pat Rotondo to Betty Smith, April 21, 1945, BSP, folder 117.

66. Viola Bell to Betty Smith, April 18, 1945, BSP, folder 116.

67. Neil C. Hartley to Betty Smith, April 20, 1944, BSP, folder 64.

68. Betty Smith to Elizabeth Lawrence, December 22, 1945, quoted in Johnson, "Life and Work," p. 216. See also "I never did care much for the company of women," Betty Smith to Jameson Bunn, December 1941, BSP, folder 46.

69. Letters from Betty Smith to Eugene Saxton at Harper and Brothers: July 31, September 30, October 7, October 13, December 9, December 10, December 26, 1942, BSP, folder 1. Elizabeth Lawrence at Harper and Brothers to Betty Smith, January 12, 1943; Smith to Lawrence January 14, 1943; Saxton to Smith, January 20, 1943, folder 2.

70. "The knowledge of sex that I brought to my marriage . . . I had acquired from filthy jingles on the walls of toilet rooms of public schools of New York City; from the conversation of other children who had received garbled versions of it from lack of privacy between their parents and from obscene things that I had overheard on street corners"; Smith, "Mr. Russell and Sex Education," pp. 96–98, in response to an article by Bertrand Russell, "Education Without Sex Taboos," *New Republic*, November 16, 1927, BSP, folder 305.

71. Smith based this incident on a 1942 newspaper article, but her choice of a "sex pervert" to represent sexual danger to young women in a poor neighborhood reflected the increasingly common representation of male sexual abusers as "dirty old men," strangers rather than family members, in social case-work records in the 1920s and 1930s; see Linda Gordon, *Heroes of Their Own Lives: The Politics and History of Family Violence, Boston 1880–1960* (New York: Viking Penguin, 1988). One reader shared a memory of a similar assault by a stranger: Sylvia Levin to Betty Smith, August 9, 1944, BSP, folder 75. In her last novel, *Joy in the Morning*, published in 1963, Smith depicts sexual danger closer to home: the female protagonist flees Brooklyn to marry her boyfriend in Ann Arbor but also to escape her stepfather's sexual attentions.

72. Letters to Betty Smith from E. Newquist, July 29, 1944, BSP, folder 74; Betty Lamb, September 7, 1943, folder 42; Mrs. S. Bakkers, January 8, 1945, folder 100.

73. Letters to Betty Smith from E. Newquist, July 29, 1944, BSP, folder 74; Mrs. Willis Johnson, December 6, 1944, folder 94; Emma Woodruff, January 8, 1945, folder 100.

74. Private Joe Dever to Betty Smith, 1945? BSP, folder 118. For Catholic critics, see letters from M. Burke, November 17, 1943, folder 50; Mrs. Martin J. Boyer, January 21, 1944, folder 57; Norine O'Toole, 1944, folder 98; support from practicing Catholics came from Father J. J. Cronin, June 28, 1944, folder 71, and Brother G. Paul, June 1945, folder 123.

75. Letters to Betty Smith from John Alexander, 5 June 1944, BSP, folder 69; Gertrude Stamp, August 24, 1944, folder 77; Beatrice Squire, September 8, 1944, folder 79; [President of the Central PTA] Roselle Park, New York, May 17, 1944, folder 1.

76. Letters to Betty Smith from Morris Luster, July 16, 1944, BSP, folder 73; James W. Somerville, June 18, 1944, folder 70; Adam Fiske, November 23, 1944, folder 92; V. Woods Kern, October 27, 1943, folder 48.

77. Letters to Betty Smith from Elmore A. Smith, February 13, 1945, BSP, folder 106; John Alexander, June 5, 1944, folder 69; James Lewis, October 21, 1944, folder 87; Bill Donohoe August 22, 1944, folder 77. Sgt. Bill Ressler also wrote that he "actually cried at the description of Francie and Neeley's grief when Johnny died," March 1, 1944, folder 60.

78. Letters to Betty Smith from Howard T. Neary, August 8, 1944, folder 75, and Albert E. McKay, February 13, 1945, folder 106.

79. Smith mentioned her "bad movie contract" in a letter to Ed Aswell, October 16, 1944, BSP, folder 10.

80. Darryl Zanuck, "Do Writers Know Hollywood: The Message Cannot Overwhelm the Technique," presented to the Writers Congress held by the University of California and the leftwing Hollywood Writers Mobilization in the fall of 1943; reprinted in *Saturday Review of Literature*, October 30, 1943, pp. 12–13.

81. Doherty, *Projections of War*, pp. 180–204.

82. The midwestern Protestant Zanuck was born in Wahoo, Nebraska, September 5, 1902, in the town's Grand Hotel, owned by his mother's wealthy family and managed by his father. After his parents divorced in 1909, he split his time between living with his mother in Los Angeles and his father in Nebraska. He served briefly in combat in World War I, tried a number of jobs, wrote pulp fiction, eventually becoming successful in 1920s Hollywood as the "writer" for Rin Tin Tin pictures and then as a producer. See Mel Gussow, *Don't Say Yes Until I Finish Talking: A Biography of Darryl Zanuck* (New York: Doubleday, 1971) and George F. Custen, *Twentieth Century's Fox: Darryl F. Zanuck and the Culture of Hollywood* (New York: Basic, 1997).

83. On the goals and accomplishments of left-wing screenwriters in the studio system, see Buhle and Wagner, *Radical Hollywood* and interviews with screenwriters in Pat McGilligan and Paul Buhle, *Tender Comrades: A Backstory of the Hollywood Blacklist* (New York: St. Martin's, 1997).

84. Slesinger, the daughter of middle-class Hungarian and Russian Jewish immigrants, had achieved both critical and commercial success with her first novel, *The Unpossessed* (1934), based on her experience with the New York left-wing literati world she had been a part of with her first husband, Herbert Solow. Her fiction pays particular attention to female sexuality and marital conflict. Frank Davis was a left-wing producer and screenwriter whom Slesinger met and married after she went to Hollywood to work as a screenwriter. Slesinger's prior credits included the first script for Pearl S. Buck's *The Good Earth* (1935); she and Davis coauthored the screenplay for Dorothy Arzner's film *Dance Girl Dance* (1940). Slesinger was an outspoken activist in the Hollywood Screen Writer's Guild and the Anti-Nazi League. See entries on Slesinger by Kim Flachmann in *Dictionary of Literary Biography: American Short Story Writers, 1910–1945*, ed. Bobby Ellen Kimball (Detroit: Gale, 1991); and in *Twentieth Century Literary Criticism*, vol. 10, ed. Dennis Poupard (Detroit: Gale, 1983); Shirley Biagi, "Forgive Me for Dying," *Antioch Review*, vol. 35 (1977).

85. Lighton began in pictures as a scenarist for silent films. Kazan's description of Lighton working on the script appeared in "The Writer and the Motion Picture," written as a preface to Budd Schulberg's script for Kazan's 1957 film, *A Face in the Crowd.* Kazan's discussion of Lighton's politics is from his autobiography, *A Life* (New York: Knopf, 1988), pp. 250–251, 253.

86. Biographical information on Kazan is drawn from his interviews with Michael Ciment in *Kazan on Kazan* (New York: Viking, 1974), and *A Life,* in which the quote about Molly Day Thatcher appears on p. 54. See also Thomas Pauly, *An American Odyssey: Elia Kazan and American Culture* (Philadelphia: Temple University Press, 1983).

87. On Kazan's relationship to the Communist Party, see Victor Navasky, *Naming Names* (New York: Penguin, 1981), pp. 199–222. Kazan's quote about the movement appears in Ciment, *Kazan on Kazan,* p. 15. He described his proletarian aspirations to Ciment on pp. 21, 23–24. See also Kazan, *A Life,* pp. 105–110, 110–133.

88. Kazan's comments about the Group Theatre are in Ciment, *Kazan on Kazan,* pp. 26–27. When the leadership of Kazan's local Communist Party unit assigned him the task of trying to "take over" the Group against his own assessment of how the Group should function, the painful split in loyalty led him to resign from the Party. *A Life,* pp. 127–33. His former colleague in the Theatre of Action, Nicholas Ray, came with him to Hollywood to work as his assistant on *A Tree Grows in Brooklyn.*

89. Ciment, *Kazan on Kazan,* p. 49; Kazan, *A Life,* p. 251. In the Ciment interview Kazan counted Lighton as one of the three most influential men in his life, ranking him just after Clurman and Strasberg, his mentors in the Group Theatre; *Kazan on Kazan,* p. 42. Lighton's control over the shape of the final film was also heightened by Kazan's inexperience as a Hollywood system filmmaker. On the advice of his cinematographer, Leon Shamroy, Kazan staged the scenes as for theater, and the cinematographer provided extensive coverage of establishing shots, close-ups and cuts that Lighton and Zanuck could later assemble; *A Life,* pp. 258–259.

90. Many reviews found McGuire miscast: Philip Hartung writes that her "face lacked the lines this suffering mother should have; her voice is too cultured for a tenement scrubwoman who is embittered but still determined to get ahead"; "It Grows," *Commonweal,* March 9, 1945, p. 518. Manny Farber found her looking more like "a respectable Junior Miss" than a working-class tenement wife; "Brooklyn Dodger," *New Republic,* March 12, 1945, p. 360.

91. Garner had been acting and modeling since the age of six. Prior film roles included a refugee child in *Pied Piper* (1942) and the young Jane in *Jane Eyre* (1944). Donaldson was ten, with credits from Broadway, radio, and other films. See Brand, "Vital Statistics on 'A Tree Grows in Brooklyn,'" Film Production File for *Tree,* Margaret Herrick Library, Academy of Motion Picture Arts and Sciences, Los Angeles, hereafter abbreviated as MHL-AMPAS.

92. Ciment, *Kazan on Kazan,* p. 51.

93. Studio publicity stressed the claim of *geographical* universality: "The charm of the book was that through the young girl, Francie Nolan, everyone relived his own childhood, no matter where that childhood had been spent." See Brand, "Vital Statistics," p. 2. Most reviewers did not attempt to date the action of the

film: of those who did, Philip Hartung placed it in 1915, the date highlighted in the publicity for the film ("It Grows," p. 517), while Manny Farber assumed that the Nolans "live poorly and indestructibly in Brooklyn during the 1920s" ("Brooklyn Dodger," p. 360).

94. James Agee, "The New Pictures," *Time,* February 19, 1945, p. 91; Farber, "Brooklyn Dodger," p. 360. Agee, who was himself involved in the 1930s project of documenting the poor, notes with ironic distance that various forms of representing poverty evoked complex responses in audiences: "The comfortable have always been able to lick their chops over the hunger of others if that hunger is presented with the right sort of humorous or pathetic charm; if certain Christian or Marxian glands are stimulated, they will drool as well"; "Films," *Nation,* February 17, 1945, p. 193.

95. Philip Hartung, "It Grows," pp. 517–518; "Green Grows the Tree," *Newsweek,* February 19, 1945, p. 100. See also Edwin Schallert, "Tree Rich in Human Qualities," *Los Angeles Times,* March 2, 1945, part 2, p. 8.

96. Kazan, *A Life,* p. 253.

97. Ibid., p. 245.

98. Ibid., p. 259.

99. The presumption that, in the absence of a male, a woman who is required to work in order to support her children and advance their class position will become "hard" also appeared in the film *Mildred Pierce,* which opened just a few months after the release of *Tree.*

100. James Agee objected to what he described as the "classic Freudian pattern" of the father-daughter and mother-son relationships ("Films," p. 193); Philip Hartung, on the other hand, found "the love between Francie and Johnny" the "most touching thing about the film" ("It Grows," p. 51).

101. Kazan's representation contradicted many women's actual wartime experience; see Karen Anderson, *Wartime Women: Sex Roles, Family Relations and the Status of Women During World War II* (Westport, Conn.: Greenwood, 1981); Susan M. Hartmann, *The Home Front and Beyond: American Women in the 1940s* (Boston: Hall, 1982); Andrea Walsh, *Women's Film and Female Experience, 1940–1950* (New York: Praeger, 1984). On wartime and postwar debates, see Barbara Melosh, *Engendering Culture: Manhood and Womanhood in New Deal Public Art and Theater* (Washington, D.C.: Smithsonian, 1991); Alan Bérubé, *Coming Out Under Fire: The History of Gay Men and Women in WWII* (New York: Free, 1990); Elaine T. May, *Homeward Bound: American Families in the Cold War Era* (New York: Basic, 1988); Feldstein, *Motherhood in Black and White;* Daniel Horowitz, *Betty Friedan and the Making of the Feminine Mystique: The American Left, The Cold War, and Modern Feminism* (Amherst: University of Massachusetts Press, 1998).

102. Farber, "The Brooklyn Dodger," p. 360; Bosley Crowther, " 'A Tree' Flourishes on Film," *New York Times,* March 4, 1945.

103. See Suzanna Danuta Walters, *Lives Together, Worlds Apart: Mothers and Daughters in Popular Culture* (Berkeley: University of California Press, 1992), pp. 61–65.

104. W. G., "The Current Cinema: Best Seller," *New Yorker,* March 3, 1945, p. 48.

105. Manny Farber was especially outraged by the ending, which he characterized in this way: "The picture then gets back to Hollywood normal with everybody eating

banana splits, the mother about to marry a Gilbralter-like policeman, the daughter starting on her first puppy love affair, the tree in the tenement court, which was cut down earlier in the film, starting to grow, and somebody announcing that they certainly had a good time being poor" ("The Brooklyn Dodger," p. 360).

106. The article quoting Betty Smith appears in *Wings*, September 1943; the UPI story was reprinted in the Shenandoah, Pennsylvania, *Herald*, January 6, 1945, and San Francisco's *People's World*, January 6, 1945; all in Smith's scrapbooks of clippings, BSP; disappointments noted in letters to Betty Smith from Joe Jones, January 8, 1945, folder 100, and "Ed," February 2, 1945, folder 104.

107. Cobbett Steinberg, *Reel Facts: the Movie Book of Records* (New York: Vintage, 1982), p. 19.

108. Edwin Schallert, "Tree Rich in Human Qualities," *Los Angeles Times*, March 2, 1945.

109. Kane, "A Tree Grows in Brooklyn," *Motion Picture Daily*, February 24, 1945; Kahn, "A Tree Grows in Brooklyn," *Variety*, January 26, 1945.

110. Johnson, "Life and Work"; Betty Smith, "Best Seller Aftermath," *Life*, June 6, 1949, pp. 7–16.

111. Cited by Johnson, "Life and Work," p. 231.

112. Smith discussed her inability to resist working on the adaptation in "That 'Tree' Keeps Growing," an article she wrote for the *New York Times*, April 15, 1951.

113. Harry Harris, "Stage Struck Novelist," *Philadelphia Sunday Bulletin*, March 25, 1951, in clipping file on Betty Smith, MHL-AMPAS. Privately, Smith may have distanced herself from the adaptation, according to a letter in response to hers. See Bob Finch to Betty Smith, May 18, 1951, BSP, folder 137: "I'm sorry it [the show] isn't important to you any more."

114. The libretto for the musical was published 1951; Betty Smith and George Abbott, *A Tree Grows in Brooklyn: a Musical Play* (New York: Harper, 1951); original Broadway cast recording, CBS, 1951; Sony Classical Recordings, SK48014, 1991.

115. "A Tree Grows in Brooklyn" (New Haven production), *Variety*, March 21, 1951; "The Theater," *Cue*, April 28, 1951; see also clippings related to the musical in Betty Smith's scrapbooks, BSP. There was a lot of competition on Broadway: *Call Me Madam, Guys and Dolls*, and *the King and I* all opened that season.

116. These comments were published in an article promoting her 1958 novel, *Maggie-Now*, "The Tree Lady's Back," *Newsweek*, February 24, 1958, pp. 109–110.

117. Johnson, "Life and Work," pp. 158, 191, 218. *Tree* sold three million copies by 1945 and four million by 1951. By the time Betty Smith died in 1972, the book had been translated into sixteen languages and had sold more than six million copies in thirty-seven hardcover printings.

3. HOME FRONT HARMONY AND REMEMBERING *MAMA*

1. Rejected by the *Atlantic Monthly*, "Mama's Bank Account" was first published in the *Toronto Star Weekly* and soon reprinted in *Reader's Digest*, February 1941, with a second installment, "Mama's Roomer," appearing two months later in response to "thousands of people writing in to demand more about Mama." See

Kathryn Forbes's entry in *Current Biography* (1944). Other Mama stories were published in *Women's Day*, October 1943, *Ladies Home Journal*, August 1944, and *Good Housekeeping*, December 1945. *Mama's Bank Account*, like *A Tree Grows in Brooklyn*, was among the first group of books to be reprinted as a special armed forces edition in the autumn of 1943.

2. Quotations from Diana Trilling, "What Has Happened to Our Novels," *Harper's Magazine*, May 1944, pp. 533–534.

3. Edith H. Crowell, *Library Journal*, March 15, 1943, p. 6.

4. Beatrice Sherman, "Family Finances," *New York Times Book Review*, March 28, 1943, p. 22.

5. *Atlantic Monthly*, May 1943, p. 129; Sherman, "Family Finances," p. 22. *Book Week*, March 21, 1943, as quoted in "Kathryn (Anderson) McLean," *Contemporary Authors—Permanent Series*, vol. 2 (Detroit: Gale, 1978), p. 362.

6. Trilling emphasized Forbes's theme of domestic strength as her contribution to the new "literary nationalism," in "What Has Happened to Our Novels"; Virginia Wright noted the novel's postwar circulation and translation, in her drama editor's column, *Daily News* (Los Angeles), July 1, 1947. By 1947 the book had been translated into ten languages.

7. Jean Baumgartner, "Meet the Author: Kathryn Forbes," *San Francisco Chronicle*, May 23, 1943, p 13.

8. In an interview with George Lipsitz, Ralph Nelson, director of the television series *Mama*, recalled reading that Forbes had grown up in foster homes and felt deserted by her family; George Lipsitz, *Time Passages: Collective Memory and American Popular Culture* (Minneapolis; University of Minnesota Press, 1990), p. 79. Robin Morgan, who played Dagmar in the television *Mama* from 1950 to 1956, described Forbes as the "neglected only child of divorced parents, raised by a mother and three critical aunts." See Robin Morgan, *Saturday's Child: A Memoir* (New York: Norton, 2001), p. 100.

9. For biographical information, see Kathryn Forbes's entry in *Current Biography* (1944); and her obituaries in the *New York Times*, May 17, 1966, and *San Francisco Chronicle*, May 17, 1966.

10. Wright, *Daily News* column, July 1, 1947.

11. Forbes apparently kept secret from her husband her radio writing for the Sperry Sunday Special. "Her loyal mother laughed at her jokes over the air, but for a long time Husband McLean took no note of there being any such a program, being totally in the dark as to its originator's identity." Fred Johnson, " 'But First of All I Remember Mama,' said Kathryn Forbes," *San Francisco Call Bulletin*, March 27, 1948. See also Baumgartner, "Meet the Author."

12. Baumgartner, "Meet the Author: Forbes"; the caption under the literary cartoon of Forbes reads "Kathryn Forbes—Fact and fiction mixes well."

13. See *Current Biography* (1944), p. 216; Johnson, " 'But First of All I Remember Mama' "; Kathryn Forbes, "Drama Author Kathryn Forbes Writes About Homecoming of a San Francisco Play," *San Francisco Chronicle*, 1947. Robin Morgan speculated that presenting the stories as fact "intensified the heartwarming factor," in *Saturday's Child*, p. 100.

14. Beatrice Sherman, "Family Finances," *New York Times Book Review*, March 28, 1943, p. 22.

15. Kathy Peiss, *Cheap Amusements: Working Women and Leisure in Turn-of-the-Century New York* (Philadelphia: Temple University Press, 1986), p. 67. On debates over familial and individual entitlement to wages, see Judith E. Smith, *Family Connections: A History of Italian and Jewish Immigrant Lives in Providence, Rhode Island, 1900–1940* (Albany: SUNY Press, 1985); and Stephen A. Lassonde, *Learning to Forget: Schooling and Family Life in New Haven's Working Class, 1870–1940* (New Haven: Yale University, 2004). On generational and gendered conflicts over wages, see Susan Porter Benson, "Living on the Margin: Working-Class Marriage and Family Survival Strategies in the United States, 1919–1941," in *The Sex of Things*, ed. Victoria De Grazia, with Ellen Furlough (Berkeley: University of California Press, 1996); and Susan Porter Benson, *Household Accounts: Working-Class Family Economies in the Interwar Years* (Ithaca: Cornell University Press, forthcoming).

16. All quotations are from the Harvest paperback edition of Kathryn Forbes, *Mama's Bank Account* (New York: Harcourt Brace, 1943).

17. *Library Journal*, March 15, 1943.

18. Wright, *Daily News* column, July 1, 1947; Louella Parsons, "Cosmopolitan's Movie Citations," in *Cosmopolitan*, April 1949; Richard Rodgers, *Musical Stages: An Autobiography* (New York: Da Capo, 1995 [1975]); Stephen Citron, *The Wordsmiths: Oscar Hammerstein II and Alan Jay Lerner* (New York: Oxford University Press, 1995).

19. Citron, *Wordsmiths*, p. 165.

20. Information on the Broadway and road company runs in William Torbert Leonard, *Theatre: Stage to Screen to Television* (Metuchen, N.J.: Scarecrow, 1981), 1:724–729. The play received three Donaldson Awards for best direction, best setting, and best costumes. Erik Barnouw wrote the radio script for the Theatre Guild on the Air adaptation; it was published in a collection of plays presented on radio, *Theatre Guild on the Air*, ed. H. William Fitelson (New York: Rinehart, 1947), pp. 357–394.

21. Van Druten, born in 1901 to a Dutch father and an English mother, grew up in an upper-middle-class family. His greatest commercial success was a play set during World War II, *The Voice of the Turtle*, celebrating the permissive heterosexuality of wartime. It opened December 1943, ran several years on Broadway, and was adapted as a film in 1947. "John Van Druten," *Current Biography* (1944); William J. Mann, *Behind the Screen: How Gays and Lesbians Shaped Hollywood, 1910–1969* (New York: Viking, 2001), pp. 207–208.

22. Joseph Wood Krutch, "Drama," *Nation*, November 4, 1944, p. 568. Stark Young, "I Remember Mama," *New Republic*, December 18, 1944, p. 836; Wolcott Gibbs, "Mama Is O.K.," *New Yorker*, October 28, 1944, pp. 38, 40. John Mason Brown used the terms "let's pretend" and noted the "liberation from realism" in "Home Fires Burning," *Saturday Review of Literature*, December 16, 1944, pp. 18, 20. George Jean Nathan commented on the use of staged fadeouts as "cinematic" and the episodic storytelling as similar to the "easy turning of the pages in the

family's album," in "'I Remember Mama,' October 19, 1944"; see his *The Theatre Book of the Year, 1944–45* (Teaneck, N.J.: Farleigh Dickinson University Press, 1972), pp. 109–112. See also Lewis Nichols's comment on the staging as cinematic, in "I Remember Mama," *New York Times*, October 20, 1944, and his noting of the "blurred focus," in "Of Mama Who Runs the Family," *New York Times*, October 29, 1944.

23. John Van Druten, *I Remember Mama: A Play in Two Acts* (New York: Harcourt Brace, 1945), pp. 128–132.

24. Being able to tip was a sign of moving from scarcity to abundance. In *A Tree Grows in Brooklyn* not being able to tip is one of the humiliations the Nolans suffer; the tip they offer for the postgraduation ice cream sodas figures prominently in the movie's finale.

25. The play was based on Clarence Day's biographical sketches of his family, *God and My Father* (1932), *Life with Father* (1935), and *Life with Mother* (1937). See *Time*, October 30, 1944, p. 68; Nichols, "Of Mama Who Runs the Family."

26. Brown, "Home Fires Burning," pp. 18, 20. Michael Rogin argues for a different set of associations between *The Jazz Singer*, "mammies," and immigrant mothers, in *Black Face, White Noise*.

27. Arthur Hopkins, "New Theatre Freedoms," *Theatre Arts*, February 1945, pp. 81–82.

28. Rosamund Gilder, "Escape to Mama," *Theatre Arts*, December 1944, pp. 697–698; Brown, "Home Fires Burning," pp. 18, 20. Rob Westbrook has argued that many appeals to wartime patriotism were couched in the language of private interests and private moral obligations in "Fighting for the American Family: Private Interests and Political Obligation in World War II," in *Power and Culture: Critical Essays in American History*, ed. Richard W. Fox and T. J. Jackson Lears (Chicago: University of Chicago Press, 1993), pp. 194–221; and "I Want a Girl, Just Like the Girl That Married Henry James: American Women and the Problem of Political Obligation in World War II," *American Quarterly* 42 (1990), pp. 587–614.

29. Brown, "Home Fires Burning," pp. 18, 20.

30. Christians was born in Vienna but moved to New York with her father, an actor and theatrical manager, and her mother, an opera and concert singer, in 1912. She returned to Europe to study acting in 1918, where she starred in classical and modern dramas and over sixty films. "Mady Christians," *Current Biography* (1945). Hazel Bruce profiled Christians when the play traveled to San Francisco, in "'I Remember Mama' Presents a Great American Family," *San Francisco Chronicle*, May 27, 1945.

31. Stark Young referred to Christians's "secret chic" in the *New Republic*, December 18, 1944, p. 836; William Lindsay Gresham mentioned wine and herring in his profile of Christians, "Mama and Papa," *Theatre Arts* 29 (April 1945), p. 215.

32. Entry on Christians in *Current Biography* (1945); Bruce, "'I Remember Mama' Presents a Great American Family," p. 15.

33. James Naremore, *More Than Night: Film Noir in Its Contexts* (Berkeley: University of California Press, 1999). Popular front leftists between 1947 and 1951 were attracted to this genre; see Thom Anderson, "Red Hollywood," in *Literature and*

the Visual Arts in Contemporary Society, ed. Suzanne Ferguson and Barbara Groseclose (Columbus: Ohio State University Press, 1985), pp. 141–196; and Buhle and Wagner, *Radical Hollywood.*

34. Linda Williams, "Feminist Film Theory: 'Mildred Pierce' and the Second World War," in *Female Spectators: Looking at Film and Television,* ed. E. Dierdre Prithbram (New York: Verso, 1988). Feldstein, *Motherhood in Black and White.*

35. "Program Notes" by Joan Cohen for the Los Angeles County Museum of Art 1977 showing of *I Remember Mama,* part of a retrospective on the RKO years, in the production files for *I Remember Mama,* MHL-AMPAS.

36. Johnson, "'But First of All, I Remember Mama.'" Parsons and Bodeen had already collaborated on *The Enchanted Cottage* (1945); see Mann, *Behind the Screen,* pp. 194–196.

37. Bruce, "'I Remember Mama' Presents a Great American Family." On Christians's blacklisting, see Lipsitz, "Why Remember Mama? The Changing Face of a Woman's Narrative," in *Time Passages.*

38. See King Kennedy, "This Entertainment World: Irene Dunne Rapidly Becoming Move Ideal Young Mother Type." *Beverly Hills Bulletin,* May 8, 1947; Barney Glazer, "The True Hollywood," *Bell Herald,* May 8, 1947; "Hollywood Marriages Are Successful," *Movieland,* June 1947; "Women Run Men, Says Miss Dunne," *Pittsburgh Press,* August 29, 1947; Philip Scheuer, "This Town Called Hollywood," *Chicago Tribune,* August 31,1947. Dunne's column in *Silver Screen* appeared at least between December 1947 and April 1948, and offered advice that stressed modern conceptions of heterosexual romance, personal improvement, women's responsibility for pleasing husbands, and personal autonomy from obligation to aging parents, among other topics also covered in middle-class magazine advice columns of the period. These articles are in Irene Dunne's scrapbooks 7, 9, 10, in box 6 of the Irene Dunne Collection, Special Collections, Cinema-Television Library, University of Southern California, hereafter abbreviated IDC, USC.

39. Elizabeth Pallette, "Hit Play Into Film," *New York Times,* October 26, 1947; Reba and Ronnie Churchill, "Hollywood Diary," *Valley Times,* June 10, 1947; Bosley Crowther, "The Screen: Irene Dunne and Oscar Homolka Head Brilliant Cast in RKO's 'I Remember Mama,'" *New York Times,* March 12, 1948; Ellen Creelman, "Picture Plays and Players: Harriet Parsons Talks of 'I Remember Mama,'" *Sun,* March 18, 1948; Louella Parsons, "Irene Dunne Conceals Glamour for New Role," *San Diego Union,* March 28, 1948.

40. "RKO Theaters Arrange Big Mama Promotion," in *Box Office Showmandiser,* April 3, 1948; see scrapbook 10, box 6, IDC, USC.

41. *Film Bulletin,* March 15, 1948.

42. Hedda Hopper, "Looking at Hollywood," *Los Angeles Times,* March 12, 1948; " 'I Remember Mama' Superb Heights: Brilliant Picture Tops Play, Novel," *Hollywood Reporter,* March 9, 1948; Lowell Redelings, "'I Remember Mama': Film Comedy a Smash Hit," *Hollywood Citizen News,* April 2, 1948. On Mama's lack of class aspirations, see Rose Pelswick, " 'I Remember Mama': Dunne, Homolka Star in a Beguiling Film," *New York Journal-American,* March 12, 1948.

43. Bosley Crowther, "Films for Easter," *New York Times,* March 28, 1948; and "The Screen: Irene Dunne and Oscar Homolka Head Brilliant Cast."

44. Richard Watts Jr., " 'I Remember Mama' Engaging Film," *New York Post,* March 12, 1948; Fred Broomfield, " 'I Remember Mama' Film to Be Long Remembered," *Valley Times,* April 3, 1948.

45. "The Current Cinema," *New Yorker,* March 20, 1948; Cecilia Anger, "Dunne Gives Depth to Sentimental Film," *PM,* March 12, 1948.

46. See "Movies—The Old Story," *New Republic,* April 19, 1948, p. 29; "Movie of the Week—I Remember Mama," *Life,* April 12, 1948; "I Remember Mama," *Hollywood Reporter,* March 9, 1948; "I Remember Mama," *Variety,* March 9, 1948; "I Remember Mama," *Cue,* March 13, 1948.

47. John Todd, "Irene Dunne Took Year to Accept 'Mama' Role," *Oakland Post-Enquirer,* July 14, 1947; Edwin Schallert, "All Three of 'Mamas' Please Play's Author," *Los Angeles Times,* July 27, 1947; Fred Johnson, "Red Carpet for Two 'Mamas,' " *Commercial News,* August 4, 1947.

48. "I Remember Mama," *Variety,* March 9, 1948; "I Remember Mama," *Cue,* March 13, 1948; Broomfield, " 'I Remember Mama' Film to Be Long Remembered."

49. "The Movies of 1948," *Life,* March 14, 1949, pp. 44–53.

50. See "In Hollywood with Louella Parsons," *Seattle Post-Intelligencer,* March 28, 1948; Parsons, "Irene Dunne Conceals Glamour," *San Diego Union,* March 28, 1948.

51. John Hobart, "Stevens: Director and Thinker," *San Francisco Chronicle,* August 17, 1947.

52. Harry McArthur, " 'I Remember Mama' Brings Joy to Screen at Keith's," *Washington Star,* March 29, 1949. See also Howard Barnes, " 'I Remember Mama' Gives Hollywood Stock a Boost," *New York Herald-Tribune,* March 14, 1948.

53. Stevens made a name for himself as a versatile and talented director of drama (*Alice Adams,* 1935), musicals (*Swing Time,* 1936), epic adventure (*Gunga Din,* 1939), and comedy (*Woman of the Year,* 1942, and *The More the Merrier,* 1943).

54. George Stevens Jr., *George Stevens: A Filmmaker's Journey* (documentary film, 1984).

55. George Stevens Jr. attributed the phrase "the confirmed period of the past" to his father in *George Stevens.* Stevens thought "it would be fun to reconstruct the period. It was at the most a play that committed itself only to the mom and family. Nothing contemporary." Patrick McGilligan and Joseph McBride, "George Stevens: A Piece of the Rock," 1974 interview, in *Film Crazy: Interviews with Hollywood Legends* (New York: St. Martin's, 2000), pp. 90–91. On Stevens's association with Liberty films, see Joseph McBride, *Frank Capra: The Catastrophe of Success* (New York: Simon and Schuster, 1993) pp. 503–507. In 1948, when the film came out, Stevens was director of the Screen Directors Guild. He attempted to hold the guild together, agitating for "freedom of the screen" against anticommunist pressures and refusing to condemn publicly Edward Dmytryk, who had been called to testify before HUAC as part of the Hollywood 10 in October 1947; Otis L. Guernsey Jr., "The Playbill: Hard Work is Stevens' Specialty," *New York Herald-Tribune,* March 14, 1948.

56. John Hobart, " 'I Remember Mama' Is a Triumph of Warm Affection and Reality," *San Francisco Chronicle*, March 31, 1948.

57. See Hobart, "Stevens: Director and Thinker"; Guernsey, "The Playbill: Hard Work Is Stevens' Specialty"; James Agee's review in *Time*, April 5, 1948. Crowther's comment appeared in his column "The Screen: Irene Dunne and Oscar Homolka Head Brilliant Cast."

58. Todd, "Irene Dunne Took Year to Accept 'Mama' Role"; Elizabeth Pallette, "Hit Play Into Film," *New York Times*, October 26, 1947. Alton Cook did note the cast's "manifold variants of Scandinavian accent" as jarring to a "Minnesota-bred ear," but he recognized this as standard procedure in pictures "where actors struggle with alien speech"; "Great Cast Sparkles in 'I Remember Mama,'" *New York World Telegram*, March 11, 1948.

59. Virginia Wright, *Daily News* column, April 13, 1948.

60. Cook, "Great Cast Sparkles."

61. This phrase was used by Watts, " 'I Remember Mama' Engaging Film."

62. "Top Grossers, 1948," *Variety*, January 5, 1949; *Time Magazine*, January 3, 1949.

63. See Kathryn Forbes, "Hurry-Up Charlie," *Colliers*, September 18, 1943; "Minstrel Boy," *Colliers*, September 15, 1945; "Mama and Dagmar," *Ladies Home Journal*, August 1944; and "Mama and the Christmas Tradition," *Good Housekeeping*, December 1945.

64. Kathryn Forbes, "I Remember the Frandsens," *Reader's Digest*, November 1946; *Transfer Point* (New York: Harcourt Brace, 1947), serialized in *Good Housekeeping*, October and November 1947. *Transfer Point* was reviewed more seriously and in more depth than *Mama's Bank Account* had been. See "Bookman's Notebook: Notes on the Margin," *San Francisco Chronicle*, February 18, 1947. The review quoted was by Mary Ross in the *New York Herald-Tribune Book Review*, January 25, 1948, p. 18.

65. Tim Brooks and Earle Marsh, *The Complete Directory to Prime-Time Network and Cable TV Shows, 1946-Present*, 6th ed. (New York: Ballantine, 1995), pp. 1170–1171, 1258.

66. The serial comedy about an ethnic family was a well-established form of popular programming on radio by the years after World War II; it drew humor and verbal style from vaudeville traditions of ethnic performance popularized by Eddie Cantor, Al Jolson, and the Marx Brothers while maintaining audience interest and loyalty with continuing story lines and characters. See Michele Hilmes, *Radio Voices*, pp. 1–4, 75–129; Robert C. Allen, *Speaking of Soap Operas* (Chapel Hill: University of North Carolina Press, 1985), pp. 110–121.

67. Max Wilk, interviewed in Jeff Kisseloff, *The Box: An Oral History of Television, 1920–1961* (New York: Viking, 1995), pp. 333–334.

68. Erik Barnouw, introduction to his radio adaptation, "I Remember Mama," in Fitelson, *Theatre Guild on the Air*, pp. 359–360.

69. Ralph Nelson, born in 1916, grew up in "lower-class circumstances" in New York City. He went from having a criminal record to winning the *New York Times* oratorical contest in 1932 and making his stage debut in 1933. During World War II, Nelson performed in Irving Berlin's all-solider show, "This Is the Army." When

he moved to the air force, he was a pilot trainer and wrote the *Air Force Acrobatics Manual.* The tensions between the demands of military and family life was the subject of Nelson's first play, *Mail Call* (1944), which won the National Theater Conference (NTC) award for the best one-act play. *The Wind Is Ninety* (1945) again won the NTC award. Fred Coe hired him to direct live drama on NBC. "Biographical Sketch of Ralph Nelson, Interview with Alan Casty," *Film Comment* 3 (Summer 1965), pp. 3–10.

70. "Theatre Guild on the Air," *Theatre Arts,* January 1949.

71. Lipsitz, "Why Remember Mama." Robin Morgan lists Gordon Webber as another left-wing writer who wrote scripts for *Mama,* in *Saturday's Child.* Wilk, who started to write regularly for *Mama* in 1952, had moved into television in the spring of 1948, writing adaptations of theatrical productions, comedy sketches, variety show and comedy series; see Max Wilk, *The Golden Age of Television: Notes from the Survivors* (New York: Delacorte, 1976), and Kisseloff, *The Box.*

72. Peggy Wood, "Actors Speak Louder Than Words," *Colliers,* April 8, 1944. Comments on the casting of Laire and Morgan appear in Lipsitz, "Why Remember Mama." Morgan has written about her working childhood in *Dry Your Smile: A Novel* (Garden City, N.J.: Doubleday, 1987) and in her memoirs, *Going Too Far: The Personal Chronicle of a Feminist* (New York: Random House, 1977) as well as in *Saturday's Child.*

73. Lynn Spigel, *Make Room for TV: Television and the Family Ideal in Postwar America* (Chicago: University of Chicago Press, 1992).

74. Max Wilk, *Golden Age of Television,* p. 49.

75. "Radio and Television: The Three Prosceniums," *Time,* December 28, 1953, p. 29.

76. CBS press release, cited by Lipsitz, "Why Remember Mama," p. 92.

77. Spigel, *Make Room for TV,* pp. 136–180.

78. Wood interviewed by Wilk, *Golden Age of Television,* p. 45.

79. Wilk, *Golden Age of Television,* pp. 45–46, 48; Kisseloff, *The Box,* pp. 333–334. According to Wilk, writers worked coffee into the show's family life, the actors performed in character for the show's opening and closing commercials, and sponsor support fended off efforts by network executives to interfere with the show's format; see also Lipsitz, "Why Remember Mama," p. 90.

80. Spigel notes the domestic settings for Lucy in *Make Room for TV;* David Marc describes how Gleason's design for the set drew on his own experience growing up in working-class Brooklyn, in *Demographic Vistas* (Philadelphia: University of Pennsylvania Press, 1984). Marc also discusses the urban and increasingly suburban settings of sitcoms in *Comic Visions: Television Comedy and American Culture* (Boston: Unwin Hyman, 1989).

81. George Lipsitz, "The Meaning of Memory: Family, Class, and Ethnicity in Early Network Television Programs," *Cultural Anthropology,* November 1986; and "Why Remember Mama."

82. These episodes are cited in Lipsitz, "Why Remember Mama," p. 91.

83. Lipsitz notes this incident in "The Meaning of Memory," p. 53, citing *TV Guide,* May 1954.

84. "Winning Women," *Newsweek,* December, 28, 1953, p. 40.

85. Lipsitz, "The Meaning of Memory," p. 61.

86. Several viewers commenting to me on the show from the vantage point of the late 1990s were unable to remember the ethnicity of the Hansens: one was sure they were Swedish, another thought they were Jewish. Ralph Nelson ruefully recalled this South Pacific reference because Yul Brynner, then a television actor and director, had called him to protest bitterly its racist implications; George Lipsitz interviews with Ralph Nelson, December 17, 1985, and January 11, 1986. Lipsitz generously provided me with a tape of these interviews.

87. Lipsitz, "Why Remember Mama," pp. 77–79. See also Morgan's account of the show, and the symposium, in *Saturday's Child*.

88. See Lipsitz's discussion of audience pleasure in *Mama* in "Why Remember Mama." See also Allen's discussion of audience pleasure in soap operas, in *Speaking of Soap Operas;* and Herman Gray's discussion of the 1980s *Cosby Show,* in "Black and White in Color," *American Quarterly* 45 (September 1993).

89. At this point the producers did make an effort to revive audience interest by returning to live performance, presenting a new play, *Here's Mama,* by writer Frank Gabrielson, based on the most popular TV episodes and performed by the actors in summer theater in Maine and Massachusetts during the summer of 1952; Morgan, *Saturday's Child,* p. 85.

90. Michele Hilmes, *Hollywood and Broadcasting From Radio to Cable* (Urbana: University of Illinois Press, 1990); Arthur Frank Wertheim, "The Rise and Fall of Milton Berle," in *American History/American Television: Interpreting the Video Past,* ed. John E. O'Connor (New York: Ungar, 1983); David Marc, "Comic Visions of the City: New York and the Television Sitcom," *Radical History Review* 42 (1988), and Marc, *Comic Visions;* Lipsitz, "The Meaning of Memory." See also Vincent Brook, "The Americanization of Molly: How Mid-Fifties TV Homogenized *The Goldbergs* (and Got "Berg-larized" in the Process)," *Cinema Journal* 38 (1999).

91. "Mama's Birthday," broadcast in 1954, cited by Lipsitz, "Meaning of Memory," p. 51.

92. Lipsitz, "Why Remember Mama," p. 89.

93. See Spigel, *Make Room for TV;* Mary Beth Haralovich, "Sit-coms and Suburbs: Positioning the 1950s Homemaker," *Quarterly Review of Film and Video* 11 (1989).

4. LOVING ACROSS PREWAR RACIAL AND SEXUAL BOUNDARIES

1. Wanger was quoted in the *Motion Picture Herald,* June 24, 1944, p. 9, as cited by Doherty, *Projections of War,* p. 200.

2. This position also surfaced in nonfiction: the popular author Margaret Halsey, for example, wrote during the war against anti-Semitism as well as racism, and kept returning to the theme of interracial marriage; see *Some of My Best Friends Are Soldiers* (1944), proposed as a dramatization for a March of Time broadcast but canceled by NBC because its sections on intolerance were "too controversial," and *Color-Blind: A White Woman Looks at the Negro* (1946), in which she devotes a chapter to attacking conservative arguments about Negro sexuality

("Sex, Jealousy, and the Negro") and a later chapter that anticipated intermarriage as an eventual result of tolerance. See Halsey's entry in *Current Biography* (1944); and Margaret Halsey, *No Laughing Matter: The Autobiography of a WASP* (Philadelphia: Lippincott, 1977).

3. See Werner Sollors, ed., *Interracialism: Black-White Intermarriage in American History, Literature, and Law* (New York: Oxford University Press, 2000); Martha Hodes, ed., *Sex, Love, and Race: Crossing Boundaries in North American History* (New York: New York University Press, 1999); Martha Hodes, *White Women, Black Men: Illicit Sex in the Nineteenth-Century South* (New Haven: Yale University Press, 1997); Kevin Mumford, *Interzones: Black/White Sex Districts in Chicago and New York in the Early Twentieth Century* (New York: Columbia University Press, 1997); Ann Holder, "Making the Body Politic: Race, Sexuality and Citizenship in the U.S., 1896–1909," Ph.D. dissertation, Boston College, 1999. Christina Simmons distinguishes between African American men's and women's public support for interracial marriage in "Women's Power in Sex Radical Challenges to Marriage in Early Twentieth-Century United States," *Feminist Studies*, April 2003.

4. The playwright Tennessee Williams was also interested in questioning the racial and sexual norms of white supremacy, particularly in such plays as *Twenty-Seven Wagons of Cotton* (1944), *The Unsatisfactory Supper* (1945), and *Battle of Angels* (1940).

5. Charles Kaiser charts this public discussion of homosexuality in the 1940s in *Gay Metropolis: 1940–1996* (Boston: Houghton Mifflin, 1997), pp. 49–50, 52–58. On the military in the Second World War, see Allan Bérubé, *Coming Out Under Fire: the History of Gay Men and Women in World War II* (New York: Free Press, 1990) and Leisa D. Meyer, *Creating GI Jane: Sexuality and Power in the Women's Army Corps During World War II* (New York Columbia University Press, 1996). For histories of homosexuality in the U.S., see George Chauncey Jr., *Gay New York: Gender, Urban Culture, and the Making of the Gay Male World, 1890–1940* (New York: Basic, 1994); John D'Emilio, *Sexual Politics and Sexual Communities: The Making of a Homosexual Minority in the U.S., 1940–1970* (Chicago: University of Chicago Press, 1983); Madeline Davis and Elizabeth Lapovsky Kennedy, *Boots of Leather, Slippers of Gold* (New York: Routledge, 1993).

6. Alfred C. Kinsey, Wardell B. Pomeroy, and Clyde E. Martin, *Sexual Behavior in the Human Male* (Philadelphia: Saunders, 1948) and *Sexual Behavior in the Human Female* (Philadelphia: Saunders, 1953). On Kinsey, see James H. Jones, "Annals of Sexology: Dr. Yes," *New Yorker*, August 25–September 1, 1997, pp. 98–113; and Jones, *Alfred C. Kinsey: A Public/Private Life* (New York: Norton, 1997).

7. See Smith's letters to Glenn Rainey, February 1941, an English professor at Georgia Tech and a supporter of her literary magazine, and to Walter White, February 21, 1942, in *How Am I to Be Heard? Letters of Lillian Smith*, ed. Margaret Rose Gladney (Chapel Hill: University of North Carolina Press, 1993), pp. 48–49, 54–55. When Smith found a publisher for the novel, she agreed to use the title made popular by the recorded blues song "Strange Fruit," a decision she later regretted because of the song's emphasis "on the lynching as opposed to her concern with the destructive nature of racial segregation as a way of life." Lillian

Smith to Frank Taylor, May 15, 1943, and Gladney's annotation, in Gladney, *How Am I To Be Heard?* pp. 70–71.

8. Lillian Smith, in a letter to her editor at Reynal and Hitchcock, Frank Taylor, July 26, 1943, in Gladney, *How Am I to Be Heard?* p. 72.

9. Lillian Smith, "Growing Into Freedom," *Common Ground*, Autumn 1943, pp. 50, 47.

10. On Smith's life, see her entry in *Current Biography* (1944), pp. 635–638; Morton Sosna, "Lillian Smith: The Southern Liberal as Evangelist," in *In Search of the Silent South: Southern Liberals and the Race Issue* (New York: Columbia University Press, 1977), pp. 172–197; Gladney, *How Am I to Be Heard?* pp. 1–16. See also Anne C. Loveland, *Lillian Smith, A Southerner Confronting the South: A Biography* (Baton Rouge: Louisiana State University Press, 1986).

11. Smith, "Growing Into Freedom," pp. 50–51. In 1945 she recounted the pain of racial separation as a break from her childhood black "nurse . . . a woman strong and wise and tender who gave my life its first meaning and on whom I leaned as I took my first steps into a new and strange world. Then one day she was sent away and I was told that I no longer needed her. And there was a great emptiness after her going;" Lillian Smith, "Author of 'Strange Fruit' Describes Home Town: Maxwell, Georgia," *New Leader*, December 1, 1945, p. 16.

12. The magazine, first called *Pseudopodia*, later changed to *North Georgia Review* and then *South Today*, began with two hundred subscribers in 1936 and expanded to ten thousand by 1946, when it ceased publication.

13. From 1942 to 1945 she served on the Executive Board of the Southern Conference for Human Welfare (SCHW), a southern popular front coalition supporting labor organizing and interracialism. Smith resigned from the SCHW board in 1945, citing political disagreements with popular front compromises. See her letter to James Dombrowski, May 7, 1945, in Gladney, *How Am I to Be Heard?* pp. 89–93.

14. Letter to the editors of *PM*, January 16, 1943, in Gladney, *How Am I to Be Heard?* pp. 65–66. Smith refused to join the board of directors of the moderate Southern Regional Council in the absence of a "firm and public stand in opposition to segregation and in defense of human equality." See her letter to Dr. Johnson, June 12, 1944, in Gladney, *How Am I to Be Heard?* pp. 85–87; and "Lillian Smith Refuses to Join Southern Council," *Chicago Defender*, March 24, 1945.

15. "Lillian Smith," *Current Biography* (1944), p. 638; Roseanne V. Camacho, "Race, Region and Gender in a Reassessment of Lillian Smith," in *Southern Women: Histories and Identities*, ed. Virginia Bernhard, Betty Brandon, Elizabeth Fox-Genovese, and Theda Purdue (Columbia: University of Missouri Press, 1992), pp. 157–176.

16. "Lillian Smith," *Current Biography* (1944), p. 638. In Detroit a United Auto Workers bookshop and the Detroit Public Library prevented an official ban on the book; Louise Blackwell and Francis Clay, *Lillian Smith* (New York: Twayne, 1971), pp. 37–38. Ruth Miller Elson suggests that *Strange Fruit* offered white readers a new path with which to enter the world of discrimination, and notes that as the first best-seller to portray the "brutality and tragedy of race relations" it stood

"alone on the bestseller list for almost two decades," in *Myths and Mores in American Best Sellers, 1865–1965* (New York: Garland, 1985), pp. 312–313.

17. Francis Downing, "Books of the Week: *Strange Fruit*," *Commonweal*, April 7, 1944, p. 626. The *Time* reviewer commented, "The same story has been told and retold, expertly or awkwardly, with Freudian variations . . . with Marxian overtones (as in proletarian novels). The main theme has been repeated in fiction almost as frequently as the lynchings that have inspired it have occurred"; "Feverish Fascination," *Time*, March 20, 1944, pp. 99–102. Henry Louis Gates Jr. and Nellie McKay have identified an African American literary tradition that reoriented "tragic mulatto" characters to represent "victimization . . . proud claiming of racial heritage . . . militant nationalism . . . [and] pathetic self-betrayal"; *Norton Anthology of African-American Literature* (New York: Norton, 1997), p. 470. See also Werner Sollors's broad survey, *Neither Black Nor White Yet Both: Thematic Explorations of Interracial Literature* (New York: Oxford University Press, 1997).

18. Cecelia Gaul, "Strange Fruit," *Christian Century*, July 19, 1944, p. 854.

19. Malcolm Cowley, "Books in Review: Southways," *New Republic*, March 6, 1944, pp. 320–322. Cowley was impressed with Smith's ability to show how "a lynching was intimately connected with the life of a whole community, that it explains and condemns a whole social order."

20. Struthers Burt, "The Making of a New South," *Saturday Review of Literature*, March 11, 1944, p. 10.

21. Diana Trilling, "Strange Fruit," *Nation*, March 18, 1944, p. 342, reprinted in Diana Trilling, *Reviewing the Forties* (New York: Harcourt Brace Jovanovich, 1978), p. 82.

22. Mary Helen Washington has argued that Smith's characterization of Nonnie falls into the most ordinary racist stereotyping of black women, in "Recovering Radicalism(s) in Alice Childress's *Wedding Band*," a paper presented at the Organization of American Historians, Toronto, Canada, April 24, 1999. In contrast, Cheryl Johnson believes that the characterization of Nonnie reflected "aesthetic and political compromises Smith confronted and negotiated as her desire to fight racism overwhelmed other considerations." Johnson interprets Nonnie's silence as Smith's strategy to combat racist definitions of black women's sexuality and compares it to the book's cryptic reference to the lesbianism of Tracey's sister: "Laura's lesbian desire or sexuality is as voiceless as Nonnie's heterosexual desire." See "The Language of Sexuality and Silence in Lillian Smith's *Strange Fruit*," *Signs* 27 (2001), pp. 1–22; quotations from pp. 9 and 17.

23. Trilling, "Strange Fruit," pp. 82–84. Similar points were made by left-wing progressives; see Earl Conrad, " 'Strange Fruit' Has Punch Above the Belt," *Chicago Defender*, December 8, 1945, p. 16; Ben Burns, "Off The Book Shelf," *Chicago Defender*, December 15, 1945, p. 12.

24. William Du Bois, "Searing Novel of the South," *New York Times Book Review*, March 5, 1944, pp. 1, 20. The prominent African American feminist educator and activist Anna J. Cooper also recommended *Strange Fruit*, in "Strange Fruit Obscene, But Lays Bare Photographic Realism, Defender Says," *Washington Tribune*, May 13, 1944; Tuskegee Institute News Clippings File, hereafter abbreviated to TINCF.

25. Langston Hughes, "Here to Yonder," *Chicago Defender*, December 16, 1944, p. 12.

26. The *Defender* published a column, "What the People Say," in which these comments appeared: Will H. Hart and Bernice Brown, May 5, 1945, p. 12; Johnnie Monroe, July 28, 1945, p. 12; Lawrence W. Henderson, April 7, 1945, p. 12. A syndicated article from Claude Barnett's Associated Negro Press also referred to this debate, mentioning criticisms from Spelman College graduates who argued that "girls with college degrees didn't go back to their small towns, take $3 a week servant jobs, and settle down to semi-serfdom for the rest of their lives. If they went back, certainly they bettered their status." *Chicago Defender*, October 13, 1945, p. 14.

27. Ralph Ellison, "Escape the Thunder," *Tomorrow*, March 5, 1945, p. 91, as cited by Mark Busby, *Ralph Ellison* (Boston: Twayne, 1991), p. 124.

28. See chapter 10 of Chester Himes's *If He Hollers Let Him Go* (New York: Doubleday, 1945) in which friends and coworkers compare *Strange Fruit* to *Native Son* in a wide-ranging discussion of "the race problem." My thanks to Eileen Boris for reminding me of this reference. Chester Himes, born in Jefferson City, Missouri, in 1909, graduated from high school and briefly attended college, beginning to write during a prison term for armed robbery in the late 1920s and early 1930s. In the later 1930s he worked as a laborer for the WPA and as a writer for the Ohio Writer's Project. When he moved to Los Angeles, he could not find work as a screenwriter and turned to the shipyards, incorporating some of his experience of the shipyards and wartime racism into *If He Hollers Let Him Go*.

29. Burns was a member of the Communist Party in the 1930s and 1940s and had previously written for the *Daily Worker* and the *People's World*. He began to work as an editor for the *Chicago Defender* in the summer of 1942, also helping John H. Johnson to edit the *Negro Digest*, first published in 1942, and *Ebony*, published beginning in 1945. See Ben Burns, *Nitty Gritty: A White Editor in Black Journalism* (Jackson: University of Mississippi Press, 1996).

30. Ben Burns, "Books—Best of the Year," *Chicago Defender*, December 30, 1944, p. 11; "Off the Book Shelf," *Chicago Defender*, June 30, 1945, p. 13; "Off the Book Shelf," *Chicago Defender*, December 15, 1945, p. 13.

31. Burns, "Off the Book Shelf," December 15, 1945, p. 13. Burns's praise included the kind of attack on the March on Washington that Lillian Smith had objected to in a letter to the left-wing tabloid *PM*, cited in note 14.

32. Burns, "Off the Book Shelf," December 15, 1945, p. 13.

33. Sumner was born in Brookhaven, Mississippi, the daughter of college professor Robert Scott and Bertha (Burnely) Ricketts; she received her B.S. from Millsaps College in Jackson, Mississippi, in 1909, and an M.A. from Columbia in 1910. "Cid Ricketts Sumner," *Contemporary Authors* (1963), p. 1118; "Cid Ricketts, Author, Is Slain," *Washington Post*, October 16, 1970, p. D6.

34. Cid Ricketts Sumner, "Quality," *Ladies Home Journal*, December 1945, p. 17 ff. Sumner's photograph, along with a paragraph in which she describes herself, appeared on the page opposite the table of contents. Published in book form as *Quality* (Indianapolis: Bobbs–Merrill, 1946).

35. Kenneth Goings, *Mammy and Uncle Mose: Black Collectibles and American Stereotyping* (Bloomington: Indiana University Press, 1994).

36. Florence Haxton Bullock, "Deep South," *New York Herald-Tribune Weekly Book Review*, September 1, 1946, section vii, p. 8.

37. Nash K. Burger, "Complacence in Dixie," *New York Times Book Review*, September 8, 1946, p. 10.

38. Sumner takes pains to caricature the black lawyer from New Orleans sent by Naughton's organization: he represents a position on social equality that is driven by pretension and revenge; Sumner describes him as speaking in an "Oxonian" accent, and saying of his white chauffeur, "I am the employer, he is the employed"; "Quality," pp. 113, 115.

39. James Baldwin, "Everybody's Protest Novel," *Partisan Review*, June 1949, reprinted in Baldwin, *The Price of the Ticket: Original Nonfiction, 1948–1985* (New York: St. Martin's, 1985), p. 29. Ann Holder brought this reference to my attention.

40. Nathan L. Rothman, "Jim Crowism," *Saturday Review of Literature*, December 7, 1946, p. 85. Some of the reviewers commented on *Quality*'s "sensationalism," melodrama, and reliance on typed characters, which they attributed to its initial appearance as women's magazine fiction. Burger, "Complacence in Dixie," p. 10; *Kirkus*, July 1, 1946, p. 303.

41. Rothman, "Jim Crowism," p. 85.

42. One exception was the left-wing white writer Jack Conroy, reviewing for the *Defender*, October 28, 1946: he recognized in *Quality* the spirit of Booker T. Washington and challenged its argument that "the future of race relations in the south depends on sentiments in the hearts of 'quality' folks both black and white, and not upon violent and drastic legal changes in the southern social pattern"; TINCF.

43. Bullock, "Deep South," p. 8. See also S. I. Hayakawa, in *Bookwork*, September 4, 1946, p. 4.

44. J. Saunders Redding commented that the story "has many of the trappings and some of the concepts that tend to cheapen and falsify the truth of colored life in America," although he found it "interesting" in having revealed "the petty meanness, the ignorance, and the hatred of the majority of white Southerners." Baltimore *Afro-American*, September 28, 1946; TINCF.

45. Black reviewers commented on the book in connection with its film adaptation in 1949; S. W. Garlington, "Amusement Row," *New York Amsterdam News*, May 28, 1949, p. 24; Lillian Scott, "Calls 'Pinky' A Realistic Film Based on a False Premise: Broadway Sees, Likes Newest Problem Sock," *Chicago Defender*, October 18, 1949, p. 26; Marjorie McKenzie, "Pursuit of Democracy," *Pittsburgh Courier*, June 4, 1949; TINCF.

46. Lillian Smith to Frank Taylor, July 26, 1943, in Gladney, *How Am I to Be Heard?* p. 73.

47. "New Plays in Manhattan—Strange Fruit," *Time*, December 10, 1945, p. 77.

48. "Strange Fruit," *PM*, November 25, 1945.

49. Autobiographical materials written by Lillian Smith ca. 1965, quoted by Gladney, *How I Am to Be Heard?* pp. 94–95; "Producer of Strange Fruit Must Cast Cautiously, Author Says," *Chicago Defender*, June 30, 1945, p. 17.

50. Wolcott Gibbs, "A Crowded Canvas," *New Yorker*, December 8, 1945, pp. 54–56. See also "Strange Fruition," *Newsweek*, December 10, 1945, pp. 92–93; *Time*, December 10, 1945, p. 77; Kappo Phelan, "Strange Fruit," *Commonweal*, December 21, 1945, p. 264. "Strange Fruit," *Life*, December 24, 1945, pp. 33–35; Stark Young, "Strange Fruit, Etc.," *New Republic*, December 15, 1945, p. 839.

51. See coverage of the play in the *Chicago Defender*, November and December 1945 and February 1946.

52. M. L. A., "A Picture Story of Strange Fruit," *Opportunity*, January-March 1946, pp. 24–35. See also Billy Rowe, "Play Means Well, Message Fails, Reviewer Says," *Pittsburgh Courier*, December 8, 1945: "The tragic tale of intolerance and miscegenation in America, talked much but said nothing." TINCF

53. The American Negro Theatre (ANT) was started in 1940 by playwright Hill and actor Frederick O'Neal with the hope of creating a permanent Harlem-based acting company.

54. Abe Hill, "Calls 'Strange Fruit' Big Disappointment," *New York Amsterdam News*, December 1, 1945, p. 23.

55. Lillian Smith, "'Strange Fruit' and White Culture," *New York Age*, December 15, 1945.

56. "Abram Hill Writes Again on 'Strange Fruit': Lillian Smith Declines Offer," *New York Amsterdam News*, January 19, 1946. Smith wrote to Snelling that month, "At present I am tired and weary and sad and bitter. I am so bitter with these damn yankees up here that I have spoken out very sharply lately and my residue of good judgement (whatever of it my weariness has left me) warns me that they'll make me pay a thousand fold for every bitter word I say aloud." Lillian Smith to Paula Snelling, January 21, 1946, in Gladney, *How Am I to Be Heard?* pp. 96–97.

57. See also Lillian Smith's piece "Addressed to White Liberals," *New Republic*, September 18, 1944, pp. 331–333, in which she asserted: "We have looked at the 'Negro problem' long enough. Now the time has come to right-about-face and study the problems of the white man: the deep-rooted needs that have caused him to seek those strange, regressive satisfactions that are derived from worshiping his own skin color. The white man himself is one of the world's most urgent problems today, not the Negro, not other colored races. We whites must learn to confess this. . . . Segregation as a way of life—or shall we say a *way of death*—is cultural schizophrenia."

58. "Abram Hill Writes Again," p. 24. An editorial in the *New York Amsterdam News*, January 19, 1946, applauding the play's closing was especially vituperative. Smith was devastated by the play's failure; she wrote, in a letter to Snelling, "The whole thing has been such a bitter and terrible fiasco that I find it hard to get free of it." Smith to Snelling, January 21, 1946, in Gladney, *How Am I to be Heard?* pp. 96–97.

59. Fredi Washington, *The People's Voice*, December 22, 1945, and "'Amsterdam' Blasts 'Fruit' in Editorial" *People's Voice*, January 26, 1946; TINCF.

60. Conrad, "'Strange Fruit' Has Punch," p. 16. Earl Conrad, born in 1912 in Auburn, New York, went to New York City in 1934, where he worked as a journalist, trade union organizer, and for several years as a writer for the Federal Writers Project. He published the first popular biography of Harriet Tubman in 1943; autobio-

graphical information in a letter from Conrad to "My Dear Friend Bowley," March 11, 1940, a copy of which was kindly provided to me by my colleague Jean Humez.

61. D'Usseau had been a well-known activist in Hollywood's radical political circles since the 1930s; he and Gow both publicly embraced the wartime popular front, describing themselves as "Win the War Democrats." During the war, both served in the military at the Army Signal Corp Photographic Center in Astoria, Queens. *Tomorrow the World* revolved around an American uncle trying to win over his Nazi-trained nephew to democratic principles and was surprisingly popular with wartime audiences, running April 1943-June 1944. D'Usseau was identified as part of the Hollywood Communist left in Bernard Gordon's oral history in *Tender Comedies,* p. 272.

62. Arnaud D'Usseau and James Gow, "Manufacturing a Problem Play," *New York Times,* October 14, 1945, as quoted by Pauley in *An American Odyssey,* pp. 66–67; Richard D. Dier, "Authors Explain 'Deep Are the Roots,' Call Racial Issue the Most Important Post-War Problem," *Afro-American,* November 17, 1945; TINCF.

63. After finishing his work on *A Tree Grows in Brooklyn* in November 1944, Kazan found someone in Hollywood to "pull strings for him" to get overseas. Kazan, *A Life,* p. 276.

64. "Everything Ernie Pyle said about the GI was true and genuine"; Elia Kazan, "Audience Tomorrow: Preview in New Guinea," *Theatre Arts,* October 1945, pp. 568–577.

65. Kazan, *A Life,* p. 293. He later identified the play as part of a cycle built on "the drama of the falsely accused," dismissing both the genre and the play as "liberal corn"; *A Life,* pp. 293–295.

66. Arnaud D'Usseau and James Gow, *Deep Are the Roots* (New York: Scribner's, 1946).

67. The playwrights were probably referring to the political platform of the SCHW (see note 13).

68. Lewis Nichols, "'Deep Are the Roots': A New Play Discusses the Question of the Negro and the South," *New York Times,* October 7, 1945; TINCF. On the disagreement among critics, see Abram Hill, "'Deep Are the Roots' Spikes N.Y. Critics," *New York Amsterdam News,* October 20, 1945. *Life* described the play as "one of the most controversial plays to reach Broadway in years," noting that "upon occasion members of the audience have arisen during the performance and stalked indignantly out of the playhouse." "Deep Are the Roots," *Life,* October 15, 1945, pp. 51–53.

69. Robert Ardrey, a protégé of Thornton Wilder, wrote two plays produced by the Group Theatre in the 1930s. *Jeb* featured the young actors Ossie Davis and Ruby Dee. See Earl Conrad, "Jeb, Another Drama on Race Issue, Hits Broadway Snag," in *Chicago Defender,* March 2, 1946; see also Ossie Davis and Ruby Dee's account of the play in *With Ossie and Ruby: In This Life Together* (New York: Morrow, 1998).

70. "Deep Are the Roots," *Life,* October 15, 1945; John Mason Brown, "Seeing Things: More Wings for God's Chillun," *Saturday Review of Literature,* October 13, 1945;

Kappo Phelan, "Deep Are the Roots," *Commonweal,* October 12, 1945, and "Brave Are the Themes," *Newsweek,* January 7, 1946.

71. Brown, "Seeing Things," pp. 38–40.

72. Phelan, "Deep Are the Roots," p. 624; "Walter Winchell Flags DAR Racial Bigotry," Chicago *Defender,* October 20, 1945, p. 4. Earl Conrad was thrilled to see the play's political range: "Questions of feudalism, capitalism, liberalism, radicalism, and social, economic and political caste are all there, coordinated into a moving vehicle that constitutes a living editorial against the modern Confederacy. Rankin and Bilbo [prominent congressional proponents of white supremacy] are denounced symbolically—if not in name." Earl Conrad, "New York Critics Predict a Hit for New Play," *Chicago Defender,* October 6, 1945, p. 15.

73. Reconsiderations included Gibbs, "A Crowded Canvas"; Young, "Strange Fruit, Etc.," p. 839; "Strange Fruit," *Life,* December 24, 1945, p. 33. Stark Young, "Serious Efforts," *New Republic,* October 15, 1945, p. 499, and "Rootless Roots," *New Republic,* April 1, 1946.

74. Abram Hill, "Hill Raves About 'Deep Are the Roots,' " *New York Amsterdam News,* September 22, 1945, p. 12. Other black reviewers were equally enthusiastic; see Al Monroe, " 'Deep Are the Roots,' Convincing Portrayal of Conditions Below Mason and Dixon Line," *Defender,* April 5, 1946; J. A. Rogers, " 'Deep Are the Roots' Finest and Boldest Race Relations Play," *Pittsburgh Courier,* October 13, 1945. Note the popular front language of Harold G. Miller's praise: "The authors are talking about today and the deep South . . . and the home-grown variety of fascism that grows there"; " 'Deep Are the Roots,' Play About Negro Soldier, Opens in Philadelphia Theatre," *Kansas City Call,* September 23, 1945; TINCF.

75. Hill, "Hill Raves," p. 12. D'Usseau and Gow, "Manufacturing a Problem Play," cited by Pauley, *An American Odyssey,* p. 67.

76. Langston Hughes, "Here to Yonder," *Chicago Defender,* October 6, 1945, p. 14.

77. "Walter White—People, Politics, and Places," *Chicago Defender,* October 20, 1945, p. 15.

78. Wolcott Gibbs, "The Theatre: What They Say About Dixie," *New Yorker,* October 6, 1945, pp. 44–45. See also Brown, "Seeing Things" and "Brave Are the Themes"; Young, "Strange Fruit."

79. H. L. S., "So Was 'Uncle Tom's Cabin': 'Deep Are the Roots,' " *Richmond Times-Dispatch,* February 24, 1946. A less inflammatory review was Boyd Martin, "Stage Plays About Negroes Not 'Quite Fair' to Whites," *Courier-Journal,* March 3, 1946.

80. Here Hughes rejected an ideological link between sexuality and citizenship—a link he had explored in his early work—proposing instead a reinstatement of clear boundaries between "private" and "public." Hughes's public persona depended on his maintaining a resolute silence about his own sexuality. "Millions of white folks in this country have never slept with a colored person," he continued in the article. "And millions of colored folks have never been near enough to touch a white person, let alone sleep with one. The real arena of the race problem is NOT a bedroom but economics. The real problem for white folks is not how to keep from marrying a Negro but how to keep from carrying the burden of a large, discontented mass of black folks on their undemocratic backs.

And the problem for the Negro is not how to get hold of a white paramour, but how to get hold of something to eat, put the kids through school, get books out of Jim Crow libraries, vote, and be treated like a citizen." Langston Hughes, "Here to Yonder," *Chicago Defender*, October 6, 1945, p. 14.

81. Hill, "Hill Raves." Hill's reference to FDR's "four freedoms" appeared in the later article, "'Deep Are the Roots' Spikes N.Y. Critics."

82. A constitutional challenge to this based on a right to privacy would not be fully established until 1967. D'Usseau and Gow's comments appear in their introduction to *Deep Are the Roots*.

83. D'Usseau and Gow, *Deep Are the Roots*, pp. xxiv–xxvi. See also D'Usseau and Gow, "'Deep Are the Roots' Authors Strike Back at Critics' Attack," *Chicago Defender*, May 4, 1946.

84. Laurents, *Original Story*, pp. 61–62, 4.

85. In his memoir Laurents interrogated his knowledge of and acceptance of homosexual desire and the development of his identity as a homosexual. He reflected that that homosexual practice did not "turn up in *Home of the Brave*, but homosexuality does—unintentionally. Finch and Coney's relationship is homosexual; the portrayal is psychologically accurate but unconscious on the author's part. Had I realized the friendship could be construed that way, I would have worked overtime to clean it out." Laurents, *Original Story*, p. 53.

86. Michael Gordon was a member of the Communist Party in the 1930s. He began to work in Hollywood films in 1940 as a dialogue director. See "Jeff Corey" in Gilligan and Buhle, *Tender Comrades*, esp. pp. 181–184, and Smith's discussion of Gordon in *Real Life Drama*, pp. 414–416. Laurents categorized the stage manager (Jimmy Gelb), "the producer [Lee Sabinson], director, and half the cast" as "Marxists" in *Original Story*, p. 3.

87. "Brave Are the Themes," *Newsweek*, January 7, 1946, p. 82; John Gassner, "The Theatre Arts" *Forum*, March 1946, p. 658.

88. "The Face" was reprinted in Barnouw, *Radio Drama in Action*. Laurents discusses his radio writing, his life in the army, and the production of *Home of the Brave* in *Original Story*, pp. 12–63.

89. Laurents appears to have experienced Jewishness as the identity of a racialized outsider; in recent interviews he has said that his experience as a victim of racialized discrimination shaped his political commitment to fighting all forms of discrimination. He has been reluctant to explain any of his work in terms of his sexual orientation. See his interview in 1991 with McGilligan in *Backstory 2*, pp. 129–156.

90. "Broadway in Review" in *Theatre Arts*, March 1946. Alan Baxter had been a member of the Group Theatre in the 1930s.

91. "Home of the Brave," *Time*, January 7, 1946, p. 88.

92. This line is from Laurents's radio play "The Face." In *The Home of The Brave*, Laurents uses this language to explain the historic forms of prejudice that are part of Coen's "problem:" "That kid's crack up goes back to a thousand million people being wrong. . . . They don't take a man for himself . . . for what he is." *Home of the Brave* (1946, rpt. in *Awake and Sing: Seven Classic Plays from the American Jewish Repertoire*, ed. Ellen Schiff (New York: Mentor, 1995)), p. 381.

93. Bérubé, *Coming Out Under Fire*. In recent interviews Laurents has described the strangeness of the military's homosocial culture from his point of view at the time. Attending an army-sponsored all-male performance of Clare Booth Luce's play *The Women*, watching the combination of straight men's drag performances and "the only one who wasn't" (obviously "the real McCoy"), all being applauded by Clare Booth Luce (in the audience that day) was like "Alice in Wonderland down the rabbit hole." Laurents described wartime New York as "the sexiest place in the world. Everybody did it—in numbers." He remembers an MP making a pass at him in basic training, and recalls his own confusion. "I was totally bewildered. And felt it was wrong. This is why later I went into analysis. . . . I felt guilty. I wanted to change—and I loved it. I never had so much sex in my life. It was incessant." Kaiser, *Gay Metropolis*, pp. 37–40.

94. Wyatt, "The Drama," p. 457.

95. The play won an award from the American Academy of Arts and Letters and the Sidney Howard Playwriting award; Laurents, *Original Story*, p. 62. When the play was published in the spring of 1946, the reviews continued to be mixed: *Kirkus*, May 1, 1946, and *Library Journal*, July 1946, recommended it as "brilliant" and "distinguished"; C. V. Terry said it "fumbles to understand the problem of discrimination in the Army," and called it a "maze of tough talk that gets nowhere"; *New York Times Book Review*, July 21, 1946, p. 8.

96. This language appeared in the review of the film in *Time*, May 9, 1949, p. 100.

5. SEEING THROUGH JEWISHNESS

1. For a discussion of shifting conceptions of the racial character of Jewishness in the U.S., see Matthew Frye Jacobson, *Whiteness of a Different Color: European Immigrants and the Alchemy of Race* (Cambridge: Harvard University Press, 1998).

2. See Stuart Svonkin, *Jews Against Prejudice: American Jews and the Fight for Civil Liberties* (New York: Columbia University Press, 1997); Peter Novick, "Holocaust Memory in America," in *The Art of Memory: Holocaust Memorials in History*, ed. James E. Young (Munich: Prestel-Verlag, 1994), and *The Holocaust in American Life* (Boston: Houghton Mifflin, 1999); Leonard Dinnerstein, *Anti-Semitism in America* (New York: Oxford University Press, 1994).

3. Arthur Miller, *Focus* (New York: Reynal and Hitchcock, 1945); Richard Brooks, *The Brick Foxhole* (New York: Harper, 1945); Laura Zametkin Hobson, *Gentleman's Agreement* (New York: Simon and Schuster, 1947).

4. Sollors comments that the earliest appearances of literary "passing" explored Jewish racial indeterminacy; see the introduction to his *Neither Black Nor White Yet Both*.

5. Miller, *Situation Normal*, p. 40.

6. Jacobson, *Whiteness of a Different Color*, p. 194; see also his discussion of *Focus*, pp. 187–199.

7. Miller, *Timebends*, p. 70. By 1943 Miller was well enough known as a leftist to be proposed for membership in the Stuyvesant 12th Assembly District of the Com-

munist Party, although he said in his HUAC testimony that he had not applied for membership at the time.

8. Miller, *Timebends*, p. 200.

9. "Arthur Miller," *Current Biography* (1947), p. 440. Miller told one interviewer that he'd been "taken for a Christian, a Jew, and an Italian"; Joseph Mackey, "Theater's Man of the Moment: Author of 'All My Sons' Tells of Hard Climb Upward to Present Success," in the clippings file of *All My Sons* in the Arthur Miller Papers, Humanities Research Center, University of Texas at Austin.

10. Miller, *Timebends*, pp. 199–202. In an introduction to *Focus* written for a 1984 edition, Miller wrote, "It is no longer possible to decide whether it was my own Hitler-begotten sensitivity or the anti-Semitism itself that so often made me wonder whether, when peace came, we were to be launched into a raw politics of race and religion, and not in the South but in New York." Arthur Miller, *Focus* (Syracuse: Syracuse University Press, 1997 [1984]), p. v.

11. Newman's belief in fixed racial boundaries was linked to his confidence in gender prescription: he assumed that a woman out at night was inviting predatory male violence.

12. Jacobson, *Whiteness of a Different Color,* pp. 194–195. Jacobson points out that Miller's attempt to undermine the notion of racialized Jewishness still depended on the categories it sought to challenge; readers had to be able to recognize what was meant by "looking Jewish."

13. Editions of *Focus* were published in Denmark, France, Italy, Germany, and England, establishing Miller's antifascist reputation among European writers and intellectuals; *Current Biography,* p. 439; Miller, *Timebends,* pp. 139, 158.

14. See reviews by Saul Bellow, *New Republic,* January 7, 1946; Edward Francis Keefe, *Commonweal,* December 7, 1946; Alfred Butterfield, *New York Times Book Review,* November 18, 1945; *Kirkus,* August 15, 1945. The King Brothers, an independent production company, had bought *Focus* for a film adaptation, but by 1947 "little had been done in the way of active preparation," according to Frank Eng's column, *Daily News,* June 20, 1947. The adaptation was not made until 2001, financed independently by New York financier (later mayor) Michael Bloomburg, directed by Neil Slavin, and distributed by Paramount.

15. Miller makes this comment in his 1984 introduction to the reissue of *Focus.* The phrase was used by Leo Kennedy, *Book Week,* November 11, 1945, p. 28.

16. Kennedy, *Book Week,* p. 28. Harrison Smith also identified Miller's theme as "familiar" in *Saturday Review of Literature,* November 17, 1945, p. 11.

17. This statement, attributed to the *Chicago Sun,* appeared on the cover of *Focus* (New York: Reynal and Hitchcock, 1945), fifth printing.

18. When Brooks's book was published his parents were still alive, and he later remembered their pride: "Greatest day in their lives, they said. They used to carry it with them when they went to work. They had read it nine times already, but they carried it with them as proof of something." See Patrick McGilligan's interview with Brooks, in *Backstory 2,* pp. 27–72.

19. Denning discusses the radical culture of cartoonists in the 1940s, in *The Cultural Front.*

20. Richard Brooks, *The Brick Foxhole* (New York: Harper, 1945).

21. Given its kinship with a passage in *Native Son,* it is probably not a coincidence that Richard Wright singled out this scene in his favorable review of the novel in *PM,* cited in note 34.

22. Keeley challenges a heroic version of the war against fascism: "It wasn't the American soldier's belief in his Bill of Rights, his Constitution, or his God which enabled him to win at Cape Gloucester and Wadke and Saipan. . . . Liberty, humanity, freedom were merely words. Many of the men who fought on Eniwetok and Kwajalein and Guadalcanal had peculiar ideas about liberty and freedom which sounded like white Supremacy and Protestant justice."

23. Jonathan Buchsbaum, "Richard Brooks," *Dictionary of Literary Biography: American Screen Writers Second Series,* ed. Randall Clark (Detroit: Gale, 1986), 44:54. In a 1991 interview Brooks said, "Servicemen used to pick up homosexuals and take their money from them and beat the shit out of them on the way into Washington"; McGilligan, *Backstory 2,* p. 41.

24. Crawford has all the markings of an enemy of the popular front. His racism embraces anti-Semitism: while serving on the Chicago police force, he had killed "two Negro suspects and one Jewish petty thief," for which he had been tried for manslaughter and acquitted. He sees Jews as "rotten refugees" who, because of Roosevelt, are "everywhere in Washington." His "Americanism" expresses itself as xenophobia. He links democratic politics with bureaucracy ("stuffed shirts in Washington") and opposes it to tough military "solutions" ("shoot all the slant-eyes you see" instead of "treating the Japs like guests in a hotel"); with the military in charge, there would be "no trouble with unions." Bowers believes that "there ain't a good nigger in the world 'less he's dead" but admits a more intimate knowledge of crossing racial lines, "some of them nigger gals ain't bad," referring to one he had raped, and conceding that "niggers're all right . . . if they know their place." Robert Corber claims that Brooks was positioning Crawford "as a representative American or 'common man'"; see his *Homosexuality in Cold War America: Resistance and the Crisis of Masculinity* (Durham: Duke University Press, 1997), pp. 87–88. I argue that Brooks intended Crawford to serve as an exemplar of domestic fascism.

25. Corber notes how Crawford and Bowers both "desire and abhor" Edwards, asserting that the book's examination of homophobia in the military was one of its most important contributions; *Homosexuality in Cold War America.* See also James Levin, *The Gay Novel: The Male Homosexual Image in America* (New York: Irvington, 1983).

26. Crawford's false account of the evening, attempting to incriminate Mitchell for the murder of Edwards, portrays Edwards as the seducer and entrapper, discrediting the stereotyping of the victim as sexual predator.

27. A number of publishers rejected Brooks's novel before it finally attracted the support of Ed Aswell at Harper and Brothers; McGilligan, *Backstory 2.* On film noir and associated forms of fiction, see Naremore, *More Than Night,* in which he discusses both *Brick Foxhole* and *Crossfire.*

28. Dan S. Norton, *New York Times Book Review,* June 3, 1945, p. 17.

29. Sgt. Walter Bernstein, "Stateside Army," *New Republic,* July 23, 1945, p. 109; Hamilton Basso, "Books—Notes from Purgatory," *New Yorker,* June 2, 1945, pp. 75–76.
30. Niven Busch, "A Yell of Pain in War," *Saturday Review of Literature,* June 2, 1945, p. 12.
31. Lewis's *Esquire* review is quoted by McGilligan, *Backstory 2,* p. 29.
32. President Truman's Committee on Civil Rights, created in 1946, would list "personal safety" and "freedom of conscience and expression" as well as "equality of opportunity" and "citizenship and its privileges" as basic civil rights in its 1947 report, *To Secure These Rights.*
33. Richard Wright, "Two Novels of the Crushing of Men, One White, One Black," *PM,* November 25, 1945; Harper and Brothers book jacket for second edition, *The Brick Foxhole,* 1945.
34. Richard Wright, "A Non-Combat Soldier Strips Words for Action," *PM,* Sunday magazine section, June 24, 1945.
35. Brooks's statement appears in Richard Schickel's documentary *The Moviemakers: Richard Brooks* (1995).
36. Buhle and Wagner, *Radical Hollywood;* Doherty, *Projections of War.*
37. Larry Ceplair and Steven Englund, *The Inquisition in Hollywood: Politics in the Film Community, 1930–1960* (Berkeley: University of California Press, 1979).
38. For a full discussion of *Crossfire,* see Jennifer Langdon-Teclaw, "Caught in the Crossfire: Anti-Fascism, Anti-Communism and the Politics of Americanism in the Hollywood Career of Adrian Scott," Ph.D. dissertation, SUNY Binghamton, 2000.
39. Naremore, "American Film Noir." Left-wing screenwriters and directors were attracted to film noir as a means to express an oppositional vision in films such as Robert Rossen's *Body and Soul* (1947), Abraham Polonsky's *Force of Evil* (1948), and Nicholas Ray's *They Live by Night* (1949). See Anderson's "Red Hollywood"; Naremore, "From Dark Films to Black Lists: Censorship and Politics," in *More Than Night;* Buhle and Wagner, *Radical Hollywood.*
40. Joan LaCoeur, active in the Hollywood Independent Citizen's Committee for the Arts, Sciences, and the Professions, who later married Adrian Scott, felt that he was included in first group subpoenaed to appear before HUAC in 1947 *because* of *Crossfire*'s explicit antifascist politics; Schwartz, *The Hollywood Writers' Wars.* On Scott as a Hollywood Communist, see Ceplair and Englund, *The Inquisition in Hollywood.*
41. On Paxton and Dymytryk, see Ceplair and Englund, *The Inquisition in Hollywood;* Navasky, *Naming Names;* Ellen Feldman, "John Paxton," *Dictionary of Literary Biography* 44.
42. Paxton Collection, MHL-AMPAS, cited in Naremore, *More Than Night,* p. 116.
43. Ceplair and Englund, *The Inquisition in Hollywood,* p. 317.
44. Adrian Scott, "Memo to Studio heads William Dozier and Charles Kormer Suggesting *Crossfire* as a Project for the Studio—RKO," reprinted in Ceplair and Englund, *The Inquisition in Hollywood,* pp. 451–454.
45. In a 1991 interview with Patrick McGilligan, Brooks recalled: "John Paxton came around with Adrian Scott to talk about the story, because they were a little afraid

of changing the book that drastically. Paxton couldn't do the story about a homosexual—because of the rules at that time. Scott asked me would I mind if they changed the character to a Jew, I said, 'No. They got the same problems. Everybody does.'" McGilligan, *Backstory 2*, p. 41.

46. Scott, "Memo to Studio Heads," in Ceplair and Englund, *Inquisition in Hollywood*, p. 453. Naremore argues that the pick-up scene in the film does "convey something of the forbidden homosexual content" of the novel, through film technique emphasizing sexual ambiguity in the intense conversation between Mitchell and Samuels, Mitchell's boyish handsomeness, and the bizarre nocturnal scenes filled with uniformed men; *More Than Night*, p. 118. On sexuality in film noir, see Richard Dyer, "Homosexuality and Film Noir," in *The Matter of Images: Essays on Representations* (London: Routledge, 1993); Corber, *Homosexuality in Cold War America*.

47. Harry Hay, a homosexual and an active member of the southern California Communist Party in the 1930s and 1940s, described the Party's stance in D'Emilio, *Sexual Politics, Sexual Communities*. In 1950–51 Hay helped to organize the Mattachine Society, one of the first organizations to challenge public discrimination against homosexuals.

48. On Hollywood representations of homosexuality see Vito Russo, *The Celluloid Closet: Homosexuality in the Movies* (New York: Harper and Row, 1981), and the 1995 documentary of the same name, directed by Rob Epstein and Jeffrey Friedman. The Breen office had initially declared Brooks's story as "thoroughly and completely unacceptable"; even after Paxton and Scott substituted the theme of race hatred for homophobia, Breen specified that there must be "nothing of a 'pansy' character about Samuels or his relationship with the soldiers"; Paxton Collection, MHL-AMPAS, as cited by Naremore, p. 117.

49. Cripps, *Making Movies Black*.

50. Paxton Collection, MHL-AMPAS, as cited by Naremore, *More Than Night*, p. 117.

51. Eric A. Goldman, "The Fight to Bring the Subject of Anti-Semitism to the Screen," *Davka* 5 (Fall 1975), p. 24.

52. Scott, "Memo to Studio Heads," p. 453. On the portrayal of cops as populist heroes, see Christopher Wilson, *Cop Knowledge: Police Power and Cultural Narrative in Twentieth-Century America* (Chicago: University of Chicago Press, 2000).

53. Paxton Collection, MHL-AMPAS, cited by Naremore, *More Than Night*, p. 117.

54. Scott, "Memo to Studio Heads," p. 454.

55. Ceplair and Englund, *Inquisition in Hollywood*, p. 318. Other progressive filmmakers had and would make brief references to this issue in, for example, *Mr. Skeffington* (1944), filmed by Vincent Sherman, according to Rogin, *Blackface, White Noise;* Orson Welles more subtly in *Citizen Kane* (1941) and *The Lady from Shanghai* (1948), according to Naremore, *More Than Night*.

56. Ceplair and Englund, *Inquisition in Hollywood*, p. 317. In the statement he prepared for the HUAC hearings in October 1947 Adrian Scott insisted that the popular front critique of anti-Semitism and racism was *the* criterion used by the HUAC in selecting its first nineteen witnesses. Many members of HUAC were

publicly identified with anti-Semitic attacks on progressive activists and with aggressive defense of southern segregation. "I would like to speak about the 'cold war' now being waged by the Committee on Un-American Activities against the Jewish and Negro people. [Scott then enumerates the antiracist productions of Hollywood radicals.] Will the American people allow this bigoted committee to sit in judgement of these men and their records?" Schwartz, *The Hollywood Writers' Wars*, pp. 273–274.

57. "Anti-Bigotry Pix [*Crossfire* and *Gentleman's Agreement*] Snare $5,000,000 Domestic Profit," *Variety*, July 7, 1948, pp. 1, 40.

58. "Crossfire," *Life*, June 30, 1947, p. 71. Finley in fact delivered two pronouncements on prejudice. The "five-minute sermon" was intended to persuade a southern soldier to help the police find the killer by showing how the hatred that once attached itself to Irish Catholic immigrants, responsible for the beating death of Finley's own grandfather, now attached itself to Jews and might in the end attack all "men with striped ties." Finley makes a second speech to Keeley: "This business of hating Jews comes in a lot of different sizes. There's the you-can't-join-our-country-club kind and you-can't-live-in-our-neighborhood kind. And yes you-can't work here kind. And because we stand for these, we get Monty's kind. He's just one guy. We don't get him very often, but he grows out of all the rest."

59. Hermione Rich Isaacs, "Films in Review," *Theatre Arts*, September 1947, pp. 15–16; James Agee, "Films," *Nation*, August 2, 1947, reprinted in *Agee on Film*, Vol. I (New York: Perigree, 1983 [1958]), pp. 269–270.

60. "Movie of the Week: Crossfire," *Life*, June 30, 1947, p. 71. *Commentary* was sponsored by the American Jewish Committee. Cohen's criticism appeared in a detailed "Letter to the Movie-Makers," *Commentary*, August 1947, pp. 110–118. Dore Schary responded with a fervent defense of the movie as an attempt to "insulate people against violent and virulent anti-semitism," in "Letter from a Movie-Maker," *Commentary*, October 1947, pp. 344–347, to which Cohen appended a rebuttal, pp. 347–349. Cohen's rebuttal included comments by reader Albert L. Furth.

61. "Crossfire," *Variety*, June 25, 1947, p. 8; "Prejudice Under Fire," *Newsweek*, July 28, 1947, p. 84. See also Shirley O'Hara, "Movies," *New Republic*, August 11, 1947, p. 34. John McCarten, "The Current Cinema—Anti-Semitism and Advertising," *New Yorker*, July 19, 1947, p. 46 called special attention to "the word 'Jew' on its sound track . . . the frankness of the dialogue."

62. John Houseman, "Violence, 1947: Three Specimens," *Hollywood Quarterly* 3 (1947), pp. 64–65. Betty Goldstein, "Movie Review: *Crossfire*," *UE News*, August 9, 1947, pp. 8–9. Daniel Horowitz provided me with a copy of this review. Goldstein also used the review to comment on mainstream Hollywood film's "censorship" of the word "CIO," and its failure too make movies about union members, or about "real problems in the lives of working people. . . . Not since 'Grapes of Wrath,' and that was a long time ago."

63. Goldstein, "Movie Review: *Crossfire*," pp. 8–9.

64. "Film to Deal with Negro," *Voice* (Oakland), June 28, 1948, TINCF; Langdon-Teclaw, "Caught in the Crossfire," pp. 477–479.

65. Richard Simon to Laura Hobson, September 26, 1944, reproduced in Hobson's first section of her autobiography, *Laura Z: A Life* (hereafter *A Life;* New York: Arbor House, 1983), p. 222.

66. Hobson noted the publishing history of *Gentleman's Agreement* in the second volume of her autobiography, *Laura Z: A Life, Years of Fulfillment* (hereafter *Years of Fulfillment;* New York: Fine, 1986).

67. Biographical information on Hobson is drawn from her entry in *Current Biography* (1947); *American Women Writers,* ed. Lina Mainiero (New York: Ungar, 1980); and her two volumes of autobiography, *A Life* and *Years of Fulfillment.*

68. *The Trespassers* drew on her affair with Ingersoll and her drawn-out struggle to obtain visas for two non-Jewish Viennese analysts in 1938–39.

69. Hobson, *A Life,* pp. 18, 9, 23.

70. Hobson's retrospective account emphasized her use of the "Z" as a Jewish marker: "The Z is for Zametkin, my maiden name, and I have clung to it through all my years because it held my identity intact before that Anglo-Saxon married name of Hobson"; *Laura Z.,* p. 7.

71. "Laura Z. Hobson," *Current Biography* (1947), p. 311. Hobson inherited this position from her father: accosted as a member of an underground socialist group, he had responded, "I have no religion. My father is a Jew." Hobson, *A Life,* p. 20.

72. Hobson, *A Life,* pp. 317–319, 320.

73. Hobson, *A Life.* The report of Rankin's speech was a first-page story in the National Affairs section of *Time,* February 14, 1944. As a promoter of FDR, the New Deal, and the fight against fascism, Winchell had battled a number of Congressional conservatives; see Neal Gabler, *Winchell: Gossip, Power and the Culture of Celebrity* (New York: Vintage, 1993).

74. Topical references in the novel include wartime incidents of crowds attacking Jewish victims; groups and individuals associated with public statements of anti-Semitism, such as Gerald L. K. Smith, the Christian Front, Congressmen Bilbo and Rankin; the anthropological theories of E. A. Hooten, Margaret Mead, and Ruth Benedict; a *Fortune* poll that found the largest incidence of anti-Semitism in the "top-income bracket."

75. Diana Trilling, "Americans Without Distinction," *Commentary,* March 1947, pp. 290–292.

76. Jacobson, *Whiteness of a Different Color,* pp. 125–131.

77. Budd Schulberg, "Kid Glove Cruelty," *New Republic,* March 17, 1947, p. 35; see also Struthers Burt, "The Poison in Our Body Politic," *Saturday Review of Literature,* March 1, 1947, p. 14. "Polite" anti-Semitism was also the subject of Philip Wylie's essay "Memorandum on Anti-Semitism," *American Mercury,* January 1945.

78. "If we [promoted equality], without the price of free speech, free opposition, free everything, then we'd really be fighting the Communists where it counts." *Gentleman's Agreement,* p. 144. On anticommunist antiracism, see Von Eschen, *Race Against Empire.*

79. Matthew Jacobson calls attention to the significance of the pseudo-scientific term *Caucasian* in *Whiteness of a Different Color.*

80. W. E. B. Du Bois, "Schuyler Green's Metamorphosis," *New York Times Book Review*, March 2, 1947, p. 5. Margaret Halsey defended the book in her essay "Mannon's Little Baby," *Saturday Review of Literature*, October 18, 1947, pp. 7–8, 34–35.

81. The phrase quoted appeared in a speech, "Do Writers Know Hollywood: The Message Cannot Overwhelm the Technique," Zanuck presented to the 1943 Writers Congress, published in *Saturday Review of Literature*, October 30, 1943, pp. 12–13.

82. See Russell Campbell, "The Ideology of the Social Consciousness Movie: Three Films by Darryl Zanuck," *Quarterly Review of Film Studies* 3 (Winter 1978), pp. 49–71.

83. On Zanuck's performance at these hearings, see Doherty, *Projections of War*.

84. Darryl Zanuck to Moss Hart, June 7, 1947, reprinted in Rudy Behlmer, *Memo from Darryl Zanuck* (New York: Grove, 1993), pp. 131–132.

85. Ciment, *Kazan on Kazan*. Bosley Crowther's column "Something About It," *New York Times*, November 16, 1947, noted Hart's account of opposition to the filming. Zanuck told Gregory Peck that the decision to do the film was challenged by Louis B. Mayer and Samuel Goldwyn, who "called him and advised him not to do it. Why rock the boat? . . . Why bring up an unpleasant, controversial subject on the screen?" Custen, *Twentieth Century's Fox*, p. 294.

86. Virginia Wright's drama column, *Daily News*, June 5, 1947.

87. Hobson, *Years of Fulfillment*.

88. Articles in *Variety* charted the film's success: " 'Agreement,' 'Naked City' 'Northside' Best Box office Performers in March," April 7, 1948, p. 6; " 'Agreement' Got Over $500,000 From 1 B'Way House, a Current Record," May 12, 1948, p. 5; "Anti-Bigotry Pix Snare $5,000,000 Domestic Profit," July 7, 1948, pp. 1, 40. An advertisement acknowledging the picture's three Academy Awards noted that *Gentleman's Agreement* had won fifty-one awards, including the New York Critics Circle Award for Best Picture; *Motion Picture Herald*, April 3, 1948.

89. Ciment, *Kazan on Kazan*; Hobson, *Years of Fulfillment*. This casting debate about who could pass as a Jew and who could not prefigured the 1949 debate over the casting of "passing" African Americans in *Lost Boundary* and *Pinky*, discussed in chapter 6.

90. Bosley Crowther, "Gentleman's Agreement," *New York Times*, November 12, 1947; Lee Mortimer, *Daily Mirror*, November 12, 1947, clippings file, AMPAS.

91. Philip Hartung, "Not for Escapists," *Commonweal*, November 21, 1947, p. 145; John Mason Brown, "Seeing Things: If You Prick Us," *Saturday Review of Literature*, December 6, 1947, p. 71. Zanuck's biographer, George Custen, credits this story to Ring Lardner in *Twentieth Century's Fox*, p. 299.

92. "Anti-Semitism—Is Hollywood's Praiseworthy Effort to Combat It Obscuring the Central Point?" *Life*, December 1, 1947, p. 44.

93. Isaacs, "Films in Review," p. 33.

94. Franklin Reeves, "Letters to the Editor: Anti-Semitism," *Life*, December 22, 1947, clippings file, AMPAS.

95. "Review of the New Film," *Film Daily*, November 11, 1947, clippings file, AMPAS; Brown, "Seeing Things," p. 69.

96. Betty Goldstein, "Movie Reviews: Gentleman's Agreement—This Movie Won't Suit UnAmericans," *UE News*, November 22, 1947, p. 11: "In these days with the Un-American Activities Committee on Hollywood's tail, its good to see that Twentieth Century Fox still has the courage to release a movie like 'Gentleman's Agreement' which is certain to displease Rankin and J. Parnell Thomas."

97. Jewell Carter, " 'The Gentleman' Shows His Hand," *Afro-American*, May 27, 1947. See also articles in the *Chicago Defender:* Lilyn [*sic*] Scott, "Broadway Witnesses Two Pictures on the Treatment of Minority Groups," November 15, 1947, p. 9; "Reveal Negroes Get Worst Deal in US," April 10, 1948, p. 3; "Lauds Movie 'Czar' for Aid to Democracy," April 17, 1948, p. 3.

98. Brown, "Seeing Things," pp. 69, 71; Scott, "Broadway Witnesses." Crowther, "Gentleman's Agreement"; Kate Cameron, "Gentleman's Agreement," *Daily News* (New York), November 12, 1947. Kazan later commented, "For the first time someone said that America is full of anti-semitism, both conscious and unconscious and among the best and most liberal people . . . In that sense, the picture broke some new ground." Ciment, *Kazan on Kazan*, p. 57.

99. Edwin Schallert, "Award-Challenging Feature Makes Debut," *Los Angeles Times*, December 26, 1947.

100. Crowther, "Gentleman's Agreement"; "Something About It."

101. "Anti-Semitism—Is Hollywood's Praiseworthy Effort?" These categories of discrimination were derived from the report from Truman's Committee on Civil Rights, *To Secure These Rights* (1947).

102. Goldstein, "Movie Review: Gentleman's Agreement," p. 11; Carter, " 'The Gentleman' Shows His Hand."

103. Laura Z. Hobson, *Cosmopolitan*, July 1947, quoted in "Program Notes," Los Angeles County Museum of Art screening of *Gentleman's Agreement*, July 24, 1980, clippings file, AMPAS.

104. This phrase comes from Jeffrey Melnick's argument about the relationship between Jews and African Americans in *A Right to Sing the Blues: African Americans, Jews, and American Popular Song* (Cambridge: Harvard University Press, 1999), p. 9; see also Rogin, *Blackface, White Noise*.

105. Jacobson, *Whiteness of a Different Color*, p. 129–31. See also George Lipsitz, *The Possessive Investment in Whiteness: How White People Profit from Identity Politics* (Philadelphia: Temple University Press, 1998) and Karen Brodkin, *How Jews Became White Folks and What That Says About Race in America* (New Brunswick: Rutgers University Press, 1998).

106. Carter, " 'The Gentleman' Shows His Hand."

107. Meredith Johns, "A New Dawn is Slowly Breaking Over Hollywood," *Chicago Defender*, July 19, 1949; A.S. "Doc' Young, "Hollywood Digs 'Black Gold,' " *Defender*, December 17, 1949.

6. HOLLYWOOD MAKES RACE (IN)VISIBLE

1. Miller, "The Year It Came Apart," *New York*, December 30, 1974, p. 31.

2. On nineteenth- and early twentieth-century passing narratives, see Hazel Carby,

Reconstructing Womanhood (New York: Oxford University Press, 1987); Gates and McKay, *The Norton Anthology of African-American Literature*. See also Sollors, *Neither White Nor Black Yet Both*.

3. See, for example, the family stories researched by Shirlee Taylor Haizlip in *The Sweeter the Juice: A Family Memoir in Black and White* (New York: Simon and Schuster, 1994); Gregory Howard Williams, *Life on the Color Line* (New York: Penguin, 1996); the profile by Henry Louis Gates Jr. of Anatole Broyard, "White Like Me," *New Yorker*, June 17, 1996.

4. Elazar Barkan, *The Retreat of Scientific Racism: Changing Concepts of Race in Britain and the U.S. Between the World Wars* (Cambridge: Cambridge University Press, 1992).

5. See chapter 1, note 80.

6. Stanley Kramer grew up in the Manhattan neighborhood of Hell's Kitchen; the multiethnic gang he belonged to included other "kikes," along with "wops," "spicks," "micks," and "niggers." His mother, daughter of Jewish immigrants, worked as a secretary in the New York offices of Paramount; his father had left soon after he was born. After graduating from NYU, he wrote for screen and radio before the war; in 1947 he set up an independent production company, Screen Plays, Inc., with Carl Foreman. Stanley Kramer with Nicholas M. Coffey, *A Mad, Mad, Mad, Mad World: A Life in Hollywood* (New York: Harcourt Brace, 1997); see also Donald Spoto, *Stanley Kramer, Filmmaker* (Hollywood: French, 1978). Carl Foreman was born in Chicago, the son of Russian Jewish immigrants. He worked on the Federal Writers Project before finding work as a screenwriter in Hollywood. Foreman joined the Communist Party in 1942, left while in the army, then rejoined it briefly after the war before allowing his membership to lapse. Ceplair and Englund, *The Inquisition in Hollywood*. Foreman dated his Communist Party membership in a letter quoted in the documentary film *Darkness at High Noon: The Carl Foreman Documents* (2002), written and directed by Lionel Chetwynd.

7. Kramer, *Mad*, pp. 35–36; Spoto, *Kramer*, p. 48; Cripps, *Making Movies Black*, p. 222. Laurents later said the Jew in his play was transposed to a black man in the movie because "the film people said Jews had been done." McGilligan, *Backstory 2*, p. 134.

8. Kramer, *Mad*, p. 36.

9. "Kramer's Negro Theme Pic May Outrace Both 20th and De Rochemont," *Variety*, March 2, 1949, pp. 2, 18. The *Chicago Defender* followed the film's progress: "Start Screening 'Home of Brave,'" March 5, 1949; "Flicks About Race New Hollywood Fad," March 26, 1949; "Story Behind 'Home of Brave,'" April 2, 1949. See also "Home of the Brave: First Film About Anti-Negro Bias Made in Secret By Hollywood Ex-GIs," *Ebony*, June 1949.

10. Lillian Scott, "A Hollywood Independent Shows Big Studios How It's Done: He's Stan Kramer, 'Brave's' Champion," *Chicago Defender*, May 14, 1949, p. 16.

11. Edwards grew up in Muncie, Indiana and attended college at Indiana University and Knoxville College in Tennessee. Joining CIO Steelworkers Local 2534 and chairing the grievance committee at the Standard Steel Plant in Hammond, Indi-

ana, Edwards was fired for a rule infraction. Entering the army as a private, he was eventually promoted to first lieutenant. He then studied acting at Northwestern University and appeared in Chicago with a local company, Skyloft Players. Edwards didn't get the part he auditioned for in New York, though he took off the yellow coat, at the request of director Elia Kazan; but he was hired as an understudy. He eventually took over the part of the returning soldier in the traveling production of *Deep Are the Roots*. Edwards's first screen part was a small role in Robert Wise's 1949 boxing exposé, *The Set-Up*. "Movie Hero is Ex-CIO Member," *News*, July 25, 1949, TINCF; "Around and About," *New York Amsterdam News*, June 1, 1949; Eugene Schrott, "Uncrowned Champion," *Negro Digest*, December 1949.

12. Cripps, *Making Movies Black*, pp. 221–226.

13. Rogin categorizes *Home of the Brave* as an example of blackface's "political unconscious" in *Blackface, White Noise*, pp. 228–242. But the culturally sanctioned wartime buddy relationship provided the context for homosexual love between Moss and Finch, a possibility denied in Rogin's reading of Moss as wholly abject, as feminine, as becoming "Mammy."

14. Cited in Cripps, *Making Movies Black*, pp. 351–352.

15. "The New Pictures," *Time*, May 9, 1949, p. 100; "Another Champion," *Newsweek*, May 16, 1949, p. 86. The *New Yorker* critic doubted that "the scars of race prejudice can be healed as neatly and briskly as 'Home of the Brave' would have us believe." "The Color Line," *New Yorker*, May 21, 1949, p. 68.

16. Meredith Johns, "'Home of the Brave' Is Brave Venture for Movie Makers," *Chicago Defender*, April 30, 1949, p. 16.

17. James L. Hicks, "'Home of the Brave' Gives the Real GI Story," *Afro-American*, May 28, 1949; Horace Cayton, "Gets Hit by Sledge Hammer and Gives Recommendation to 'Home of the Brave,'" *Pittsburgh Courier*, May 28, 1949; "Citizens Enthusiastic After Preview of 'Home of the Brave' at Jewel Theatre," *Black Dispatch* (Oklahoma City), August 6, 1949.

18. S. W. Garlington's column, "Amusement Row," *New York Amsterdam News*, June 4, 1949, p. 24. An editorial praised Edwards's citizen-solider as undermining older Hollywood representational systems by showing the Negro "as he is—like other people—and not as a clown, a jester, a bum, or a menial worker." The editorial hailed Edward as a "crusader" who has "broken down the barriers of race, color, creed, and national origin" and the film itself as the production in which "Uncle Tomism in major screen production died in the United States." "A Great Step Forward," *New York Amsterdam News*, June 1, 1949, p. 11.

19. Johns, "'Home of the Brave' Is Brave Venture."

20. See the "Around and About" column in the *New York Amsterdam News*, June 11, 1949, and June 18, 1949, and accompanying photographs. See also the photographs in "These Figures Thrilled the World in 1949," *Chicago Defender*, December 31, 1949.

21. "A Great Step Forward," p. 11.

22. Ralph Ellison, "The Shadow and the Act," *Reporter*, December 9, 1949, reprinted in *Shadow and Act* (New York: Random House, 1972), p. 278.

23. " Our Opinions: Home of the Brave?" *Chicago Defender,* June 18, 1949, p. 6.

24. " 'Home of the Brave' Movie May Set Record in D.C.," *New York Amsterdam News,* August 6, 1949, p. 20. After black members of the "interracial theater party" were denied entrance, the sponsoring organizations demanded to meet with theater management; "Groups Meet to Discuss Bias in Capital Theater," *New York Amsterdam News,* August 27, 1949, p. 20.

25. " 'Home of the Brave' to Play Key Cities," *Chicago Defender,* May 14, 1949, p. 25; " 'Brave' On Big Time Dixie Tour," July 30, 1949, p. 25. Passing the censorship board in Memphis opened the film to bookings in Tennessee and Kentucky; Garlington, "Amusement Row," August 6, 1949, p. 19. The *Defender* also touted mainstream press praise for the film: "Memphis Scribe Praises 'Home of the Brave,' " August 27, 1949, p. 25; "Atlanta Church Groups Call 'Home of the Brave' the Year's Best," October 15, 1949, p. 26.

26. William L. White, *Lost Boundaries* (Harcourt Brace, 1948). The book was well reviewed by Orville Prescott in the *New York Times,* March 23, 1948; Walter White, *New York Times Book Review,* March 28, 1948; as well as in the *New Republic,* March 15, 1948; *Commonweal,* May 21, 1948; and the *Daily Worker,* March 31, 1948.

27. Raymond Fielding, *The March of Time, 1935–1951* (New York: Oxford University Press, 1978); Denning, *The Cultural Front.* De Rochemont produced *March of Time* features from 1934–1943, and then became a feature film producer for Twentieth Century-Fox, producing the popular war documentary *The Fighting Lady* (1945) and the commercial films *House on 92nd Street* (1945), *Thirteen Rue Madelaine* (1946), and *Boomerang* (1947), directed by Elia Kazan. The quotes from De Rochemont appear in his entry in *Current Biography* (1949), pp. 144–146.

28. Johnson was born in 1900. His father grew up in Michigan, son and grandson of northern free blacks. His mother was the daughter of Mississippi slaves. Johnson's father had passed as white in order to hold a job as a Chicago real estate agent. Johnson attended a black church until he was eight, when his family shifted to a white Presbyterian church. Rush Medical College did not give credit for internships at the four Negro hospitals that trained Negro interns, so Johnson applied for a "blind" placement, which did not require an interview. When Maine General Hospital accepted him, he was thought to be "a Filipino or maybe a Hawaiian or a Jew." After he finished his internship, he was offered a job as a pathologist by the hospital but decided instead to buy a practice from a doctor retiring in Gorham, New Hampshire. Albert Johnson's obituary, *New York Times,* June 28, 1988, p. D 25; White, *Lost Boundaries,* pp. 11–18.

29. Thyra Baumann was the granddaughter of a German shipping commissioner of the Port of New Orleans, and the daughter of a postal clerk. She and her sisters attended "colored public schools" in New Orleans until 1912, when their father, fearing that Woodrow Wilson's election would segregate federal offices, moved the family to Boston, where Thyra and her siblings were "the only Negroes in their class." After finishing a commercial course in high school, she applied for a job as a stenographer as "white." Thyra Johnson's obituary, *New York Times,* November 29, 1995, p. D 19; White, *Lost Boundaries;* see also "Lost Boundaries," *Ebony,* May 1948.

30. See White, *Lost Boundaries*; Ann Johnson also mentioned her continuing relationship with her white boyfriend in "Real Life 'Lost Boundaries' Principal Visits Los Angeles," *Los Angeles Tribune*, January 21, 1950. Dr. Albert Johnson described his practice as unchanged, except for the addition of his first Negro patients, in "Dr. Johnson, of 'Lost Boundaries' Fame, Here, Says His Revelation 'Helped Things,'" *Los Angeles Tribune*, July 22, 1950.

31. Johnson's disillusioned remarks appear in White, *Lost Boundaries*, pp. 83–85. "Dr. Johnson . . . Says His Revelation 'Helped Things.'" The comment to Ellis is cited in Cripps, *Making Movies Black*, p. 230.

32. Cripps, *Making Movies Black*, p. 227, based on his research in the NAACP manuscript papers at the Library of Congress, and in Louis De Rochemont's papers at the American Heritage Center in Laramie, Wyoming. Ellison, *Shadow and Act*, p. 277.

33. Cripps, *Making Movies Black*, pp. 227–228.

34. Charles Palmer, Virginia Shaler (De Rochemont's wife), Eugene Ling, Lothar Wolfe, and the radio and film documentary writer Ormonde de Kay all worked on the screenplay; Cripps, *Making Movies Black*; Obituary for De Kay, *New York Times*, October 23, 1998. The actor Mel Ferrer rejected an ending in which Dr. Carter showed "he had made a mistake in trying to pass . . . [and would] be punished, slapped on the wrists, and be allowed to return to his home town but on terms dictated by his white neighbors." Ferrer wanted the doctor to be able to say, "Yes, I had lived a false life but now was the time to say to everyone I am a human being, that I am a Negro but I am not ashamed . . . that the same blood courses through my body as it does yours. . . . We'll pick up where we left off on our terms, not theirs"; Al Weinstein, "He Passed as a Negro," *Negro Digest*, October 1951, p. 20.

35. Cripps, *Making Movies Black*, p. 230.

36. Lillian Scott, "White Is Black in Hollywood," *Chicago Defender*, March 19, 1949, p. 1. Scott quoted Fredi Washington, Tallulah Bankhead, Jane White, director Henry Wagstaff Gribble, Frederick O'Neal, and Canada Lee, all protesting the casting of white actors as the passing family in *Lost Boundaries* and of Jeanne Crain as the eponymous character in *Pinky*. Bankhead called the casting decisions "a setback for all the things liberals are fighting for." Washington criticized the *Lost Boundaries* producers for not even interviewing Negro actors, noting that "the social impact of both films will be greatly weakened and miss its mark by a wide margin if whites are to play Negro roles."

37. Werker was quoted in Darr Smith's column in the *Daily News*, July 15, 1949. His remarks were reprinted in an article in the *Amsterdam News* with a reply from the Committee for the Negro in the Arts, a coalition of African American cultural activists based in New York. Ernest Crichlow was the chairman; others active in the organization included Fredi Washington, Canada Lee, and Shirley Graham; "Attack 'Lost Boundaries' Director for 'Race Slur,'" *New York Amsterdam News*, August 6, 1949, p. 19.

38. "Attack 'Lost Boundaries' Director for 'Race Slur,'" p. 19.

39. Ibid. Cripps found letters from Fredi Washington to Darr Smith and to Carleton

Moss, telling them to expect nothing from Werker and De Rochemont. She was particularly critical of the "Harlem and the Southern Negro hospital scenes" in the final film. Cripps, *Making Movies Black*, pp. 230–231.

40. Ellison, *Shadow and Act*, pp. 278–279. See also the criticism of this point by Lillian Scott, "De Rochemont's Powerful Picture Pierces Age-Old Hate Boundaries," *Chicago Defender*, July 9, 1949; and Carlton Moss, "Does 'Lost Boundaries' Say I'd Give Anything Just to Be White?" (National Negro Press Association), *Afro-American*, August 20, 1949; José Iglesias, "'Lost Boundaries' Shallow, Patronizing Film on Negro," *Daily Worker*, July 1, 1949 ("The film apologizes for white supremacists by accusing Negroes of 'anti-Negro' discrimination too").

41. Ellison, *Shadow and Act*, pp. 278–279. Although Walter White publicly praised the script as "the most courageous treatment of the Negro in motion pictures today," after seeing a rough cut of the film he privately expressed criticisms to De Rochemont of the stereotypes in the Harlem sequence, featuring "a zoot-suited shifty-looking character paring his finger nails in front of the boarding house." Walter White to "Dear Louis," February 25, 1949, and May 23, 1949, cited by Cripps, *Making Movies Black*, pp. 227–228; Walter White, "Do Race Pictures Denote a New Hollywood Attitude?" *Chicago Defender*, August 20, 1949, p. 7.

42. These comments appeared in a letter Ellison wrote to De Rochemont, cited by Cripps, *Making Movies Black*, p. 227, cited in note 32.

43. White, *Lost Boundaries*, pp. 83–85, as cited in note 31.

44. Thyra Johnson obituary, p. D19.

45. Crowther was aware of the film's omissions: "This film is not a picture of the whole complex problem of race and racial discrimination. . . . It touches the immediate anxieties of only a limited number of Negroes at best, and locates its drama in an area which is virtually free of the economic tensions of race. . . . It may even be regarded by some Negroes with a certain distaste because of the curiously sensitive implications towards color." Bosley Crowther, "Lost Boundaries," *New York Times*, July 1, 1949, section 4, p. 14.

46. Cited in "Movies: New Films," *Newsweek*, October 10, 1949, p. 90.

47. "Library Gets Script of 'Lost Boundaries,'" *New York Amsterdam News*, August 30, 1949.

48. White, "Do Race Pictures Denote New Hollywood Attitude?" p. 7.

49. Scott, "De Rochemont's Powerful Picture Pierces Age-Old Hate Boundaries," p. 25.

50. Al Anderson, "Three Films Reflect Anti-Discrimination," *Afro-American*, December 31, 1949. Carleton Moss's review for the National Negro Press Association linked these "shortcomings" (the talk of tolerance, black color prejudice, the white casting), to the film's "false" premise that black people shared white attitudes of white superiority and to its effort to avoid offending the "white supremacists in the audience who might object to seeing anybody with bona fide colored ancestry masquerading as white—eating, working, fraternizing, and giving orders to white people." "Does 'Lost Boundaries' Say I'd Give Anything to Be White?"

51. Anderson mentions advertising for *Lost Boundaries* in "Three Films Reflect Anti-Discrimination." Although the Supreme Court let stand the decisions of the

southern courts that upheld the censors, by the early 1950s the film opened in the last of the markets to which it had been denied access. Cripps notes that censorship unified support from the NAACP, the ACLU, and other groups, and probably increased the film's viewership; *Making Movies Black,* pp. 231–232. Southern audiences were mentioned in "Movies: New Films," pp. 89–90.

52. Walter White noted Zanuck's hopes to do "as great a picture about the Negro as Twentieth Century Fox had done about the Jewish question in 'Gentleman's Agreement.'" Walter White, "Regrets He Has No Words of Praise for 'Pinky,'" *Chicago Defender,* October 29, 1949, p. 7.

53. Russell Campbell, "The Ideology of the Social Consciousness Movie: Three Films by Darryl Zanuck," *Quarterly Review of Film Studies* 3 (Winter 1978), pp. 49–71; memo from Philip Dunne to Darryl F. Zanuck, April 19, 1948, in *Pinky* file, Philip Dunne Collection, University of Southern California, Cinema-Television Library, hereafter PDC USC CTL.

54. "Race Conscious," *New York Times,* May 25, 1948; "General Comments by Zanuck," Conference on Screenplay, May 25, 1948; *Pinky* file, PDC USC CTL.

55. Philip Dunne memo to Darryl Zanuck, April 19, 1948, in *Pinky* file, PDC USC CTL.

56. The quote appeared in the coverage of the 1942 NAACP convention, held in Hollywood in the NAACP monthly, the *Crisis;* cited by Doherty, *Projections of War,* p. 208.

57. *Pinky* was the first Hollywood "message" movie in which African Americans were consulted, according to Cripps, citing over twenty drafts of the script in the Twentieth Century-Fox Film Archive at USC, and extensive correspondence with White and others. Philip Dunne saw Jane White's involvement as "valuable insurance"; *Making Movies Black,* pp. 232–236.

58. Cripps quoted letters written by White to his fiancée, journalist Poppy Cannon, in January 1949, suggesting that the script would face criticism from Hollywood Negroes, the left, and the African American press; *Making Movies Black,* p. 235.

59. Formerly a newspaper reporter, Nichols had been in Hollywood since 1929, and had written numerous scripts for Ford, including *The Informer* (1935) and *Stagecoach* (1939).

60. Philip Dunne, *Take Two: A Life in Movies and Politics* (New York: Limelight, 1992 [1980]), pp. 60–61; Cripps, *Making Movies Black,* pp. 234–236.

61. "Drop Message Pix," *Variety,* August 18, 1948, cited by Pauley, *An American Odyssey,* pp. 106–107. Zanuck's memo articulated his use of the trading places formula: he wanted to make "the white majority of the audience experience emotionally the humiliation and hurt and evil of segregation and discrimination . . . [and] carry away a sense of shame. . . . Their feeling and thinking will be changed." Darryl Zanuck to Walter White, September 21, 1948, cited by Cripps, *Making Movies Black,* pp. 233–234.

62. Philip Dunne was educated at Harvard, worked in Hollywood from the early 1930s, and was, like Nichols, a respected screenwriter known for his commitment to the Screenwriters' Guild and pro-FDR politics. He worked closely with Zanuck at Fox in the late 1930s. During the war he worked for the Motion Picture Bureau

of the OWI and in 1947 he was one of the originators, with William Wyler and John Huston, of the Committee for the First Amendment, which protested the 1947 Hollywood HUAC hearings and the threatened black list; Dunne, *Take Two*.

63. Philip Dunne to Darryl Zanuck, October 25, 1948; *Pinky* file, PDC USC CTL. Dunne consulted with Elia Kazan about the screenplay months before the latter agreed to direct it; Dunne to Zanuck, November 5, 1948; *Pinky* file.

64. Dunne, *Take Two*, pp. 60–62. Zanuck and Dunne privately noted a contradiction between Nichols's objection and his reputation as a liberal. Philip Dunne's notes, November 30, 1948; *Pinky* file, folder 3, PDC USC CTL.

65. Ellison, *Shadow and Act*, p. 279.

66. Jane White, "Suggested Changes and Additions to Jan. 12, 1949, Screenplay of *Pinky*"; *Pinky* file, folder 4, PDC USC CTL.

67. Darryl Zanuck to Jane White, February 1, 1949; *Pinky* file, PDC USC CTL; Philip Dunne to Darryl Zanuck, February 2, 1949; *Pinky* file.

68. Philip Dunne to Darryl Zanuck, February 2, 1949; *Pinky* file, PDC USC CTL.

69. Casting lists in William Gordon Collection, folder 228 (*Pinky*), AMPAS.

70. " 'Pinky' Message Pic Zanuck's 49 Film," *Variety*, January 26, 1949, p. 26. "The studio is officially describing it as an original story by Nichols . . . nor is its connection with *Quality* even admitted," *New York Times*, January 30, 1949, in *Pinky* production files, AMPAS. Black critics were not fooled: S. W. Garlington noted, "according to reports from out Hollywood way, they are having a bit of difficulty shooting Pinky. . . . Nevertheless, regardless of the 'changes' they make, the outcome will be the same—anti-Negro—[as] the book *Quality*." "Amusement Row," May 28, 1949, p. 24.

71. Darryl Zanuck to Dudley Nichols, November 1, 1948; in *Pinky* file, PDC USC CTL.

72. Francis Harmon, "Notes on the Picture, March 18, 1949," in Motion Picture Association of America (MPAA) files on *Pinky*, AMPAS. Harmon provided several examples of known interracial sexual relationships among the southern political elite who most actively condemned "social equality."

73. Darryl Zanuck to Francis Harmon, March 30, 1949, in MPAA files on *Pinky*, AMPAS. Zanuck's claim to be elevating social responsibility over business interests ("I am sure this would increase the box office of the picture by a considerable amount") further indicated that he could only imagine interracial sexuality as illicit sensationalism.

74. Philip Dunne to Darryl Zanuck, February 7, 1949; *Pinky* file, PDC USC CTL.

75. Darr Smith, column, *Daily News*, March 23, 1949, p. 29.

76. Philip Dunne to Darryl Zanuck, February 11, 1949, "Re Conference with John Ford About Pinky"; Zanuck to Mr. John Ford, March 15, 1949; *Pinky* file, folder 4, PDC USC CTL. Ethel Waters, with Charles Samuels, *His Eye is on the Sparrow: An Autobiography* (Westport, Conn: Greenwood, 1978), pp. 270–272; Gussow, *Darryl F. Zanuck*, p. 151.

77. Dunne, *Take Two*, p. 98. See also Gussow, *Darryl Zanuck*, pp. 151–152; "Pinky Finished," *New York Times*, May 29, 1949. Kazan described his involvement with *Pinky* in *A Life*, pp. 373–376.

78. "The New Pictures: Pinky," *Time*, October 10, 1949, p. 98. Other reviews that noted these aspects included "Pinky," *Hollywood Reporter*, September 30, 1949; *Variety*, September 30, 1949; and "New Films: Pinky," *Newsweek*, October 10, 1949. Kazan later described the film as "a total dodge . . . not about a black girl but about a charming little white girl"; Ciment, *Kazan on Kazan*, pp. 59–61.

79. Marjorie McKenzie, "Pursuit of Democracy," *Pittsburgh Courier*, June 4, 1949.

80. Scott, "White Is Black in Hollywood," p. 1; Garlington, "Amusement Row," p. 24; "Here's the Lowdown on Pinky," *Chicago Defender*, June 11, 1949, p. 25.

81. "Here's the Lowdown," p. 25.

82. Meredith Johns, "A New Dawn Is Slowly Breaking Over Hollywood: Filmland Focuses on Plight of Minorities," *Chicago Defender*, July 9, 1949, p. 12.

83. Dunne's statement was published in the *New York Times*, May 1, 1949.

84. Kazan's and Crain's remarks appeared in an article on *Pinky* in *Ebony*, September 1949, pp. 23–25; Crain's comment also appears in studio promotional materials distributed by Harry Brand, director of publicity for Fox, in the *Pinky* production files at AMPAS.

85. Ethel Waters quoted in Lena Brown, "The Tragedy of Race Prejudice: Movie Critics, Public Await Premiere of Picture, 'Pinky,'" *New York Amsterdam News*, September 17, 1949, p. 16.

86. Edwin Schallert, "'Pinky' Fascinates as Race Issues Film," *Los Angeles Times*, October 22, 1949; *Pinky* production files, AMPAS.

87. "Pinky," *Hollywood Reporter*, September 30, 1949; see also "Zanuck Scores with 'Pinky,'" *Los Angeles Examiner*, October 22, 1949, which described Pinky's work in building "a home and a school for Negro children" as enabling her to "forget her desire to go back North to the man she loves." The camera work establishing the shift in the relationship between Pinky and Miss Em from racial and class antagonism to warmth and intimacy briefly suggests the possibility of a wider range of desire than the heterosexual romance foregrounded by the film.

88. "Who Is Happy," *Commonweal*, October 14, 1949, p. 15; "A Woman's Problem," *Life*, October 17, 1949, pp. 112–115.

89. Robert Hatch, "Pinky," *New Republic*, October 3, 1948, p. 23. David J. Bethea answered Hatch in his defense of *Pinky*: "the story of 'Pinky' concerns the terrible sickness of race prejudice in a poor white community where bigotry is not threatened by sentimentality and falsehood but thrives on them"; "Play Attacks Race Bias with Honesty," *Afro-American*, October 8, 1949.

90. "Pinky," *Variety*, September 30, 1949; "The New Pictures," *Time*, October 10, 1949, p. 86.

91. Ezra Goodman, "Film Review," undated New York newspaper, from the *Pinky* file, PDC USC CTL; Bosley Crowther, "'Pinky,' Zanuck's Film Study of Anti-Negro Bias in Deep South, Shown at Rivoli," *New York Times*, September 30, 1949, section 2, p. 28; "Pinky," *Variety*, October 5, 1949; *Pinky* production files, AMPAS.

92. Seymour Peck, "Today's Movie: Screen Moves Forward with Story of Pinky," *Daily Compass*, September 30, 1949. Peck read the film as encouraging individuals to fight rather than pass, and he applied this message to Jews and liberals: "It

might confront the Jew who considers the economic and social advantages of concealing his religion, it might confront the liberal who, in these difficult times, looks for safety in denying he is a liberal or has ever been one."

93. White, "Regrets He Has No Words of Praise for 'Pinky,'" p. 7; Lillian Scott, "Calls 'Pinky' a Realist Film Based on False Premises: Broadway Sees, Likes, Newest Problem Sock," *Chicago Defender*, October 8, 1949, p. 26.

94. John McCarten, "Darryl in the Old Southland," *New Yorker*, October 1, 1949, pp. 50–51.

95. Crowther, "'Pinky'. . .Shown at Rivoli"; untitled clipping, *New York Times*, October 9, 1949; *Pinky* production files, AMPAS.

96. Crowther, "'Pinky'. . . Shown at Rivoli."

97. "The casting of Ethel Waters as an out-and-out Dixie mammy and Nina May McKinney as a razor-toting hussy is sure to offend Negroes." "Pinky," *Ebony*, September 1949, pp. 23–25. These criticisms appeared also in White's and Scott's columns in the *Chicago Defender*.

98. Scott, "Calls 'Pinky' A Realistic Film Based on False Premises," p. 26.

99. Cab Calloway, "Cab Calloway Finds No Problem Solved in 'Pinky,' 'Lost Boundaries,'" *Chicago Defender*, November 19, 1949, p. 26.

100. Alice Childress, "About Those Colored Movies," *Freedom*, June 1952, revised in *Like One of the Family: Conversations from a Domestic's Life* (Boston: Beacon Press, 1986 [1956]), pp. 123–124. Thanks to Rachel Rubin for calling my attention to this sketch. "What's Your Story? Pinky Has One," *Chicago Defender*, November 12, 1949, p. 25; "Women at Defender Premiere Agree: 'Pinky" Is Very Good Movie Fare," *Chicago Defender*, November 26, 1949, p. 10.

101. Some of these posters appear in the *Pinky* production files, AMPAS; a copy of the complete pressbook is part of Special Collections, USC CTL. See also the ad in the *New York Amsterdam News*, September 24, 1949, p. 29, with the tag lines "Soon You Will Know Why They Call Her 'Pinky'" and "This is the personal story of a girl who passed for white."

102. Archer Winston, "Movies: 'Pinky' Documents Southern Customs," *New York Post*, September 30, 1949; "Pinky," *Ebony*, pp. 23–25.

103. Scott, "Calls 'Pinky' A Realistic Film Based on False Premises," p. 26; Childress, "About Those Colored Movies," pp. 123–124; Ellison, *Shadow and Act*, pp. 279–280.

104. The Atlanta cuts were detailed in "Approved," *New York Times*, November 6, 1949; the Marshall, Texas, objections were listed in "Law Banning Film in Texas Overruled," *Los Angeles Times*, June 3, 1952.

105. Resistance to censorship in Marshall may have been related to the presence of Wiley College, thought to be the center of black intellectual life in Texas in the 1930s, or to Marshall's 1946 voting rights challenge. For coverage in the trade press, see "On Appeal, Tex. Convicts Exhib Showing 'Pinky,'" *Variety*, January 31, 1952; "'Pinky' Ban Ruled Legal," *Motion Picture Herald*, February 2, 1952; "Exhib Fights Censorship to Hi Court," *Variety*, March 11, 1952; "Texas Court Reversal Paves Way for Appeal on 'Pinky,'" *Hollywood Reporter*, March 14, 1952;

"'Pinky' Hearing to High Court," *Motion Picture Herald,* March 22, 1952; "Supreme Court Gives 'Pinky' Texas Freedom," and "The 'Pinky' Case," *Motion Picture Herald,* June 7, 1952; "Trade Brings Guns to Bear in Censor Fight," *Motion Picture Herald,* June 21, 1952.

106. Translation into Turkish, Arabic, Chinese, Japanese, Hindustani, and three other Indian dialects, Tagalog, and Bantu suggested that *Pinky* was considered a cultural weapon in the U.S. battle against Communism around the world; *Variety,* May 2, 1949. The critic Gerald Weales noted special black and white enthusiasm for the courtroom scene: "Pro-Negro Films in Atlanta," *Phylon* 13 (1962), pp. 298–304. Exhibition was covered as news in *Variety:* "Atlanta DeLuxer Opens Balcony to Negroes for 'Pinky,'" November 17, 1949; "'Pinky' Gets More Southern Dates," November 21, 1949; "'Pinky' Eases by That Censor in Memphis," December 2, 1949; and in the *Chicago Defender:* "Pinky Does All Right in New Orleans," December 17, 1949.

107. A. S. "Doc" Young, "Hollywood Digs 'Black Gold:' Once Feared Films About Race Now Box Office Hits," *Chicago Defender,* December 17, 1949, p. 1.

108. Ibid.

109. Anderson, "Three Films Reflect Anti-Discrimination."

110. "New Award to Outstanding Film Annually," *Argus* (St. Louis), November 25, 1949, TINCF. The critics included Lillian Scott of the *Chicago Defender;* James Hicks, NAACP correspondent in New York and feature writer for the *Afro-American* and the *Norfolk Journal and Guide,* Bill Chase (*New York Age*), George Schuyler (*Pittsburgh Courier*), Julius Adams (*Amsterdam News*), Dick Campbell (*Sphinx*), Ludlow Werner (*Oracle*).

111. Faulkner's novel highlighted the southern case for states' rights, according to Lewis Gannett, "Books and Things: 'Intruder in the Dust,'" *New York Herald-Tribune,* September 28, 1948; J. Saunders Redding, "Book Review: 'Intruder in the Dust,'" *Afro-American,* October 9, 1948. Cripps documented black and white input and responses to making *Intruder in the Dust* in *Making Movies Black,* pp. 240–244. Maddow's account appeared in McGilligan, *Backstory 2,* pp. 157–192.

112. Lawrence LaMar, "Hernandez in Leading Role," *Afro-American,* November 19, 1949; Lillian Scott, "'Intruder in the Dust' Puts Hernandez in the Tops Class," *Chicago Defender,* November 26, 1949; Ellison, *Shadow and Act,* p. 281.

113. Bosley Crowther, "'Intruder in the Dust,' MGM's Drama of Lynching in the South, at the Mayfair," *New York Times,* November 23, 1949; Crowther, "A Great Film: 'Intruder in the Dust' Commands High Praise," *New York Times,* November 27, 1949. See also Cripps, *Making Movies Black,* pp. 243–244.

114. Zanuck described *Pinky* as "tea" and *No Way Out* as "dinner;" in Kenneth Geist, *Pictures Will Talk: The Life and Films of Joseph L. Mankiewicz* (New York: Da Capo, 1978), p. 153. Philip Yordan also worked on the script, developed from an original story by Lesser Samuels.

115. Billy Rowe, "Zanuck Blazed Way in Changing View Toward Racial Themes," *Pittsburgh Courier,* August 12, 1950; "No Way Out: Story of Negro Doctor Is Strongest of Race-Themed Movies," *Ebony,* March 1950, pp. 31–34.

116. "'No Way Out' at Rivoli New View of Race Bias," *New York Herald-Tribune,* August 13, 1950. See also Thomas Pryor, "'No Way Out' Latest Chapter in Screen's Extended Study of Anti-Negro Bias," *New York Times,* August 20, 1950.

117. On the censorship efforts, and the NAACP organization against censorship see Cripps, *Making Movies Black,* pp. 346–347.

118. The filmmakers initially included anti-Semitism as well as racism among the crimes of the white working-class villains; June 20, 1949, "Conference on Screenplay, June 16, 1949," in Twentieth Century-Fox Archive, Legal Files and Production Files, 1915–1982, box 010, FX PRS-700, Special Collections, UCLA Arts Library.

119. One ending that was filmed entailed having the racist lure Luther Brooks into a coal cellar and force him to dig his own grave, emphatically restoring racial boundaries. See Geist, *Pictures Will Talk,* p. 156; Custen, *Twentieth Century's Fox,* pp. 335–336. Another ending, described in the feature on the film for *Ebony,* pictured the white working-class woman sacrificing herself so that the black doctor could live, with dialogue assessing Brooks's color-blind medical capacity as more valuable than her working-class life: "We never built anything, we never healed anybody—we never even cooked a supper for friends. He's a human being. He lives for everything and we live for nothing"; quoted in "'No Way Out': Story of Negro Doctor," p. 31.

120. *Variety,* August 30, 1950, as cited by Geist, *Pictures Will Talk,* p. 157.

121. Early notes on the film from Philip Yordan to Zanuck, January 28, 1949, in Twentieth Century-Fox Archive, Legal Files and Production Files, 1915–1982, box 010, FX PRS-700, Special Collections, UCLA Arts Library.

122. The full list of organizations provides a snapshot of progressive-liberal support for civil rights in 1950. It included the Anti-Nazi League, the New York State CIO Council, the Synagogue Council of America, the American Jewish Committee, the American Jewish Congress, the Anti-Defamation League of B'Nai Brith, the Jewish Labor Committee, the Phelps Stokes Fund, the National Community Relations Advisory Council; the National Probation and Parole Association; Exhibitors' Campaign Book, *No Way Out,* pp. 14–15, in Special Collections, USC CTL. The production also received many awards, including from the Negro Actors' Guild and the New York Foreign Language Press Film Critics' Circle.

123. Geist, *People Will Talk,* p. 157; see also "'No Way Out' Draws Protest," *Afro-American,* October 21, 1950.

124. See Buhle and Wagner, *Radical Hollywood;* Peter Roffman and Jim Purdy, *The Hollywood Social Problem Film* (Bloomington: Indiana University Press, 1981).

125. On Robinson's life, see Arnold Rampersad, *Jackie Robinson: A Biography* (New York: Ballantine, 1987); on the film, see pp. 223–226. State Department interest in the film, and plans to send it to "far-away places like China, India, and parts of Africa where there has been heavy communistic infiltration" were noted in Herman Hill, "Cameras Grind Out Life Story of Jackie Robinson," *Pittsburgh Courier,* February 18, 1950; "Robinson an Admirable Hero of His Own Screen Biography," *Washington Post,* June 14, 1950.

126. Aline Mosby, "Robinson Says Movie of Life Is Toned Down," *Louisville Courier-Journal*, April 18, 1950.

7. COMPETING POSTWAR REPRESENTATIONS OF UNIVERSALISM

1. Quoted by Hugh Cordier, "A History and Analysis of *Destination Freedom*," unpublished seminar paper, Northwestern University, summer 1949, p. 26. Fred MacDonald cites this interview in *Richard Durham's "Destination Freedom": Scripts from Radio's Black Legacy, 1948–1959* (New York: Praeger, 1989), and generously provided me with a copy of Cordier's paper as well as tapes of several *Destination Freedom* broadcasts. On Durham's career, see also Savage, *Broadcasting Freedom;* Barlow, *Voice Over.*

2. Canada Lee was the keynote speaker at the "Conference on Radio, Television, and the Negro People" (July 6, 1949), convened by the Committee for the Negro in the Arts and attended by "300 radio and TV writers, actors, directors, representatives of unions, and colored organizations." Lee pleaded not for the promotion of "tolerance" but for black stories: "A virtual Iron Curtain exists against the entire Negro people as far as radio is concerned." "Negro Stereotypes on Air, Lack of Job Chances Scored by Canada Lee," *Variety*, July 13, 1949, p. 35.

3. Paul Neimark, "The Man Who Knows Muhammad Ali Best," *Sepia*, May 1976, pp. 22–30.

4. Bill V. Mullen, *Popular Fronts: Chicago and African-American Cultural Politics, 1935–1946* (Urbana: University of Illinois Press, 1999).

5. The regional and ethnographic orientation of the Federal Writers' Project supported a racially inclusive panethnic Americanism; Denning, *Cultural Front.* Telephone conversation with Clarice Durham, Chicago, Illinois, July 9, 1999. Although the South Side Writers' Group disbanded shortly before Wright left Chicago in 1937, left-wing literary formations continued into the 1940s; Mullen, *Popular Fronts.* Oscar Brown Jr., later to achieve renown as a rhythm and blues and jazz singer, was a progressive activist and actor affiliated with the Chicago left in the late 1940s and early 1950s. Jack Gibson, who helped to develop "black appeal" radio in the years after World War II, had studied drama in college but could not find work as an actor in the early 1940s, since he was "too light to play a Negro but [too] dark to pass as white." Barlow, *Voice Over*, p. 135. Janice Kingslow won the lead in the Chicago production of *Anna Lucasta* in the late 1940s but also had difficulty finding work as a light-skinned black actress, until she found radio work with Durham; Kingslow, "I Refuse to Pass," *True Experiences,* January 1950, reprinted in *Negro Digest,* May 1950, pp. 22–31. The young lawyer Louis Terkel, who named himself "Studs" after James T. Farrell's character, said in an interview that being in a workers' theater group production of *Waiting for Lefty* led to his first jobs as a radio actor on soap operas, his own radio show from 1945 to 1947, and his television show from 1949 to 1952; Tony Parker, *Studs Terkel: A Life in Words* (New York: Holt, 1996).

6. Neimark, "The Man Who Knows Muhammad Ali Best," p. 25.

7. The film *Black Press: Soldiers Without Swords* (1999) emphasizes the significance of this period for the black press, a point also made by Von Eschen, *Race Against Empire*. Within a few months of the *Pittsburgh Courier* announcement on February 7, 1942, of the Double V campaign, J. Edgar Hoover presented Roosevelt's attorney general, Francis Biddle, with a report urging the indictment for treason of a group of black press publishers. John Sengstacke, publisher of the *Chicago Defender*, negotiated a compromise with Biddle to avoid legal action.

8. Von Eschen refers to this focus as a "diasporic consciousness"; *Race Against Empire*, pp. 7–21.

9. Burns, *Nitty Gritty*, pp. 19–20; Durham quoted by Neimark, "The Man Who Knows Muhammad Ali Best," p. 24. At the *Chicago Defender* Durham became friends with Langston Hughes, who helped him publish his first book of poetry.

10. From the statement by Metz Lochard, editor in chief of the *Defender*, May 5, 1945. Durham's front-page contribution that day was part of an article headlined "Delegates Juggle Colonial Question: White, Du Bois Ask for Equality of Races"; Von Eschen, *Race Against Empire*, p. 215.

11. The *Pittsburgh Courier* sponsored the first radio show devoted to "Negro Journalism," an hour-long news show, in 1927. In the early 1930s Jack Cooper initiated a late-evening news roundup, in conjunction with the *Defender*'s news show, the *Defender Newsreel*, and later with the *Pittsburgh Courier*; Barlow, *Voice Over*.

12. Neimark, "The Man Who Knows Muhammad Ali Best," p. 28; Durham interviewed by Cordier, "A History and Analysis," p. 6.

13. *Here Comes Tomorrow* provided an entry into broadcasting for actor Jack Gibson and for actress Janice Kingslow, who also worked on *Democracy USA;* Barlow, *Voice Over*.

14. In the popular 1934 film *Imitation of Life*, based on the best-selling Fannie Hurst novel, Louise Beaver plays a housekeeper devoted to Claudette Colbert's working mother, and Fredi Washington plays her passing daughter.

15. Durham interview with Cordier, "A History and Analysis," pp. 24–25.

16. The *Defender* urged the station to share the costs; its support decreased after the 1948 campaign of *Destination Freedom* actor Oscar Brown Jr. on the Progressive Party ticket, in opposition to the *Defender*-backed candidate, a Democrat. WMAQ picked up the costs after the show won numerous awards. Cordier, "A History and Analysis," pp. 15–21.

17. The *Defender* "paid the writer and all the talent cost." Ibid., p. 7. See also MacDonald, *Richard Durham's "Destination Freedom"*, pp. 2–4.

18. Durham may have demanded this control as a result of his dissatisfaction with *Democracy USA*, cited by Cordier, "A History and Analysis," p. 8. Cordier cited Durham's memos rejecting a station proposal assigning various NBC staff writers for some of the programs. See also Barlow, "Commercial and Non-Commercial Radio," p. 205. WMAQ did reject Durham's proposals to do scripts on Nat Turner and Paul Robeson and demanded cuts in the script for "Segregation USA"; see MacDonald, *Richard Durham's "Destination Freedom"*, p. 6.

19. This memo is attached to Cordier, "A History and Analysis," and excerpted in Barlow, "Commercial and Non-Commercial Radio," pp. 205–206.

20. The titles and broadcast dates of Durham's ninety-one scripts for *Destination Freedom* appear in MacDonald, *Richard Durham's "Destination Freedom"*, pp. ix–xii. Durham's original proposal to the station appears in Cordier, "A History and Analysis," pp. 49–54.

21. Cordier, "History and Analysis," p. 31.

22. Durham quoted by Cordier, "A History and Analysis," p. 25. Durham returned to the atomic age in a script about scientist Dr. Ossborg ("Boy with a Dream," script no. 13) in which the protagonist declares: "We beat [Germany and Japan] because we built a team no bigots could stop. Now, we men of science have a bigger assignment. It is to show men that there is only one race in this one world and with our discovery of the atomic bomb we will either learn to live together as free and equal people or die together" (p. 35).

23. Durham quoted by Cordier, "A History and Analysis," pp. 25–26.

24. "The Story of 1875," broadcast August 29, 1948, reprinted in MacDonald, *Richard Durham's "Destination Freedom"*, pp. 101–116.

25. African American progressives have often credited popular antifascism with increasing their understanding of racial discrimination. For example, Ossie Davis, a Georgia-born college student at Howard from 1935 to 1939 who came to Harlem in 1939 to become a playwright and found a job in a women's clothing factory, recalled learning from the Jewish cutters "a new, international dimension to the struggles of my own people. Anti-Semitism and racism were one and the same . . . the struggles of the Jewish people in Germany, the colonization of the people in Africa, and the persecution of Negroes in America all overlapped." Ossie Davis and Ruby Dee, *With Ossie and Ruby: In This Life Together* (New York: Morrow, 1998), pp. 109–111.

26. This speech is quoted by MacDonald, *Richard Durham's "Destination Freedom,"* p. 7.

27. "Peace Mediator," broadcast February 20, 1949, reprinted in MacDonald, *Richard Durham's "Destination Freedom"*, pp. 145–161; quotations from pp. 148, 150. In Bunche's story Durham also called attention to Du Bois and the NAACP's attempt to use the UN charter's protection of civil rights as the grounds for an international protest against racial discrimination in the U.S.; the script ends with Bunche's refusal to serve as assistant secretary of state as a protest against segregation in the nation's capital.

28. Born in 1863, the year of the Emancipation Proclamation, Mary Church Terrell was a writer, educator, and lecturer who championed women's rights and racial equality.

29. "The Long Road," broadcast August 7, 1949, reprinted in MacDonald, *Richard Durham's "Destination Freedom"*, pp. 131–144; quotations from pp. 139, 141. Durham also wrote a militant speech for Terrell in which she declared: "The only protection women need is protection by equality under the law. Equalities of opportunities and the right to share the benefits of this land, alongside men. Equality to chose their own associates without fear of intimidation from bigots and the hissing of cowards. That is why I am staying in the South and getting Negro and white women together to find their freedom together. In the right to

vote and the right to work—will freedom be found—for once a white woman bows down before white masculinism—she is ready for slavery" (p. 141).

30. "Segregation Incorporated," broadcast August 28, 1949, reprinted in MacDonald, *Richard Durham's "Destination Freedom"*, pp. 163–179; censorship noted on p. 6; quotations from p. 178.

31. Richard Durham, Interview with John Dunning, January 1983, cited by MacDonald, *Richard Durham's "Destination Freedom"*, p. 5.

32. *Destination Freedom* was commended by the South Central Association of Chicago for "a splendid contribution . . . towards the achievement of democracy in our time," honored by the Institute for Education by Radio at Ohio State University, praised by Norman Corwin, and specially commended by then governor of Illinois Adlai Stevenson.

33. Richard Durham to Langston Hughes, November 19, 1949, in Langston Hughes Papers, James Weldon Johnson Manuscripts 26, series 1: Personal Correspondence, box 57, Beinecke Library, Yale University. My thanks to Rachel Rubin for transcribing this letter. For the pressures on Hughes, see Rampersad, *The Life of Langston Hughes,* vols. 1 and 2. Savage also cited this letter in *Broadcasting Freedom,* p. 269.

34. MacDonald, *Richard Durham's "Destination Freedom"*, pp. 3, 5, 6–7; Barlow, "Commercial and Non-Commercial Radio," p. 204–205.

35. By the early 1950s Durham was working in the labor movement, as the national program director of the United Packinghouse Workers of America, until he was forced out in 1957; Roger Horowitz, *"Negro and White: Unite and Fight": A Social History of Industrial Unionism in Meatpacking, 1930–1990* (Urbana: University of Illinois Press, 1997). In the 1960s he edited Elijah Muhammad's weekly publication, *Muhammad Speaks,* one of the most sophisticated sources of information on Africa available in the U.S. in the 1960s and 1970s, according to Von Eschen, *Race Against Empire.* He did freelance writing for television, including *Playhouse 90,* and in the 1970s created and wrote scripts for an award-winning PBS drama series, *Birds of the Iron Feather* (from a 1847 speech by Frederick Douglass). In the 1970s he recorded hundreds of hours of interviews with Muhammad Ali for his life story, Muhammad Ali with Richard Durham, *The Greatest: My Own Story* (New York: Random House, 1975), which he helped Ali to write. Durham died in 1984.

36. *Death of a Salesman* was the first play to win all four major drama awards including the Pulitzer Prize, as well as prizes from the Theatre Club and the American Newspaper Guild. Published in book form in May (New York: Viking Press, 1949), *Salesman* was the first play ever to be chosen as a Book-of-the-Month Club selection. By the summer of 1949 touring companies set off for London and across the U.S., and theater companies all over the country mounted productions. By 1950 productions were staged in Europe, Israel, Mexico, Latin America, and Australia. The book was translated into six foreign languages. Charles Grutzner, " 'Salesman' is Pulitzer Play; Sherwood, Cozzens Cited," *New York Times,* May 3, 1949, p. 1; Luke P. Carroll, "Birth of a Legend: First Year of 'Salesman,' " *New York Herald-Tribune,* February 5, 1950. See also the program for the 1950 touring production, in the Kermit Bloomgarden Papers, box 72, folder 5,

Death of a Salesman programs and flyers, the Wisconsin Historical Society. John Lahr recently estimated that the eleven million copies of the play sold make it "probably the most successful modern play ever published," running "somewhere in the world almost every day of the year" since it opened; Lahr, "Life and Letters: Making Willy Loman," *New Yorker*, January 25, 1999, p. 42.

37. Miller, *Timebends*, p. 231. Miller was referred to as a "non-Hollywood writer" by Joseph Mackey, "Theater's Man of the Moment," *New York Times*, February 23, 1947.

38. The Abbey Theatre production of *Juno*, featuring Sara Allgood and Barry Fitzgerald, played in New York in January 1940; Miller later commented that this production "humbled the heart as though before an unalterable truth" and came closest to the Group Theatre's combination of the "natural and surreal." *Juno* also provided an important theatrical model for Tennessee Williams, who was also deeply moved by seeing the 1940 production, and for Lorraine Hansberry; see chapter 9.

39. Although Miller described himself in *Timebends* as a mimic from childhood, his work collecting American dialect speech for the Library of Congress and in radio contributed to his sensitivity to language. In a 1970 interview with British critic Ronald Hayman, Miller commented, "I can speak in any dialect I've ever heard. . . . A playwright writes with his ears." *Conversations with Arthur Miller*, ed. Matthew C. Roudane (Jackson: University Press of Mississippi, 1987), p.190.

40. Reynal and Hitchcock, Miller's publisher for *Situation Normal* in 1944 and *Focus* in 1945, published the book of *All My Sons*.

41. John Wilson, "Broadway Report: Miller Upholds the Morality Theme," *PM*, January 29, 1947.

42. Miller, *Timebends*, p. 244.

43. Kazan and Miller began to spend time together in the fall of 1946. Rehearsals for *All My Sons* began in December 1946.

44. Kazan's *A Life* is filled with descriptions of competitive triangles of attachment, both personal and professional, to which he was drawn throughout his life.

45. Kazan, *A Life*, pp. 318–319. Kazan had begun psychoanalysis in 1945.

46. Miller admired Kazan's performance of the gangster Fuseli in the Group Theatre 1937 production of Odets's *Golden Boy:* "Ah, what glamour, what hard clear strokes of theatrical characterization!" Miller, *Timebends*, p. 271. By 1946, when they met, Kazan had directed ten plays on Broadway, of which five had been major critical and commercial successes.

47. Miller, *Timebends*, pp. 270, 273–274.

48. Miller, *Timebends*, pp. 299, 332. "I was never sure what I meant to him, but he had entered my dreams like a brother and there we had exchanged a smile of understanding that had blocked others out" (p. 333).

49. Arthur Pollock, "Theater," *Brooklyn Eagle*, January 30, 1947; Brooks Atkinson, "Welcome Stranger: Arthur Miller's 'All My Sons' Introduces a New Talent to the Theatre," *New York Times*, January 30, 1947.

50. The Boston reviews were quoted by Wilson, "Broadway Report." By August 1947 Catholic War Veterans had organized to block a production of the play for U.S.

troops stationed in Germany, on the grounds that it was a "Party-line propaganda vehicle." As Miller's 1947 *Current Biography* entry commented, "The play
may not be presented in United States occupied zones in Europe as a result of a
charge that it contained Communist propaganda: the criticism has been rejected
by Brooks Atkinson and by other theater goers" (p. 439).

51. Howard Barnes, "The Theater's 'All My Sons' Finds Critics Taking Sides," *New
York Herald-Tribune,* in the clipping files for *All My Sons* in the Arthur Miller
Papers, Harry Ransom Humanities Research Center, University of Texas at
Austin, hereafter abbreviated as AMP HRHRC UTA.

52. "Theater," *Time,* February 10, 1947. See also Stark Young, "Theatre," *New Republic,* February 10, 1947.

53. Samuel Sillen, "'All My Sons' a Powerful New Play by Arthur Miller," *Daily
Worker,* January 31, 1947. A second, more critical, review also appeared in the
Daily Worker; Miller, *Timebends,* p. 237.

54. Pollock, "Theater." A number of the critics were pleased with Miller's depiction
of the Kellers as an ordinary family. William Hawkins called them "usual people
with usual ambitions" in the *New York World-Telegram,* January 20, 1947; Joseph
Wood Krutch said that the family and the neighbors "seemed to come from
some real back yard," in "Drama," *Nation,* February 15, 1947, p. 191.

55. Bigsby, "Early Plays," in *Cambridge Companion,* pp. 21–47; Miller, *Timebends,* p.
73. Miller described his own radicalism as affirmed by his wife Mary's Ohio
grandmother—her socialist identification, Farmer-Labor vote and support for
the Nazi-Soviet pact as the common sense of "so authentic a native of the heart-
land" (pp. 80–86).

56. Atkinson, "Welcome Stranger"; Krutch, "Drama." Some critics objected to
Miller's occasional lapses from the ordinary: Kappo Phelan, "All My Sons,"
Commonweal, February 14, 1947, p. 446; John Mason Brown, "Seeing Things: New
Talents and Arthur Miller," *Saturday Review of Literature,* March 1, 1947, p. 23.

57. Steve Vineberg, *Method Acting: Three Generations of an American Acting Style*
(New York: Schirmer, 1991), p. 3. As Joe, Kazan cast Ed Begley, a radio actor
whose voice could communicate Keller's clichéd language. As Kate, Kazan cast
Beth Merrill, because of her non-Method theatrical style; "as a long-unemployed
leading lady," she had a "certain pathetic pretension"; Miller, *Timebends,* p. 133.

58. Isidor Schneider, "Sights and Sounds: 'All My Sons,'" *New Masses,* February 18,
1947, p. 28–29; William Hawkins, "'All My Sons' a Tense Drama," *New York
World-Telegram,* January 20, 1947. John Beaufort, "'All My Sons' Excoriates Profiteering in Materiel" (undated, unidentified clipping for *All My Sons*—likely to
have appeared in the *Christian Science Monitor,* where Beaufort was writing drama
reviews in 1949), refers to the "older tradition" which puts "family loyalty above
individual integrity," and looks forward to the day when "human relations are
purged of such false family ideals and when world concepts are cleansed of similar
monolithic ideals of nationalism." *All My Sons* clippings, AMP HRHRC UTA.

59. "Arthur Miller," *Current Biography* (1947), p. 440.

60. These phrases were used by Stark Young in the *New Republic,* Joseph Wood
Krutch in the *Nation,* and William Hawkins in the *New York World-Telegram.*

61. Harold Clurman, "The Meaning of Plays: 'All My Sons,'" *Tomorrow,* June 1947; Atkinson, "Welcome Stranger."

62. John Chapman, "'All My Sons' Takes Critics Prize: 'No Exit,' 'Brigadoon,' Cited"; Louis Calta, "Critics Laurels: Arthur Miller's Play Is Named Best of the Season," *New York Times;* both in *All My Sons* clippings file, AMP HRHRC UTA.

63. The purchase price of $150,000 was reported in the *New York Times,* June 22, 1947.

64. Miller does not mention the film *All My Sons* in his memoir. Hollywood progressives shaping the production included the director Irving Reis, who came to Hollywood after founding and directing CBS radio's Columbia Workshop; producer and screenwriter Chester Erskine; Edward G. Robinson and Burt Lancaster, cast as Joe and Chris Keller; Mady Christians, cast as Kate Keller; and Lloyd Gough, cast as the doctor neighbor. Many people in *All My Sons* signed the Committee for the First Amendment's petition opposing the 1947 HUAC hearings: Irving Reiss, Burt Lancaster, Henry Morgan, Howard Duff, Edward G. Robinson, and Arlene Francis. Promotional strategies for the film built on the play's critical and commercial acclaim, emphasizing its break from Hollywood genre film, typecasting, and appeal to vets and noting its use of folk music; pressbook for *All My Sons,* AMPAS. For pressures on the production, see the MPAA file on *All My Sons,* AMPAS Special Collections. The FBI comment was quoted by Kate Buford, *Burt Lancaster: An American Life* (New York: Knopf, 2000), p. 79.

65. See, for example, reviews in *Variety* and *Hollywood Reporter,* February 19, 1948, and in the *Daily News* (Los Angeles), April 1, 1948. Bosley Crowther, "The Screen in Review," *New York Times,* March 29, 1948; when Crowther discussed the film in "Observed in Passing," *New York Times,* April 18, 1948, he called attention to the importance of its antiwar message amidst the intensifying militarism of the cold war, "in these uneasy times when the clang and clatter of the armorers is sounding more loudly on the winds."

66. Miller, *Timebends,* p. 265; Wilson, "Broadway Reports."

67. Miller described his 1947 factory work in *Timebends,* pp. 138–139, 276. He was "attempting to be part of a community instead of formally accepting my isolation" (p. 276).

68. "Arthur Miller," *Current Biography,* p. 440.

69. The Civil Rights Congress was formed in 1946 as the result of a merger between the International Legal Defense Fund, which had defended the Scottsboro Boys, the National Negro Congress, and the National Federation for Constitutional Liberties. Its specialty was mobilizing support for "black" and "red" cases, including defending Willie McGee, a black truck driver from Laurel, Mississippi, convicted of rape for a four-year relationship with a white woman, and eleven leaders of the Communist Party, convicted in 1949 under the Smith Act (1940), which made teaching or advocating the overthrow of the government a federal crime. The Congress of American Women, also an interracial organization, was formed in 1946 as the U.S. branch of the Women's International Democratic Federation, a postwar antifascist alliance of women in forty-one countries dedicated to women's equality, security, opportunities for children, and peace.

Miller's support of the left was detailed in claims presented to him, to which he assented, at his hearing before HUAC in June 1956.

70. Miller, *Timebends*, 237–238.

71. Looking back on 1943 in his memoir, Miller commented that sexual desire "was nearly absent" from his marriage (p. 279); the quoted description is from *Timebends*, p. 145.

72. For details of Longhi's life before he met Miller, see his oral history in Tamiment Library and his memoir of his wartime years in the Merchant Marines with his buddies Woody Guthrie and Cisco Huston, *Woody, Cisco, and Me: Seamen Three in the Merchant Marine* (Urbana: University of Illinois, 1997). He also spoke as one of the "common men" on the 1944 Democratic National Committee broadcast for Roosevelt in November 1944, discussed in chapter 1.

73. Miller, *Timebends*, pp. 148–150. The only celebrity Miller was able to influence to contribute to Longhi's campaign was Tennessee Williams. In Miller's account it was Williams's lover Frank Merlo who knew the waterfront, explained the social issues and indignities to Williams, and insisted that Williams make a sizable contribution ($500). Merlo was a self-educated navy veteran who was just ending an affair with the progressive lyricist John LaTouche when Williams met him in June 1947. *Timebends*, pp. 154–155; Donald Spoto, *The Kindness of Strangers: The Life of Tennessee Williams* (New York: Ballantine, 1985), p. 146.

74. Miller, *Timebends*, pp. 149–150, 155. His examples of "unreality" included Levittown suburban housing that "made the previous generation's homes seem primitive" and "old atheist friends and cousins . . . contributing to something they called 'temple'; before the war I would not have imagined that anyone of my generation would ever go to shul again" (pp. 155–156).

75. Miller, *Timebends*, pp. 158–164, 166–167, 176, 195.

76. Miller and Williams were aware of each other's work before they met. Miller had won a playwriting award from the Theatre Guild in 1938; Williams had won a special award from the Group Theatre in 1939. Both Miller and Williams had work published in the *Best One-Act Plays of 1944*. Miller's first Broadway play, *The Man Who Had All the Luck*, opened and closed after four performances at the end of November 1944. In contrast, Williams's family memory play, *The Glass Menagerie*, opened in Chicago in December 1944 and went on to Broadway, running for 561 performances and winning various awards. Williams and Miller competed for Kazan's directorial attention; Miller spoke of his "envious curiosity" in *Timebends*, p. 181. Barbara Leaming has called attention to the triangulation between Miller, Williams, and Kazan as part of her larger analysis of the triangulation between Kazan, Miller, and Marilyn Monroe, with whom Kazan initially had an affair and whom Miller later married; Leaming, *Marilyn Monroe* (New York: Crown, 1998).

77. Miller wrote in *Timebends* about Williams as "the only other writer with the same approach" and about the impact of *Streetcar*'s use of language (pp. 180–182). *Streetcar* was also popular, running for 855 performances, a year longer than *Glass Menagerie*.

78. Two contemporary literary examples included Eudora Welty's short story, "Death of a Traveling Salesman" (1941), and Tennessee Williams's short play, "The Last of the Solid Gold Watches" (1945). In early interviews Miller identified a familial context for *Salesman;* see Murray Schumach, "Arthur Miller Grew Up in Brooklyn," *New York Times,* February 6, 1949, section 2, pp. 1, 3; Robert Sylvester, "Brooklyn Boy Makes Good," *Saturday Evening Post,* July 16, 1949, rpt. in Roudane, *Conversations with Arthur Miller,* p. 12. Miller describes one salesman uncle in particular as the model for Willy, in *Timbends,* pp. 121–131.

79. "In Memoriam" is with the *Death of a Salesman* notebooks, AMP HRHRC UTA.

80. Miller, *Timebends,* pp. 177–179.

81. Ibid., p. 184.

82. Jo Mielziner wrote about creating the stage and lighting design for *Salesman* in *Designing for the Theatre* (New York: Atheneum, 1965).

83. Robert Sylvester noted how the staging differentiated *Salesman* from that "cliché of playwriting, the living room. Miller hates living room scenes almost as much as he despises scenery itself"; "Brooklyn Boy Makes Good," pp. 11–12.

84. *Death of a Salesman* notebook, April 1948, p. 30, AMP HRHRC UTA.

85. The use of overlapping voices and sounds in the scene changes in Orson Welles's *Citizen Kane* (1941) may have provided a model for Miller, who uses overlapping laughter to move between the Laughing Woman and Linda. One critic noted Miller's use of "familiar screen and radio techniques," especially flashbacks and musical bridges between scenes; see William Beyer, "The State of the Theatre: The Season Opens," *School and Society,* December 3, 1949, pp. 363–364.

86. Miller, *Timebends,* pp. 184; Miller, "The 'Salesman' Has a Birthday," *New York Times,* February 5, 1950, section 2, pp. 1, 3; Miller, *Timebends,* pp. 194–195.

87. Miller, *Timebends,* p. 180.

88. See Murray Schumach, "Arthur Miller Grew in Brooklyn," *New York Times,* February 6, 1949.

89. Steve Vineberg identified these different forms of colloquialism as Charley's, although he also noted that Willy also occasionally speaks in this way. George Ross also identified Miller's language as Yiddish-inflected, suggesting that Miller's efforts to make the "Loman family anonymous" deprived Miller of "one of the resources of his experience"; "'Death of a Salesman' in the Original," *Commentary,* February 1951, pp. 184–186.

90. Peter Applebome, "Present at the Birth of a Salesman," *New York Times,* January 29, 1999, p. B1. In an article on theater for *Holiday,* January 1955, Miller described what the production had sought in Linda: "We needed a woman who looked as though she had lived in a house dress all her life, even somewhat coarse, and certainly less than brilliant"; reprinted in *Death of a Salesman: Text and Criticism,* ed. Gerald Weales (New York: Penguin, 1996), p. 151.

91. *Death of a Salesman* notebook, April 1948, p. 3, AMP HRHRC UTA. According to Miller, it wasn't until 1999 that a Linda performed this rage openly: Elizabeth Franz "mounted a kind of wonderful outrage I've never quite seen before"; quoted by Applebome, "Present at the Birth of a Salesman," p. B27.

92. See, for example, Janice Radway, *A Feeling for Books: The Book-of-the-Month Club, Literary Taste, and Middle-Class Desire* (Chapel Hill: University of North Carolina Press, 1997).

93. *Death of a Salesman* notebook, p. 3, AMP HRHRC UTA.

94. I explored this transformation of immigrant family life in Smith, *Family Connections*.

95. Miller, *Timebends*, p. 185.

96. This attribution is cited in Lahr, "Making Willy Loman," p. 49.

97. Miller, "The 'Salesman' Has a Birthday," pp. 1, 3; Miller, "Introduction to *Collected Plays* (1957)," reprinted in *The Theater Essays of Arthur Miller*, ed. Robert A. Martin (New York: Penguin, 1985), p. 142. In *American Drama Since World War II* (New York: Harcourt, Brace and World, 1962), Weales noted that the "system of love" that Miller discusses in this introduction is never mentioned in his early comments on *Salesman* and suggests that this language might be the product of his concurrent work on "The Misfits" (*Esquire*, November 1957). I would argue, rather, that Miller developed an abstract language for talking about the work in the many drafts he wrote for the introduction in 1956; those drafts are in AMP HRHRC UTA.

98. Kronenberger likened the advance excitement to that which awaited *The Iceman Cometh* in 1946, O'Neill's first play since winning the Nobel Prize for literature in 1936; Louis Kronenberger, "The Theatre," *Town and Country*, p. 65, in *Death of a Salesman* clipping file, AMP HRHRC UTA. See also "Death of a Salesman," *Time*, February 21, 1949, p. 74; "Eighty Backers Have 100G in 'Death of a Salesman,'" *Variety*, December 15, 1948.

99. Weales, *Death of a Salesman*, pp. xii–xiii.

100. Miller, *Timebends*, p. 191. See descriptions of the New York opening, in Lahr, "Making Willy Loman," p. 49. Douglas Watt, New York *Daily News*, as quoted on *All Things Considered*, February 10, 1999. Richard Garland, *New York Journal-American*, February 11, 1949, rpt. in Weales, *Death of a Salesman*, p. 199. George Currie, *Brooklyn Eagle*, February 11, 1949, p. 10.

101. Howard Fuller, "A Salesman is Everybody: The Broadway Hit—*Death of a Salesman*—Has Less to Do with Selling Than with Life," *Fortune*, May 1949, pp. 79–80; Miller, "The Year It Came Apart," p. 30.

102. Gabriel, *Theatre Arts*, April 1949, pp. 15–16. See also David Savran, *Communists, Cowboys, and Queers: The Politics of Masculinity in the Work of Arthur Miller and Tennessee Williams* (Minneapolis: University of Minnesota Press, 1992).

103. Arthur Miller, "Tragedy and the Common Man," *New York Times*, February 27, 1949, rpt. in Weales, *Death of a Salesman*, pp. 143–145.

104. Brooks Atkinson, "'Death of a Salesman': Arthur Miller's Tragedy of an Ordinary Man," *New York Times*, February 20, 1949, section 2, p. 1. John Gassner, "Aspects of the Broadway Theatre," *Quarterly Journal of Speech*, February 1949, rpt. in Weales, *Death of a Salesman*.

105. Harold Clurman reviewed the play twice: "Attention!" *New Republic*, February 28, 1949, and "The Success Dream on the American Stage," *Tomorrow*, May 1949; rpt. in Marjorie Loggia and Glenn Young, eds., *The Collected Works of Harold*

Clurman: Six Decades of Commentary on Theatre, Dance, Music, Film, Arts and Letters (New York: Applause, 1994).

106. Weales observed that the "majority of critics from the beginning have voted for Linda as the character the audience should admire"; Weales, *Death of a Salesman,* p. xix.

107. Robert Garland, "Audience Spellbound by Prize Play of 1949," New York *Journal American,* February 11, 1949, p. 24; Atkinson, "Death of a Salesman," p. 1. John Mason Brown, "Seeing Things—Even as You and I," *Saturday Review of Literature,* February 26, 1949, pp. 30–32.

108. Coverage of the play's success noted that "salesmen's wives also write to the author. Most of them say they think of the play as having been written about them—how tough it is to be s salesman's wife"; Luke P. Carroll, "Birth of a Legend: First Year of 'Salesman,'" *New York Herald-Tribune,* February 5, 1950.

109. Ross, "*Death of a Salesman* in the Original," pp. 184–186. Jewish ethnicity was not a requisite for audience identification: Miller reported that Boston critics termed one production "the best Irish play ever," with a national touring company featuring Thomas Mitchell as Willy, Darren McGavin as Happy, Kevin McCarthy as Biff, and June Walker as Linda; *Timebends,* p. 322. Ivor Brown, "As London Sees Willy Loman," *New York Times Magazine,* August 28, 1949; T. C. Worsley, "Poetry Without Words," *New Statesman and Nation,* August 6, 1949; rpt. in Weales, *Death of a Salesman,* pp. 224–227.

110. John Beaufort, "American Dreamer Wakens—Arthur Miller's New Play an Absorbing Experience," *Christian Science Monitor,* February 19, 1949, p. 10.

111. William Hawkins, "Death of a Salesman Powerful Tragedy," *New York World-Telegram,* February 11, 1949, rpt. in Weales, *Death of a Salesman,* p. 202. Louis Kronenberger, "The Theatre," *Town and Country,* p. 65, in *Death of a Salesman* clipping file, AMP HRHRC UTA. Brown, "Seeing Things—Even As You and I," p. 31.

112. "Magnificent Death," *Newsweek,* February 21, 1949, p. 78; "Death of a Salesman: Fine Tragedy Becomes a Critical and Box-Office Sensation," *Life,* February 21, 1949, pp. 115, 117–118, 121.

113. Joseph Wood Krutch, "Drama," *Nation,* March 5, 1949, pp. 283–284; "Death of a Salesman," *Time,* February 21, 1949, p. 75; Worsley, "Poetry Without Words," p 225.

114. Other participants included the composer Aaron Copeland, "literary stars" Lillian Hellman, Norman Mailer, Mark Van Doren, Louis Untermeyer, and Norman Cousins, the "radical Odets," and "real live Soviets" Dmitri Shostakovich and the writer A. A. Fadayev, according to Miller, *Timebends* p. 234.

115. Ibid., p. 234.

116. Some twelve hundred delegates, a quarter of whom were black, attended the CRC Bill of Rights conference. These affiliations were enumerated at Miller's HUAC hearing in June 1956.

117. On the Millers' relationship to Jaffe, see *Timebends,* p. 182–183. Mary Grace Slattery Miller is only briefly mentioned in *Timebends,* but Miller did note her midwestern populist radical roots and hinted at their shared commitment to the left at Michigan in the 1930s. His only other reference to her politics was his memory

of her weeping for the heroic Yugoslavs (then suffering a Nazi invasion) while in labor with their first child, Jane, during the winter of 1944. *Timebends*, pp. 69–86, 159.

118. "Red Visitors Cause Rumpus," *Life*, April 4, 1949, pp. 39–43; the two-page picture spread that included Miller was on pp. 42–43.

119. Miller, *Timebends*, p. 234.

120. Ibid., 269. Kelton was part of Jackie Gleason's supporting cast on the *Cavalcade of Stars*, and originated the role of Alice Kramden in Jackie Gleason's *Honeymooners*' sketches, but she was fired when the show moved to CBS in 1952. Untermeyer was a poet and anthologist who was fired in 1951 after gaining national acclaim as one of the original panelists on the popular show *What's My Line?*

121. Eleanor Clark, "Old Glamour, New Gloom," *Partisan Review*, June 1949, rpt. in Weales, *Death of a Salesman*, pp. 217–223.

122. Sylvester, "Brooklyn Boy Makes Good," p. 17. Miller's retrospective comment appeared in *Timebends*, p. 239.

123. Miller described this period in "The Year it Came Apart," pp. 30–44 and in *Timebends*. In the Dramatists' Guild meeting Miller hoped for support from the chairman, Moss Hart, fellow dramatists Oscar Hammerstein, and former FDR speechwriter Robert Sherwood, but his proposal for a counter picket was dashed by Arthur Schwartz, Broadway producer and composer of musicals, including *A Tree Grows in Brooklyn*, who threatened to form a new organization if any guild money was spent defending a Communist. Miller, *Timebends*, pp. 321–322; "The Year it Came Apart," p. 40.

124. Miller, *Timebends*, pp. 321–322.

125. Ibid., pp. 310–311; "The Year it Came Apart," p. 40. Miller does not date these meetings precisely, but Senator Joe McCarthy made his sensational accusations about Communists in the state department on February 9, 1950; the group was organized some time after that. Miller noted that less than a year after the meetings ceased Goodman was investigated by HUAC, "not accused of Communism but called to explain why these gatherings had been held and how as a non-red he could have sponsored such an anti-American campaign involving so many first class authors and editors" on the basis of a detailed account provided by a participant who must have been an informer; *Timebends*, p. 311.

126. *Red Channels* ironically verified the success of progressives in gaining access to the airwaves; Smith, "Radio's 'Cultural Front,'" in Hilmes and Loviglio, *Radio Reader*.

127. Hartnett's speech expressed particular outrage at the participation of left-wing actors in radio shows in which they played ordinary Americans. He singled out Jean Muir's performance as Mrs. Aldrich in *The Aldrich Family*. "Red Channels Author in Challenge," *Peoria Journal-Star*, October 15, 1950.

128. "Legion, JC Show Charges Branded 'Outright Lie,'" *Peoria Journal*, October 21, 1950; Dekker's statement in the *Peoria Journal*, October 23, 1950; *Variety*, October 23, 1950; an undated copy of a letter to Miller from Gabriel (probably Gilbert Gabriel, on the Council of the League of American Writers) mentions that "last night with the Jack Goodman bunch. We talked considerably about the Peoria

incident: what pallid things we (at the League) did to fight it, and what we ought to have done, instead." Kermit Bloomgarden Papers, box 72, folder 4, "Peoria Boycott *Death*" file, Wisconsin State Historical Society.

129. Miller, *Timebends*, pp. 312–313, 195, 299–308.

130. This was also the beginning of their complex competition over Marilyn Monroe—who slept with Kazan first and later married Miller—played out against the background of the HUAC hearings, according to Leaming, *Marilyn Monroe*. Kazan's account is in *A Life*, pp. 383–415. In 1952 Kazan would give testimony to HUAC, dating his Communist Party membership and naming various associates from the Group Theatre and other left-wing theatrical groups. On April 12 he loudly proclaimed his opposition to Communism and defended his cooperation with HUAC in a paid advertisement in the *New York Times*. Miller was subpoenaed by HUAC in 1956; he managed to talk about his own left-wing activities without naming names, partly deflecting HUAC's scrutiny by his surprise announcement to the press—and to Monroe—of their plans to marry.

131. Miller, *Timebends*, p. 195.

132. "The studios then were in full command. . . . I took it for granted that we were headed into a struggle in the coming days but the prize was worth it: a truthful film about a dark cellar under the American Dream." Miller, *Timebends*, p. 299.

133. Ibid., pp. 311–312.

134. Weales, *Death of a Salesman*, pp. xiii–xv.

135. Sylvester, "Brooklyn Boy Makes Good," pp. 17–18.

136. Fuller, "A Salesman Is Everybody," pp. 79–80.

137. See Daniel Schneider, "Play of Dreams," *Theater Arts*, October 1949, rpt. in Schneider, *The Psychoanalyst and the Artist* (New York: Farrar Strauss, 1950). Miller began his own psychoanalysis with Rudolph Lowenstein in 1950; *Timebends*, pp. 320–321.

138. See MPAA files, *Death of a Salesman*, special collections, AMPAS. The film was seen in Hollywood as a prestige production, winning five Academy Award nominations, though no awards. Miller, *Timebends*, pp. 314–316; Kramer, *A Mad, Mad, Mad, Mad World*, pp. 74–90. Columbia Pictures made a short feature to accompany the film *Salesman*, "proving that the selling career was in reality both emotionally and financially remunerative and secure." But it was never circulated, Miller later speculated, either because of his threat of a suit or because "they were ridiculing their own two-million-dollar film"; Miller, "The Year It Came Apart," p. 32.

139. Murray Schumach, "Arthur Miller Grew in Brooklyn," *New York Times*, February 6, 1949.

140. Sylvester, "Brooklyn Boy Makes Good," p. 9.

141. Arthur Miller, "A Boy Grew in Brooklyn," *Holiday* 17 (March 1955), pp. 54–55, 117, 119–120, 122–124. The discarded drafts for the introduction are in AMP HRHRC UTA.

142. Philip Gelb, "Morality and Modern Drama," *Educational Theatre Journal* (1958), rpt. in Roudane, *Conversations with Arthur Miller*, pp. 35–51.

143. Olga Carlisle and Rose Styron, "The Art of the Theater II: Arthur Miller, an

Interview," from *Paris Review* 10 (1966), pp. 51–98; rpt. in Roudane, *Conversations with Arthur Miller,* p. 100.

144. Arthur Miller to George, April 28, 1975, in box 24, *Death of a Salesman* correspondence, AMP HRHRC UTA.

8. MARITAL REALISM AND EVERYMAN LOVE STORIES

1. May, *Homeward Bound.*

2. Mario Puzo, "Choosing a Dream," in *The Godfather Papers and Other Confessions* (New York: Dial, 1972), pp. 25–26.

3. Westbrook, "Fighting for the American Family: Private Interests and Political Obligations During World War II," in *The Power of Culture: Critical Essays in American History,* ed. Richard W. Fox and T. J. Jackson Lears (Chicago: University of Chicago Press, 1993), pp. 195–221; Elaine May, "Rosie the Riveter Gets Married," in *The War in American Culture: Society and Consciousness During World War II,* ed. Lewis A. Erenberg and Susan E. Hirsch (Chicago: University of Chicago Press, 1996), pp. 128–143.

4. John D'Emilio and Estelle Freedman, *Intimate Matters: A History of Sexuality in America* (New York: Harper and Row, 1988); Davis and Kennedy, *Boots of Leather;* Chauncey, *Gay New York;* May, *Homeward Bound;* Nancy Cott, *Public Vows: A History of Marriage and the Nation* (Cambridge: Harvard University Press, 2000).

5. On the film, see the oral histories of John Berry and Jean Rouveral Butler in McGilligan and Buhle, *Tender Comrades,* pp. 55–89, 154–176. Berry described RKO producer William Pereira's pitch on p. 69.

6. The son of Jewish immigrants, Berry grew up in the Bronx. Both he and Butler had been members of the Communist Party. Although Bell had worked for MGM as a writer from 1936–1937, he did not write the screenplay, as he considered writing dialogue for films "conveyor-type work"; John Berko, "Thomas Bell: Slovak-American Novelist," *Slovak Studies* 15 (1975), pp. 143–157.

7. After the early 1930s Bell's career as a writer was subsidized by his wife's employment; when she got home from work, he had dinner ready; Berko, "Thomas Bell," p. 145.

8. Florence Milner, *Boston Transcript,* December 26, 1936, p. 1; Frances Woodward, *Saturday Review of Literature,* November 7, 1936, p. 6. See also Alfred Kazin, "Love Without Money," *New York Times Book Review,* November 1, 1936, p. 7

9. MPAA PCA files on *From This Day Forward,* MHL AMPAS. Breen objected to revealing "the sacred intimacies of married life" in his correspondence in April 1946 with Goldwyn about *The Best Years of Our Lives;* cited by Leonard Leff and Jerold L. Simmons, *The Dame in the Kimono: Hollywood, Censorship and the Production Code from the 1920s to the 1960s* (New York: Doubleday, 1991), p. 136.

10. These ads for the film appeared in mass-market publications, women's magazines, and fan magazines; pressbook for *From This Day Forward* at USC CTL.

11. Philip T. Hartung, "The Screen," *Commonweal,* April 26, 1946, p. 47; "Movies: Love Out of Uniform," *Newsweek,* April 29, 1946, p. 89. James O'Farrell, " 'From This Day Forward' at Two Houses," *Los Angeles Examiner,* May 31, 1946. The

New York reviewers included John McCarten, "The Current Cinema," *New Yorker,* April 20, 1946; J. T. M., "At the Palace" (n.d.); "Saturday's Children," *New York Times,* April 21, 1946; all from the clippings file on *From This Day Forward* at AMPAS.

12. "Garson Kanin," *Current Biography* (1941), pp. 453–454, and (1952), pp. 294–296. Kanin was from a left-wing Jewish family. He described his father as a revolutionary from Vitebsk, Russia, who immigrated to escape arrest, a tinsmith by trade, a poet and playwright by avocation. His mother was a buttonhole maker from Kovno, Lithuania, who met his father when her amateur Yiddish theatrical society performed his play. Kanin's father eventually became a builder, moving from Buffalo to Detroit and in 1922 to Brooklyn, building up and losing his business twice during the Depression years; Jerry Tallmer, "Garson and Kate and Spencer," *New York Post,* November 13, 1971. Kanin mentions his relationships with Trumbo and Jarrico in his memoir, *Hollywood* (New York: Limelight, 1984 [1967]). Kanin's postwar activism was catalogued in *Red Channels* (1950). The Committee for the Negro in the Arts (CNA) 1949 conference call, on which Kanin's name appeared, is in the *Counterattack* files on the CNA at the Tamiment Library, New York University; my thanks to Terry Signaigo for providing me with a copy.

13. "Ruth Gordon," *Current Biography* (1943), pp. 238–241. Gordon's postwar affiliations were catalogued in *Red Channels* (1950). See also her memoirs *Myself Among Others* (New York: Atheneum, 1971); *My Side: The Autobiography of Ruth Gordon* (New York: Harper and Row, 1976); *Ruth Gordon: An Open Book* (New York: Doubleday, 1980).

14. George Cukor, born in 1899 into a middle-class Jewish family with an American-born father and a Hungarian-born mother, had directed stars on Broadway and then in Hollywood film through the 1920s and 1930s, developing a reputation as an actor's director and more specifically as a women's director (perhaps a coded reference to his widely known homosexuality). Patrick McGilligan, *George Cukor: A Double Life* (New York: St Martin's, 1991).

15. Holliday's New York urban ethnic background infused her star persona as a working-girl heroine. Born in 1921 to a family with ties to the Jewish immigrant left, she worked as a switchboard operator for Orson Welles's Mercury Theater Company in 1938–1939. She performed with Adolph Green and Betty Comden as the Revuers at Max Gordon's Village Vanguard and at various popular front benefits. Holliday's Greenwich Village roommate and lover in the early 1940s was a woman active in the left; their friendship would sustain Holliday for the rest of her life. In the years of her *Born Yesterday* celebrity, she campaigned for Wallace, supported the Hollywood Ten, lent her name as a sponsor of the World Peace Conference held in New York City in the spring of 1949, and protested the attack on Paul Robeson's Peekskill concert. Gary Carey, *Judy Holliday: An Intimate Life Story* (New York: Seaview, 1982); Will Holtzman, *Judy Holliday* (New York: Putnam, 1982).

16. Kanin's exposé of Washington, D.C., politics became associated with its lead female character, Billy Dawn, who represented the promise of the postwar social contract. The play, set in 1945, inscribed Billy Dawn's political emergence with popular front references: she allies herself with the hotel cleaner who compares

402 8. Marital Realism and Everyman Love Stories

the price of a hotel room to her weekly earnings, she invokes Tom Paine and the Bill of Rights. The play also refers to Henry Wallace, and jabs at the rhetoric of "free enterprise" used by conservatives to oppose social welfare.

17. Garson Kanin to George Cukor, July 12, 1951, and September 9, 1951; Cukor to Kanin and Gordon, July 27, 1951, in *The Marrying Kind* folder, Correspondence with Kanin, George Cukor Collection, MHL AMPAS. See also casting notes filed with the screenplay for *The Marrying Kind* at AMPAS.

18. "Marrying Blonde," *New York Times*, April 22, 1951; Philip Scheuer, "We've No System," *Los Angeles Times*, June 29, 1952.

19. McGilligan, *Cukor*, p. 194. Cukor directed the films Kanin and Gordon wrote, *A Double Life* (1947) and *Adam's Rib* (1948), as well as the film version of *Born Yesterday* (1950).

20. Cukor was quoted in Ezra Goodman's column, *Los Angeles Daily News*, July 16, 1951.

21. Cary, *Holliday*, pp. 128–129.

22. Brandon French discussed this aspect of the film in *On the Verge of Revolt: Women in American Films of the Fifties* (New York: Ungar, 1978), p. 25. Although French did not mention the social context of the writers and directors she identified as introducing themes later associated with second-wave feminism, nearly all the films she analyzed were created by people associated with the Hollywood left.

23. The attack on Kanin by a conservative columnist syndicated in Catholic newspapers across the country, and Parson's response, was noted in Kanin's obituary; Marilyn Berger, "Garson Kanin, a Writer and Director of Classic Movies and Plays, Is Dead at 86," *New York Times*, March 14, 1999. Holtzman discussed specific attacks on Holliday in *Judy Holliday*, pp. 144–147.

24. Kanin listed his memberships in the Screenwriters', Directors', and Dramatists' Guilds, and the American Veterans' Committee, in *Current Biography* (1952), pp. 294–296; Scheuer, "We've No System."

25. Carey, *Judy Holliday*, p. 143; "Wage Earners Committee Pickets 'Marrying Kind,'" *Variety*, April 14, 1952.

26. Howard Thompson, "The Local Scene," *New York Times*, September 25, 1951.

27. Pressbook for *The Marrying Kind* at USC CTL; "You're in for a surprise. . . . It's a far different—and far better—movie than its advertising would lead you to believe. From the newspaper ads, anyone logically could and would conclude that 'The Marrying Kind' is broad farce of the parlor-bedroom-and-bath variety." Kay Proctor, "Marrying at Three Theaters," *Los Angeles Examiner*, April 12, 1952.

28. John L. Scott, "New Film Blends Comedy and Drama," *Los Angeles Times*, April 12, 1952.

29. "The Marrying Kind," *Variety*, March 12, 1952.

30. The letter from Rosalind Hochbaum of New York City was noted in the *Hollywood Citizen News*, April 12, 1952. Stuart Svonkin discusses the racial discrimination suit against Stuyvesant Town in *Jews Against Prejudice*, pp. 98–104. Although the court case was ultimately unsuccessful, it prompted public meetings, hearings, and the passage of local fair housing laws that supported the move of ten African American families into Stuyvesant Village in 1950 and 1951.

31. Arthur Knight, "The Month's Films: Manhattan Makes It Real," *Theater Arts,* April 1952, p. 40. Bosley Crowther identified Florence Keefer as a "Brooklyn-Bronx-Manhattan type" in "More on Miss Holliday and the Marrying Kind," *New York Times,* March 23, 1952. Gilbert Seldes found that "the parts as written and played . . . strike me as second generation of various stocks, and it would have been appropriate to let that come out instead of being glossed over." "SR Goes to the Movies," *Saturday Review of Literature,* March 22, 1952, p. 31. Manny Farber termed Judy Holliday's performance an "uncomfortable spectacle . . . a cautious and intelligent highbrow squeezing herself into the dumb role of a Bronx yenta"; *Nation,* April 26, 1952, p. 410.

32. John L. Scott, "New Film Blends Comedy and Drama," *Los Angeles Times,* April 12, 1952; "New Films," *Newsweek,* March 24, 1952, pp. 109–110.

33. Crowther, "Three New Films Measure Up to the Test of Detailed Accuracy," *New York Times,* March 16, 1952; "More on Miss Holliday and 'The Marrying Kind' "; Kay Proctor, " 'Marrying' at Three Theaters," *Los Angeles Examiner,* April 12, 1952; "The New Pictures," *Time,* March 17, 1952, p. 102.

34. Carey, *Judy Holliday,* p. 143.

35. "Judy Holliday Not Red, Just 'Slightly More Than Stupid,' " *Daily News* (Los Angeles), September 23, 1952; "Was Duped by Reds, Says Judy Holliday," *Los Angeles Times,* September 25, 1952. The red-baiting of Judy Holliday is covered most extensively in Holtzman's biography.

36. See "Oscar Winner's Life No Cinch, Says Judy," *Mirror,* June 13, 1953; Betty Randolph, "An Intimate Talk with Judy Holliday," *TV and Movie Screen,* 1955; Virginia Bird, "Hollywood's Blonde Surprise," *Saturday Evening Post,* December 31, 1955; William Peters, "Judy Holliday," *Redbook,* 1957, from Judy Holliday clipping file, AMPAS.

37. McGilligan described Kanin's dissatisfaction with the filmed version of his critique of advertising hype, *It Should Happen to You* (1954), and the end of the collaboration between Kanin and Gordon, in *George Cukor,* pp. 212–215, 209.

38. David L. Goodrich, *The Real Nick and Nora: Frances Goodrich and Albert Hackett, Writers of Stage and Screen Classics* (Carbondale: Southern Illinois University Press, 2001), pp. 211–215.

39. Kanin's statement to Goodrich and Hackett appeared in a letter to them in November 1954, quoted by Lawrence Graver in *An Obsession with Anne Frank: Meyer Levin and the Diary* (Berkeley: University of California Press, 1995), p. 89. The play opened in October 1955, with a long New York run and various traveling companies; it won the 1956 Pulitzer Prize for drama, among other awards. Goodrich and Hackett also wrote the script for the film.

40. Author's interview with Delbert Mann, Los Angeles, March 3, 1986. Shaun Considine, *Mad as Hell: The Life and Work of Paddy Chayefsky* (New York: Random House, 1994), pp. 57–58; 84–87, 97–100. Steiger's comment quoted in Barnouw, *Tube of Plenty,* p. 159.

41. Chayefsky commented on "Marty" in *The Collected Works of Paddy Chayefsky: The Television Plays* (New York: Applause, 1995 [1955]) p. 183.

42. In the late 1930s Coe had produced *Waiting for Lefty* and a modern-dress, antifascist *Julius Caesar;* Jon Krampner, *The Man in the Shadows: Fred Coe and the*

Golden Age of Television (New Brunswick, N.J.: Rutgers University Press, 1997), pp. 12–19. Minor noted that "throughout the thirties I was known in Hollywood as 'the red director of New York,'" adding, "I was all but blacklisted"; Directors' Guild of America (DGA), *Worthington Minor: Interviewed by Franklin J. Schaffner* (Metuchen, N.J.: DGA and Scarecrow, 1985), p. 29. Harry Castleman and Walter J. Podrazik, *Watching Television: Four Decades of American Television* (New York: McGraw Hill, 1982), pp. 21–72.

43. The Actors Studio was founded as an actor's training workshop by former Group Theatre members Elia Kazan, Cheryl Crawford, and Robert Lewis in October 1947. David Garfield, *The Actors Studio: A Players Place* (New York: Collier, 1984 [1980]), pp. 72–73.

44. Krampner, *Man in the Shadows,* pp. 35–42.

45. Television's early critics discussed these issues; see, for example, Jack Gould, "Television in Review," *New York Times,* October 9, 1949, section 10, p. 11; Nat Kahn, "TV Must Develop Camera Technique to Capture Big Shows—Liebman," *Variety,* March 2, 1949, pp. 29, 40.

46. "The Julian Houseman Story," in *The Best Television Plays of the Year,* ed. Walter I. Kaufman (New York: Merlin, 1950). The fluid boundaries of television drama were also apparent in Harriet Van Horne's review, "The Living Theater on Television," in *Theatre Arts,* September 1951, pp. 52–53, 77.

47. Flora Rheta Schreiber, "Television: A New Idiom," *Hollywood Quarterly* 4 (1949), pp. 188–189. *Hollywood Quarterly* was a left-wing publication, and Schreiber specifically mentioned Liss's adaptations of the left-wing writer Millan Brand's *The Outward Room, The Light that Failed,* and Liss's own play "Time Is a Kind Friend." Worthington Minor also described the successful defense of Liss's work in *The Light that Failed* in DGA, *Worthington Minor,* pp. 201–204.

48. DGA, *Worthington Minor,* p. 219.

49. Schreiber, "Television: A New Idiom," p. 192.

50. O'Neal, interviewed by Estelle Edmerson for her M.A. thesis, "A Descriptive Study of the American Negro in U.S. Professional Radio, 1922–1953," UCLA, 1954, p. 389; see also J. Fred McDonald, *Blacks and White TV: African Americans in Television Since 1948* (Chicago: Nelson-Hall, 1992), pp. 46–48. Elsewhere on early television variety formats provided limited openings to talented black entertainers, including Ethel Waters, Louis Armstrong, Cab Calloway, Lena Horne, and Hazel Scott; MacDonald, *Blacks and White TV,* pp. 11–21; Bogle, *Prime Time Blues,* pp. 9–19. Ethel Waters and Louise Beavers starred as the maid when *Beulah* made the move from radio to television from 1950 to 1953. *Amos 'n' Andy* was on television with an all-black cast from 1951 to 1953, until an NAACP suit forced them off the air.

51. Many scholars have called attention to the centrality of blacklisting in shaping television's early history. See Barnouw's *Tube of Plenty;* Castleman and Podrazik, *Watching TV;* Kisseloff, *The Box;* Murray Schumach, *The Face on the Cutting Room Floor: The Story of Movie and TV Censorship* (New York: De Capo, 1974 [1964]), pp. 233–252.

52. Erik Barnouw, *The Sponsor* (New York: Oxford University Press), pp. 42–55; Kisseloff, *The Box.*

53. Rose's comment appeared in the foreword to his published plays, p. xi. Vidal quoted in "They Never Had It So Good," *TV Guide,* August 6, 1955, cited by Tom Stempel, *Storytellers to the Nation: A History of American Television Writing* (New York: Continuum, 1992), p. 48.

54. Schreiber, "Television: A New Idiom," p. 183.

55. Ibid., pp. 184–186, 189–191. See also Lynn Spigel's discussion of "Television in the Family Circle" and "The Home Theater," in *Make Room for TV.*

56. Robert Hatch, "Review of *The Bachelor Party,*" *Nation,* April 27, 1957, p. 379. Al Hine, movie critic for *Holiday,* wrote that "a good Chayefsky show gives you the uncanny sensation of eavesdropping on life itself—a sensation so acute as to be almost uncomfortable"; in "Cheers for Chayefsky," *TV Week,* January 22, 1955, p. 31.

57. See Krampner, *The Man in the Shadows,* pp. 45–53; Liss, *Radio's Best Plays,* pp. 369–370; "Robert Alan Aurthur," *Variety* obituary, November 22, 1978; Merle Miller, "In Memoriam: Remembering Bob Aurthur," *Esquire,* January 1, 1979, pp. 21–22. On Foote, see Marion Castleberry, "Remembering Wharton, Texas," in *Horton Foote: A Casebook,* ed. Gerald C. Wood (New York: Garland, 1998), pp. 13–33. On original-drama television writers, see "Coe's Brain Trust," *New York World-Telegram and Sun* Saturday magazine, October 9, 1954, p. 5; and "A New Era for Playwrights," *Life,* July 25, 1955, pp. 31–34.

58. Copies of scripts produced on *Philco* and *Goodyear Playhouse* by Fred Coe are collected in his papers at the Wisconsin State Historical Society (WSHS), boxes 13–19. Files with NBC promotional materials for the television dramas are also collected at the WSHS. Examples of early "obstacles-to-marriage" plays included David Swift's adaptation of Mary Jane Ward's novel *A Little Night Music* (November 18, 1951) and Horton Foote's "The Travelers" (April 27, 1952).

59. Early scripts of merit included Robert A. Aurthur's account of D. W. Griffith's rise and fall in "Birth of the Movies" (April 22, 1951) and Max Wilk's portrait of an aging Wall Street financier trying for one last killing in "The Fast Dollar" (June 10, 1951). Actors and scripts appearing on *Television Playhouse* before Chayefsky were described by Krampner, *Man in the Shadow,* pp. 40–62.

60. "Waterfront Boss" discussed in Wilk, *Golden Age,* and in DGA, *Worthington Minor.* After Minor left *Studio One* in 1952 the show shifted from adaptations to original drama, produced by antifascist German émigré Felix Jackson and later Herbert Brodkin, directed by Franklin Schaffner and Paul Nickell.

61. Biographical information comes from John M. Clum's study, *Paddy Chayefsky* (Boston: Twayne, 1975), pp. 15–57; Considine, *Mad as Hell,* pp. 3–68. Both authors rely on Helen Dudar's four-part profile of Chayefsky published in the *New York Post,* January 4–7, 1960. See also John Brady's interview with Chayefsky in the late spring of 1981, shortly before his death, in *The Craft of the Screenwriter: Interviews with Six Celebrated Screenwriters* (New York: Simon and Schuster, 1982), pp. 29–83.

62. Considine, *Mad as Hell,* p. 17; Brady, *The Craft of the Screenwriter,* p. 33.

63. On the Actors' Lab School, see the interviews with Jeff Corey and Betsy Blair in *Tender Comrades,* ed. Buhle and McGilligan and Buhle and Wagner's *The Hollywood Left.* Hecht was part of the Federal Theatre Project and a Communist Party

member, 1935–39. Lancaster was briefly employed with the FTP as a circus performer, 1936–38. Hecht and Lancaster are identified as part of Hollywood left circles in Kate Buford, *Burt Lancaster: An Intimate Life* (New York: Knopf, 2000). The progressive circle around Gene Kelley and Betsy Blair is discussed in her interview in *Tender Comrades* and in Arthur Laurents's memoir, *Original Story*, p. 92. See also Considine, *Mad as Hell*, pp. 30–32.

64. Considine, *Mad as Hell*, p. 41.

65. On the basis of Chayefsky's FBI files, Considine noted that four of the other signatories were subpoenaed to testify in front of HUAC; *Mad as Hell*, p. 386.

66. Betsy Blair described Chayefsky as "a Social Democrat" in Considine, *Mad as Hell*, p. 386. In her interview in *Tender Comrades*, Blair said that Chayefsky and Gene Kelly "were the same politically," "good left-wing people who believed in all the right things—trade unions, anti-racism"; pp. 549, 543.

67. Brady, *The Craft of the Screenwriter*, p. 50. Chayefsky often spoke of his indebtedness to Odets: "It would be difficult to find a writer of my generation, especially a New York writer, who doesn't owe his very breath—his entire attitude toward the theater—to Odets"; "Paddy Chayefsky," in *Masters of Modern Drama*, ed. Haskell M. Block and Robert G. Shedd (New York: Random House, 1962), p. 1055.

68. Going on the air in September 1950, *Danger* shows were directed initially by Yul Brenner, an actor protégé of Michael Chekhov. After 1951, when Brenner left to take the lead part in *The King and I* on Broadway, former Group Theatre child actor Sidney Lumet became the director. (Blacklisted writer Walter Bernstein wrote for the show both under his own name and using a pseudonym.) A picture of *Danger* as a left-wing enclave in early television emerges from Gabriel Miller, *The Films of Martin Ritt: Fanfare for the Common Man* (Jackson: University Press of Mississippi, 2000); Walter Bernstein, *Inside Out: A Memoir of the Blacklist* (New York: De Capo, 2000); the chronology prepared for Jay Boyer, *Sidney Lumet* (New York: Twayne, 1993).

69. Paul Deutschman, "It Happened on the Brooklyn Subway," *Reader's Digest*, May 1949; Chayefsky, *Television Plays*, p. 41. Jeffrey Shandler discusses early television references to the Holocaust in *While America Watches: Televising the Holocaust* (New York: Oxford University, 1999). A video copy of the original kinescope is in the collection at the Museum of Radio and Television, New York.

70. Chayefsky, *Television Plays*, p. 41.

71. Irving Howe, *The World of Our Fathers* (New York: Harcourt Brace, 1976), pp. 489–490; Nahma Sandrow, *Vagabond Stars: A World History of Yiddish Theater* (New York: Harper and Row and Jewish Publication Society, 1977), pp. 282, 251–302. My thanks to Rachel Rubin for this reference.

72. Krampner, *Man in the Shadows*, pp. 62–63; Chayefsky, *Television Plays*, p. 41. Susskind was born in 1920 to a middle-class Jewish family in Brookline, Massachusetts, and educated at University of Wisconsin and Harvard. In 1942 he began to work as a press and talent agent. In 1953 he served briefly in Coe's place as producer of *Philco Television Playhouse*; "David Susskind," *Current Biography*

(1960), pp. 412–414. Buloff had performed in Europe with the Russian Theatre and the Vilna Troupe, in the U.S. with Yiddish theater groups, in Yiddish film, and as the peddler Ali Hakim in *Oklahoma* during its long run on Broadway.

73. Considine, *Mad as Hell*, p. 48. David Opatoshu, whose career began in Artef, also had a part.

74. See the Philco publicity release for "Reluctant Citizen," NBC files, WSHS. See also "As Recorded Philco Television Playhouse Script February 8, 1953," in NBC Papers, Broadcast Promo for Television Playhouse, 1952–53, folder 16, box 134, WSHS. Although this play won an award from the Freedom Foundation in 1954, Chayefsky chose not to publish it in his collected plays. A copy is in Chayefsky's papers, WSHS. Peter Novick pointed out that, prior to the 1960s, it was the "marginalized sections of American Jewry that were nostalgic for the popular front" who "talked most about Nazism and the Holocaust"; "Holocaust Memory in America," in *The Art of Memory*, pp. 160–161.

75. " 'Printer's Measure' Story Idea ca. 1953 [*sic*]," Paddy Chayefsky Papers, folder 11, box 9, WSHS, hereafter abbreviated as PCP WSHS. The play was published in *Television Plays* and reprinted in the high school magazine *Literary Cavalcade* in March 1957. "So he [Chayefsky] made them Irish in "The Printer's Measure" and Italian in "Marty" but they were all Jewish—they were all about himself"; author's interview with Delbert Mann, March 3, 1986.

76. "Marty" was reprinted in *Television Plays;* a video copy of the original kinescope is in the Museum of Radio and Television in NYC. Author's interview with Delbert Mann, March 3, 1986. Considine, *Mad as Hell*, pp. 58–61.

77. Chayefsky, *Television Plays*, pp. 183–188.

78. "The Big Deal" (July 19, 1953), featured a once successful building contractor, not unlike Willy Loman, trying to finance one last development deal, even if he has to borrow money from his daughter and disrupt her own marriage plans; its characters had names with no discernible ethnicity, though David Opatoshu was cast as the father. "The Bachelor Party" (October 11, 1953) exposed the marital claustrophobia of an aspiring bookkeeper with a newly pregnant wife, commuting to the city from a New Jersey suburb, joining his office mates for a night on the town. No particular ethnicity was attached to the lead, Eddie Albert, an experienced radio and stage actor who also appeared in films after 1938, or to Joe Mantell, (who had played Marty's friend Angie), cast as a playboy bachelor.

79. For an account of Marlene Dietrich's admiration of "The Mother," see Tad Mosel, "In Search of the Untouched Moments of Life," *New York Times*, December 10, 1989, p. H7.

80. Chayefsky's other television plays included "In the Middle of the Night" (September 9, 1954), exploring the triumph of love's redemption for an unlikely couple, a middle-aged Jewish garment manufacturer (played by the stage and film actor E. G. Marshall) and a young divorced woman who works for him (Actor's Studio actress Eva Marie Saint). "Catch My Boy on Sunday" (December 12, 1954), featured a frustrated mother, played by the stage and 1930s film actress Sylvia Sidney, disappointed by her marriage, who pushes her ten-year-old son into an act-

ing career. Copies of the scripts for "In the Middle of the Night" and "Catch My Boy on Sunday" in PCP WSHS. A copy of the kinescope of "In the Middle of the Night" is at the Museum of Radio and Television, New York.

81. J. P. Shanley, "Big Decision on a Bronx Gridiron," *New York Times,* December 12, 1954, section 2, p. 15. See also "TV's Golden Boy," *CCNY Alumnus,* April 1955; "A New Era for Playwrights," *Life,* July 25, 1955; in clippings files, PCP WSHS.

82. Chayefsky quoted in Shanley, "Big Decision," December 12, 1954. Chayefsky told Brady in 1981: "Everybody came out crying. I was startled the first couple of times in television where I would call home and ask, 'How'd you like it?' 'Oh God, we cried our eyes out.' I didn't believe it. It amazed me. And then I realized that in television we were writing for criers, not for laughers"; *The Craft of the Screenwriter,* p. 50. Marchand's comment quoted by Considine, *Mad as Hell,* p. 54.

83. Al Hine, "Cheers for Chayefsky," *TV Week,* January 22, 1955; J. P. Shanley, "He Celebrates the Bronx," *Saturday Review of Literature,* April 16,1955, pp. 13–14, 56; Walter Goodman, "The Drama of the Ordinary," *New Republic,* June 20, 1955, pp. 20–21; Gerald Weales, "Marty and His Friends and Neighbors: The 'Little Man' of the 50s," *Commentary,* September 1955, pp. 265–269.

84. Goodman, "The Drama of the Ordinary," p. 20. Gerald Weales was struck with this same quality, although he identified the characters as lower middle class (this is the language Chayefsky used). "Sometimes his characters are Italian, as in 'Marty,' sometimes Jewish, as is the author, and sometimes Irish. It makes little difference whether the characters reach for a cup of coffee, a glass of tea, or a drop of whiskey, because the essential ingredient is the same"; "Marty and His Friends," p. 265.

85. Weales, "Marty and His Friends," p. 265.

86. Chayefsky credited Foote's "Trip to Bountiful" (March 1, 1953) with expanding the possibilities of television drama exploring family and place; Wilk, *The Golden Age of Television,* pp. 129–130. Mosel's plays were reprinted in *Other People's Houses: Six Television Plays* (New York: Simon and Schuster, 1956). "Twelve Angry Men" was reprinted in Reginald Rose, *Six Television Plays* (New York: Simon and Schuster, 1957). Krampner identified two other "imitation Martys" on Coe's *Playwrights '56,* "Adam and Evening" (March 13, 1956) and "Nick and Letty" (June 5, 1956); *Man in the Shadows,* p. 105.

87. Ceplair and Englund, *Inquisition in Hollywood,* pp. 361–366; Castleman and Podrazik, *Watching Television,* p. 52.

88. Ceplair and Englund, *Inquisition,* p. 367; Considine, *Mad as Hell,* p. 387.

89. Considine, *Mad as Hell,* pp. 387–388, 390. Eric Albertson, son of blacklisted William Albertson, who worked with Chayefsky on *The Hospital* in 1971, told Considine that Chayefsky had admitted to him that he had cooperated with investigators in order to clear his own name after the *Firing Line* listing and that he had followed Kazan's example; *Mad as Hell,* pp. 389–390.

90. Krampner, *Man in the Shadows,* pp. 58, 71–72. From a left-wing Jewish family, Bernstein joined the Communist Party in the late 1930s as a Dartmouth College student, and worked as a dramatist and writer, for the *New Yorker,* and after he was drafted, as a correspondent for *Yank.* See "Walter Bernstein" in *Tender Com-*

rades, pp. 43–54, and Bernstein's memoir, *Inside Out: A Memoir of the Blacklist* (New York: Da Capo, 2000 [1996]). See also "Fade to Black" in Kisseloff, *The Box,* pp. 403–429.

91. Ring Lardner Jr., *I'd Hate Myself in the Morning: A Memoir* (New York: Thunder's Mouth, 2000), pp. 138–139; Krampner, *Man in the Shadows,* pp. 71–73. Delbert Mann Interview in Gorham Kindem, *The Live Television Generation of Hollywood Film Directors: Interviews with Screen Directors* (Jefferson, N.C.: McFarland, 1994), pp. 150–153.

92. *Variety* supported "realistic" drama on *Playhouse* in "A Case for TV Drama," March 17, 1954, p. 23; April 21, 1954, p. 29. These criticisms of TV drama were reported in "Radio and Television: The Week in Review," *Time,* August 30, 1954, p. 55; and in Terry Barr, "Horton Foote's TV Women: The Richest Part of a Golden Age," in *Horton Foote: A Casebook,* ed. Gerald C. Wood (New York: Garland, 1998) pp. 44–45; Krampner, *Man in the Shadows,* pp. 72–73.

93. Elmer Rice, "The Biography of a Play," *Theatre Arts,* November 1959, pp. 59–64, 94–95. The producer's letter was quoted on p. 95.

94. Chayefsky's CBC interview quoted by Gerald Weales, "Marty and His Friends and Neighbors," *Commentary,* September 1955, p. 268; Chayefsky, *Television Plays,* p. 138.

95. Weales, "Marty and His Friends and Neighbors," p. 268; Lardner, "TV's New Realism: Truth Sans Consequences," *Nation,* August 13, 1955, pp. 132–134. The *Masses and Mainstream* reviewer of Chayefsky's collected plays dismissed them as "introspective drama with a myopic social outlook." V. H. F., "TV: Electronic Bard," *Masses and Mainstream* (1955), pp. 48–52.

96. "A New Era for Playwrights," *Life,* July 25, 1955.

97. Billy Rowe, "Zanuck Blazed Way in Changing View Toward Racial Tolerance," *Pittsburgh Courier,* August 12, 1950.

98. Rose's listing of his concerns appeared in his commentary in *Six Television Plays.* On Rose's political alliances, see Kindem, *The Live Television Generation of Hollywood Film Directors,* p. 168.

99. Rose described self-censorship and sponsor pressure in *Six Television Plays* and in Kisseloff, *The Box,* pp. 516–517. Serling described the pressures in writing "Noon on Doomsday" in a 1959 interview with Mike Wallace, cited in Gordon F. Sander, *Serling: The Rise and Twilight of Television's Last Angry Man* (New York: Plume, 1994) pp. 116–117; see also Joel Engel, *Rod Serling: The Dreams and Nightmares of Life in the Twilight Zone* (Chicago: Contemporary Books, 1989), pp. 125–16L; "Dixie Pressure on TV Talent," *Variety,* June 20, 1956, p. 17.

100. Serling interviewed by Wallace, in Sander, *Serling,* p. 117; Rose, *Six Television Plays,* pp. 107–108.

101. Rose explored many themes of the progressive left: "Tragedy in a Temporary Town" (for *Alcoa Aluminum Hour,* February 19, 1956) concerned the threatened lynching of a Mexican migrant worker; "The Sacco-Vanzetti Story" (NBC *Sunday Showcase*) won an Emmy in 1960. Progressive themes and compromises in Serling's work have been traced in Sander, *Serling.*

102. The writers were invited to speak on David Susskind's late-night television show,

Open End, in November 1958. Forbidden subjects Chayefsky mentioned that he would have liked to dramatize included fears of sexual inadequacy ("a woman going through . . . change of life . . . 49, 50 . . . who throws a pass at a friend of her son") and left-wing political identity ("a wonderful drama of what-in-heaven's-name-makes-a-man-become-a-Communist, and then, let's say, abandon it"); "Top TV Writers Say Taboos of Nets, Sponsors, Agencies Drive Them Away," *Advertising Age,* December 1, 1958, p. 76. See also Leo Rosten's account of network censorship ("television can't touch stories about segregation"), based on a prize-winning set of true stories of grassroots activism against social injustice, "Wanted: Men," *Harper's,* October 1957, and the response from a CBS executive in "Letters" *Harper's,* December 1957.

103. Aurthur had written and published a story about Tommy, "On the Docks" in a little magazine; this would serve as the basis of his play. Poitier discussed the experience in *This Life* (New York: Ballantine, 1981), pp. 173–178; *The Measure of a Man: A Spiritual Autobiography* (New York: Harper Collins, 2000), pp. 90–94. Aurthur wrote about it in "Fifty-Two Plays a Year, All Original, All Live," *TV Guide,* March 17, 1973, pp. 6–20. See also Ethel Winant, casting director for *Studio One* and a vice president of CBS, in Kisseloff, *The Box,* p. 516.

104. Aurthur, "Fifty-Two Plays a Year," p. 20.

105. Later a film adaptation, *The Edge of the City* (1957), was part of a small-scale renewal of social filmmaking in the late 1950s, produced by Susskind's independent production company, screenplay by Aurthur, and directed by Martin Ritt, modestly financed, grudgingly released, and haltingly distributed by MGM. Miller, *The Films of Martin Ritt,* pp. 17–22; Lindsay Anderson, "Ten Feet Tall," *Sight and Sound,* Summer 1957, pp. 34–37; Colin Young, "The Hollywood War of Independence," *Film Quarterly,* Spring 1959, pp. 4–15.

106. Hollywood's interest in television plays was described in "The Perils of an Oscar," and "Small Screen to Big," *Newsweek,* April 2, 1956, pp. 60–62. By 1956 the success of *Marty* encouraged the sale of thirty hour-long television dramas to Hollywood, including Chayefsky's "The Bachelor Party" and "The Catered Affair" and Serling's "Patterns," Rose's "Twelve Angry Men" and "Crime in the Streets." Author's interviews with Mann, March 3, 1986, and Ernest Borgnine, March 4, 1986, Los Angeles.

107. Hecht's testimony was described by Buford, *Burt Lancaster,* pp. 130–132; Betsy Blair detailed her temporary clearance in her interview in *Tender Comrades,* pp. 54–55.

108. Considine, *Mad as Hell,* pp. 78–87; Buford, *Burt Lancaster,* pp. 143–150.

109. "Marty," *Variety,* March 23, 1955.

110. Oscar Godbout, "Hollywood Dossier: 'Marty' Hits Jackpot—Team—On the Set," *New York Times,* September 14, 1955"; "The Promotion of 'Marty,'" *Time,* March 19, 1956; Author's interview with the film's publicist, Walter Seltzer, March 4, 1986, Los Angeles.

111. The head of the prize jury in Cannes was Marcel Pagnol, whose film had provided the model conception for Chayefsky's first television play. "The distin-

guished audience that packed the Palais du Festival interrupted the showing of the American entry seven times with applause"; "'Marty' is Cheered at Cannes Festival," *New York Times,* May 1, 1955.

112. The film cost $343,000 to produce; the promotion budget was $350,000; "The Promotion of Marty," *Time,* March 19, 1956. "Box Office Champions for July 1955," *Motion Picture Herald,* August 6, 1955, p. 17; Edwin Schallert, "'Marty' Proves Simple Values Still Hold the Greatest Impact," *Los Angeles Times,* July 16, 1955.

113. Jack Moffitt, "Marty," *Hollywood Daily Reporter,* March 21, 1955; Tom O'Reilly, "'Marty' an Artistic Gem of a Movie," *Morning Telegraph,* April 27, 1955.

114. Chayefsky, *Television Plays,* pp. 184–186.

115. Howard Thompson, "Bivouac with 'Marty' in the Bronx," *New York Times,* September 12, 1954; John McCarten, "Current Cinema," *New Yorker,* April 23, 1955; "Marty," *Time,* April 18, 1955, p. 110; Jack Moffitt, "Marty," *Hollywood Daily Reporter,* March 21, 1955. Another Los Angeles reviewer made the comparison with O'Henry: Hazel Flynn, "'Marty' Is Miracle Film With O'Henry-Like Pathos, Humor," *Daily News* (Los Angeles), July 9, 1955.

116. William Zinsser, "Marty," *New York Herald-Tribune,* April 12, 1955; Robert Hatch, "Marty," *Nation,* April 30, 1955, pp. 381–382.

117. Moira Walsh, "Films," *America,* April 30, 1955, p. 139; "Viewing Movies," *Catholic View,* July 1955, p. 28. See also "Film and TV," *Catholic World,* April 1955, p. 63; Philip T. Hartung, "Boy Meets Girl, 1955," *Commonweal,* April 22, 1955, p. 77; Robert Bingham, "Movies: Passion in the Bronx," *Reporter,* May 1955, pp. 36–38.

118. *Marty* won awards from the New York Film Critics, the Critics' Circle of the Foreign Language Press, the National Board of Review, the Directors' Guild, and the Writers' Guild. Walter Seltzer's sophisticated promotional campaign helped bring the film to the attention of Academy voters who awarded it four Oscars in March 1956, for best picture, director, screenplay, and actor.

119. Philip Scheuer, "'Marty' Once a TV Hit, Scores as a Movie Too," *Los Angeles Times,* February 20, 1955; Lowell E. Redelings, "UA Releases Smash Hit in LA," *Hollywood Citizen News,* July 16, 1955. Miller described his date with Monroe in the summer of 1955 in *Timebends,* p. 374. Robert Hatch, "Marty," *Nation,* April 30, 1955, pp. 381–382. *Photoplay,* June 1955, p. 35.

120. "'Marty' Impresses Critics in Moscow," *New York Times,* November 13, 1959.

121. I discussed these films in "The Marrying Kind: Working-Class Courtship and Marriage in 1950s Hollywood," in *Multiple Voices in Feminist Film Criticism,* ed. Diane Carson, Linda Dittmar, and Janice R. Welsch (Minneapolis: University of Minnesota Press, 1994) pp. 226–242.

122. The sexual explicitness and sensationalism with which these films were promoted, in order to stimulate declining ticket sales throughout the period, eclipsed the more complex social contexts in which their authors and directors intended to situate the sexual narrative. See Barbara Klinger's discussion of this process in relationship to the films of Douglas Sirk, *Melodrama and Meaning: History, Culture and the Films of Douglas Sirk* (Bloomington: University of Indiana Press, 1994).

123. On the battles over the making and censoring of *Salt of the Earth,* see Herbert

412 8. Marital Realism and Everyman Love Stories

Biberman, *Salt of the Earth: the Story of a Film* (Boston: Beacon, 1965); Michael Wilson, *Salt of the Earth,* ed. Deborah Rosenfelt (New York: Feminist, 1978); Ellen Schrecker, *Many Are the Crimes: McCarthyism in America* (Boston: Little, Brown, 1998) pp. 316–340. On IATSE, see Gerald Horne, *Class Struggle in Hollywood, 1930–1950: Moguls, Mobsters, Stars, Reds and Trade Unionists* (Austin: University of Texas, 2001). See also James Lorence, *The Suppression of "Salt of the Earth": How Hollywood, Big Labor and Politicians Blacklisted a Movie in Cold War America* (Albuquerque: University of New Mexico Press, 1999).

9. RERACIALIZING THE ORDINARY AMERICAN FAMILY: RAISIN IN THE SUN

1. Doris Abramson, *Negro Playwrights in the American Theatre, 1921–1959* (New York: Columbia University Press, 1969), p. 241. See also Loften Mitchell's account of *Raisin* in *Black Drama: The Story of the American Negro in the Theatre* (New York: Hawthorne, 1967); Philip Rose's memoir, *You Can't Do That on Broadway! A Raisin in the Sun and Other Theatrical Improbabilities* (New York: Limelight, 2001).

2. The group of 147 investors included Juanita Poitier, Harry Belafonte, and playwright William Gibson. See Shauneille Perry, "How 'Raisin' Got Started to Stage," *Chicago Defender,* February 21, 1959, pp. 1–2; Michael Anderson, "A Landmark Lesson in Being Black Made Its Way to Broadway," *New York Times,* March 7, 1999, pp. A7, 28.

3. Gerald Weales, "Thoughts on 'A Raisin in the Sun,'" *Commentary,* June 1959, p. 528; Sidney Poitier, *This Life* (New York: Ballantine, 1981), p. 232; Abramson, *Negro Playwrights,* p. 253. See also Rose's account in *You Can't Do That on Broadway,* p. 12; "'Raisin in Sun' Among Broadway's Fastest Hits," *Afro-American,* May 2, 1959, p. 15.

4. FBI memo, February 5, 1959, quoted by Ben Keppel, *The Work of Democracy: Ralph Bunche, Kenneth B. Clark, Lorraine Hansberry, and the Cultural Politics of Race* (Cambridge: Harvard University Press, 1995), p. 177.

5. Hansberry's papers are not yet available to the public. The following account relies on information provided to biographers by her late husband, Robert Nemiroff, or published by Hansberry's biographer, Margaret Wilkerson, drawing on these papers.

6. E. B. White, "Talk of the Town," interview with Lorraine Hansberry, *New Yorker,* May 9, 1959, p. 34; Anne Cheney, *Lorraine Hansberry* (Boston: Twayne, 1984), p. 2.

7. Patricia C. McKissack and Frederick L. McKissack, *Young, Black, and Determined: A Biography of Lorraine Hansberry* (New York: Holliday House, 1998), pp. 4–6.

8. Nannie Perry's brother, Graham Perry, also came to Chicago, where he eventually worked as a lawyer, becoming assistant attorney general for the state of Illinois; Catherine Scheader, *Lorraine Hansberry: Playwright and Voice of Justice* (Berkeley: Enslow, 1998), p. 26.

9. With regard to this and the quotes from Hansberry that follow, note Adrienne Rich's caution concerning the difficulty in separating Hansberry's voice from

Nemiroff's edited presentation of her voice in "The Problem with Lorraine Hansberry," *Freedomways* 19 (1979), pp. 247–248.

10   Lorraine Hansberry, *To Be Young, Gifted, and Black: An Informal Autobiography*, adapted by Robert Nemiroff (New York: Signet, 1970), pp. 48, 63.

11. Hansberry, *To Be Young, Gifted, and Black*, p. 50.

12. Cheney, *Lorraine Hansberry*, p. 9.

13. Hansberry, *To Be Young, Gifted, and Black*, pp. 63–64.

14. James R. Grossman, *Land of Hope: Chicago, Black Southerners, and the Great Migration* (Chicago: University of Chicago Press, 1991), p. 174. In 1910 25 percent of Chicago blacks lived in areas that were 95 percent white, and none lived in areas that were over 90 percent black. By 1934 less than 5 percent lived in areas that were primarily white, while 65 percent lived in areas that were 90 percent or more black. By the late 1920s 85 percent of Chicago real estate was covered by restrictive covenants. Allen R. Kamp, "The History Behind Hansberry v. Lee," *University of California at Davis Law Review* 120 (1987), pp. 483–485. My thanks to James D. Smith's legal research assistance in finding this article, which clarified the legal limits of the *Hansberry v. Lee* decision.

     Restrictive covenants made a special exception for residence by janitors, chauffeurs, and house servants employed in white-owned households, while also expressing confidence in firm and enforceable racial boundaries, defining the "excepted class of owners" as "every person having one-eighth part or more of Negro blood, or having any appreciable admixture of Negro blood, and every person who is what is commonly known as a colored person."

15. Kamp, "The History Behind," p. 487.

16. Hansberry Enterprises is described in "The Hansberrys of Chicago: They Join Business Acumen with Social Vision," *Crisis* 48 (April 1941), p. 106. Mamie Hansberry was quoted by Cheney, *Lorraine Hansberry*, p. 2. On Hansberry's title as "kitchenette king," see Margaret Wilkerson, "Lorraine Hansberry," in *Black Women in America: An Historical Encyclopedia*, ed. Darlene Clark Hine (New York: Carlson, 1993), p. 524.

17. Theodore Ward, "Big White Fog," in *Black Theater USA: Forty-Five Plays by Black Americans, 1847–1974*, ed. James V. Hatch (New York: Free, 1974), pp. 278–319; "The Hansberrys of Chicago," 106.

18. Lorraine Hansberry, unpublished "Letter to the Editor," *New York Times*, April 23, 1964, reprinted in Hansberry, *To Be Young, Gifted, and Black*, p. 51.

19. Cheney, *Lorraine Hansberry*, pp. 2–3; Keppel, *The Work of Democracy*, pp. 23–24.

20. "The Hansberrys of Chicago," pp. 106–107.

21. Cheney, *Lorraine Hansberry*, p. 4.

22. Kamp, "The History Behind," pp. 487–488.

23. McKissack and McKissack, *Young, Black, and Determined*, pp. 22–27; Kamp, "The History Behind," pp. 487–490.

24. White, "Talk of the Town," pp. 33–35; Hansberry, *To Be Young, Gifted, and Black*, p. 51. See also Cheney's "Chronology" and McKissack and McKissack, *Young, Black, and Determined*, pp. 25–26.

25. Hansberry, *To Be Young, Gifted, and Black*, p. 51.

26. Not until after the war in 1948, in the Supreme Court decision *Shelley v. Kraemer*,

would the Court finally rule that judicial enforcement of restrictive covenants constituted state action and thus violated the Fourteenth Amendment; Kamp, "The History Behind," pp. 489–493.

27. Keppel, *The Work of Democracy*, p. 24.

28. McKissack and McKissack, *Young, Black, and Determined*, pp. 27–29; Cheney, *Lorraine Hansberry*, p. 22. Later Hansberry Enterprises would file suit against Mayor Daley and the City of Chicago.

29. Steven R. Carter, "Lorraine Hansberry," in *Dictionary of Literary Biography 38: African-American Writers After 1955: Dramatists and Prose Writers*, ed. Thadius Davis and Trudier Harris (Detroit: Gale, 1986), p. 122; Scheader, *Lorraine Hansberry*, p. 30.

30. Merl E. Reed, *Seedtime for the Modern Civil Rights Movement: The President's Committee on Fair Employment Practice, 1941–46* (Baton Rouge; Louisiana State University Press, 1991), pp. 321–343.

31. White, "Talk of the Town," p. 34; Mamie Hansberry Mitchell interview, January 2, 1976, as cited by Cheney, *Lorraine Hansberry*, p. 8.

32. Keppel, *The Work of Democracy*, p. 24; Carter, "Lorraine Hansberry," p. 122.

33. Hansberry, *To Be Young, Gifted, and Black*, p. 51.

34. The account of the lynching of Dr. Lewis Harrison Johnson and his brothers appeared in Robert Nemiroff, "From These Roots: Lorraine Hansberry and the South," *Southern Exposure*, September-October 1984, p. 33.

35. Hansberry, *To Be Young, Gifted, and Black*, pp. 48, 50, p. 53; Harold R. Isaacs, *The New World of Negro Americans* (New York: Viking, 1966 [1963]), pp. 283–285; Scheader, *Lorraine Hansberry*, p. 26.

36. Isaacs, *The New World*, p. 283. On the role of the black press and the black church generally in publicizing the Ethiopian crisis in these terms, see Von Eschen, *Race Against Empire*, p. 11.

37. Isaacs, *The New World*, p. 285.

38. Hansberry, *To Be Young, Gifted, and Black*, p. 61. Pearl Buck used her literary celebrity to speak out as "one of the most tenacious white opponents of America's systematic wartime discrimination" as well as the "leading American spokesman for Indian independence"; Peter Conn, *Pearl Buck: A Cultural Biography* (New York: Cambridge University Press, 1996), pp. 259, 268.

39. Mullen, *Popular Fronts*, pp. 1–15. On the relationship between Communism and race radicalism, see Smethurst, *The New Red Negro*; and William Maxwell, *New Negro, Old Left: African American Writing and Communism Between the Wars* (New York: Columbia University Press, 1999).

40. Hansberry, *To Be Young, Gifted, and Black*, p. 67.

41. Margaret Burroughs identified this important relationship in Lerone Bennett Jr. and Margaret G. Burroughs, "A Lorraine Hansberry Rap," *Freedomways* 19 (1979), p. 228.

42. On the coverage of Azikiwe, see Von Eschen, *Race Against Empire*, pp. 54–56.

43. White, "Talk of the Town," p. 34; Isaacs, *The New World*, p. 283.

44. Cheney, *Lorraine Hansberry*, p. 10; McKissack and McKissack, *Young, Black, and Determined*, pp. 32–38.

45. Margaret Wilkerson, "Political Radicalism and Artistic Innovation in the Works of Lorraine Hansberry," in *African-American Performance and Theater History*, ed. Harry Elam Jr. and David Krasner (New York: Oxford University Press, 2001), p. 45.

46. John C. Culver and John Hyde, *American Dreamer: A Life of Henry Wallace* (New York: Norton, 2000), p. 457.

47. Gerald Horne, *Black and Red: W. E. B. Du Bois and the Afro-American Response to the Cold War, 1944–1963* (Albany: State University of New York Press, 1986), pp. 83–95; Horne, *Race Woman: The Lives of Shirley Graham Du Bois* (New York: New York University Press, 2000), pp. 113–114; Lewis, *W. E. B. Du Bois*, pp. 532–557; Duberman, *Paul Robeson*, pp. 316–414.

48. Horne, *Black and Red*, pp. 87–88. Coretta Scott was a member of the Antioch chapter of the NAACP and the Young Progressives of America; Clayborn Carson, *The Papers of Martin Luther King*, vol. 2 (Berkeley: University of California Press, 1992), p. 13 and photograph.

49. Lorraine Hansberry, radio interview with Studs Terkel, Chicago, May 12, 1959, published as "Make New Sounds," *American Theatre*, November 1984, pp. 6–7.

50. Rose, *You Can't Do That on Broadway*, pp. 41–43. Rose and Hansberry were both working at Camp Unity, a left-wing vacation camp in upstate New York. Others on the staff that summer were the actor Herschel Bernardi and the African American writer, Lonnie Elder Jr. Paul Mishler discusses Camp Unity in *Raising Reds: The Young Pioneers, Radical Summer Camps, and Communist Political Culture in the U.S.* (New York: Columbia University Press, 1999), p. 84.

51. McKissack and McKissack, *Young, Black, and Determined*, pp. 43–44; Cheney, *Lorraine Hansberry*, p. 11.

52. Lewis, *W. E. B. Du Bois*, pp. 455–457; Du Bois, *Black Folk: Then and Now*, as cited by Lewis, p. 457.

53. Hansberry, *To Be Young, Gifted, and Black*, p. 93.

54. Hansberry, "Flag from a Kitchenette Window," *Masses and Mainstream*, September 1950, pp. 38–40.

55. The Southern Negro Youth Congress lasted from 1936 to 1948; the Southern Conference on Human Welfare from 1938 to c. 1948; the National Negro Congress from 1935 to c. 1945; the Civil Rights Congress from 1946 to 1956. For more on these organizations, see Robin D. G. Kelley, *Hammer and Hoe: Alabama Communists During the Great Depression* (Chapel Hill: University of North Carolina Press, 1990); Linda Reed, *Simple Decency and Common Sense: The Southern Conference Movement, 1938–1963* (Bloomington: Indiana University Press, 1991); Patricia Sullivan, *Days of Hope: Race and Democracy in the New Deal Era* (Chapel Hill: University of North Carolina Press, 1996); Mark Naison, *Communists in Harlem During the Great Depression* (Urbana: University of Illinois Press, 1983); Gerald Horne, *Communist Front? The Civil Rights Congress, 1946–1956* (Rutherford, N.J.: Farleigh Dickinson University Press, 1987).

56. Duberman discusses this period, 1949–50, in *Paul Robeson*, pp. 336–403.

57. Duberman, *Paul Robeson*, 381–403; MacDonald, *Blacks and White TV*, pp. 60–62.

58. Hansberry, *To Be Young, Gifted, and Black*, pp. 99–100.

59. On Burnham, see Kelley, *Hammer and Hoe,* pp. 221–224; Sullivan, *Days of Hope,* pp. 252–274; Kelley, "SNYC," in *Encyclopedia of the American Left,* pp. 785–787; Duberman, *Paul Robeson,* pp. 392–393; Horne, *Black and Red,* p. 137. After *Freedom* folded, Burnham would write for the *National Guardian.*

60. Du Bois's moves to the left are documented by Lewis, *W. E. B. Du Bois,* pp. 523–547; Horne, *Black and Red,* pp. 83–149; Horne, *Race Woman,* pp. 89–133. For Hunton's background, see Von Eschen, *Race Against Empire,* pp. 57–60.

61. Horne, *Black and Red,* pp. 125–136, 151–158. *Family* was the term used in the newspaper to refer to those affiliated with and supporters of *Freedom.*

62. Cheney, *Lorraine Hansberry,* pp. 14–15; [Lorraine Hansberry], "Frederick Douglass School Opens Its Doors in Harlem," *Freedom* 2 (March 1952), pp. 2, 7. Photographs of Du Bois and Hansberry, captioned with their names and the titles of their courses, appeared in an ad for the tenth anniversary fall term of the Jefferson School, *Freedom* 3 (September 1953), p. 8.

63. Horne quoted Graham Du Bois on Du Bois's relationship to Hansberry in *Race Woman,* p. 18.

64. Duberman, *Paul Robeson,* pp. 392–393; Terry Signaigo, "Committee for the Negro in the Arts," notes for M.A. final project on the CNA, University of Massachusetts, Boston, 2002. The CNA led the public opposition to "white" casting for mixed-race character in the 1949 Hollywood movies discussed in chapter 6.

65. LaVinia Delois Jennings, *Alice Childress* (New York: Twayne, 1995) pp. xv–xvi, 1–55; Elizabeth Brown-Guillory, "Alice Childress," *Black Women in America,* ed. Darlene Clark Hine (New York: Carlson, 1993), pp. 233–235; Trudier Harris, "Alice Childress," *Dictionary of Literary Biography 38,* p. 67–68; Roberta Maguire, "Alice Childress," *Dictionary of Literary Biography 249: Twentieth Century American Dramatists* (2001), pp. 30–39. Sidney Poitier wrote of Childress as his political mentor in *This Life,* p. 119.

66. See "Dick Campbell," "Abram Hill," "Frederick O'Neal," in Loften Mitchell, *Voices of Black Theatre* (Clifton, N.J.: White, 1975), pp. 99–100, 117–118, 176–179.

67. On the CNA theater at Club Baron, see Duberman, *Paul Robeson,* p. 703; Hughes and Meltzer, *Black Magic,* p. 212. *Just a Little Simple* played until January 31, 1951, to a total audience estimated at eight thousand. *Florence* was published in *Masses and Mainstream* in October 1950; CNA presented *Florence* as part of a February Negro History Program for the American Labor Party, and *Just a Little Simple* for the Fur Workers Union in February 1951; see Signaigo, "Committee for the Negro in the Arts."

68. Alice Childress, "Knowing the Human Condition," papers from a conference held November 30–December 1, 1978, at the University of Tennessee, Knoxville, and published as *Black American Literature and Humanism,* ed. R. Baxter Miller (Lexington: University Press of Kentucky, 1982), p. 10.

69. The columns in *Freedom* (1951–1955) contained more topical and explicit political references than those collected in *Like One of the Family: Conversations from a Domestic's Life* (Boston: Beacon, 1986 [1956]).

70. The *Freedom* tour was described in Duberman, *Paul Robeson,* pp. 400–403.

71. Letter (unsent) to a Madison classmate, in Hansberry, *To Be Young, Gifted, and*

Black, p. 98; John O. Killens, "Lorraine Hansberry: On Time!" in *Freedomways* 19 (1979), p. 274.

72. Du Bois to Hunton, September 26, 1952, both cited by Von Eschen, *Race Against Empire,* p. 142. See also Horne, *Black and Red,* p. 186.

73. George B. Murphy Jr., "In the Freedom Family," *Freedom* 1 (December 1951), p. 3; Cheney, *Lorraine Hansberry,* 19. According to Julian Mayfield, Hansberry also wrote the script for the variety show honoring Robeson at the Renaissance Ballroom in May 1954: Mayfield, "Lorraine Hansberry: A Woman for All Seasons," *Freedomways* 19 (1979), p. 266.

74. "Negroes Cast in Same Old Roles in TV Shows," June 1951, p. 7; "Old Timers' Eyes Grow Misty Remembering Florence Mills," July 1952, p. 7; "Songs of Clarence Williams Inspire Today's Musicians," August 1952, p.7; " 'Medal for Willy' Deserves a Medal," November 1951, p. 7; " 'Gold Through the Trees,' CNA Presents Exciting Dramatic Review," May 1952, p. 7; "Alice Childress Brightens a Fine Off-Broadway Theatre Piece," October 1953, p. 7; "New York Theatre Fans Enjoy 'The Big Deal,' by Ossie Davis," April 1953, p. 7. Hansberry also reviewed *A Medal For Willie* in *Masses and Mainstream* 4 (December 1951), pp. 59–60. She reviewed the Japanese-produced protest film *Hiroshima* in *Freedom* 5 (May–June 1955).

75. See her "Books" column: June 1952, p. 7; April 1953, p. 7; March 1953, p. 11; February 1953, p. 3.

76. These statements appeared in the second part of the article, published in March 1955.

77. These articles appeared in May 1951, January, February, August 1952, and March 1953; McKissack and McKissack, *Young, Black, and Determined,* p. 62.

78. These articles appeared in May and November 1951, February 1955, and February 1954. In March 1955 *Freedom* also covered the failed legal challenge to segregation in the Pennsylvania Levittown development.

79. NNLC conventions were covered extensively in November 1951 and December 1952. Other labor movement coverage included the West Coast Marine Cooks and Stewards Union antidiscrimination efforts (June 1951) and vulnerability to anticommunist attacks (July 1953); a special UAW supplement for a convention in Atlantic City in March 1953; and a Louisiana sugar cane workers strike in December 1953.

80. *Freedom* articles on the NYC NLC appeared in April and August 1952, and April 1955; the newspaper also covered a national NLC campaign against Sears in 1952.

81. Cheney, *Lorraine Hansberry,* p. 10; Nemiroff, "From These Roots," p. 33.

82. Lorraine Hansberry, "Lynchsong," *Masses and Mainstream* 4 (July 1951), pp. 19–20. On the McGee campaign, see Horne, *Communist Front?*; Jessica Mitford, *A Fine Old Conflict* (New York: Vintage, 1978), pp. 160–194.

83. Hansberry, "Why the Drum-Beaters Fear Roosevelt Ward," *Freedom* 1 (August 1951), p. 2; Douglas Turner Ward, who later renamed himself, identified himself as the subject of the profile in "Lorraine Hansberry and the Passion of Walter Lee," *Freedomways* 19 (1979), p. 224.

84. "Noted Lawyer Goes to Jail: Says Negro Fight Menaced," *Freedom* 2 (May 1952),

p. 3; "Student Killing Exposes NYU Bias," *Freedom* 2 (June 1952), p. 5. See also Cheney, *Lorraine Hansberry*, p. 18.

85. Cheney, *Lorraine Hansberry*, p. 20. Mamie and Nanny Hansberry attended one rally late in 1952.

86. On Sojourners, see Kate Weigand, *Red Feminism: American Communists and the Making of Women's Liberation* (Baltimore: Johns Hopkins University Press, 2001), p. 111; Horne, *Race Women*, p. 144.

87. These articles appeared in May 1951; September 1953; June, 1952; May, 1953; July 1953; October, 1953. Hansberry's attack on HUAC in 1952 was noted by Mayfield, "Lorraine Hansberry," p. 265.

88. Thelma Dale had worked in labor and left organizations in the 1930s and 1940s, and she was the last general manager trying to hold *Freedom* together, taking over in March 1955.

89. The article by Marshall appeared in November 1951; articles by E.G. Robeson in June, 1951 and April 1952; Hansberry's articles appeared in December 1951; March, 1952; and December 1952. Hunton's article on South Africa was in March 1953; reports on Bandung appeared in March and April 1955; the Freedom Charter was reprinted in July-August 1955.

90. Hansberry's conference report, "Illegal Conference Shows Peace is Key to Freedom," in *Freedom* 2 (April 1952), p. 3; Cheney, *Lorraine Hansberry*, p. 19; Tripp, *The Importance of Lorraine Hansberry*, pp. 39–40.

91. Weigand, *Red Feminism*, pp. 102–104. Jones's essay "An End to the Neglect of the Problems of the Negro Woman" (1949) is reprinted in *Words of Fire: An Anthology of African-American Feminist Thought*, ed. Beverly Guy-Sheftall (New York: Free, 1995), pp. 107–123.

92. Alice Childress, "For a Negro Theatre," *Masses and Mainstream* 4 (February 1951), p. 63.

93. Hansberry, *To Be Young, Gifted, and Black*, p. 105.

94. Nemiroff's left-wing parents were former garment workers who later opened a series of small restaurants and nightclubs. Wilkerson identified Nemiroff as having "an earlier involvement with Communist Party activities" on the basis of Hansberry's FBI file, in "Political Radicalism and Artistic Innovation in the Works of Lorraine Hansberry," p. 45.

95. Nemiroff was a camper at Camp Wo-Chi-Ca in the "wartime forties," according to a personal correspondence from his counselor, Irwin Silber, to the author, September 24, 2001. On the camp history, see Paul Mishler, *Raising Reds*, pp. 94–99.

96. Cheney, *Lorraine Hansberry*, pp. 20, 21, 24.

97. On the Village in the 1940s, see Baldwin, *The Price of the Ticket;* Anatole Broyard, *Kafka Was the Rage: A Greenwich Village Memoir* (New York: Vintage, 1997); Henry Louis Gates Jr., "Broyard: White Like Me," *New Yorker,* June 17, 1996, reprinted as "The Passing of Anatole Broyard," *Thirteen Ways of Looking at a Black Man* (New York: Vintage, 1998). The artist Beauford Delaney, his brother, the artist Joe Delaney, Alain Locke, and the jazz musician Frankie Newton commented on the increasing dangers and continuing appeals of the Village in 1949 in Allan Morrison, "Twilight for Greenwich Village," *Negro Digest*, January 1949, pp. 29–34.

98. Cheney, *Lorraine Hansberry* p. 22; Scheader, *Lorraine Hansberry*, p. 46. Hansberry worked briefly at Arnold Perl's Rachel productions, in the company of Ruth Jett and Ruby Dee, and part time for a number of months at the leftwing folk music magazine *Sing Out*, tracking subscriptions and renewals and writing some record reviews.

99. Unpublished script staged in New York, May 26, 1954; Tripp, *The Importance of Lorraine Hansberry*, p. 27. The salute was held at the Renaissance Casino, with an overflowing crowd of a thousand filling a nearby church. Duberman, *Paul Robeson*, pp. 424–425.

100. Hansberry, *To Be Young, Gifted, and Black*, pp. 105–106.

101. Nemiroff, "From These Roots," p. 34.

102. On the Greenwich Mews Theatre, supported by the Village Presbyterian Church and the Brotherhood Synagogue, see Rampersad, *Langston Hughes*, vol. 2, p. 265. Hughes and Meltzer, *Black Magic*, p. 220; Loften Mitchell, *Black Drama*, pp. 158–180. *In Splendid Error* was published in Hatch, *Black Theater USA*, pp. 587–618; *Trouble in Mind* was published in *Black Theater: A Twentieth-Century Collection of the Works of Its Best Playwrights*, ed. Lindsay Patterson (New York: Dodd and Mead, 1971).

103. Carter, "Lorraine Hansberry," p. 123. Hansberry's notes on her Toussaint project were reprinted with a short excerpt in *To Be Young, Gifted, and Black*, pp. 138–143. An excerpt from *Toussaint* appeared in Margaret Wilkerson, ed., *Nine Plays by Black Women* (New York: New American Library, 1986).

104. "Mother to Son" was written in 1920; Rampersad, *Langston Hughes*, vol. 1, pp. 43–44. On "Montage of a Dream Deferred," see Rampersad, *Langston Hughes*, vol. 2, pp. 151–153, 187.

105. Hansberry, *To Be Young, Gifted, and Black*, p. 107.

106. Hansberry, notes dated November 16, 1955, cited by Margaret Wilkerson in the introduction to Lorraine Hansberry, *Les Blancs: The Collected Last Plays*, ed. Robert Nemiroff (New York: Vintage, 1994 [1972]), p. 7.

107. Letter in *Women in Theatre: Compassion and Hope*, ed. Karen Malpede (New York: Drama, 1983), pp. 171–173. *Village Voice* began publishing at the end of October 1955, and by the late 1950s, it was the primary venue for Hansberry's nonfiction writing.

108. Lorraine Hansberry, "Simone De Beauvoir and *The Second Sex*: An American Commentary," introduction by Margaret Wilkerson, in Guy-Sheftall, *Words of Fire*, pp. 125–142. See also Hansberry's unpublished "Defense of the Equality of Men" written in 1961, excerpted in *The Norton Anthology of Literature by Women: The Tradition in English*, ed. Sandra Gilbert and Susan Gubar (New York: Norton, 1985), p. 2064.

109. The Mattachine Society was founded by a Communist Party activist, Harry Hay. On the history of Mattachine, DOB, and *The Ladder*, see D'Emilio, *Sexual Politics, Sexual Communities*, pp. 57–125.

110. Letter from LHN, NY, NY, to the *Ladder*, vol. 1, no. 8 (May 1957), p. 28.

111. Wilkerson wrote that Hansberry "condemned homophobia both in essays and letters," in "Political Radicalism and Artistic Innovation," p. 53; letter from LHN, NY, NY, to the *Ladder*, vol. 1, no. 11 (August 1957), p. 27.

112. Nemiroff quoted by Steven R. Carter, *Hansberry's Drama: Commitment and Complexity* (Urbana: University of Illinois Press, 1991), p. 6.

113. Letter to the *Ladder,* May 1957, pp. 26–27.

114. In Hansberry's words, "to formulate a new and possible concept that homosexual persecution and condemnation has at its roots not only social ignorance, but a philosophically active anti-feminist dogma"; letter to the *Ladder,* August 1957, p. 30. Before she knew him personally, Hansberry publicly defended James Baldwin's explorations of homosexuality at an Actor's Studio reading of a dramatization of *Giovanni's Room* in the winter of 1957–58, standing up to the Broadway and Hollywood celebrities there who seemed to hate it; Baldwin, "Sweet Lorraine" (1969), reprinted in *The Price of the Ticket,* p. 444.

115. Hansberry's entry in *Current Biography* (1959), p. 166.

116. Rose and Hansberry signed the original option agreement on December 3, 1957; Rose, *You Can't Do That on Broadway,* p. 62. Hansberry, *To Be Young, Gifted, and Black,* p. 108.

117. According to Yordan's account, he based his play loosely on Eugene O'Neill's *Anna Christie* (1920); "Philip Yordan: the Chameleon," interviewed by Patrick McGilligan in *Backstory 2,* pp. 330–381. See also Bernard Gordon's account in *Hollywood Exile* (Austin: University of Texas Press, 1999), pp. 101–109. Harry Wagstaff Gribble, playwright, screenwriter, and director, began to work with ANT in 1943 and to adapt *Anna Lucasta* in 1944. See Harry W. Gribble, "'Anna Lucasta' is Not His Dream Play About Negroes, Director Says," *Chicago Defender,* February 9, 1946, p.16.

118. Marjorie Greene, "No Hesitance in Acclaim of Performance," *World* (Memphis), September 15, 1944, TINCF; E. B. Rea, "'Anna Lucasta' Reveals Fine Dramatic Ability of Actors," *Afro-American,* September 9, 1944; Sara Ann Herman, "Simms, O'Neal Give 'Anna Lucasta' Genius, But Its Moral Is Yordan's," *Chicago Defender,* October 6, 1945, p. 16.

119. Lewis Nichols, "Visitor from Harlem," *New York Times,* September 10, 1944; Louis Kronenberger, "'Anna Lucasta' Scores Again," *PM,* September 1, 1944; Burton Rascoe, *New York World Telegram,* as cited by Carl D Lawrence, "Play Depicts Sameness of Problems in Living Among All Peoples," Norfolk (Virginia) *Journal and Guide,* September 9, 1944.

120. Peterson quoted in Seymour Peck, "The Man Who Took a Giant Step," *New York Times,* September 20, 1953, section 2, p. 1; Nan Robertson, "Dramatist Against the Odds," March 8, 1959. Louis Peterson, born in Hartford, Connecticut in 1922, grew up in a mixed immigrant neighborhood where he and his friends defended one another from ethnic and racial insults: "You were a gang linked against that sort of thing," in marked contrast with the "awful destructive incidents as today [1953] when Negroes move into white neighborhoods in some places." He developed *Take a Giant Step* working closely with Clifford Odets. The play is anthologized in Hatch, ed., *Black Theater USA,* pp. 547–584.

121. "Brooks Atkinson, "'Giant Step' Negro Dramatist Tells an American Story," *New York Times,* October 4, 1953. Atkinson's review directly opposed "racial" to "universal."

122. Jack Garvin [UPI Drama Editor], "'Raisin in the Sun' Author Has Her Say About

Route to Broadway," *Chicago Defender,* April 4, 1959, p. 18; Margaret Wilkerson, "The Dark Vision of Lorraine Hansberry: Excerpts from a Literary Biography," *Massachusetts Review* 28 (Winter 1987), p. 646. See also Rose, *You Can't Do That on Broadway,* pp. 56–68.

123. See the Huntington Theatre Company's restored thirtieth anniversary edition of *Raisin in the Sun,* with notations from the 1959, 1983, and 1988 versions, prepared by Jayme Zoszyn. Mary Helen Washington generously shared with me her copy of the annotated script, prepared for the Huntington production in June 1995.

124. Isadora Rowe, "Lorraine Hansberry Goes into B'Way Orbit with Socko 'Raisin in the Sun,'" *Pittsburgh Courier,* February 14, 1959, p. 23. See also Jesse Walker's profile "Meet Miss Hansberry," *New York Amsterdam News,* March 14, 1959. What Hansberry called a "misquote" originally appeared in a profile written by Nan Robertson, "Dramatist Against the Odds," *New York Times,* March 8, 1959, section 2, p. 3: "I told them this wasn't a 'Negro play.' It was a play about honest-to-God, believable, many-sided people who happened to be Negro." The *Times* then repeated the comment: "Miss Hansberry, whose play is about Negroes, is exasperated by producers who think of plays with Negro characters as 'Negro plays.' Her play, she says, is about believable, many-sided people, who happen to be Negroes." "Her Dream Came True: Lorraine Hansberry," *New York Times,* April 9, 1959, p. C 37. It was repeated and revised in Hansberry's listing in *Current Biography* (1959), p. 165: "In her work she is trying to break down the racial stereotype of the Negro by writing plays about people who 'happen to be Negroes' rather than 'Negro plays.'" Hansberry attempted to correct the "misquote" in her TV interview with Mike Wallace, May 8, 1959, and in her radio interview with Studs Terkel, May 12, 1959.

125. Ted Poston, "Lorraine Hansberry: We Have So Much to Say," *New York Post,* March 22, 1959, p. M2,

126. Hansberry, "Make New Sounds," pp. 7–8. Whatever Hansberry's political intentions, the literary critic Mary Helen Washington has called attention to missteps in Hansberry's effort to depict working-class family life, especially the references to Beneatha's riding lessons and Ruth's suggestion that Lena might want to use the insurance money to travel. Mary Helen Washington, unpublished comments prepared for the American Studies Association, Pittsburgh, November, 1995.

127. The *Courier* also mentioned the leadership of Autherine Lucy, Daisy Bates, Rosa Parks, Harriet Tubman, and Sojourner Truth; "The Weaker Sex," *Pittsburgh Courier,* April 11, 1959, p. 8.

128. Hansberry, "Make New Sounds," pp. 5–6; Hansberry, "Willy Loman, Walter Younger, and He Who Must Live," *Village Voice,* August 12, 1959, reprinted in Malpede, *Women in Theatre,* pp. 166–167.

129. Hansberry, "Make New Sounds," p. 41. Von Eschen discusses the significance of anticolonialism within civil rights coalitions in *Race Against Empire.*

130. Hansberry, "Willy Loman, Walter Younger, and He Who Must Live," p. 167.

131. Ibid., p. 170. Henry T. Murdock, "Second Time Around: 'Raisin in the Sun' Earned Its Laurels," *Philadelphia Inquirer,* April 12, 1959, pp. 1, 6.

132. Accounts of first nights were included in Al Monroe, "Blackstone Tenant Real 'Theatre' With Socksational Punch," *Chicago Defender,* February 21, 1959, p. 18; Jesse H. Walker, "'Raisin in the Sun' Raising Cain Among Broadway Critics," *New*

York Amsterdam News, March 21, 1959, pp. 1, 9; "Raisin in the Sun Raises Rave Comment," *New York Amsterdam News,* March 21, 1959, p. 10; Izzy Rowe, " 'Raisin in the Sun' Captures Broadway," *Pittsburgh Courier,* March 21, 1959, p. 23. See also memoirs by Sidney Poitier, *This Life,* pp. 229–232; *The Measure of a Man: A Spiritual Autobiography* (San Francisco: Harper San Francisco, 2000), pp. 156–157; Davis and Dee, *With Ossie and Ruby,* p. 282. Louis Kronenberger referred to the "self-mocking humor" in Kronenberger, ed., *The Best Plays of 1958–1959* (New York: Dodd, Mead, 1959), p. 16. The significance of *Raisin* for a generation of aspiring black actors was documented by Woodie King Jr., "Lorraine Hansberry's Children: Black Artists and *A Raisin in the Sun,*" *Freedomways* 19 (1979), pp. 219–222.

133. Henry Murdock, "Raisin is Sturdy Drama," *Philadelphia Inquirer,* February 1, 1959, pp. 1, 10. Murdock identified himself as a partisan of left-wing theater: "If the true functions of drama are to stimulate, perhaps harass the conscience, mourn defeat, cheer aspirations and sing to courage—and we believe they are— then Lorraine Hansberry's 'A Raisin in the Sun' meets these obligations in fuller measure than any play we've seen this season." Murdock, "Second Time Around," pp. 1, 6.

134. Kenneth Tynan, *New Yorker,* March 21, 1959, pp. 100–102. Tynan's vote was one of the six that gained Hansberry the New York Drama Critics award. The *Saturday Review* critic, Henry Hewes, also gave his vote to *Raisin:* "Here we see the glimmer of a condemnation of today's America in which life seems to abound with accidental successes and sudden acquisition of wealth. In the past, the American Negro had less opportunity to fancy himself part of this illusion than he does now. Like the rest of us, some will be destroyed by it. But *Raisin* would seem to suggest that when the bubble bursts, the families with the most courageous pasts will be best equipped to pick up the pieces." "Broadway Postscript: A Plant Grows in Chicago" *Saturday Review* 42 (April 4, 1959), p. 28.

135. "Izzy Rowe's Notebook," *Pittsburgh Courier,* February 7, 1959, p. 22. See also Rowe, "Lorraine Hansberry Goes Into B'Way Orbit," p. 23; Shauneille Perry, "Miss Hansberry Makes History," *Chicago Defender,* February 14, 1959, pp. 1, 2, and "How 'Raisin' Got to Stage," February 21, 1959, pp. 1, 2.

136. The *Defender's* banner headline of its arts section read, "Broadway, Get Ready: 'A Raisin in the Sun' Shines Brightly." Underneath were Al Monroe's rave review, "Blackstone Tenant Real 'Theatre' With Socksational Punch," and the article quoted, Rob Roy, "Prediction: All Who See Play to Sing Its Praise," March 7, 1959, p. 18. See also Roy, "Let Us Be Factual About 'Raisin in the Sun,' " *Chicago Defender,* March 21, 1959, p. 19. Letter to Hansberry reprinted in *To Be Young, Gifted, and Black,* p. 128.

137. "With a Wallop," *Newsweek,* March 23, 1959, p. 76; "Surprise," *Newsweek,* April 20, 1959, p. 75; *Time,* March 2, 1959, pp. 58–59; Brooks Atkinson, " 'A Raisin in the Sun': Negro Drama Given at the Barrymore," *New York Times,* March 12, 1959, p. C 24.

138. Harold Clurman, "Raisin in the Sun," *Nation,* April 4, 1959, pp. 301–302. Clurman assumed that as a "young Negro woman" Hansberry "simply wants to say

what she has seen and experienced," distinguishing her from neorealist writers, who produced "art and literature."

139. Quotes drawn from reviews cited in previous footnote, and reviews in *Time*, March 23, 1959, pp. 58–60; Marya Mannes, "Sour Bird, Sweet Raisin," *Reporter*, April 16, 1959, pp. 34–35; Richard Hayes, "The Weathers of the Heart," *Commonweal*, April 17, 1959, pp. 81–82.

140. Jack Garvin for UPI, Joseph Shipley for the *New Leader*, Kenneth Tynan for the *New Yorker*, Henry Hewes for the *Saturday Review*, Emory Lewis of *Cue*, and Whitney Bolton of the *Morning Telegraph*. Compare white and black coverage: "Drama Critics Award Given to First Negro," *Philadelphia Inquirer*, April 8, 1959, p. 34; " 'Raisin' Cops Prize Despite 'Boycott,' " *Afro-American*, April 9, 1959, p. 15.

141. Tom F. Driver, "A Raisin in the Sun," *New Republic*, April 13, 1959, p. 21.

142. Nelson Algren, "Is 'Raisin in the Sun' a Lemon in the Dark?" *Tone*, April 1961.

143. In addition to reviews by Driver and Hayes, see Gerald Weales, "Thoughts on 'A Raisin in the Sun': A Critical Review," *Commentary*, June 1959, pp. 527–530; Kronenberger, "The Season on Broadway," in *The Best Plays of 1958–1959*, pp. 15–17.

144. Hansberry, "Make New Sounds," p. 41.

145. Mayfield, "Lorraine Hansberry," p. 263.

146. Interview with Mike Wallace, May 8, 1959.

147. Hansberry, "Me Tink Me Hear Sounds in De Night," *Theatre Arts*, October 1960, 9–11; letter to Miss Oehler in *To Be Young, Gifted, and Black*, pp. 131–132.

148. Wallace interview, 8 May 1959. Her irritation leaked through in "People Are Talking About" in *Vogue*: "What tires, her, however, is the recurrent label, 'the first Negro woman to have a smash Broadway play.' In addition, she is thoroughly sick of the idea that she traced her characters out of her life. She did not. She created them." *Vogue*, June 1959, pp. 78–79.

149. Hansberry, "Me Tink Me Hear Sounds in De Night," pp. 9–11, 69–70.

150. Hansberry, "The Negro Writer and His Roots: Toward a New Romanticism," speech delivered March 1, 1959, to the "First Conference of Negro Writers" convened by the American Society of African Culture, New York City, February 29-March 1, 1959; in *Black Scholar*, March-April 1981, pp. 2–12.

151. Hansberry, "Make New Sounds," p. 7.

152. "Lorraine Hansberry on Mama," from interview with Terkel, May 12, 1959, typescript.

153. Hansberry, "Playwriting: Creative Constructiveness," in *Annals of Psychotherapy Monograph*, no. 8: *The Creative Use of the Unconscious by the Artist and the Psychotherapist*, eds. Jules Barron and Renee Nell, vol. 5, no. 1 (1964), p. 14. The last quote from Hansberry was cited by McKissack and McKissack, *Young, Black, and Determined*, p. 86.

154. On the new scenes, and their rejection by the Hollywood team, particularly Columbia producer Samuel Briskin, see Margaret Wilkerson, "Introduction," *Raisin in the Sun: The Original Unfilmed Screenplay*, ed. Robert Nemiroff (New York: Plume, 1992), pp. xxx–xxxviii; Eugene Archer, " 'Sun' On the Chicago

Landscape," *New York Times,* July 17, 1960; " 'Raisin the Sun,' " *Ebony,* April 16, 1961, pp. 53–56.

155. Archer, " 'Sun' On the Chicago Landscape"; "Hollywood: Susskind in Gomorrah," *Time,* September 12, 1960; " 'Raisin the Sun,' " *Ebony,* April 1961, pp. 53–56.

156 Lorraine Hansberry, "What Could Happen Didn't," *New York Herald-Tribune,* March 26, 1961.

157. Steve Duncan, " 'A Raisin in the Sun' Keeps Artistic Honesty," *Afro-American,* March 11, 1961, p. 15; Jesse Walker, "Hit Stage Play Now Film Hit," *New York Amsterdam News,* March 11, 1961, p. 17; Bosley Crowther, "Screen: Stagelike Version: Poitier Heads Cast of Fine Adaptation," *New York Times,* March 28, 1961, p. C 24; Paul Beckley, "Raisin in the Sun," *New York Herald-Tribune,* March 30, 1961; Philip K. Scheuer, "A Strong Argument for the Human Race," *Los Angeles Times,* March 26, 1961, calendar section, p. 3. Dick Williams, " 'Raisin in the Sun' Equals the Stage Original," *Los Angeles Mirror,* April 20, 1961; John L. Scott, " 'Raisin in the Sun' Stirring Film Play," *Los Angeles Times,* April 21, 1961.

158. "A Raisin in the Sun," *Variety* [weekly], March 29, 1961; Edith Oliver, "The Sun Still Shines," *New Yorker,* April 8, 1961, pp. 164–165.

159. On Petrie's camera work, see Arthur Knight, "SR Goes to the Movies—Theatre into Film," *Saturday Review,* March 25, 1961, p. 34.

160. Ted Poston, "We Have So Much to Say," *New York Post,* March 22, 1959, p. M2.

161. Hansberry quoted ibid.; "Movie Review: 'Raisin in the Sun,' " *Look,* May 9, 1961, pp. 45–46; Moira Walsh, "Films: A Raisin in the Sun," *America,* April 8, 1961, pp. 133–134. See also "Listen, Don't Look," *Newsweek,* April 10, 1961, p. 103; "Angry Young Black Man," *Commonweal,* April 7, 1961, pp. 46–47 ; "New Fame for Raisin," *Life,* April 21, 1961, p. 52. Hansberry's next play after *Raisin* was "The Drinking Gourd," commissioned by NBC for a Civil War centennial, in which she tried again to link family to nation. She used the disintegrating relationship between a slave-owning family and a family of their slaves to show the poison of systemic racism and to dramatize the mother's redefinition of familial survival as resistance; the play was "shelved" by the network. Mary Helen Washington discussed *Raisin* and *Drinking Gourd* in a lecture presented in association with the Huntington Theatre Company production of *Raisin,* Boston, June 4, 1995.

162. Harold Cruse, *The Crisis of the Black Intellectual: From Its Origins to the Present* (New York: Morrow, 1967) pp. 267–284, quotes on pp. 278, 283.

163. Nikhil Singh, "The Paradox of Negro Exceptionalism: Reading Harold Cruse," unpublished paper; Mayfield, "Lorraine Hansberry," pp. 164–165. Hansberry defended the Nation of Islam in her television interview with Mike Wallace, May 8, 1959, and in her text for *The Movement: Documentary of a Struggle for Equality* (New York: Simon and Schuster, 1964), pp. 46–49. Ossie Davis introduced Hansberry to Malcolm X at this social gathering; McKissack and McKissack, *Young Black and Determined,* p. 116.

164. Horowitz, *Betty Friedan;* Weigand, *Red Feminism.*

INDEX